The History and Theology of the
New Testament Writings

The History and Theology of the New Testament Writings

Udo Schnelle

Translated by M. Eugene Boring

Fortress Press
Minneapolis

THE HISTORY AND THEOLOGY
OF THE NEW TESTAMENT WRITINGS

English translation copyright © 1998 Augsburg
Fortress Publishers. Translated by M. Eugene Boring
from the German *Einleitung in das Neue Testament*,
copyright © 1994 Vandenhoeck & Ruprecht,
Göttingen.

Cover design by Nora Koch, Gravel Pit Publications.

Library of Congress Cataloging-in-Publication Data
Schnelle, Udo.
    [Einleitung in das Neue Testament.   English]
    The history and theology of the New Testament
writings / Udo Schnelle ; translated by M. Eugene
Boring.
    p.   cm.
Includes bibliographical references (p.   ) and
indexes.
ISBN 0-8006-2952-3 (alk. paper)
    1. Bible.   N.T.—Introductions.   I. Title.
BS2330.2.S613   1998
225'.06—dc21   98-35932
                                                        CIP

Manufactured in Great Britain   AF 1-2952
02 01 00 99 98 1 2 3 4 5 6 7 8 9 10

Contents

Preface

This book is intended to introduce the reader to the basic historical and theological dimensions of the New Testament documents. The conception on which this presentation is based has been worked out and tested during the last ten years in numerous lectures, classes, and seminars in Göttingen, Erlangen, and Halle; I hope that this conception will prove to be helpful for the readers of this book as well.

I express my sincere gratitude to Prof. Dr. Otto Merk (Erlangen), who carefully read the manuscript and offered valuable suggestions. I would also like to thank my co-workers in Halle, M. Lang, my Academic Assistant, and Th. Spielmann, E. Maurer, and T. Nagel, theology students, for their help in correcting the proofs.

Udo Schnelle

Bibliographical Note

When bibliographical references are made in abbreviated form, the complete documentation is always found in the bibliography preceding the section or in the footnotes of the same subsection. Otherwise, full documentation is given, or the reader is referred to the first occurrence (see above/see below). Full documentation for introductions to the New Testament is given only in section 1.1. Abbreviations generally correspond to those of TRE and EDNT. [Translator's note: minor adjustments have sometimes been made to correspond to English style.]

Translator's Note

At the author's request, I have added English titles to the bibliographies and occasionally amplified a footnote with bibliography and comment. Many thanks are here extended to Lana N. Byrd, Kate Hawthorne, Edward J. McMahon, Joseph A. Weaks, and Brenda Wilson, without whose help in editing, indexing, and proofreading, this project could not have been completed.

M. Eugene Boring

I

Introduction

1.1. Literature

Canon and the Academic Discipline 'Introduction to the New Testament'

Merk, Otto. 'Bibelwissenschaft II,' TRE 6 (1980) 375–409; Kümmel, Werner G. 'Einleitungswissenschaft II,' TRE 9 (1982) 460–482 (additional literature!).

History of Research

Kümmel, Werner G. *The New Testament: the History of the Investigation of Its Problems*, tr. S. McLean Gilmour and Howard Clark Kee. London: SCM Press, 1972. Vielhauer, Philipp. 'Einleitung in das NT,' ThR 31 (1965/66) 97–155, 193–231; 42 (1977) 175–210; Fischer, Karl-Martin. 'Zum gegenwärtigen Stand der neutestamentlichen Einleitungswissenschaft,' VF 24/1 (1979) 3–35; Epp, Elton J. and MacRae, George W., eds. *The New Testament and Its Modern Interpreters*. Atlanta: Scholars Press, 1989; Roloff, Jürgen. 'Neutestamentliche Einleitungswissenschaft,' ThR 55 (1990) 385–423; Baird, William. *History of New Testament Research. Vol. 1: From Deism to Tübingen*. Minneapolis: Fortress Press, 1992.

Introductions

Holtzmann, Heinrich Julius. *Lehrbuch der historisch-kritischen Einleitung in das Neue Testament*. Freiburg: J. C. B. Mohr, 1885, 1892³; Jülicher, Alfred. *An Introduction to the New Testament* tr. Janet Penrose Ward. New York: G. P. Putnam's Sons, 1904; Moffatt, James. *Introduction to the Literature of the New Testament*. Edinburgh: T. & T. Clark, 1918³; Jülicher, Alfred and Fascher, Erich. *Einleitung in das Neuen Testament*. Tübingen: J. C. B. Mohr (Paul Siebeck), 1931⁷; Dibelius, Martin. *A Fresh Approach to the New Testament and Early Christian Literature*. New York: Scribner, 1936; Knopf, Rudolf, Lietzmann, Hans, Weinel, Heinrich. *Einführung in das Neue Testament*. Giessen: 1923; Berlin: Töpelmann, 1949⁵; Wikenhauser, Alfred. *New Testament Introduction*. New York: Herder and Herder, 1958; Marxsen, Willi. *Introduction to the New Testament*. Philadelphia: Fortress Press, 1970; Wikenhauser, Alfred and Schmid, Josef. *Einleitung in das Neue Testament*. Freiburg: Herder, 1973; Kümmel, Werner. *Introduction to the New Testament*, tr. Howard Clark Kee. Nashville & New York: Abingdon Press, 1975; Vielhauer, Philipp. *Geschichte der urchristlichen Literatur*. Berlin: Walter de Gruyter, 1975; Schenke, Hans Martin and Fischer, Karl-Martin. *Einleitung in die Schriften des Neuen Testaments*, 2 vols. Berlin/Gütersloh, 1978, 1979;

Koester, Helmut. *Introduction to the New Testament*. Philadelphia: Fortress Press;
Berlin and New York: Walter de Gruyter, I 1995 (2ed.); II 1980; Lohse, Eduard. *The
Formation of the New Testament*, tr. M. Eugene Boring. Nashville: Abingdon, 1981;
Schmithals, Walter. *Einleitung in die drei ersten Evangelien*. Berlin: Walter de Gruyter,
1985; Johnson, Luke Timothy. *The Writings of the New Testament*. Minneapolis:
Fortress Press, 1986; Schweizer, Eduard. *A Theological Introduction to the New
Testament*, tr. O. C. Dean, Jr. Nashville: Abingdon, 1991; Wright, N. T. *The New
Testament and the People of God*. Minneapolis: Fortress Press, 1992; Pregeant, Russell.
Engaging the New Testament. Minneapolis: Fortress Press, 1995.

1.2 The Canonical New Testament and the Academic Discipline 'Introduction to the New Testament'

The history of the discipline 'Introduction to the New Testament' has
been determined from the very beginning by the problematic of the New
Testament canon. The fundamental issue continues into the present: how
are historic *theological* affirmations derived from studying the New
Testament as canonical Scripture to be related to the results of a purely
historical study of the twenty-seven documents of the New Testament?
The founder of the German academic discipline 'Introduction to the New
Testament,' the Göttingen Orientalist *Johann David Michaelis* (1717–
1791) was faced with the central problem posed by the claim to inspiration
made for the New Testament writings. In his 1750 publication *Einleitung
in die Göttlichen Schriften des Neuen Bundes* (Introduction to the Divine
Scriptures of the New Covenant)[1], his first section was a general treatment
of the questions of text criticism and ancient manuscripts. Proceeding
on the basis of apostolic authorship of the majority of New Testament
documents which must therefore be regarded as inspired, he then turned
his attention to the circumstances involved in the composition of the individual documents. Since, however, the Gospels of Mark and Luke as well
as the Acts of the Apostles were not written by apostles, and so could not
be considered inspired, the question was raised for Michaelis why they
were accepted into the canon. 'Taking all this into consideration, I can
regard the writings of Mark and Luke as approved, to be sure, by eyewitnesses and apostles; Peter and John, not as inspired, but as written
with supernatural help and infallibility.'[2] Thus for Michaelis, apostolicity,
inspiration, and canonicity all belong together as a matter of cause and

---

[1] Later editions appeared in dramatically changed form in the years 1765[2], 1777[3], 1788[4].

[2] J. D. Michaelis, *Einleitung in die göttlichen Schriften des Neuen Bundes* (Göttingen, 1788[4])
1.100; translation from Kümmel, *The New Testament* 71–72.

effect. If there are historical grounds for doubt concerning the apostolic authorship of a writing, then this has persistent consequences for how the document is to be understood. Doubt concerning the Pauline authorship of Hebrews led Michaelis to make the judgment, '. . . If then the epistle . . . was written by the apostle Paul, it is canonical. But if it was not written by an apostle, it is not canonical: for, however excellent its contents may be, they alone will not oblige us to receive it as a work inspired by the Deity.'[3] So also, the canonical authority of the Letter of James depends on whether it was written by the Apostle James or only by James, the half-brother of Jesus. In the latter case, the Letter of James can no longer be numbered among the reliable sources on which the Christian religion is based. In the same way, Michaelis entertained doubts on the apostolic character of the Letter of Jude, with the result that he had to declare it non-canonical. Thus already with Michaelis the fundamental problem of the academic discipline 'Introduction to the New Testament' becomes clear: insight into the historical circumstances of the composition of the New Testament writings leads necessarily to the dissolution of a concept of canon that is bound to a dogma of inspiration and apostolic authorship. Already for Michaelis the New Testament is no longer a whole, but falls apart into apostolic and non-apostolic documents, a judgment made on the basis of combining historical insights with theological value judgments.

If the work of Michaelis illustrates the first efforts toward a historical understanding of the New Testament writings, the discipline of 'Introduction' was substantially advanced by the Halle theologian *Johann Salomo Semler* (1725–1791), who published his *Abhandlung von freier Untersuchung des Canon* (Treatise on the Free Investigation of the Canon) in 1771. Semler subjected the New Testament to investigation from a strictly historical point of view, thereby distinguishing between Word of God and Holy Scripture, since in the Holy Scripture there are found elements that were only of significance in the past, and no longer serve to address a message of 'moral improvement' to the present. 'Holy Scripture and the Word of God are clearly to be distinguished, for we know the difference. If one has not previously been aware of this, that is no prohibition that keeps us from making the distinction. To Holy Scripture (using the particular historical expression that originated among the Jews) belong Ruth, Esther, the Song of Songs, etc., but not all these books that are called Holy belong to the word of God, which at all times makes all men wise unto salvation . . .'[4] The distinction between Word of God and Holy Scripture became

---

[3] Ibid. 72.

[4] J. S. Semler, *Abhandlung von freier Untersuchung des Canon* (Halle, 1771) 1.75; Kümmel, *New Testament* 63.

the principle of a new hermeneutic that totally canceled the doctrine of verbal inspiration and dissolved the understanding of canon that had been based on it, since this presupposition meant that not all parts of the canon could be inspired. Rather, Semler saw the canon to be a purely historical entity that had resulted from the compromises of competing elements in early Christian history, and which must stand open to a free, unprejudiced investigation. Moreover, by means of his distinction Semler set in motion a process of sorting out the contents of the Bible into historically relative elements and the abiding Word of God, the criterion being what served the 'moral improvement' of humanity. 'Since we are not made morally better by any of the twenty-four books of the Old Testament, we are not able to persuade ourselves that they are divine.'[5] Semler's equating 'divine' and 'moral improvement' thus led to his separating the Old Testament from the New. Likewise important was his distinction between religion and theology. While 'religion' includes the proper piety to be practiced by all Christians, Semler understood 'theology' to designate the academic methods necessary for the theological education of specialists. By this means he carved out space for academic freedom in which critical scholarly work could be done that was by no means typical of his time, but whose methods and results did not fundamentally challenge religion as practiced by the masses.

Another scholarly differentiation that was to have an effect on the academic discipline 'Introduction to the New Testament' was that made by *Johann Philipp Gabler* (1753–1826). In his inaugural lecture at the University of Altdorf in 1787, he developed the distinction between biblical theology and dogmatic (systematic) theology. 'Biblical theology bears a historical character in that it hangs on what the sacred writers thought about divine things; dogmatic theology, on the other hand, bears a didactic character in that it teaches what every theologian through use of his reason philosophizes about divine things in accordance with his understanding, with the circumstances of the time, the age, the place, the school to which he belongs, and similar matters of this sort. Considered by itself the former always remains the same, since its arguments are historical (although represented this way by one person and that way by another), while the latter, on the other hand, as constant and assiduous observation over so many centuries more than demonstrates, is subjected along with other human disciplines to manifold change. . . .'[6]

---

[5] Semler, *Abhandlung* 3.26.

[6] J. Ph. Gabler, 'Von der richtigen Unterscheidung der biblischen und der dogmatischen Theologie und der rechten Bestimmung ihrer beiden Ziele,' in *Das Problem der Theologie des Neuen Testaments*, ed. Georg Strecker. WdF 367. (Darmstadt: Wissenschaftliche Buchgesell-

The task of biblical theology thus lies in the delineation of the *sensus scriptorum*, which must be based on the process of historical exegesis. Dogmatic theology, on the other hand, is characterized by rational, systematic thought, confessional orientation, a philosophical conceptuality relevant to the current situation. Biblical passages may no longer be used simply as proofs for dogmatic theses (*dicta probantia*), but as *genus historicum* biblical theology is an independent academic discipline and the presupposition to dogmatic theology. By conceiving biblical theology as a purely historical discipline, Gabler thought it important to lay aside the doctrine of the divine inspiration of Scripture as a means of attaining the *sensus literalis*. The ideas, concepts, and views of the 'holy men' must be precisely distinguished and compared, which means that Old and New Testaments are to be separated from each other, and that in exegesis a differentiation is to be made between grammatical exposition and the subsequent explanation of the text that follows. While the grammatical exposition is oriented toward the ancient meaning of the text itself, based on what the author understood and intended as he composed the text, the subsequent explanation of the text involves a sharp historical and philosophical critical analysis.

The Tübingen theologian *Ferdinand Christian Baur* (1792–1860) understood the discipline of 'Introduction to the New Testament' as a critical analysis of the traditional claims to authorship and the historical and dogmatic implications of these claims. 'Now, the actual object of criticism is just this dogmatic element associated with them, the principle of their canonical authority. The science of introduction, therefore, has to investigate whether these writings are also by their own right what they are said to be by virtue of the dogmatic idea that is held of them. Since the first presupposition of such a dogmatic view is that they are actually written by the authors to whom they are ascribed, it follows that the first task is to answer the question, by what right they represent themselves as apostolic writings.'[7] Consequently, after F. C. Baur it was clear that New Testament documents had been provided with titles on the basis of theological claims made for them, and it became the task of the discipline 'Introduction to the New Testament' to subject these claims to historical criticism in order to attain an objective as possible assessment of the nature of these documents. As a determining factor within the history of earliest Christianity, Baur

---

schaft, 1975) 35–36; Kümmel, *New Testament* 98–99. On the significance of Gabler's work, cf. Otto Merk, *Biblische Theologie des Neuen Testaments in ihrer Anfangszeit*, MThSt 9. (Marburg: Elwert, 1972).

[7] F. Chr. Baur, 'Die Einleitung in das Neuen Testament als theologische Wissenschaft,' *ThJb* (T) 9 (1850), (463–566) 478; Kümmel, *New Testament* 140.

recognized the clash between Gentile Christianity (especially as represented by Romans, 1–2 Corinthians, and Galatians), and a rigid Jewish
Christianity (represented by the Apocalypse, supposedly written by the
Apostle John). All the other New Testament writings belong to a period in
which the conflicts between Gentile and Jewish Christianity began to be
evened out. With the help of this principle of opposition as a point of
orientation, Baur attempted to unlock the history of early Christianity, and
to allocate the individual writings to a place in this history depending on
their tendency [*Tendenz*] with regard to this conflict. Baur's schematic
conception of the history of early Christianity is no longer accepted, but
nevertheless an insight deriving from his approach is still valid: every
document of the New Testament stands in a concrete historical context
from which it must be understood.

If F. C. Baur's standpoint must be described as critical of the concept of
canon, the Strasbourg New Testament scholar *Heinrich Julius Holtzmann*
(1832–1910) understood the tensive relation between the concept of canon
and a purely historical analysis of the New Testament writings in another
way. In his 1885 *Lehrbuch der historisch-kritischen Einleitung in das Neue
Testament*, he emphasized that the limitation of the discipline 'Introduction
to the New Testament' to the twenty-seven New Testament writings is
justified only by the concept of canon. 'As an organic member of the
academic theological disciplines, the biblical "Introduction" is to be understood only from the concept of the canon; its internal coherence is found
only in this concept.'[8] To be sure, Holtzmann explicitly excludes the
dogmatic dimension of the concept of canon from consideration (inspiration, the divine character of the writings). 'Our task is the history of the
canon, not the doctrine of the canon.'[9] Thus the historical assignment of
studying the collection and selection of the New Testament documents,
and their formation into one book, was included in the responsibilities of
the discipline 'Introduction to the New Testament.' From this understanding of the goals of the discipline organically evolved the division that
was already customary prior to Holtzmann, but was executed by him in
exemplary fashion, namely the division of the discipline into 'General
Introduction' and 'Special Introduction.' 'General Introduction' has as its
subject matter the growth of the New Testament canon and the history of
the New Testament text, while 'Special Introduction' is devoted to the
investigation of each of the twenty-seven New Testament books.

If the work of Heinrich Julius Holtzmann represents the summation of

---

[8] H. J. Holtzmann, *Einleitung* (1892³) 11.
[9] Ibid. (1886²) 15.

introductory research of the nineteenth century, around the turn of the century approaches and issues were formulated that continue to set the agenda of the discipline today. On the one hand the demand arose for a more consistent understanding of the task of the discipline than is permitted by the canonical boundaries. Thus the Giessen church historian *Gustav Krüger* (1862–1940), in his 1896 book *Das Dogma vom Neuen Testament* insists, 'for the "history of New Testament Times" and the "history of the apostolic age" . . . there should be substituted a general history of early Christianity; for "introduction," a history of early Christian literature; for "New Testament theology," a history of early Christian theology.'[10] For Krüger, the abandonment of the dogma of the New Testament resulted from the historical fact that there never was a specifically New Testament thought world, and that the canonical New Testament documents are not to be separated from the writings that originated at the same time as the New Testament, but never attained canonical status. 'I challenge the idea that one can be justified in operating with a concept of the "New Testament" in any form whatsoever in the historical study of a time which does not yet know of a "New Testament."'[11]

Like Krüger, the Breslau New Testament scholar *William Wrede* (1859–1906), in his 1897 'Über Aufgabe und Methode der sogenannten neutestamentlichen Theologie,' insisted that the exegete may not limit himself or herself to the canonical documents. If New Testament scholarship is to understand itself as a truly historical discipline, then the existence of the canon presents a problem. 'When once the doctrine of inspiration is given up, the dogmatic idea of the canon cannot be retained.'[12] The problem posed by the concept of the canon consists in the fact that the New Testament documents originated with no canonical claim attached to them, but they were later declared to be canonical. To that may be added, 'It is very difficult to define the boundaries at all points between the canonical and adjacent noncanonical literature.'[13] It is not the fact that a document belongs to the canon, but its own literary structure that provides the appropriate entré to understanding it. Wrede issued a challenge to a Biblical Theology that conceives its task in dogmatic terms, and wanted to replace it with a history of early Christian religion that takes into consideration the whole of early Christian literature, an approach that intentionally abandons the concept of a canon, and so for the first time will

---

[10] Gustav Krüger, *Das Dogma vom Neuen Testament* (Giessen, 1896) 37; Kümmel, *New Testament* 303.   [11] *Ibid.* 10.

[12] W. Wrede, 'Über Aufgabe und Methode der sogenannten neutestamentlichen Theologie,'; translation from Kümmel, *New Testament* 304.   [13] *Ibid.*

accept the assignment of working out a purely historical understanding of the New Testament.

A different conception of the task was advocated by *Adolf Jülicher* (1857–1938), whose *Introduction to the New Testament* first appeared in 1894. Jülicher conceived the discipline 'Introduction to the New Testament' as a strictly historical discipline and treated serially the history of the individual New Testament writings, the history of the New Testament canon, and the history of the New Testament text. He was not fundamentally opposed to the approach of writing a history of early Christian literature, but declared that in his opinion 'unfortunately this is not to be attained by studying the New Testament.'[14] Jülicher's reason for limiting the materials he treats to the twenty-seven canonical books is based on their later influence [*Wirkungsgeschichte*]: from the body of early Christian literature, only they later attained a universally historical significance, and this justifies their treatment as a separate collection.

The opposite positions advocated by G. Krüger and W. Wrede on the one side, and A. Jülicher on the other are reflected in significant Introductions by two contemporary Protestant scholars. Thus we have the *Introduction to the New Testament* by *Werner Georg Kümmel* (1905–1995) in the tradition of H. J. Holtzmann and A. Jülicher. On the one hand, Kümmel understands the 'science of introduction' as a 'strictly historical discipline,'[15] while on the other hand emphasizing that 'through their belonging to the canon demarcated by the early church the NT writings possess a special character . . . '.[16] It is not the scholarly methods, but the concept of the canon that is the basis for the theological character of the discipline 'Introduction to the New Testament.' For Kümmel, the concept of the canon also determined the structure of his work, in that he first discussed the narrative books (Gospels and Acts), and then the Letters and the Apocalypse. Kümmel thus represents a moderately conservative standpoint that is open to the full application of the historical–critical method for determining the historical foundation of the New Testament writings.

A comparable position is assumed by a leading Roman Catholic introduction by *A. Wikenhauser* and *J. Schmid*. On the one hand, the authors emphasize the significance of the church that received into the canon only inspired Scriptures. On the other hand, 'all introductory issues are to be investigated and answered with the tools of historical method, to the extent that this is permitted by the source materials.'[17]

---

[14] Jülicher- Fascher, *Einleitung* 6.
[15] W. G. Kümmel, *Introduction* 28.
[16] *Ibid.* 29.
[17] Wikenhauser and Schmid, *Einleitung* 3.

The ideal of a history of early Christian literature was realized by *Philipp Vielhauer* (1914–1977) in his *Geschichte der Urchristlichen Literatur* published in 1975. Vielhauer thereby took up the fundamental insight of the church historian Franz Overbeck (1837–1905), who emphasized: 'The history of a literature is located in its forms, so every real history of literature will be a history of its forms [*Formgeschichte*, literally 'form history,' usually translated 'form criticism'].'[18] Above all, Vielhauer joined the program of his teacher *Martin Dibelius* (1883–1947), who already in 1926 had published a concise *Geschichte der urchristlichen Literatur* in which early Christian literature was surveyed from a form-critical point of view and briefly analyzed. Like Dibelius, Vielhauer also followed the lead of Krüger and Wrede in ignoring the concept of canon, since a history of literature oriented to forms and genres cannot stop at the canonical boundaries, but has as its task the investigation of both extra-canonical and canonical writings of the same generic categories. Thus alongside the writings of the New Testament Vielhauer includes in his presentation discussions of the later letters (1 Clement, the Letters of Ignatius, the Letter of Polycarp, the Letter of Barnabas), the apocryphal Gospels, apocryphal Acts, and church orders (Didache). It is not the canon that determines the boundary for the material to be investigated; it is rather the case that this boundary is formed where it is recognized that early Christian forms die out and the transition to Graeco-Roman literature becomes visible.[19]

The Introduction to the New Testament by *Willi Marxsen* (1963) occupies a special position. He understands the writings of the New Testament as a record of the history of proclamation, so that the New Testament 'could . . . be described as the earliest volume of sermons in the church that has come down to us.'[20] Since this proclamation makes the claim to preach Jesus Christ to each generation with binding force, the New Testament is as such a matter of theological documents, and 'Introduction to the New Testament' is a theological discipline. It is not the concept of canon, but the claim made by the New Testament documents themselves that determines the theological character of the discipline 'Introduction to the New Testament'. Although Marxsen denies a normative function to the canon,

---

[18] Franz Overbeck, *Über die Anfänge der patristischen Literatur*, (Darmstadt: Wissenschaftliche Buchgesellschaft, 1954 [=1882]) 12.

[19] Georg Strecker acknowledges that he is committed to this position, *History of New Testament Literature* (Harrisburg, PA: Trinity Press International, 1997) 224: 'In raising questions of literary history, slighting extra-canonical writings is misguided, for historical interpretation is compelled on grounds of form and content to include this wider circle of writings in its purview.' However, on practical grounds Strecker limits his presentation to the writings of the New Testament.

[20] Marxsen, *Introduction* 282.

he restricts his treatment to the writings found in the New Testament on the grounds of their later influence [Wirkungsgeschichte]. 'The New Testament has now become the church's book.'[21] By defining the subject matter of the discipline 'Introduction to the New Testament' as the history of proclamation, he combines historical, exegetical, and hermeneutical ways of formulating the issues and broadens the range of the discipline's significance.

The American Old Testament scholar *Brevard S. Childs* shifts the concept of canon to the center of the discipline 'Introduction.' In his introduction published in 1984 he makes the concept of canon the hermeneutical and historical key to New Testament interpretation. He uses the concept of canon in an expanded sense, so that 'canon' serves to describe a comprehensive traditioning process that already begins in the New Testament and extends itself organically throughout the whole development. 'There is an organic continuity in the canon of sacred writings of the earliest stages of the scope.'[22] Such a development is by no means conceived by Childs only as a historical phenomenon, but also as a work of the exalted Lord.[23] Childs also extends this approach to the methodological plane, in that he speaks of a 'methodology of canonical exegesis,'[24] which always takes its point of departure from the canonically fixed final form of the text, and is very reserved toward the results of source analysis and form criticism on the prehistory of the text. By making the concept of canon into the historical and dogmatic key to exegesis and thereby subjecting exegetical work to a norm that transcends its own methodology, he again takes up that standpoint which the academic discipline 'Introduction to the New Testament' believed it had overcome in the 250 years of its history.

1.3 The Structure and Goal of this Introduction

How does the historical character of the discipline 'Introduction to the New Testament' relate to its subject matter, the New Testament/early Christian writings? Is it possible to combine a secular historical-literary-critical method with a concept of canon that has theological implications? The resolution of this central problem depends on how the goal of the discipline 'Introduction to the New Testament' can be attained. This goal is the illumination of *both* the historical origin of the New Testament/

---

[21] Marxsen, *Einleitung* 23. (Translator's note: the citation does not appear in the English translation from an earlier edition.)

[22] Brevard S. Childs, *The New Testament as Canon: An Introduction* (Philadelphia: Fortress Press, 1984) 21.

[23] Cf. *ibid.* 29.

[24] Cf. *ibid.* 48–53.

early Christian documents in their own contexts *and* the theological intention of these writings. When the goal is so defined, the discipline 'Introduction to the New Testament' must be understood as a strictly historical discipline which is at the same time a theological discipline. The historical dimension of introductory studies is inseparably bound up with the character of the literature under investigation. So too the theological orientation of introductory studies is a necessary consequence of the testimony of the New Testament documents themselves. They claim to declare the saving act of God in Jesus Christ as valid for and binding upon their readers. The *canonical concept* is only a later focusing and concentration of a claim already implicit within the documents themselves. It is therefore possible for one to dispense with the specific concept of the canonicity of the documents being studied without surrendering a concern for the substance of their message or negating the theological dimension of the discipline 'Introduction to the New Testament.' To be sure, even a purely historical perspective cannot regard the formation of the canon as a historical accident, since already in the pre-canonical tradition of early Christian literature a tendency toward the assumption of particular forms and their collection is discernible, and since from the very beginning the question of the appropriate understanding of the Christ event was reflected on and discussed in controversial settings that tended toward selectivity.

It is also the case that the formation of the canon is not to be conceived as an inevitable process that had the oldest traditions in its grasp. On the one hand, we know that there were very old traditions irretrievably lost, before the canonizing process could include them (including at least one letter of Paul, cf. 1 Cor. 5.9; 2 Cor. 2.4), one letter from the Pauline school (Col. 4.16), and to some extent the literary sources of the Synoptic Gospels. So too, the author of the Gospel of John had considerably more traditions available than he in fact integrated into his composition (cf. John 20.30). On the other hand, one can ask on both historical and theological grounds why it was that writings such as 2 Peter and Jude found a place in the canon, while 1 Clement and the Letters of Ignatius were not considered canonical. To be sure, the criterion of apostolicity provides a historical explanation, but such an explanation cannot pass judgment on the theological rectitude of this action. Finally is to be noted that the history of the formation of the canon makes clear that for a long time the canonical status of a whole series of early Christian writings was disputed (e.g. Hebrews, Revelation, the Catholic Letters, the Shepherd of Hermas, the Letter to the Laodiceans, the Letter of Barnabas, the Acts of Paul). It is not, however, a concept of the canon derived secondarily that is the basis for the historical and theological character of 'Introduction to the New

Testament', but only the testimony of the documents that are being studied themselves. It is not possible, in the interest of illuminating the historical and theological structures of the New Testament writings, to subordinate them to a foreign, external norm. It would make even less sense to derive the special character of the New Testament writings within early Christian literature from the concept of the canon as if this decision had no consequences for carrying out the exegetical task. Because 'canon' describes and comprises those early Christian documents that became the normative New Testament for all of Christianity, it is a historical given that the subject is important for 'Introduction to the New Testament.' Even though in principle the academic discipline 'Introduction to the New Testament' reserves the right to extend its investigation beyond the canonical boundaries, it still makes sense for 'Introduction to the New Testament' to limit its specific subject matter to the twenty-seven books of the canon, both on pragmatic grounds and due to the influence that the concept of the canon has had in history. In the church, a normative status is attributed only to these twenty-seven books, and in the broad spectrum of theology, only they play a significant role. The concept of canon determines the contemporary use of early Christian literature.

If the historical influence of the concept of canon is in itself sufficient to justify the inclusion of the concept of canon within the purview of 'Introduction to the New Testament,'[25] then certain consequences for the structure and scope of an Introduction follow. If the history of the formation of the canon has no effect on the study of the introductory issues connected with the origins of the particular documents in the New Testament, then the usual division of an Introduction into a 'General Introduction' (text, canon) and a 'Special Introduction' (the individual documents themselves) can be allowed to fall aside. The history of New Testament studies in the twentieth century also suggests such a proceeding, since for a long time both textual criticism[26] and the history of the canon have been independent academic disciplines. Throughout the New Testament writings themselves are scattered passages where issues of text criticism and the history of the canon need to be discussed, but a comprehensive treatment of the history of the New Testament canon and of New Testament text

---

[25] Thus the absolutely essential elements of the history of the formation of the canon are presented in Excursus 2 (The Collection of the Pauline Letters and the Formation of the Canon), from the perspective of the history of their influence [*Wirkungsgeschichte*].

[26] Indispensable for text criticism and the history of the New Testament text: Bruce M. Metzger, *The Text of the New Testament* (New York: Oxford University Press, 1992[3]), and Kurt and Barbara Aland, *The Text of the New Testament: An Introduction to the Critical Editions and to the Theory and Practice of Modern Textual Criticism*, tr. Eroll F. Rhodes (Grand Rapids: Wm. B. Eerdmans, 1987).

criticism abstracted from concrete significance for particular writings would not be meaningful.

The historical orientation of 'Introduction to the New Testament' suggests a *structure* that begins with the undisputed Pauline letters as the oldest writings of the New Testament. Then the second coherent category of writings is formed by the Synoptic Gospels. Acts will be treated in conjunction with the Gospel of Luke. The third interrelated block of traditions is the Deuteropauline letters, all of which claim to be from Paul himself. The Letter to the Hebrews belongs to a special category, for it was accepted into the canon as a letter of Paul, but its contents set it apart from both the undisputed Pauline letters and the Deuteropaulines. Separate treatment is appropriately reserved for those letters that are not written to a particular community and thus are known as Catholic Letters (καθολικός = 'general,' 'universal'). The Johannine literature concludes the discussion.

In the *individual chapters* the questions of authorship, place, and date of composition of each New Testament writing are discussed first. Since the New Testament documents are always integral elements of a communications process, it is necessary to reflect thoroughly on the situation of the intended readership. The literary structure of a New Testament writing must be investigated from the perspectives of form criticism, literary criticism, source analysis and the perspective of the history of traditions. Then follows the delineation of the streams of Hellenistic religion that might have influenced the composition of a New Testament document. A particular space is reserved for the presentation of the basic theological ideas of each New Testament writing. Since form and content constitute a unity, the literary structure of a document is the direct expression of the intended theological content. The theology of a New Testament writing is also of decisive significance for its understanding as a whole. 'Introduction to the New Testament' may not restrict itself to the classical issues (authorship, date, etc.), but must take into account the theological intentions of a New Testament author in order to do justice to all the other dimensions of a New Testament writing.[27]

> Historical data inevitably have an effect on the theological interpretation of a New Testament document. Historical insights, however, must not lead to theological prejudices and value judgments. Historical facticity is not simply to be identified with theological truth! Rather, the valid approach will value both history and theology, and will attempt to determine both the facts of the historical situation *and* the theological intention of the text. If a

---

[27] Cf. Kümmel, 'Einleitungswissenschaft' 480.

Letter or Gospel was in fact not written by the author attributed to it by early church tradition or by the writing itself, then this is a historical datum. It does not decide anything about the validity of the theological truth-claims made by the text, for already the earliest document of the New Testament exhibits a self-understanding that transcends being dominated by a narrow understanding of historical events (1 Thess. 2.13: 'We also constantly give thanks to God for this, that when you received the word of God that you heard from us, you accepted it not as a human word but as what it really is, God's word, which is also at work in you believers.'). Issues of historical probability do not have the final say as to whether God by the Holy Spirit may speak to people through the New Testament and call them to faith. This event is not a matter of human research and knowledge, but is in the exclusive province of the God who makes himself known in the Holy Spirit, and according to the conviction of the ancient church is valid for every document of Scripture. Insight into the historical circumstances of the writing of the New Testament documents, which, like all historical know-ledge can achieve only an approximation of what really happened, does not by itself provide a full understanding. Rather, the affirmations of the New Testament writings are referred to the self-interpretation through the Spirit, in order to be understood in all their dimensions.

The conclusion of each chapter is formed by a brief survey of the tendencies of recent study, intended to introduce the reader into the current discussion and to open further perspectives for the understanding of a New Testament document.

Thus each chapter follows the same outline: [28]

    1. Literature
    2. Author
    3. Place and Time of Composition
    4. Intended Readership
    5. Outline, Structure, Form
    6. Literary Integrity
    7. Traditions, Sources
    8. History-of-religions Standpoint
    9. Basic Theological Ideas
    10. Tendencies of Recent Research

---

[28] In cases where data is insufficient for the discussion of a particular topic, it is skipped.

2

The Letters of Paul

Comprehensive Interpretations of Pauline Theology

Bultmann, Rudolf. *Theology of the New Testament*, tr. Kendrick Grobel. New York: Charles Scribner's Sons, 1951, 185–352; Davies, W. D. *Paul and Rabbinic Judaism.* London: SPCK, 1962; Conzelmann, Hans. *An Outline of the Theology of the New Testament*, tr. John Bowden. London: SCM Press, 1969, 153–286; Bornkamm, Günther. *Paul*, tr. D. M. G. Stalker. New York: Harper & Row, 1971; Stendahl, Krister. *Paul among Jews and Gentiles and Other Essays.* Philadelphia: Fortress Press, 1976; Sanders, E. P. *Paul and Palestinian Judaism.* Philadelphia: Fortress Press, 1977; Beker, J. Christian. *Paul the Apostle.* Philadelphia: Fortress Press, 1984; Segal, Alan E. *Paul the Convert: The Apostolate and Apostasy of Saul the Pharisee.* New Haven: Yale University Press, 1990; Bassler, Jouette, ed. *Pauline Theology, Volume I: Thessalonians, Philippians, Galatians, Philemon.* Minneapolis: Fortress Press, 1991. (important collection of essays); Wright, N. T. *The Climax of the Covenant.* Minneapolis: Fortress Press, 1992. (important collection of essays); Stuhlmacher, Peter. *Biblische Theologie des Neuen Testaments* I. Göttingen: Vandenhoeck & Ruprecht, 1992, 221–392; Becker, Jürgen. *Paul: Apostle to the Gentiles*, tr. O. C. Dean, Jr. Louisville: Westminster/John Knox, 1993; Hübner, Hans. *Biblische Theologie des Neuen Testaments* II: *Die Theologie des Paulus.* Göttingen: Vandenhoeck & Ruprecht, 1993.

Anthology of Key Contributions to Pauline Research

Rengstorf, Karl H., ed. *Das Paulusbild in der neueren deutschen Forschung.* Darmstadt: Wissenschaftliche Buchgesellschaft, 1982³ (contains fundamental essays by W. Wrede, A. Schweitzer, R. Bultmann and others).

History of Pauline Research

Hübner, Hans. 'Paulusforschung seit 1945' *ANRW* 25.4. Berlin: Walter de Gruyter, 1987, 2649–2840; Merk, Otto. 'Paulus-Forschung 1936–1985', ThR 53 (1988) 1–81.

2.1 The Chronology of Paul's Life and Ministry

Rigaux, Beda. *The Letters of St. Paul*, tr. Stephen Vonickle. Chicago: Franciscan Herald Press, 1968; Suhl, Alfred. *Paulus und seine Briefe*, StNT 11. Gütersloh: Gütersloher Verlagshaus (Gerd Mohn), 1975; Hengel, Martin. *Acts and the History of Earliest Christianity*, tr. John Bowden. Philadelphia: Fortress Press, 1979; Jewett,

Robert. *A Chronology of Paul's Life*. Philadelphia: Fortress Press, 1979; Lüdemann, Gerd. *Paul, Apostle to the Gentiles. Studies in Chronology*, tr. F. Stanley Jones. Philadelphia: Fortress Press, 1984; Hyldahl, Niels. *Die paulinische Chronologie*, AthD. Leiden: E. J. Brill, 1986; Knox, John. 'On the Pauline Chronology: Buck-Taylor-Hurd Revisited,' in *The Conversation Continues: Studies in Paul and John*. (FS J. Louis Martyn), ed. Robert T. Fortna and Beverly R. Gaventa. Nashville: Abingdon, 1990, 258–274; Söding, Thomas. 'Zur Chronologie der paulinischen Briefe,' BZ 56 (1991) 31–59; Suhl, Alfred. 'Der Beginn der selbständigen Mission des Paulus,' NTS 38 (1992) 430–447; Riesner, Rainer. *Die Frühzeit des Apostels Paulus*. WUNT 71. Tübingen: J. C. B. Mohr (Paul Siebeck), 1994; Goulder, Michael. *St. Paul vs. St. Peter. A Tale of Two Missions*. Louisville: Westminster/John Knox, 1995.

The extant Pauline letters name neither the time nor place of their composition. Acts, of course, gives an extensive description of Paul's missionary work, but here too we find no indications of when or where he might have composed his various letters. Events that were important for the history of early Christianity such as the Apostolic Council or the conversion of Paul are not arranged chronologically by Luke. So too the year in which the apostle to the Gentiles was born and the date of his death can be surmised only from indirect evidence.[1] This illustrates the great difficulties in constructing a chronology of Paul's life and ministry and explains why precisely on this subject there is such great divergence in the opinions of scholars. We must therefore begin this discussion of Pauline chronology with a discussion of methodology.[2] The point from which all further considerations must proceed is the principle obvious to every historian, namely that preference is always to be given to primary sources. The usable chronological data of the authentic Pauline letters are thus always to be preferred, when they stand in tension or contradiction to other reports in the New Testament. This is not necessarily to demean the historical value of Acts, but when Acts and the undisputed Pauline letters are in conflict on chronology, it is the letters that must be followed. On the other hand, when it is possible to combine information from Acts and the letters, we then are on the most solid ground for ascertaining the Pauline chronology. When Acts is alone in reporting events in the life of Paul, we must investigate to what extent Luke has trustworthy old tradition at his disposal or whether his presentation originates from his own redactional work.

The natural beginning point for obtaining the absolute chronology of Paul's life are the few events mentioned in the New Testament that make

---

[1] On the year of his death see below 2.1.2. He was apparently born about the middle of the first decade of the first century CE. In Philemon 9 (written about 61 CE) Paul describes himself as a πρεσβύτης ('old man'); he would have been about fifty-five years old at this point in time.

[2] Cf. the methodological reflections of Hyldahl, *Chronologie* 1–17, which deserve serious consideration.

contact with dates in general world history, known either from extra-canonical authors or from archaeological discoveries. Then the relative chronology of Paul's life must be coordinated with the basis established for the absolute chronology.

2.1.1 Absolute Chronology

Two events facilitate the reconstruction of an absolute chronology of Paul's ministry: the expulsion of the Jews from Rome under Claudius (cf. Acts 18.2b) and the dates when the proconsul Gallio held office in Achaia.

The *edict of Claudius* (Suetonius, *Life of Claudius* 25: 4) reports concerning Claudius: Iudaeos impulsore Chresto assidue tumultuantis Roma expulit ('He drove the Jews out of Rome because they, incited by Chrestus, were continually disturbing the peace'). This event is dated in the ninth year of Claudius' reign (= 49 CE) by the later Christian historian Orosius (5th cent.).[3]

An earlier dating of the edict of Claudius in the year 41 CE is advocated by Lüdemann.[4] He considers the date given in Orosius as secondary and connects Claudius' edict with an event reported by Dio Cassius 60.6.6 for the year 41: 'The population of the Jews, however, had increased to the extent that their great numbers made it difficult to expel them from Rome without riots, so he did not expel them (οὐκ ἐξήλασε μέν), but let them continue to live by their own customs, except that he forbid them to assemble.' Lüdemann refers this report to the events connected with 'Chrestus,' postulating a common source used by Suetonius and Dio Cassius that had reported the expulsion of all Jews from Rome by Claudius but had been corrected by Dio Cassius, using a source that was concerned with an uproar about 'Chrestus' in a synagogue. Claudius is supposed to have forbidden the other members of the synagogue to meet together, i.e. to have withdrawn their right to assemble as a legal association. The weak point in this argument lies in the postulated common source for Dio Cassius and Suetonius, which Lüdemann then interprets to fit his theory. Furthermore, the comment of Dio Cassius that Claudius did not drive out all the Jews is not a correction of a source, but rather Dio Cassius is referring to the expulsion of the Jews from Rome by Tiberius previously mentioned in 57.18.5. Obviously οὐκ ἐξήλασε μέν in 60.6.6 is taking up the expression τοὺς πλείονας ἐξήλασεν (he drove out the majority).[5] Finally, the dating of

---

[3] Cf. Orosius, *Historia adversum paganos* 8.6.15.

[4] Cf. Lüdemann, *Chronology* 164–170.

[5] Cf. Peter Lampe, *Die stadtrömischen Christen* (see below 2.8.1) 8. For critiques of Lüdemann see also Andreas Lindemann, ZKG 92 (1981) 344–349; Jewett, *Chronology* 164–71;

Claudius' edict in 49 CE fits better the data in Acts 18.1–17, which reports the arrival of the married couple Prisca and Aquila in Corinth after they had been driven from Rome, and Paul's hearing before the proconsul Gallio.

The *Gallio inscription.* The time of office of the proconsul of Achaia Lucius Gallio mentioned in Acts 18.12 may be determined with a fair degree of precision by the letter of the emperor Claudius to the city of Delphi, since the letter was preserved in an inscription. The text dates itself with reference to the 26th acclamation of Claudius as emperor. To be sure, the 26th acclamation itself can no longer be exactly dated, but data from other inscriptions document that the 27th acclamation had already occurred by 1 August 52.[6] The letter is addressed to Gallio's successor (Gallio is mentioned in the text in the nominative case, 6th line from above, Γαλλίων)[7] and so must have been written in the summer of 52. From that it may be inferred that Gallio's time in office was from the early summer of 51 to the early summer of 52, since proconsuls of senatorial provinces normally served one year. Priscilla and Aquila arrived from Rome not long before Paul's own arrival (Acts 18.2 προσφάτως = recently), so the apostle arrived in Corinth in the year 50 CE. If one combines the information in Acts 18.11, that Paul remained in Corinth a year and a half, with the assumption that the Jews would have made their charges against Paul soon after the arrival of the new proconsul, the result is that the scene before Gallio (Acts 18.12–16) is to be dated in the summer of 51.[8]

The arrival of Paul in Corinth at the beginning of the year 50 thus provides a firm basis for calculating the relative chronology of Paul's life forwards and backwards from that point.

2.1.2 *Relative Chronology*

The events prior to Paul's arrival in Corinth must first be reconstructed. According to the account in Acts, Paul's visit to Corinth was a segment of the larger Pauline mission in Asia Minor and Greece (= the 'second missionary journey' of Acts 15.36–18.22). The tradition used by Luke

---

Traugott Holtz, *1 Thess* (see below 2.4.1) 18 note 18. Lüdemann's response, 'Das Judenedikt des Claudius (Apg 18,2),' in *Der Treue Gottes trauen* (FS G. Schneider [see below 3.6.1]) 289–298, brings no new arguments of substance. Here Lüdemann supposes that Orosius derived his chronology from Acts (cf. *ibid.* 296).

[6] Cf. Adolf Deissmann, *Paul: A Study in Social and Religious History* (New York: Harper & Brothers, 1957) 274–275; Schenke and Fischer, *Einleitung* 1.52.

[7] The best Greek text of the Gallio inscription, newly edited by A. Plassart and J. H. Oliver, is available with a German translation in Schenke and Fischer, *Einleitung* 1.50–51.

[8] This datum represents the only point on which there is consensus in the recently renewed discussion of Pauline chronology. Cf. Suhl, *Paulus* 325; Lüdemann, *Chronology* 169–70; Jewett, *Chronology* 40; Hyldahl, *Chronologie* 122.

facilitates the reconstruction of the individual stations of Paul's missionary tour. The trip first took Paul and Silas to the churches that had already been established in Syria and Cilicia (cf. Acts 15.40–41; cf. also Acts 15.23/ Gal. 1.21). Then came Derbe and Lystra (Acts 16.1) where he converted Timothy (cf. 1 Cor. 4.17). Next Paul and his coworkers journeyed through Phrygia and the Galatian country (Acts 16.6) on the way to beginning their mission in Europe. Philippi was the first station (Acts 16.11–12a; Phil. 4.15ff.), from which Paul went to Thessalonica (Acts 17.1), and subsequently via Berea to Athens (cf. Acts 17.10, 15). Then early in the year 50 Paul traveled from Athens to Corinth (cf. Acts 18.1). The major outlines of this itinerary are confirmed by Paul's letters. Paul himself reports that he established the church in Thessalonica after coming from Philippi (cf. I Thess. 2.2). Paul's stay in Athens is also documented by 1 Thess. 3.1, so that according to both Acts and 1 Thessalonians the stations on Paul's missionary tour were Philippi, Thessalonica, Athens, Corinth.[9] Paul's missionary activity as here portrayed would take about a year and a half,[10] which would bring the account near the time of the confrontation between Paul and Peter in Antioch and the Apostolic Council that had preceded it. Both events are thus to be located in the first half of the year 48 CE.

The occasion for the *Apostolic Council* was the dispute about the role of the Law in the Gentile mission (cf. Gal. 2.3–5). Paul formulates the results of the meeting in Galatians 2.9b: ἡμεῖς εἰς τὰ ἔθνη, αὐτοὶ δὲ εἰς τὴν περι-τομήν ('. . . we should go to the Gentiles and they to the circumcised'). A division of the world mission along ethnographic lines was decided upon. This division of responsibilities did not mean for Paul, however, that he must abandon the Jewish mission in his own churches (cf. 1 Cor. 9.20–22). Furthermore, it was agreed that an offering of money was to be collected by the newly formed Gentile churches for the support of the original Jerusalem church (Gal. 2.10). Paul's dialogue partners at the Apostolic Council were James the brother of Jesus, Cephas, and John son of Zebedee (cf. Gal. 2.9).

F. Hahn[11] and A. Suhl[12] date the Apostolic Council in 43/44, based on the references to the death of both James and John the sons of Zebedee in Mark

---

[9] On the persisting differences between Acts and the letters, cf. Suhl, *Paulus* 96ff.; Lüdemann, *Chronology* 13—14.

[10] Jewett, *Chronology* 96–100, points out that Paul's travels between the Apostolic Council and his arrival in Corinth could have lasted as long as three or four years. However, he also considers eighteen months as possible (cf. *ibid.* 100). The chronology presupposed here allows a maximum travel time of two years.

[11] Cf. Ferdinand Hahn, *Mission in the New Testament*, tr. F. Clarke, SBT 47 (London: SCM Press, 1965) 77–78.

[12] Cf. Suhl, *Paulus* 316ff.

10.38–39 and Acts 12.2. The latter text refers to the execution of James son of Zebedee by Herod Agrippa I (41–44). The tradition used by Luke knows nothing of the death of John son of Zebedee at the same time, however – otherwise it could hardly have used the expression Ἰάκωβον τὸν ἀδελφὸν Ἰωάννου (James the brother of John). To be sure, Mark 10.38–39 does look back on the death of both brothers, but this does not necessarily mean that John too had been killed in the time of Herod Agrippa I. Acts 12.2 and Galatians 2.9 presuppose only the death of James son of Zebedee, which speaks in favor of dating the Apostolic Council in 48.[13] It is likely that Peter left Jerusalem for a while during Herod's persecution of Christians (cf. Acts 12.18–19), but then returned to Jerusalem after Herod's death.

According to Paul's own account in Galatians 2.1–14, the *confrontation at Antioch*[14] occurred in immediate proximity to the Apostolic Council. To be sure, no explicit temporal connection for the two events is given by Paul, but the order of the narration in Galatians and Paul's line of argument both suggest that the two events happened close together. Just as Paul had previously withstood the people from James and the hypocrisy of Peter and Barnabas, so the Galatian churches must now withstand the Judaistic false teachers. This argument could only be effective if it were known by the Galatian churches that the agreements of the Apostolic Council attained only recently had already been broken by the militant Jewish Christians. Thus the confrontation in Antioch falls in the summer of 48, as Paul and Barnabas spent some time in Antioch after their return from Jerusalem (cf. Acts 15.35).

Suhl[15] places the Antioch confrontation in 47, quite distant from his dating of the Apostolic Council (44 CE). But no three year gap can be inserted between Galatians 2.10 and 2.11. G. Lüdemann regards the Antioch confrontation as the event that triggered the Apostolic Council, and thus dates

---

[13] The council is dated in 48 by e.g. Adolf v. Harnack, *The Mission and Expansion of Christianity in the First Three Centuries* (New York: G. P. Putnam & Sons, 1908) 1.60–61; Kümmel, *Introduction* 255; Leonhard Goppelt, *Apostolic and Post-Apostolic Times*, tr. Robert A. Guelich (New York: Harper & Row, 1962) 222; Bornkamm, *Paul* 31; Hans Conzelmann, *History of Primitive Christianity*, tr. John E. Steely (Nashville and New York: Abingdon Press, 1973) 32; Jürgen Roloff, *Neues Testament* (Neukirchen: Neukirchener Verlag 1982³) 49. Besides Hahn and Suhl, others who vote for 44 as the date of the council are Ph. Vielhauer, *Urchristliche Literatur* 78; Marxsen, *Introduction* 22; and Wilhelm Schneemelcher, *Das Urchristentum* (Stuttgart: Kohlhammer, 1981) 53 (though cf. already Eduard Schwartz, *Gesammelte Schriften* 5, Berlin: Walter de Gruyter, 1963 [= 1904] 131).

[14] Cf. here Andreas Wechsler, *Geschichtsbild und Apostelstreit. Eine forschungsgeschichtliche und exegetische Studie über den antiochenischen Zwischenfall (Gal. 2,11–14)*. BZNW 62 (Berlin: Walter de Gruyter, 1991).

[15] Cf. Suhl, *Paulus und seine Briefe* 322–323.

it earlier.[16] The order of these events in the text of Galatians is clearly against such an assumption; the confrontation at Antioch belongs to the problems that resulted from the Apostolic Council.

In their portrayal of Paul's work from his conversion to the Apostolic Council, Acts and the undisputed Pauline letters diverge considerably. In Galatians 1.6–2.14 Paul gives a survey of his missionary activity up to the time of the Apostolic Council. He first emphasizes in Gal. 1.17 that after his conversion he did not go to Jerusalem, but to Arabia, and then returned to Damascus.[17] With this comment the apostle wants to underscore his independence from the earliest church in Jerusalem, so that the temporal connections in Galatians 1.18 (ἔπειτα μετὰ ἔτη τρία = 'three years later') probably refer to his conversion. It was only after this relatively long period of time that Paul came to Jerusalem, in order to stay fifteen days with Peter and also to see James the Lord's brother. After the first visit to Jerusalem Paul spent considerable time in Syria and Cilicia, far removed from Jerusalem, and then 'afterwards, fourteen years later' (Gal. 2.1 ἔπειτα διὰ δεκατεσσάρων ἐτῶν) in the company of Barnabas and Titus made a second visit to Jerusalem for the Apostolic Council.

The temporal expression in Galatians 2.1 raises the question of the reference point for 'after fourteen years.' Paul uses the adverb ἔπειτα ('afterwards, following, then') in series and lists (cf. 1 Thess. 4.17; 1 Cor. 15.5, 6, 7, 23, 46). It has a predominately temporal sense (1 Cor. 12.28 is an exception), and connects to the preceding. There are three possibilities for understanding Galatians 2.1: (a) the reference point is the conversion of Paul;[18] (b) it connects directly to the immediately preceding, i.e. the apostle's trip to Syria and Cilicia;[19] (c) the reference point is the first visit to Jerusalem.[20] The first possibility is to be rejected, because it subsumes the three years of Galatians 1.18 under the fourteen years of Galatians 2.1. Since Paul designates two periods of time, there is no reason to suppose that the first is then included in the second.[21] As for the second possibility, if ἔπειτα ('then,' 'later') is intended to make a close connection with what

---

[16] Cf. Lüdemann, Chronology 57–59, 75ff., Theodor Zahn, *Der Brief des Paulus an die Galater*, KNT 9 (Leipzig: Deichert, 1922³) 112–113, and others who place the confrontation at Antioch before the Apostolic Council. On this cf. Wechsler, *Geschichtsbild* 153ff.

[17] This early mission of Paul is also indicated by Paul's flight from the soldiers of the Ethnarch of the Nabatean King Aretas IV (ca. 9 BCE–38–39 CE) mentioned in 2 Corinthians 11.32–33; on the problems with this cf. Suhl, *Paulus und seine Briefe* 314–315; A. Knauf, 'Zum Ethnarchen des Aretas 2Kor 11,32,' ZNW 74 (1983) 145–147.

[18] So Suhl, *Paulus und seine Briefe* 46ff.

[19] This position is advocated by Lüdemann, *Chronology* 61–63.

[20] So for example Traugott Holtz, *1 Thess* (see below 2.4.1) 19.

[21] For a critique of Suhl cf. especially Lüdemann, *Chronology* 61–63.

immediately precedes, in Galatians 1.18 with the return to Damascus and in 2.1 with the trip to Syria and Cilicia (Gal. 1.21), then the Pauline line of argument loses its persuasive power. But the temporal data in Galatians 1.18 are obviously intended to support the apostle's demonstration of his independence, so that their reference point is not to the return to Damascus (relatively unimportant in this context), but to the call and commissioning of Paul. So too in Galatians 2.1, ἔπειτα does not count from the immediately preceding events, but rather refers to the first visit to Jerusalem. Paul confirms this himself by his statement that he 'went up again' (πάλιν ἀνέβην) to Jerusalem. The designation of the temporal period with the preposition διά instead of μετά is noticeable (cf. previously Gal. 1.18). Even if διά emphasizes the duration of the period of time more than μετά or πρό, still no fundamental difference in meaning can be derived from this distinction.

Since in the ancient manner of counting the year in progress is reckoned as a full year, Paul's activities from his conversion to the Apostolic Council may be charted as follows: Prior to the Apostolic Council in the spring of 48 Paul had engaged in missionary work in Syria and Cilicia for about thirteen years. Paul's first visit in Jerusalem would then have occurred in 35. The sojourn in Arabia then probably was in 34, so that between his conversion in 33 and the first visit to Jerusalem there was a period of about two years. The year 33 for the call and commissioning of Paul in Damascus fits well with the presumed date for the death of Jesus, the 14th of Nisan (7 April) of the year 30.[22] Two arguments may be presented for this date for the crucifixion: (1) Both the astronomical calculations and the traditions about the date of Jesus' death speak in favor of accepting the view that in 30 CE the 14th of Nisan fell on a Friday. (2) According to Luke 3.1–2, John the Baptist began his public ministry in the year 27/28. This datum would also signal the beginning of the public ministry of Jesus, which lasted about two or three years. A period of about three years between the crucifixion of Jesus and the conversion of Paul can be inferred from the history of the early Christian mission, since Paul's activity as a persecutor presupposes that Christianity had already experienced a significant expansion.

The central problem of Pauline chronology consists of the contradictions between the statements of Galatians 1–2 and testimony of Acts. In Galatians 1.17 Paul insists that after his conversion at Damascus he had not gone immediately to Jerusalem, but according to Acts 9.26 he does go directly to Jerusalem after his flight from Damascus. This portrayal of events corresponds to Lucan ecclesiology, for the evangelist is interested in

---

[22] For the basic evidence cf. August Strobel, 'Der Termin des Todes Jesu,' ZNW 51 (1960) 69–101.

the unity of the developing church, which is symbolized by Paul's immediately making contact with the Jerusalem apostles.[23] In Galatians 1.18 Paul reports only one trip to Jerusalem before the Council (11.27–30). Here too, the apostle's own testimony is to be followed, especially since the second trip to Jerusalem fits in so well with Luke's own theology. In Acts 11.27–30 Luke edits individual units of tradition into his own composition in order to emphasize the continuity of salvation history and the unity of the church. Since in Acts 11.19–26 he had just reported the founding of the important Antioch church, he immediately adds a story depicting its contact with the original church in Jerusalem.[24] For Luke, the various trips of Paul to Jerusalem are a compositional means of illustrating the spread of the gospel in the world. They stand in the service of his ecclesiology and facilitate his use of a wide range of traditional material within his own editorial framework. For Luke, the one great journey of Jesus to Jerusalem in the Gospel (cf. Luke 9.51–19.27), the five trips by Paul, missionary to the Gentiles, to Jerusalem (Acts 9.26; 11.27–30; 15.2, 4; 18.22; 21.15), and the procession of the martyr Paul to Rome comprise a unity. In terms of actual history, however, Paul's own testimony that he was in Jerusalem only three times as a Christian missionary is undoubtedly correct.

Numerous problems are connected with the *first missionary journey* of Paul in Acts 13–14. While in Galatians 1.21 Paul speaks of missionary activity prior to the Apostolic Council only in the regions of Syria and Cilicia, Acts goes beyond this by reporting missionary work on Cyprus and in the regions of Pamphylia, Pisidia, and Lycaonia in Asia Minor. Is the 'first missionary journey' then only a matter of a Lucan construction of a 'model mission?'[25] This question cannot be answered with a clear 'yes' or 'no.' While it is true that especially Acts' portrayal of a mission in Pamphylia, Pisidia, and Lycaonia is difficult to harmonize with the statement of Galatians 1.21,[26] it is also true that in this passage Paul is not giving an exhaustive list of the individual stations of his mission, but only emphasizing his independence from Jerusalem. Furthermore, the Lucan account in Acts 13–14 contains numerous traditions that speak for the historicity of the 'first missionary journey.'[27] Differently than in the later

---

[23] Cf. Jürgen Roloff, *Apostelgeschichte* (see below 4.1) 154.

[24] For analysis cf. Georg Strecker, 'Die sogenannte Zweite Jerusalemreise des Paulus (Act. 11, 27–30),' in *Eschaton und Historie*, ed. G. Strecker (Göttingen: Vandenhoeck & Ruprecht, 1979) 132–141.

[25] So Hans Conzelmann, *Acts* (see below 4.1) xlii.

[26] Cf. Martin Hengel, 'The Origins of the Christian Mission,' in *Between Jesus and Paul*, tr. John Bowden (Philadelphia: Fortress Press, 1983) 48–64, 50 note 16, who indicates that Syria and Cilicia (including Tarsus) formed one Roman province at the time of Paul.

[27] Cf. Roloff, *Apostelgeschichte* (see below 4.1) 194ff.

missionary trips, Paul appears here merely as a missionary commissioned by the Antioch church who is still a subordinate of his associate Barnabas (cf. especially Acts 14.12). In addition, it is Antioch and not Jerusalem that is both the point of origin and the place to which this first significant missionary trip returns, which does not correspond to Luke's intention in the composition of the other missionary journeys. One may then assume that there was a Pauline mission in Syria and Cilicia that included Cyprus and south Galatia prior to the Apostolic Council, even though the account in Acts and Paul's own statements in Galatians 1.21 may not be completely reconciled.

Ph. Vielhauer and A. Suhl combine their early dating of the Apostolic Council with the assumption that the mission of Paul on Cyprus and in south Galatia took place between the Apostolic Council and the confrontation in Antioch.[28] But the 'first missionary journey' does not belong to the results of the Apostolic Council but is its presupposition. The issue of how Jewish and Gentile Christians could live together was first raised by organized and authorized missionary work.

According to G. Lüdemann, there was also an early mission of Paul in Europe prior to the Apostolic Council that is not reported in Acts.[29] In addition to the early dating of the Claudius edict, Lüdemann also presents Acts 18.1–17 as evidence, according to which vv. 1–8 are supposed to refer to Paul's first visit to Corinth within the framework of an early mission to Greece in the year 41 CE, but vv. 12–17 are assigned to Paul's third visit to Corinth in 51. The expression ἐν ἀρχῇ τοῦ εὐαγγελίου (NRSV 'in the early days of the gospel') in Philippians 4.15, translated by Lüdemann as 'in the beginning of my proclamation of the gospel,'[30] is also taken to refer to an early mission in Greece at the beginning of Paul's missionary career. So too, the serious differences between the eschatological statements of 1 Thessalonians 4.13–18 and 1 Corinthians 15.51ff. are in Lüdemann's view more easily understood if 1 Thessalonians is dated in the year 41 and interpreted as evidence for Paul's early mission in Europe.

To begin with, the dating of the Claudius edict in 41 is problematic in itself (see above), but there are also other objections to Lüdemann's hypothesis: (1.) Why does Paul not mention an earlier independent mission in Europe in Galatians 1? Would this not have been additional evidence of his independence from the Jerusalem church? (2.) The different synagogue leaders mentioned in Acts 18.8 and 17 are not evidence for Lüdemann's view, but are necessitated by the situation: since v. 8 explicitly refers to

---

[28] Cf. Vielhauer, *Urchristliche Literatur* 76ff.; Suhl, *Paulus und seine Briefe* 43ff.
[29] Cf. Lüdemann, *Chronology* 157–58.
[30] *Ibid.* 106.

the conversion of Crispus (cf. 1 Cor. 1.14), the following reference to the 'synagogue ruler' must be a different person. (3.) The expression ἐν ἀρχῇ τοῦ εὐαγγελίου in Philippians 4.15 hardly refers to the beginning of the Pauline mission, since in Lüdemann's chronology the supposed early European mission would have been preceded by missionary activity in Syria, Cilicia and Galatia. (4.) The acknowledged differences between 1 Thessalonians 4.13–18 and 1 Corinthians 15.51 ff. may be explained without difficulty if 1 Thessalonians is dated in 50 CE (see below 2.4.3) and there are thus four years between the composition of the two letters.

As we have taken the Gallio scene as providing a relatively sure basis for dating the main stations of Paul's missionary journeys back to his conversion, so we may now proceed from the fixed chronological point of Paul's stay in Corinth as pictured in Acts 18.1–17 to construct the chronology for the events of the Pauline mission that happened after this. We already meet big problems, however, in the summarized travel narrative of Acts 18.18–23. This report states that Paul spent several days in Corinth, after which he sailed for Syria. In Ephesus, he leaves behind the married couple Priscilla and Aquila who had accompanied him, engaged the Jews in the synagogue in discussion, but in order to continue his journey declined the opportunity they presented for further mission work in Ephesus.

Although Acts 18.18 had designated Syria as Paul's real destination for this trip, in Acts 18.22 he lands at Caesarea, goes up (ἀναβάς is regularly used for going to Jerusalem), and then proceeds on from Jerusalem to Antioch.[31] The stations on this journey that come after the move of Priscilla and Aquila to Corinth are not confirmed by Paul's own letters. Nor can satisfactory explanations be found either for this trip's course of events or for its motivation. Why did Paul want to go to Antioch in the middle of his successful missionary work in Macedonia and Asia Minor? Finally, there is no explanation for the landing at Caesarea and the visit to Jerusalem, for according to Acts 18.18 Syria, and according to 18.22 Antioch, is the trip's real destination. To attempt to explain the landing at Caesarea as a result of unfavorable winds[32] is scarcely more than an embarrassed effort to provide some sort of explanation. Furthermore, the fourth visit of Paul to Jerusalem (in Luke's enumeration) can hardly be

---

[31] For the analysis of Acts 18.18–23 cf. especially Alfons Weiser, *Apostelgeschichte* (see below 4.1) 2.496ff. The separation of redaction and tradition results in the following picture: vv. 18a–c, 19a, 21b–23 probably contain tradition elements, while vv. 18d, 19b–21a correspond to Luke's own picture of Paul.

[32] So for example Ernst Haenchen, Acts (see below 4.1) 547; Jürgen Roloff, *Apostelgeschichte* (see below 4.1) 276.

considered historical,[33] since it conflicts with statements in the undisputed Pauline letters. But what would be the justification for striking Jerusalem from 18.22 and considering Caesarea and Antioch still to be original? On the other hand, the pre-Lucan tradition spoke of a trip by the apostle to Antioch, from which he left for Ephesus, visiting the Galatian country and Phrygia en route. After all attempts to fit the traditions worked over in Acts 18.18–23 into another trip to Jerusalem have failed,[34] we must be satisfied with the insight that according to the tradition used by Luke, after staying a while in Corinth Paul first returned to Antioch, and from there left again for Ephesus. While the data in this tradition may have some claim to be considered historical, a visit to Jerusalem on this trip remains excluded.

The reconstruction of Paul's mission in Ephesus is burdened with less uncertainty (Acts 19). The trips described in Acts 18.18–23 would occupy the time from the summer of 51 to the spring of 52, after which Paul remained in Ephesus about two years and nine months (cf. Acts 19.8, 10; 20.31), from the summer of 52 to the spring of 55. Then Paul left Ephesus for the tour through Macedonia and Achaia to raise money for the collection to be taken to Jerusalem. According to Acts 19.21 and 1 Corinthians 16.5 Paul intended to go to Corinth through Macedonia. From Acts 20.1–3 one can also see Corinth as the destination, where the apostle probably arrived at the beginning of 56 CE and stayed three months (cf. Acts 20.3). Originally Paul intended to sail by ship directly to Syria. This plan was thwarted by Jews, however, so that he had to go back through Macedonia. This data from Acts 20.3 stand in tension with Romans 15.25, where Paul announces his return to Jerusalem in order to deliver the collection. But Romans 15.25 does not speak of a direct Corinth–Jerusalem trip, so that it is not necessary to find a conflict here between Acts and Paul's letter. According to Acts 20.6 Paul traveled from Corinth to Philippi, then to Troas, then via Assos to Miletus. From there the apostle continued his trip to Caesarea by ship, in order to reach Jerusalem by Pentecost of 56 CE (cf. Acts 20.16).

Decisive for the later chronology is the date of the replacement of the procurator Felix by Festus reported in Acts 24.27. According to Acts 24.10 Felix had already been procurator for several years, and Paul had already been in custody for two years when the change of procurators took place. Felix probably began his administration in the year 52/53 (cf. Josephus, *War* 2.247),[35] but the year of his leaving office is disputed (55[36] or 58 CE).

---

[33] Cf. Weiser, *Apostelgeschichte* 2.502; Roloff, *Apostelgeschichte* 277.

[34] Cf. Weiser, *Apostelgeschichte* 2.495–502.

[35] Cf. Peter Schäfer, *Geschichte der Juden in der Antike* (Neukirchen: Neukirchener Verlag, 1983) 131.   [36] So Lüdemann, *Chronology* 172 n. 104, 192–93.

Josephus (*War* 2.250–270) places the events connected with Felix in the reign of Nero. Nero became emperor in October of 54, so all the events mentioned by Josephus would have had to have occurred in a rather short time if he left office in 55.[37] It is thus better to proceed on the basis that Felix left office in 58,[38] which also fits in well with Acts 24.1, since the high priest Ananias mentioned there was in office from 47 to 59.[39] Since during his hearing before the procurator Festus Paul appealed to Caesar (cf. Acts 25.11), he was probably sent to Rome the same year (58) in a prisoner transport under the command of a centurion (cf. Acts 27.1–28.16).[40] If the trip to Rome fell in the winter of 58/59, then Paul would have arrived in the capital of the world in the spring of 59. According to Acts 28.30 Paul could move about with some freedom, and he preached two years in his residence without hindrance. The year of Paul's death is unknown, but it may be assumed that he died as a martyr in Rome in the persecution of Christians under Nero in 64 CE (cf. 1 Clement 5.5–7).

From the preceding considerations the following *Chronology of Paul's Ministry* may be derived:

Death of Jesus	30
Conversion of Paul	33
Apostolic Council	48
	(spring)
Confrontation in Antioch	48
	(summer)
Paul in Corinth	50/51
Gallio in Corinth	51/52
Trip to Antioch	51/52
Stay in Ephesus	52–54/55
Last stay in Corinth	55/56
Arrival in Jerusalem	spring 56

---

[37] Cf. the thorough discussion of all related problems by Jewett, *Chronology* 40–44.

[38] Cf. S. Safrai and M. Stern, *The Jewish People in the First Century*, CRINT 1/1 (Philadelphia: Fortress Press, 1974) 74–76. Felix entered office in 52/53, so ten years are available for him and Festus together, since in 62 Albinus was already in the procurator's office (cf. Josephus *War* 6.301ff.). It may be inferred from Josephus' delineation (*War* 2.247–276) and Acts 24.10 that Felix was procurator the major part of this period.

[39] Cf. Emil Schürer, *The History of the Jewish People in the Age of Jesus Christ*, rev. and ed. Geza Vermes, Fergus Millar, and Matthew Black (Edinburgh: T. & T. Clark, 1979) 2.231.

[40] Heinz Warnecke, *Die tatsächliche Romfahrt des Paulus*, BS 127 (Stuttgart: Katholisches Bibelwerk, 1987) does not identify the island named Μελίτη in Acts 28.1 with Malta but thinks the place where Paul's boat was wrecked is to be sought off a peninsula of the west Greek island of Cephallenia. For a justified critique of this thesis cf. Jürgen Wehnert, 'Gestrandet. Zu einer neuen These über den Schiffbruch des Apostels Paulus auf dem Wege nach Rom (Apg 27–28),' ZThK 87 (1990) 67–99 (reply by Alfred Suhl, 'Gestrandet! Bemerkungen zum Streit über die Romfahrt des Paulus,' ZThK 88 [1991] 1–28).

Change of office Felix/Festus	58
Arrival in Rome	59
Death of Paul	64

The establishment of this chronology merely creates the framework within which the letters written by Paul during his missionary activity may be dated. The discussion of the date of each letter included in the sections below devoted to each letter.

2.2 The Pauline School

Literature

Conzelmann, Hans. 'Paulus und die Weisheit', in *Theologie als Schriftauslegung*, ed. H. Conzelmann. BEvTh 65. Munich: Chr. Kaiser Verlag, 1974, 177–190; Ludwig, Helga. *Der Verfasser des Kolosserbriefes* (1974; see below 5.2.1) 201–229; Conzelmann, Hans. 'Die Schule des Paulus,' in *Theologia Crucis – Signum Crucis* (FS Erich Dinkler) ed. Carl Andresen and Günter Klein. Tübingen: J. C. B. Mohr (Paul Siebeck), 1979, 85–96.

The theological and historical complexity of Paul's life and thought can only be rightly apprehended when it is thought of as embedded within the tradition of the Pauline school. There is no doubt that Paul was the outstanding theologian of his time, who went his own way in developing a new compelling theology that was widely influential. At the same time, he both came out of a particular school tradition and founded a school of thought himself, from which both the undisputed and the Deuteropauline letters became different branches.[41]

2.2.1 The Pauline School Tradition

Paul himself passed through a particular school tradition. In Philippians 3.5–6 he emphasizes that as a Pharisee he had been blameless with regard to the Law. According to Galatians 1.14 he surpassed his contemporaries in the study of the Law, which in any case points to some sort of academic education as a Pharisee.[42] According to Acts 22.3 Paul received his education in Jerusalem from the Pharisee Gamaliel I, a descendent of Hillel, who was active as a respected scribal leader ca. 25–50 CE. Against the historicity

---

[41] So far as I know, the first one to speak of a 'Pauline school' was Heinrich J. Holtzmann, Die *Pastoralbriefe* (see below 5.5.2) 117.

[42] On this cf. Martin Hengel, *The Pre-Christian Paul*, tr. John Bowden. (Philadelphia: Trinity Press International, 1991); Karl W. Niebuhr, *Heidenapostel aus Israel*, WUNT 62 (Tübingen: J. C. B. Mohr [Paul Siebeck] 1992).

of this account it is objected that Paul himself never refers to his education in Jerusalem and that Galatians 1.22 excludes a residence of the Pharisee Paul in Jerusalem. However, Pharisaic schools outside Jerusalem are not evidenced before 70 CE, so that a thorough education in the Torah for a Pharisaic student was obviously only possible in Jerusalem. The presence in Paul's writings of materials typical of a Hellenistic education is no refutation of this, since Hellenistic materials had been an element of education in Jewish schools since the third century BCE.[43]

After his conversion Paul worked long years as a coworker of the church in Antioch. Acts 13.1 mentions others who worked alongside Paul in Antioch as prophets and teachers: Barnabas, Simeon Niger, Lucius of Cyrene, and a certain Manaen who had been a fellow student with Herod the tetrarch. It was probably in Antioch that Paul himself was introduced to the basic elements of the Christian faith. The apostle emphasizes the importance of the delivered tradition for his own theology (1 Cor. 11.23a; 15.3a). Paul's close connection with previous tradition is documented by his incorporation of eucharistic traditions (cf. 1 Cor. 11.23b–25), baptismal traditions (cf. 1 Cor. 1.30; 6.11; 12.13; 2 Cor. 1.21–22; Gal. 3.26–28; Rom. 3.25; 4.25; 6.3–4), the integration of elements of christological traditions (cf. Rom. 1.3b–4a), and the use of early Christian hymns (cf. Phil. 2.6–11), which at the same time lets us see that to a considerable extent he wants his theology to be understood as the exposition of this tradition.[44]

2.2.2 *The School Founded by Paul*

Before beginning his own missionary work Paul was shaped and influenced by school traditions in a two-fold manner, so that the founding of his own school tradition was merely being consistent with his previous experience. Several observations point to the existence of such a school:

(a) To a considerable extent, the Pauline mission was carried and shaped by the presence of several *coworkers*.[45] The undisputed Pauline letters mention about forty persons who are to be reckoned among the number of Paul's coworkers. The inner circle of this group was at first comprised of

---

[43] Cf. Martin Hengel, *Judaism and Hellenism*, tr. John Bowden. (London: SCM Press, 1974) 1.65ff.; Henry A. Fischel, *Rabbinic Literature and Graeco-Roman Philosophy*. (Leiden: E. J. Brill, 1973).

[44] That Paul worked in Antioch as a coworker in the mission based there by no means implies that most of the pre-Pauline traditions found in Paul's letters also originated in Antioch, contra Peter Stuhlmacher, *Romans* (see below 2.8.1) 22–25; Jürgen Becker, *Paul* (see above 2) 125ff.

[45] Here the basic work is Wolf-Henning Ollrog, *Paulus und seine Mitarbeiter*, WMANT 50 (Neukirchen: Neukirchener Verlag, 1979); in addition cf. Reinhold Reck, *Kommunikation und Gemeindeaufbau. Eine Studie zu Entstehung, Leben und Wachstum paulinischer Gemeinden in den Kommunikationsstrukturen der Antike*, SBB 22 (Stuttgart: Katholisches Bibelwerk, 1991).

Barnabas, then at the beginning of his independent mission Silas and Timothy, and then later, Titus. Silas (1 Thess. 1.1) and Timothy (1 Thess. 1.1; 2 Cor. 1.1; Phil. 1.1; Phlm. 1.1) functioned as co-senders of particular letters (cf. also Sosthenes in 1 Cor. 1.1), which documents their sharing the responsibility for the work in different Pauline churches. In particular, both Timothy and Titus emerge as independent missionaries, dispatched by Paul to resolve problems in the mission churches (cf. 1 Cor. 4.17; 2 Cor. 8). There were also missionaries independent of Paul with whom the apostle occasionally cooperated in joint projects, among whom may be mentioned especially Apollos (cf. 1 Cor. 1–4) and the Christian married couple Priscilla and Aquila (cf. 1 Cor. 16.19; Rom. 16.3–4).

Most of those mentioned in Paul's letters as coworkers were commissioned by various churches. They came from the churches founded by Paul and then participated in the Pauline mission as delegates of these churches (e.g. Erastus, Gaius, Aristarchus, Sosipater, Jason, Epaphras and Epaphroditus). They maintained their relationship with their home churches, supported Paul's work in many ways, and conducted their own missionary work in proximity to the churches founded by Paul. The large number of such coworkers sent forth by the churches has a causal connection with the new missionary methods inaugurated by Paul. He did not further extend the kind of missionary journeys that had been practiced previously, but developed an independent *missionary center*. While other missionaries or early Christian prophets wandered from place to place, Paul attempted to found a series of stable churches in the provincial capitals. He stayed with each until it could stand on its own feet and did not need his own presence any longer. From this central church as a missionary center, there grew independent congregations that for their part became the basis for further Pauline missions and undertook missionary work on their own responsibility (cf. 1 Thess. 1.6–8). This hardly means that within this large circle of coworkers Paul himself will have been limited to purely managerial and organizational concerns. We must rather presuppose an intensive theological work, especially within the inner circle of his colleagues.[46]

(b) This supposition is confirmed by the presence within the Pauline letters of texts that stand out from the letter by their particular form, their theology, and their position. Thus 1 Cor. 13 seems to have only a rather loose connection with its particular context; the transition from 1 Cor. 12.31 to 14.1 is seamless.[47] The content also shows distinctive features, for

---

[46] On this cf. Ludwig, *Der Verfasser des Kolosserbriefes*, 210ff.

[47] Cf. Hans Conzelmann, *1 Corinthians* (see below 2.5.1) 217ff.

in this section the charismatic gifts of faith, hope, and love stand above all other gifts and graces. First Corinthians 13 was already conceived before the composition of 1 Corinthians; it is an evidence of the work of the Pauline school. Comparable texts are found in 1 Corinthians 1.18ff.; 2.6ff.; 10.1ff.; 2 Cor. 3.7ff.; Rom. 1.18ff.; 7.7ff. All these texts are distinguished by their unpolemical character, their thematic tightness, and, from the perspective of the history of traditions, their rootedness in Hellenistic Judaism. Their proximity to Wisdom literature also suggests that Paul here draws upon materials from his pre-Christian time.[48]

(c) The *Deuteropaulines* (Colossians, Ephesians, 2 Thessalonians, the Pastorals)[49] specifically confirm the existence of a Pauline school that endured beyond the death of the apostle himself. This literary and theological bequest from four students of Paul clarifies for us how the inheritance of Pauline theology was elaborated and applied in changed situations. One notable feature is that in all the Deuteropaulines the specific Pauline doctrine of justification found in Galatians and Romans recedes into the background.[50] Also, the apocalyptic motifs in Christology decline in importance, and a realized eschatology becomes dominant. The central elements become those of church discipline and Christian ethics that have emerged as issues due to the changed situation of the church (the appearance of heretical teachers, coming to terms with the diminishing expectation of the parousia). In this situation, Paul as the suffering apostle (Colossians, Ephesians, and 2 Timothy are all represented as prison letters) becomes *the* authority of the period of beginnings, when the church was founded. His students appealed to Paul as the authority, and attempted to elaborate the meaning of his theology under changed conditions. To be sure, the Pastorals diverge from authentic Pauline theology in essential points, but one can nonetheless perceive familiarity with the apostle's own thinking. In particular, the author of Colossians is strongly influenced by the Pauline school tradition, especially by the letter to the Romans. He seems to have learned the basic themes of Pauline theology within the Pauline school, and then to have developed them independently and appropriately to respond to the challenges of his own time.

Ephesus presents itself as a likely candidate for the setting of the Pauline school.[51] This city, influenced by many cultural streams (the Artemis

---

[48] Cf. Conzelmann, 'Paulus' 179; for a critique of Conzelmann's thesis of a Pauline school see Ollrog, *Paulus* 115–118.

[49] Peter Müller, *Anfänge der Paulusschule* (see below 5) 270–320, limits the phenomenon of a Pauline school to the Pastorals.

[50] On this cf. Ulrich Luz, 'Rechtfertigung bei den Paulusschülern,' in *Rechtfertigung* (FS Ernst Käsemann), ed. J. Friedrich et al. (Tübingen: J. C. B. Mohr [Paul Siebeck], 1976) 365–383.

[51] Cf. Conzelmann, 'Paulus' 179.

temple, mystery religions, an important Jewish community, the emperor cult, Hellenistic philosophy) was the center of the early Christian mission.[52] This was the location of the work of Priscilla and Aquila (cf. Acts 18.19–21; 1 Cor. 16.19), the Alexandrian Apollos (cf. Acts 18.24–28; 1 Cor. 16.12), and of Paul himself from the summer of 52 until the spring of 55. Paul spent a longer time here than in any other city, gathered a large staff of coworkers around himself, preached two years in the lecture hall of the rhetorician Tyrannus (according to Acts 19.9–10). Not only was 1 Corinthians written in Ephesus, but probably some of the Deuteropauline letters as well (Colossians, Ephesians [?], the Pastorals).

The Pauline letters are part of a comprehensive *communications process* that occurred between the apostle, his coworker-students, and the various missionary congregations. Paul presented his coworkers and churches with resolutions for their disputed questions, corrective theological reflections, and ethical instructions, while at the same time being strongly influenced by his coworkers and the changing situations in the churches. In conclusion, it should be noted that the assumption of a Pauline school gives us insight into the process of the formation of theology, as it is mirrored in the Pauline letters where argumentation conditioned by particular situations, is woven together with general instruction and foundational tradition.

2.3 Ancient Letters

2.3.1. *The Genre of the Ancient Letter*

Deissmann, Adolf. *Light from the Ancient East*, tr. L. M. R. Strachan. London: Hodder & Stoughton, 1911; Koskenniemi, Heikki. *Studien zu Idee und Phraseologie des griechischen Briefes bis 400 n. Chr.* AASF B 102,2. Helsinki: Suomalainen Tiedeakatemia, 1956; Thraede, Klaus. *Grundzüge griechisch-römischer Brieftopik.* Zetemata 48. Munich: C. H. Beck, 1970; Doty, William G. *Letters in Primitive Christianity.* Philadelphia: Fortress Press, 1973; Stowers, Stanley K. *Letter Writing in Greco-Roman Antiquity.* Philadelphia: Westminster Press, 1986; White. L. John. *Light from Ancient Letters.* Philadelphia: Fortress Press, 1986; Malherbe, Abraham J. *Ancient Epistolary Theorists.* Atlanta: Scholars Press, 1988; Probst, Hermann. *Paulus und der Brief.* WUNT 2.45. Tübingen: J. C. B. Mohr (Paul Siebeck), 1991; Strecker, Georg. *History of New Testament Literature* (see above 1.2) 44–68.

In this century the understanding of the form of the epistolary literature in the New Testament has been essentially determined by A. Deissmann's

---

[52] On Ephesus, cf. especially Winfried Elliger, *Ephesos. Geschichte einer antiken Weltstadt* (Stuttgart: Verlag Katholisches Bibelwerk, 1985).

distinction between 'letter' and 'epistle.' Deissmann saw the ancient letter as a rather unliterary form that served as 'a means of communication between persons who were separated from each other.'[53] In contrast, the epistle was a literary compositional form, 'a species of literature, just like the dialogue, the oration, or the drama.'[54] 'The letter is a piece of life, the epistle is a product of literary art.'[55] Deissmann classifies Paul's letters as real, unliterary letters, but describes the Catholic Epistles (James, Peter, Jude), the Epistle to the Hebrews, and Revelation as epistles. The alternative 'unliterary letter/literary epistle' must be regarded as overdrawn, for so stated it is inappropriate both for ancient letters in general and New Testament letters in particular. The Pauline letters manifest an outline that has been thought through in advance, and except for Philemon are much longer than typical ancient letters. They were written to be read in worship and thus have a certain public character. Furthermore, Paul often makes use of literary compositional forms in his letters. Some elements of Pauline argumentation are antitheses, typologies, comparisons, irony, similitudes, logical chains, inclusions, digressions, chiasmus, sentences, examples, catalogues of vices, peristasis catalogues, citations from the LXX, words of the Lord, interposed questions, supposed objections of opponents, evaluative address, and several others.[56] Finally, we may note that the letters to the Galatians and to Philemon manifest a rhetorical structure, so that his letters may be classified somewhere in the literary spectrum in terms of both form and content.

Ancient letters, including those of Paul, were a form of communication in which the communication partners were separated in time and space. The letter served as substitute for face to face communication (cf. Seneca, *Epistles* 75). The author of the letter takes from his or her repertoire of literary forms of expression whatever seems to serve best the kind of communication being attempted.[57] There is a relationship of interdependence

---

[53] Deissmann, *Light* 194.

[54] *Ibid.* 229.

[55] *Ibid.* 230.

[56] Cf. Rudolf Bultmann, *Der Stil der paulinischen Predigt und die kynisch-stoische Diatribe*, FRLANT 13 (Göttingen: Vandenhoeck & Ruprecht, 1910 [= 1985]); Stanley K. Stowers, *The Diatribe and Paul's Letter to the Romans*, SBL.DS 57 (Chico: Scholars Press, 1981); Folker Siegert, *Argumentation bei Paulus gezeigt an Röm 9–11*, WUNT 34 (Tübingen: J. C. B. Mohr [Paul Siebeck], 1985); Thomas Schmeller, *Paulus und die 'Diatribe'*, NTA 19 (Münster: Aschendorff, 1987); Johannes Schoon-Janßen, *Umstrittene 'Apologien' in Paulusbriefen*, GTA 45 (Göttingen: Vandenhoeck & Ruprecht, 1991).

[57] A communications theory that could be adapted by exegesis is presented by F. Schulz von Thun, *Miteinander reden: Klärungen und Störungen. Psychologie der zwischenmenschlichen Kommunikation* (Hamburg: Rowohlt, 1986). This theory distinguishes four aspects: content, connection, self-disclosure, and appeal. All these elements are found in Paul's letters, with different intensity and in a variety of forms.

between the available literary forms of expression and particular stylistic means available to a particular author, their specific application and the different possibilities of written communication between separated author and reader(s), just as the intended goal of the communication constitutes a variable factor.[58] Only in comparison with the usual literary means at the author's disposal in handling a particular communications situation does the specific accomplishment of the author become visible.

Ancient letters can be classified basically into public (e.g. official or business) letters and private (familiar) letters. From among the many letter genres available to the ancient writer,[59] two that are important for understanding the Pauline letters are the *friendship letter* and the *philosophical letter*. The friendship letter[60] serves to cultivate personal contact between friends. Of course, the letter is only an imperfect substitute for bridging the distance between writer and reader, but there is also a sense in which the author is present with his or her letter. The letter calls to memory the basis of the friendship, the relationship is renewed by means of the letter, and the preview of a speedy reunion lessens the pain of separation. So Paul too repeatedly reminds the churches to whom he writes of the foundations of their common relationship (1 Cor. 15.1; Gal. 3.1), he longs to see the churches (1 Thess. 2.17; Gal. 4.20), and hopes to be able to come to them soon in person (1 Thess. 2.18; Rom. 1.11; 15.32; Phil. 2.24). To make up for his absence, he sends messengers or letters (1 Thess. 3.1–2; 1 Cor. 5.3–4). He is concerned to justify his delay and to remove hindrances that still stand in the way of his coming to them soon (2 Cor. 1.15–22).

In the philosophical letters[61] (e.g. letters of the Cynics, of Epicurus, and Seneca's *Epistulae morales ad Lucilium*) are found sections that combine doctrinal and ethical instruction, just as in Paul's letters. Philosophical reflections are related to practical issues of life. So too, the author's own self-description and testimony to his own life plays a considerable role. Seneca repeatedly sets forth Socrates as an example, as well as becoming an example to his readers himself.[62] This corresponds to Paul's commending himself as an example to his churches (1 Thess. 1.6; 1 Cor. 11.1; 4.16–17;

---

[58] Cf. Karl Ermert, *Briefsorten. Untersuchungen zu Theorie und Empirie der Textklassifikation*, RGL 20 (Tübingen: J. C. B. Mohr [Paul Siebeck], 1979).

[59] Stowers, *Letter Writing* 49ff., suggests six types of letters; 1. friendship letters, 2. family letters, 3. letters of praise, and accounting or blame, 4. letters of exhortation and advice, 5. letters of meditation, 6. apologetic letters. Other classifications are offered by Doty, *Letters* 5ff.

[60] On friendship letters cf. Koskenniemi, *Studien* 115ff.

[61] Cf. here Hubert Cancik, *Untersuchungen zu Senecas Epistulae morales*, Spudasmata 18 (Hildesheim: Georg Olms, 1967) 46–68; Klaus Berger, 'Hellenistische Gattungen und Neues Testament,' ANRW 25.2 (Berlin: Walter de Gruyter, 1984), (1031–1432) 1132–1138.

[62] Cf. Seneca, *Epistles* 20.34.35 et passim; an interpretation of the relevant texts is given by Cancik, *Untersuchungen* 68ff.

Gal. 4.12; Phil. 3.17; 4.9), and including distinctive biographical passages as part of his argumentation (Gal. 1.13ff.; Phil. 1.12–26; 3.4ff.).

As further elements of the features typically found in Greco–Roman letters that reappear in Paul's letters, one may mention: praise, blame, admonition, consolation, accusation and defense. Paul does not simply adopt some particular ancient letter genre, but he is both dependent on the conventions of ancient letter writing and at the same time gives his independent variations of them.[63]

2.3.2 *The Form of the Pauline Letter*

Roller, Otto. *Das Formular der paulinischen Briefe*, BWANT 4.6. Stuttgart: Kohlhammer, 1933; Schubert, Paul. *Form and Function of the Pauline Thanksgiving*, BZNW 20. Berlin: Walter de Gruyter, 1939; Bjerkelund, Carl J. *PARAKALÔ. Form, Funktion und Sinn der parakalô-Sätze in den paulinischen Briefen*, BNT 1. Oslo: Universitetsforlaget, 1967; Berger, Klaus. 'Apostelbrief und apostolische Rede,' ZNW 65 (1974) 190–231; White, L. John. 'New Testament Epistolary Literature in the Framework of Ancient Epistolography,' *ANRW* II 25.2. Berlin: Walter de Gruyter, 1984, 1730–1756; Schnider, Franz and Stenger, Werner. *Studien zum neutestamentlichen Briefformular*, NTTS XI. Leiden: E. J. Brill, 1987; Taatz, Irene. *Frühjüdische Briefe. Die paulinischen Briefe im Rahmen der offiziellen religiösen Briefe des Frühjudentums*, NTOA 16. Göttingen: Vandenhoeck & Ruprecht, 1991; Vouga, Francois. 'Der Brief als Form der apostolischen Autorität,' in *Studien und Texte zur Formgeschichte*, TANZ 7. Tübingen: Francke, 1992, 7–58; Dormeyer, Detlev. *Das Neue Testament im Rahmen der antiken Literaturgeschichte*. Darmstadt: Wissenschaftliche Buchgesellschaft, 1993, 190–198.

2.3.2.1 *The Introduction to the Pauline Letter*

The *introduction* includes the prescript, the thanksgiving, and the self-commendation.

In the *prescript* a distinction must first be made between the external and internal address of the letter. The external address stands on the outside of the papyrus roll and names the addressees, the sender, and often also the place of destination.[64] The external address for all New Testament letters has been lost. The internal address corresponds to the modern letterhead

---

[63] Cf. here the good methodological reflections by David Aune, *The New Testament in Its Literary Environment* (Philadelphia: Westminster, 1987) 203: 'Early Christian letters tend to resist rigid classification, either in terms of the three main types of oratory or in terms of the many categories listed by the epistolary theorists. Most early Christian letters are multifunctional and have a 'mixed' character, combining elements from two or more epistolary types. In short, each early Christian letter must be analyzed on its own terms.' On the whole, the Pauline letters stand closest to the ancient deliberative letters of friendship, but Paul in no case restricts himself to the ideal genres of the ancient rhetoricians and their successors.

[64] Cf. Deissmann, *Light* 149ff.

and always follows a fixed formula. The prescripts of New Testament letters have been divided into two types based on their macrostructure, a Greek and an oriental form. The Greek form combines the three basic elements of the prescript (sender, addressee, greeting) into one sentence, with the sender as the grammatical subject standing in the nominative case and the addressee in the dative. The basic form is, 'A (says) to B, he should rejoice (ὁ δεῖνα τῷ δεῖνι χαίρειν).'[65] The conventional form of the Greek letter prescript is found in the New Testament in James 1.1 and in the letters cited in Acts 15.23–29; 23.26–30. The conventional oriental prescript is documented especially in Hebrew and Aramaic letters.[66] The characteristic form has two members, the first of which names only the addressee ('to A') or the sender and the addressee ('from A to B'). The introductory greeting, usually 'peace' (שָׁלוֹם), follows in the second part of the prescript. While the addressee is always named by name, sometimes with a descriptive or titular addition, the sender must not appear in the prescript. If the sender is placed before the prescript, it is introduced by a preposition. When placed at the beginning of the prescript, the sender is introduced by a preposition. In the New Testament the conventional oriental form is predominant, which has, however, already been modified. The two part prescript of the oriental form is adjusted to the Greek form in that the name of the sender is placed first in the nominative form as the subject.

> Hellenistic influence in eastern Mediterranean areas resulted in the coining of mixed forms used in letter formulae. Such a mixed form is found in Daniel 3.31 in Theodotion's translation (there as 4.1): 'Nebuchadnezzar the king, to all peoples, tribes, and languages on the whole earth: peace be with you in abundance;' Syriac Baruch 78.2: 'Thus says Baruch, the son of Neriah, to the brothers who are imprisoned: mercy and peace be with you.'[67] In contrast, 2 Maccabees 1.1 is more oriented to the conventional oriental form, where the addressee in the dative precedes the sender in the nominative: 'To the Jewish kindred in Egypt, our greetings. The brothers, the Jews in Jerusalem and in Judea wish good peace.'[68]

The Pauline letter formula represents a mixed form in that, on the one hand, he maintains the two-membered prescript, but on the other hand in

---

[65] On the prescript of the Greek letter, cf. Koskenniemi, *Studien* 155ff.

[66] Cf. Denis Pardee, 'An Overview of Ancient Hebrew Epistolography,' JBL 97 (1978) 321–346; and *Handbook of Ancient Hebrew Letters*, SBL S. 15 (Chico: Scholars Press, 1982); Taatz, *Frühjüdische Briefe*, passim.

[67] For analysis, cf. Taatz, *Frühjüdische Briefe* 66–67, who, however, classifies the prescript within the general oriental formula.

[68] For analysis, cf. Taatz, *Frühjüdische Briefe* 18–19.

the first member he names the sender in the nominative case prior to the addressees in the dative. Finally, it is to be noticed that Paul merely takes up the macrostructure of a letter formula common in his environment, on the basis of which he develops a *distinctively independent* letter formula. For Paul the apostolic letter is obviously the appropriate means for maintaining or initiating (Rome) contact with the churches and preaching his gospel,[69] in addition to personal visits and sending of messengers. From a pragmatic view of the function of texts, the letters serve as an essential means of guiding his churches within the framework of the Pauline mission work taken as a whole.

The prescript of the Pauline letters begins with the *sender* (superscriptio). Only in Romans 1.1 does Paul's name stand alone as the sole sender of the letter; otherwise there are always cosenders (cf. 1 Thess. 1.1; 1 Cor. 1.1; 2 Cor. 1.1; Phil. 1.1; Phlm. 1).[70] In Galatians 1.2 Paul names no individuals as cosenders, but formulates it 'all the brothers with me.' With the exception of 1 Thessalonians 1.1 the sender's name 'Paul' is always followed by some sort of title. Thus Paul calls himself 'apostle' (Rom. 1.1; 1 Cor. 1.1; 2 Cor. 1.1; Gal. 1.1), 'servant/slave' (Rom. 1.1; Phil. 1.1), and 'prisoner' (Phlm. 1.1). Titles are also provided for the cosenders, thus 'the brother' (1 Cor. 1.1; 2 Cor. 1.1; Phlm. 1) and 'servant/slave of Jesus Christ' (Phil. 1.1).

Following the sender comes the *addressee* (adscriptio). For the most part the adscriptio has the form 'the church of God' (1 Cor. 1.2; 2 Cor. 1.1) or 'the church in God the Father and the Lord Jesus Christ' (1 Thess. 1.1) or simply 'the churches' (Gal. 1.2) in a certain town or area. Philippians 1.1 is addressed 'to all the saints in Christ Jesus at Philippi.' The good relationship between the apostle and the church in Philippi is emphasized by the special form of the adscriptio. Paul omits the term ἐκκλησία (assembly, church) from the prescript of the letter to the Romans, and addresses the letter 'to all those in Rome,' since he cannot allude to his authority as founder of the Roman church. In the Pauline letters the addressees are always addressed as a collective and never as individual persons. Even in Philemon, alongside the real addressee Philemon there appears additional coworkers of Paul and the congregation that meets in Philemon's house

---

[69] The relative independence of the Pauline letter formula is undisputed among scholars. It is disputed, however, whether Paul stands more under the influence of the Greek or the early Jewish tradition of letter writing. While American scholarship has primarily stressed the lines of connection to the Greek letter tradition, I. Taatz emphasizes 'a certain continuity between the early Jewish letters written as direction to communities and the letters of Paul' (*ibid.* 114).

[70] Taatz, *ibid.* 113, sees therein a parallel to early Jewish letters: 'In the group of letters directed to communities several cosenders are named that represent or function as leaders of the Jewish community.'

(Phlm. 1.2). When in the prescripts of 1 Corinthians, 2 Corinthians, and Philemon Paul names other coworkers alongside the real addressees ('to the church of God'), he is thereby broadening the circle of influence within which the letter will have an effect, not undertaking some sort of individualizing of the addressees.

Following the first part of the Pauline epistolary prescript that contains the sender and addressees comes the second part that comprises the introductory greeting (salutatio). Six times this salutation has exactly the same wording: 'grace to you and peace from God our Father and the Lord Jesus Christ' (1 Cor. 1.3; 2 Cor. 1.2; Gal. 1.3; Rom. 1.7b; Phil. 1.2; Phlm. 3). The pair of concepts χάρις (grace) and εἰρήνη (peace) designates a gift of God given to the church through Jesus Christ. With this salutatio Paul is following a custom documented in both Jewish and Greek letters in which opening and concluding greetings invoke salvation on the addressees. Thus in Paul the opening greeting is always to be understood in view of the addressees and their particular church situation (cf. Gal. 1.4).[71]

In almost all Pauline letters (the only exception: Galatians) the prescript is immediately followed by a formally and functionally independent section of the letter called the *epistolary thanksgiving* (proemium), from the main verb εὐχαριστέω (I give thanks) found in the opening sentence of each section. While the beginning of the thanksgiving section can be clearly determined in each case, the transition from thanksgiving to the following section is not always so clear.[72] A step forward has been made here by the suggestion of F. Schnider and W. Stenger, that the Pauline thanksgiving ends at the point where the perspective changes and the apostle no longer has the addressees in view, but wants to direct the attention of the hearer/ readers back to the writer of the letter himself. This transition is 'always introduced with the following constitutive elements: (1) address "brothers and sisters;" (2) reference to some knowledge that the writer of the letter wants the addressees to attain by his admonitory gesture of sending the letter.'[73] If one understands this change in perspective as a signal in the text that marks the beginning of a new section, then the thanksgiving sections of the Pauline letters can be delineated as follows: 1 Thess. 1.2–10; 1 Cor. 1.4–9; 2 Cor. 1.3–7; Rom. 1.8–12; Phil. 1.3–11; Phlm. 4–7. The Pauline proemium has been transmitted to us in two types. In the first formulation, following the main clause with the verb εὐχαριστέω comes one or more

---

[71] On the salutation in the Pauline letters cf. especially Schnider and Stenger, *Studien* 25–33. Taatz, *Frühjüdische Briefe* 112 regards the Pauline salutatio as standing in the tradition of Syriac Baruch 78.2.

[72] Cf. the table in Schnider and Stenger, *Studien* 42.

[73] *Ibid.* 43.

participles that modify the verb. To these participles a concluding purpose clause can be subordinated (cf. Phil. 1.3–11; 1 Thess. 1.2–10; Phlm. 4–7). The subject of εὐχαριστέω is always the writer of the letter, who continually gives thanks to God for the addressees. In the second type the main clause with εὐχαριστέω is followed by a ὅτι (because, for) clause, to which another coordinate clause may be joined (cf. 1 Cor. 1.4–9). These two types may not be rigidly distinguished from each other; Romans 1.8–12 has a combination of elements of both types. Second Corinthians 1.3–7 is a special case, where the thanksgiving begins with εὐλογητός (blessed). The extended blessing here has the same function as the proemium in the other Pauline letters. In the proemium the apostle thanks God for the salvation that has come from God to the church to which he is writing. The proemium thus has an ecclesial function, placing the congregation being addressed in the worldwide ἐκκλησία θεοῦ (church of God). Through the mission of the apostle Paul and the existence of this congregation God creates a church for himself, a church that is to proclaim and bear witness to the gospel of Jesus Christ.

In addition to the prescript and the epistolary thanksgiving, F. Schnider and W. Stenger consider yet a third distinct element to be included in the Pauline letter introduction: the *epistolary self commendation*.[74] It makes a theme of the presence of the letter writer with the addressees, whether it is the future presence (Rom. 1.13–15) or the continuing effect of the first visit that founded the church (1 Thess. 2.1ff.). Under the heading of the epistolary self commendation they also include an explanation for the visit of the apostle that has so far been delayed (Rom. 1.13; 1 Thess. 2.8), the mention of the church's prayer for the writer of the letter (2 Cor. 1.11; Phil. 1.19), the emphasis on good relations between the apostle and the church being addressed (1 Cor. 4.14; 1 Thess. 2.1–11; 2.17), the reference to the particular manner in which the apostle conducted his preaching in the community (1 Cor. 2.1–5.2; 2 Cor. 1.12), and finally the model character of his conduct (1 Thess. 4.1; 1 Cor. 4.15). The epistolary self commendation functions to generate and strengthen the addressees' belief in the trustworthiness of the author of the letter. This is also the purpose of the address that always introduces this section, 'brothers and sisters.' The problem is to define the limits of the 'self commendation,' for while it is clear in Romans (Rom. 1.13–15), 2 Corinthians (2 Cor. 1.8–2.17), Galatians (Gal. 1.8–10), Philippians (Phil. 1.12–30) and Philemon (Phlm. 7–9), it is difficult to discern in 1 Thessalonians and 1 Corinthians.[75] Even if it is possible to

---

[74] *Ibid.* 50ff.

[75] Schnider and Stenger, *Studien* 53ff. unduly extend the epistolary self commendation in 1 Thessalonians (2.1–12; 2.17–3.8) and 1 Corinthians (1.10–4.21).

discover a distinctive section within the Pauline letter introduction, the 'epistolary self commendation,' the apostle must be granted a great deal of freedom in the application of this form.

While the one hand, the Pauline letter introduction is bound to the contemporary conventions, on the other hand his independent adaptation of this convention testifies to the hermeneutical function of this section of the Pauline letter: it signals the current communications situation between Paul and the addressees, and it names in advance key words that will form the central theological themes to be developed in the body of the letter.

2.3.2.2 *The Conclusion of the Pauline Letter*

The Pauline letter conclusion is composed of two elements: (1) closing parenesis and (2) postscript.

The *closing parenesis* is marked off from the body of the letter by particular expressions that set the following section off as an independent part of the text (cf. 1 Thess. 4.1; 1 Cor. 16.15; 2 Cor. 13.11).[76] The style of the concluding parenesis is characterized by addressing the readers directly in the form of imperatives. The use of both second-person singular and plural forms shows that Paul seeks direct contact with his addressees. The concrete relations in the church's situation or the particulars of the writer's situation can also influence the content of the closing parenesis. Alongside exhortations and admonitions the closing parenesis may also contain the following themes: (1) Request for prayers (1 Thess. 5.17; Rom. 15.30–32; Phil. 4.6). (2) The importance of church leadership can also be emphasized (cf. 1 Thess. 5.12; 1 Cor. 16.15–18). (3) The parenesis can be concluded with an intercessory prayer for blessing (cf. 1 Thess. 5.23; Gal. 6.16; Rom. 15.13, 33; Phil. 4.7). (4) The apostolic parousia: in five Pauline letters the closing section includes a unit in which the apostle presents his travel plans (cf. 1 Cor. 16.5–12; 2 Cor. 12.14–13.10; Rom. 15.14–29; Phil. 2.19–30; Phlm. 22). Paul here takes up and elaborates an epistolary motif of the Hellenistic letter of friendship.[77] In the Hellenistic friendship letter the parousia motif comes to expression in a variety of forms to express the presence of the letter writer with the readers by means of the letter, not merely his or her future arrival. In Paul's letters too, the motif of apostolic parousia is intended to overcome the distance that separates writer and readers, while at the same time expressing the presence of the apostle's authority and mandate within the church addressed by the letter. Since Paul thinks of himself being present in the congregation either personally,

---

[76] Cf. ibid. 76–107.
[77] Cf. Klaus Thraede, *Grundzüge griechisch-römischer Brieftopik* (see above 2.3.1) 95–106.

by means of a messenger, or through his letter, the letter brings his apostolic authority to bear on the congregation (example: 2 Cor. 13.10).[78] The apostolic parousia can be regarded as an integral part of the closing parenesis, since the parousia motif is either integrated fully in the closing parenesis (1 Cor. 16.5–12; Rom. 15.14–29) or mostly appears in immediate conjunction with it. Thus the closing parenesis sections of the Pauline letters may be delineated as follows: 1 Thess. 5.12–25; 1 Cor. [15.58]; 16.1–18; 2 Cor. 12.14–13.10, 13.11; Gal. 6.1–10; Rom. 15.7–13, 30–33; Phil. 4.2–9; Phlm. 21, 22.

The *postscript* in the Pauline letters is as a rule comprised of three elements: (1) a greetings instruction, in which the letter writer instructs the addressees to convey greetings to other members of the church; (2) greetings from other people are conveyed to the addressees through the letter writer; (3) the letter writer himself greets the addressees, which is the letter's real concluding farewell.

In the Pauline letters the *greetings instruction* is introduced by the imperative ἀσπάσασθε (greet, welcome) and is found in 1 Thess. 5.26; 1 Cor. 16.20b; 2 Cor. 13.12a; Rom. 16.3–16a; Phil. 4.21a. The greetings instruction is often connected with the motif of the 'holy kiss' (cf. 1 Thess. 5.26; 1 Cor. 16.20b; 2 Cor. 13.12a; Rom. 16.16a). The greetings instruction facilitates the letter's overcoming the distance that separates writer and addressees, while it also assures the circulation of the letter to all those to whom it is addressed.

The greetings from other people (*greetings communication*) to the addressees is found in 1 Cor. 16.19–20a; 2 Cor. 13.12b; Rom. 16.16b.21–23; Phlm. 23, 24. The greetings to 'all the saints' (2 Cor. 13.12b; Phil. 4.22), to all the churches in the province of Asia (1 Cor. 16.19), from 'all the churches of Christ' (Rom. 16.16b) or from Paul's individual coworkers show that it is not only the apostle and the churches to which he writes that know themselves to be bound together into one comprehensive community of faith, but the churches have this same mutual understanding of their relation to each other. Furthermore, the greetings communication is always nuanced to fit the particular situation of the church, as seen not only in the mentioning of individual names, but in the absence of the form in 1 Thessalonians and Galatians.

As in ancient letters generally, so also in the Pauline letter the *final farewell* forms the real conclusion of the letter (cf. 1 Thess. 5.28; 1 Cor. 16.23–24; 2 Cor. 13.13; Gal. 6.11–18; Rom. 16.24[?]; Phil. 4.23; Phlm. 25).

---

[78] For details, cf. Robert W. Funk, 'The Apostolic Presence: Paul,' in *Parable and Presence*, ed. R. W. Funk (Philadelphia: Fortress Press, 1982) 81–102.

In Hellenistic personal letters the final word was often simply 'farewell' (ἔρρωσσο or εὐτύχει). In addition, the closing words of ancient letters contained the date, and the final greeting is sometimes written by the author himself and not by the scribe. As in other elements of the letter, so too in the farewell Paul adopts the customs of his time and place, but also elaborates them. The simple 'farewell' is transformed into an extensive benediction, which in 1 Thess. 5.28; 1 Cor. 16.23; Rom. 16.20b reads: ἡ χάρις τοῦ κυρίου ἡμῶν Ἰησοῦ Χριστοῦ μεθ' ὑμῶν (the grace of our Lord Jesus Christ be with you), in Gal. 6.18; Phlm. 25 is augmented by τοῦ πνεύματος (of the spirit) and in 2 Cor. 13.13 it is expanded into a trinitarian form.

E. Lohmeyer explains the introductory and concluding forms in the Pauline letters in terms of early Christian worship.[79] They were the forms with which worship began and ended. Our knowledge of the liturgy of early Christian worship services is too fragmentary, however, to postulate that here is the *Sitz im Leben* for various forms of early Christian tradition. It is likely that the epistolary function led Paul to the particular form he coined for his concluding blessing. As in ancient letters in general, so too in Paul the concluding greeting had the task '(1) at the close of the letter once again to express the continuing relationship between writer and addressees in a wish that things will go well for them, and (2) at the same time to vouch for the authenticity of the letter's contents by writing something in his own hand, so that at least in this section his addressees could experience a bit of his personal presence.'[80] Parallels in both Jewish and Hellenistic letters indicate that the personal signature at the conclusion of a letter served also to give it a certain legal significance.[81] Paul sometimes wrote the closing words in his own hand (cf. 1 Cor. 15.21; Gal. 6.11). In 1 Cor. 16.21 he signs the letter with his own name explicitly to underscore the authority of what he has said to the Corinthians. In Philemon 19 this reference to Paul's own name and hand is not found in the postscript, but at the end of the body of the letter, Paul's signal to Philemon that he is really willing to assume responsibility for the damages caused by Onesimus.

---

[79] Cf. Ernst Lohmeyer, 'Probleme paulinischer Theologie,' ZNW 26 (1927) 158–173.
[80] Schnider and Stenger, *Studien* (see above 2.3.2) 133.
[81] *Ibid.* 137–144.

2.4 The First Letter to the Thessalonians

2.4.1 Literature

Commentaries

Dobschütz, Ernst v. *Die Thessalonicherbriefe*, KEK 10. Göttingen: Vandenhoeck & Ruprecht, 1909; Dibelius, Martin. *An die Thessalonicher*, HNT 11. Tübingen: J. C. B. Mohr (Paul Siebeck), 1937³; Best, Ernest. *The First and Second Epistles to the Thessalonians*, HNTC. New York: Harper, 1972; Marxsen, Willi. *Der erste Brief an die Thessalonicher*, ZBK 11.1. Zürich: Theologischer Verlag, 1979; Bruce, Frederick F. *1 and 2 Thessalonians*, WBC 45. Waco: Word Books, 1982; Marshall, I. Howard. *1 and 2 Thessalonians*, NCeB. Grand Rapids: Eerdmans, 1983; Friedrich, Gerhard. *Die Briefe an die Galater, Epheser, Philipper, Kolosser, Thessalonicher, und Philemon*, NTD 8. Göttingen: Vandenhoeck & Ruprecht, 1990³; Holtz, Traugott. *Der erste Brief an die Thessalonicher*, EKK 13. Neukirchen: Neukirchener Verlag, 1990²; Wanamaker, Charles A. *The Epistles to the Thessalonians*, NIGTC. Grand Rapids: Wm. B. Eerdmans, 1990.

Monographs

Harnisch, Wolfgang . *Eschatologische Existenz*, FRLANT 97. Göttingen: Vandenhoeck & Ruprecht, 1973; Laub, Fritz. *Eschatologische Verkündigung und Lebensgestaltung nach Paulus*, BU 10. Regensburg: Pustet, 1973; Schade, Hans-Heinrich. *Apokalyptische Christologie bei Paulus*, GTA 18. Göttingen: Vandenhoeck & Ruprecht, 1984²; Jewett, Robert. *The Thessalonian Correspondence*. Philadelphia: Fortress Press, 1986; Johanson, Bruce C. *To All the Brethren. A Text-Linguistic and Rhetorical Approach to 1 Thessalonians*, CB.NTS 16. Stockholm: Almquist & Wiksell, 1987; Malherbe, Abraham J. *Paul and the Thessalonians*. Philadelphia: Fortress Press, 1987; Donfried, Karl P. 'The Theology of 1 Thessalonians,' in *The Theology of the Shorter Pauline Letters*, eds. Karl P. Donfried and I. Howard Marshall. Cambridge University Press, 1993, 1–79.

Articles

Kümmel, Werner G. 'Das literarische und geschichtliche Problem des Ersten Thessalonicherbriefes,' in *Heilsgeschehen und Geschichte 1*, ed. Werner G. Kümmel. Marburg: Elwert, 1965, 406–416; Demke, Christoph. 'Theologie und Literarkritik im 1.Thessalonicherbrief,' in *FS Ernst Fuchs*, ed. Gerhard Ebeling et. al. Tübingen: J. C. B. Mohr (Paul Siebeck), 1973, 103–124; Friedrich, Gerhard. '1 Thessalonicher 5, 1–11, der apologetische Einschub eines Späteren,' ZThK 70 (1973) 288–315; Collins, Raymond F. *Studies on the First Letter to the Thessalonians*, BETL 66. Leuven: Leuven University Press, 1984; Schnelle, Udo. 'Der Erste Thessalonicherbrief und die Entstehung der paulinischen Anthropologie,' NTS 32 (1986) 207–224; Collins, Raymond F., ed. *The Thessalonian Correspondence*, BETL 87. Leuven: University Press, 1990. (important collection of essays); Merk, Otto. 'Zur Christologie im ersten Thessalonicherbrief,' in *Anfänge der Christologie* (FS F. Hahn), eds. Cilliers

Breytenbach and Henning Paulsen. Göttingen: Vandenhoeck & Ruprecht, 1991,
97–110; Söding, Thomas. 'Der Erste Thessalonicherbrief und die frühe paulinische
Evangeliumsverkündigung. Zur Frage einer Entwicklung der paulinischen Theologie,'
BZ 35 (1991) 180–203.

2.4.2 *Author*

The Pauline authorship of 1 Thessalonians has never been seriously
doubted. Ignatius of Antioch already knew 1 Thessalonians (cf. 1 Thess.
5.17/IgnEph 10.1), and the Muratorian Canon adduces it as a Pauline
letter.

2.4.3 *Place and Time of Composition*

Paul founded the church in Thessalonica after having come from Philippi
(cf. 1 Thess. 1.9–10; 2.2). He lived and worked in the church for a considerable time (cf. 1 Thess. 2.1–12). After his departure, he twice wanted
to return but was hindered by Satan (cf. 1 Thess. 2.17–20). From Athens
he sent Timothy to them (1 Thess. 3.1–2, 6), who brought a good report
about the way things were going in the church (1 Thess. 3.6–8). Paul's
location at the time he wrote 1 Thessalonians is unknown, and can be
inferred only hypothetically. One indication is provided by the reference to
Silvanus and Timothy in 1 Thessalonians 1.1, whom Paul met in Corinth
according to Acts 18.5. Supposing that the letter was written in *Corinth*
would also permit the date of its composition to be determined, for Paul
arrived in Corinth in *50* CE (see above 2.1.1), and in this year composed 1
Thessalonians.[82]

2.4.4 *Intended Readership*

The city of Thessalonica was newly founded ca. 315 BCE. Its favorable
location in the innermost corner of the Thermaic Gulf and on the Via
Egnatia accounts for the great significance it has enjoyed through all the
centuries as a harbor city and center for commerce and transportation.[83] As

---

[82] 1 Thessalonians is dated in 50 (51) by among others Dibelius, *1 Thess.* 33; Kümmel,
Introduction 257; Vielhauer, *Urchristliche Literatur* 88; Friedrich, *1 Thess.* 206; Marxsen, 1 Thess.
14; Koester, *Introduction*, 2.112; Holtz, *1 Thess.* 19; Jewett, *Thessalonian Correspondence* 60. Other
opinions that diverge from this consensus are reviewed by Holtz, *1 Thess.* 20–23. John Knox,
Chapters in a Life of Paul (New York/Nashville: Abingdon, 1950) 86, dates 1 Thessalonians at
the beginning of the 40s ('not long after AD 40'), followed by among others Lüdemann,
Chronology (see above 2.1) 238; Donfried, 'Theology' 12.

[83] On the history of the city cf. Winfried Elliger, *Paulus in Griechenland* (Stuttgart:
Katholisches Bibelwerk, 1990²) 78–116.

a cultural and religious center, Thessalonica also attracted many people. Archaeological excavations and literary witnesses document the worship of cultic deities such as Serapis, Isis, Dionysus, or the Cabiri.[84]

Most of those who had joined the church in Thessalonica were Gentile Christians (cf. 1 Thess. 1.9; 2.14). Acts 17.1 indicates there was a synagogue in the city, so that one must reckon with the presence of Jewish Christians and Gentile sympathizers of the Jewish religion in the church. Although at the time of the letter the church had been in existence only a short while (cf. 1 Thess. 2.17), the news about its founding had penetrated all parts of Greece (cf. 1 Thess. 1.7–8). Despite the good report conveyed by Timothy (1 Thess. 3.6), Paul reveals his concern about circumstances in the church.[85] The Christians in Thessalonica stand before a prolonged experience of suffering that began when they accepted the message of the gospel (cf. 1 Thess. 1.6) and is obviously continuing at the time Paul writes to them. The church in Thessalonica is suffering the same kind of things from their Gentile compatriots as the churches in Palestine suffer from the Jews (cf. 1 Thess. 2.14–16). The sharp polemic suggests that Paul saw the Jews as the real cause of the persecution in Thessalonica as well. In addition to religiously motivated conflicts with Jews and Gentiles, the church was also burdened with continual friction of an everyday sort between themselves and their surroundings (cf. 1 Thess. 4.10b–12). The young church was also beset with troubling theological questions (cf. 1 Thess. 3.10). Thus the repeated περί (concerning) in 1 Thess. 4.9, 13; 5.1 obviously refers to concrete questions raised by the Thessalonians. In particular, the unanticipated death of members of the community before the parousia of the Lord caused anxiety and occasioned Paul's discussion of the manner and date of God's eschatological act at the parousia of Christ.

2.4.5 Outline, Structure, Form

1.1	Prescript	
1.2–3.13	PART ONE	
1.2–10	Proemium	—Introduction
2.1–12	Epistolary Self Commendation	

---

[84] Cf. Karl P. Donfried, 'The Cults of Thessalonica and the Thessalonian Correspondence,' NTS 31 (1985) 336–356; Jewett, *Thessalonian Correspondence* 126ff.

[85] On the various theses of older scholarship concerning 'gnostic' or 'enthusiastic' streams in Thessalonica, cf. *Ibid.* 135–157. On Jewett's theses cf. section 2.4.10.

2.13–2.16	Thanksgiving for Reception of the Gospel	
2.17–3.13	The Church's Testing during the Time of the Apostle's Absence	
4.1–5.11	PART TWO	⎤ Body
4.1–12	Living in Holiness	
4.13–18	Assurance of Salvation for Dead and Living	
5.1–11	The Eschatological Existence of the Believers	

5.12–25	Closing Parenesis	
5.26–27	Greetings Instruction	⎤ Conclusion
5.28	Final Farewell (Eschatokoll)	

The macrostructure of 1 Thessalonians manifests a clear division into two major parts, chapters 1–3 and chapters 4–5. Corresponding to the comprehensive theological perspective of the letter, each chapter concludes with a look to the future parousia of Christ (cf. 1.9–10; 2.19; 3.13; 4.13–18; 5.23), a clear indication of the manner in which the structure of the letter as a whole has been thought through in advance. The term εὐχαριστέω or εὐχαριστία characteristic for the thanksgiving section is found in 1 Thessalonians 1.2; 2.13; 3.9. One might therefore consider whether the proemium extends through 3.13.[86] Such a division is too schematic, for the whole first major part of the letter has as its theme the thanksgiving that Paul offers to God in behalf of the community. This central theological motif is taken up again in 1 Thessalonians 2.13 and 3.9, but this does not mean that the proemium is begun afresh. Moreover, it must be remembered that Paul's use of εὐχαριστέω or εὐχαριστία is by no means restricted to the proemium of his letters (cf. 1 Thess. 5.18; 1 Cor. 14.16; 2 Cor. 4.15; 9.11; Phil. 4.6). The letter's conclusion lacks greetings from Paul's coworkers to the church in Thessalonica. Obviously there are as yet no close contacts between the church from which Paul is writing and the addressees that would have made such greetings meaningful.[87]

---

[86] Cf. Schnider and Stenger, *Studien* (see above 2.3.2) 42ff.

[87] Cf. for different understandings of the letter's structure Jewett, *Thessalonian Correspondence* 68–71 ('traditional' outline); 71–78 (outline from rhetorical point of view). In Jewett's view, 'the rhetorical genre most closely associated with 1 Thessalonians is demonstrative/epideictic . . .' (71). Cf. further J. Schoon-Janßen, Umstrittene *'Apologien' in den Paulusbriefen* (see above 2.3.1) 39–53, who discusses different attempts at classification ('paraenetic letter', 'epideictic letter') and categorizes 1 Thessalonians as a 'friendship letter.' Detlev Dormeyer, *Das Neue Testament im Rahmen der antiken Literaturgeschichte* (see above 2.3.2) 193–194, sees in 1 Thessalonians the standard Pauline letter formula: prescript 1.1, exordium 1.2–10; argumentatio 2.1–3.13; exhortatio 4.1–5.22; postscript/ salutatio 5.23–28. Donfried, 'Theology' 3–7 classifies 1 Thessalonians as an 'epideictic letter' and outlines it I Exordium 1.1–10; II Narratio 2.1–3.10; III

2.4.6 Literary Integrity

The literary unity of 1 Thessalonians has often been disputed. Among the numerous partition hypotheses[88] may be named:

(a) K. G. Eckart finds two letters combined in our 1 Thessalonians, one complete letter and one with an abbreviated beginning.[89] The first letter is supposed to have been written in Athens as a letter of recommendation for Timothy, as was the second letter, but only after Timothy's return. An unknown redactor then composed canonical 1 Thessalonians from these two letters, in the process of which he added a series of texts he himself had composed. Letter 1:1 Thess. 1.1–2.12; 2.17–3.4; 3.11–13. Letter 2:1 Thess. 3.6–10; 4.9–10a; 4.13–5.11; 5.23–26; 5.28. Non-Pauline texts: 1 Thess. 2.13–16; 3.5; 4.1–8; 4.10b–12; 5.12–22.

(b) Chr. Demke proceeds on the basis of the peculiarities of the language and subject matter as compared with later Pauline letters and considers only 1 Thess. 2.17–3.2a, 5b–11; 4.9–10a, 13–17; 5.1–22 to have belonged to the original Pauline letter.[90] A post-Pauline author close to the author of the Gospel of Luke then composed the extant 1 Thessalonians, having himself formulated 1.2–2.16; 3.2b–5a; 3.12–4.8; 4.10b–12; 5.23–27.

(c) According to W. Schmithals, a later redactor had five authentic letters of Paul, which he edited into our 1 and 2 Thessalonians, including several redactional contributions of his own.[91]

Thessalonians A: 2 Thess. 1.1–4a, 11–12; 3.6–16

Thessalonians B: 1 Thess. 4.13–14, 5.1–28

Thessalonians C: 2 Thess. 2.13–14,1–4, 8b, 15–17; 3.1–2, 17–18

Thessalonians D: 1 Thess. 1.1–2.12; 4.2–12; 2 Thess. 3.3–5

Thessalonians E: 1 Thess. 2.13; 2.17–4.1

Redactional Supplements: 1 Thess. 2.14–16; 4.15–18; 2 Thess. 1.4b–10; 2.5–8a, 9–12.

There are no compelling arguments for any of these partition hypo-

---

Partitio 3.11–13; IV Probatio 4.1–5.3; V Peroratio 5.4–11; VI Exhortatio 5.12–22; VII Final prayers and greetings 5.23–28.

[88] A comprehensive presentation and critique of individual hypotheses is found in Peter Beier, 'Geteilte Briefe? Eine kritische Untersuchung der neueren Teilungshypothesen zu den paulinischen Briefen' (Diss. theol., Halle 1984) 159–181, 326–339. Cf. further Jewett, *Thessalonian Correspondence* 33–46.

[89] Cf. Karl Gottfried Eckart, 'Der zweite echte Brief des Apostels Paulus an die Thessalonicher,' ZThK 58 (1961) 30–44.

[90] Cf. Demke, 'Theologie und Literarkritik.'

[91] Cf. most recently Walter Schmithals, *Die Briefe des Paulus in ihrer ursprünglichen Form* (Zürich: Theologischer Verlag, 1984) 111–124; and 'The Historical Situation of the Thessalonian Epistles,' in *Paul and the Gnostics*, tr. John E. Steely (Nashville: Abingdon, 1972) 123–218.

theses. For instance, there is no real evidence for different situations addressed by 1 Thessalonians. Neither is 1 Thess. 2.13 the beginning of a letter, nor is 1 Thess. 3.11–13 a letter's conclusion, but Paul merely here takes up the dominant motif of thanksgiving once again.[92] Praise and blame must not be considered mutually exclusive in the same letter, and disruptions in the train of thought or repeated reflections on the same theme are by themselves not methodologically controllable criteria for partition hypotheses. Likewise, the theologically peculiarities of 1 Thessalonians present no arguments that a critical method may use, since in this case later Pauline letters would then have to provide the standard of what could be considered Pauline – a completely unhistorical method.

1 Thess. 2.14–16 has often been regarded as a post-Pauline interpolation.[93] The following arguments have been based on the content: (1) the contradiction between Romans 9–11 and 1 Thess. 2.14–16. (2) The references to what has happened to Jews as a model for a Gentile Christian church. (3) There were no extensive persecutions of Christians by Jews in Palestine prior to the first Jewish war. (4) The use of the concept of imitation in 1 Thessalonians 2.14 is singular. (5) The aorist ἔφθασεν (has overtaken) refers to the destruction of Jerusalem. These arguments cannot be considered persuasive.[94] (1) The tension between 1 Thessalonians 2.14–16 and Romans 9–11 goes back to Paul himself. It is a problem that needs to be explained, not a problem to be set aside by interpolation hypotheses. (2) Paul's ecclesiology presupposes a church of Jewish and Gentile Christians, so that Jewish Christians in Palestine can in fact serve as a model for Gentile Christians elsewhere. (3) Prior to 70 CE there were already conflicts between Jews and Christians in Palestine (cf. Luke 6.22). (4) The concept of imitation in 1 Thessalonians 2.14 is found already in 1 Thessalonians 1.6. (5) 1 Thessalonians 2.16c does not have the destruction of Jerusalem in view, but Paul sees in the hostile conduct of the Jews that the wrath of God has come to completion.

G. Friedrich considers 1 Thess. 5.1–11 as a post-Pauline insertion that has many features of Lucan language and theology that serves as an apologetic correction to the Pauline expectation of the parousia and thus already reflects the problem of the delay of the parousia.[95] The untypical linguistic

---

[92] Cf. Holtz, *1 Thess.* 24

[93] Cf. for example Birger A. Pearson, '1 Thessalonians 2,13–16: A Deuteropauline Interpolation,' HThR 64 (1971) 79–94.

[94] Cf. Ingo Broer, "Antisemitismus' und Judenpolemik im Neuen Testament. Ein Beitrag zum besseren Verständnis von 1 Thess. 2,14–16,' in *Religion und Verantwortung als Elemente gesellschaftlicher Ordnung* (FS K. Klein), ed. B. B. Gemper (Siegen 1983²) 734–772; Gerd Lüdemann, *Paulus und das Judentum.* TEH 215 (Munich: Chr. Kaiser Verlag, 1983) 25–27.

[95] Cf. Friedrich, '1 Thessalonicher 5,1–11.'

features of 1 Thess. 5.1–11 are the result, however, of the fragments of pre-Pauline tradition that are incorporated, and the great similarity to Rom. 13.11–14 confirms the Pauline character of 1 Thess. 5.1–11.[96]

Thus 1 Thessalonians is a literary unity; the distinctive features of the letter call for a theological clarification, not an explanation in terms of the supposed literary history of the document.

2.4.7 Traditions, Sources

Two central passages in 1 Thessalonians represent Paul's editing of early Christian traditional material. A summary of early Christian missionary proclamation is found in 1 Thess. 1.9b–10.[97] Against the background of ancient polytheism, the conversion of Gentiles from idols that were no gods to the one living God appears as a decisive turn in salvation history. Now the Christians place their hope in the coming of the Son from heaven, who will deliver them from the eschatological judgment that is already breaking in.

Paul also took up traditional material in the eschatological section *1 Thess. 4.13–18.*[98] In v. 16–17 he quotes a saying of the Lord that circulated in early Christian tradition (cf. 1 Cor. 7.12, 25; 9.14; 11.23ff.); the traditional character can be verified on the linguistic level as well as within the history of motifs.[99] The saying of the Lord pictured the course of the eschatological events and was edited into his composition by Paul with a view to the situation in Thessalonica.

2.4.8 History-of-religions Standpoint

1 Thessalonians testifies to the broad spectrum of religious ideas and practices present in Paul's environment that formed the background for his own thought. In 1 Thess. 2.1–12 the apostle describes his own troubles and his concern to convince the Thessalonians of his own point of view with

---

[96] Extensive evidence in Lars Aejmelaeus, *Wachen vor dem Ende*, SFEG 44 (Helsinki: Finnish Exegetical Society, 1985) 13–98.

[97] The linguistic form shows the text 1 Thess. 1.9b–10 to be pre-Pauline. A thorough analysis of the text is found in C. Bussmann, *Themen der paulinischen Missionspredigt auf dem Hintergrund der spätjüdisch-hellenistischen Missionsliteratur*, EHS.T 3 (Bern – Frankfurt: Peter Lang, 1971) 38–56.

[98] Comprehensive analyses of 1 Thess. 4.13–18 are found e.g. in Ulrich Luz, *Das Geschichtsverständnis bei Paulus* (see below 2.8.1) 318–331; Peter Siber, *Mit Christus leben*, AThANT 61 (Zürich: Theologischer Verlag, 1971) 13–59; Gerd Lüdemann, *Chronology* (see above 2.1) 205–238. Schade, *Apokalyptische Christologie* 157–172; Helmut Merklein, 'Der Theologe als Prophet,' NTS 38 (1992) 402–429.

[99] Cf. Lüdemann, *Chronology* 221.

ideas that have close parallels in Dio Chrysostum's (ca. 40–120 CE) portrayal of the true (Cynic) philosopher.[100] The true philosopher will help other people without having any hidden agenda or financial interests (*Or* 32.10.11); he says what he thinks, because he loves the masses like his own children (*Or* 77/78.40–43). He is their father, brother, and friend, but without flattery, and is unwilling to become a burden to them. He is not interested in increasing his own reputation, but the insight of his hearers (*Or* 32.14–16).

The most impressive (and almost the only) parallel to the dualistic-eschatological expression 'children of light' documented at Qumran is found in 1 Thess. 5.4–9.[101] Particularly in 1QS 3.13–4.26, the contrast between the 'children of light' and the 'children of darkness' is developed. As in Paul, this idea is connected with predestination or election, and in each case the fact that one belongs to a particular elect group is the basis for a particular ethical demand. The proximity of the views adopted here by Paul to those of Qumran is here especially great, but at the same time it is also true that 'There is no evidence that Paul is directly dependent on any Qumran text [here or anyplace else].'[102]

2.4.9 *Basic Theological Ideas*

The effort to construct a theological profile of 1 Thessalonians seems at first to yield only negative results. Key words in Pauline theology are entirely missing, including the anthropological terms σάρξ (flesh), ἁμαρτία (sin)[103], θάνατος (death); σῶμα (body), ἐλευθερία (freedom) and ζωή (life) as well as words from the δικ-root (righteous) and the σταυρ-root (cross). Neither the word νόμος (law) nor the doctrine of justification as found in Galatians and Romans is evidenced in Paul's oldest letter. So too the theology of the cross and the idea of the church as the body of Christ or baptism as burial with Christ are obviously unknown to 1 Thessalonians. Faith is not set in opposition to works of the Law, 'but is understood as steadfastness in the face of troubles, as faithfulness.'[104] The Old Testament is not explicitly cited, the polemic against the Jews in

---

[100] Cf. Abraham Malherbe, 'Gentle as a Nurse': The Cynic Background to 1 Thessalonians 2,' in *Paul and the Popular Philosophers* (Minneapolis: Fortress Press, 1989) 35–48.

[101] Cf. Heinz-Wolfgang Kuhn, 'Die Bedeutung der Qumrantexte für das Verständnis des Ersten Thessalonicherbriefes,' in *The Madrid Qumran Congress*, STDJ IX/1, eds. J. T. Barrera and L. V. Montaner (Leiden: E. J. Brill, 1992) 1.339–353.

[102] *Ibid.* 351. On Qumran cf. the foundational work of Hartmut Stegemann, *Die Essener, Qumran, Johannes der Täufer und Jesus* (Freiburg: Herder, 1994³).

[103] In 1 Thess. 2.16 ἁμαρτία has no significance in terms of Paul's theological anthropology.

[104] Söding, 'Der Erste Thessalonicherbrief' 185.

1 Thess. 2.14–16 is singular, and the eschatological statements of 1 Thessalonians diverge considerably from Paul's later statements.[105] Of course Paul cannot be expected to say everything in every letter, the letters are not complete compendia of his doctrine, and the origin of an idea is not always identical with its application. Still, the particular features of 1 Thessalonians cannot be accounted for merely by referring to the situation in which the letter was composed or the circumstances of the church in Thessalonica. Rather, Paul's oldest letter itself contains a coherent theological conception.

There is a basic *apocalyptic-eschatological tone* that permeates 1 Thessalonians, which comes to explicit expression in 4.13–18; 5.1–11. Occasioned by unanticipated deaths among the congregation, in 4.13–18 Paul connects the ideas of the Lord's parousia and the resurrection of dead Christians. Within the framework of the traditional word of the Lord of vv. 16–17, the portrayal of the final events begins with the triumphal coming of the Lord, followed first by the resurrection of the dead ἐν Χριστῷ (in Christ) who then with the living are caught up in the clouds to meet the Lord. Within this course of events the resurrection of the dead members of the church plays only a minor role, for the goal of the whole event is 'being with the Lord.' For this to happen, all must be caught up to meet him as he returns, and the precondition of this is the resurrection of those 'in Christ.' The unexpected death of members of the community before the Lord's parousia had given rise to the Thessalonians' question, so that the idea of the resurrection of the dead was probably unknown to them. But for Paul, the former Pharisee, it was a common idea, which indicates that in his initial preaching in Thessalonica that founded the church Paul had omitted the idea of the resurrection of dead believers, since he was convinced of the nearness of the Lord's return. It was the death of some members of the church that made it necessary for him to introduce this idea. 1 Thess. 4.13–18 confirms this supposition, for the concept of the resurrection of dead Christians functions only in an auxiliary manner, and Paul remains faithful to his original idea that all Christians will be caught up to meet the Lord at his return. Paul counts himself and the church at Thessalonica among those who will be alive at the parousia (vv. 15, 17: ἡμεῖς οἱ ζῶντες = we who are alive), probably with the conviction that the advent of the Lord would occur in the immediate future. In 1 Thess. 5.1–11 the apostle proceeds from a discussion of the 'how' of the eschatological events to the question of 'when.' He adopts traditional motifs in

---

[105] Cf. Udo Schnelle, *Wandlungen im paulinischen Denken*, (SBS 137) (Stuttgart: Katholisches Bibelwerk, 1989) 37–48.

rejecting speculations about an exact date (5.1–3), and admonishes
the faithful to live their lives in view of the Day of the Lord that will
certainly come, but the date of which cannot be calculated (vv. 4–8). The
content of the Christian life is characterized by its orientation to the future
advent of the Lord, and is thus eschatological existence. The pregnant
expression in 1 Thess. 5.10 connects with 4.17 in naming the goal of
Christian existence as a 'being with Christ' that endures even beyond
death.

The eschatological orientation that dominates the final two chapters of
1 Thessalonians is also found in the first chapter of the letter. Thus, in
contrast to the missionary sermons in Acts, 1 Thess. 1.9b–10 speaks only
of Jesus' resurrection, as that which makes possible his function as savior,
not however of a general resurrection of the dead. So too the concept of
living one's life in imitation of others who have been persecuted during
the present time of troubles must be understood within an eschatological-
apocalyptic horizon of meaning.[106] By accepting the word during the time
of eschatological distress the Thessalonians become imitators of the Lord
and of the apostles (cf. 1 Thess. 1.6; 2.13–14; 3.3–5), and thereby become
themselves models for others. In 1 Thessalonians Paul understands the
imitatio concept not primarily in an ethical sense; for him it rather serves
to describe the church's standing within the saved community and as a
comprehensive interpretation of Christian existence. In any case, the ethic
of 1 Thessalonians is oriented completely to the Lord's parousia.[107] The
apostle repeatedly challenges the church to be a holy people ready to meet
the returning Lord (cf. 1 Thess. 3.13; 4.3, 4, 7; 5.23). Appearing before
God's throne (cf. 1 Thess. 1.3; 2.19; 3.13) and the judgment according to
one's works (1 Thess. 4.6; 5.9) are connected with the parousia. For the
grounding and motivation of the ethical demands of the Christian life, Paul
does not point primarily to the Christ event of the past, but to the eschatological events that are shortly to break in (cf. 1 Thess. 5.11). As those who
have been elected and called by God (cf. 1 Thess. 1.4–5; 2.12; 4.7; 5.9, 24),
the Thessalonians place their hope on the future saving act of God.[108] The
pneumatology of the letter is also distinctive, for '1 Thessalonians does not

---

[106] Cf. Schade, *Apokalyptische Christologie* 117–134. The accents are placed differently by Otto
Merk, 'Nachahmung Christi,' in *Neues Testament und Ethik* (FS R. Schnackenburg), ed. Helmut
Merklein (Freiburg: Herder, 1989) 172–206.

[107] Cf. Udo Schnelle, 'Die Ethik des 1 Thessalonicherbriefes,' in *The Thessalonian Correspondence*, ed. Raymond F. Collins, 295–305; Siegfried Schulz, *Neutestamentliche Ethik* (Zürich:
Theologischer Verlag, 1987) 301–333.

[108] On the concept of election in 1 Thessalonians, cf. Schade, *Apokalyptische Christologie*
117–134; in this connection Merk, 'Christologie' 104ff. rightly emphasizes the close relationship
between theo-logy and Christ-ology.

know the idea of a pneumatic Christ–realm, into which the Christian is sacramentally incorporated.'[109]

The expectation of the imminent parousia is stamped on the theology of 1 Thessalonians throughout, from the way in which the letter is structured to the manner in which ethical instructions are given. It is no accident that four of the five Pauline references to the παρουσία (coming, presence) are found in 1 Thessalonians (2.19; 3.13; 4.15; 5.23)! There is thus a tightly-coherent theological conception: in faith in Jesus Christ who has been raised from the dead and in the present power of the Spirit sent from God (1 Thess. 4.8; 5.19), the church awaits the coming of the Son from heaven who will deliver them from the wrath to come. It is thus both historically and theologically misguided to introduce views from Paul's later letters into this oldest document of Pauline theology. Such an exegetical approach has the effect of leveling out the independent theology of 1 Thessalonians, which can be described as *early Pauline*, since it obviously forms the beginning point for a consideration of Pauline theology from both a historical and theological point of view. So regarded, it stands in continuity with the theology of Paul's Hellenistic mother church, but does not presuppose the central themes and conflicts of the later letters.

2.4.10 Tendencies of Recent Research

During the last ten years the first letter of Paul to the Thessalonians has emerged from its previous existence in the shadows and become a new focus for Pauline studies. There are two reasons for this: (1) attention has shifted from key individual texts (cf. 1 Thess. 1.9–10; 2.14–16; 4.13–18; 5.1–11) to the letter as a whole as an independent witness to Pauline theology. At the commentary level, such a study was carried through for the first time by W. Marxsen. (2) Of great heuristic relevance is the thesis advocated in somewhat different ways by, among others, G. Strecker,[110] H. H. Schade, U. Schnelle, S. Schulz,[111] K. P. Donfried,[112] W. Thüsing[113] and F. W. Horn,[114] namely that 1 Thessalonians represents an early stage of Pauline thinking. The distinctive elements of 1 Thessalonians in com-

---

[109] Friedrich W. Horn, *Angeld des Geistes* (see below 2.5.8) 147.

[110] Cf. Georg Strecker, 'Befreiung und Rechtfertigung,' in *Eschaton und Historie*, ed. G. Strecker (Göttingen: Vandenhoeck & Ruprecht, 1979) 229–259.

[111] Cf. Siegfried Schulz, 'Der frühe und der späte Paulus,' ThZ 41 (1985) 228–236.

[112] Cf. Karl P. Donfried, '1 Thessalonians, Acts and the Early Paul,' in *The Thessalonian Correspondence*, ed. Raymond F. Collins, 3–26.

[113] Cf. Wilhelm Thüsing, *Gott und Christus in der paulinischen Soteriologie*, NTA 1/I (Münster: Aschendorff, 1986³) 1.viii–ix.

[114] Cf. Horn, *Angeld des Geistes* (see below, 2.5.8), 119–160.

parison with later Pauline letters are no longer considered to be incidental or minor, but to reflect the independent theological substance of the oldest Pauline letter. From this point of view there emerges a new perspective for understanding and portraying Pauline thought as a whole, since now one must reckon with developments and changes in Paul. W. Wiefel[115] pointed to changes in the realm of Pauline eschatology by a comparison of 1 Thess. 4.13–18; 1 Cor. 15.51–52; 2 Cor. 5.1–10 and Phil. 1.23; 3.20–21. For G. Strecker, U. Wilckens,[116] U. Schnelle,[117] S. Schulz and others, the doctrine of justification found in Galatians and Romans is not characteristic of the thinking of 1 Thessalonians, but represents a later stage of Pauline theology. In the judgment of many scholars, the statements about Israel in 1 Thess. 2.14–16 cannot be harmonized with those in Romans 9–11, so that here too a change in Paul's thought can be discerned.[118]

In a second direction that Pauline research has taken, 1 Thessalonians is integrated into the corpus of Pauline theology taken as a whole. Paul is understood to have received his gospel that was critical of the Law already at Damascus,[119] so that all the important theological topics of the later Pauline letters are already to be presupposed in the interpretation of 1 Thessalonians. The distinctive features of 1 Thessalonians are mostly explained as a result of the specific situation of the church to which the letter is addressed, which does not call for an elaboration of the doctrine of justification, for example. On eschatology and the relation of the church to Israel, scholars with this point of view speak of a shift of accents rather than substantial changes in Paul's thought. As representative of this approach one may count the commentary of T. Holtz, the works of G. Klein on the law and eschatology in Paul,[120] the studies of O. Merk, and (with different emphases) the Pauline interpretation of P. Stuhlmacher[121] within the framework of his biblical theology. A mediating position is assumed by Th. Söding, who on the one hand emphasizes the relative continuity between 1 Thessalonians and the following letters, 'on the other hand Philippians 3

---

[115] Cf. Wolfgang Wiefel, 'Die Hauptrichtung des Wandels im eschatologischen Denken des Paulus,' ThZ 30 (1974) 65–84.

[116] Cf. Ulrich Wilckens, 'Zur Entwicklung des paulinischen Gesetzesverständnisses' (see below 2.8.1) 154–190.

[117] Cf. Udo Schnelle, *Gerechtigkeit und Christusgegenwart. Vorpaulinische und paulinische Tauftheologie*, GTA 24 (Göttingen: Vandenhoeck & Ruprecht, 1986²).

[118] Cf. most recently Peter Stuhlmacher, *Romans* (see below 2.8.1) 177ff.

[119] Cf. Ulrich Luck, 'Die Bekehrung des Paulus und das Paulinische Evangelium,' ZNW 76 (1985) 187–208; Christian Dietzfelbinger, *Die Berufung des Paulus als Ursprung seiner Theologie*, WMANT 58 (Neukirchen: Neukirchener Verlag, 1985). A different interpretation of the Damascus event is offered by Udo Schnelle, *Wandlungen* (see above 2.4.9) 15–21.

[120] Cf. Günter Klein, 'Eschatologie IV,' TRE 10 (1982) 277–285; 'Gesetz,' TRE 13 (1984) 64–75.

and Galatians present not only new forms of expression for a basically unchanged theological substance. They rather signal a qualitative new level of Pauline theology (as 1 Corinthians had already done in a different way).'[122]

J. Becker interprets 1 Thessalonians as a witness for the theology of the Antioch church.[123] Accordingly, the central theological conception of the oldest Pauline letter is a theology of election,[124] in which the awareness of God's gracious choice of the eschatological community comes to expression. 'The called will not be subjected to wrath with the rest of humanity, but will immediately experience final deliverance.'[125]

Recent American research has been dominated by sociological and history-of-religions perspectives. Thus the significance of pagan cults for the situation of the church is discussed (K. P. Donfried,[126] R. Jewett). Jewett supposes that among the members of the church from the lower social stratum were many earlier adherents of the Cabirus cult. Phenomena within the congregation such as ecstasy, sexual freedom, and intense eschatological expectation are explained in terms of this background. Moreover, Jewett sees substantial elements of the congregation as advocates of a kind of millennialism already at the time of 1 Thessalonians, against whom Paul then directs 2 Thessalonians. A. J. Malherbe interprets Paul's missionary strategy in the context of contemporary philosophy and ethics. He points to parallels between Paul and the wandering philosophers in the process of community formation: persuasion or conversion of the hearers, formation of small groups, training in doctrine, ethics, and cultic praxis, and maintenance of contact by visits, sending messengers, and letters.

2.5 The First Letter to the Corinthians

2.5.1 Literature

Commentaries

Weiss, Johannes. *Der erste Korintherbrief.* KEK 5. Göttingen: Vandenhoeck & Ruprecht, 1910[5]; Lietzmann, Hans. *An die Korinther I, II.* HNT 9. Tübingen: J. C. B.

---

[121] Cf. Peter Stuhlmacher, *Biblische Theologie* (see above 2) 1.334: 'From the very beginning Paul's theology as a whole is characterized by the doctrine of justification.'

[122] Söding, 'Der Erste Thessalonicherbrief' 201.

[123] Cf. Becker, *Paul* (see above 2) 130–140.

[124] The significance of the concept of election for 1 Thessalonians was already clearly recognized by Schade, *Apokalyptische Christologie* 117ff.

[125] Becker, *Paul* 132.

[126] Cf. Donfried, 'Cults of Thessalonica' 336–356.

Mohr (Paul Siebeck), 1969⁵; Conzelmann, Hans. *1 Corinthians*, tr. James W. Leitch. Philadelphia: Fortress Press, 1975; Fascher, Erich. *Der erste Brief des Paulus an die Korinther* (Chs. 1–7), ThHK 7/I. Berlin: Evangelische Verlagsanstalt, 1980²; Wolff, Christian. *Der erste Brief des Paulus an die Korinther* (Chs. 8–16), ThHK 7/II. Berlin: Evangelische Verlagsanstalt, 1982; Klauck, Hans-Joseph. *1 Korintherbrief*, NEB. Würzburg: Echter Verlag, 1984; Lang, Friedrich. *Der Briefe an die Korinther*, NTD 7. Göttingen: Vandenhoeck & Ruprecht, 1986; Fee, Gordon D. *The First Epistle to the Corinthians*, NIC. Grand Rapids: William B. Eerdmans, 1987; Strobel, August. *Der erste Brief an die Korinther*, ZBK 6.1. Zürich: Theologischer Verlag, 1989; Merklein, Helmut. *1 Korintherbrief*, (Chs. 1–4) ÖTK 7.1. Gütersloh: Gütersloher Verlagshaus (Gerd Mohn), 1992; Schrage, Wolfgang. *Der Erste Brief an die Korinther*, EKK VII/1–2. Neukirchen-Vluyn: Neukirchener Verlag, 1991, 1995

Monographs

Lütgert, Wilhelm. *Freiheitspredigt und Schwarmgeister in Korinth*, BFChTh 12.3. Gütersloh: Bertelsmann, 1908; Wilckens, Ulrich. *Weisheit und Torheit*, BHTh 26. Tübingen: J. C. B. Mohr (Paul Siebeck), 1959; Schmithals, Walter. *Gnosticism in Corinth*, tr. John E. Steely. Nashville: Abingdon, 1971; Winter, M. *Pneumatiker und Psychiker in Korinth*, MThST 12. Marburg: Elwert, 1975; Schreiber, Alfred. *Die Gemeinde in Korinth*, NTA 12. Münster: Aschendorff, 1977; Sellin, Gerhard. *Der Streit um die Auferstehung der Toten*, FRLANT 138. Göttingen: Vandenhoeck & Ruprecht, 1986; Klauck, Hans-Joseph. *Herrenmahl und hellenistischer Kult*, NTA 15. Münster: Aschendorff, 1987²; Marshall, Peter. *Enmity in Corinth*, WUNT 2.23. Tübingen: J. C. B. Mohr (Paul Siebeck), 1987; Mitchell, Margaret M. *Paul and the Rhetoric of Reconciliation*, HUTh 28. Tübingen: J. C. B. Mohr (Paul Siebeck), 1991; Hay, David, ed. *Pauline Theology, Volume II: 1 and 2 Corinthians*. Minneapolis: Fortress, 1993.

Articles

Soden, Hans v. 'Sakrament und Ethik bei Paulus,' in *Das Paulusbild in der neueren deutschen Forschung*, ed. Karl H. Rengstorf. Darmstadt: Wissenschaftliche Buchgesellschaft, 1964, 338–379; Friedrich, Gerhard. 'Christus, Einheit und Norm der Christen,' in *Auf das Wort kommt es an*, ed. G. Friedrich. Göttingen: Vandenhoeck & Ruprecht, 1978, 147–170; Vielhauer, Philipp. 'Paulus und die Kephaspartei in Korinth,' in *Oikodome*. TB 65, ed. P. Vielhauer. Munich: Chr. Kaiser Verlag, 1979, 169–182; Theißen, Gerd. 'Social Stratification in the Corinthian Community,' in *The Social Setting of Pauline Christianity*, ed. John H. Schütz. Philadelphia: Fortress Press, 1982, 69–119; Theißen, Gerd. 'The Strong and the Weak in Corinth,' in *The Social Setting of Pauline Christianity*, ed. John H. Schütz. Philadelphia: Fortress Press, 1982, 121–43; Merklein, Helmut. 'Die Einheitlichkeit des ersten Korintherbriefes,' in *Studien zu Jesus und Paulus*, WUNT 43, ed. H. Merklein. Tübingen: J. C. B. Mohr (Paul Siebeck), 1987, 345–375; Schniewind, Julius. 'Die Leugner der Auferstehung in Korinth,' in *Reden und Aufsätze*, ed. E. Kähler. Wuppertal: R. Brockhaus, 1987², 110–139; Barth, Gerhard. 'Zur Frage nach der in 1 Korinther 15 bekämpften Auferstehungsleugnung', ZNW 83 (1992) 187–201.

History of Research

Sellin, Gerhard. 'Hauptprobleme des Ersten Korintherbriefes', *ANRW* 25.4. Berlin: Walter de Gruyter, 1987, 2940–3044.

2.5.2 *Author*

The Pauline authorship of 1 Corinthians is undisputed. The author of 1 Clement reminds the church at Corinth of this letter they have received from Paul (cf. 1 Clem. 47.1–3), and Ignatius of Antioch quotes four times from 1 Corinthians (cf. 1 Cor. 4.4/IgnRom. 5.1; 1 Cor. 1.19–20/IgnEph. 18.1; 1 Cor. 6.9–10/IgnEph. 16.1; IgnPhld. 3.3; 1 Cor. 5.7a/IgnMag. 10.2). The high regard in which the Corinthian letters were held in the early church is shown by the fact that in the Muratorian Canon, 1 and 2 Corinthians stand at the head of the Pauline letters.

2.5.3 *Place and Time of Composition*

1 Corinthians was written in *Ephesus* (cf. 1 Cor. 16.8), presumably around Easter (cf. 1 Cor. 5.7–8).[127] The apostle's travel plans (cf. 1 Cor. 16.5–8) point to the last year of his stay in Corinth as the year in which the letter was composed, i.e. *spring of 55* CE,[128] even if the previous year cannot be completely excluded as a possibility. The collection for the poor among the saints in Jerusalem was already arranged (cf. 1 Cor. 16.1), though it remains unclear whether this had happened by means of a letter (1 Cor. 5.9?) or by a messenger (1 Cor. 16.15, 17: Stephanas?). Timothy was already en route to Corinth (1 Cor. 4.17), but is not expected to arrive there until after they have received Paul's letter. 1 Corinthians should be dated prior to Galatians for the following reasons: (1) The investigation of specific points of contact in language and content between the two letters points clearly to the order 1 Corinthians → Galatians.[129] (2) There is no trace in the Corinthian correspondence of the understanding of the Law set forth in Galatians. The word νόμος (law) does not occur in 2 Corinthians, and only eight times in four passages in 1 Corinthians (cf. 1 Cor. 9.8, 9, 20–22; 14.21; 15.56). None of these texts contains either the level of discussion or the complex of metaphors and line of argument associated with reflection on the Law in Galatians. Only 1 Cor. 15.56 points in the

---

[127] Cf. among others Lietzmann, *1 Korintherbrief* 89; Conzelmann, *1 Corinthians* 4; Wolff, *1 Korintherbrief* 222; Merklein, *1 Korintherbrief* 1.51.

[128] Cf. Lang, *1 Korintherbrief* 4; Conzelmann, *1 Corinthians* 4 note 31; Fee, *1 Corinthians* 4–5; Kümmel, *Introduction* 279; Lohse, *Formation* 67; Jülicher – Fascher, *Einleitung* 85; Schrage, *1 Korintherbrief* 1.36; Merklein, *1 Korintherbrief* 51.

[129] Cf. Udo Borse, *Der Standort des Galaterbriefes* (see below 2.7.1) 58–70.

direction of Paul's later line of argument.[130] (3) So too, the Pauline doctrine of justification found in Galatians (and Romans) is missing from the Corinthian letters. Should we think of Paul as having regarded the understanding of the Law and of justification expressed in Galatians as so unimportant that he failed to employ it in his disputes with the Corinthian opponents? Can one imagine that the very precise ideas of Galatians sank into the background of Paul's thought, only then to reemerge with vehemence shortly thereafter in Romans? But the doctrine of justification as found in Galatians (and Romans) would have been for Paul a very appropriate theological instrument with which to pull the rug out from under the perfectionist self-consciousness of the Corinthian enthusiasts. (4) The extensive agreements between Galatians and Romans indicate that Galatians was written immediately prior to Romans (see below 2.7.3).

2.5.4 Intended Readership

In 146 BCE Corinth had been destroyed, but continued to be inhabited. In 44 BCE Caesar refounded the city as a Roman colony for veterans[131] which then became the capital of the senatorial province of Achaia in 27 BCE. Thus alongside a powerful Roman element, the Greek and oriental segments of the population were also large and important. Philo indicates that there was a notable Jewish colony in Corinth (cf. *Embassy to Gaius* 281), and Acts 18.4 reports the existence of a synagogue. [132] The unique location of the city with its two harbors of Cenchrea and Lecheum explains why the city became such an important commercial center between Asia and Rome/Greece. Corinth was considered a wealthy city, in which business, finance, and manufacturing flourished. A number of Hellenistic-Oriental religious cults were found in Corinth. Pausanias reports that in the second century CE Corinth had altars and shrines of Poseidon, Dionysus, Isis and Serapis, the Ephesian Artemis, and a temple to Asclepius.[133] Apuleius describes an Isis initiation that took place in Corinth (cf. *Metamorphoses* 11.22.7ff.).[134] Corinth was certainly a center of the Cynic movement that

---

[130] Cf. for a more detailed argument, Udo Schnelle, *Wandlungen* (see above 2.4.9) 49–54.

[131] On Corinth cf. especially J. Wiseman, 'Corinth and Rome I. 228 BC–AD 267,' ANRW II 7.1 (Berlin: Walter de Gruyter, 1979) 438–548; W. Elliger, *Paulus in Griechenland* (see above 2.4.4) 200–251; J. Murphy-O'Connor, St. Paul's Corinth. Texts and Archaeology (Wilmington: Michael Glazier, 1983); D. W. J. Gill, 'Corinth: a Roman Colony in Achaea,' BZ 37 (1993) 259–264.

[132] Inscriptional evidence for a synagogue in Corinth comes only from the 2–3 century CE; cf. Klauck, *Herrenmahl* 234 note 3.

[133] Cf. Pausanias, *Description of Greece* 2.1.7–5.5.

[134] On the worship of Egyptian gods in Corinth, cf. Dennis E. Smith, 'Egyptian Cults at Corinth,' HThR 70 (1977) 201–231.

experienced a revival in the first century CE. Already Diogenes liked to stay there (Dio Chrysostom *Or* 6.3), and later the famous Cynic Demetrius lived and taught in Corinth[135] (cf. Lucian, *Indoct* 19; Philostratus, *Life of Apollonius* 4.25). Moreover, Corinth was the site of the Isthmian Games (cf. 1 Cor. 9.24–27), after the Olympic Games the most important athletic contest in antiquity. We may note finally that in the north part of the city an Asclepius temple has been excavated with three banquet rooms, illustrating the kind of problem in the background of 1 Corinthians 8–10.[136]

Paul founded the church in Corinth after his work in Philippi, Thessalonica, Berea, and Athens in the year 50. He arrived in Corinth alone (cf. Acts 18.5), but was soon joined by Silas and Timothy. Paul remained there about a year and a half (cf. Acts 18.11), so that Corinth became a center of the Pauline missionary work alongside Ephesus. The cultural, religious, and social pluralism of the city is also reflected in the composition of the Corinthian church. That most of its members had come from the gentile population (cf. 1 Cor. 12.2) is illustrated by the problems and issues the church had to deal with (participation in cultic banquets, trials before pagan courts, prostitution). The report of the conversion of Crispus, the leader of the synagogue (cf. Acts 18.8) as well as 1 Cor. 1.22–24; 7.18; 9.20; 10.32; Rom. 16.21 testify to the presence of a significant Jewish element in the church. Proselytes and Godfearers also joined the Corinthian church (cf. Acts 18.7). The majority of the church belonged to the lower socio-economic class (cf. 1 Cor. 1.26; 7.21; 11.22b). The church also included some wealthy members, such as the synagogue leader Crispus already mentioned (cf. 1 Cor. 1.14), or Erastus, who held a high office in the Corinthian city administration (cf. Rom. 16.23). Some Corinthian Christians owned houses (cf. 1 Cor. 1.16; 11.22a; 16.15ff.; Rom. 16.23; Acts 18.2, 3, 8), and the church was intensively involved in the collection for the saints in Jerusalem (cf. 1 Cor. 16.1–4; 2 Cor. 8.4; 9.1, 12; Rom. 15.31).[137]

In the church there existed a number of tensions dealing with theological, ethical, and social issues. Thus in 1 Cor. 1–4 Paul challenges their divisions into theologically motivated groups. There were obviously in Corinth four groups, named after their postulated founders Paul, Apollos, Cephas, and Christ.[138] In 1 Corinthians 1.12 ἐγὼ δὲ Χριστοῦ (I belong to Christ) is parallel to the preceding group designations. There seems to be

---

[135] Cf. Margarethe Billerbeck, *Der Kyniker Demetrius. Ein Beitrag zur Geschichte der frühkaiserlicher Popularphilosophie*, (PhAnt 36) (Leiden: E. J. Brill, 1979).

[136] Cf. Murphy-O'Connor, *St. Paul's Corinth* 161–167.

[137] On the social structure in Corinth, cf. most recently Merklein, *1 Korintherbrief* 1.31–42.

[138] Cf. here Schrage, *1 Korintherbrief* 1.142–152.

no change of emphasis or nuance in the listing of the four groups, so that we must reckon with the existence of a 'Christ party' in Corinth.[139] Moreover, μεμέρισται ὁ Χριστός (has Christ been divided?) in v. 13a presupposes ἐγὼ δὲ Χριστοῦ of v. 12! Paul challenges this tendency toward division by pointing to the unity of the church grounded in Christ and appropriated in baptism. In 1 Cor. 5 Paul responds to a case of incest in the congregation, while 1 Cor. 6.1–11 presupposes court cases between Corinthian Christians held before pagan judges. Warning against (cultic) prostitution prevalent in Corinth (1 Cor. 6.12–20) is followed in 1 Cor. 7 by the recommendation of sexual asceticism. The conflict about eating food sacrificed to idols is evoked by both religious and social factors (cf. especially 1 Cor. 8.1–3; 10.14–23). The *'strong'* in Corinth certainly belonged in part to the upper social stratum, for whom it was possible to abandon traditional religious ideas on the basis of superior religious knowledge (cf. 1 Cor. 8.1, 4; 10.23). Nevertheless, the 'strong' are not simply to be identified with those church members who belonged to the upper social class, for the knowledge that only one God exists and that gods and demons are nothing is the expression of a monotheism claimed by both Jews and Gentiles regardless of social rank (cf. 1 Thess. 1.9–10). Cynic traditions could also be of significance here, for Cynics, corresponding to their monotheistic confession, claimed the freedom to eat any kind of food[140] – as did some of the Corinthian church. Both Gentile Christians and liberal Jewish Christians were numbered in the group of the 'strong.' They were invited to dinners by their non-Christian Gentile associates (cf. 1 Cor. 10.27), and their social position made it impossible to completely avoid meat that had been dedicated to an idol. The *'weak'* in the Corinthian church were mainly a minority among the Gentile Christians, since it is only of Gentile Christians that Paul could speak of a συνήθεια τοῦ εἰδώλου (cf. 1 Cor. 8.7, still being accustomed to idols). Some members of this group, out of fear of the gods, probably gave up eating meat dedicated to idols altogether. Others, under the material necessity to take part in public religious festivals, felt that on such occasions they must eat meat within a cultic context, but did so only with damage to their own conscience. Still others were misled by the conduct of the 'strong' into voluntarily eating meat contrary to their own conscience, for the 'strong'

---

[139] Among those who see the fourth slogan as a gloss are Weiß, *1 Korintherbrief* 15ff. and Wilckens, *Weisheit und Torheit* 17 note 2. Merklein, *1 Korintherbrief* 1.146–147, speaks not of a 'Christ party' but of a 'Christ motto' that Paul thinks all the groups should adopted.

[140] Thus Epictetus, *Discourses* 3.22.50, can designate 'eating anything you give them' as a characteristic of the Cynics. Further texts with interpretations are found in F. Stanley Jones, *'Freiheit' in den Briefen des Apostels Paulus*, GTA 34 (Göttingen: Vandenhoeck & Ruprecht, 1987) 59–61.

participated in pagan banquets when under no pressure to do so, and without giving it a second thought (1 Cor. 10.14–22).

In 1 Cor. 11.17–34 Paul engages in debate concerning problems that had arisen in connection with their abuse of the Lord's Supper.[141] In Corinth the sacramental act was connected with a regular meal the church shared in common (1 Cor. 11.23–25), whereas originally the breaking of bread and the drinking of the wine formed the framework around the whole meal (cf. μετὰ τὸ δειπνῆσαι in 1 Cor. 11.25, literally = 'after dining'). This original practice had been replaced by meals that preceded the real sacramental act. This allowed the real differences between poor and rich members of the church to emerge openly, for some feasted while others went hungry (cf. 21–22, 33–34). At the pagan banquets held in connection with sacrifice to a god, table groups were formed among the wealthy from which the poor were excluded.

There were also arguments among the Corinthian Christians over the relative value of the different spiritual gifts (cf. 1 Cor. 12–14). Finally, whether there was to be a future resurrection of the dead was a disputed issue within the Corinthian church (cf. 1 Cor. 15.12b).

The structure and line of argument of 1 Corinthians corresponds to this complex situation within the Corinthian church.

2.5.5 Outline, Structure, Form

1.1–3	Prescript	Introduction
1.4–9	Proemium	
1.10–4.21	Divisions in the Church	
5.1–6.20	Ethical Problems in the Church	
7.1–40	Various Groups in the Church	
8.1–11.1	Eating Meat Sacrificed to Idols	Body
11.2–14.40	Problems of Worship	
15.1–58	Resurrection of the Dead	
16.1–18	Closing Parenesis (vv. 5–12 Apostolic Parousia)	
16.19–20	Greetings Instruction	Conclusion
16.21–24	Final farewell (Eschatokoll)	

---

[141] On the possible history-of-religions backgrounds, cf. Peter Lampe, 'Das korinthische Herrenmahl im Schnittpunkt hellenistisch-römischer Mahlpraxis und paulinischer Theologia Crucis,' ZNW 82 (1991) 183–213.

In contrast to other Pauline letters, 1 Corinthians cannot be divided into two major sections, a doctrinal part followed by a parenetic part. The line of argument is determined throughout by the situation in Corinth and the previous communication between the apostle and the church. In 1 Cor. 5.9 Paul refers to a previous letter that has been lost, to which the church is obviously responding. Their letter contains a series of questions, which the apostle takes up and answers one by one. Each such response is signaled by an introductory περὶ δέ 'now concerning': 7.1 (concerning marriage and celibacy); 7.25 (concerning virgins); 8.1 (concerning meat sacrificed to idols); 12.1 (concerning spiritual gifts); 16.1 (concerning the gift for Jerusalem); and 16.12 (concerning Apollos). In addition, Paul has information communicated by word of mouth at his disposal (cf. 1.11; 5.1; 11.18) to which he is responding especially in 1 Cor. 1–4; 5; 6, and 11.17–34. 1 Corinthians is thus distinctive among the Pauline letters in that it has no recognizable line of thought that structures the letter as a whole. Rather, the parenesis that characterizes the whole letter begins already with the παρακαλέω (I appeal) clause of 1.10.[142]

In the first major section (chapters 1–4) Paul relativizes the Corinthian striving after wisdom with this theology of the cross, which manifests itself as the reversal of all worldly values. Then the apostle goes into the issues raised by their letter and the current problems and abuses in the church (5.1–13; 6.1–11, 12–24; 7.1–40; 8.1–10.33). Chapter 11 stands in a close thematic connection to chapters 12–14, and the series spiritual gifts – eschatological expectation has already been prepared for in 1 Cor. 1.7. There is a clear connection between the subject matter of chapters 12–14 and chapter 15, since the discussion of the future resurrection was called forth by the extreme pneumatic enthusiasm of the Corinthians that emphasized present fulfillment (cf. 1 Cor. 15.46).

2.5.6 Literary Integrity

The distinctive literary structure of 1 Corinthians has repeatedly given the occasion for the development of theories that the document is composed of

---

[142] For a possible rhetorical structure connecting 1 Corinthians 1–4 and 15, cf. Michael Bünker, *Briefformular und rhetorische Disposition im 1. Korintherbrief*, GTA 28 (Göttingen: Vandenhoeck & Ruprecht, 1984). A survey of recent attempts to ascertain a literary-rhetorical structure in 1 Corinthians is presented by Schrage, *1 Korintherbrief* 1.71–94. For Schrage 1 Corinthians is primarily a 'parenetic-symbuleutic' letter. Mitchell, *Rhetoric of Reconciliation* 20–64, understands 1 Corinthians as an instance of deliberative rhetoric. Against the background of the political rhetoric of the times, 1 Corinthians appears as a call for unity and concord.

more than one letter.[143] Only the most important hypotheses are named here:

(1.) J. Weiß[144] (Letter A: 10.1–23; 6.12–20; 9.24–27; 11.2–34; 16.7b–9, 15–20; 2 Cor. 6.14–7.1. Letter B: 7.1–8.13; 13; 10.24–11.1; 9.1–23; 12; 14; 15; 16.1a–7a, 10–14, 21–24. Letter C: 1.1–6.11).

(2.) E. Dinkler[145] (Letter A: 6.12–20; 9.24–10.22; 11.2–34; 12–14. Letter B: 1.1–6, 11; 7.1–9.23; 10.23–11.1; 15; 16).

(3.) W. Schenk[146] (Letter A: 1.1–9; 2 Cor. 6.14–7.1; 6.1–11; 11.2–34; 15; 16.13–24; Letter B: 9.1–18; 9.24–10.22; 6.12–20; 5.1–13; Letter C: 7.1–8.13; 9.19–23; 10.23–11.1; 12.1–31a; 14.1c–40; 12.31b–13.13; 16.1–12; Letter D: 1.10–4.21).

(4.) H. J. Klauck[147] (Letter A: 6.12–20; 9.1–18; 9.24–10.22; 11.2–34; 13 [?]; 15 [?]; Letter B: 1.1–6.11; 7.1–8.13; 9.19–23; 10.23–11.1; 12; 14; 16).

(5.) G. Sellin[148] (Letter A: 11.2–34; 5.1–8; 6.12–20; 9.24–10.22; 6.1–11; Letter B: 5.9–13; 7.1–9.23; 10.23–11.1; 12.1–14.33a, 37–40; 15; 16; Letter C: 1.1–4.21).

(6.) In his most recent publication W. Schmithals divides the Corinthian correspondence into a total of 13 letters.[149]

Despite their difference in detail, all partition hypotheses proceed from certain phenomena in the text of 1 Corinthians:

In 1 Cor. 1.11 Paul mentions 'Chloe's people,' but says nothing about Stephanas and his companions (cf. 1 Cor. 16.15–18). On the other hand, 'Chloe's people' are not mentioned at all at the conclusion of the letter. But situations that are the occasions for different letters may not be inferred from this, for Paul mentions 'Chloe's people' only because he had heard about disputes in the congregation from them. Thus in the context of 1 Cor. 1.16 it was not necessary for Paul to refer to the presence of Stephanas, since he played no role in vouching for the accuracy of the report of the debates pictured in 1 Cor. 1–4. On the other hand, Paul does name Stephanas and his companions in the closing parenesis, since they were of great importance for continuing contact with the church. It is also

---

[143] Cf. the surveys in P. Beier, 'Geteilte Briefe?' (see above 2.4.6) 103–158, 301–326; Sellin, 'Hauptprobleme' 2965ff.; Merklein, 'Einheitlichkeit' 346–348.

[144] Cf. Weiß, *1 Korintherbrief* xli–xlii; and *Earliest Christianity*, 2 vols. tr. F. C. Grant (New York: Harper & Bros., 1937) 340–341.

[145] Cf. Erich Dinkler, 'Korintherbriefe,' RGG³ IV (1960) 18.

[146] Cf. Wolfgang Schenk, 'Der 1. Korintherbrief als Briefsammlung,' ZNW 60 (1969) 219–243.

[147] Cf. Klauck, *1 Korintherbrief* 10–11.

[148] Cf. Sellin, 'Hauptprobleme,' 2968; Cf. also his, '1Korinther 5–6 und der "Vorbrief" nach Korinth,' NTS 37 (1991) 535–558.

[149] Cf. Walter Schmithals, *Briefe des Paulus* (see above 2.4.6) 19–85.

possible that Stephanas and the other coworkers arrived only after Paul had already written much of the letter.[150]

Literary criticism has found no reason to question the unity of 1 Cor. 1.1–4.21 as a coherent text. Thus this section is often regarded as an independent letter, for which 1 Cor. 4.14–21 is supposed to form the conclusion. However, the elements of a letter conclusion are not found here, but rather the epistolary self commendation[151] (v. 14: presence of the letter writer with the addressees; v. 15: the first visit that founded the church; v. 17: sending of apostolic emissaries; v. 19: prospective presence of the letter writers with the addressees).

The beginning point of almost all theories of multiple documents in 1 Corinthians is the assumption that Paul's letter mentioned in 1 Cor. 5.9 was not lost, but has been transmitted as a part of our present 1 Corinthians. In 1 Cor. 5.9–13 Paul corrects a misunderstanding that had arisen on the basis of his previous letter concerning the association of believers with sexually immoral people; people have looked for the elements of such a letter in our extant letters to the Corinthians. The following have been identified as possible texts: 1 Cor. 6.1–11[152]; 6.12–20[153]; 5.1–8[154]; 2 Cor. 6.14–7.1[155] and 1 Cor. 5.1–8; 6.1–11.[156] None of these texts really deals with the problem referred to in 1 Cor. 5.9–13, so that here literary analysis can produce no unambiguous evidence for the letter mentioned in 5.9.[157]

In 1 Cor. 5.1–13; 6.1–11 Paul deals with two concrete issues in the church, then in 6.12 he takes up the Corinthian catchword ἐξουσία (authority), in order to name foods in 6.13a and immorality in 6.13b as examples of the right use of Christian freedom.[158] The problem of immorality is dealt with in terms of basic principles up through 1 Cor. 6.20, and then in chapter 7 in terms of practical issues (marriage, asceticism). In chapter 8 Paul seizes on the catchword βρώματα (food) from 1 Cor. 6.13a in order to reflect on the concrete example of meat sacrificed to idols. Within this section 1 Cor. 8.10 already refers to 1 Cor. 10.14–22, so that one must speak of a pragmatic coherence between the two

---

[150] Cf. Conzelmann, *1 Corinthians* 298 note 9.

[151] Cf. Schnider and Stenger, *Studien* (see above 2.3.2) 54.

[152] Cf. Günter Bornkamm, 'Vorgeschichte' (see below 2.6.1) 189 note 131.

[153] Cf. Weiß, *1 Korintherbrief* xli, 138–139; Schenke and Fischer, *Einleitung* 1.94.

[154] Cf. Alfred Suhl, *Paulus und seine Briefe* (see above 2.1) 206ff.

[155] Cf. Schmithals, *Gnosticism in Corinth* 94–95.

[156] Cf. Sellin, 'Hauptprobleme' 2969ff.

[157] Cf. Merklein, 'Einheitlichkeit' 371ff.

[158] Cf. Dieter Lührmann, 'Freundschaftsbrief trotz Spannungen. Zu Aufbau und Gattung des Ersten Korintherbriefes' in *Studien zum Text und zur Ethik des Neuen Testaments* (FS H. Greeven), ed. Wolfgang Schrage, BZNW 47 (Berlin: Walter de Gruyter, 1986) 308.

sections.[159] So too the Pauline argumentation in 1 Cor. 9.1–23 is appropriate to the subject being discussed, for Paul here illustrates his maxim of 8.13 from his own personal experience. The freedom he practices is not a matter of weakness, but freedom exercised in love for others.[160] Although the connection between 1 Cor. 9.24–27 and 10.1–22 is uncontested, 10.23–11.1 is often taken to belong to a different literary unit. But the changed line of argument is rather to be explained as due to the example that Paul here takes up: here it is no longer a matter of participation in pagan cultic banquets, but concerns contact with meat sacrificed to idols when one is purchasing meat in the marketplace or is invited to dinner in people's homes. So too the differing evaluations of divisions within the congregation found in 1 Cor. 1.12ff. and 11.18ff. do not justify the assignment of 11.2–34 to the 'previous letter.' Whereas in 1 Cor. 1.10–12 theological and personal motives led to the formation of groups, the conflict addressed in 11.18 is a matter of the rigid social distinctions that have been made within the congregation.

The numerous partition hypotheses for 1 Corinthians represent at the most a vague possibility, by no means a compelling necessity. From the positive side it may be said that the literary integrity[161] of 1 Corinthians is indicated in two ways that transcend the individual arguments: (1) The distinctive manner in which the line of argument is a loosely constructed series of topics corresponds to the special communications situation between apostle and the Corinthian church. (2) The series 1 Cor. 12–14 and 15 (spiritual gifts; parousia) is already telegraphed in advance by the structure of 1.4–6, 7–8.[162]

It is probably the case that in the course of the transmission process glosses were introduced into 1 Corinthians.[163] One such possibility is 6.14, since this verse stands in opposition to the eschatological statements in 15.51–52. In 1 Cor. 6.14 the personal pronoun ἡμεῖς (we) includes Paul himself, indicating that he reckons on his own death before the parousia. That contradicts 15.51–52, where Paul explicitly counts himself among those who will still be alive at the parousia.[164]

Another gloss is found in 1 Cor. 14.33b–36. Whereas in 11.5 Paul presupposes the active participation of women in the worship service by prayer

---

[159] Cf. Merklein, 'Einheitlichkeit' 356–365.

[160] Cf. Wolff, *1 Korintherbrief* 16–17.

[161] On the unity of 1 Corinthians in the most recent research, cf. in addition to Merklein and Lührmann especially Jürgen Becker, Paul (see above 2) 187–197 ; Schrage, *1 Korintherbrief* 1.63–71; Mitchell, *Rhetoric of Reconciliation* 184ff.

[162] Cf. Wolff, *1 Korintherbrief* 149.

[163] Cf. Jerome Murphy-O'Connor, 'Interpolations in 1 Corinthians,' CBQ 48 (1986) 81–94.

[164] Cf. Udo Schnelle, '1 Cor. 6,14 – eine nachpaulinische Glosse,' NT 25 (1983) 217–219.

and prophecy, 14.33b–36 requires that they be silent. Moreover, this gloss interrupts the train of thought concerning prophecy, and is introduced here because of the point of contact with the word σιγάω (to be silent) (1 Cor. 14.28, 30). The content of this text corresponds to the tendency of the Pastoral Letters to subordinate women completely to men (cf. 1 Tim. 2.11–15).[165]

2.5.7 *Traditions, Sources*

Paul integrates numerous traditions in his argumentation in 1 Corinthians. In 1 Cor. 1.30; 6.11; 12.13 are found prepauline *baptismal traditions* that describe the new being of the baptized in its soteriological and ethical dimensions.[166] In the confessional formula of 1 Cor. 8.6, a philosophical monotheism is combined with faith in Jesus Christ as the mediator of creation and redemption. In 1 Cor. 11.23b–26 a *eucharistic tradition* is quoted as a word of the Lord (11.23a).[167] The foundation for his own position in the dispute with those who deny the resurrection in chapter 15 is provided by a confessional formula Paul introduces with the terms παραδίδωμι (I deliver, NRSV I hand on) and παραλαμβάνω (I receive), as he does with the eucharistic tradition in 11.23a. This confessional formula comprises *1 Cor. 15.3b–5*[168] and portrays the saving work of Christ. The formula has a clear structure, the subject ὁ Χριστός (Christ) having four verbal clauses that affirm the death, burial, resurrection and appearance of Jesus Christ as the fundamental elements of the saving event. The first and third affirmations are each elaborated by a reference to the scripture, which suggests a bipartite structure for the tradition.

2.5.8 *History-of-religions Standpoint*

There are very different opinions among scholars on how to classify the religious phenomena that may be perceived in 1 Corinthians in the categories of the history of religions.[169] Thus W. Schmithals, adopting and elaborating the view of W. Lütgert, sees the opponents of Paul as Christian Gnostics who feel that they have been freed from all earthly restrictions by their new knowledge and are oriented exclusively to the Spirit-Christ.

---

[165] On this, cf. most recently Jürgen Roloff, *1 Timothy* (see below 5.5.1) 128ff.

[166] Cf. Udo Schnelle, *Gerechtigkeit und Christusgegenwart* (see above 2.4.10) 37–46, 139–142.

[167] Cf. Helmut Merklein, 'Erwägungen zur Überlieferungsgeschichte der neutestamentlichen Abendmahlstraditionen,' in *Studien zu Jesus und Paulus*, ed. H. Merklein, WUNT 43 (Tübingen: J. C. B. Mohr [Paul Siebeck], 1987) 157–180.

[168] Cf. here Wolff, *1 Korintherbrief* 153–168.

[169] On this cf. the instructive reflections by Schrage, *1 Korintherbrief* 1.38–63.

Schmithals can point to a series of agreements between statements of I Corinthians and Gnostic texts (flesh/spirit dualism, sophia speculation, devaluing of bodily existence, the resurrection experienced as already having happened to them). But the presence of a dualistic anthropology is not sufficient in itself to postulate Gnostic influence (see below 8.5.8). Nor can Paul's opponents be shown to have had the idea of a consubstantiality between the real self and the deity. The creation does not appear as the realm of a power hostile to God (cf. 1 Cor. 8.6; 10.26), so that the opponents do not distinguish between the highest God and a lesser creator God.[170] But one can only speak meaningfully of Gnosticism as present when God and the creation are understood within the same system in terms of a protological dualism. Moreover, for the reconstruction of Gnostic theology Schmithals must constantly draw his materials from Patristic traditions that are to be dated at least half a century later than the Corinthian letters. The model of a pre-Christian redeemer myth that Schmithals has taken over from R. Bultmann can now be considered obsolete,[171] so that it remains very questionable whether the Gnosticism reconstructed from second-century CE texts existed at all at the time when I Corinthians was written.

The opinion of F. C. Baur[172] that Jewish Christians were Paul's real opponents in Corinth is still often advocated.[173] Particularly the Cephas party as those who deny Paul's apostleship then appears as the bearer of Jewish Christian criticism of Paul in Corinth (cf. 1 Cor. 9.1–18; 15.1–11). However, typical Jewish Christian demands such as Torah observance and circumcision are missing in I Corinthians, and the conflict over Paul's apostleship need not have been caused by militant Jewish Christians. Moreover, the pneumatic-enthusiastic phenomena in Corinth open up the

---

[170] Cf. S. Arai, 'Die Gegner des Paulus im 1. Korintherbrief und das Problem der Gnosis,' NTS 19 (1972/73) 430–437.

[171] Cf. Carsten Colpe, *Die religionsgeschichtliche Schule. Darstellung und Kritik ihres Bildes vom gnostischen Erlösermythos*, FRLANT 78 (Göttingen: Vandenhoeck & Ruprecht, 1961). Differently now Hans M. Schenke, 'Die Rolle der Gnosis in Bultmanns Kommentar zum Johannesevangelium aus heutiger Sicht,' in *Protokoll der Tagung 'Alte Marburger'* (1991), (49–83) 74, who would like to rehabilitate the 'myth of the redeemed redeemer as a modern scholarly category to describe the essence of Gnosticism' from the perspective of the Nag Hammadi texts. A critical introduction to the problem is offered by Karlmann Beyschlag, *Grundriß der Dogmengeschichte* (Darmstadt: Wissenschaftliche Buchgesellschaft, 1988²) 1.130–152.

[172] Cf. F. C. Baur, 'Die Christuspartei in der korinthischen Gemeinde, der Gegensatz des petrinischen und paulinischen Christenthums in der ältesten Kirche, der Apostel Petrus in Rom,' TZTh (1831) 61–206.

[173] Cf. for this understanding (with differences in individual arguments), e.g. Weiß, *1 Korintherbrief* xxxv–xliii; Vielhauer, 'Paulus und die Kephaspartei;' Lüdemann, *Opposition to Paul* 75–80. Vielhauer and Lüdemann also reckon with spiritualists in Corinth, but do not regard them as opponents of Paul. On the hypothesis of 'multiple fronts,' cf. Sellin 'Hauptprobleme' 301 1ff.

possibility of other history-of-religions connections. The sophia theology in 1 Cor. 2.6–16, the flesh/spirit dualism, the high evaluation of knowledge (cf. 1 Cor. 8.1–6; 13.2), the denigration of the body (cf. 1 Cor. 6.12–20) and the concept of two archetypes of humanity in 1 Cor. 15.45 point to the influence of Hellenistic-Jewish wisdom theology in Corinth.[174] Paul himself, of course, comes from Hellenistic Judaism,[175] so that his theology and the position of the Corinthian opponents could not be distinguished in every case. In addition, the texts in which Paul obviously criticizes and corrects the Corinthians would not be easy to explain. Thus G. Sellin[176] supposes that through Apollos an Alexandrian-Jewish wisdom theology had penetrated the predominately Gentile Christian church in Corinth. Sellin can point to remarkable agreements between Philo and the Corinthian theology, but nonetheless there are objections to this hypothesis: (1) The theology of the Alexandrian Christian Apollos (cf. Acts 18.24) is unknown, so that all postulated agreements would be purely hypothetical. (2) If Apollos had been the cause of the conflict between Paul and the Corinthians, then it can hardly be explained why Paul not only does not criticize him but accepts him as an independent and equal missionary (cf. 1 Cor. 3.5, 8). (3) According to 1 Cor. 16.12 Paul had several times urged Apollos to make another visit to Corinth, which would mean that Paul repeatedly attempted to get the cause of the Corinthian troubles to leave Ephesus and go back to Corinth!

There is no denying the influence of Hellenistic-Jewish wisdom theology on both Paul and the Corinthians, but this is not the source of the conflict between them. Rather, the theology that is developing in Corinth and reflected in 1 Corinthians must be understood as the *independent* achievement of the Corinthians themselves,[177] which may not be discussed in terms of a single cause. The Corinthians developed central elements of Paul's own theology further, at the same time remaining open to influences from their immediate context. In this process a kind of thinking oriented to the sacraments formed the real starting point of their theology.[178] Thus

---

[174] Cf. here for example Karl G. Sandelin, *Die Auseinandersetzung mit der Weisheit in 1.Korinther 15* (Åbo: Åbö Akademi, 1976); Richard A. Horsley, 'Wisdom of Word and Words of Wisdom in Corinth,' CBQ 39 (1977) 224–239; Merklein, *1 Korintherbrief* 1.119–133.

[175] On this cf. Egon Brandenburger, *Fleisch und Geist. Paulus und die dualistische Weisheit*, WMANT 29 (Neukirchen: Neukirchener Verlag, 1968); Gerd Theißen, *Psychological Aspects of Pauline Theology*, tr. John P. Galvin (Philadelphia: Fortress Press, 1987) 355ff.

[176] Cf. Sellin, Auferstehung der Toten, passim.

[177] In contrast Marshall, *Enmity in Corinth*, supposes that it was not theological motives, but purely social ones that were behind the conflict between Paul and the Corinthians. In his view Paul declined the offer of financial help from wealthy Corinthians, which they took as an affront, and resulted in the formation of the different groups.

[178] v. Soden, 'Sakrament und Ethik' 364, rightly emphasizes that 'all the participants were

baptism played a decisive role in the formation of the different groups in the Corinthian church; it determined which group one belonged to (cf. 1 Cor. 1.13–17). Obviously the authority of the real or claimed baptizer was transferred to the baptizee, so that the baptizee's participation in the life of the church was influenced by the regard in which the baptizer was held. From the perspective of the history of religions, here as in Romans 6.3–4 one must reckon with influence from the mystery religions, where the concept of a shared fate between the initiates and the deity is found. The problems and abuses associated with the Lord's Supper (cf. 1 Cor. 11.17–34) also point to the mystery cults that were well represented in the city. Probably the Corinthians applied Hellenistic sacral ideas (e.g. theophagy) to the Lord's Supper. The high regard for sacraments and the spiritual gifts that were associated with them (cf. 1 Cor. 12.13) comes to explicit expression in the Corinthians' consciousness of perfection and fulfillment (cf. 1 Cor. 2.6; 4.8, 10, 18–20; 5.2; 6.12; 10.1ff., 23; 15.12). For them the sacrament was the absolute guarantee of salvation, because through it the gift of the Spirit accomplished the ultimate transition into a new state of being that could never be lost (1 Cor. 5.5). As spiritual beings, some members of the Corinthian church felt that they had obviously already been taken out of ordinary fleshly existence and were no longer bound by moral or religious norms (cf. 1 Cor. 6.12–20; 10.1–13). The discussion of the ecstatic-enthusiastic phenomena taken up by Paul in 1 Cor. 12–14 underscores the value that the Corinthians place on the Spirit and its gifts. So too the denial of the resurrection of the dead mentioned in 1 Cor. 15.12 is connected to the Corinthian sacramentalism. Since the resurrection had already taken place in baptism (cf. Col. 2.12–13; 3.1–4; Eph. 2.6), affirmations of the resurrection as a future event and the nature of the resurrection body were seen as pointless. The attainment of life was accomplished for the Corinthians not by the overcoming of death at the parousia of the Lord, but by the conferral of the spirit received in baptism. The practice of vicarious baptism of 1 Cor. 15.29 illustrates their faith in the potency of baptism to overcome death and is a drastic illustration of how it was understood: as a saving sacrament, as the beginning and completion of redemption.[179]

Since the Corinthians also applied this perfect-tense time frame to the

---

thinking in sacramental terms.' He characterizes the Corinthians as 'over-excited enthusiasts of the pneuma-faith' (ibid. 361); Hans Conzelmann, Chr. Wolff, G. D. Fee, and F. Lang are among those whose commentaries argue for an indigenous development in this sense. Cf. further the comprehensive analyses by Friedrich W. Horn, *Angeld des Geistes*. FRLANT 154 (Göttingen: Vandenhoeck & Ruprecht, 1992) 160–301.

[179] A further example of the realistic terms in which some early Christians understood the sacraments is found in 1 Corinthians 11.30!

eschatological realities, they exchanged future and present and disregarded the course of eschatological events willed by God. In contrast, Paul emphasizes that the eschatological events too will unfold according to God's sovereign plan (1 Cor. 15.23ff.), when the spiritual body will follow the physical one, and not the other way around (1 Cor. 15.46).

2.5.9 Basic Theological Ideas

In view of its factual divisions, the one great theme that occupies Paul's thought in 1 Corinthians is the *unity of the church* founded in Jesus Christ. Already with his reference in 1.13 to ὁ Χριστός (Christ), as an abbreviation for σῶμα Χριστοῦ (body of Christ)[180] the apostle introduces the idea of the church as the body of Christ in order to make clear that it is not the possession of the Spirit by various individuals that assures the unity of the church, but that this is something that can only be done by Jesus Christ himself. In 1.18ff. Paul then criticizes the Corinthians' individualistic consciousness of their own fulfillment with his theology of the cross.[181] The cross shatters all supposed security; by the cross human wisdom is overcome by the foolishness of God. For Paul the criterion for the truth of the Gospel is not found in human wisdom; he anchors the identity of faith in the cross. When the Corinthians subordinate God's loving deed to their own individual knowledge, they mislead themselves about salvation itself, for Jesus Christ alone is the foundation of faith and the church (cf. 1 Cor. 3.11; 4.15).

By baptism the Corinthians become the holy and righteous community (cf. 1 Cor. 6.11), so that as members of the body of Christ they cannot at the same time live in impurity (cf. 1 Cor. 6.15, 19). Immorality, court disputes, and traffic with prostitutes endanger the unity of the church just as does leaving the state in which one entered the church (cf. 1 Cor. 5–7). So too, arguments about eating meat sacrificed to idols places the unity of the church in danger. Since Christians have only one Lord (cf. 1 Cor. 8.6), eating meat sacrificed to idols is possible in principle. But when this correct knowledge wounds the conscience of one's brother or sister in the church and leads to disputes, it does not serve the building up of the church (cf. 1 Cor. 8.1, 10; 10.23–24). It is precisely not the case that Christian freedom is realized in boundless self expression and self-realization, but is in its very essence a relational concept: it attains its true

---

[180] Cf. Friedrich, 'Christus' 153.

[181] On the Pauline theology of the cross, cf. Hans Weder, *Das Kreuz Jesu bei Paulus*, FRLANT 125. (Göttingen: Vandenhoeck & Ruprecht, 1981).

character only in relationship with one's fellow Christians and with the Christian community.[182]

Paul also clarifies the fundamental idea of the unity of the church that dominates 1 Corinthians by using spiritual gifts as an example (1 Cor. 12–14).[183] For him, the variety and number of spiritual gifts is a manifestation of the unity of the church. The church is the body of Christ (1 Cor. 12.27), the space in which the crucified and risen one is still effectively and concretely present. That is why the charisms are to serve not individual self-expression, but are there only for building up the church as a whole (cf. 1 Cor. 14.3–5, 17, 26). Paul values the spiritual gifts, but he offers the Corinthians a still more excellent way: Christian love. It is no accident that 1 Cor. 13[184] stands between the two chapters that deal with the misuse of spiritual gifts. Love is the opposite of egoism and antagonism, it does not seek its own, but reveals its true nature precisely in the bearing of evil and in the doing of good. Knowledge without love tears the community down rather than building it up (cf. 1 Cor. 13.2). To the warning against an exaggerated pneumatic enthusiasm in 1 Cor. 12–14 Paul adds in chapter 15 the issue of the resurrection, since the Corinthian misunderstanding of the resurrection also rests on an overvaluation of spiritual gifts (cf. 1 Cor. 15.46). The transition to a spiritual body does not happen until the Lord's return (cf. 1 Cor. 15.50ff.). Christians have not yet attained the state of perfection; full knowledge and direct vision are still in the eschatological future (cf. 1 Cor. 13.12; 2 Cor. 4.7; 5.7).

Neither 1 Cor. 15[185] nor 1 Cor. 13[186] are the center or high point of 1 Corinthians, but one fundamental principle of Pauline ecclesiology permeates the whole letter: Christ is the foundation, the architect, the present Lord and final goal of the Christian Church.

2.5.10 Tendencies of Recent Research

The issue of the literary structure and unity of 1 Corinthians continues to be a point on which research is concentrated. While the commentaries of

[182] On the Pauline concept of freedom, cf. the different positions of F. Stanley Jones, *'Freiheit' in den Briefen des Apostels Paulus* (see above 2.5.4), and Samuel Vollenweider, *Freiheit als neue Schöpfung*. FRLANT 147 (Göttingen: Vandenhoeck & Ruprecht, 1989).

[183] Cf. Ulrich Brockhaus, *Charisma und Amt* (Wuppertal: R. Brockhaus, 1987²).

[184] On 1 Corinthians 13 cf. especially Oda Wischmeyer, *Der höchste Weg. Das 13. Kapitel des 1. Korintherbriefes*. StNT 13 (Gütersloh: Gütersloher Verlagshaus [Gerd Mohn], 1981); further Thomas Söding, *Die Trias Glaube, Hoffnung, Liebe bei Paulus*, SBS 150 (Stuttgart: Katholisches Bibelwerk, 1992).

[185] So Karl Barth, *The Resurrection of the Dead*, tr. H. J. Stenning (New York: Fleming H. Revell, 1933).

[186] So Rudolf Bultmann, 'Karl Barth, "Die Auferstehung der Toten",' in *Glauben und Verstehen* I (Tübingen: J. C. B. Mohr [Paul Siebeck], 1980⁸) 1.38–64.

Conzelmann, Wolff, Lang, Fee, Strobel and Schrage proceed on the basis of the unity of 1 Corinthians, Klauck and Sellin have recently argued once again for the partitioning of 1 Corinthians into several letters. In contrast, Merklein and Lührmann, with particular attention to methodological considerations, have shown yet once more the unity of 1 Corinthians.[187]

A second area in which research has focused is the history-of-religions classification of Paul's opponents in 1 Corinthians. A modified form of the Gnostic hypothesis is advocated by L. Schottroff[188] and M. Winter. They see the essence of the Corinthian Gnosis in a dualism that not only regards the world as the negative counterpart to the human 'I,' but understands it as a power hostile to human existence. The Corinthians are described as 'pre-Gnostic' or 'early Gnostic' by e.g. J. M. Robinson and R. McL. Wilson.[189] On the other hand, G. Sellin has presented a careful argument showing the problem of defining the multifaceted phenomenon 'Gnosticism' and of locating it precisely on a temporal scale.[190] As the Gnostic hypothesis continues to lose plausibility, there remain the two explanatory models already mentioned (see above 2.5.8), which partly overlap: (1) The influence of Jewish-Hellenistic wisdom theology on the Corinthians (and on Paul). (2) The Corinthians independently developed their own theology oriented to the sacraments and the gift of the Spirit, a theology that elaborated what they had received from Paul as well as what they had inherited from their own religious environment.

There are numerous individual studies of 1 Cor. 15. The analyses of H. Conzelmann advanced the understanding of the pre-Pauline tradition in 1 Cor. 15.3b–5,[191] and P. v. d. Osten-Sacken worked out the apologetic tendency of 1 Cor. 15.1–11.[192] The Pauline line of argument in 1 Cor. 15.12ff., and thus the opponents' position that is to be presupposed, is

---

[187] Hermann Probst, *Paulus und der Brief* (see above 2.3.1) 108ff., advocates a mediating position between unity of the letter and partition hypotheses. He sees 1 Corinthians as a collection of originally independent letters that were joined in chronological order to form our 1 Corinthians.

[188] Cf. Louise Schottroff, *Der Glaubende und die feindliche Welt* (see below 8.5.1) 115ff.

[189] Cf. James M. Robinson. 'Kerygma and History in the New Testament,' in *Trajectories through Early Christianity*, eds. James M. Robinson and Helmut Koester (Philadelphia: Fortress Press, 1971) 20–70; Robert McL. Wilson, 'How Gnostic were the Corinthians?' NTS 19 (1972/73) 65–74.

[190] Cf. Sellin, *Auferstehung der Toten* 195–209.

[191] In addition to the exposition in his commentary on 1 Corinthians, cf. especially Hans Conzelmann, 'On the Analysis of the Confessional Formula 1 Corinthians 15.3–5,' Interpretation 20 (1966) 15–25.

[192] Cf. Peter v. d. Osten-Sacken, 'Die Apologie des paulinischen Apostolats in 1.Kor. 15,1–11,' in *Evangelium und Tora*, TB 77 (Munich: Chr. Kaiser Verlag, 1987) 131–149.

studied in different ways by G. Brakemeier,[193] B. Spörlein,[194] K. G. Sandelin, H. H. Schade,[195] and G. Sellin (among others). Recent research has been particularly interested in the relation of 1 Cor. 15.51ff. to 1 Thess. 4.13–18, in which the question of possible lines of development in Paul's eschatology is the center of attention (see above 2.4.10).

1 Corinthians is especially important in understanding the genesis of Paul's way of thinking. Can the doctrine of justification as expressed in Galatians and Romans be simply presupposed for 1 Corinthians, or equated with its theology of the cross?[196] The answer to this question depends to a considerable extent on the interpretation of 1 Cor. 15.56, where a basic principle of Paul's doctrine of justification as found in Romans flashes forth from this context without any preparation.[197]

Excursus 1: Methodological Considerations on Partition Hypotheses of Pauline Letters

The great importance of partition hypotheses for the understanding of the Pauline letters and the course of the Pauline mission makes it necessary to insert here a discussion of the formulation of basic methodological principles. The partition hypotheses proceed on the basis of the classical methods of literary criticism and source analysis (internal tensions, breaks, lapses in logical flow, contradictions, items that disagree with their context, additions that disrupt the line of thought, theological statements that depart from the context, the reflection of different historical situations)[198] and apply them with different arguments, sometimes arriving at strongly divergent results. In the process exaggerated logical strictness is sometimes demanded of the texts. This is a rationalism that prejudices perception and is hostile to the text, since what is to be considered a contradiction useful for source analysis is essentially a subjective judgment of the exegete. But

---

[193] Cf. Günter Brakemeier, 'Die Auseinandersetzung des Paulus mit den Auferstehungsleugnern in Korinth', Diss. theol., Göttingen 1968.

[194] Cf. Bernhard Spörlein, *Die Leugnung der Auferstehung*, BU 7 (Regensburg: Pustet, 1971).

[195] Cf. Hans H. Schade, *Apokalyptische Christologie* (see above 2.4.1) 191–212.

[196] So for example Eduard Lohse, *Grundriß der neutestamentlichen Theologie* (Stuttgart: W. Kohlhammer, 1989⁴); contra Udo Schnelle, *Wandlungen* (see above 2.4.9) 49–54.

[197] For differing interpretations of 1 Cor. 15.56 cf. Friedrich W. Horn, '1 Cor. 15,56 – ein exegetischer Stachel,' ZNW 82 (1991) 88–105, and Thomas Söding, '"Die Kraft der Sünde ist das Gesetz" (1 Cor. 15,56),' ZNW 83 (1992) 74–84.

[198] A listing and discussion of all relevant criteria for partitioning the Pauline letters is found in Beier, 'Geteilte Briefe?' (see above 2.4.6) 190–223. The upshot of the discussion is that for every argument introduced to support partition theories, a valid counter argument can also be introduced.

despite the thought-through structure and the high level of reflection present in the Pauline letters, they are still writings determined by particular occasions, not consistent (and sterile) treatises in the modern sense. Therefore a gap in the line of thought in something written by a personality such as Paul is no argument for literary critical judgments about source analysis. Praise and blame can alternate, new themes can be introduced, without necessarily implying that a different situation is addressed. Partition hypotheses can thus only be considered plausible when the present form of the text of a Pauline letter cannot be understood as a coherent unit. The methodological principle must be to establish not the possibility but the unconditional necessity of a partition theory. What must be shown is that the text only gives a good sense in its purportedly original location. But absolute proof has not yet been presented for any Pauline letter that it can only be understood on the basis of partition hypotheses. Moreover, what is denied to Paul is always attributed to an unknown redactor: the composition of the letters in their present form. Finally, the assumption is often made in partition hypotheses that in the redactional process the beginnings and endings of Paul's original letters were lost, which cannot be proved at all. There are no parallels for such a procedure, for the redactors would have had to wait on the letter fragments (the reconstructed units cannot be described as letters), in order then to construct new artificial letters that were then sent on to other churches. Historically, this is a very unlikely event, as the letter to the Galatians proves. It has only been preserved because it was quickly sent forth by the Galatians to other churches. Moreover, the extant manuscripts of the Corpus Paulinum presents us with a unified text (with explainable differences), from which we may conclude that the letters that stood in the individual collections at the beginning also had the same text.[199] They were probably never transmitted in any form other than their present one.

Partition hypotheses are thus methodologically justified only when no explanation for the present form of the text can be given at the Pauline level, proceeding on the principle of *textual coherence* and its different dimensions such as syntactical coherence, semantic coherence, and pragmatic coherence.

---

[199] Cf. Kurt Aland, 'Die Entstehung des Corpus Paulinum,' (see below, excursus 2) 348ff.

2.6 The Second Letter to the Corinthians

2.6.1 Literature

Commentaries

Lietzmann, Hans. *An die Korinther* I, II. HNT 9, Tübingen: J. C. B. Mohr (Paul Siebeck), 1969,[5] 97–164; Windisch, Hans. *Der zweite Korintherbrief,* KEK 6. Göttingen: Vandenhoeck & Ruprecht,1924[9] (= 1970 reprint); Furnish, Victor P. *II Corinthians,* AncB 32A. Garden City: Doubleday & Company, 1984; Betz, Hans. *2 Corinthians 8 and 9.* Philadelphia: Fortress Press 1985; Bultmann, Rudolf. *The Second Letter to the Corinthians,* tr. Roy A. Harrisville. Minneapolis: Augsburg, 1985; Klauck, Hans-Joseph. *2 Korintherbrief,* NEB. Würzburg: Echter Verlag, 1986; Lang, Friedrich. *Die Briefe an die Korinther,* NTD 7. Göttingen: Vandenhoeck & Ruprecht, 1986; Martin, Ralph. *2 Corinthians,* WBC 40. Dallas: Word, 1986; Danker, Frederick. *II Corinthians.* Minneapolis: Augsburg, 1989; Wolff, Christian. *Der zweite Brief des Paulus an die Korinther,* ThHK 8. Berlin: Evangelische Verlagsanstalt, 1989; Thrall, Margaret. *A Critical and Exegetical Commentary on the Second Epistle to the Corinthians,* Vol. 1. Edinburgh: T. & T. Clark, 1994.

Monographs

Rissi, Mathias. *Studien zum zweiten Korintherbrief,* AThANT 56. Zürich: Zwingli Verlag, 1969; Betz, Hans D. *Paulus und die sokratische Tradition,* BHTh 45. Tübingen: J. C. B. Mohr (Paul Siebeck), 1972; Baumert, Norbert. *Täglich sterben und auferstehen,* StANT 34. Munich: Kösel, 1973; Georgi, Dieter. *The Opponents of Paul in Second Corinthians* (with an Epilogue by D. Georgi). Philadelphia: Fortress Press, 1986; Aejmelaeus, Lars. *Streit und Versöhnung. Das Problem der Zusammensetzung des 2.Korintherbriefes,* SES 46. Helsinki: Finnish Exegetical Society, 1987; Breytenbach, Cilliers. *Versöhnung,* WMANT 60. Neukirchen-Vluyn: Neukirchener Verlag, 1989; Sumney, Jerry L. *Identifying Paul's Opponents. The Question of Method in 2 Corinthians,* JSOT.S 40. Sheffield: Sheffield University Press, 1990; Murphy-O'Connor, Jerome. *Theology of the Second Letter to the Corinthians.* Cambridge: Cambridge University Press, 1991; Zeilinger, F. *Krieg und Friede in Korinth.* Wien, 1992; Hay, David, ed. *Pauline Theology, Volume II: 1 and 2 Corinthians.* Minneapolis: Fortress, 1993.

Articles

Käsemann, Ernst. 'Die Legitimität des Apostels,' in *Das Paulusbild in der neueren deutschen Forschung,* ed. K. H. Rengstorf (see above 2.) 475–521; Bornkamm, Günther. 'Die Vorgeschichte des sogenannten zweiten Korintherbriefes,' in *Geschichte und Glaube* II, ed. Günther Bornkamm, BEvTh 53. Munich: Kaiser (1971) 162–194; Hyldahl, Niels. 'Die Frage nach der literarischen Einheit des Zweiten Korintherbriefes,' ZNW 64 (1973) 288–306; Friedrich, Gerhard. 'Die Gegner des Paulus im 2.Korintherbrief,' in *Auf das Wort kommt es an,* ed. Gerhard Friedrich. Göttingen: Vandenhoeck & Ruprecht, 1978, 189–223; Hofius, Otfried. 'Gesetz und Evangelium nach 2. Korinther 3,' in *Paulusstudien,* ed. O. Hofius, WUNT 51.

Tübingen: J. C. B. Mohr [Paul Siebeck] (1989) 75–120; Strecker, Georg. 'Die Legitimität des paulinischen Apostolats nach 2 Korinther 10–13,' NTS 38 (1992) 566–586.

2.6.2 Author

The authenticity of 2 Corinthians was disputed by some of the hypercriti-
cal scholars of the nineteenth century (e.g. Bruno Bauer), but is today
doubted by no one. The first reflection of 2 Corinthians (9.12) is found in
1 Clement 38.2.

2.6.3 Place and Time of Composition

This letter can only be approached by surveying the events that happened
between the writing of 1 Corinthians and 2 Corinthians. In 2 Cor. 12.14
and 13.1 Paul had announced a third visit to Corinth, so he must already
have been in Corinth once after writing 1 Corinthians. In 2 Cor. 1.15–16
the apostle speaks of a planned trip directly to Corinth, then to Macedonia,
from Macedonia back to Corinth and from there to Judea. Which trip does
this refer to? Information thereon is provided by 2 Cor. 2.1, where Paul
mentions that he does not want to make another painful visit to Corinth.
There was thus a second visit after the one on which the church was
founded, during which Paul was mistreated, and after which he wrote the
'tearful letter' (cf. 2 Cor. 2.4; 7.8, 12). This is the visit mentioned in 2 Cor.
1.15, which took place as a result of a change of the travel plans expressed
in 1 Cor. 16.5ff. Furthermore, after the incident Paul did not carry through
with his travel plans mentioned in 2 Cor. 1.16, but probably returned to
Ephesus and wrote the 'tearful letter.' Finally, during the painful second
visit Paul had obviously announced that he would make a third visit (cf. 2
Cor. 1.23). Instead of this promised visit, he sent the 'tearful letter.'
(cf. 2 Cor. 2.3, 4), which Titus presumably brought with him to Corinth
(cf. 2 Cor. 7.5–9). It was especially this changing of his travel plans that
provoked the charge that he was not dealing straightforwardly with them
(cf. 2 Cor. 1.17).

  From Ephesus the apostle then began a trip that was fraught with
danger (cf. 2 Cor. 1.8) via Troas (2 Cor. 2.12) to Macedonia, where he met
Titus (2 Cor. 7.6–7). Titus conveyed the good news from Corinth, which
formed the presupposition for the third visit announced in 2 Cor. 12.14
and 13.1. The gathering of the collection in Macedonia was successful (cf.
2 Cor. 8.1ff.; Rom. 15.26); this was probably facilitated by Timothy, who
traveled overland to Macedonia (1 Cor. 4.17; 16.10) and is mentioned as
cosender of 2 Corinthians (2 Cor. 1.1).

Thus in the period between the writing of 1 Corinthians and that of 2 Corinthians the following events took place:

(1) The trip from Ephesus to Corinth, the apostle's second visit (cf. 2 Cor. 12.14; 13.1).

(2) Precipitous return to Ephesus, due to Paul's having been grievously offended by a member of the Corinthian church (cf. 2 Cor. 2.3–11; 7.8, 12).

(3) Writing the 'tearful letter,' which was brought to Corinth by Titus (cf. 2 Cor. 7.5–9).

(4) Paul's life endangered in Asia (2 Cor. 1.8).

(5) The apostle travels from Troas to Macedonia (cf. 2 Cor. 2.12, 13).

(6) In Macedonia Paul meets Titus who is on his way back from Corinth (2 Cor. 7.5ff.). This course of events would have required a period of more than six months, so 2 Corinthians was probably written in the *late fall of 55 CE in Macedonia* (cf. 2 Cor. 7.5; 8.1–5; 9.3–4).[200]

2 Cor. 8.10 indicates that a new year had begun between the writing of 1 Corinthians and 2 Corinthians. If Paul is following the usual Macedonian calendar, this new year would have begun in the fall.[201] On the other hand, if one reckons with the two letters being separated by a year and a half,[202] there are two possible results: (1) 1 Corinthians had already been written in the spring of 54. (2) Paul wrote 1 Corinthians in the spring of 55, 2 Corinthians in the fall of 56, and did not arrive in Jerusalem until the spring of 57.

2.6.4 Intended Readership

2 Corinthians is addressed not only to the Corinthian church but also to 'all the saints throughout Achaia' (2 Cor. 1.1). Through this *expansion* of the circle of addressees the character of the letter itself is changed, since Paul at once addresses a local church and all Christians in Achaia (cf. 2 Cor. 9.2; 11.10). This double purpose is also important in determining the literary structure of 2 Corinthians.

In contrast to the situation of the church pictured in 2.5.4 a drastic change has been brought about by the incursion into the church from outside (cf. 2 Cor. 11.4) of false teachers who quickly gained influence and defamed Paul (cf. 2.6.8). The apostle speaks of these opponents in the third

---

[200] Cf. Lietzmann, *2 Korintherbrief* 135; Lang, *2 Korintherbrief* 320 (2 Cor. 1–9); Furnish, *2 Corinthians* 55 (2 Cor. 1–9); Wolff, *2 Korintherbrief* 10.

[201] Cf. Jack Finegan, *Handbook of Biblical Chronology* (Princeton: Princeton University Press, 1964) 59ff.; Lietzmann, *2 Korintherbrief* 135.

[202] So for example Windisch, *2 Korintherbrief* 255–256 (18 months); Lüdemann, *Chronology* 98 (16 months).

person, in order clearly to distinguish them from the Corinthian Christians themselves (cf. 2 Cor. 10.1–2, 7, 10, 12; 11.4–5, 12–13, 18, 20, 22–23).

2.6.5 Outline, Structure, Form

1.1–2	Prescript	
1.3–7	Proemium	— Introduction
1.8–2.17	Epistolary Self Commendation	
3.1–4.6	The Ministry of the Apostle as Ministry of the Spirit	
4.7–5.11	Suffering with Christ and the Apostle's Hope	
5.12–21	The Ministry of Reconciliation	
6.1–10	The Glory of the Apostle's Suffering	
6.11–7.16	Reconciliation with the Corinthians	— Body
8.1–23	The Collection for Jerusalem	
9.1–15	The Blessing of the Collection	
10.1–11	The Opponents Accusations	
10.11–18	The Criteria of Apostleship	
11.1–15	The Unselfish Ministry of the Apostle	
11.16–12.13	The 'Fools Speech'	
12.14–13.10	The Apostolic Parousia	
13.11	Closing Parenesis	
13.12	Greetings	— Conclusion
13.13	Final Farewell (Eschatokoll)	

While the prescript of 2 Corinthians corresponds completely to the usual form of the Pauline letter (cf. 1 Cor. 1.1–3), the thanksgiving section of 1.3–7 is introduced not with εὐχαριστέω but with εὐλογέω. The first major part of 2 Corinthians is usually taken to begin at 1.8. However, F. Schnider and W. Stenger[203] point out that 2 Cor. 1.8–2.17 contains all the typical elements of the epistolary self commendation (mention of the apostle's first visit that founded the church, 1.19; the presence of the letter writer among the addressees, 1.11; the prospective presence of the letter writers with the addressees/travel plans, 1.15–16, 23; 2.1; the sending forth and return of messengers, 2.14; safeguarding of the apostle's authority, 1.17–18; 2.17;

---

[203] Cf. Schnider and Stenger, *Studien* (see above 2.3.2) 52ff.

2.5–11; an appeal to the readers' emotions, 1.23–24; 1.13). Moreover, in 2 Cor. 3.1 Paul characterizes the preceding section as an epistolary self commendation! Finally, a new subject begins not in 2.14 but in 3.1. The thanksgiving in 2.14 is certainly a surprise, but there is a parallel to it in 1 Cor. 15.57 (cf. further 2 Cor. 8.16; 9.15; Rom. 6.17; 7.25a). In 2 Cor. 2.14–17 Paul makes a transition to the first major part of the letter.[204]

The transition with a παρακαλέω-sentence in 2 Cor. 10.1 corresponds to the Pauline letter style (cf. 1 Thess. 4.1; Rom. 12.1; Phil. 4.2; Phlm. 8–10). The closing parenesis in 2 Cor. 13.11 refers to the content of the whole letter (cf. χαίρετε and καταρτίζεσθε). The final farewell in 2 Cor. 13.13 manifests a tripartite form, whereas elsewhere the monopartite form prevails (cf. 1 Thess. 5.28; 1 Cor. 16.23; Gal. 6.18; Rom. 16.20; Phil. 4.23; Phlm. 25).

2.6.6 Literary Integrity

The unity of 2 Corinthians is very disputed. The following phenomena of the text are presented as arguments for partition hypotheses:

(1) The break between 2 Cor. 1–9 and 2 Cor. 10–13 is so striking that Paul must be presumed to have a different attitude toward the church in the two sections. This supposition is often joined with the assumption that 2 Cor. 10–13 is to be seen as a fragment of an independent letter.

(2) In 2 Cor. 2.13 the discussion of an incident in Corinth is supposed to be obviously interrupted by a defense of Paul's apostolic office (2 Cor. 2.14–7.4), which then clarifies the connection between 2 Cor. 7.5 with 2.13.

(3) The two sections of instructions about the collection in 2 Cor. 8 and 9 appear not to belong together originally.

(4) 2 Cor. 6.14–7.1 is quite different from Paul's other letters in language and content, so that the Pauline origin of this section must be doubted.

Letters or letter fragments must therefore be reconstructed from 2 Cor. 1.1–2.13; 2.14–6.13; 7.2–4; 7.5–16; 8; 9 and 10–13. The most important variations of these efforts may be named here:[205]

(a) Taking up the suggestion of J. S. Semler, A. Hausrath saw in 2 Cor. 10–13 a part of the lost 'tearful letter.'[206] He thus moved chapters 10–13

---

[204] Cf. Wolff, *2 Korintherbrief* 51: '2.14–17 can best be understood as a transition to a new, major line of thought concerned with theological reflections on the apostolic ministry.'

[205] A survey of research is given by Windisch, *2 Korintherbrief* 11–21; Martin, *2 Corinthians*, xl–lii; Betz, *2 Corinthians* 3–36; Roland Bieringer, 'Der 2. Korintherbrief in den neuesten Kommentaren,' EThL LXVII (1991) 107–130.

[206] Cf. Adolf Hausrath, *Der Vier-Capitelbrief des Paulus an die Korinther* (Heidelberg: Bassermann, 1870).

from the end of the extant letter to the beginning of the correspondence
preserved in 2 Corinthians. This partition-hypothesis was widely accepted
and in a modified form is still important today. Thus H. J. Klauck and L.
Aejmelaeus attribute 2 Cor. 10–13 to the 'tearful letter'[207] and advocate the
following chronology: (1) 'tearful letter' (2 Cor. 10–13); (2) 'letter of
reconciliation' (2 Cor. 1–9). F. Lang also sees in 2 Cor. 10–13 a part of the
'tearful letter' written by Paul after his experience during his second,
painful visit to Corinth. After the 'tearful letter' Paul wrote the 'letter
of reconciliation' of 2 Cor. 1–8, to which he added an accompanying
document giving instructions about the collection (2 Cor. 9). A further
modification of Hausrath's hypothesis is advocated by G. Dautzenberg,
who regards 2 Corinthians as a collection of three letters or letter fragments. He places 2 Cor. 9 at the beginning of the correspondence, followed
by 2 Corinthians 10–13, then 2 Cor. 1–8.[208]

(b) The second important variation of the partition hypothesis likewise
proceeds on the basis of chapters 10–13 as an independent letter, but does
not understand them as a part of the 'tearful letter.' Rather, 2 Cor. 1–9
is seen as representing an intermediate stage in the relationship of the
apostle to the Corinthian church. Then 2 Cor. 10–13 follows as the last
letter, by which Paul attempted to establish his own authority in Corinth.
The series 2 Cor. 1–9, 10–13 is advocated, to some extent with different
arguments, by H. Windisch, A. Jülicher,[209] F. F. Bruce,[210] C. K. Barrett,[211]
V. P. Furnish und R. P. Martin, among others.

(c) R. Bultmann followed J. Weiss[212] in extracting 2 Cor. 2.14–7.4 from
the 'letter of reconciliation' and included it along with chapter 9 and
chapters 10–13 with the 'tearful letter.'[213] Bultmann thus advocated the
order: (1) 'tearful letter' 2.14–7.4; 9; 10–13; (2) 'letter of reconciliation'
1.1–2.13; 7.5–16; 8.

(d) G. Bornkamm regards the apologia in 2 Cor. 2.14–7.4 as the section
of 2 Corinthians that was composed the earliest, with which Paul sought to

---

[207] Cf. further Frances Watson, '2 Cor. X–XIII and Paul's Painful Letter to the Corinthians,'
JThS 35 (1984) 324–346; Strecker, 'Legitimität' 566; Zeilinger, *Krieg und Friede* 36. Zeilinger
(23–24) divides 2 Corinthians into four letters: a) 2 Cor. 10–13; b) 2 Cor. 1.1–2.13; 7.5–16; c) 2
Cor. 8 and 9; d) 2 Cor. 2.14–7.4.

[208] Cf. Gerhard Dautzenberg, 'Der zweite Korintherbrief als Briefsammlung,' ANRW 25.5
(Berlin: Walter de Gruyter, 1987) 3045–3066.

[209] Cf. Jülicher and Fascher, 98ff.

[210] Cf. F. F. Bruce, *1 and 2 Corinthians* (Grand Rapids: Eerdmans, 1980) 117ff.

[211] Cf. C. K. Barrett, *2 Corinthians* (NY: Harper & Row, 1973) 21.

[212] Cf. Johannes Weiss. *Earliest Christianity*, ed. F. C. Grant (New York: Harper & Brothers,
1937) (see above 2.5.6) 345, 355–56.

[213] Cf. Rudolf Bultmann, 'Exegetische Probleme des zweiten Korintherbriefes,' in *Exegetica*,
ed. R. Bultmann (Tübingen: J. C. B. Mohr [Paul Siebeck], 1967) 298–322.

increase his influence on the state of affairs in Corinth. Despite his efforts the situation became so bad that the apostle sent the 'tearful letter,' part of which Bornkamm thinks has been preserved in chapters 10–13. After the success of the 'tearful letter' and the mission of Titus, Paul then wrote the 'letter of reconciliation,' to which Bornkamm reckons 2 Cor. 1.1–2.13; 7.5–16. He classifies 8.1–24 as a postscript to the 'letter of reconciliation' and 9.1–15 as an independent circular letter to the churches of Achaia. The original course of events of the correspondence now contained in 2 Corinthians was thus as follows: (1) 2.14–7.4; (2) 10–13; (3) 1.1–2.13; 7.5–16; (4) 8.1–24; (5) 9.1–15.[214]

For an appropriate evaluation of the partition-hypotheses that have been applied to 2 Corinthians, the first issue that must be clarified is whether or not 2 Cor. 10–13 could have been part of the 'tearful letter.' In 2 Cor. 2.3ff.; 7.8, 12 Paul gives a very precise description of what caused the incident in Corinth, his precipitous departure, and the 'tearful letter:' he had somehow been grievously offended by a member of the Corinthian church, the details of which can no longer be reconstructed. After receiving the 'tearful letter' the church punished the offender, so that Paul asked the congregation to forgive him (cf. 2 Cor. 2.6–8). If chapters 10–13 are part of the 'tearful letter,' then it is very remarkable that Paul does not mention the incident that had caused such pain and was supposed to have occasioned this letter in the first place. The opponents whom he battles in 10–13 have no connection to the individual member of the congregation in 2.3ff. While Paul forgives the ἀδικήσας (the one who had done the wrong) and the matter for him is over and done with (cf. 2 Cor. 2.6–10), the debate with the opponents essentially continues to determine the Pauline line of argument also in 2 Cor. 1–9 (cf. 2 Cor. 3.1–3 with 10.12, 18; further 2 Cor. 4.2, 3, 5; 5.12; 2.17). The 'super-apostles' are 'false apostles' and 'deceitful workers' (2 Cor. 11.13) to whom Paul does not extend his hand for reconciliation in the way he does to the offending individual. While the ἀδικήσας doubtless belonged to the local church, the opponents invaded it from outside (cf. 2 Cor. 11.4: ὁ ἐρχόμενος [the one who comes]).

The 'tearful letter' was written as a substitute for the promised return from Macedonia to Corinth, a visit that failed to materialize (cf. 2 Cor. 1.16; 1.23–2.4), while chapters 10–13 have a third visit in prospect. So also,

---

[214] The position of Betz, *2 Corinthians* 141–144 is close to Bornkamm's, since Betz regards 2 Corinthians as composed from the following letters or letter fragments: 2.14–6.13; 7.2–4 (fragment of an apologetic letter); 10.1–13.10 (fragment of the 'tearful letter'); 1.1–2.13; 7.5–16, 13.11–13 (letter of reconciliation); chapter 8 (fragment of an administrative letter to the Corinthians); chapter 9 (fragment of an administrative letter to the churches of Achaia); 6.14–7.1 (post-Pauline interpolation).

the objection thrown in Paul's face that his personal appearance before the congregation was weak, while his letters are powerful and impressive (10.1, 9–11; 13.2) speaks against relegating 10–13 to the 'tearful letter.' These reproaches refer to the conflict with the individual member of the church and the following 'tearful letter;' therefore they presuppose the 'tearful letter' and cannot be a part of it. The plural αἱ ἐπιστολαί (his letters) in 2 Cor. 10.10 includes both 1 Corinthians and the 'tearful letter'![215] The second visit mentioned in 2 Cor. 13.2 also fits into this interpretation, for it is this visit in which the painful incident occurred that led to the 'tearful letter.' At that time Paul spared the congregation, but when he arrives for his third visit he will spare them no longer.

Finally, if one considers chapters 10–13 to be part of the 'tearful letter,' then the reference to Titus in 12.17–18 presupposes that Titus was already in Corinth before the occasion on which he delivered the 'tearful letter' to them. This would be a clear contradiction of 2 Cor. 7.14, for if Paul here in connection with the 'tearful letter' mentions that his boasting about the Corinthians to Titus had paid off, then Titus had not been in Corinth prior to delivering the 'tearful letter.' Besides Paul, especially Silvanus (cf. 2 Cor. 1.19) and Timothy (cf. 1 Cor. 4.17; 16.10–11; 2 Cor. 1.1, 19) had maintained contact with the church and accompanied the first phase of the collection of the offering. Titus did not participate in the organization of the collection prior to the delivery of the 'tearful letter' (cf. 2 Cor. 8.6). In order to justify including 2 Cor. 10–13 in the 'tearful letter,' scholars have often taken refuge in the idea that passages are lost from it that deal with the apostle's being hurt by an individual in the congregation.[216] It is also not the case that a reference to this incident is found in 2 Cor. 10.1–11,[217] since the Pauline line of argument in this section presupposes the 'tearful letter.' Moreover, the procedure of the putative redactor could hardly be explained, since contrary to the postulated historical course of events he placed chapters 10–13 at the end of the Corinthian correspondence and thus evokes the impression that Paul had finally been defeated in Corinth. Summary: 2 Cor. 10–13 cannot be considered the 'tearful letter' or a fragment thereof.[218]

---

[215] Whoever reckons 2 Cor. 10–13 to the 'tearful letter' must refer the plural of 10.10 to 1 Corinthians and the letter mentioned in 1 Cor. 5.9. Cf. for example Klauck, *2 Korintherbrief* 79. This 'previous letter,' however, had nothing at all to do with the problems dealt with in 2 Corinthians.

[216] For this understanding cf. for example Vielhauer, *Urchristliche Literatur* 152.

[217] So Watson, '2 Cor. X–XIII and Paul's Painful Letter to the Corinthians' 343ff.; Klauck, *2 Korintherbrief* 8.

[218] It is also the case that the characterization of the 'tearful letter' in 2 Cor. 2.4 does not fit 1 Corinthians, as again argued recently by Udo Borse, '"Tränenbrief" und 1. Korintherbrief,' SNTU 9 (1984) 175–202.

A further central problem of the literary-critical analysis of the unity of 2 Corinthians is represented by the section 2.14–7.4. The first consideration that speaks against the hypothesis that this is part of an independent letter is the observation that a series of thematic connections bind it together with 1.1–2.13: the theme of εἰλικρινεία (sincerity) (2 Cor. 1.12) is taken up again in 2.17; 4.2; 6.3–10. The statements about suffering and comfort in 1.4ff. are expanded and deepened in 4.8ff. 2 Cor. 5.12 is related to 1.14b in that Paul makes 'proper καύχησις' (boasting) the theme of each. The problematic of 5.1–10 (the death of the apostle before the parousia) is already hinted at in 1.8–10. Not only in 1.1–2.13 but also in 2.14–7.4 Paul deals with a central theme: the ministry of the apostle and its relation to the Corinthian church. Precisely the discussions of the essence of the Pauline apostolate in 2 Cor. 3–5 serve to refute the objections that have been raised against the apostle and to lead the church to a deepened understanding of the apostolic ministry.

Moreover, 2 Cor. 7.5 cannot be considered the immediate continuation of 2.13.[219] Thus there are linguistic connections between 7.4 and 7.5–7. (The παρακλήσει of v. 4 is continued by the παρακαλῶν and παρεκάλεσεν of v. 6 and the παρακλήσει of v. 7 ['consolation' vocabulary]; χαρῆναι in v. 7 takes up the χαρᾷ in v. 4 while θλιβόμενοι in v. 5 takes up the θλίψει in v. 4 [joy, rejoicing).[220] Also 7.4 and 7.5–7 belong closely together in terms of their content, for the cause of the boundless joy of 7.4 is the arrival of Titus with good news from Corinth mentioned in 7.5–7 (cf. also 7.4 with 7.16!). The travel report that begins in 7.5 with καὶ γάρ is not intended primarily as information about the circumstances of the trip, but to portray the reason for the joy. The content of 7.4 is thus referred directly to the context that immediately follows, so that the connection between 2 Cor. 7.4 and 7.5ff. must be regarded as original. Finally, the statement of the apostle in 2 Cor. 6.11 ('We have opened our mouth to you, Corinthians, our heart is wide open to you') shows that Paul was fully aware of his unusual procedure in 2 Cor. 3–6. In order to refute the objections that had been raised against him, Paul had to set forth a full elaboration of his self-understanding as a minister of the new covenant and preacher of reconciliation with God.[221]

The Pauline authorship of 2 Cor. 6.14–7.1 is disputed. This brief text contains numerous hapax legomena for both Paul and the New Testament

---

[219] Cf. also Wolff, *2 Korintherbrief* 155–156.

[220] Cf. Lietzmann, *2 Korintherbrief* 131.

[221] There is a certain parallel here to the seventh letter of Plato, where Plato also interrupts the chronological representation of events with a rambling discussion. (Cf. *Ep.* 7 330b with 337e; in 344d Plato describes the manner of his presentation as 'a rambling narrative.')

(μετοχή [partnership], μέρις [agreement], καθαρίζω [cleanse], συμφώνη-σις [agreement], συγκατάθεσις [agreement], Βελιάρ [Beliar], παντο-κράτωρ [Almighty], μολυσμός [defilement], ἑτεροζυγέω [mismatched], ἐμπεριπατέω [walk among]). Moreover, there are rare concepts and expressions. Elsewhere Paul never describes Satan as 'Beliar' (cf. 1QM 13.11–12; Test Sim 5.3; Test Lev 19.1; Test Iss 6.1), and the description of God as the 'Almighty' is found only here. The expression 'defilement of flesh and spirit' is in tension with the other places in Paul where flesh and spirit are related antithetically, rather than coordinated as here. In addition, 7.2 joins seamlessly to 6.13. The linguistic and thematic peculiarities of this text, in particular its nearness to the Qumran documents, to Jubilees and the Testaments of the Twelve Partriarchs, have repeatedly led to the supposition that 2 Cor. 6.14–7.1 was written by a post-Pauline Jewish Christian and inserted into 2 Corinthians.[222] Those who regard the text as original usually explain its peculiarities as the adoption of traditional concepts and motifs by the apostle.[223]

2 Cor. 8 and 9 are often considered to be doublets, so that they are regarded as separate documents, as postscripts, or as part of different letters to the Corinthians.[224] The main arguments introduced for this sort of partition-hypotheses are as follows: [225] (1) The fresh beginning in 9.1. (2) In 8.1ff. the Macedonians are an example for the Corinthians, while in 9.2ff. it is Achaia that is to be an example to the Macedonians. These cannot be persuasive arguments, since, while it is true that 9.1 is a fresh beginning, it cannot be the beginning of an independent letter.[226] Paul writes 2 Corinthians to the congregations of Corinth and Achaia (2 Cor. 1.1), so that it is not surprising if in 9.1 as he discusses the important issue of the collection he turns directly to address Achaia. Moreover, the γάρ

---

[222] Extensive evidence for the secondary character of 2 Cor. 6.14–7.1 has been given by Joseph A. Fitzmyer, 'Qumran and the Interpolated Paragraph in 2 Cor. 6.14–7.1,' CBQ 23 (1961) 271–280; Joachim Gnilka, '2 Cor. 6,14–7,1 im Lichte der Qumranschriften und der Zwölf-Patriarchen-Testamente,' in *Ntl. Aufsätze* (FS J. Schmid), ed. (Regensburg: Pustet, 1963) 86–99.

[223] Cf. for this interpretation Martin, *2 Corinthians* 189–212; Wolff, *2 Korintherbrief* 146–154 (Paul takes over a baptismal parenesis); Jerome Murphy-O'Connor, 'Philo and 2 Cor. 6.14–7.1' in *The Diakonia of the Spirit* (2 Co 4,7–7,4), ed. L. de Lorenzi, SMBen 10 (Rome, 1989) 133–146 (all the expressions and motifs of this section have parallels in Hellenistic Judaism); R. Reck, *Kommunikation und Gemeindeaufbau* (see above 2.2.2) 290–294. That Paul is the author of this section as a whole is now once again advocated by Gerhard Saß, 'Noch einmal: 2 Cor. 6,14 – 7,1,' ZNW 84 (1993) 36–64; Franz Zeilinger, 'Die Echtheit von 2 Cor. 6,14–7,1,' JBL 112 (1993) 71–80.

[224] On the individual hypotheses cf. Lang, *2 Korintherbrief* 317.

[225] Cf. also the listing of arguments in Bultmann, *2 Korintherbrief* 258.

[226] One can understand 2 Cor. 9.1 as a paralipsis, cf. Friedrich Blass and Albert Debrunner, *A Greek Grammar of the New Testament and Other Early Christian Literature*, tr. and rev. Robert W. Funk (Chicago and London: The University of Chicago Press, 1961) §495 (1), 262: 'The orator pretends to pass over something which he in fact mentions.'

of 9.1 refers directly to the preceding; after the excursus about the messengers in 8.16–24 Paul again takes up the main theme of the collection, this time with all Achaia in view. Paul wants to animate both the Corinthian church and the other churches in Achaia to a renewed and stronger effort to complete the collection. Thus to the Corinthians he effusively praises the Macedonians' sacrificial giving (8.1–5) so that Titus can now achieve the same results in Corinth (8.6). Paul chooses a different approach in addressing Achaia. He mentions his boasting to the Macedonians (9.2) and thus encourages Achaia to live up to what he has said about them (9.4–5). There is no contradiction here, but rather Paul very skillfully appeals to the sense of honor and self understanding of the Christians in Corinth and Achaia respectively so that he can bring the work of raising the offering to a successful conclusion.

Further observations speak for the unity of 2 Cor. 8 and 9: (a) In 8.10 and 9.2 the same point in time is named for the beginning of the collection of the offering, namely the spring. (b) The reference to the brothers in 9.3 presupposes that the congregations know of them from 8.16ff. (c) The coming of Titus to be with Paul, named in 7.5ff., is the presupposition for the whole line of argument in 2 Cor. 8 and 9. (d) There is a clear internal connection between chapter 8 and chapter 9, for Paul sends Titus and the coworkers (8.16ff.) so that the procedures for collecting the offering will already be complete when he arrives with the Macedonians (9.3–4).

Can the two main parts of 2 Corinthians be regarded as a literary unity? W. Bousset sees 2 Cor. 1–9 as directed to the church, with 10–13 directed not to the church but to the opponents,[227] so that the change in tone is not an argument for partition hypotheses. H. Lietzmann also argues for the unity of 2 Corinthians and explains the dramatic change in mood between chapters 9 and 10 as the result of 'a sleepless night.'[228] In more recent times, W. G. Kümmel, U. Borse, N. Hyldahl and Chr. Wolff have voted for the unity of 2 Corinthians. W. G. Kümmel supposes that Paul did not dictate 2 Corinthians at one sitting, and that the unevenness is to be explained on the basis of interruptions.[229] U. Borse also suggests that an interruption accounts for the strong break between chapters 9 and 10. These chapters are not to be assigned to the 'tearful letter' or other letter between 1 and 2 Corinthians, however, but after some time Paul appended them to the letter of chapters 1–9 that had not yet been sent, after a new situation had

---

[227] Cf. Wilhelm Bousset, *Der zweite Brief an die Korinther*, SNT 2. (Göttingen: Vandenhoeck & Ruprecht, 1917³) 171–172.

[228] Lietzmann, *2 Korintherbrief* 139.

[229] Kümmel, *Introduction* 292: 'Paul dictated the letter with interruptions, so the possibility of unevenness is antecedently present.'

arisen in Corinth.[230] N. Hyldahl regards 1 Corinthians as the 'tearful letter, and disputes that there was a 'second visit' before the writing of 2 Corinthians, which he regards as a literary unity on this basis. In Chr. Wolff's opinion, 2 Cor. 8–9 was the planned conclusion of 2 Corinthians, but Paul added chapters 10–13 after he received new and unhappy reports from Corinth.[231]

For the reconstruction of the relationship between 2 Cor. 1–9 and 10–13, it is especially important to keep in view the reports about Titus and his companion in both parts of the letter. Paul mentions in both 2 Cor. 8.17, 18, 22 and in 9.3, 5 that he had sent Titus and 'the brother' to Corinth. Often ἐξῆλθεν (he is going, 8.17) and συνεπέμψαμεν (we are sending 8.18) are regarded as epistolary aorists.[232] However, if they are true aorists,[233] then this would presuppose that Paul first dictated 2 Cor. 1–9 after Titus and his companion had left for Corinth. Obviously Paul wanted to send the letter as quickly as possible to his coworkers who had gone on ahead (cf. προέρχομαι in 2 Cor. 9.5). This had not yet been done, however, and 2 Cor. 1–9 was still in his hands as new reports from Corinth reached him through the Titus group. That the Titus group was back with Paul again is indicated by 2 Cor. 12.17–18, for here the visit announced in 2 Cor. 8.16ff. and 9.3, 5 is already seen in retrospect. These verses cannot be referred to some other visit, for Titus had not been in Corinth prior to the delivery of the 'tearful letter' (cf. 2 Cor. 7.14).[234] In 2 Cor. 12.18 Paul names only the brother commissioned by the churches in Macedonia, but not his coworker mentioned in 2 Cor. 8.22. This is appropriate in the context of the accusations made against him in Corinth that he was using the collection to enrich himself personally (cf. 2 Cor. 8.20; 12.14, 16, 17), for only Titus and the brother commissioned from Macedonia were officially responsible for the administration of the collection. Moreover, in 2 Cor. 12.17–18 it was not necessary for Paul once again to give the exact personnel list of the Titus group.

Obviously Titus and 'the brother' brought new information about the situation in Corinth, which occasioned Paul's writing of 2 Cor. 10–13. In the meantime the opponents in Corinth had probably gained the majority position; Paul deals with them in chapters 10–13 in an unusually sharp form, and hopes thereby to win many members of the church back to

---

[230] Cf. Udo Borse, *Der Standort des Galaterbriefes* (see below 2.7.1) 114ff.

[231] Cf. Wolff, *2 Korintherbrief* 193–194; similarly Danker, *2 Corinthians* 147–148.

[232] Cf. for example Windisch, *2 Korintherbrief* 262; Furnish, *2 Corinthians* 421–422.

[233] Blass and Debrunner § 334 rightly do not list any of the places named as epistolary aorists.

[234] Whoever counts 2 Cor. 10–13 as part of the 'tearful letter' must of course refer 12.17–18 to an earlier visit of Titus to Corinth in connection with the collection; cf. for example Lang, *2 Korintherbrief* 354; Klauck, *2 Korintherbrief* 98.

himself. The invective passages in 2 Cor. 10–13 are not unusual in the context of ancient literature, for invective content is found especially in tragedy, comedy, and in such famous speakers as Cicero.[235] Paul adds chapters 10–13 to 2 Cor. 1–9, because it is precisely under the presupposition of increasing influence of the apostles' opponents that the problems dealt with in 1–9 (delay of his announced visit, the 'tearful letter,' the collection project) must be persuasively clarified. Parallels for a change of tone within a Pauline letter are 1 Cor. 8/9; Gal. 2/3; Rom. 11/12. The polemic in 2 Cor. 10–13 is not directed toward the Corinthian church, but against the opponents that are seen as a third group (cf. 2 Cor. 10.1–2) that has interposed itself into the relationship between the apostle and the Corinthian church. Thus there exists no fundamental difference in the relationship between apostle and church in the two major parts of the epistle 1–9/10–13. In both sections Paul attempts to persuade uncommitted members of the congregation to his own cause. In favor of the unity of 2 Corinthians, presupposing that there was a change in the church's situation between 2 Cor. 1–9 and 10–13, we may also adduce the letter's conclusion in 13.11–13. It remains surprisingly positive and unites in itself both parts of the letter (cf. 2 Cor. 13.11a). Obviously Paul won the church back to his own view by means of this letter, for in the spring of 56 he spent some time in Corinth and there wrote the letter to the Romans, in which he notes (Rom. 15.26) that the gathering of the collection in Macedonia and Achaia had been successfully completed.

No reconstruction of the historical course of events preceding and behind the composition of 2 Corinthians can get by without hypothetical elements. The explanatory model here chosen has two advantages: (1) The reference to Titus and his companion is the only clear indication, contained in the letter itself, that can be utilized for the reconstruction of these events. (2) The thesis of the unity of 2 Corinthians, presupposing a changed situation in the church between chapters 1–9 and 10–13, has the great advantage that it does not require the postulation of additional letters or letter fragments, the beginning and endings of which can no longer be recognized.[236]

---

[235] On this cf. Severin Koster, *Die Invektive in der griechischen und römischen Literatur*, Beiträge zur Klassischen Philologie 99. (Meisenheim, 1980) 354: 'The invective is a structured literary form, but one that manifests at least the main point of the πράξεις [Acts], whose goal it is with all available means to disparage in a way that annihilates forever a person explicitly named or that could be named, either as an individual or as representative of a group, openly against the background of the dominant values in the consciousness of the group addressed.'

[236] In addition to the authors already named (Bousset, Lietzmann, Kümmel, Borse, Hyldahl, Danker, Wolff), among other scholars that vote for the unity of 2 Corinthians we may list Georg Heinrici, *2. Korintherbrief*, KEK 6. (Göttingen: Vandenhoeck & Ruprecht, 1883) 7–10; Philipp Bachmann, *Der zweite Brief des Paulus an die Korinther*, KNT 8 (Leipzig: Deichert,

2.6.7 *Traditions, Sources*

Extensive pre-Pauline traditional elements cannot be discovered in 2 Corinthians. A pre-Pauline baptismal tradition is found in 2 Cor. 1.21–22,[237] and it is likely that traditional elements are also included in 3.7ff.[238] and 5.19ab.[239]

2.6.8 *History-of-religions Standpoint*

W. Lütgert saw the opponents of Paul in 2 Corinthians, like the opponents of Paul elsewhere, as libertinistic pneumatics and Gnostics.[240] This position was adopted by R. Bultmann[241] and W. Schmithals,[242] among others. In contrast, E. Käsemann argued against equating the opponents in the two letters to the Corinthians, maintaining that 2 Corinthians presupposes a new, advanced situation. For him the opponents in 2 Corinthians are missionaries close to the Jerusalem mother church who undertook to establish the authority of the original apostles over against that of Paul (cf. ὑπερλίαν ἀπόστολοι [super apostles] in 2 Cor. 11.5; 12.11). According to Käsemann, the issue in 2 Corinthians was the debate between two different understandings of official authority within early Christianity, the Pauline idea of apostleship over against the claims to church leadership made by the Jerusalem authorities. There is not a single passage in 2 Corinthians, however, where it is clear that the opponents were agitating as real or presumed delegates of the mother church in Jerusalem. Already 2 Cor. 3.1b speaks against this (πρὸς ὑμᾶς ἢ ἐξ ὑμῶν [to you or from you]), for if the opponents had come with letters of recommendation from Jerusalem, they would hardly have also claimed letters of recommendation from the

---

1909[12]) 6–19, 414–419; Adolf Schlatter, *Paulus der Bote Jesu* (Stuttgart: Calwer Verlag, 1956[2]) 612; Carl J. Bjerkelund, *PARAKALO* (see above 2.3.2) 145–155; Erich Fascher, *1 Korintherbrief* (see above 2.5.1) 25; Nils A. Dahl, *Studies in Paul* (Minneapolis: Fortress Press, 1977) 38–39 (Unity of 2 Cor. 1–9); Klaus Berger, *Bibelkunde des Neuen Testaments* (Heidelberg: Quelle u. Meyer, 1986[3]) 380ff.; Gerd Lüdemann, *Chronology* (see above 2.1) 98; P. Beier, 'Geteilte Briefe?' (see above 2.4.6) 79–103; Karl Th. Kleinknecht, *Der leidende Gerechtfertigte*, WUNT 2.13 (Tübingen: J. C. B. Mohr [Paul Siebeck], 1984) 303–304.

[237] Cf. Udo Schnelle, *Gerechtigkeit und Christusgegenwart* (see above 2.4.10) 124–126.

[238] Cf. Windisch, *2 Korintherbrief* 112ff.

[239] Cf. Breytenbach, *Versöhnung* 118–119.

[240] Cf. Wilhelm Lütgert, *Freiheitspredigt* (see above 2.5.1) 79. A comprehensive survey of the question of Paul's opponents in 2 Corinthians is presented by Sumney, *Identifying Paul's Opponents* 13–73. John J. Gunther, *Paul's Opponents and their Background*, NTS 35 (Leiden: E. J. Brill, 1973) 1, lists thirteen different classifications that have been suggested for identifying Paul's opponents.

[241] Cf. Bultmann, *2 Korintherbrief* 216.

[242] Cf. most recently Walter Schmithals, *Gnosis und Neues Testament* (Darmstadt: Wissenschaftliche Buchgesellschaft, 1984) 28–33.

Corinthians themselves. Probably the opponents appeared on the scene with letters of recommendation written indirectly by themselves (cf. 2 Cor. 10.12) and a high level of self-praise (cf. 2 Cor. 10.12–18).

D. Georgi judges the opponents in 2 Corinthians to be early Christian missionaries that are to be classified within the type widespread in late antiquity that comprised wandering prophets, goetes and bringers of healing and salvation. They already honored the earthly Jesus as the triumphant pneumatic and made no distinction between the earthly and exalted Jesus. Like the pagan miracle workers who presented themselves as having been sent by their deities and who boasted of their own powers, these early Christian missionaries put themselves on display by means of revelations and miracles. The indications of the opponents' militant Jewish Christian position are clearly undervalued by Georgi, while in other reconstructions they form the primary basis of the argument.

Thus G. Lüdemann,[243] following F. C. Baur, describes the opponents as Jewish Christians from Jerusalem who had participated in the Apostolic Council, but who then did not hold to the agreement reached there, since they attacked Paul in his own churches. This is an inadequate characterization of the opponents, for while it places proper value on their Jewish origin (cf. 2 Cor. 11.22), the decisive criterion of their credibility was their possession of the Spirit that came to expression in signs and wonders (cf. 2 Cor. 12.12). They invaded the Corinthian church from outside (2 Cor. 11.4), represented themselves as true apostles of Jesus Christ (2 Cor. 10.7; 11.5, 13; 12.11), contested Paul's own apostleship with their letters of recommendation (2 Cor. 11.7b, 20), and charged Paul with a lack of integrity (changing his travel plans) and greed (lining his own pockets with the collection). They allowed themselves to be supported by the church (2 Cor. 11.7b, 20), were gifted speakers (2 Cor. 11.6a), boasted of their extraordinary revelations (cf. 2 Cor. 12.1–6), and taught a different gospel than Paul's (2 Cor. 11.4). Probably they advocated a *theology of glory* that could not be reconciled with Paul's theology of the cross. However, Paul never mentions that the opponents demanded circumcision. Since the apostle goes into considerable detail in describing the activities and objections of the opponents, he would certainly have named circumcision if they had been propagating it. Thus the opponents in 2 Corinthians cannot be described as Judaizers in the same sense as the opponents in Galatians.[244] Circumcision, and therefore the issue of the Law in general, are not the

---

[243] Cf. Gerd Lüdemann, *Opposition to Paul* (see above 2.5.8) 80–97. This position, with small modifications, is also advocated Klauck, *2 Korintherbrief* 11.

[244] Cf. Windisch, *2 Korintherbrief* 26; Furnish, *2 Corinthians* 53; Lang, *2 Korintherbrief* 357–359.

disputed issues in 2 Corinthians; it is characteristic of this that the word νόμος (law) does not occur in 2 Corinthians. It is also not the case that the opponents appeal to a special relationship to the historical Jesus, for otherwise Paul could hardly have responded to the opponents' slogan 'I belong to Christ' with his οὕτως καὶ ἡμεῖς (so do we). Paul's opponents in 2 Corinthians were early Christian wandering missionaries of Hellenistic-Jewish origin who charged Paul especially with being deficient in his possession of the Spirit and who sought to legitimize themselves as true apostles and bearers of the Spirit by their speaking and by miracles.[245] To what extent they were associated with Jerusalem, if at all, may no longer be determined.

2.6.9 Basic Theological Ideas

Second Corinthians discloses to the readers the configuration of Paul's own *existence as an apostle*.[246] The legitimacy and essential character of Paul's apostleship are the themes that permeate the whole letter. Following the introductory greeting and thanksgiving for deliverance from deadly peril (2 Cor. 1.1–11) Paul defends himself against the charge that he had not dealt straightforwardly with them (2 Cor. 1.12–2.1). He then develops the essential character of the apostolic office in 2 Cor. 2.14–7.4. The apostolic ministry carried out by Paul includes both glory (2 Cor. 3.7–4.6) and suffering (2 Cor. 4.7–5.10), just as Jesus Christ himself passed through suffering to glory. Paul understands himself to be a minister of the new covenant, the eternal glory of which is grounded in Jesus Christ. The apostle knows that he is bound to Jesus Christ in suffering as well as in glory, and that it is the power of Christ that works in him to overcome external problems that befall him (cf. the peristasis catalogues in 2 Cor. 4.7–12; 6.4–10; 11.23–29).[247] As an apostle called by God (cf. 2 Cor. 2.16–17; 3.5–6) Paul proclaims the message of reconciliation (cf. 2 Cor. 5.11–21). His ministry is a part of the reconciliation given by God in Jesus Christ (cf. 2 Cor. 5.19–21). He proclaims the one who 'died and was raised again' (2 Cor. 5.15) and whose 'power is made perfect in weakness' (2 Cor. 12.9). The doxological tone is characteristic of 2 Corinthians (cf. 2 Cor. 1.3–4, 11; 2.14; 8.16; 9.12–13, 15); the existence of both apostle and church

---

[245] Cf. Sumney, *Identifying Paul's Opponents* 190; differently Friedrich W. Horn, *Angeld des Geistes* (see above 2.5.8) 302–309, who does not regard pneumatism as an essential aspect of Paul's opponents in 2 Corinthians.

[246] Cf. Wolff, *2 Korintherbrief* 11–14; Strecker, 'Legitimität' 573–582.

[247] Cf. Erhardt Güttgemanns, *Der leidende Apostel und sein Herr*, FRLANT 90 (Göttingen: Vandenhoeck & Ruprecht, 1966); Martin Ebner, *Leidenslisten und Apostelbrief*, Fzb 66 (Würzburg: Echter Verlag, 1991).

is determined by the grace of God. The apostle lives for the church (2 Cor. 5.13; 11.28–29), which he wants to present to Christ at the parousia (2 Cor. 11.2).

The dispute between Paul and the opponents that had invaded the Corinthian church also concerned the nature and authority of Paul's apostleship. Obviously the opponents made personal accusations against the apostle (2 Cor. 10.1–18) and contrasted his apparent weakness with their own pneumatic and ecstatic abilities. In contrast, the apostle boasts of his own weakness, for it is through the weakness of the apostle that the power of Christ works. The extravagant self-praise of the opponents shows that they represent and proclaim themselves, but not the Jesus Christ who died for our sins and for the reconciliation of the world.

One's whole existence is decided in the encounter with the gospel (2 Cor. 2.15); the preaching ministry has eschatological dimensions. This is why Paul struggles with and for his church.

2.6.10 *Tendencies of Recent Research*

The literary-critical analysis of the unity of 2 Corinthians manifests three tendencies: (1) 2 Cor. 1–9 is mostly regarded as a literary unity (e.g. Furnish, Lang, Klauck, Martin, Wolff). (2) The authenticity and integrity of 2 Cor. 6.14–7.1 continues to be disputed by many exegetes (e.g. Lang, Klauck). However, the suggestion is gaining support in the most recent studies that 2 Cor. 6.14–7.1 is a non-Pauline traditional text, partly reworked by the apostle, whose position in its present context is original (e.g. Furnish, Martin, Wolff). (3) The majority of exegetes consider 1–9 and 10–13 to belong to different letters. At the same time, within the framework of a temporal partition-hypothesis, the unity of 2 Corinthians with the presupposition of a changed situation between 2 Cor. 1–9 and 10–13 is again being seriously considered (Wolff, Danker). On the issue of the identity of Paul's opponents a consensus is emerging, inasmuch as the opponents are mostly described as Hellenistic Jewish Christians (Furnish, Lang, Wolff), while most scholars have rejected the θεῖος ἀνήρ ('divine man') model of D. Georgi.

At the center of the theological interpretation of 2 Corinthians stand two complexes of texts: chapters 3 and 5. In 2 Cor. 3 the disputed issues concern the real subject matter being discussed (freedom from the Law? the surpassing of the Old Testament and the disclosure of its real meaning by the Christ event?), the Pauline line of argument, and the history of traditions that stand in the background. Several different models of interpretation may be distinguished: D. Georgi explains Paul's line of argument mainly in terms of a text that Paul has taken over from his opponents.[248] O. Hofius derives far-reaching inferences for Pauline theology from his historical-systematic interpretation of 2 Cor. 3. 'Our analysis of 2 Cor. 3.7–18 shows that in these verses Paul elaborates the antithesis of Law and gospel formulated in 3.6, making clear and precise distinctions, and does so in fact under the premise that the Torah that condemns and kills the sinner has found its "end" in Christ and the verdict of acquittal announced in the gospel.'[249] In her primarily tradition-critical oriented analysis of 2 Cor. 3, Carol Kern-Stockhausen thoroughly works out the structures of the Pauline argumentation and comes to the conclusion 'that II Cor. 3.1–4.6 is a unified and integral text containing a single coherent argument in support of Paul's authentic apostleship in conformance to a Mosaic paradigm.'[250] In 2 Cor. 5.1–10 the main question is how this text is to be incorporated in the larger complex of Paul's eschatological statements. Does this text document a Hellenizing and individualizing of Paul's eschatology?[251]

The traditions that stand in the background of Paul's doctrine of reconciliation are hotly disputed (cf. 2 Cor. 5.11ff.; Rom. 5.1–11). According to C. Breytenbach Paul adopted essential elements of his doctrine of reconciliation from the language and conceptual world of Hellenistic diplomacy. In classical and Hellenistic texts both διαλάσσω and καταλάσσω describe conciliatory behavior in the political, social realm of everyday relations, without any religious or cultic component. 'The Pauline καταλάσσω-concept and the Old Testament כפר-tradition have no connections in the history of tradition that can be made the foundation of a biblical theology.'[252] Paul himself is the first to make this connection by adopting a traditional element in 2 Cor. 5.19ab. In contrast, O. Hofius emphasizes what is in his view a firm connection already made prior to Paul between 'reconciliation' and cultic 'atonement.' Paul accordingly made use of a way of speaking that had already developed in ancient Judaism. 'The Pauline idea of reconciliation is . . . decisively influenced by the message of Deutero-Isaiah.'[253]

---

[248] For the reconstruction, cf. Georgi, *Opponents* 271–272.
[249] Hofius, 'Gesetz und Evangelium' 120.
[250] Carol Kern-Stockhausen, *Moses' Veil and the Glory of the New Covenant*, AB 116 (Rome: Pontifical Biblical Institute, 1989) 175.
[251] Cf. Wolfgang Wiefel, 'Die Hauptrichtung des Wandels' (see above 2.4.10) 76; Udo Schnelle, *Wandlungen* (see above 2.4.9) 42–44, and the survey of research in F. G. Lang, *2. Korinther 5,1–10 in der neuen Forschung*. BGBE 16 (Tübingen: J. C. B. Mohr [Paul Siebeck], 1973); Wolff, *2 Korinther* 101–106.   [252] Breytenbach, *Versöhnung* 221.
[253] Otfried Hofius, 'Erwägungen zur Gestalt und Herkunft des paulinischen Versöhnungsgedankens,' in *Paulusstudien*, ed. O. Hofius, WUNT 51 (Tübingen: J. C. B. Mohr [Paul Siebeck], 1989) 14; cf. in the same volume pp. 15–32, 33–49.

2.7 The Letter to the Galatians

2.7.1 Literature

Commentaries

Lietzmann, Hans. *An die Galater*, HNT 10. Tübingen: J. C. B. Mohr (Paul Siebeck), 1971[4]; Schlier, Heinrich. *Der Brief an die Galater*, KEK 7. Göttingen: Vandenhoeck & Ruprecht, 1971[5]; Betz, Hans D. *Galatians*. Hermeneia. Philadelphia: Fortress Press, 1979; Mußner, Franz. *Der Galaterbrief*, HThK 9. Freiburg: Herder, 1981[4]; Borse, Udo. *Der Galaterbrief*, RNT. Regensburg: Pustet, 1984; Lührmann, Dieter. *Galatians*, tr. O. C. Dean, Jr. ZBK 7. Minneapolis: Fortress Press, 1984; Rohde, Joachim. *Der Brief des Paulus an die Galater*, ThHK 9. Berlin: Evangelische Verlagsanstalt, 1989; Becker, Jürgen. *Der Brief an die Galater*, NTD 8. Göttingen: Vandenhoeck & Ruprecht, 1990[3]; Longenecker, Richard N. *Galatians*, WBC 41. Dallas: Word, 1990.

Monographs

Lütgert, Wilhelm. *Gesetz und Geist*, BFChTh. Gütersloh: Bertelsmann, 1919; Eckert, Jost. *Die urchristliche Verkündigung im Streit zwischen Paulus und seinen Gegnern im Galaterbrief*, BU 6. Regensburg: Friedrich Pustet, 1971; Borse, Udo. *Der Standort des Galaterbriefes*, BBB 41. Köln: Hanstein, 1972; Hübner, Hans. *Law in Paul's Thought*, tr. James C. G. Greig. Edinburgh: T. & T. Clark, 1984; Bachmann, Michael. *Sünder oder Übertreter. Studien zur Argumentation in Gal. 2,15ff*, WUNT 59. Tübingen: J. C. B. Mohr (Paul Siebeck), 1992.

Articles

Kertelge, Karl. 'Zur Deutung des Rechtfertigungsbegriffs im Galaterbrief,' BZ 12 (1968) 211–222; Blank, Josef. 'Warum sagt Paulus: "Aus Werken des Gesetzes wird niemand gerecht?"' *EKK.V 1*. Neukirchen-Vluyn: Neukirchener Verlag, 1969, 79–95; Klein, Günter. 'Individualgeschichte und Weltgeschichte bei Paulus,' in *Rekonstruktion und Interpretation*, ed. G. Klein. BEvTh 50. Munich: C. Kaiser, 1969, 180–224; Merk, Otto. 'Der Beginn der Paränese im Galaterbrief,' ZNW 60 (1969) 83–104; Hahn, Ferdinand. 'Das Gesetzesverständnis im Römer- und Galaterbrief,' ZNW 67 (1976) 29–63; Vielhauer, Philipp. 'Gesetzes- und Stoicheiadienst im Galaterbrief,' in *Oikodome*, ed. Ph. Vielhauer. TB 65. Munich: C. Kaiser, 1979, 183–195; Schmithals, Walter. 'Judaisten in Galatien?' ZNW 74 (1983) 27–58; Hübner, Hans. 'Galaterbrief.' *TRE* 12 (1984) 5–14; Suhl, Alfred. 'Der Galaterbrief – Situation und Argumentation,' *ANRW* II 25.4. Berlin: Walter de Gruyter, 1987, 3067–3164; Söding, Thomas. 'Die Gegner des Apostels Paulus in Galatien,' MThZ 42 (1991) 305–321.

2.7.2 Author

The Pauline authorship of Galatians is now uncontested.

2.7.3 *Place and Time of Composition*

Two possibilities must be seriously considered for the time and place of the letter's composition: (1) Galatians was written during Paul's stay in Ephesus, either before or after 1 Corinthians, which was sent from Ephesus in any case.[254] (2) Paul wrote Galatians during his journey through Macedonia (cf. Acts 20.2), so that it is to be placed after 1 and 2 Corinthians and just before Romans.[255] The only criteria for deciding between these options are the noticeable similarity to Romans and the references to the collection in Galatians 2.10 and 1 Corinthians 16.1.

Close contacts between Galatians and Romans are seen first of all in their respective structures:[256]

Gal. 1.15–16	Rom. 1.1–5	Set apart as apostle to the Gentiles
Gal. 2.15–21	Rom. 3.19–28	Justification by faith
Gal. 3.6–25, 29	Rom. 4.1–25	Abraham
Gal. 3.26–28	Rom. 6.3–5	Baptism
Gal. 4.1–7	Rom. 8.12–17	Slavery and freedom
Gal. 4.21–31	Rom. 9.6–13	Law and promise
Gal. 5.13–15	Rom. 13.8–10	Freedom in love
Gal. 5.17	Rom. 7.15–23	Conflict between willing and doing
Gal. 5.16–26	Rom. 8.12ff.	Life in the Spirit

The train of thought found in Romans already appears in a preliminary form in Galatians. The polemic of Galatians, conditioned by the particular situation, becomes in Romans a way of posing the issues that is based more on fundamental principles. In Romans the argumentation is more

---

[254] So for example Albrecht Oepke, *Der Brief des Paulus an die Galater*, ThHK 9 (Berlin: Evangelische Verlagsanstalt, 1973³) 211–212 (Galatians after 1 Corinthians); Schlier, *Galaterbrief* 18; Vielhauer, *Urchristliche Literatur* (110–111); Lührmann, *Galatians* 10 (Galatians after 1 Corinthians); Hübner, 'Galaterbrief' 11.

[255] So for example J. B. Lightfoot, *Saint Paul's Epistle to the Galatians* (London: Macmillan, 1890¹⁰) 55; Otto Pfleiderer, *Das Urchristentum* (Berlin: 1902) 1.138; Borse, *Galaterbrief* 9–17; Mußner, *Galaterbrief* 9ff.; Ulrich Wilckens, *Römerbrief* (see below 2.8.1) 1.47–48; Lüdemann, *Chronology* (see above 2.1) 263; Becker, *Galater* 4ff.; Dieter Zeller, *Römerbrief* (see below 2.8.1) 13; F. Stanley Jones, *'Freiheit' in den Briefen des Apostels Paulus* (see above 2.5.4) 25–26; Samuel Vollenweider, *Freiheit als neue Schöpfung* (see above 2.5.9) 20 note 40; Heikki Räisänen, *Paul and the Law* (see below 2.8.1) 8; Rohde, *Galaterbrief* 10–11; Georg Strecker, *Neues Testament* (Stuttgart: Kohlhammer 1989) 78; Eduard Schweizer, *Theological Introduction* 74; Thomas Söding, 'Chronologie der paulinischen Briefe' (see above 2.1) 58; Friedrich W. Horn, *Angeld des Geistes* (see above 2.5.8) 346. Even when Galatians is seen as standing in close proximity to Romans, the relation of this letter to 2 Corinthians and Philippians may be regarded in different ways. For example, Mußner (*Galaterbrief* 10–11), following Borse, places Galatians between 2 Cor. 1–9 and 10–13, as does Rohde (*Galaterbrief* 11). Jürgen Becker, *Paul* 314 (see above 2), on the basis of Philippians, argues for the order Galatians, Philippians B, Romans, while describing Philippians B (see below 2.9.6) as a supplementary 'little Galatians.'

[256] Cf. Borse, *Standort* 120–135; Ulrich Wilckens, *Römerbrief* (see below 2.8.1) 1.48.

reflective, the introduction of evidence to support the argument is more stringent. Also, new questions bothersome to Paul are taken up, as shown by Rom. 1.18–3.21 and chapters 9–11. Above all, the doctrine of justification common to the two letters speaks for some kind of connection between them. Only here do we find the alternative 'by faith, not by works of the Law'; only here is there a reflective, worked-out understanding of the Law. The differences in the way the Law is understood in Galatians and Romans derive from the manner in which Galatians is conditioned by the particular situation to which it is directed, while it is precisely these particular ideas that receive a further development in Romans.

According to 1 Cor. 16.1 Paul also organized a collection in Galatia for the saints in Jerusalem, probably not long before the composition of 1 Corinthians. There is here no trace of a crisis between the apostle and the Galatian churches, a clear indication that Galatians was at least written after 1 Corinthians. Gal. 2.10 mentions the collection completely unpolemically within the framework of the agreements worked out at the Apostolic Council. Since the collection was not a matter of debate between the apostles and his opponents or the church and is otherwise not mentioned in Galatians, we may suppose that the project of gathering the collection in Galatia was already complete at the time Galatians was composed. When Paul explicitly emphasizes in Gal. 2.10b that he had fully discharged the obligations accepted when he agreed to the collection at the Jerusalem conference, he thereby presupposes the arrangements for gathering the collection mentioned in 2 Corinthians (cf. Rom. 15.26).[257]

Both the proximity to Romans and the reports about the collection in Galatians speak in favor of the view that Galatians was written after the two Corinthian letters and immediately before Romans *in the late fall of 55* CE *in Macedonia*. Considerations as to the location of the addressees confirm this late dating, although it was attained by data from the letter itself.

2.7.4 *Intended Readership*

The Letter to the Galatians could be written either to the churches in the region of Galatia (the north Galatian/ regional hypothesis) or those in the southern part of the Roman province of Galatia (south Galatian/ provincial hypothesis). The Galatians are descendants of the Celts who invaded Asia Minor in 279 BCE, and who settled in the area around present day Ankara.

---

[257] Cf. Rohde, *Galaterbrief* 94. The use of the first aorist ἐσπούδασα (I was eager) by Paul indicates 'that he himself "sought strenuously" to honor the commitment' (G. Harder, TDNT 7.564). In any case Gal. 2.10b excludes dating Galatians early, as the oldest Pauline letter, as advocated by Theodor Zahn, *Der Brief des Paulus an die Galater*, KNT 9 (Leipzig – Erlangen: Deichert, 1922³) 20–21.

In 25 BCE the region of Galatia was incorporated into the Roman province of Galatia, which included also parts of the southern districts Pisidia, Lycaonia, Isauria, Paphlagonia, Pontus Galaticus, and part of Pamphylia.

According to the *south Galatian theory* the addressees of the letter were Christians in the districts of Lycaonia, Pisidia and Isauria, where according to Acts 13.13–14, 27 Paul founded churches that he also probably visited later (cf. Acts 16.2–5). The following arguments can be brought forward for the south Galatian theory.[258] (1) The Galatian churches participated in the offering made for Jerusalem (cf. 1 Cor. 16.1); Acts 20.4 mentions as members of the delegation sent with the offering only Christians from southern Asia Minor, including Gaius from Derbe. (2) The successful agitation of Paul's opponents in Galatia points toward the presence of Jewish Christians in the churches. There was a Jewish element in the population of the southern region of the province of Galatia, but this is not clear for the northern district.[259] (3) Paul frequently uses the provincial names (Asia, Achaia, Macedonia); he does not orient his mission on a regional basis, but to the important large cities of the provinces.[260] (4) The order of the travel note in Acts 18.23 ('. . . from place to place through the region of Galatia and Phrygia') can be understood as evidence for the province hypothesis.

Weighty arguments can also be presented for the *north Galatian theory*.[261] (1) The south Galatian theory presupposes that the churches of Galatia were founded on the first missionary journey. Paul mentions nothing of this in Gal. 1.21, although this would have provided strong support for his argument. The addressees thus know that Paul did not found churches in their area until later.[262] (2) Acts 16.6; 18.23 presuppose as Luke's view that Paul did missionary work in the region of Galatia (and not only in the southern area of the province Galatia).[263] (3) With the exception of Philemon, Paul elsewhere always directs his letters to concrete local churches. The lack of a place name and the use of an ethnic term for the

---

[258] A comprehensive argument for the south Galatian theory is found in Theodor Zahn, *Introduction* (see below 2.9.3) 1.173–193; Carl Clemen, *Paulus. Sein Leben und Wirken* (Gießen: J. Ricker, 1904) 1.24–38; it has recently again been advocated by Peter Stuhlmacher, *Biblische Theologie des Neuen Testaments* (see above 2) 1.226.

[259] Here the argument is from silence, and cannot bear the weight of such far-reaching hypotheses.

[260] Cf. W. H. Ollrog, *Paulus und seine Mitarbeiter* (see above 2.2.2) 55–56.

[261] Cf. the extensive argument in Ph. Vielhauer, *Urchristliche Literatur* (see above) 104–108.

[262] This argument is not vitiated by referring to the expression τὰ κλίματα (τῆς Συρίας καὶ τῆς Κιλικίας) (the regions [of Syria and Cilicia]), for otherwise Paul argues very precisely in Gal. 1. That the Galatian churches had already been founded before the Apostolic Council would have clearly demonstrated his independence from Jerusalem.

[263] Cf. Mußner, *Galaterbrief* 3–5.

addressees (Gal. 1.2; 3.1) speak in favor of the regional hypothesis. (4) The peoples included by the Romans in the province of Galatia maintained their individual cultural and linguistic heritage, so that for example the Lycaonians still used their own language (cf. Acts 14.11). It would therefore be extraordinary for Paul to address people of Lycaonia or Pisidia as 'foolish Galatians' (3.1).[264] (5) In the contemporary use of the term, ἡ Γαλατία was used primarily to refer to the region of Galatia, not the province.[265] (6) It is by no means the case that Paul always used the official Roman provincial names, but he often used the older regional terms (cf. Gal. 1.17, 21; 1 Thess. 2.14; Rom. 15.24).

On the whole the arguments for the north Galatian hypothesis are stronger. In particular, the absence of the addressees in Gal. 1.21, the Lucan statement about Paul's work in 'the region of . . . Galatia' and the address in Gal. 3.1, along with the well thought out arrangement of the letter as a whole, speak against the south Galatian theory.[266]

When were the Galatian churches founded? According to Acts 16.6 and 18.23, Paul traversed 'the region of . . . Galatia' at the beginning of both his second and third missionary journeys. Acts 16.6 is often regarded as the time during which the Galatian churches were founded, followed by a second visit to strengthen the churches (Acts 18.23). Gal. 4.13 is understood as evidence for this view, where τὸ πρότερον is translated as 'the first time' and thus implies a later second visit already in the letter's past. The Galatian churches would then have been founded on the second missionary journey.[267] But of course both Acts texts are at least for the most part Lucan redaction,[268] so that nothing certain can be said about Paul's

---

[264] In this argument one must of course also notice that a mixed population is to be reckoned with not only in the south, but also in the north.

[265] Documentation in Rohde, *Galaterbrief* 1–2. Since the region of Galatia also belonged to the province of Galatia, the reference to the province cannot be played off against the regional hypothesis as though province and region were alternatives.

[266] The positions of individual exegetes on the north vs. south Galatian theories are listed by Rohde, *Galaterbrief* 6–7. Cf. for the north Galatian theory most recently and extensively Betz, *Galatians* 3–5; further Ulrich Wickert, 'Kleinasien,' TRE 19 (1990) (244–265) 251: 'The north Galatian theory is to be decisively preferred.' He says nothing about the theological reason at work in those who prefer the south Galatian theory.

[267] So among others, Schlier, *Brief an die Galater* 17–18; Oepke, *Galaterbrief* 25, 142; Mußner, *Galaterbrief* 3–9, 306–307,

[268] Acts 18.23c ('strengthening all the disciples') is often regarded as evidence for a previous mission in Galatia. Cf. Hübner, 'Galaterbrief' 6. But precisely this expression is clearly redactional; cf. Luke 22.32; Acts 14.22; 15.32, 41; 16.5. Moreover, in Acts 18.23 certainly redactional are ποιεῖν χρόνον τινά (to spend some time) (cf. Acts 15.33); καθεξῆς ('from place to place') is found in the New Testament only in Luke 1.3; 8.1; Acts 3.24; 11.4. Acts 16.6 must be understood as entirely a note composed by Luke himself, that brings to expression the apostle's path toward Europe as his goal. For detailed analysis cf. A. Weiser, *Apostelgeschichte* (see below 4.1) 2.404, 500. The different order of the stations in Acts 16.6 and 18.23 is to be noted. On the great problems of Acts 18.18–23 see above 2.1.2.

missionary activity in 'the region of Galatia' beyond the bare fact that he did missionary work there. Thus if one chooses to work only on the basis of the data supplied by the letter itself, other possibilities of interpretation arise. Galatians 1.6 presupposes that the visit on which Paul founded the churches lies not very long in the past, since the Galatians at first were 'running well' (5.7), but Paul is now 'astonished' that they 'so quickly' have fallen away from his gospel (1.6). A second visit of the apostle in Galatia is neither mentioned nor in any way presupposed. It is not necessary to understand the temporal designation τὸ πρότερον in Gal. 4.13 as 'the first time,' but it may be translated as 'first' in the sense of 'then.'[269] Moreover, Gal. 4.13–15, 18–19 refer in any case only to the visit on which the churches were founded, so that a second visit can be inferred only hypothetically from the letter itself.[270] A reflection of the origin of the Galatian churches is thus found only in Acts 18.23. The founding of the churches on the beginning of Paul's third missionary journey in the spring of 52 fits the internal data of the letter itself, takes into account the statements of Acts, and agrees with the dating of Galatians shortly before Romans presupposed above.

The Galatians were predominately Gentile Christians (cf. Gal. 4.8; 5.2–3; 6.12–13) and probably belonged to the hellenized population of the cities. The reception of Galatians presupposes a certain level of education, and the preliminary effect of the Pauline message of freedom points to circles that were interested in cultural and religious emancipation.

2.7.5 Outline, Structure, Form

1.1–5	Prescript	— Introduction
1.6–10	Occasion for the letter	

1.11–2.14	Autobiographical report: the independence of the Pauline gospel	
2.15–2.21	Thesis: Justification by Faith	
3.1–4.7	Law: Spirit and sonship	— Body
4.8–4.31	Warning against falling back into slavery	
5.1–5.12	Conclusion: slavery or freedom	
5.13–5.26	Love as fruit of the Spirit	

---

[269] Cf. Borse, *Galaterbrief* 150.

[270] Borse, *Galaterbrief* 8ff. and Betz, *Galatians* 10–11 also vote against a second visit by Paul to the Galatian churches.

6.1–10	Concluding parenesis	
6.11–18	Final farewell [Eschatokoll]	Conclusion

The peculiar features of the structure of Galatians are explained by the special situation in which the letter was composed. Thus the introduction lacks the proemium [thanksgiving], since Paul sees no reason to give thanks in view of the situation in Galatia. Paul explicitly brings his authority to bear by referring to his apostolic title in Gal. 1.1. The sharp polemic at the very beginning of the letter is unique (1.6–9), and determines the line of argument for extended sections of the first two chapters. In 3.1–4.11, 21–31 Paul attempts by means of a multi–layered argument to convince the Galatians of the foolishness of their behavior. Topoi of the friendship letter prevail in 4.12–20, as Paul reminds the church of their previous good conduct and encourages them to return to the former basis of their Christian life. In 5.1–6.11 Paul advises the Galatians not to casually abandon the freedom they have been given. The letter's conclusion omits any sort of greeting and instead enters into a fresh debate with his opponents (cf. Gal. 6.12–14). The macrostructure of Galatians resembles that of other Pauline letters, with a more doctrinal main section (chapters 1–4) followed by a more parenetic section (from 5.13 on), with 5.1–12 functioning as summary and transition.

H. D. Betz outlines Galatians according to the criteria of Greco-Roman rhetoric and epistolography.[271] He regards Galatians as an apologetic letter structured according to the following typical sections:

1.1–5	praescriptum (prescript)
1.6–11	exordium (introduction)
1.12–2.14	narratio (narrative)
2.15–21	propositio (proposition)
3.1–4.31	probatio (proof)
5.1–6.10	exhortatio (exhortation)
6.11–18	conclusio (conclusion)

Galatians appears to be a particularly good candidate for the analysis of a Pauline letter from the rhetorical point of view, since the debate with the opponents and the relationship to the church explain the form of the

---

[271] Cf. Betz, *Galatians* 83–105. The accents are placed differently in the rhetorical analysis of George A. Kennedy, *New Testament Interpretation through Rhetorical Criticism* (Durham: University of North Carolina, 1984) 144–152 and in Joop Smit, 'The Letter of Paul to the Galatians: A Deliberative Speech,' NTS 35 (1989) 1–26, who classify Galatians as belonging to the genus deliberativum.

letter. The letter takes the place of the absent Paul and represents the apologetic speech he would give if present. However, the letter may not be fully explained as an apologetic letter. Doubtless in Gal. 1 and 2 an apologetic tendency prevails, but 5.13–6.18 is deliberative and 3.1–5.12 is adjusted to both the symbuleutic and epideictic patterns.[272] So also the place of parenesis within an 'apologetic letter' remains unclear. When presenting a defense speech before the court, who would add parenetic elaborations to the real argument for the defense?

A further problem is presented by the relation between ancient epistolography and rhetoric, for here there are only minor points of contact.[273] When the apostle in 2 Cor. 11.6 agrees that he was untrained in speech (ἰδιώτης τῷ λόγῳ), but not in knowledge, this should be an advance warning against attempting to explain the Pauline line of argument strictly in terms of rhetorical elements (cf. further 1 Thess. 2.4–6; 1 Cor. 2.1–3; 2 Cor. 3.5; 13.3–4). In addition, Paul wrote his letters in situations that were considerably more complex than the settings assumed by textbooks of ancient rhetoric.[274] Paul did adopt rhetorical conventions as *elements* of his *cultural environment*, but they never became the determining factor of his argumentation.

2.7.6 Literary Integrity

The literary integrity of Galatians is undisputed. The unpauline expressions in Galatians 2.7–8 (εὐαγγέλιον τῆς ἀκροβυστίας/τῆς περιτομῆς [gospel to the uncircumcised/to the circumcised] Πέτρος [Peter]) do not suggest a non-Pauline interpolation, but are an indication of pre-Pauline tradition.[275]

---

[272] Cf. J. Schoon-Janßen, *Umstrittene 'Apologien' in den Paulusbriefen* (see above 2.3.1) 66–113, who also offers a thorough critique of Betz.

[273] For critique of Betz's view cf. especially from the point of view of ancient philology: Carl Joachim Classen, 'Paulus und die antike Rhetorik,' ZNW 82 (1991) 1–33. Classen points to the difference between rhetoric and epistolography in the ancient understanding, doubts that there was a 'genre of apologetic letter,' and in regard to the 'captivity to theory' of ancient authors states that 'precisely the dissimulatio artis belongs to the central requirements that theory makes on every practitioner, i.e. the requirement of not allowing the praecepta to becoming obvious, so that the clearly discernable use of the rules was considered a sign of inexperience or deficient ability, especially in the realm of dispositio and elocutio' (31).

[274] David E. Aune, *Literary Environment* (see above 2.3.1) 203 appropriately comments: 'Paul in particular was both a creative and eclectic letter writer. The epistolary situations he faced were often more complex than the ordinary rhetorical situations faced by most rhetoricians.'

[275] Evidence in Gerd Lüdemann, *Chronology* (see above 2.1) 64–69.

2.7.7 Traditions, Sources

In Gal. 2.7–8 (ὅτι πεπίστευμαι . . . τὰ ἔθνη [I had been entrusted . . . the Gentiles]) and 2.9e (ἡμεῖς εἰς τὰ ἔθνη, αὐτοὶ δὲ εἰς τὴν περιτομήν [we to the Gentiles, but they to the circumcision]) is found a pre-Pauline tradition stamped by personal recollections of the Apostolic Council.[276] Galatians 3.26–28 represents a pre-Pauline *baptismal tradition*.[277] Here the new situation of the baptized is expansively portrayed. They are ἐν Χριστῷ (in Christ), as the new relationship between the baptized and Christ is constituted by baptism. The baptismal candidate puts on Christ like a garment, is completely surrounded by Christ and precisely for this reason can be said to be ἐν Χριστῷ. The results of this εἶναι ἐν Χριστῷ (being in Christ) are described more closely in 3.28 in their history-of-salvation and political-social dimensions: the history-of-salvation distinction between Jews and Greeks and the political-social differentiation between slave and free, male and female are no longer valid. Because in baptism there is only a being-in-Christ, Christians are delivered from these ancient fundamental alternatives. Traditional material is also reworked by Paul in the catalogues of vices and virtues in Gal. 5.19–23.[278]

2.7.8 History-of-religions Standpoint

Who were the opponents against whom Paul struggles in Galatians? What was their teaching, and how should they be classified in history-of-religion categories?[279] In 1919 W. Lütgert gave an answer to these questions that has endured until the present in some circles, namely that Paul struggled on two fronts at the same time: on the one hand against Judaizers, on the other hand against pneumatics. It is not demonstrable from Galatians, however, that there are two groups of opponents with whom Paul disputes, so that contemporary research mostly reckons with one group. W. Schmithals[280] classifies the opponents as representatives of a Jewish or Jewish Christian enthusiasm of gnostic provenience. He points out that the

---

[276] Lüdemann, *Chronology* 48–75.

[277] For analysis, cf. Udo Schnelle, *Gerechtigkeit und Christusgegenwart* (see above 2.4.10) 57–62, 191–195.

[278] Cf. as parallels 1QS 3, 25–4, 14; for an analysis cf. Heinz-Wolfgang Kuhn, 'Die drei wichtigsten Qumranparallelen zum Galaterbrief,' in *Konsequente Traditionsgeschichte* (FS K. Baltzer), ed. R. Bartelmus et al. OBO 126 (Göttingen: Vandenhoeck & Ruprecht, 1993) (227–254) at 238–249.

[279] A survey of research is presented by Eckert, *Verkündigung* 1–18; Mußner, *Galaterbrief* 11–29; Rohde, *Galaterbrief* 14–21

[280] Cf. Walter Schmithals, 'The Heretics in Galatia,' in *Paul and the Gnostics*, tr. John E. Steely (Nashville and New York: Abingdon Press, 1972) 13–64.

Judaizer hypothesis would mean that Paul's opponents of a Gentile mission would themselves be carrying on such a mission. Moreover, for Schmithals texts such as Gal. 4.9–10; 5.3 and especially 6.12–13 can only be properly interpreted from gnostic-enthusiastic presuppositions. In his view the opponents only pushed the demand for circumcision in order to win the approval of the synagogue; neither they themselves nor the Galatians had in view a complete adoption of the Law.[281] But it cannot be established that there was any sort of danger for the churches from the side of the synagogue. In addition, it is very doubtful that at the time of the writing of Galatians there was any such thing as Christian gnostics. Finally, Schmithals does not do justice to the statements in the letter that imply that the Galatians were adopting the Law (cf. 4.21; 5.1, 4).

The most persuasive thesis is thus that posed by F. C. Baur and still advocated by the majority of exegetes, namely that the opponents are *Jewish Christian missionaries* (from a strict background).[282] They intrude into the churches and interfere with the good relationship between them and the apostle (cf. Gal. 4.13–15; 5.7). The opponents demand the practice of circumcision (cf. Gal. 5.3; 6.12–13, as well as 2.2; 6.15)[283] and the observation of cultic times (cf. Gal. 4.3, 9, 10).[284] Both features point to Jewish Christians,[285] for especially the Qumran texts testify to the great significance of calendrical issues in ancient Judaism and the firm connection between Law and attending to correct dates for festivals and holy days (cf. e.g. 1QS 1.13–15; 9.26–10.8; 1QM 2.4; 10.15; CD 3.12–16; 16.2–4;

---

[281] Cf. Schmithals, 'Judaisten in Galatien?' 55: 'The circumcision party want the Galatians to be circumcised only as a protection from Jewish persecution; they no more advocate an adoption of the Law as a whole than does Paul or the Galatians themselves.'

[282] For this understanding cf. among others, A. Oepke, *Galaterbrief* (see above 2.7.3) 27ff.; Kümmel, *Introduction* 298–301; Mußner, *Galaterbrief* 25; Merk, 'Paränese' 95; Lührmann, *Galatians* 104–108; Hübner, 'Galaterbrief' 7–8; Betz, *Galatians* 5–9; Gerd Lüdemann, *Opposition to Paul* (see above 2.5.8) 101; Friedrich W. Horn, *Angeld des Geistes* (see above 2.5.8) 346–350.

[283] Peder Borgen, 'Observations on the Theme "Paul and Philo". Paul's preaching of circumcision in Galatia (Gal. 5.11) and debates on circumcision in Philo,' in *Die Paulinische Literatur und Theologie*, ed. S. Pedersen (Århus: Forlaget Aros – Göttingen: Vandenhoeck & Ruprecht, 1980) 85–102, points out the distinction between 'ethical' and physical circumcision in Philo *Migration* 86–93; *Questions on Exodus* 2.2, and from this infers with regard to Galatians that Paul's opponents had persuaded some of the church members that Paul's preaching was to be understood as calling for 'ethical' circumcision, which now must be followed by physical circumcision.

[284] On the possible history-of-religions background of στοιχεῖα τοῦ κόσμου (elements of the world) cf. Eduard Schweizer, 'Die "Elemente der Welt" Gal. 4,3.9; Kol 2,8.20,' in *Beiträge zur Theologie des Neuen Testaments*, ed. E. Schweizer (Zürich: Zwingli Verlag, 1970) 147–163; cf. further 5.2.8.

[285] Differently Nikolaus Walter, 'Paulus und die Gegner des Christusevangeliums in Galatien,' in *L'Apôtre Paul*, ed. A. Vanhoye, BETL LXXIII (Leuven: Leuven University Press, 1986) 351–356, according to which Paul is debating with a Jewish counter mission.

1QH 1.24; 12.4–9; Jub 6.32, 36, 37; 1 Enoch 72.1; 75.3–4; 79.2; 82.4, 7–10). The honoring of particular days, months, seasons, years, and the elemental spirits/ principles of the universe thus is not out of step with a Jewish Christian interpretation of the opponents, but rather supports it.[286] At the same time, the complex interconnections between service to the *stoicheia*, a kind of piety connected to the calendar, and observance of the Law point to Hellenistic Jewish Christians.[287] Obviously significant numbers of Christians in the Galatian churches had accepted the demands of the Jewish Christian missionaries (cf. Gal. 1.6–9; 4.9, 17, 21; 5.4; 6.12–13), which calls forth sharp criticism from the apostle. Paul hopes, however, to win the community back by his arguments (cf. Gal. 3.4; 4.11–12, 19–20). The preservation and handing on of Galatians shows that this hope was not without basis.

What was the relationship between the opponents and the Jerusalem authorities, especially to James? A connection to the 'certain people from James' (Gal. 2.12) cannot be established, since there is no evidence that they demanded circumcision.[288] Recently the thesis has again been energetically advocated that Paul's opponents were identical with the 'false brethren' that attempted unsuccessfully to compel Titus to be circumcised at the Apostolic Council.[289] They did not go along with the agreement reached at the Council, and then intruded into the Pauline churches in Galatia and insisted on observation of the Law and the cultic calendar. Here too the scanty sources at our disposal do not permit a firm judgment. If there was some sort of connection between the Jerusalem authorities and the opponents of Paul in Galatia, then the 'pillars' had intentionally engineered the breaking of the agreement reached at the Apostolic Council. This would be an inference that cannot be verified by the texts, but must remain in the twilight of historical speculation. We will therefore have to be satisfied with the statement that Paul's opponents were Jewish Christian missionaries (from Palestine) who regarded the Law-free Gentile mission

---

[286] Cf. the extensive evidence in Dieter Lührmann, 'Tage, Monate, Jahreszeiten, Jahre (Gal. 4,10),' in *Werden und Wirken des Alten Testaments* (FS C. Westermann), ed. Rainer Albertz et al (Göttingen: Vandenhoeck & Ruprecht, 1980) 428–445.

[287] Cf. for example Söding, 'Gegner des Paulus' 315–316; like many other exegetes, he considers the opponents to be 'Hellenistic Jewish Christians who advocate a Christian nomism that has been synchretistically influenced' (316).

[288] Among those who present a different view is Francis Watson, *Paul, Judaism and the Gentiles*. SNTSMS 56 (Cambridge: Cambridge University Press, 1986) 59ff.

[289] Cf. Gerd Lüdemann, *Opposition to Paul* (see above 2.5.8) 99–103; this thesis was previously advocated by, among others, Oepke, *Galaterbrief* 212–213. Of course Gal. 2.3–4 shows that there were influential groups within Jewish Christianity that programatically advocated the circumcision of Gentile Christians. Their appearance at the Apostolic Council indicates that they claimed authority beyond the Palestine/ Syria area.

as carried on by Paul as a blatant offense against the saving will of God as revealed in the Torah. They must be seen within the framework of a movement that pursued the Pauline mission, a movement that attempted in different ways to make the combination of faith in Jesus Christ *and* observance of the Law to be binding not only for Jewish Christians, but for Gentile Christians as well. Of course there was no Jewish Law that Gentiles should be circumcised, but in the view of Paul's opponents these who once had been Gentiles had by their entrance into the Christian community become part of the people of God, which then raised the issue of circumcision and other aspects of the Law.

2.7.9 *Basic Theological Ideas*

Paul refutes those who are attacking him by first presenting an autobiographical (Gal. 1.13–24) and 'church-history' argument (Gal. 2.1–14). He did not receive the gospel of Jesus Christ from human beings, but only through the revelation of God. He thus had no reason to hurry to Jerusalem in order to be instructed by the Jerusalem authorities. So too, the agreement worked out at the Jerusalem Council and the conflict with Peter at Antioch testify to the independence of Paul's gospel. In Gal. 2.15 Paul shifts to a discussion of the role of the Law for Christians in God's plan of salvation. The core thesis of his *doctrine of justification* that emerges for the first time in Gal. 2.16 is based on an anthropological premise: no human being will be justified before God by works of the Law (Gal. 2.16d). No human being is capable of fulfilling all the requirements of the Law, so that falling short of the Law's demand results in every human being's coming under the curse of the Law (cf. Gal. 3.10–12). In this Paul is viewing the fulfillment of the requirements of the Law from a purely quantitative aspect in which every single transgression makes a person completely unrighteous.[290] Paul thereby separates the attainment of salvation from works of Torah.[291]

The human experience of being shattered by the Law's demand is not yet the real foundation of Paul's argument, however, which appears in Gal. 3.22: συνέκλεισεν ἡ γραφὴ τὰ πάντα ὑπὸ ἁμαρτίαν (the Scripture has imprisoned all things through the power of sin). Through the power of sin the Law loses its quality as a way of salvation; Paul declares the Law to

---

[290] Cf. Hübner, *Law in Paul* 24–25.

[291] Cf. the interpretation of Habakkuk 2.4b in Galatians 3.11 and 1QpHab 7.17–8.3. Kuhn, 'Qumranparallelen zum Galaterbrief' (see above 2.7.8) 249 rightly emphasizes: 'With this interpretation of the important prophetic passage Hab 2.4 in terms of his theology the Pharisee Paul has doubtless taken a step beyond Judaism—and that by referring to the biblical text they held in common.'

be inadequate in the face of the power of sin. The agitation of Paul's opponents has therefore brought the Galatians in danger of falling away from the state of salvation they have already reached. By baptism and the conferral of the Spirit the Galatians have already been delivered from the realm of the Law that brings the curse. In order to remain in the people of God, they must not subject themselves to the Jewish regulations. After all, they received the Spirit through the preaching of the gospel and not through works of the Law (cf. Gal. 3.3–5). Furthermore, they are already υἱοὶ θεοῦ (sons of God) and thus the true heirs of the promise (cf. Gal. 3.26; 4.6–7). In the Spirit the Galatians await the righteousness that is the object of their hope (Gal. 5.5); they live and walk in the Spirit, so that the saying applies, 'If you are led by the Spirit, you are not subject to the Law' (Gal. 5.18). As those who are gifted with the Spirit (Gal. 6.1 πνευματικοί) the Galatians are no longer subject to the power of the flesh and sin (Gal. 6.8). Christ is formed in them (Gal. 4.19); they have put on Christ and now in Christ they transcend all ethnic, religious and social distinctions (Gal. 3.26–28).

The Galatians are called to freedom (cf. Gal. 5.1, 13), so that adopting the practice of circumcision and the observation of a cultic calendar would as *pars pro toto legis* transform their freedom back into slavery. Paul wants to set forth the foolishness of the opponents' demands and their own conduct in view of the saved state in which they already live. He thus utilizes a detailed line of argument with several different levels in order to demonstrate that his doctrine of justification is biblical and therefore true. In Galatians Paul's evaluation of the Law is entirely negative.[292] It is secondary in relation to the promise, since it was not given until 430 years after the promise was given to Abraham (cf. Gal. 3.15–18). The Law only served to provoke sin, and became effective on the human scene only by being transmitted through angels and by the mediator Moses (Gal. 3.19–20).[293] Before the revelation of Christ, human beings lived under the Law and the cosmic powers; they were ὑπὸ νόμον (under the law) (Gal. 3.23), ὑπὸ παιδαγωγόν (under a custodian) (Gal. 3.25), ὑπὸ ἐπιτρόπους καὶ οἰκονόμους (under guardians and trustees) (Gal. 4.2) and ὑπὸ τὰ στοιχεῖα τοῦ κόσμου (under the elemental spirits of the universe) (Gal. 4.3). From this slavery believers have been freed by Christ and now live a life of freedom in the power of the Spirit.

---

[292] For a detailed analysis cf. Hübner, *Law in Paul* 15–50.

[293] The interpretation of Gal. 3.19–20 is extremely disputed. For the recent discussion cf. Rohde, *Galaterbrief* 152ff. In Gal. 3.19 Paul virtually denies the divine origin of the Law, for it is only under this presupposition that the distinction made in 3.20 makes sense. To be sure, Gal. 3.21; Rom. 7.22; 8.7; 9.4 show that Paul was neither able nor willing to maintain this idea consistently, but these other passages should not determine the exegesis of Gal. 3.19–20.

2.7.10 *Tendencies of Recent Research*

Among the classic introductory issues, most exegetes continue to vote for the North Galatian hypothesis and to regard the opponents in Galatia as strict Jewish Christians. With regard to form criticism, the proposal of H. D. Betz that Galatians should be seen as an 'apologetic letter' at first received a generally positive reception, but in the recent discussion this has become increasingly problematic. There is a clear trend in regard to the date of Galatians: almost all recent studies place Galatians immediately before Romans. This is connected with the central problem that has occupied research on Galatians in recent years: the understanding of the Law in Galatians vis-à-vis Romans. Thus Hans Hübner sees considerable difference between Paul's argumentation in Galatians and his line of argument in Romans. In Galatians the function of the Law is above all to provoke transgressions (cf. Gal. 3.19a). Paul defames it as given (merely) by angels, and sees it in an entirely negative light. In Romans however it serves to make one aware of sin (cf. Rom. 3.20; 7.7), for it is holy, just, and good (cf. Rom. 7.12). The differentiation between ἁμαρτία (sin) as an independent power opposed to salvation and the νόμος (law), whereby a distinction is made between the Law's original intent and its actual function, is not found in this way in Galatians. On the basis of this and other observations Hübner concludes that there was significant theological development in Paul's thought between the writing of the two letters.

For U. Wilckens the issue of the Law first became acute in Paul's thought as a result of the work of the Judaizer opponents in Galatia.[294] Previously, freedom from the Law had been the more or less self-evident basis for the Pauline missionary churches. If Galatians and Philippians represent the polemical position of Paul in the midst of battle on the salvific function of the Law, then in Romans Paul revised his stance in a matter that was not insignificant. In a manner that corresponds to the occasion of the letter to Rome, the apostle here presents his understanding of the Law in a comprehensive and balanced manner.

Of course, in contemporary scholarly discussion the question remains vigorously debated whether it was in fact the demand for the circumcision of Gentile Christian converts made by his opponents in Galatia that first compelled Paul to move the problem of the role of the Law from the periphery to the center of his theology. This judgment arises at first glance from the preceding letters (1 Thess.; 1 & 2 Cor.), where one can hardly speak of a doctrine of justification and understanding of the Law in the

---

[294] Cf. Ulrich Wilckens, 'Zur Entwicklung des paulinischen Gesetzesverständnisses' (see below 2.8.1) 164ff.

sense of Galatians and Romans. But neither does Galatians evoke the impression that the argumentation brought forth here by Paul was the result of twenty years of reflection on the role of the Torah for Christians. Paul obviously struggles with a problem that was new for him, as shown by the very different reasons given for the abrogation of the Torah in Galatians. If on the one hand Galatians documents changes in Paul's thought,[295] on the other hand the peculiarities of Galatians can be understood as the situational application of the coherent core of the Pauline doctrine of justification already received in his Damascus experience. Thus the hypothesis of a sharp turn in Paul's understanding of the Law is rejected by, among others, G. Klein,[296] F. Hahn,[297] K. Kertelge[298] and J. Rohde.[299] Moreover, the doctrine of justification of Galatians and Romans is often seen as in material agreement with the theology of the cross in 1 Corinthians, so that the doctrine of justification is an actualization of the same subject matter with which the theology of the cross is concerned.[300]

2.8 The Letter to the Romans

2.8.1 Literature

Commentaries

Lietzmann, Hans. *An die Römer*, HNT 8. Tübingen: J. C. B. Mohr (Paul Siebeck), 1971[5]; Schmidt, Hans Wilhelm. *Der Brief des Paulus an die Römer*, ThHK 6. Berlin: Evangelische Verlagsanstalt, 1972[3]; Michel, Otto. *Der Brief an die Römer*, KEK 14. Göttingen: Vandenhoeck & Ruprecht, 1978[5]; Cranfield, C.E.B. *A Critical and Exegetical Commentary on the Epistle to the Romans*, 2 vols. ICC. Edinburgh: T. & T. Clark, 1975, 1979; Schlier, Heinrich. *Der Römerbrief*, HThK VI. Freiburg: Herder, 1979[2]; Käsemann, Ernst. *Commentary on Romans*, tr. G. R. Bromiley. Grand Rapids: Wm. B. Eerdmans, 1980; Wilckens, Ulrich. *Der Brief an die Römer*, EKK 6.1–3. Neukirchen: Neukirchener Verlag, 1978, 1980, 1982; Zeller, Dieter. *Der Brief an die Römer*, RNT. Regensburg: Pustet, 1984; Dunn, James D. G. *Romans*, WBC 38A B.

---

[295] Cf. Udo Schnelle, *Wandlungen* (see above 2.4.9) 54–61.

[296] Cf. Günter Klein, 'Gesetz' (see above 2.4.10) 64–65; 'Werkruhm und Christusruhm im Galaterbrief und die Frage nach einer Entwicklung des Paulus,' in *Studien zum Text und zur Ethik des Neuen Testaments* (FS H. Greeven), ed. Wolfgang Schrage. BZNW 47 (Berlin: Walter de Gruyter, 1986) 196–211.

[297] Cf. Hahn, 'Gesetzesverständnis' 60–61, who, to be sure, sees the difference between Galatians and Romans, but nevertheless proceeds from an 'inner' understanding of the unified concept of the Law he finds in Paul. Cf. further his article 'Gibt es eine Entwicklung in den Aussagen über die Rechtfertigung bei Paulus?,' EvTh 53 (1993) 342–366.

[298] Cf. Karl Kertelge, 'Gesetz und Freiheit im Galaterbrief,' NTS 30 (1984) 382–394.

[299] Cf. Rohde, *Galaterbrief* 175–178.

[300] So among others Jürgen Becker, *Paul* (see above 2), 289–290.

Dallas: Word, 1988; Schmithals, Walter. *Der Römerbrief.* Gütersloh: Gütersloher Verlagshaus (Gerd Mohn), 1988; Stuhlmacher, Peter. *Paul's Letter to the Romans*, tr. Scott J. Hafemann. Louisville: Westminster/John Knox, 1989; Fitzmyer, Joseph. *Romans*, AncB 33. New York: Doubleday, 1993.

Monographs

Brandenburger, Egon. *Adam und Christus*, WMANT 7. Neukirchen-Vluyn: Neukirchener Verlag, 1962; Stuhlmacher, Peter. *Gerechtigkeit Gottes bei Paulus*, FRLANT 87. Göttingen: Vandenhoeck & Ruprecht, 1966²; Luz, Ulrich. *Das Geschichtsverständnis des Paulus*, BEvTh 49. Munich: Kaiser, 1968; Kertelge, Karl. *Rechtfertigung bei Paulus*, NTA 3. Münster: Aschendorff, 1971²; Kümmel, Werner Georg. *Römer 7 und das Bild des Menschen im Neuen Testament.* TB 53. Munich: Kaiser, 1974; Paulsen, Henning. *Überlieferung und Auslegung in Römer 8*, WMANT 43. Neukirchen-Vluyn: Neukirchener Verlag, 1974; Osten-Sacken, Peter v. d. *Römer 8 als Beispiel paulinischer Soteriologie*, FRLANT 112. Göttingen: Vandenhoeck & Ruprecht, 1975; Schmithals, Walter. *Der Römerbrief als historisches Problem*, StNT 9. Gütersloh: Gütersloher Verlagshaus (Gerd Mohn), 1975; Zeller, Dieter. *Juden und Heiden in der Mission des Paulus*, Fzb 8. Stuttgart: Katholisches Bibelwerk, 1976²; Wolter, Michael. *Rechtfertigung und zukünftiges Heil*, BZNW 43. Berlin: Walter de Gruyter, 1978; Kettunen, M. *Der Abfassungszweck des Römerbriefes*, AASF 18. Helsinki: Suomalainen Tielenkatemia, 1979; Hübner, Hans. *Gottes Ich und Israel*, FRLANT 136. Göttingen: Vandenhoeck & Ruprecht, 1984; Hübner, Hans. *Law in Paul's Thought* (1984; see above 2.7.1); Räisänen, Heikki. *Paul and the Law*, WUNT 29. Tübingen: J. C. B. Mohr (Paul Siebeck), 1987²; Lampe, Peter. *Die stadtrömischen Christen in den beiden ersten Jahrhunderten*, WUNT 2.18. Tübingen: J. C. B. Mohr (Paul Siebeck), 1989²; Bindemann, Walter. *Theologie im Dialog.* Leipzig: Evangelische Verlagsanstalt, 1992; Hay, David M., and Johnson, E. Elizabeth, eds. *Pauline Theology, Volume III.Romans.* Minneapolis: Fortress, 1995 (important collection of essays).

Articles

Borse, Udo. 'Die geschichtliche und theologische Einordnung des Römerbriefes,' BZ 16 (1972) 70–83; Conzelmann, Hans. 'Die Rechtfertigungslehre des Paulus.Theologie oder Anthropologie?' in *Theologie als Schriftauslegung*, ed. Hans Conzelmann. BEvTh 65. Munich: Kaiser, 1974, 191–206; Hahn, Ferdinand. 'Das Gesetzesverständnis im Römer- und Galaterbrief' (see above 2.7.1); Wilckens, Ulrich. 'Christologie und Anthropologie im Zusammenhang der paulinischen Rechtfertigungslehre,' ZNW 67 (1976) 64–82; Wilckens, Ulrich. 'Zur Entwicklung des paulinischen Gesetzesverständnisses,' NTS 28 (1982) 154–190; Stuhlmacher, Peter. 'Der Abfassungszweck des Römerbriefes,' ZNW 77 (1986) 180–193; Räisänen, Heikki. 'Römer 9–11: Analyse eines geistigen Ringens,' *ANRW* 25.4. Berlin: Walter de Gruyter, 1987, 2891–2939; Haacker, Karl. 'Der Römerbrief als Friedensmemorandum,' NTS 36 (1990) 25–41; Meyer, Paul W. 'The Worm at the Core of the Apple: Exegetical Reflections on Romans 7,' in *The Conversation Continues. Studies in Paul and John.* (FS J. Louis Martyn), eds. Robert T. Fortna and Beverly R. Gaventa. Nashville: Abingdon, 1990, 62–84; Bornkamm, Günther. 'The Letter to the Romans as Paul's Last Will and

Testament,' in *The Romans Debate*, ed. Karl P. Donfried (Minneapolis: Augsburg Publishing House, 1991 rev. ed.) 17–31 (important collection of essays); Wiefel, Wolfgang. 'The Jewish Community in Ancient Rome and the Origins of Roman Christianity,' in *The Romans Debate*, ed. Karl P. Donfried (Minneapolis: Augsburg Publishing House, 1991 rev. ed.) 100–119; Lohse, Eduard. 'Summa Evangelii – zu Veranlassung und Thematik des Römerbriefes,' NAWG.PH (1993) 89–119.

2.8.2 Author

The Pauline authorship of Romans is undisputed.

2.8.3 Place and Time of Composition

The letter to the Romans was written at a turning point in the missionary work of Paul. The apostle regards his work in the eastern part of the Empire as finished and wants now to continue preaching the gospel in the west, especially in Spain (cf. Rom. 15.23–24). He is about to depart for Jerusalem to deliver the offering he has gathered from Macedonia and Achaia (cf. Rom. 15.28–29). Romans was probably composed in *Corinth*, where Paul wrote [i.e. dictated] the letter in the house of Gaius in the *spring of 56 CE* (cf. Acts 20.2–3; Rom. 16.1, 22, 23; 1 Cor. 1.14).[301] The letter was probably delivered by the deaconess Phoebe (cf. Rom. 16.1–2).

The occasion and goal of Romans are closely related to the situation in which Paul found himself. The apostle needed the personal and material support of the Roman church in order to carry through his planned mission to Spain. This is why Paul, who was personally unknown to most of the Roman Christians, introduces himself with such an extensive presentation of his theology. Associated with this immediate occasion for the letter which Paul mentions in the letter (Rom. 15.24) are two other problematic areas that led Paul to write to the Romans. Paul is obviously not certain that the collection he has taken will be accepted by the Jerusalem church, for this is the only way one can understand the doubts that continue to plague him and his request for the prayers of the Roman church (cf. Rom. 15.30–31). The apostle understands the collection both as material support for the distressed Jerusalem Christians and an acknowledgment of the priority of the earliest church from the point of view of the history of salvation (cf. Rom. 15.27). Above all, however, the offering is to strengthen the bond between Jewish Christians and Gentile Christians, and thereby strengthen the agreements worked out at the Apostolic Council (Gal. 2.9).

---

[301] On this relatively large consensus of scholarship cf. for example Zeller, *Römerbrief* 15; Stuhlmacher, *Romans* 5.

The increasing agitation of Jewish opponents in the Pauline churches shows that the position of this group had gained considerable influence, especially in Jerusalem, so that Paul sees himself compelled to renew his opposition against these streams. Romans too must be read as a witness to this debate, for Paul's line of argument is still visibly influenced by the dispute in Galatia in the immediate background, and the church in Rome will already have heard something about Paul and his gospel from the mouth of his opponents (cf. Rom. 3.8, 31a; 6.1, 15; 7.7; [16.17–18?]). The conflict between 'strong' and 'weak' taken up by Paul (Rom. 14.1–15.13) may well have something to do with to the work of rigorous Jewish Christians. And finally, there is yet another element which influenced the argumentation of the apostle in Romans, problems in the way his theology had been represented that led to misunderstandings and allegations. Thus the struggle of the apostle concerning Israel in Rom. 9–11 derives logically from his doctrine of justification. If Paul proclaims faith in the one God who justifies the godless (Rom. 4.5), then the question arises most sharply concerning those to whom the promises have belonged, but who according to Paul have broken faith with God. Further, one must ask how, within the Pauline doctrine of justification, God's grace and human action are related to each other. If all are guilty as they stand before the divine judgment (Rom. 2.1) and no one can appeal to his or her deeds, then the question of the meaning and function of ethical conduct arises. On the one hand it seems that one's deeds have no significance for one's salvation, and yet one can lose salvation precisely by one's deeds!

Thus four factors determine the composition and goal of Romans: (1) The help needed from the Roman church for the planned mission to Spain. (2) The apostle's wish for prayer (and support) during the anticipated debate in Jerusalem when he presents the offering. (3) The agitation of Judaizing opponents to Paul's mission, whose influence he must presuppose in both Jerusalem and Rome. (4) Problems in understanding the Pauline theology. These aspects are obviously woven together: only by refuting Judaizing objections and a persuasive elaboration of his own position can Paul count on having the collection accepted in Jerusalem and the Romans adopting 'his' gospel as their own.

The modern discussion of the goal of Romans was opened by F. C. Baur.[302] Baur supposed that there was an anti-Pauline party in Rome that rejected Paul's universalism and wanted to exclude the Gentiles from God's grace.

---

[302] Cf. Ferdinand Chr. Baur, 'Über Zweck und Veranlassung des Römerbriefes und die damit zusammenhängenden Verhältnisse der römischen Gemeinde,' in *Ausgewählte Werke*, ed. K. Scholder (Stuttgart 1963 [= 1836]) 1.147–266.

Paul wrote Romans in order to oppose the false particularism of this Jewish Christian group.[303] The classical position of Baur has been followed by a discussion that continues today and has generated an immense number of hypotheses, only a few of which can be named here.[304] (1) G. Klein infers from the lack of the ἐκκλησία-concept in Rom. 1–15 that Paul regarded the Roman church as still in need of an apostolic foundation, so that the letter to the Romans is to be understood as the anticipatory act of the εὐαγγελίζεσθαι (preaching the gospel) still to be accomplished in Rome.[305] Against this one must object that Paul acknowledges Roman Christianity without reservation, and that there is no reference in Romans to such a lack in the Roman congregation. (2) G. Bornkamm, J. Jervell and U. Wilckens see the whole of Romans as overshadowed by the worry expressed in 15.30–31[306] that the collection might not be received by the Jerusalem church due to the opposition of the Judaizers. Paul will then have formulated in Romans a kind of defense speech of the kind he will have to give in Jerusalem. Jerusalem would then be the secret address of Romans. Here, a point that is doubtless important for understanding the composition of Romans is over-estimated. (3) For M. Kettunen and P. Stuhlmacher, Romans must be understood as a great apologia over against his Judaizing opponents. They follow him everywhere, and he must suppose that they are already agitating against him in Rome. The letter to the Romans would then be the apostle's attempt to refute the objections brought by his opponents and thereby to win the Roman church over to support his mission to Spain. (4) K. Haacker interprets Romans in the context of the increasing tensions between Rome and Jerusalem in advance of the first Jewish war (66–73/74 CE). The Pauline thesis of the equality of Jews and non-Jews is to be understood 'as an intentionally aimed word of reconciliation in a time of growing polarization between Jerusalem and Rome.'[307] (5) E. Lohse understands Romans as a 'summary of the gospel' and thus to some extent as its timeless and only appropriate exposition.[308] Paul here presents a critical accounting

---

[303] A. J. M. Wedderburn, *The Reasons for Romans* (Edinburgh: T. & T. Clark, 1988), takes up the view of F. C. Baur. He explicitly emphasizes that there are several reasons for the composition of Romans, but considers the Jewish Christians in Rome to be the ones Paul is really addressing. They had charged that Paul's gospel offends and violates the righteousness of God.

[304] Surveys of research are found in Otto Kuss, *Paulus* (Regensburg: Pustet, 1976²) 178–204; Schmithals, *Römerbrief als historisches Problem* 24–52; Kettunen, *Abfassungszweck* 7–26. Important essays are reprinted in K. P. Donfried, *The Romans Debate*.

[305] Cf. Günter Klein, 'Der Abfassungszweck des Römerbriefes' in *Rekonstruktion und Interpretation*, ed. G. Klein, BEvTh 50 (Munich: Kaiser, 1969) 129–144.

[306] Cf. Bornkamm, 'Der Römerbrief als Testament' 136–139; Jacob Jervell, 'Der Brief nach Jerusalem. Über Veranlassung und Adresse des Römerbriefes,' StTh 25 (1971) 61–73; Ulrich Wilckens, 'Über Abfassungszweck und Aufbau des Römerbriefes,' in *Rechtfertigung als Freiheit*, ed. U. Wilckens (Neukirchen: Neukirchener Verlag, 1974) 110–170.

[307] Haacker, 'Römerbrief als Friedensmemorandum' 34.

[308] Cf. Lohse, 'Summa Evangelii' 113ff.

and summary of his previous preaching, without going into actual current problems.

2.8.4 Intended Readership

The origin of Christianity in Rome cannot be understood apart from the history of the Jewish community in Rome, which is mentioned for the first time in 139 BCE. The Jews in Rome had lived through many ups and downs. The community grew very rapidly; Josephus (*Ant* 17.300) refers to 8000 Roman Jews who accompanied the Jewish delegation that came to Rome after the death of Herod. It is reported of Claudius that in 41 CE, because of the large number of Jews he did not expel them from the city, but did prohibit their assembly (Dio Cassius 60.6.6). The Jews in Rome were organized in independent congregations with their own assembly halls and their own administration.[309] The Roman Jews had been severely struck by the expulsion under Tiberius in 19 CE[310] and under Claudius in 49 CE.[311] The edict of Claudius presupposes disputes between Jews and Christians in Rome about 'Chrestus' and indicates that there had been a successful Christian mission within the sphere of the synagogues.

As had been the case with Judaism previously, so also Christianity came to Rome by means of the *trade routes and business*. It is hardly coincidental that there were pre-Pauline Christian congregations in Puteoli (Acts 28.13) and Rome (Acts 28.15). Not only were two large Jewish communities found here, but the primary trade route between the eastern part of the Empire and the city of Rome ran through Puteoli. Probably the gospel was brought to Rome by tradesmen and business people who were also Christian missionaries. The edict of Claudius, however, affected not only the Jews in Rome, but was also important for the Christian community in a twofold way: (1) It accomplished the final separation between the Christian community and the synagogue. (2) The expulsion of Jews and Jewish Christians from Rome dramatically affected the composition of the Roman church. While prior to Claudius' edict the majority of the Christian community in Rome had been Jewish Christians, after 49 CE they were a minority. In the persecution of Christians under Nero in 64 CE, the authorities were already making the distinction between Jews and Christians.[312]

---

[309] Cf. Wiefel, 'Jewish Community' 105–108; Lampe, *Die stadtrömischen Christen* 367ff.

[310] Cf. Tacitus, *Annals* 2.85; Suetonius, *Tiberius* 36.

[311] On the edict of Claudius cf. section 2.1.1.

[312] Cf. Tacitus, *Annals* 14.44; Cf. here Hermann Lichtenberger, 'Josephus und Paulus in Rom. Juden und Christen in Rom zur Zeit Neros,' in *Begegnungen zwischen Christentum und Judentum in Antike und Mittelalter* (FS H. Schreckenberg), eds. Dietrich A. Koch and Hermann Lichtenberger (Göttingen: Vandenhoeck & Ruprecht, 1993) 245–261.

At the time the letter was written, the congregation was already comprised of a majority of Gentile Christians (cf. Rom. 1.5, 13–15; 10.1–3; 11.13, 17–32; 15.15, 16, 18). However, we must also reckon with the presence and influence of a significant Jewish Christian minority in the Roman church, as indicated especially by Rom. 9–11 and 16.7, 11 (Andronicus, Iunia[s] and Herodion as συγγενής [relatives] of Paul). The conflict between 'strong' and 'weak' (cf. Rom. 14.1–16.13) also involved Jewish Christians, and many of the Gentile Christians will surely have belonged to the group of σεβόμενοι ('God fearers') before they were baptized.

The 28 persons mentioned (26 by name) in Rom. 16.3–16 gives some information regarding social strata within the Roman church. Thus Prisca and Aquila (16.3–4) were independent practitioners of their craft, who may have had other employees or slaves in their business.[313] Rom. 16.10b, 11b names as fellow Christians those who belonged to the household (so NIV; NRSV 'family;' there is no noun at all in the Greek text, only the possessive 'those of . . .') of Aristobulus and Narcissus, i.e. people who were slaves or freed slaves who worked in the household of a non-Christian master. The analysis of the names from Rom. 16 that occur in inscriptions indicates that of 13 comparable names, 4 refer to free persons and 9 to slaves.[314] Many of the tasks of community life were undertaken by women, for only of them is it said that they 'worked hard' (κοπιάω; Rom. 16.6, 12; cf. also 13b). Of the 26 persons mentioned by name in 16.3–16, 12 came to Rome from the East and are known personally by Paul, which points to a steady stream of Christians from the eastern part of the Empire who had found their way into the Roman church.

Romans 16.3–16 also provides information about the form of organization among the Roman Christians. Paul not only mentions the house church of Prisca and Aquila (Rom. 16.5), but at least 16.14 and 16.15 document the existence of several independent house churches in Rome.[315] So too, after his own arrival in Rome, Paul met with gatherings of fellow Christians in his own residence (cf. Acts 28.30–31). Thus at this time in Rome the church did not exist as a single congregation that all met together in one large assembly hall. This is why Paul does not direct his letter to the one ἐκκλήσια (church) in Rome, but 'to all those in Rome who are beloved of God and called to be saints' (Rom. 1.7a).

The Christian community in Rome at the time when the letter was

---

[313] Cf. here Lampe, *Die stadtrömischen Christen* 156–164.

[314] Cf. *ibid.* 141–153.

[315] On this cf. Hans-Joseph Klauck, *Hausgemeinde und Hauskirche im frühen Christentum*, SBS 103 (Stuttgart: Katholisches Bibelwerk, 1981) 26ff.; Lampe, *Die stadtrömischen Christen* 301ff.

written must have already been quite large, since Paul expected it to supply both money and people for his further work. Nero's persecution in 64 CE also presupposes an expanding community known throughout the city.

2.8.5 *Outline, Structure, Form*

1.1–7	Prescript	
1.8–12	Proemium	—Introduction
1.13–15	Epistolary Self Commendation	
1.16–11.36	PART ONE	
1.16–8.39	The Righteousness of God	
1.16, 17	The Thesis of the Letter	
1.18–3.20	The necessity of the righteousness of God (1.18–32, Gentiles; 2.1–29, Jews; 3.1–8, Priority of the Jews; 3.9–20, The guilt of the Jews)	
3.21–4.25	The possibility of God's righteousness (3.21–31.The righteousness of God that has appeared in Jesus Christ; 4.1–25, The righteousness of God promised to Abraham)	
5.1–8.39	The reality of the righteousness of God (5.1–11, Assurance of salvation; 5.12–21, Adam-Christ typology; 6, Baptism; 7, Law, sin, and the believer; 8, Life in the Spirit)	—Body
9.1–11.36	The righteousness of God and Israel (anticipated in 1.16; 2.9–10; 3.1–8)	
9.1–5	The problem	
9.6–29	The promise was not made to empirical Israel, but to the true Israel	
9.30–10.21	The rejection of empirical Israel	
11.1–36	The mystery of God's saving plan and the salvation of Israel	
12.1–15.13	PART TWO	
12.1–13.14	General exhortations (worship, congregational life, living by love, the state)	
14.1–15.13	Particular instructions ('strong' and 'weak')	

15.14–15.29	Apostolic parousia	
15.30–15.33	Closing parenesis	— Conclusion
16.1–16, 21–23	Greetings	
16.24 (?)	Final Farewell (Eschatokoll) (?)	

The macrostructure of Romans is easily recognizable, with a predominately *doctrinal* Part One (1.16–11.36) followed by a predominately *hortatory* Part Two (12.1–15.13).[316] This division may not be taken too schematically, however, for Part One also contains some basically hortatory material (e.g. 6.11–12, 19).

Within the structure of Part One,[317] 5.1–11 and chapters 9–11 have a special significance. Romans 5.1–11 does not just round off the argument of 3.21–4.25 but develops it further. This is seen in the new central theological concepts of 5.1–11 (ἐλπίς [hope], ζωή [life], ἀγάπη [love], πνεῦμα [spirit], θάνατος [death]), which are taken up again in chapter 8, so that one can speak of a ring composition in Rom. 5–8. The thematic of Rom. 9–11 is not a digression, but follows necessarily from the apostle's doctrine of justification, underscoring the problematic already anticipated in 1.16; 2.9–10; 3.1–8.

The parenetic Part Two begins with παρακαλῶ (I appeal to you) so that 12.1–2 both forms the title for this section and announces its theme. The unity of the church as the body of Christ is dealt with first in 12.3–8, then in 12.9–21 Paul already makes a transition to particular parenesis, which is developed in a special way in 13.1–7.[318] Romans 13.8a both takes up 13.1–7 and refers back to 12.9–21. The eschatological perspective in 13.11–14 concludes the line of argument and corresponds to 12.1–2. The admonitions to 'strong' and 'weak' in 14.1–15.13 must be understood as concretions of the love command in 12.9; 13.8–10.

The letter to the Romans contains the usual elements of a Pauline writing; it strives for communication and is therefore to be classified in the letter category. At the same time, however, for extensive sections it functions like an instructive monologue not directed to a concrete situation in one church. This characteristic feature is explained by the particular communication situation between the apostle and the church in Rome. The attempts to classify Romans more precisely within rhetorical and literary categories have had differing results. Thus Romans has been designated

---

[316] Sometimes Romans 9–11 is regarded as a separate major section, for example by Stuhlmacher, *Romans* 15.

[317] Cf. on this especially Ulrich Luz, 'Zum Aufbau von Rom. 1–8,' ThZ 25 (1969) 161–181.

[318] On the Pauline line of argument cf. Otto Merk, 'Handeln aus Glauben,' MThSt 5 (1968) 157–167.

as a 'logos protreptikos,'[319] by which is meant a didactic letter seeking followers to engage in a specific discipline, usually philosophy. Additional classifications include 'epistolary letter' (A. Deissmann), 'letter essay' (D. Zeller), 'didactic writing' (W. Schmithals).[320]

2.8.6 Literary Integrity

The central problem for both text criticism and literary criticism of Romans is constituted by chapter 16. The very complex text critical circumstances can be perceived by the following data presented in basic outline.[321]

a) 1.1–16.23 + 16.25–27: P[61vid] $\aleph$ B C
b) 1.1–14.23 : Marcion (according to Origen)
c) 1.1–15.33 + 16.25–27 + 16.1–23: P[46]
d) 1.1–16.23 + 16.24: D 06 (Greek original) F 010gr G
e) 1.1–16.23 + 16.24 + 16.25–27: D 06 F 010lat Pel
f) 1.1–14.23 + 16.25–27 + 15.1–16.23 + 16.24: $\mathfrak{M}$ l sy[h]
g) 1.1–14.23 + 16.25–27 + 15.1–16.23 + 16.25–27: A

From this data we may draw three conclusions: (1) Romans 16.24 was not found in the oldest textual tradition (Marcion, P[46]). It clashes with the concluding doxology that usually follows it as 16.25–27, and is probably to be considered a secondary addition that intruded into the text because it had become the prevailing conclusion of Romans in the western text. (2) The very different locations in which the concluding doxology of vv. 25–27 are found in the textual tradition, the fact that they are missing entirely in Marcion's text, and the parallels in the deuteropauline writings (cf. Col. 1.26–27; 2.2; 4.3; Eph. 1.9; 3.3–4, 9; 6.19; further Jude 24–25[!]) make it likely that these verses did not belong to the original text of

---

[319] Cf. Stanley K. Stowers, *Letter Writing* (see above 2.3.1) 112–114; David E. Aune, 'Romans as a Logos Protreptikos in the Context of Ancient Religious and Philosophical Propaganda,' in *Paulus und das antike Judentum*, eds. Martin Hengel and Ulrich Heckel, WUNT 58 (Tübingen: J. C. B. Mohr [Paul Siebeck], 1991) 91–121; Klaus Berger, *Formgeschichte des Neuen Testaments* (Heidelberg: Quelle & Meyer, 1984) 217–220. Cf. further Hans Hübner, 'Die Rhetorik und die Theologie. Der Römerbrief und die rhetorische Kompetenz des Paulus,' in *Die Macht des Wortes*, eds. C. J. Classen and H. J. Müllenbrock, *Ars Rhetorica* 4 (1992) 165–179, who emphasizes the rhetorical quality of Romans but at the same time rejects a rhetorical classification of the letter as a whole.

[320] Cf. Adolf Deissmann, *Paul* (see above 2.1.1) 19; Zeller, *Römerbrief* 10; Schmithals, *Römerbrief* 43–44, in reference to his 'Romans A'.

[321] A complete listing of the data can be found in Kurt Aland, 'Der Schluß und die ursprüngliche Gestalt des Römerbriefes,' in *Neutestamentliche Entwürfe*, TB 63 (Munich: Kaiser, 1979) (284–301) 287–290.

Romans.[322] Probably 16.25–27 formed the usual conclusion to Romans in the east. Obviously the position of the concluding doxology and v. 24 were flexible, since each of the textual traditions currently extant placed them according to their own decisions. But whether such a weighty and well organized letter as Romans concluded with 16.23 must of course be very doubtful. (3) No manuscript ends with chapter 15. Either chapter 15 and 16.1–23 are entirely missing (Marcion) or both are transmitted. There is no text critical evidence for a seam between Romans 15 and 16.[323]

Of course, for more than 150 years a case has been made on grounds of both content and literary criticism to separate chapter 16 from the rest of the letter to the Romans and to understand it as an independent letter to the church in Ephesus.[324] The following arguments are brought forward for the Ephesian hypothesis:[325] (a) In 16.3–16a Paul greets a remarkably large number of people in a church that according to Romans 1.13 still is unacquainted with him. (b) Among those greeted are found several whom we may assume belong in Asia, especially in Ephesus. Thus Prisca and Aquila live in Ephesus at the time when 1 Corinthians was composed (cf. 1 Cor. 16.19), and in 2 Tim. 4.19 they are still live there. Epaenetus, the 'first convert in Asia' (Rom. 16.5), also fits Ephesus better than Rome. The manner in which several of them are greeted presupposes an intensive contact with them. (c) The polemic against false teaching in Rom. 16.17–20 does not fit the tone of the rest of Romans and is more likely directed to a different church. (d) The variations in the manuscript tradition indicate that chapter 16 did not belong to the original letter.

These arguments cannot be regarded as compelling. Romans 15.33 presupposes that greetings will follow and the δέ of 16.1 picks up on the preceding text. The long list of those greeted in 16.3–16a may be explained

---

[322] Contra Stuhlmacher, *Romans* 240–242, who counts vv. 25–27 as belonging to the authentic original letter to the Romans. Against this cf. Zeller, *Römerbrief* 251: 'The compressed allusion to the beginning of the letter, the exalted view of Paul's work and the language akin to that of the deuteropauline letters make it certain that in these final verses a redactor from the Pauline school has given the Epistle to the Romans a final worshipful note that directs the reader's gaze back to God.'

[323] On the minuscule MS 1506 cf. Lampe, *Die stadtrömischen Christen* 125. On the possibility of arranging the extant MSS of Romans in a genealogical pattern, cf. Aland, 'Schluß des Römerbriefes' 291ff.; Peter Lampe, 'Zur Textgeschichte des Römerbriefes,' NT 27 (1985) 273–277.

[324] A survey of research is presented by Wolf-Henning Ollrog, 'Die Abfassungsverhältnisse von Rom 16,' in *Kirche* (FS G. Bornkamm), eds. Dieter Lührmann and Georg Strecker (Tübingen: J. C. B. Mohr [Paul Siebeck], 1980) 221–244.

[325] Cf. here especially Schmithals, *Römerbrief* 543–565, who regards 16.1–20 as a separate writing. In addition to Schmithals, the Ephesus hypothesis has been advocated recently by, for example Marxsen, *Introduction* 108 ; Käsemann, *Romans* 409ff.; Ph. Vielhauer, *Urchristliche Literatur* 190; Schenke – Fischer, *Einleitung* 1.136ff., who however combine Romans 14.1–15.13 and 16.1–20 into a letter from Paul to Ephesus.

in a two-fold manner: (1) After the death of Claudius in 54 CE those
Christians who had been driven out of Rome returned to their home
(Prisca and Aquila). To these may be added those members of the Roman
Christian community who had previously worked with Paul in Asia. They
are carrying out a plan that Paul had also had in mind for a long time (cf.
Rom. 1.3). Of the 26 persons named by name, Paul was personally
acquainted with at least 12.[326] They had worked with him earlier in the East
(cf. vv. 3–9, 10a, 11a, 12b, 13). In the case of 14 of those mentioned, the
greetings are more general, and Paul seems not to have known them
personally (cf. vv. 10b, 11b, 12a, 14, 15). Paul had probably been informed
by his former co-workers about this group and the circumstances in Rome.
In favorable circumstances the mail between Corinth and Rome took not
much more than a week, so that one can readily imagine an intensive
contact between the apostle and the members of the Roman church known
to Paul. Thus it is not at all the case that the list of greetings would have
to presuppose 'a kind of mass migration from the Pauline churches of the
East.'[327] On the contrary, there is nothing surprising about the presence of
approximately twelve people whom the apostle knows well in the Roman
church after the death of Claudius, given the mobility of early Christian
missionaries and the drawing power of the capital city of the world. So also
the list of those who send greetings (Rom. 16.16b, 21–23) is more easily
understood as directed to Rome than to Ephesus. The singular expression
'all the churches of Christ greet you' in v. 16b points to Rome, for it is the
churches of the previous missionary territory of Paul who now greet their
sister congregations in Rome. Moreover, the description of Timothy in v.
21 as 'my co-worker' suggests a Roman address, for the church in Ephesus
had long since been acquainted with him. Finally, the greeting of the scribe
Tertius in 16.22 can be taken as a clear item of evidence that Rom. 1–15
and 16 originally belonged together: taking the dictation and writing a letter the length of Romans was no small accomplishment, which would
account for the fact that only here in the Pauline letters is the secretary
mentioned by name. (2) The whole tendency of Romans explains why it is
precisely in this letter that Paul greets so many members of the church and
sends greetings from so many co-workers. Paul wants to come to an agreement with the Roman church about supporting his mission to Spain. He
therefore makes use of all the contacts he already has, and attempts to
establish contact with Roman Christians still personally unknown to him

---

[326] For an analysis of the names, cf. Ollrog, 'Abfassungsverhältnisse' 234ff.; Lampe, *Die
stadtrömischen Christen* 128ff.

[327] Adolf Jülicher, *Einleitung in das Neue Testament* (Tübingen [3.4]1901) 85; but cf. the much
more hesitant argument in Jülicher – Fascher, *Einleitung* 108ff.

by sending them greetings. He thus shows the whole Roman church that many of their members already know him and that he is well informed about circumstances in the church.

Additional arguments may be introduced against the Ephesus hypothesis: (a) Romans 16 cannot be understood as an independent letter, for within the Pauline corpus there are no parallels to such a letter.[328] (b) Romans 1–15 and Rom. 16 presuppose the same historical situation, for both 15.19b–29 and 16.21–23 (cf. Acts 20.4) point to the end of the third missionary journey as the time, and Corinth as the place, where the letter was composed. (c) There is no convincing explanation why a letter of recommendation originally sent to Ephesus would now be appended to a letter sent to Rome. If 16.1–16, 21–23 belong to the original letter to Rome, then one must reflect deeply on the significance of its concluding parenesis in the form of a polemic against false teachers in 16.17–20a.[329] In Paul's letters such an admonition always precedes the final greetings, while here it interrupts the list of greetings. Furthermore, this admonition stands after the command for the holy kiss! In this brief text there are six Pauline *hapax legomena* (ἐκκλίνειν [avoid] [Rom. 3.12 is a citation], χρηστολογία [smooth talk], ἄκακος [naive], ἀφικνεῖσθαι [to be known], συντρίβειν [crush], ἐν τάχει [soon]). Elsewhere Paul never uses διδαχή as a term for the summary of Christian doctrine. The manner of argumentation does not correspond to that used by Paul elsewhere against his opponents, but is reminiscent of the polemic against heretics in the deuteropauline letters (cf. 2 Tim. 3.1–9). To be sure, in Romans too Paul debates with the objections of his opponents (cf. Rom. 3.1–8; 3.31; 6.1, 15; 7.7, 12, 14), but in a completely different manner than in 16.17–20a.

Often Rom. 7.25a is considered to be a post-Pauline gloss.[330] In the line of argumentation, 7.25b falls back prior to 7.25a, for in this comment the situation of unredeemed humanity is thematized once again, while 25a already reflects the situation of the redemption accomplished in Jesus Christ, which is then developed in Rom. 8 as the new life in Christ.

---

[328] To be sure, Schmithals, *Römerbrief* 128ff., can point to ancient letters of recommendation as parallels, but this does not remove the fact that Rom 16 as an independent letter would be unique within the Pauline letter corpus. In Philippians we do have a Pauline letter of recommendation, and it is very different from Rom 16!

[329] These verses are considered a post-Pauline interpolation especially by Ollrog, 'Abfassungsverhältnisse' 229–234; Schnider and Stenger, *Studien* (see above 2.3.2) 82–83. In recent times the originality of these verses has been advocated by, for example, U. Wilckens, D. Zeller and P. Stuhlmacher in their commentaries. A form-critical analysis is presented by Ulrich B. Müller, *Prophetie und Predigt im Neuen Testament*. StNT 10 (Gütersloh: Gütersloher Verlagshaus, 1975) 185–190 (Rom. 16.17–20 as a 'prophetic pronouncement of judgment').

[330] Most recently, Stuhlmacher, *Romans* 113–114 has voted for the originality of Romans 7.25b.

Furthermore, in 7.7–25a there is no reference to serving the Law, for sin prevents this. Obviously 7.25b is a gloss expressing a scribe's understanding of Romans 7.

W. Schmithals[331] first divides the extant letter into two (Rom. A: 1.1–4.25; 5.12–11.36; 15.8–13, Rom. B: 12.1–21; 13.8–10; 14.1–15.4a, 7, 5–6; 15.14–23; 16.21–23; 15.33). To this was added the writing to Ephesus in 16.1–20. A redactor then put the whole together and integrated texts of different origins (Rom. 5.1–11; 13.1–7; 13.11–14; 15.4b; 16.25–27). Schmithals then regards 2.16; 6.17b; 7.25b; 8.1 as glosses. These theories cannot persuade, especially since a new section of Romans begins with 12.1, but not a new letter.[332] In addition, Schmithals' judgments about what constitutes a meaningful line of argumentation, disturbing intrusions, and differing historical situations remain very subjective.

2.8.7 Traditions, Sources

In a way that distinguishes it from all the other letters of Paul, the letter to the Romans presents itself as an unfolding of the early Christian kerygma. This is another indication of Paul's wish to come to an agreement with the Roman church and to present his own theology as an appropriate exposition of their common faith. Already in Rom. 1.3b–4a Paul cites a Jewish Christian tradition in which Jesus Christ is seen as Son of David during his fleshly existence, and Son of God in his spiritual existence.[333] Neither the preexistence of Christ nor the existence of Jesus as Son of God during his earthly life are here presupposed, but Jesus first becomes Son of God by his inthronization through the resurrection. In the description of the path of the earthly Jesus to exaltation and inthronization, σάρξ (flesh) and πνεῦμα (spirit) give the respective spheres in which Jesus lived and by which he was determined. Paul does not buy into this tradition sight unseen, but with the addition of περὶ τοῦ υἱοῦ αὐτοῦ (concerning his son) in v. 3a he includes his own preexistence Christology.

In Rom. 3.25–26a Paul integrates a Jewish Christian baptismal tradition into his line of argument.[334] Jesus Christ appears as the publicly established

---

[331] Cf. Schmithals, *Römerbrief* 25–29.

[332] For a critique of Schmithals cf. especially Wilkens, *Römerbrief* 27–29.

[333] For analysis, cf. the commentaries, and especially Eduard Schweizer, 'Rom. 1,3f und der Gegensatz von Fleisch und Geist bei Paulus,' in *Neotestamentica*, ed. E. Schweizer (Zürich: Zwingli Verlag, 1963) 180–189.

[334] An extensive survey of the state of present research is provided by Wolfgang Kraus, *Der Tod Jesu als Heiligtumsweihe. Eine Untersuchung zum Umfeld der Sühnevorstellung in Rom. 3,25–26a*, WMANT 66 (Neukirchen: Neukirchener Verlag, 1991).

means of reconciliation (ἱλαστήριον) that God has instituted, through whose blood the sins of humanity are forgiven and the divine forbearance is demonstrated. Through the forgiveness of sins grounded in the atoning death of Jesus Christ, justification is conferred on the baptized, by which God's righteousness is shown in the rightwising of sinners. The Pauline interpretative addition διὰ τῆς πίστεως (through faith) connects the tradition with the central thesis of the doctrine of justification in Rom. 3.21–22. Thereby the apostle documents the anchoring of his doctrine of justification in the foundational traditions of the earliest Christian faith: in the rightwising of sinners in baptism through faith in Jesus Christ, God's own righteousness is revealed. Another baptismal tradition is found in Rom. 4.25. In baptism the death and resurrection of Jesus Christ are made present to the believer as the forgiveness of sins and the rightwising act of God. With the doubled ἡμῶν the tradition pointedly emphasizes the soteriological dimension of the Christ event.

In 6.1 Paul takes up an objection from his opponents, in order to refute it in 6.3–4 with the help of another baptismal tradition.[335] Baptism appears as a sacramental reexperiencing of the death of Jesus, resulting in one's own death to sin (v. 3). The paralleling of the death of Jesus with the death of the baptized is developed further in v. 4a, as the one who is baptized experiences being buried together with Christ, which shows the total unity between Christ and his own. Paul avoids, however, the idea associated logically in the tradition that the baptized are already risen with Christ. Rather, in v. 4c the apostle portrays the future of the one who has been baptized in ethical terms. As baptism into the death of Christ, baptism is in reality an actual dying out from under the power of sin, so that the Christian no longer lives in the realm of sin, but in the realm of grace. The relation between grace and sin postulated by Paul's opponents in Rom. 6.1 has nothing to do with the Pauline doctrine of justification, because the appropriation of the saving event in baptism radically withdraws the one who is baptized from the power of sin.

2.8.8 History-of-religions Standpoint

Romans 6.3–4 describes the unity between Christ and the baptized with ideas dependent on the mystery religions.[336] Thus in Apuleius, *Meta-*

---

[335] For an analysis of Romans 6 and discussion and debate with recent literature, cf. Udo Schnelle, *Gerechtigkeit und Christusgegenwart* (see above 2.4.10) 74–88, 203–215; A. J. M. Wedderburn, *Baptism and Resurrection*, WUNT 44 (Tübingen: J. C. B. Mohr [Paul Siebeck], 1987).

[336] This is disputed by, for example, Günter Wagner, *Das religionsgeschichtliche Problem von Rom. 6,1–11*, AThANT 39 (Zürich: Zwingli, 1962); Wedderburn, *Baptism and Resurrection*. On

morphoses 11.23.8 the initiate reports the central event of an Isis initiation: 'I drew near to the confines of death, treading the very threshold of Proserpine. I was borne through all the elements and returned to earth again. At the dead of night I saw the sun shining brightly. I approached the gods above and the gods below, and worshipped them face to face.' In Firmicus Maternus, *The Error of Profane Religions* 22, a priest of the mystery cult proclaims: "Rejoice, O mystai! Lo, our god appears as saved! And we shall find salvation (σωτηρία), springing from our woes.' The common element between these texts and Rom. 6.3–4 lies in the concept of an identification of the initiates or baptized with the destiny of the deity, so that they participate in the power of the deity. At the same time, there is a basic difference between the mystery religions and the understanding of baptism in Rom. 6.3–4. The repeated initiations of the mystery cults are only one part of a comprehensive cultic system of promotion from one degree to another, while Christian baptism is not merely one part of an initiation ritual, but once and for all confers participation in the whole saving act of God in Christ.

A further problem with regard to the historical context of Romans is the classification of the conflict between the '*strong*' and the '*weak*' in terms of the history of religions (Rom. 14.1–15.13). This conflict is by no means merely a reflection of the Corinthian debate about eating meat sacrificed to idols, but reflects a current conflict in the Roman church. In Rome the 'weak' obviously not only avoid meat sacrificed to idols, but reject the eating of meat as such (cf. Rom. 14.2, 21a). Furthermore, the 'weak' also seem to have rejected the drinking of wine (14.21b), and they observed certain days (14.5). Several different models from the history of religions may be introduced to explain the conduct of the 'weak.'[337] Thus the Pythagoreans were vegetarians because they rejected the practice of eating the flesh of beings that have souls (cf. Philostratus, *Life of Apollonius* 1.1.5–8). In the mystery religions too, the practice of temporary abstention from flesh (and wine) is documented (Apuleius, *Metamorphoses* 11.28). The Therapeutai of Egypt used only bread, salt, and water as nourishment (Philo, *Contemplative Life* 37). Similarly, abstention from flesh and wine is also reported of later Jewish Christian and Gnostic groups, but the

---

the other side cf. the argument of Dieter Zeller, 'Die Mysterienkulte und die paulinische Soteriologie,' in *Suchbewegungen*, ed. H. P. Siller (Darmstadt: Wissenschaftliche Buchgesell-schaft, 1991) 42–61. A critical introduction to the history and thought of the ancient mystery cults is offered by Walter Burkert, *Ancient Mystery Cults* (Cambridge: Harvard University Press, 1987). He rejects the concept of 'mystery religions,' 'as though it was a matter of a closed system segregated from other systems. The mysteries were a personal option within the framework of a general polytheistic system' (*ibid.* 17).

[337] Cf. also the summary in Schmithals, *Römerbrief als historisches Problem* 98–101.

practice of the 'weak' in the Roman church cannot be derived from these late texts. The Greek version of the Old Testament, while to be sure not making general prohibitions of meat and wine, still provides numerous examples of abstinence from meat and wine by pious Jews in a Gentile environment, since in this situation there was always the possibility that the meat had been sacrificed to idols and the wine was used in libations (cf. Dan. 1.3–16; 2Macc. 5.27; Additions to Esther 3.28; and further Josephus, *Life* 13, 14).

The observing of certain days and seasons likewise points to (former) Jews (see above 2.7.8), so that among the 'weak' in Rome there must have been some Jews. Alongside these, those who had been associated with the synagogue without actually converting to Judaism (Sebomenoi, 'God fearers') must also be counted among the 'weak.'[338] The observance of certain holy days and the Jewish food regulations is explicitly documented for Sebomenoi in Rome (cf. Juvenal, *Saturnalia* 14.96–106; Horace, *Saturnalia* 1.9.68–72). In Rome too it was difficult for Christians who had been Jews or Sebomenoi to obtain kosher meat, and they could never be certain that the meat and wine they were buying had not been consecrated in a pagan ritual.

The conduct of the 'weak' obviously led to conflicts within the Roman church, conflicts in which it is no longer discernible whether the Eucharist was a contributing factor. The 'strong' despised the 'weak,' while the 'weak' pronounced judgment on the 'strong' (Rom. 14.3). Since for Christians there is only one Lord and Judge, in Paul's view the individual Christian by no means has the right to pronounce judgment on brothers and sisters in the church. Christians should rather give attention to avoiding the placing of stumbling blocks in the path of the Christian brother or sister (cf. Rom. 14.13; 1 Cor. 8.9). Paul counts himself among the 'strong' (cf. Rom. 14.14; 15.1), but he is not ready to sacrifice love for the brother or sister in order to put into practice the position that he considers right in itself. The 'strong' must be willing and able to bear with the 'weak.' Thereby they serve the peace of the church and further its edification (cf. Rom. 14.19; 15.2). Just as Christ in his passion did not consider himself and did not pursue his own agenda (Rom. 15.3), so the 'strong' should be willing to renounce their own right and freedom for the sake of the 'weak' brothers and sisters. Both groups should accept each other in order to overcome the conflict (cf. Rom. 15.7).

---

[338] On this, cf. Folker Siegert, 'Gottesfürchtige und Sympathisanten,' JSJ 4 (1973) 109–164.

2.8.9 Basic Theological Ideas

The argumentation of Romans cannot be understood apart from the specific situation to which the letter is directed and the agreement that Paul wanted to work out with the Roman church. Paul's concern is already visible in the effusive praise of the faith of the Roman Christians (Rom. 1.8) and his apology for not having visited them sooner (1.13). In the letter's thesis statement in 1.16–17 the central theological themes of the letter are already bundled together. Only in the gospel of salvation is the righteousness of God revealed to all those who believe in Jesus Christ, whether Jews or Greeks. The letter's thesis is developed in a twofold manner in 1.18–3.20, with 1.18 providing the heading for the whole section. Paul first reflects on the possibility of the knowledge of God available to the gentiles from the works of creation, but which they did not accept. Thus the wrath of God came upon the gentiles, God gave them up to idolatry and the errors of their instincts (cf. Rom. 1.21–32). From Rom. 2.1 on Paul turns to direct his argument to the Jews (cf. 2.17). He does not dispute their position in God's saving plan as the elect people of God but emphasizes the contrast between orthodoxy and orthopraxis among the Jewish people. Since in reality the Jews by no means fulfill the will of God, but in fact do those things that they condemn in others, in the future judgment they will not be helped at all by the Law and circumcision. Their election will in fact be their undoing, for the gentiles who instinctively do what God commands and thus are circumcised in their hearts will accuse the Jews. When people are judged justly by their works, neither Jews nor gentiles can stand (2.7–13); both must count on being condemned. Paul's point is the negative equality of Jews and gentiles before God, for in each case they stand condemned by the Law. The first extensive line of argument reaches its goal in Rom. 3.20, where Paul names the anthropological premise of his doctrine of justification: the universal power of sin (cf. Rom. 3.9; Gal. 3.22) makes every human striving after salvation hopeless. Even obedience to the Law does not save, for in reality the Law leads not to life but only to the awareness of sin.

In sharp contrast to this situation of humanity from which there is no escape, the saving act of God now appears, whose righteousness has been revealed in Jesus Christ χωρὶς νόμου (apart from law) (Rom. 3.21). The righteousness that comes from God and is appropriated by faith is revealed in the Christ event alone,[339] so that a human being is justified before God

---

[339] In Rom. 1.17; 3.21, 22 and 10.3 δικαιοσύνη θεοῦ appears as a power and gift proceeding forth from God (= genitive of source, genitivus auctoris); in Rom. 3.5 in contrast we have a subjective genitive (cf. Rom. 3.25, 26). Cf. here Günter Klein, 'Gottesgerechtigkeit als Thema der

by grace alone, which removes any soteriological significance from the Law. In that Paul, differently from Galatians, here describes the *righteousness of God* as δικαιοσύνη θεοῦ διὰ πίστεως but χωρὶς νόμου (the righteousness of God through faith apart from law) and abrogates the Law as a way of salvation, he achieves a partially-new evaluation of the Law. Thus his doctrine of the Law can no longer be interpreted as a pure antinomism that endangers the fellowship of the church, while at the same time he preserves the positive theological results of the debate with the Galatian Judaizers (cf. on the one hand Rom. 3.27, 31; 7.12; 8.2; 13.8–10, on the other hand Rom. 3.21; 6.14; 10.4).

In Rom. 4 Paul illustrates the Old Testament foundation of his doctrine of justification by pointing to the figure of Abraham. In the ring composition Rom. 5–8 the apostle then turns to the present reality of salvation experienced by the church. Peace and reconciliation with God are grounded in the saving act of God in Jesus Christ, who has overcome the power of sin that entered the world through Adam's fall (Rom. 5). The dramatic turn from the death-dealing yoke of sin to the life-giving unity with Christ is accomplished for the individual Christian in baptism (Rom. 6). Here the Christian dies once for all to sin and is made free for a life in the power of the Spirit. In Rom. 7.5–6 Paul contrasts the old and new existence of the Christian, in order then in 7.7–25a to elaborate on the situation over which the Christian now stands victorious (7.5), while the theme of Rom. 8 is the new life determined by the Spirit (7.6). The ἐγώ in Rom. 7 and 8 must be understood in a general sense, for Paul is describing here the situation of unbelief as it appears from the perspective of faith.[340] In Rom. 8.1–11 Paul sketches a contrasting picture to that of Rom. 7. The Spirit gives life and delivers the Christian from the inescapable vicious circle of sin and death. In Rom. 8.12–17, the reference to sharing the hope of the glory of God takes up again the theme of 5.1–11. He develops it further in 8.18–30, working in magnificent perspectives on the hopes of the unredeemed creation. In the triumphal finale of 8.31–39 the apostle underscores once again faith's assurance of salvation even when the sufferings of the present are clearly in view.

The theme of Rom. 9–11[341] derives both as the consequence of the

---

Paulusforschung,' in *Rekonstruktion und Interpretation*, ed. G. Klein, BEvTh 50 (Munich: Kaiser, 1969) 225–236; Udo Schnelle, *Gerechtigkeit und Christusgegenwart* (see above 2.4.10) 92–103, 217–224.

[340] Cf. here in addition to Kümmel, *Römer 7*, especially Gerd Theißen, *Psychological Aspects* (see above 2.5.8); Udo Schnelle, *The Human Condition*, tr. O. C. Dean, Jr. (Minneapolis: Fortress, 1996) 66ff.

[341] In addition to the monographs by Luz and Hübner and the essay by Räisänen listed in the bibliography, cf. Werner G. Kümmel, 'Die Probleme von Römer 9–11 in der gegenwärtigen

Pauline doctrine of justification and from the specific communication situation with the Roman church, in which the relation of gentile Christians and Jewish Christians was obviously a problem. The righteousness of God himself is at stake if the election of Israel, the promises to the ancestors, and the covenant decisions of the past are no longer valid (Rom. 9.5). The word of God would then have failed (9.6). However, Paul affirms the opposite: the election of Israel is still valid, the promises still apply, but Israel has now fallen into a crisis in view of the revelation of God in Jesus Christ. For Paul, this revelation is the basis and beginning point of every discussion concerning the crisis that it generates for every falsely-understood doctrine of priority or advantage.

In Rom. 9–11 Paul wants to demonstrate the faithfulness of God over against the unfaithfulness of Israel. He presents his convictions in a train of thought that is conceived dialectically, constantly adopting new perspectives and alternating angles of vision. He first distinguishes between Israel as 'children of the flesh' and Israel as 'children of the promise,' with only the latter being the true Israel (Rom. 9.6–8). Then he affirms that only a remnant of Israel is elected, the rest are hardened (Rom. 11.5ff.). Finally he proceeds to the idea that the election of the gentiles will lead Israel to salvation to the grand finale of his argument in Rom. 11.26a: πᾶς 'Ἰσραὴλ σωθήσεται (all Israel will be saved). It is precisely the number of solutions that shows how vigorously Paul has struggled with this problem that affected not only the apostle's personal life and the fulfillment of his missionary plans, but is the test case for the δικαιοσύνη θεοῦ (righteousness of God): if God does not hold true to the continuity of his promises, then how can the gospel be credibly preached at all? Ultimately, the theme of Rom. 9–11 is the Godness of God, his faithfulness in view of human unfaithfulness.

In the parenetic Part Two Paul bases his exhortation especially on Rom. 6–8.[342] As there he had developed the basis and possibility of a new life in the Spirit, so here he is concerned about how to make this new life the concrete experience of the Roman church. Romans 12.1–2 functions as a programmatic opening text in the light of which the following ethical

---

Forschungslage,' in *Heilsgeschehen und Geschichte*, eds. Erich Grässer and Otto Merk, MThSt 16 (Marburg: N. G. Elwert, 1978) 2.245–260; Nikolaus Walter, 'Zur Interpretation von Römer 9–11,' ZThK 81 (1984) 172–195; Egon Brandenburger, 'Paulinische Schriftauslegung in der Kontroverse um das Verheißungswort Gottes (Rom. 9),' ZThK 82 (1985) 1–47; Folker Siegert, *Argumentation bei Paulus* (see above 2.3.1); Otfried Hofius, 'Das Evangelium und Israel,' ZThK 83 (1986) 297–324; Hans Martin Lübking, *Paulus und Israel im Römerbrief*, EHS.T 260 (Frankfurt: Lang, 1986).

[342] On the Pauline argumentation, cf. Otto Merk, *Handeln aus Glauben* (see above 2.8.5) 157–173.

instructions are to be understood.[343] Paul designates the Christian's bodily existence as the location where spiritual/ reasonable worship to God is performed, and challenges the Romans to understand their whole life as a life acceptable to God. God claims the whole person, who is to serve God precisely in the concrete reality of his or her bodily life. For Paul there is no realm of life that is excluded from worship-service to God (Gottes-Dienst); in every situation the Christian is challenged to perceive the will of God and to follow it.

In Rom. 12.3–13.14 are found general admonitions concerning life together in the church and the relation to the state. The context is important for the interpretation of Rom. 13.1–7: Paul is not here proposing some sort of Christian theory of the state, some dogmatic compendium about the divine legitimization of governmental authority; on the contrary, Rom. 13.1–7 is parenesis.[344] If the Pauline exhortation in 12.9–13.14 is already centered upon the concept of Christian love, so also it determines the apostle's line of argument in the conflict between the 'strong' and 'weak' in 14.1–15.13. Paul himself shares the position of the 'strong' (Rom. 15.1), but for love's sake challenges the 'strong' to be considerate of the 'weak.' Both groups live from the fact that Christ has accepted them, so they should accept each other (Rom. 15.7). The extensive list of greetings in Rom. 16 signals once again that the apostle wants to work out an agreement with the Roman church in order to continue his work of preaching the gospel in the western part of the Empire.

2.8.10 *Tendencies of Recent Research*

Among the classical introductory issues a clear consensus is emerging: that Romans was written from Corinth in 56 CE is now no more disputed than the view that 16.1–23 belonged to the original letter. A plurality of reasons is usually assigned for writing the letter, for a monocausal explanation does not do justice to the situation of the complex discussion between Paul, the Roman church, Paul's opponents and the Jerusalem authorities (Kettunen, Stuhlmacher, Wedderburn).

On the other hand, the understanding of the Law represented by Romans continues to be the object of vigorous dispute. Both the juxtaposition of negative (cf. e.g. Rom. 3.20, 21, 28; 5.20; 6.14b) and positive (cf. e.g. Rom. 3.31; 7.12; 13.8–10) statements about the Law and the relation

---

[343] Cf. Ernst Käsemann, 'Worship in Everyday Life: A Note on Romans 12,' *New Testament Questions of Today*, tr. W. J. Montague (London: SCM Press Ltd., 1969) 188–195.

[344] Cf. Ernst Käsemann, 'Principles of the Interpretation of Romans 13,' *New Testament Questions of Today*, tr. W. J. Montague (London: SCM Press Ltd., 1969) 196–216.

of the way the Law is understood in Romans to that of Galatians need clarification. Especially the meaning of the term νόμος (law) in the expressions νόμος πίστεως (law of faith) in Rom. 3.27 and νόμος τοῦ πνεύματος (law of the spirit) in Rom. 8.2 are still debated. Νόμος is referred to the Torah by, among others, E. Lohse, P. v. d. Osten-Sacken, F. Hahn, and H. Hübner,[345] while for example E. Käsemann, H. Paulsen, H. Räisänen, D. Zeller and R. Weber[346] understand νόμος here in the non-specific sense as 'rule, norm, order.' Paul would then be playing with the concept νόμος,[347] in order to clarify the fundamental change in the plan of salvation that had taken place between Sinai and Christ. Similarly, the interpretation of Rom. 10.4 remains controversial, where τέλος is translated with 'end' or 'goal.' Thus P. v. d. Osten-Sacken[348] vigorously advocates the interpretation that through Christ the Law has been fulfilled, so that τέλος must be translated with 'fulfillment' or 'goal.' In contrast, H. Lietzmann, R. Bultmann, E. Käsemann, and O. Michel[349] among many others translate τέλος with 'end,' which corresponds to the usual Pauline usage (cf. e.g. Rom. 6.21, 22) and the immediate context. A medial position is adopted by U. Wilckens, when he understands Christ to be 'end and goal of the Torah in faith.'[350] Additional hot spots of the recent discussion are the internal consistency of Romans statements about the Law (H. Räisänen) and their relation to the way the Law is understood in Galatians (H. Hübner).

The interpretation of the ἐγώ of Rom. 7 continues to be determined by W. G. Kümmel's analysis, according to which 'we have in Rom. 7 a portrayal of the non-Christian from the perspective of the Christian,'[351] and the 'I' is thus to be understood in the non-specific, typical sense. In contrast, G. Theissen emphasizes: 'Anyone who denies to Paul the ἐγώ in Romans 7 has to bear the burden of proof for this claim. What suggests itself most readily is to think of an "I" that combines personal and typical

[345] Cf. Eduard Lohse, 'ὁ νόμος τοῦ πνεύματος τῆς ζωῆς,' in *Die Vielfalt des Neuen Testaments*, ed. E. Lohse (Göttingen: Vandenhoeck & Ruprecht, 1982) (128–136) 134; Osten-Sacken, *Römer 8*, 226ff.; Ferdinand Hahn, 'Gesetzesverständnis' (see above 2.7.1) 57 note 89; Hübner, *Law in Paul* 146.

[346] Cf. Käsemann, *Romans* 215; Paulsen, *Römer 8* 64; Heikki Räisänen, 'Das "'Gesetz des Glaubens" (Rom. 3,27) und das "Gesetz des Geistes" (Rom. 8,2),' NTS 26 (1980) (101–117) 113ff.; Zeller, *Römerbrief* 152; R. Weber, 'Die Geschichte des Gesetzes und des Ich in Römer 7,7–8,4,' NZSTh 29 (1987) (147–179) 166–167.

[347] On this point cf. the linguistic evidence in Heikki Räisänen, 'Sprachliches zum Spiel des Paulus mit Nomos,' in *Glaube und Gerechtigkeit* (FS R. Gyllenberg). SFEG 38 (Helsinki 1983) 131–154.

[348] Cf. Osten-Sacken, *Römer 8* 250ff.

[349] Cf. Lietzmann, *Römerbrief* 96; Rudolf Bultmann, *Theology* (see above 2) 263; Käsemann, *Romans* 282; Michel, *Römerbrief* 326.

[350] Wilckens, *Römerbrief* 2.223.

[351] Kümmel, *Römer 7* 138.

traits.'[352] T. Laato goes a step further and affirms on the basis of Rom. 6.12 and 8.10 that Rom. 7.14–25 does not picture the person under the Law, but the Christian under grace. 'Rom. 7 does not cover anything which is not suited to the Christian, or – to formulate it to the point – everything covered in Rom. 7 is only suitable for the Christian.'[353]

Among the interpretative issues of Rom. 9–11, the meaning of πᾶς 'Ισραὴλ σωθήσεται (all Israel shall be saved) in 11.26a is especially disputed. Does πᾶς 'Ισραὴλ refer to all of ethnic Israel, or only that part of Israel that will be converted to faith in Jesus Christ in the salvific eschatological events? In favor of the latter possibility one may bring forward Rom. 11.20, 23 and the Pauline use of σῴζειν/σωτηρία (save; salvation).[354] A different interpretation is advocated by F. Mußner: 'The parousia of Christ saves all Israel, and that *sola gratia*, without works of the Law, but also without any previous "conversion" of the Jews to the gospel. God saves Israel in a "special way," but still not without reference to the gospel, for Christ, who according to Rom. 10.12 is "Lord of all" will also be Israel's "savior."'[355]

2.9 The Letter to the Philippians

2.9.1 Literature

Commentaries

Dibelius, Martin. *An die Thessalonicher I, II; An die Philipper*, HNT 11. Tübingen: J. C. B. Mohr, 1937³, 59–98; Ernst, Josef. *Der Brief an die Philipper, an Philemon, an die Kolosser, und an die Epheser*, RNT. Regensburg: Pustet, 1974; Lohmeyer, Ernst. *Der Brief an die Philipper, und die Kolosser und an Philemon*, KEK 9.1. Göttingen: Vandenhoeck & Ruprecht, 1974⁷; Barth, Gerhard. *Der Brief an die Philipper*, ZBK 9. Zürich: Theologischer Verlag, 1979; Gnilka, Joachim. *Der Philipperbrief*, HThK X .3. Freiburg: Herder, 1980³; Hawthorne, Gerald F. *Philippians*, WBC 43. Waco: Word, 1983; Schenk, Wolfgang. *Die Philipperbriefe des Paulus*. Stuttgart: Kohlhammer, 1984; Friedrich, Gerhard. *Der Brief an die Philipper*, NTD 8. Göttingen: Vandenhoeck & Ruprecht, 1990³; O'Brien, Peter T. *The Epistle to the Philippians*, NIGTC. Grand

---

[352] Gerd Theißen, *Psychological Aspects* (see above 2.5.8) 201.

[353] Timo Laato, *Paul and Judaism: An Anthropological Approach* (Atlanta: Scholars Press, 1995) 129.

[354] Cf. Ferdinand Hahn, 'Zum Verständnis von Rom. 11, 26a: . . . und so wird ganz Israel gerettet werden',' in *Paul and Paulinism* (FS C.K. Barrett), eds. Morna D. Hooker and Stephen G. Wilson (London: S. P. C. K., 1982) 221–236.

[355] Franz Mußner, '"Ganz Israel wird gerettet werden" (Rom. 11,26),' *Kairos 18* (1976) (241–255) 251. For a critique of a 'special way' for Israel cf. especially Erich Grässer, 'Zwei Heilswege?' in *Der Alte Bund im Neuen*, ed. E. Grässer, WUNT 35 (Tübingen: J. C. B. Mohr [Paul Siebeck], 1985) 212–230; Räisänen, 'Römer 9–11' 2917–2918.

Rapids: Wm. B. Eerdmans, 1991; Müller, Ulrich B. *Der Brief des Paulus an die Philipper*, ThHK 11.1. Leipzig: Evangelische Verlagsanstalt, 1993.

Monographs

Lohmeyer, Ernst. *Kyrios Jesus*, SAH 4. Heidelberg: Heidelberger Akademie der Wissenschaften, Phil.-hist. Kl., 1928; Schmid, Josef. *Zeit und Ort der paulinischen Gefangenschaftsbriefe*. Freiburg: Herder, 1931; Mengel, Berthold. *Studien zum Philipperbrief*, WUNT 2.8. Tübingen: J. C. B. Mohr (Paul Siebeck), 1982; Martin, Ralph P. *Carmen Christi. Philippians 2.5–11 in Recent Interpretation and in the Setting of Early Christian Worship*. Grand Rapids: Wm. B. Eerdmans, 1967; rev. 1983; Hofius, Otfried. *Der Christushymnus Philipper 2.6–11*, WUNT 17. Tübingen: J. C. B. Mohr (Paul Siebeck), 1991².

Articles

Bornkamm, Günther. 'Der Philipperbrief als Briefsammlung,' in *Geschichte und Glaube* II, ed. G. Bornkamm (1968; see above 2.8) 195–205; Käsemann, Ernst, 'Kritische Analyse von Phil. 2,6–11,' in *Exegetische Versuche und Besinnungen* I, ed. E. Käsemann. Göttingen: Vandenhoeck & Ruprecht, 1970⁶, 51–95; Baumbach, Günther. 'Die von Paulus im Philipperbrief bekämpften Irrlehrer,' in *Gnosis und Neues Testament*, ed. Karl Wolfgang Tröger. Berlin: Walter de Gruyter, 1973, 293–310; Walter, Nikolaus. 'Die Philipper und das Leiden,' in *Die Kirche des Anfangs* (FS H. Schürmann), ed. Rudolf Schnackenburg and others. Freiburg: Herder, 1978, 417–434; Strecker, Georg. 'Redaktion und Tradition im Christushymnus Phil. 2,6–11,' in *Eschaton und Historie*, ed. G. Strecker. Göttingen: Vandenhoeck & Ruprecht, 1979, 142–157; Klein, Günter. 'Antipaulinismus in Philippi,' in *Jesu Rede von Gott und ihre Nachgeschichte im frühen Christentum* (FS W. Marxsen), eds. Dietrich A. Koch, Gerhard Sellin and Andreas Lindemann. Gütersloh: Gütersloher Verlagshaus (Gerd Mohn), 1989, 297–313; Meeks, Wayne A. 'The Man from Heaven in Paul's Letter to the Philippians,' in *The Future of Early Christianity* (FS Helmut Koester), ed. Birger A. Pearson. Minneapolis: Fortress, 1991, 329–336.

2.9.2 Author

The Pauline authorship of Philippians is uncontested in contemporary exegesis.[356]

2.9.3 Place and Time of Composition

Paul wrote the letter to the Philippians during a time of imprisonment (Phil. 1.7, 13, 17), but which did not prevent him from carrying on a vigorous missionary activity (1.12ff.). From Philippi he had received a gift through Epaphroditus (4.18; cf. further 2.25; 4.14), and he now sends

---

[356] Those who have disputed the authenticity of the letter (especially in the nineteenth century) are listed by Mengel, *Studien* 317–324.

Epaphroditus back (with the letter) in order to communicate his gratitude (Phil. 2.25, 28). In the meantime Epaphroditus had become seriously ill while visiting Paul at the prison, which had caused the church at Philippi much anxiety (Phil. 2.26–30). Paul would like to visit the church himself (1.26; 2.24), although the outcome of his trial is still an open question. One hearing has already taken place (1.7), and Paul counts on a speedy resolution (2.23). He thinks either acquittal or death are possible results (1.19–24), but hopes for a good outcome (1.25). In any case he wants to send Timothy to Philippi (2.19–23) in order to learn how things are in the church.

Which place of imprisonment corresponds to this situation in the apostle's life? Of the three suggestions that have been made by scholars (Rome, Caesarea, Ephesus),[357] Rome is the most likely location. The portrayal of the Roman imprisonment in Acts 28.30–31 fits very well with the mild form of imprisonment presupposed by Philippians.[358] Moreover, the most direct way to understand the references to the Pretorian Guard (Phil. 1.13)[359] and the imperial slaves (Phil. 4.22) is in terms of a Roman imprisonment. Additional reasons favoring Rome as the place of composition and therefore for a relatively late dating of Philippians are: (1) The lack of reference to the offering indicates that at the time Philippians was written the collection had already been concluded.[360] (2) Philippians presupposes an imprisonment that had lasted some time. If the letter had been written in Ephesus, there would be no explanation for the silence of Acts about such a long imprisonment in Ephesus,[361] while the two years of the

---

[357] For arguments pro and con, cf. Kümmel, *Introduction* 324–32; Gnilka, *Philipperbrief* 18–25; Hans H. Schade, *Apokalyptische Christologie* (see above 2.4.1) 182ff. The Ephesus hypothesis, founded by Adolf Deissmann (cf. *Paul* [see above 2.1.1], 17–18 note 1), is shared by many exegetes today (for example Günter Bornkamm, *Paul* [see above 2] 246–247; Friedrich, *Philipperbrief* 129ff.; Gnilka, *Philipperbrief* 199; Barth, *Philipperbrief* 8–9; Schenk, *Philipperbriefe* 338; Müller, *Philipperbrief* 17–21). Caesarea as Paul's place of imprisonment is argued especially by Lohmeyer, *Philipperbrief* 3–4. The Roman hypothesis was renewed in this century by Schmid, *Gefangenschaftsbriefe passim*, and Charles H. Dodd, 'The Mind of Paul II' in *New Testament Studies* (Manchester: Manchester University Press, 1954²) (83–128) 85–108. In the most recent research it is again winning adherents. Cf. Otto Merk, *Handeln aus Glauben* (see above 2.8.5) 174; C. H. Hunzinger, 'Die Hoffnung angesichts des Todes im Wandel der paulinischen Aussagen,' in *Leben angesichts des Todes* (FS H. Thielicke), ed. Bernhard Lohse et al. (Tübingen: J. C. B. Mohr [Paul Siebeck], 1968) (69–88) 85 note 30; Wolfgang Wiefel, 'Hauptrichtung des Wandels' (see above 2.4.10) 79; Georg Strecker, 'Befreiung und Rechtfertigung' (see above 2.4.10) 230; Gerd Lüdemann, *Chronology* (see above 2.1) 104 note 186; Schade, *Apokalyptische Christologie* 190; Jürgen Roloff, *Apostelgeschichte* (see below 4.1) 372; O'Brien, *Philippians* 19–26.

[358] Cf. however Acts 24.23 for Caesarea.

[359] On this cf. Theodor Zahn, *Introduction to the New Testament* (Grand Rapids: Kregel Publications, 1953) 1.389 note 2, 551–554.

[360] Cf. Schade, *Apokalyptische Christologie* (see above 2.4.1) 190.

[361] On the difficulties of the Ephesus hypothesis, cf. especially Schmid, *Gefangenschaftsbriefe* 10ff., 72ff.

Roman imprisonment (Acts 28.30) fits very well with the situation presupposed in the letter. Paul's allusion to mortal danger he had experienced
in the province of Asia (2 Cor. 1.8) is not necessarily evidence for the
Ephesian hypothesis, since this report indicates only the fact of the mortal
danger, not the circumstances it involved.[362] So also the fighting with 'wild
animals' in 1 Cor. 15.32 is no evidence for an extended imprisonment in
Ephesus.[363] (3) The somewhat distant manner in which relationships are
described at the place where Paul is presently imprisoned (Phil. 1.12–18,
esp. vv. 15, 17, and cf. 1 Clem. 5.5!) suggests that the church there had not
been founded by the apostle himself. (4) The term ἐπίσκοπος (overseer)
that appears in the authentic Pauline letters only in Phil. 1.1 (cf. further
Acts 20.28; 1 Tim. 3.2; Titus 1.7) presupposes a development in the
church situation in the direction of the Pastoral letters.[364] (5) The
investigation of the Pauline language of Philippians by H. H. Schade[365]
shows that the linguistic features of the proemium, in the use of the title
'Christ,' in the use of 'we' and 'I,' and in the presence of rare words (cf.
esp. Βενιαμίν [Benjamin] only Rom. 11.1; Phil. 3.5; Ἑβραῖος (Hebrew)
only 2 Cor. 11.22; Phil. 3.5; ἐργάτης (worker) only 2 Cor. 11.13; Phil. 3.2;
φυλή (tribe) only Rom. 11.1; Phil. 3.5) all indicate that Philippians is to be
located chronologically after Romans.

Objections to the Roman origin of Philippians are the great distance
between Paul's place of imprisonment and the church to which he writes,
which supposedly would not allow for the brisk traffic back and forth presupposed by the letter. In addition, the Roman location would mean that
Paul had changed his travel plans announced in Rom. 15.24, 28, since he
now plans to visit Philippi after being released. Neither objection is
compelling. Paul could change his travel plans, as shown by the Corinthian
correspondence (cf. 1 Cor. 16.5–8 with 2 Cor. 1.15f.). When Paul wrote
Romans, he could not foresee the years of imprisonment in Caesarea and
Rome, new contacts with the older churches could have been the occasion
for Paul's changing (not giving up!) his plans for future missions. The
mission planned for Spain would then have been postponed, but not
abandoned, by the occasion that calls for his visiting Philippi. Besides, the
wish for a future visit belongs to the formal elements of a Pauline letter (cf.
1 Thess. 2.17ff.; 1 Cor. 16.5–6; 2 Cor. 13.1; Gal. 4.20; Rom. 15.23–24;

---

[362] Contra Victor P. Furnish, *2 Corinthians* (see above 2.6.1) 123; Helmut Koester,
Introduction 2.130–131.
[363] Contra Hans Conzelmann-Andreas Lindemann, *Interpreting The New Testament* (Peabody,
Massachusetts: Hendrickson Publishers, Inc., 1988) 176–177.
[364] Cf. Jürgen Roloff, 'Amt' (see below 5.5.1) 522.
[365] Cf. Schade, *Apokalyptische Christologie* 184–190.

Phlm. 22). The transportation connections between Philippi and Rome were very good (on the Via Egnatia to Dyrrhachium, by ship to Brundisium, then further on the Via Appia).[366] A boat trip from Philippi to Rome required about two weeks,[367] while the predominantly land route covered about 1084 km[368] at an average of about 37 km per day[369] would mean a maximum of four weeks to cover the distance. The trip could be made significantly more quickly when one considers the good road conditions, if one had favorable winds, and traveled by wagon part of the way. Philippians presupposes four trips: (1) The Philippians hear of Paul's imprisonment. (2) They send Epaphroditus. (3) The Philippians learn of Epaphroditus' illness. (4) Paul sends Epaphroditus back to Philippi. This is no difficulty within the span of Paul's extended imprisonment in Rome. Thus Philippians was probably written in *Rome* about *60* CE.[370]

2.9.4 *Intended Readership*

The city of Philippi was founded about 356 BCE by Philip II of Macedon.[371] In 42 BCE an intensive Roman settlement of the city began, which gained great momentum in 31 BCE (Octavian's victory over Anthony). Philippi evolved into a Roman military colony settled particularly by veterans. The economic importance of the city derived from its location on the Via Egnatia, the main traffic artery connecting the east and west of the Roman empire. Philippi is an example of the religious syncretism of the first century CE (cf. Acts 16.16–22), for alongside Greek, Roman, and Egyptian deities the older local cults of the native Thracian population, especially fertility gods, still enjoyed great popularity.

The first Pauline Christian community in Europe thus originated in Philippi (cf. Acts 16.11ff.; Phil. 4.15), founded by the apostle in 49/50. The church was mostly composed of Gentile Christians (cf. Acts 16.33b, and the Gentile names in 2.25ff.; 4.2–3, 18: Euodia, Syntyche, Clement, Epaphroditus), but also sebomenoi ("God fearers"; cf. Acts 16.14) and Jewish Christians (cf. Acts 16.13) seemed to have been included. The

---

[366] On this cf. Schmid, *Gefangenschaftsbriefe* 77–83. On the very good condition of Roman roads, cf. Gerhard Radke, 'Viae publicae Romanae,' PW.S 13 (1417–1686) col. 1477.

[367] Cf. Ludwig Friedländer, *Sittengeschichte Roms* (Leipzig: 1919⁹) 1.337ff.

[368] Cf. Alfred Wikenhauser, *New Testament Introduction* 436.

[369] L. Friedländer, *Sittengeschichte* 333, calculates 37.5 km per day. Other calculations are found in R. Reck, *Kommunikation und Gemeindeaufbau* (see above 2.2.2) 85–8.

[370] When Ephesus is regarded as the place where Philippians was composed, it is mostly dated at the end of Paul's Ephesian period. Thus for example Müller, *Philipperbrief* 22 argues for the year 55.

[371] On the city and its history cf. Walter Elliger, *Paulus in Griechenland* (see above 2.4.4) 23–77.

relationship between the church and Paul was very good, for the apostle granted it the privilege of being permitted to support his work financially (cf. Phil. 4.18). After the trip on which he founded the church Paul visited Philippi at least once more (cf. Acts 20.6, as well as 1 Cor. 16.5–6). Also at the time of the composition of the letter there was lively and friendly contact between the church and Paul, even though opponents had intruded into the church (cf. Phil. 1.27–30; 2.21) whom the apostle sharply attacks in Phil. 3.2ff. There were also some tensions within the community itself (cf. 2.1–4), so that Paul mentions a dispute between two women who were coworkers with the apostle (4.2–3).

2.9.5 Outline, Structure, Form

1.1–2	Prescript	
1.3–11	Proemium	Introduction
1.12–1.30	Epistolary Self Commendation	
2.1–4	Admonitions to church unity	
2.5–11	The Christ Hymn	
2.12–18	Appended admonitions	
2.19–24	The sending of Timothy	Body
2.25–30	The sickness of Epaphroditus	
3.1–4.1	Dispute with false teachers	
4.2–9	Closing parenesis	
4.10–20	Thanks for the community	
4.21–22	Greetings	Conclusion
4.23	Final Farewell (Eschatokoll)	

In contrast to 1–2 Corinthians, Galatians, and Romans, the apostolic title is lacking, and Paul describes himself and Timothy in Phil. 1.1 as δοῦλοι Χριστοῦ Ἰησοῦ (servants of Christ Jesus). This is a clear signal of the tenor of the letter as a whole, in which Paul never raises the claim of apostolic authority over against the Philippians. So too the proemium introduced by εὐχαριστῶ (I give thanks) documents the friendly relationship between Paul and the church. When Paul uses the ἀπών/πάρων (absent/present) motif in 1.7, 27; 2.12, 18, 24, he is adopting a topos of the ancient friendship letter.[372] Paul engages the church as a friend

---

[372] On this cf. J. Schoon-Janßen, *Umstrittene 'Apologien' in den Paulusbriefen* (see above 2.3.1) 136–146, who affirms a symbuleutic/deliberative orientation for Philippians.

and interprets their and his sufferings as a sign of their common salvation.

On the macro level the letter to the Philippians exhibits a tight structure.[373] At the center of the letter stand the admonitions to church unity and the dispute with false teachers. There is a connection between the subject matter of these two sections, for the unity of the church is the presupposition for its rejection of false teachers. It is hardly an accident that the Christ hymn stands at the letter's center. It is Jesus Christ himself who both originally lived out this model of conduct in his own life and still holds it before both apostle and church (*Urbild* and *Vorbild*). The note of thanksgiving at the letter's conclusion is by no means unusual, as 1 Thess. 5.16–18 shows.

2.9.6 Literary Integrity

The unity of Philippians is a disputed point among scholars.[374] Numerous exegetes regard Philippians as a letter collection and distinguish three letters that have been combined: Letter A, 4.10–20, a letter of gratitude for the gift from Philippi; Letter B, 1.1–3.1; 4.4–7; 4.21–23, a report on the situation of the apostle; Letter C, 3.2–4.3, 8–9, a debate with false teachers.[375] Others divide Philippians into two letters (e.g. G. Friedrich: a letter from prison, Phil. 1.1–3.1a; 4.10–23 and a letter against false teachers, 3.1b–4.9; J. Gnilka: a letter from prison 1.1–3.1a; 4.2–7, 10–23 and a letter against false teachers 3.1b–4.1, 8–9; J. Becker: Letter A: 1.1–3.1; 4.1–7, 10–23: Letter B: 3.2–21; 4.8–9).[376] The arguments presented for this thesis are: (1) the change in mood between 3.1 and 3.2; (2) the lack of reference to a prison situation in 3.2–4.3; (3) the comparable structure of 4.4–7 and 4.8–9 as an indication of two different concluding admonitions; (4) the tight thematic coherence of 4.10–20 as pointing to a separate letter of thanksgiving.

---

[373] Duane F. Watson, 'A Rhetorical Analysis of Philippians and its Implications for the Unity Question,' NT 30 (1988) 57–80, outlines Philippians from the perspective of rhetorical criticism: 1.3–26 exordium; 1.27–30 narratio; 2.1–3.21 probatio; 4.1–20 peroratio.

[374] A comprehensive history of research on Philippians is found in Mengel, *Studien* 82–221.

[375] Among others who argue for three letters, but with different assignment of individual verses, are Walter Schmithals, *Die Briefe des Paulus in ihrer ursprünglichen Form* (see above 2.4.6) 99–108; Helmut Koester, 'The Purpose of the Polemic of a Pauline Fragment,' NTS 8 (1961/62) 317; Günter Bornkamm, 'Philipperbrief als paulinische Briefsammlung;' Marxsen, *Introduction* 61–62; Barth, *Philipperbrief* 11; Vielhauer, *Urchristliche Literatur* 164–165; Wolfgang Schenk, *Die Philipperbriefe des Paulus*; various scholars surveyed in W. G. Kümmel, *Introduction* 332–333; Gnilka, *Philipperbrief* 6ff.; W. Schenk, 'Der Philipperbrief in der neueren Forschung (1945–1985),' ANRW 25.4 (Berlin: Walter de Gruyter, 1987) 3280–3313.

[376] Cf. Jürgen Becker, *Paul* (see above 2) 305ff.

These arguments cannot persuade. On (1): While it is not to be denied that there is a change of mood between 3.1 and 3.2, it is not so abrupt as is often affirmed. In 1.15–18 Paul mentions missionaries in his place of imprisonment who preach the gospel from insincere motives, and in 1.28 refers to opponents in Philippi by whom the church should not be intimidated. Paul announces the destruction of these opponents, but the salvation of the church. Paul also alludes to opponents in Philippi in 2.21, when he speaks of those who seek their own interests, not those of Jesus Christ. Moreover, the church is called to unity in 1.27 and 2.1–5, so that the reference to κύνες (dogs) in 3.2 is by no means without advance notice.[377] Finally, the χαρά (joy) that is the central motif of the letter is not a matter of feelings, but is that which endures precisely amid conflicts. The τὰ αὐτά (same things) of 3.1 clearly takes up 2.18[378] and as in 1.18b–26 intentionally precedes his declarations with this affirmation of joy. Just as in 1.18b–26, so also in 3.1–11 nothing is said to encourage the kind of joy based entirely on subjective feelings. Rather, Paul first strengthens the church in the joy of its salvation before discussing the threatening problems.

On (2): references to the apostle's situation of imprisonment are of course lacking in 3.2–4.3, but only if these verses have previously been separated from their present context and considered as a fragment of an independent letter.[379] Methodologically, such a procedure can only be described as petitio principii [begging the question], and thus has no argumentative value.

On (3): In Phil. 4.1 Paul concludes the argument with the opponents with the admonition 'stand firm in the Lord.' Then in 4.2–3 there follows the challenge to settle a dispute between two women. The general parenesis resumes in 4.4–6,[380] in which the exhortations and the motivations in which they are grounded are not specific to the situation, but still must be seen against the background of the disputes that threaten the church. The superior eschatological grounding of the apostle's claim appears in the ὁ κύριος ἐγγύς (the Lord is near) of v. 5b, on which all the

---

[377] The βλέπετε in Philippians 3.2 is not a warning against new external dangers, but is to be translated with 'watch yourselves;' see G. D. Kilpatrick, 'ΒΛΕΠΕΤΕ Phil 3,2,' in *In Memoriam Paul Kahle*, eds. Matthew Black and Georg Fohrer, BZAW 103 (Berlin: Walter de Gruyter, 1968) 146–148. According to David E. Garland, 'The Composition and Unity of Philippians,' *NT* 27 (1985) 164–165, 3.2 begins a digressio that is to make clear to the Philippians that they are basing too much confidence on the 'flesh.'

[378] Cf. Dibelius, *Philipperbrief* 86. On the repeated references to χαίρω (rejoice) or χαρά (joy) in Philippians cf. especially J. Schoon-Janßen, *Umstrittene 'Apologien' in den Paulusbriefen* (see above 2.3.1) 129–136.

[379] Cf. Kümmel, *Introduction* 332–333.

[380] Cf. Otto Merk, *Handeln aus Glauben* (see above 2.8.5) 194.

following admonitions are based. V. 7 is then not a concluding wish, but a promise with which Paul grounds the admonition of v. 6.[381] A catalogue of virtues follows in v. 8, introduced with τὸ λοιπόν (finally) (cf. 1 Cor. 7.29). V. 9 then takes up v. 8 and makes the apostle's own life the basis for the instructions just communicated. One can thus see a tightly connected chain of thought in 4.4–9, so that the assumption of two originally independently transmitted concluding admonitions is not probable.

On (4): If 4.10–20 is a separate letter of thanksgiving, then it is very remarkable that the thanks for the concrete monetary gift recedes so much into the background,[382] for Paul expresses his joy over the state of the church and its support in very general terms.[411] In addition, the sickness of Epaphroditus, who had brought the Philippians gift to Paul, remains unmentioned.[384]

Finally, chapter 3 of Philippians is connected with the rest of the letter in several ways. Thus 3.20–21 refers to 2.6–11 in both language and content. The following linguistic contacts are clear: a) The predication κύριος 'Ιησοῦς Χριστός (the Lord Jesus Christ) in 2.11/3.20; b) ταπεινοῦν (humble) 2.8/ταπείνωσις (humility) 3.21; c) σχῆμα (form) 2.7/μετασχηματίζεσθαι (transform) 3.21; d) μορφή (form) 2.6, 7/ σύμμορφος (conformed) 3.21; e) πᾶν (all) 2.9, 10; πᾶσα (every) 2.11/τὰ πάντα (all things) 3.21; f) ἐπουράνιος (heavenly) 2.10/οὐρανός (heaven) 3.20; g) δόξα (glory) 2.11/3.21. In terms of content, the inthronization of Jesus Christ is the presupposition for the eschatological action of the almighty one described in 3.20–21. The motif of the 'right mind' connects 2.2, 5 and 3.15; 4.2.

In summary, it may be affirmed that the letter to the Philippians must be understood as both a literary and theological *unity*.[385]

Polycarp *Philippians* 3.2, in which it is said that Paul 'also wrote letters to you when he was absent,' is repeatedly brought forth as an argument for the

---

[381] *Ibid.* 195.

[382] Cf. Wolfgang Schrage, *Die konkreten Einzelgebote in der paulinischen Paränese* (Gütersloh: Gütersloher Verlagshaus [Gerd Mohn], 1961) 60.

[383] For analysis, cf. Merk, *Handeln aus Glauben* 198ff.

[384] Barth, *Philipperbrief* 75 is among those who, on the basis of their partition hypothesis, must affirm that the 'letter' of Philippians 4.10–20 was written before Epaphroditus had become sick.

[385] In addition to E. Lohmeyer, M. Dibelius, A. Jülicher and E. Fascher, *Einleitung* 123, scholars who have recently argued that Philippians is a unity are (among others) Kümmel, *Introduction* 332–335; Gerhard Delling, 'Philipperbrief', RGG³ 5 (1961) 335; Merk, *Handeln aus Glauben* 200; Mengel, *Studien* 297ff.; Andreas Lindemann, *Paulus im ältesten Christentum* (see below 5) 24–25; W. Egger, *Philipperbrief*, NEB 11 (Würzburg: Echter, 1985) 49; Duane F. Watson, 'Rhetorical Analysis' 80–83; David E. Garland, 'Composition and Unity' 162; J. Schoon-Janßen, *Umstrittene 'Apologien' in den Paulusbriefen* (see above 2.3.1) 119–138; O'Brien, *Philippians* 10–18; Müller, *Philipperbrief* 4–14 (he reckons with a pause in dictation after 1.1–3.1; then new information from Philippi and a change in his own trial situation occasion 3.2– 4.23).

existence of several letters to the Philippians and thus as support for the partition hypotheses. But this plural stands in contrast to Polycarp *Philippians* 11.3, where Polycarp explicitly proceeds on the basis of a single letter of Paul to the Philippians.[386]

2.9.7 Traditions, Sources

Since the analyses of E. Lohmeyer[387] it can be considered as established that in Phil. 2.6–11 we have a pre-Pauline *hymn*.[388] Evidence that this is tradition rather than Pauline composition is provided by the vocabulary (ὑπερυψοῦν [highly exalted], καταχθόνιος [under the earth] only here in the New Testament; μορφή [form], ἁρπαγμός [something to be exploited] only here in Paul), the heaping up of participial and relative clauses, the strophic construction of the text, and the interruption of the Pauline line of thought in Philippians. The phrase in v. 8c θανάτου δὲ σταυροῦ (even death on a cross) is usually regarded as Pauline redaction, but G. Strecker argues that all of v. 8 comes from Paul,[389] and O. Hofius reckons includes 8c as part of the original hymn.[390] The arrangement of the pre-Pauline textual unit is debated. E. Lohmeyer subdivides the tradition into six strophes of three lines each, all of which is divided into two equal units by the διό of v. 9. In contrast, J. Jeremias[391] advocated a division into three major parts of four lines each (6–7a; 7b–8; 9–11), a reconstruction that proceeds on basis of parallelismus membrorum as the formal principle involved. All other reconstructions must be considered as variations of these two basic suggestions of Lohmeyer and Jeremias.

From the point of view of the history of religions, the hymn is not a unity; while the second part (vv. 9–11) points to a Jewish background with its allusions to Old Testament passages and material from Jewish liturgical forms, the first part (vv. 6–7) contains strong conceptual parallels to

---

[386] Cf. Kurt Aland, 'Die Entstehung des Corpus Paulinum' (see below Excursus 2) 349–350; Walter Bauer – Henning Paulsen, *Die Briefe des Ignatius von Antiochia und der Polykarpbrief*, HNT 18 (Tübingen: J. C. B. Mohr [Paul Siebeck], 1985) 116. Probably Polycarp understood Paul's statement in Philippians 3.1 'to write the same things to you. . .' to imply more than one letter, and hence used the plural in 3.2 of his own letter to the Philippians.

[387] Cf. Ernst Lohmeyer, *Kyrios Jesus*.

[388] For the history of research cf. Martin, *Carmen Christi* 97ff. A critical evaluation of recent discussion is found in Jürgen Habermann, *Präexistenzaussagen im Neuen Testament*, EHS 23.362 (Frankfurt: Lang, 1990) 91–157.

[389] Cf. Strecker, 'Redaktion und Tradition' 150.

[390] Cf. Hofius, *Christushymnus* 4–17; previously Otto Merk, *Handeln aus Glauben* (see above 2.8.5) 179 note 23.

[391] Cf. Joachim Jeremias, 'Zur Gedankenführung in den paulinischen Briefen' (4. Der Christushymnus Phil 2,6–11), in *Abba* (Göttingen: Vandenhoeck & Ruprecht, 1966) 274–276; 'Zu Philipper 2,7. ἑαυτὸν ἐκένωσεν', in *Abba* 308–313.

Hellenistic religio–philosophical writings. The hymn's 'setting in life' (Sitz im Leben) is in the church's liturgy. The first strophe sings of the descent of the preexistent one, the second strophe of his inthronization. For the Pauline understanding of the hymn, the crucial factors are its location in this context and the redactional additions. Paul imbeds this traditional piece in a parenetic train of thought, as shown by Phil. 2.1–4. There are both compositional and terminological connections between this section and its context. Thus the descent of Christ in v. 8 is expressed with ταπεινόω (humbled himself), which corresponds to the ταπεινοφροσύνη (humility) to which the church is called (v. 3). The obedience of the lowly Christ appears as the contrasting picture to the self-seeking and quarreling that is to be overcome in the life of the community (v. 3). Finally, the summarizing formulation of the preexistent one's descent (v. 7: ἑαυτὸν ἐκένωσεν [emptied himself]) points to the fundamental instruction of v. 4, according to which Christians are not to seek their own interests, but that which serves others. So too there is a connection with the following v. 12; there Paul takes up the idea of the obedience of Christ and makes it the basis of the ethical attitude to which the church is called. For the apostle, it is an ethical understanding of the tradition, not a mythical one, that is important. The church is challenged to duplicate in its own ethical life what the Kyrios had accomplished in the saving event of his incarnation, death on the cross and inthronization. Christ is thus portrayed in Phil. 2 as the one who both originally lived out this model of conduct in his own life and still holds it before the church as a model to be followed (*Urbild* and *Vorbild*).

It is also possible that Paul also took over another fragment of tradition in Phil. 3.20–21.[392]

2.9.8 History-of-religions Standpoint

There is a wide range of opinions regarding the identification of Paul's opponents in Philippians, both as to how they are to be classified from a history of religions perspective and whether they represent a united front or more than one group. The following explanatory models are the most important that have been proposed (with some differences among individual proponents).[393] (1) Paul struggles against only one front, whether

---

[392] For discussion of the problems, cf. Gnilka, *Philipperbrief* 208ff.; Jürgen Becker, 'Erwägungen zu Phil 3,20–21,' ThZ 27 (1971) 16–29.

[393] For a brief survey of the history of research, cf. Klein, 'Antipaulinismus in Philippi,' 297–300. John J. Gunther, *St. Paul's Opponents* (see above 2.6.8) 2, lists eighteen different suggestions on the history-of-religions classification of Paul's opponents in Philippi.

Judaizers (G. Delling,[394] G. Klein, G. Lüdemann[395]), Jewish Christian gnostics (W. Schmithals,[396] G. Bornkamm, Ph. Vielhauer[397]), or Jewish Christian missionaries like the opponents in 2 Corinthians (J. Gnilka, G. Friedrich). (2) The Pauline polemic is directed against two fronts, in 3.1–11(–16) against Jews, after 3.12 (17) against Hellenistic libertines (M. Dibelius, G. Baumbach). (3) Three different sets of opponents in Phil. 3 are proposed by E. Lohmeyer, who sees 3.2–11 against the danger of Judaism, 3.12–15 against libertines, and 3.17–21 as a warning against the danger of apostasy from either internal or external threats (similarly H. D. Betz[398]).

It is mostly undisputed, however, that in 3.2–11 Paul struggles against *Jewish Christian missionaries*.[399] The apostle describes them as 'dogs,' in order to characterize the malignant and destructive intentions of his opponents.[400] The expression βλέπετε τοὺς κακοὺς ἐργάτας (beware of the evil workers) is explained from 2 Cor. 11.13, where ἐργάται δόλιοι (deceitful workers) is used as a polemical term for 'apostle.' Clearly early Christian missionaries used ἐργάτης (worker) as a term to describe themselves (cf. Matt. 9.37–38; 10.10), but Paul here qualifies it with the negative adjective κακός (evil). The position of his opponents is clearly recognizable in the word κατατομή (mutilation), which means the same as 'circumcision' (cf. Gal. 5.12). When in 3.3a Paul reclaims the concept in a positive sense for the Christian community, he puts his finger on the key issue in the debate: Jewish Christian missionaries had penetrated into the church at Philippi and insisted that Gentile Christians be circumcised. In his polemic in 3.4ff. Paul intentionally refers to the advantages of his Jewish ancestry, his belonging to the Pharisees and his blameless fulfilling of the Law. So too his terminology in 3.9, reminiscent of his doctrine of justification in Galatians, suggests that his opponents are to be regarded as militant Jewish Christians.

In his first train of thought in 3.12–16 Paul draws ethical consequences from the preceding argumentation. He turns to the church (cf. vv. 13, 15) and clarifies his understanding of Christian maturity. He numbers himself

---

[394] Cf. Delling, 'Philipperbrief' 334.

[395] Cf. Lüdemann, *Opposition to Paul* 104–109 (Jewish Christians from Jerusalem).

[396] Walter Schmithals, 'The False Teachers of the Epistle to the Philippians,' *Paul and the Gnostics*, tr. John E. Steely (Nashville and New York: Abingdon Press, 1972) 65–122.

[397] Cf. Ph. Vielhauer, *Urchristliche Literatur* 165.

[398] Cf. Hans D. Betz, *Nachfolge und Nachahmung Jesu Christi im Neuen Testament*, BHTh 37 (Tübingen: J. C. B. Mohr [Paul Siebeck], 1967) 151.

[399] So most recently Müller, *Philipperbrief* 186–191.

[400] Cf. Billerbeck, *Kommentar* 3.621: 'The ignorant, godless and non-Israelites were described as "dogs".'

among the 'mature' (v. 15), i.e. he considers himself to be one of the 'spiritual' people (cf. 1 Cor. 2.6; 3.1). This 'maturity' or 'perfection' does not mean for him, however, the fulfillment of salvation in the present, but it rather derives from the future fulfillment, as underscored by the eschatological reservation in Phil. 3.12. The notable agreements between Phil. 3.12–16 and 1 Cor. 2.6–10; 4.8; 9.24 in both subject matter and language show that here too Paul must debate with an enthusiastic stream within the church. In 3.17 Paul again explicitly addresses the church, but it is difficult to determine whether he still has the enthusiastic stream within the community in view, or takes up the argument in 3.2–11 again. The description of his opponents as 'enemies of the cross of Christ' in 3.19, which can hardly refer to the internal group, favors the latter possibility. The clear anti-libertine orientation of 3.19 and the parallel statement in 2 Cor. 12.21 thus make it likely that Paul's opponents in Philippi were Hellenistic Jewish Christian missionaries that combined Judaizing and enthusiastic elements. In Phil. 3 Paul struggles against a united front of opponents that also initiated or strengthened enthusiastic tendencies within the Philippian church.

2.9.9 *Basic Theological Ideas*

In Philippians Paul expresses the *paradox of Christian existence* in terms of his own person. The point of departure is his gratitude to God whose faithfulness keeps the Philippians in their faith and nourishes it (1.3–11; 4.6) and even brings good from the present situation of the apostle. Thus the tone of both thanksgiving and joy permeates the whole letter (cf. 1.3, 18; 2.29; 3.1a; 4.1, 4–6, 19–20). It is precisely the threatening situation of Paul in prison that leads to a more extensive and courageous preaching of the gospel (1.12, 14). Although he must reckon with the possibility of the death sentence, the apostle is filled with joy as he contemplates the future, for he lives in the certainty of glorifying Christ whether he lives or dies (1.18ff.). He would choose to live for the sake of preaching the gospel and nurturing the church in the faith, although he would really rather die and be with the Lord (1.22–26; 3.10–11). Thus emerges the conclusion that by human standards must be paradoxical: in the suffering of the apostle the faithfulness and grace of God is revealed.

The Christian community responds to the goodness of God when they live their lives in such a manner that they correspond to Jesus Christ (1.27–30). In 2.1–5, 6–11, 12–18 the apostle makes clear that the orientation of Christian existence is to the Lord Jesus Christ, the founder, guarantor, and fulfiller of salvation. As the founder who himself first lived out the new kind of life to which Christians are called, he both makes it possible and shows what it is in his own life. Just as Christ did not look after his own interests but gave himself over to death for others, so Christians must not live in selfishness and competitive strife, but in humility and unity. The church is to follow Christ with the awareness that they, like the apostle, are not yet in the state of final salvation, but that they are living toward the day of Christ's return, the final judgment, and the resurrection (3.12ff.). This possibility is given by God, for it is God who enables Christians both to will and to do (2.13). The Pauline ethic is not rooted in an idealistic striving after perfection, but in the knowledge of the power of God that is present in the Spirit (1.19, 4.12–13).

A further insight into the apostle's self-understanding is given in 3.4–11. Paul evaluates his splendid Jewish past from the perspective of Christian faith, and considers it 'rubbish.' Righteousness cannot be attained by the Law, but only received in faith (3.9). As in all Paul's letters, so too in Philippians the acute expectation of the nearness of the parousia comes to expression (cf. 4.5b; 1.6, 10; 2.16; 3.20b). In contrast to preceding letters, here Paul reckons with the possibility that he might die before the Lord's coming and directly after death be with the Lord (1.23; 3.20–21).

2.9.10 *Tendencies of Recent Research*

The Letter to the Philippians as a whole has played only a subordinate role in previous Pauline research. For the most part, individual passages of the letter have been studied, especially 2.6–11. The two key issues regarding the letter as a whole continue to be its provenance and unity. There is no developing consensus on these points, for on the one hand many exegetes regard Ephesus as the place of composition and the present document to be composed of more than one letter, while on the other hand in the most recent research a growing number of scholars vote for Rome and the unity of the letter. Recent studies have also concentrated on the eschatology of Philippians, especially the comparison of 1.23 and 3.20–21 with other statements of the apostle on eschatology and the significance of the σὺν Χριστῷ-expression (with Christ).[401] The new interest on the pre-Christian Paul[402] has drawn Philippians more toward the center of Pauline studies, for no text contains so much information about the apostle's pre-Christian period and his self-understanding during this time as does Phil. 3.4b–11. 'Even if Paul . . . represents his turn from an exemplary advocate of Jewish

---

[401] On this cf. Peter Siber, *Mit Christus leben* (see above 2.4.8).

[402] Cf. Martin Hengel, *The Pre-Christian Paul* (see above 2.2.1); Karl W. Niebuhr, *Heidenapostel aus Israel* (see above 2.2.1).

life to apostle of Christ as a radical about-face, he still does not evaluate this turn as a turning away from the content of Jewish faith in God and understanding of salvation.'[403]

The increasing interest in the individual texts of Philippians cannot disregard the fact that a comprehensive historical and theological assessment of this letter does not yet exist. That will not happen until Philippians is accepted and interpreted as a witness from the *late period* of Paul's life and work.

2.10 The Letter to Philemon

2.10.1 *Literature*

Commentaries

Dibelius, Martin. *An die Kolosser, Epheser, an Philemon*, HNT 12. Tübingen: J. C. B. Mohr (Paul Siebeck), 1953³, 101–108; Lohse, Eduard. *Colossians and Philemon. A Commentary on the Epistles to the Colossians and to Philemon*, tr. William R. Poehlmann and Robert J. Karris; ed. Helmut Koester, Hermeneia. Philadelphia: Fortress Press, 1971, 186–208; Lohmeyer, Ernst. *Colossians and Philemon*, tr. W. R. Poehlmann and R. J. Karris, Hermeneia. Philadelphia: Fortress, 1971; Ernst, Josef. *Der Brief an die Philipper, an Philemon, an die Kolosser, an die Epheser*, RNT. Regensburg: Pustet, 1974. Stuhlmacher, Peter. *Der Brief an Philemon*, EKK 18. Neukirchen: Neukirchener Verlag, 1981²; Suhl, Alfred. *Der Philemonbrief*, ZBK 13. Zürich: Theologischer Verlag, 1981; Gnilka, Joachim. *Der Philemonbrief*, HThK X. 4. Freiburg: Herder, 1982; O'Brien, Peter T. *Colossians. Philemon*, WBC 44. Waco: Word, 1982; Binder, Hermann (Joachim Rohde). *Der Brief des Paulus an Philemon*, ThHK 11/II. Berlin: Evangelische Verlagsanstalt, 1990; Friedrich, Gerhard. *Die Brief an Philemon*, NTD 8. Göttingen: Vandenhoeck & Ruprecht, 1990³; Wolter, Michael. *Der Philemonbrief*, ÖTK 12. Gütersloh: Gütersloher Verlagshaus (Gerd Mohn), 1993.

Monographs

Petersen, Norman. *Rediscovering Paul: Philemon and the Sociology of Paul's Narrative World* (Philadelphia: Fortress, 1985)

Articles

Wickert, Ulrich. 'Der Philemonbrief- Privatbrief oder apostolisches Schreiben?' ZNW 52 (1961) 230–238; Suhl, Alfred. 'Der Philemonbrief als Beispiel paulinischer Paränese,' *Kairos* 15 (1973) 267–279; Lampe, Peter. 'Keine "Sklavenflucht" des Onesimus,' ZNW 76 (1985) 135–137; Schenk, Wolfgang. 'Der Brief des Paulus an Philemon in der neueren Forschung (1945–1987),' *ANRW* 25.4. Berlin: Walter de Gruyter, 1987, 3439 3495; Winter, Sara C. 'Paul's Letter to Philemon,' NTS 33

---

[403] *Ibid.* 110.

(1987) 1–15; Barclay, J.M.G. 'Paul, Philemon and the Dilemma of Christian Slave-Ownership,' NTS 37 (1991) 161–186; Rapske, Brian M. 'The Prisoner Paul in the Eyes of Onesimus,' NTS 37 (1991) 187–203.

2.10.2 *Author*

The authenticity of Philemon was occasionally disputed in the 19th century (F. C. Baur), but today there is no longer any doubt that it is an authentic letter of Paul.

2.10.3 *Place and Time of Composition*

The time and place of Philemon seems to be very close to that of Philippians, for Paul is in prison (Phlm. 1, 9, 13), and Timothy and other coworkers are with him, as in the case of Philippians (Phlm. 1, 23, 24). The moderate prison conditions are also comparable, for Paul has his coworkers around him (Phil. 1.23–24) and can continue his missionary activity (Phlm. 10). These circumstances, as well as the singular self-description πρεσβύτης (elder)[404] in Phlm. 9 point to *Rome* as the place where Philemon was composed.[405] The temporal relationship to Philippians cannot be determined with certainty, but the irony in Phlm. 19 suggests that in comparison to Philippians Paul finds himself in a better situation and mood, so that Philemon is probably to be dated after Philippians (ca. 61 CE).

The occasion of the letter is the sending of the slave Onesimus back to his master Philemon, a Christian from Colossae (cf. Col. 4.9, Onesimus; Col. 4.17/ Phlm. 2, Archippus). Why is Onesimus with Paul? Possibly Onesimus ran away from his master after having stolen something from him (cf. Phlm. 18), then became acquainted with Paul and was converted by him to the Christian faith (cf. Phlm. 10). In that case Onesimus would have had the status of a runaway slave (*fugitivus*), and would have to reckon with the corresponding punishment, which Paul seeks to prevent.

---

[404] Πρεσβύτης is not an official title, but indicates Paul's age (cf. Luke 1.18; Tit 2.2); Cf. M. Wolter, *Philemonbrief* 260.

[405] Among those who vote for Rome are J. B. Lightfoot, *The Epistles of Paul III* (London 1890³) 310–311; Johannes Weiß, *Earliest Christianity* (see above 2.5.6) 382; Albert Schweitzer, *The Mysticism of Paul the Apostle*, tr. William Montgomery (New York: Seabury Press, 1968) 47; Jülicher – Fascher, *Einleitung* 124–125; Henneke Gülzow, *Christentum und Sklaverei in den ersten drei Jahrhunderten* (Bonn: R. Habelt, 1969) 29–30; Schenke – Fischer, *Einleitung* I, 156. In favor of Caesarea (tendentiously): Dibelius, *Philemonbrief* 107; Lohmeyer, *Philemonbrief* 172; Kümmel, *Introduction* 348–49; Claus-Jürgen Thornton, *Der Zeuge des Zeugen* (see below 4.1) 212. The majority of scholars consider Ephesus to be the place where Philemon was composed, among whom are Stuhlmacher, *Philemonbrief* 21; Lohse, *Colossians and Philemon* 188; Gnilka, *Philemonbrief* 4–5; Binder, *Philemonbrief* 21–29; Wolter, *Philemonbrief* 238. In this case Philemon would have been written between 53 and 55 CE.

This hypothesis cannot satisfactorily explain why it is that Onesimus appears with Paul in his situation of imprisonment (accident? did he already know the apostle?) and did not try to preserve the freedom he sought in a large city in a foreign country. Thus it has recently been argued (P. Lampe) that Onesimus was no runaway slave, but that he had sought out Paul as his advocate in a household conflict. Onesimus' goal would then be to return to the household of Philemon. In this case Onesimus' stay with Paul would be plausible, but Phlm. 13, which presupposes a longer time of service by the slave Onesimus with Paul, still poses a problem. Why does Onesimus remain with Paul a considerable time, if he only wants Paul to provide (a written) intercession for him? Thus why Onesimus is with Paul is still not clear; what is clear is only that some event in the household of Philemon occasioned the departure of Onesimus,[406] he met Paul in prison, helped him, and now debates whether to stay with Paul or to return to the household of Philemon.

2.10.4 Intended Readership

The letter is directed primarily to Philemon, who is addressed as ἀδελφός (brother) and συνεργός (fellow worker) (Phlm. 1). But the letter is also addressed to Apphia, Archippus, and the congregation that meets in Philemon's house. Since the 'your' in the expression 'your house' is singular, Philemon, Apphia, and Archippus are not a family group, but Apphia and Archippus are prominent coworkers in the congregation to which the letter is addressed. It must remain an open question whether Archippus worked in the congregation as a deacon, as suggested by Col. 4.17. Philemon was a Christian (Phlm. 5, 7) who was active in the work of the congregation, owned at least one slave, and his house served as the meeting place for the church, so that he apparently belonged to the middle class of craft workers or business people. In Phlm. 19b Paul mentions that Philemon was someway in Paul's debt. It is thus quite possible that they were personally acquainted with each other, but this is by no means necessary, since v. 19b can also be an element of the subtle Pauline argument that alternates between deferential showing of favor and hidden directives.[407] On the other hand, it could be the case that Paul had converted Philemon and alludes to it in v. 19b. In determining the location of the addressees, the agreements between Phlm. 23–24 and Col. 4.10ff. are of great significance.

---

[406] According to Wolter, *Philemonbrief* 231, we may assume 'that Onesimus was charged with some offense in the household of his master, but maintained his innocence and sought Paul's help in mediating the case.'

[407] Cf. Suhl, *Philemonbrief* 20.

All those named in the epistolary conclusion of Philemon appear in a different order and with supplementary elements in Col. 4.10ff. (exception: Jesus Justus, Col. 4.11). Thus most scholars consider Colossae as the place of Philemon's residence.[408]

2.10.5 Outline, Structure, Form

1–3	Prescript	— Introduction
4–7	Proemium	
8–16	The Apostle's Concern	— Body
17–20	Epilogue	
21	Closing Parenesis	
22	Apostolic Parousia	— Conclusion
23–24	Greetings	
25	Final Farewell (Eschatokoll)	

The structure of Philemon is heavily influenced by rhetorical elements.[409] As in ancient rhetoric, so also in Paul the proemium has the function of creating a receptive mood in the hearers or readers. That becomes very clear in Phlm. 7, a verse that as *captatio benevolentiae* leads into the apostle's real argument. So too the main body of Philemon manifests elements of rhetorical structure. Thus Phlm. 9, 10; 11, 13; 11, 14 exhibit the rhetorical argumentation figures of pathos, logos (rational grounds)) and ethos (considerations of usefulness; appeal to honor). Especially the identification of the apostle with Onesimus in Phlm. 12 (17) has its goal of winning over the addressees' emotions. The epilogue in ancient rhetoric has the function of summarizing and underscoring what has been said previously, with increased pathos. As v. 17 pulls together the preceding argument of the apostle, so in vv. 19–20 the element of pathos is intensified.

Philemon is *not* a private letter, since it is written not only to Philemon but also to the church that meets in his house. As in other letters, Paul appeals here to his apostolic authority. In terms of form criticism,

---

[408] Cf. for example Kümmel, *Introduction* 349; Vielhauer, *Urchristliche Literatur* 173–174; Lohse, *Colossians and Philemon* 188; Stuhlmacher, *Philemonbrief* 20; Gnilka, *Philemonbrief* 6 (a congregation in the Lycus valley). Schenk votes for Pergamon as the location of the addressees, *Philemon* 3843.

[409] Cf. F. F. Church, 'Rhetorical Structure and Design in Paul's Letter to Philemon,' HThR 71 (1978) 17–33; Gnilka, *Philemonbrief* 7–12.

Philemon must be classified as a letter of request (παρακαλῶ in v. 9, 10a, explicit request in v. 17), with elements of a letter of recommendation (cf. Phlm. 10b–13).

2.10.6 Literary Integrity

The literary integrity of Philemon is uncontested.

2.10.7 Traditions, Sources

In this letter Paul integrates no previously-existing traditions.

2.10.8 History-of-religions Standpoint

From the point of view of the history of religions, Philemon is significant as a witness to the stance of early Christianity over against *ancient slavery*.[410] Slavery was a phenomenon that extended throughout the whole ancient world. People became slaves by birth, by being taken captive in war, by being exposed as babies, by selling themselves into slavery, or by kidnapping, and generally spent most of their lives in slavery. The numbers of slaves in antiquity is difficult to estimate; the percentage of the whole population was probably between 25% and 50%. These figures make clear the great economic significance of the institution of slavery in the ancient world. Slavery was really never a disputed issue in antiquity. Both Plato and Aristotle considered slavery to be a necessity on economic grounds. In contrast, Philo stated pointedly ἄνθρωπος γὰρ ἐκ φύσεως δοῦλος οὐδείς (for no one is a slave by nature) (*Special Laws* II 69). Moreover, he reports of the Therapeutai (*Contemplative Life* 70) and the Essenes (*Every Good Man is Free* 79) that they did not know the institution of slavery and/or had no slaves. The Damascus Document, however, is acquainted with prescriptions dealing with slaves (CD 11.11; 12.10ff.), so that the absence of slavery apparently applied to the Qumran community at the Dead Sea. A fundamentally humane attitude toward slaves and slavery is found in Stoic philosophy, where slave-existence is a matter of internal desires rather than external circumstances. Slavery and freedom were conceived exclusively as internal values, since only the right relationship to things makes one truly free (cf. Epictetus, *Diss* 4.4.33; Seneca, *Epistles* 47). So too in ancient

---

[410] As an introduction to the problem, cf. Franz Laub, *Die Begegnung des frühen Christentums mit der antiken Sklaverei*, SBS 107 (Stuttgart: Katholisches Bibelwerk, 1982). All texts relevant to the study of ancient slavery are found in Thomas E. J. Wiedemann, *Greek and Roman Slavery* (Baltimore: Johns Hopkins University Press, 1981); *Sklaven und Freigelassene in der Gesellschaft der römischen Kaiserzeit*, eds. W. Eck and J. Heinrichs (Darmstadt: Wissenschaftliche Buchgesellschaft, 1993).

Judaism, slavery was an unquestioned reality.[411] Slaves are often mentioned in the parables of the synoptic tradition (cf. Mark 12.1–12par; 13.34–35; Matt. 18.23–35; 22.1–14par; 24.45–51par; 25.14–30par; Luke 15.22; Lk 17.7–10). Jesus never said anything with regard to the problematic of slavery as such, although he obviously used the term δοῦλος or its Aramaic equivalent.

In early Christianity, the question of slavery first became a theme in the pre-Pauline and Pauline churches, as shown in the baptismal traditions 1 Cor. 12.13 and Gal. 3.26–28. Baptism cancels basic religious and social distinctions and constitutes the status of believers on a fundamentally new basis (slave/free; Jew/Greek; male/female: in the church all are one 'in Christ' (Gal. 3.28). The model of domination and subjection is dissolved by the practice of brother/sister relationships within the family of God. In the church this Christian freedom draws back from social demonstration, as 1 Cor. 7.21–24 shows. Paul here advises slaves to remain in their present state, even if they have the opportunity to gain their freedom. Paul defines freedom as inner freedom, which has its power and goal in Jesus Christ alone. Social structures are not important for this concept of freedom, since they neither guarantee freedom nor are able to remove bondage. But the preservation of the prevailing law does not exclude the possibility of a fundamental change in the situation of slaves, as the argumentation of Philemon shows.

2.10.9 *Basic Theological Ideas*

At first glance Philemon might give the impression of a theologically insignificant document. This would be an inadequate evaluation, for it is precisely the letter to Philemon that permits us an insight into the characteristic special features of Pauline argumentation. In the proemium (vv. 4–7) Paul is clearly seeking to win Philemon over to his own point of view. He addresses him at the point of his existence as a Christian, suggesting that he do the good that he is able to do (Phlm. 6–7). While to this point he has appealed only to Philemon's own sense of responsibility, in vv. 8–9 he subtly brings his own authority into play. He explicitly emphasizes that he does not want to make any use of his own authority, and refrains from using his apostolic title (Phlm. 8, 8b, 9), but precisely thereby makes the power of his position all the more effective. The real concern of the letter does not become clear until v. 10; Paul pleads for the slave Onesimus, whose master in the legal sense Philemon was and is. The central theologi-

---

[411] Cf. Billerbeck IV 698–744.

cal motif of the letter appears in v. 11: the conversion of Onesimus not only has consequences for himself, but also for the relationship of the slave Onesimus to his master Philemon. Philemon is to recognize and accept the new status of the slave Onesimus as a beloved brother καὶ ἐν σαρκὶ καὶ ἐν κυρίῳ (both in the flesh and in the Lord) (Phlm. 16). The apostle thereby encourages Philemon to break through the social structure of the ancient household and to acknowledge Onesimus has having a new social status as a beloved brother even as he continues in the same legal status.[412] By explicitly identifying with Onesimus (Phlm. 12, 16, 17–20), Paul clarifies for Philemon what the new situation means. Philemon is to learn from his relationship to Paul how he should configure his new relationship to Onesimus. When Paul, in accord with the civil law but contrary to Deut 23.16 (!) sends Onesimus back to his master (Phlm. 12, 14), a part of Paul himself comes to Philemon. The real goal of Paul's argument becomes clear in v. 13: He would like for Onesimus to remain with him, to assist him in his work of proclaiming the gospel. Paul will not avail himself of this service of Onesimus without the voluntary agreement of Philemon (v. 14), which, however, he de facto presupposes (v. 21). To be sure, Paul hopes to be able to visit Philemon soon himself (v. 22), but this does not make the present and future service of Onesimus superfluous. According to the witness of Philemon, Christian freedom does not accomplish the abolition of social structures, but is concretely realized within the sphere of the Christian community.

The Letter to Philemon allows us to see something of the early Christian organizational form of the *house church*.[413] The household, which was also the central location of religious life, had a long tradition in antiquity. Not only the Jewish house synagogue, but also private cultic associations, mystery circles, and philosophical schools in the immediate environs of Christian congregations testify to the integrative and missionary force of this form of religious organization. Philemon is not the only document that testifies to the existence of early Christian house churches. The married couple Prisca and Aquila founded house churches in both Ephesus (cf. 1 Cor. 16.19–20) and Rome (cf. Rom. 16.3–5). House churches formed around Stephanas (cf. 1 Cor. 16.15) and Gaius (cf. Rom. 16.23). So too the greetings in Rom. 16.14–15 indicate there were several house churches in Rome, with others being mentioned in Col. 4.15 and Acts 12.12; 18.7. The house church was an especially appropriate setting for the practice of a communal Christian life in the midst of a partially hostile environment.

---

[412] Cf. Wolter, *Philemonbrief* 233–234.

[413] In addition to Klauck, *Hausgemeinde und Hauskirche im frühen Christentum* (see above 2.8.4), see especially the commentaries of P. Stuhlmacher and J. Gnilka.

Here the community joined in prayer (cf. Acts 12.12), the word was proclaimed (cf. Acts 16.32; 20.20), baptism and the eucharist were celebrated, and missionaries were provided with lodging (cf. Acts 16.15). 1 Corinthians 14.23 documents congregational meetings in a house, and Paul's letters were read aloud in house churches (cf. 1 Thess. 5.27; further Col. 4.16). The house church was a center of early Christian mission, permitting a relatively undisturbed practice of religious life and made possible an efficient competition to the synagogue congregations and ancient cultic associations. Finally, the house church offered the setting in which ancient traditional understandings of the world and society could be broken through and the new existence in Christ lived out in practice.

2.10.10 *Tendencies of Recent Research*

One focus of the recent discussion concerns the legal issue raised by Philemon: was Onesimus a runaway slave or was he only absent from the household of Philemon for a brief period in order to seek out Paul's advocacy in a household conflict. Will Onesimus have to count on punishment for larceny, or does a dispute that does not fall in the legal category determine the way matters will develop in the future life of the slave? M. Wolter interprets the letter to Philemon within the context of the social structure of the ancient household: 'Philemon is to see precisely in the slave Onesimus his Christian brother (vv. 15–16), indeed without the radicality of this demand being mitigated by a change in his legal status in which he is granted his freedom.'[414]

The name Onesimus is also mentioned in Col. 4.9. There it is said that Paul will send the loyal and dear Onesimus to Colossae. If this is the same person as in Philemon, it can be inferred that Philemon not only forgave his slave Onesimus, but also set him free to serve Paul personally and within the framework of the Pauline mission. P. Stuhlmacher affirms this, and infers even beyond this that the Bishop Onesimus of Ephesus mentioned three times by Ignatius (IgnEph. 1.3; 2.1; 6.2) is identical with the slave Onesimus of Philemon.[415] This hypothesis is rejected by, among others, E. Lohse and J. Gnilka,[416] who rightly see no compelling argument for such an extensive hypothesis in the mere fact of identical names. It also continues to be disputed among scholars, whether Paul called for the freeing of Onesimus or (only) challenged Philemon to receive his slave as one who is now a beloved brother in Christ.

---

[414] Wolter, *Philemonbrief* 233–234.
[415] Cf. Stuhlmacher, *Philemonbrief 18*, 57.
[416] Cf. Lohse, *Colossians and Philemon* 186; Gnilka, *Philemonbrief* 6.

3

The Synoptic Gospels

3.1 The Gospel Genre

3.1.1 Literature

Bultmann, Rudolf. *The History of the Synoptic Tradition*, tr. John Marsh. New York & Evanston: Harper & Row, 1963; Dibelius, Martin. *From Tradition to Gospel*, tr. Bertram Lee Woolf. New York: Charles Scribner's Sons, n. d; Talbert, Charles. *What is a Gospel?* Philadelphia: Fortress Press, 1977; Schmidt, Karl Ludwig. 'Die Stellung der Evangelien in der allgemeinen Literaturgeschichte,' in *Neues Testament-Judentum-Kirche*, ed. K. L. Schmidt. TB 69. Munich: Kaiser 1981 (=1923) 37–130; Strecker, Georg. 'εὐαγγέλιον.' *Exegetical Dictionary of the New Testament* II, eds. Horst Balz and Gerhard Schneider. Grand Rapids: Wm. B. Eerdmans, 1982, 170–74; Dihle, Albrecht. 'Das Evangelium und die biographischen Traditionen der Antike,' ZThK 80 (1983) 33–49; Cancik, Hubert, 'Die Gattung Evangelium', in *Markus-Philologie*, ed. Hubert Cancik. WUNT 33. Tübingen: J. C. B. Mohr (Paul Siebeck), 1984, 85–113; Reiser, Marius. 'Der Alexanderroman und das Markusevangelium,' in *Markus-Philologie* ed. Hubert Cancik. WUNT 33. Tübingen: J. C. B. Mohr (Paul Siebeck), 1984, 131–165; Aune, David E. 'Greco-Roman Biography,' in *Greco-Roman Literature and the New Testament*, ed. David E. Aune. Atlanta: Scholars Press, 1988, 107–126; Hock, Ronald F. 'The Greek Novel,' in *Greco-Roman Literature and the New Testament*, ed. David E. Aune. Atlanta: Scholars Press, 1988, 127–146; Frankemölle, Hubert. *Evangelium. Begriff und Gattung*. SBB 15. Stuttgart: Katholisches Bibelwerk, 1988; Dormeyer, Detlev. *Evangelium als literarische und theologische Gattung*. Darmstadt: Wissenschaftliche Buchgesellschaft, 1989; Koester, Helmut. *Ancient Christian Gospels*. London/Philadelphia: Trinity Press International, 1990; Stuhlmacher, Peter, ed. *The Gospel and the Gospels*. Grand Rapids: Wm. B. Eerdmans, 1991; Theißen, Gerd. *The Gospels in Context*, tr. Linda M. Maloney. Minneapolis: Fortress Press, 1991; Strecker, Georg. *Literaturgeschichte* (1992; see above 1.2) 122–148; Burridge, Richard A. *What are the Gospels? A Comparison with Graeco-Roman Biography*, SNTSMS 70. Cambridge: Cambridge University Press, 1992.

3.1.2 The Concept 'Gospel'

The substantive εὐαγγέλιον (usually translated 'gospel') originally signified not a literary genre, but the good news of Jesus Christ. In Paul εὐαγγέλιον appears as an unliterary concept that has as its content the saving message mediated through the living, spoken word. The pre-Pauline understanding of εὐαγγέλιον is reflected in the traditions of 1 Thess. 1.9b–10; 1 Cor. 15.3b–5; Rom. 1.3b–4a. Paul here unites individual units of traditions that had been handed on to him with the absolute use of the term εὐαγγέλιον (cf. 1 Thess. 1.5; 1 Cor. 15.1; Rom. 1.1, 9) and pre-supposes that this terminology is familiar to his hearers/readers. The filling of the term 'gospel' with christological-soteriological content that is dominant in Paul also goes back to the early Christian pre-Pauline Hellenistic churches. With regard to its origin and authority, the gospel is the εὐαγγέλιον τοῦ θεοῦ ('gospel of God') (cf. 1 Thess. 2.2, 8, 9; 2 Cor. 11.7; Rom. 1.1; 15.16), while with regard to its content it is the εὐαγγέλιον τοῦ Χριστοῦ ('gospel of Jesus Christ;' cf. 1 Thess. 3.2; 1 Cor. 9.12; 2 Cor. 2.12; 9.13; 10.14; Gal. 1.7; Rom. 15.19; Phil. 1.27).

The history-of-religions background of the early Christian missionary term 'gospel' is disputed. While P. Stuhlmacher advocates a derivation from the Semitic-Palestinian linguistic field and sees Matt. 11.2–6 and Rev. 14.6; 10.7 as belonging to the earliest stratum of the tradition,[1] G. Strecker sees the primary history-of-tradition background of the term to be the use of εὐαγγέλιον in the penumbra of the Caesar cult.[2] Stuhlmacher can point especially to the verb εὐαγγελίζομαι (to proclaim good news), whose linguistic history reveals a predominantly Old Testament-Jewish background. It appears in the LXX as well as in the writings of ancient Judaism and must be translated as 'to announce eschatological salvation.' To be sure, εὐαγγελίζομαι also appears in Hellenistic literature in a religious sense (cf. Philostratus, *Life of Apollonius* 1.28; Philo *Embassy to Gaius* 18, 231). The following arguments speak in favor of Strecker's view: (1) The substantive εὐαγγέλιον appears in the LXX without theological meaning (cf. 2 Kings 4.10; 18.22, 25). (2) Along with instances in the inscriptions,[3] especially Philo (*Embassy to Gaius* 18, 99, 231) and Josephus (*Jewish War* 4. 618, 656) document the use of εὐαγγέλιον in the context of Hellenistic emperor worship. Significant in this regard is the connection made by Josephus between εὐαγγέλια, the elevation of Vespasian to emperor, and the presentation of offerings. (3) Probably εὐαγγέλιον, εὐαγγελίζομαι or their Hebrew/Aramaic equivalents were not elements of the preaching of the historical Jesus, for the quotation from Isa 61.1 LXX in Matt. 11.5/ Luke 7.22 already presupposes a post-Easter Christology.[4]

[1] Cf. Peter Stuhlmacher, *Das paulinische Evangelium I. Vorgeschichte*, FRLANT 95 (Göttingen: Vandenhoeck & Ruprecht, 1968) 218ff.

[2] Cf. Georg Strecker, 'Das Evangelium Jesu Christi,' in *Eschaton und Historie*, ed. G. Strecker (Göttingen: Vandenhoeck & Ruprecht, 1979) 183–228.

[3] Cf. *ibid.* 189ff.

[4] Cf. the evidence in Migaku Sato, *Q und Prophetie* (see below 3.3.1) 141–144.

If the traditional roots of the New Testament concept εὐαγγέλιον lie in the Hellenistic ruler cult, then the early Christian communities adopted a term current in their context, while at the same time distinguishing their own usage by the singular τὸ εὐαγγέλιον over against the plural τὰ εὐαγγέλια typical of their Hellenistic environment.

3.1.3 The Literary Genre 'Gospel'

How did it happen that the unliterary term εὐαγγέλιον became the designation for the macro-genre 'gospel?' The evangelist Mark created this new genre, so that his historical and theological insights associated with his concept of the gospel can also give us information about the origination of the gospel genre as a distinct literary form. All seven instances of εὐαγγέλιον come from the redactional hand of the evangelist (cf. Mark 1.1, 14–15; 8.35; 10.29; 13.10; 14.9).[5] If prior to Mark εὐαγγέλιον was always understood as the preaching about Jesus Christ, such that an objective genitive Ἰησοῦ Χριστοῦ was to be supplied, a fundamental transformation is now manifest. In Mark 1.1 Jesus Christ is at one and the same time both the proclaimer and the content of the gospel, with the genitive Ἰησοῦ Χριστοῦ expressing both the subject and the object of the gospel.[6] The correspondence between Mark 1.1 and Mark 1.14–15 makes clear that for Mark the Jesus proclaimed in the gospel is at the same time himself the proclaimer of the gospel. The pre-Easter εὐαγγέλιον τοῦ θεοῦ (gospel of God, Mark 1.14) has now become the εὐαγγέλιον Ἰησοῦ Χριστοῦ (gospel of Jesus Christ, Mark 1.1), in such wise that for Mark the theo-logical proclamation of Jesus and the christological confession of the church are not opposed to each other. The deeds and words of Jesus Christ are the content of the gospel, while at the same time for Mark Jesus Christ is not merely a figure of past history, but the crucified and risen Son of God and therefore also the speaking subject in the gospel. Mark underscores the representation of the gospel through Jesus and the representation of Jesus in the gospel by the addition of 'and for the sake of the gospel' to 'for my sake' in Mark 8.35 and 10.29. The evangelist thereby binds the past and present works of Jesus Christ inseparably to the gospel as both proclaimed

---

[5] Evidence in Georg Strecker, 'Literarkritische Überlegungen zum εὐαγγέλιον-Begriff im Markusevangelium,' in *Eschaton und Historie*, ed. G. Strecker (Göttingen: Vandenhoeck & Ruprecht, 1979) 76–89.

[6] Cf. Joachim Gnilka, *Markus* I (see below 3.4.1) 43. Contra Hans Weder, '"Evangelium Jesu Christi" (Mk 1,1) und "Evangelium Gottes" (Mk 1,14),' in *Die Mitte des Neuen Testaments*, eds. Ulrich Luz and Hans Weder (FS Eduard Schweizer) (Göttingen: Vandenhoeck & Ruprecht, 1983) 399–411, who prefers to understand Mark 1.1 only as objective genitive (402). Cf. M. Eugene Boring, 'Mark 1.1–15 and the Beginning of the Gospel,' *Semeia* 52 (1990) 33ff.

message and literary genre. At the same time the internal and external textual levels that are constitutive for the gospel genre are fused into each other. The call to decision announced by Jesus on the internal level of the Markan text points to the level of the Markan church exterior to the text, making the Jesus Christ of the gospel accessible and present to the church.

By presenting in his gospel the earthly way of Jesus the Son of God, Mark takes up a tendency already discernible in 1 Cor. 15.3b–5: the confession of the crucified and risen Jesus Christ is not possible apart from the fundamental union with the way of the earthly Jesus. The earthly way of Jesus is, however, at the same time the way of the Son of God, for this Jesus is equally in union with heaven and earth, so that his story is both heavenly and earthly. Mark makes this fundamental connection clear by the narrative of Jesus' baptism (Mark 1.9–11), the story of the transfiguration (Mark 9.2–9) and the confession of the centurion under the cross (Mark 15.39). These three texts form the basic compositional framework of the gospel, in that in each case they present heavenly and earthly figures, and that each time Jesus' belonging to the divine world is expressed by the use of the title υἱός (son). Baptism, transfiguration, and confession under the cross are the three foundational pillars around which Mark groups his traditions in the form of a *vita Iesou*.

The title υἱός thus designates the central element of Mark's material, for by it Mark is able equally to express both Jesus' divinity and his giving himself over to his destiny of suffering and death. Jesus' being and essential nature are firmly fixed from the beginning: he is God's son and does not change his essential nature. But for human beings it is a matter of his first *becoming* God's son, for they need a process of recognition.[7] This process is the *vita Iesou*, as presented by Mark in the new literary genre of the gospel. This recognition process reaches its goal only at the end of the gospel, at the cross, for it is here that for the first time a human being, not God, recognizes and confesses Jesus as υἱὸς θεοῦ (Son of God, 15.39). This is knowledge previously shared only by God (Mark 1.11; 9.7), the demons (Mark 3.11; 5.7), and the Son himself (Mark 12.6; 13.32). A human being must first stride through the whole life of Jesus from baptism to cross in order to attain a legitimate recognition of the divine sonship of Jesus. In that the literary genre 'gospel' sets forth this way of the Son of God with the intention of leading the reader to a right understanding of his person, it is nothing other than the *literary expression* of the *theological recognition* that the crucified Jesus of Nazareth went his way from the very beginning

---

[7] Cf. R. Weber, *Christologie und 'Messiasgeheimnis'* (see below 3.4.1) 115–116.

as the divine Son of God.[8] The literary genre 'gospel' is thus a form *sui generis* that owes its being to the theological insight that in the once for all and irreplaceable history of Jesus of Nazareth God himself was present and active. There is thus for Mark no tension between pre- and post-Easter, history and kerygma, or the internal and external levels on which the text is presented and understood, but his theological accomplishment consists precisely in the fact of having resolutely understood and presented each pair as an inseparable unity.[9] By firmly holding together historiographical-biographical narrative text and kerygmatic address and presenting Jesus' way to the cross as dramatic event, he preserves what he regards as the historical and theological identity of Christian faith.

The theological intentions at work in the generation of the gospel form and writing the gospel were formed within a framework of historical conditions. The pre-Markan collections and the passion stories testify to the tendency within the material itself to form larger complexes, and Luke 1.1 confirms that there were preliminary stages of gospel writing. Mark as the creator of the gospel form thus stands within a process that was already underway before him. Besides, a new orientation to time and history is called for by the fading expectation of the imminent parousia, the variety of theological streams emergent in first-century Christianity, and the concrete questions of Christian ethics. The evangelists meet these challenges especially by the taking up of salvation-historical traditions, the working out of practical ethical norms, and the introduction of offices into the community charged with order and instruction. The tendencies toward historicizing, ethicizing, and institutionalizing of the traditional material are obvious in Matthew and Luke, but can also be clearly discerned in the Gospel of Mark. Thus the literary character of the Gospels corresponds to their function within the life of the church as the foundation for preaching and their use in worship and instruction.

3.1.4 The Place of the 'Gospel' Genre in the History of Literature

Even though the literary genre 'gospel' owes its existence primarily to a theological insight, this does not yet answer the question of whether and how the evangelists may also have oriented their work in the conception

---

[8] The declaration of Hans Conzelmann regarding Mark's Messianic secret is thus still fundamentally appropriate, that 'the secrecy theory is the hermeneutical presupposition of the genre "Gospel",' in 'Present and Future in the Synoptic Tradition,' *Journal for Theology and Church* 5, ed. Robert W. Funk (New York: Harper & Row, 1968) 26–44

[9] On this point cf. H .F. Weiß, *Kerygma und Geschichte* (Berlin: Evangelische Verlagsanstalt, 1983).

of their gospels to the forms of secular or religious literature of their times.[10]

The classification of the gospel as a distinct literary genre inaugurated by Franz Overbeck (1837–1905) was hesitant to see lines of connection to general literary history, or rejected them altogether. The literature of earliest Christianity 'is a literature, which Christianity so to speak created from its own means, to the extent that it developed exclusively on the native soil and for the internal interests of the Christian community prior to its becoming mixed with the surrounding world.'[11] Overbeck supposed that the literature of earliest Christianity developed at some distance from the secular literature of its time. The work of the earliest form critics adopted this judgment, in that they emphasized the special status of the macro-genre 'gospel' from the perspective of the sociology of literature. According to M. Dibelius the Synoptic Gospels are to be counted as *Kleinliteratur* (minor literature). Their 'composers are only to the smallest extent authors. They are principally collectors, vehicles of tradition, editors.'[12] Even if John and Luke in Acts can be regarded as somewhat literary authors, this is not the case particularly for Mark. Karl Ludwig Schmidt formulated the point programatically in his influential study of the place of the gospels in general literary history: 'The gospel is by nature not truly a *Hochliteratur* (literary work), but *Kleinliteratur* (minor literature), not a matter of individual literary achievement, but a folk-book, not biography, but cult legend.'[13] Originally isolated units of tradition or sequences of sayings and pericopes were gathered, joined to kerygmatic traditions and interpretations, and recast in a new form. The process was more unconscious than an intentional transformation. Since the New Testament gospels originated in this way, it is impossible to compare them with the categories of contemporary Hellenistic literature.

Redaction criticism, which came into its own after 1945,[14] modified this picture considerably. In contrast to classical form criticism the evangelists

---

[10] For detailed histories of the investigation of the problem, in addition to the standard works of Frankemölle and Dormeyer cf. especially W. S. Vorster, 'Der Ort der Gattung Evangelium in der Literaturgeschichte,' VuF 29 (1984) 2–25; David Aune, *The New Testament in Its Literary Environment* (see above 2.3.1) 17–45; and Folkert Fendler, *Studien zum Markusevangelium* (see below 3.4.1) 14–35.

[11] Franz Overbeck, *Über die Anfänge der patristischen Literatur* (Darmstadt: Wissenschaftliche Buchgesellschaft, 1954, (= 1882) 36.

[12] Martin Dibelius, *Tradition to Gospel* 3. While Rudolf Bultmann evaluates the authorial and compositional work of the evangelists higher than does Dibelius, he remains basically within this explanatory paradigm. Cf. Bultmann, *History of the Synoptic Tradition* 368–374.

[13] Karl Ludwig Schmidt, 'Die Stellung der Evangelien' 66–67.

[14] For a history of this methodological approach, cf. Joachim Rohde, *Rediscovering the Teaching of the Evangelists* (London: SCM Press, 1968).

were no longer regarded as mere tradents and collectors, but as authors who intentionally composed their writings to express their theology. The present form of the gospels does not go back to an immanent growth process; the gospels owe their literary and theological form to the evangelists. The goal of redaction criticism is to make apparent the historical and theological standpoint of the evangelist. Redaction criticism worked out the understanding of history that had been a constituent element of composing the gospels, which in Matthew and Luke can be characterized as a periodizing of (salvation-) history. Mark's understanding of history[15] is portrayed as the integration of historical and kerygmatic traditions and their redactional interpretation, in which the (awareness of the) significance of the advent of Jesus in the past is determinative for the present. A weakness of many redaction-critical works is that they see the achievement of the evangelists as exponents of their communities primarily on the theological plane, and neglect their literary activity, including their relation to possible parallels in ancient literature. This neglect has provided the opportunity for recent investigations in linguistics, the history of religions and literary history.

Parallels from ancient literature have always been advanced for the explanation of the new literary genre 'gospel.'[16] After redaction criticism had demonstrated the theological independence of the evangelists, there need be no hesitation about investigating their literary products from the perspective of possible parallels in ancient literature. From the realm of Semitic literature the following explanatory models (among others) were considered:

(1) *Old Testament ideal biography*. In this genre worked out by Klaus Baltzer,[17] the ideal traits of towering figures of the Old Testaments (kings, prophets) are taken over, with the following topoi considered as typical: report of their inauguration into office, the securing of internal and external peace, the establishment of social justice in all important realms of life, the purity of the cult. Baltzer sees the Gospel of Mark as well as the later gospels as standing in the tradition of the Old Testament ideal biographies. As evidence he can especially point to the parallels in the inauguration into office (Mark 1.9–11), the miracle tradition (Elijah-Elisha cycle of tradition), and the resolution of legal and practical issues in the

---

[15] Cf. here James M. Robinson, *The Problem of History in Mark and Other Markan Studies* (see below 3.4.1) 5–104; Jürgen Roloff, 'Das Markusevangelium als Geschichtsdarstellung,' EvTh 29 (1969) 73–93.

[16] Cf. among others Johannes Weiß, *Das älteste Evangelium* (Göttingen: Vandenhoeck & Ruprecht, 1903); Hermann v. Soden, *Urchristliche Literaturgeschichte* (Berlin, 1905); Clyde W. Votaw, *Gospels and Contemporary Biographies in the Greco-Roman World* (Philadelphia: Fortress Press, 1970² = 1915).

[17] Cf. Klaus Baltzer, *Die Biographie der Propheten* (Neukirchen: Neukirchener Verlag, 1975).

conflict stories. On the other hand, the extensive Markan passion story cannot be integrated into this genre. In addition, the evangelists portray Jesus neither as a returned Moses or Elijah, nor as a Davidic king, with the result that the appeal to Old Testament motifs to explain the macro-genre 'gospel' is inadequate.

(2) *Biography of the righteous one.* D. Lührmann[18] took up the thesis of Baltzer and modified it: the background of the Gospel of Mark is not the biography of the prophets, but the biography of the (suffering) righteous man. Lührmann finds the motif of the suffering righteous one especially in Wis 2.12–20, and supposes that Mark took up elements of the tradition of the suffering servant of Yahweh as well as elements from the passion Psalms under the influence of the tradition of the suffering righteous one (cf. Ps 22 in Mark 15). Mark presents the story of Jesus as the life of a righteous man who must suffer. He thereby created for his readers the possibility of identifying with Jesus by finding their own story in the story of Jesus. This model does explain central elements of the passion story and related texts, but not the gospel genre with its narrative substructure.

From the broad spectrum of possible Hellenistic parallels to the gospel genre, the following have emerged as significant in recent research:

(1) *Aretalogy.* Particularly in North American research (J. M. Robinson, H. Koester, M. Smith, P. J. Achtemeier and others) the attempt has been made to understand the gospel form in terms of aretalogy (= a biographical writing that treats the wonders of a 'divine man'). Thus H. Koester supposes that independently of each other Mark and John integrated collections of aretalogical miracle stories into their writings and structured the new genre on this basis.[19] To be sure, the term 'aretalogy' as the designation for a macro-genre is very disputed, for in classical philology aretalogy describes not the form, 'but the content and the purpose of very different literary genres.'[20] Aretalogical motifs are found in hymns, letters, dedicatory inscriptions, and novels, so that 'one can by no means speak of an established literary genre.'[21] Thus the attempt to relate the New Testament gospels to the concept 'aretalogy' in the sense of a firm form-critical literary genre should be abandoned.

---

[18] Cf. Dieter Lührmann, 'Biographie des Gerechten als Evangelium,' WuD 14 (1976) 25–50.

[19] Cf. Helmut Koester, 'One Jesus and Four Primitive Gospels,' in James M. Robinson and Helmut Koester, *Trajectories through Early Christianity* (Philadelphia: Fortress Press, 1971) 158–204; Helmut Koester, 'Formgeschichte/Formenkritik' II, *TRE* 11 (1983) (286–299) 295.

[20] Ph. Vielhauer, *Urchristliche Literatur* 310, in conjunction with D. Esser, *Formgeschichtliche Studien zur hellenistischen und frühchristlichen Literatur unter besonderer Berücksichtigung der vita Apollonii des Philostrat und der Evangelien*, Diss. theol., Bonn 1969, 98ff. Cf. Carl R Holladay, *Theios Aner in Hellenistic-Judaism: A Critique of the Use of This Category in New Testament Christology*, SBLD.S.40. Missoula, MT: Scholars Press, 1977.

[21] Esser, *ibid.* 101.

(2) *Greek novel.* M. Reiser derives the gospel genre from the Greek novel. 'In more than one regard the Alexander novel perhaps forms the closest analogy to the Gospels. This is indicated not only by the results of tradition criticism and redaction criticism, but much that is comparable is also presented by composition and narrative techniques, as well as language and style. And since the content, the manner in which sources are used, and the manner of presentation as a whole show great similarities, the Alexander novel presents the closest parallel to the Gospel genre.'[22] Reiser counts both the Gospels and the Alexander novel as belonging to Hellenistic folk literature, and locates them on the fluid boundary that separates unliterary works from real literature. Nonetheless, the Alexander novel is distinct from the Gospels in a two-fold manner: 1. There are no miracle stories in the Alexander novel. 2. In contrast to the Gospels, legends and fairy-tale motifs do play a great role in the Alexander novel.

(3) *Hellenistic biography.* In the most recent research once again the ancient Hellenistic biography is regarded as a possible model for the kind of text represented by the Gospels. In his debate with R. Bultmann,[23] C. H. Talbert shows that both ancient biographies and the New Testament Gospels have a mythical character, can be understood as cult legends, and display world-negating characteristics. As in the Gospels, so too in ancient biographies, traditions were taken up that were foreign to their authors but which received a new interpretation by being incorporated into the work as a whole. Talbert names as a common goal of the Gospels and ancient biography the intention to correct an erroneous picture of a departed teacher, in order to replace it with a more appropriate understanding and to present a model of the teacher's life and work for imitation by his disciples. Classifying the Gospels in the genre of Hellenistic biography is meaningful, since for the gospel genre too a historigraphical and biographical interest is constitutive, a message is enclosed within the framework of a chronological course of events. Over against these formal similarities, however, stand differences in content, for in ancient biography it is a matter of representing possibilities of human existence to be evaluated morally, while the Gospels present the way of the Son of God from baptism in the Jordan to the cross on Golgotha and the appearance of the resurrected one.

The continuity between oral and written tradition, a fundamental assumption on which both form criticism and redaction criticism were based, was

---

[22] Reiser, 'Der Alexanderroman und das Markusevangelium' 131.

[23] Bultmann's view was that the history of Greek literature provided no analogies to the form of the Gospels, *History of the Synoptic Tradition* 371–372.

called in question by E. Güttgemanns.[24] A new written project such as the gospel genre may not be explained simply on the basis of its parts. Rather, the previous oral traditions experience a qualitative change when they are incorporated in the new written macro-genre 'Gospel.' They lose their character as oral tradition and receive now in the realm of written materials a new independent form and function. The Gospel did not arise automatically out of the kerygma, but was rather the work of an individual and of an autosemantic linguistic form. Güttgemanns rightly shows the problematic nature of the relation orality/ written form as it had been understood in the older scholarship, but fails to make a convincing case against the possibility that illumination of written texts may be provided by analysis of their oral antecedents. It is rather the case that it is precisely the insight into the oral tradition phase, as uncertain as this may be in details, that facilitates a better understanding of the distinctive literary character of New Testament texts and the manner in which units of tradition received their characteristic form of expression at various phases in the tradition process.[25] The gospel genre emerged as a distinctively new text type, the final product of a process of tradition and redactional composition, but the kind of thing it turned out to be can hardly be understood apart from the process by which it came to be. The present compositional form of the Gospels and therefore the kind of composition represented by a Gospel as such can then only be adequately understood when the historical course of formation of the individual textual units is worked out, i.e. when diachronic and synchronic perspectives are conceived not as alternatives, but when their interdependent relationship is grasped.[26]

A mono-causal explanation of the Gospel genre in terms of the history of literature is not possible. Among the comparable types of texts in the Hellenistic world, the Hellenistic biography stands closest to that of the Gospel genre.[27] The combination of historiographical and biographical

---

[24] Cf. Erhardt Güttgemanns, *Candid Questions Concerning Gospel Form Criticism* (Pittsburgh: Pickwick, 1979).

[25] On this issue cf. Georg Strecker, 'Schriftlichkeit oder Mündlichkeit der synoptischen Tradition?,' in *The Four Gospels*, ed. F. Van Segbroeck et al., (FS F. Neirynck) BETL 100. (Leuven: Leuven University Press, 1992) 159–172.

[26] Cf. Eugenio Coseriu, *Synchronie, Diachronie und Geschichte* (Munich: Fink, 1974).

[27] Among recent scholars who adopt this interpretation are Klaus Berger, *Formgeschichte des Neuen Testaments* (see above 2.8.5) 367–371; Aune, *The New Testament in Its Literary Environment* (see above 2.3.4) 64 (Gospel as a sub-genre of ancient biography); Ludger Schenke, *Markusevangelium* (see below 3.4.1) 146; Philip L. Shuler, 'The Genre(s) of the Gospels,' in *The Interrelations of the Gospels* (see below 3.2.1) 459–483 (Gospel as 'encomium biography'); Fendler, *Studien* (see below 3.4.1) 80 (the Gospel of Mark as a special form of ancient biography, 'anonymous biography'); Detlev Dormeyer, *Das Neue Testament im Rahmen der antiken Literaturgeschichte* (see above 2.3.2) 199–228 (the Gospels as 'kerygmatic ideal biographies'); Burridge. *What are the Gospels?* ('The genre of the form canonical gospels is to be found in βίος literature.' 254).

declarations with kerygmatic intent is also found in the Gospels. Characteristic for the Gospel form is the *interweaving of narrative text and kerygmatic address* in which a narrative substructure[28] is combined with biographical, historiographical, dramatic,[29] and kerygmatic elements. However, the Gospels do take a distinctive place within ancient literature on the grounds of their content: only they declare that in a concrete and limited event of the past, a decisive turn has been made in history so that now both present and future are determined by this event. In this respect the Gospel is in fact sui generis, and cannot be incorporated as a subgenre into any higher category.

In the first half of the second century the word εὐαγγέλιον also became the designation of a book (cf. Did 11.3; 15.3–4;[30] 2 Clem. 8.5; Justin Apology I.66.3). At about this same time the titles of the Gospels were added, in which εὐαγγέλιον undoubtedly refers to a book. M. Hengel dates these titles in the time between 70 and 100 CE. He does not claim that the evangelists themselves used the word εὐαγγέλιον in the literary sense, but that as soon as the first Gospels were copied and distributed in other churches, the titles would have come into being as their designations, since it would have been necessary to distinguish one Gospel from another by their titles. These titles 'with a considerable degree of probability can be traced back to the time of origin of the four Gospels between 69 and 100, and are connected with their circulation in the communities.'[31]

3.2 The Synoptic Problem

3.2.1 *Literature*

Holtzmann, Heinrich Julius. *Die synoptischen Evangelien*. Leipzig: W. Engelmann, 1863; Wernle, Paul. *Die synoptische Frage*. Freiburg i. Br.: J. C. B. Mohr (Paul

---

[28] Cilliers Breytenbach, 'Das Markusevangelium als episodische Erzählung,' in *Erzähler des Evangeliums*, ed. Ferdinand Hahn (see below 3.4.1) 137–169, evaluates the Gospel of Mark as an 'episodic' narrative, in which the global themes recur repeatedly in the individual pericopes. On the narrative substructure of the oldest Gospel cf. also Reinhold Zwick, *Montage im Markusevangelium. Studien zur narrativen Organisation der ältesten Jesuserzählung*, SBB 18 (Stuttgart: Katholisches Bibelwerk, 1989), who sees the distinctiveness of the narrative technique of the evangelist in a specific system 'of placing things in a spatial perspective and montages of spatial elements' (*ibid.* 620).

[29] On this cf. F. G. Lang, 'Kompositionsanalyse des Markusevangeliums,' ZThK 74 (1977) 1–24, who comes to the conclusion 'that Mark has consciously composed his Gospel in analogy to an ancient drama' (*ibid.* 22).

[30] According to Klaus Wengst, *Schriften des Urchristentums* II (Darmstadt: Wissenschaftliche Buchgesellschaft, 1984) 24ff., εὐαγγέλιον in such cases refers to the Gospel of Matthew.

[31] Martin Hengel, 'The Titles of the Gospels and the Gospel of Mark,' *Studies in the Gospel of Mark*, tr. John Bowden (Philadelphia: Fortress Press, 1985) 84.

Siebeck), 1899; Streeter, B. H. *The Four Gospels*. London: Macmillan, 1924; Schmid, Josef. *Matthäus und Lukas*. BSt 23.2–4. Freiburg i. Br: Herder, 1930; Farmer, William R. *The Synoptic Problem*. London: Macmillan, 1964; Fuchs, Albert. *Sprachliche Untersuchungen zu Matthäus und Lukas*, AnBibl 49. Rome: Biblical Institute Press, 1971; Tuckett, C. M. *The Revival of the Griesbach Hypothesis*, SNTSMS 44. Cambridge: Cambridge University Press, 1983; Bellinzoni, Arthur J. *The Two-Source Hypothesis. A Critical Appraisal*. Macon: Mercer University Press, 1985; Schmithals, Walter. *Einleitung in die drei ersten Evangelien*. Berlin: Walter de Gruyter, 1985; Stoldt, Hans H. *The History and Criticism of the Marcan Hypothesis*. Macon: Mercer University Press, 1987; Dungan, David L., ed. *The Interrelations of the Gospels*. BETL XCV. Leuven: Leuven University Press, 1990 (important collection of essays); Neirynck, Frans. *Evangelica* II, BETL XCIX. Leuven: Leuven University Press, 1991; Strecker, Georg, ed. *Minor Agreements*, GTA 50. Göttingen: Vandenhoeck & Ruprecht, 1993 (important collection of essays).

3.2.2 The History of the Synoptic Problem

So long as the authors of the Gospels were considered eyewitnesses of the life of Jesus and the traditions from the ancient church were uncritically accepted, the differences between the Gospels were problematic for only a few.[32] Only Augustine was concerned with the literary interdependence of the Gospels and in his writing *De consensu evangelistarum* 4.10–11 set forth the thesis that the Gospels originated in their canonical order (cf. 3.2.6 below). The real investigation of the Synoptic Problem did not begin until the second half of the eighteenth century. Of the numerous hypotheses that emerged, four are worthy of particular note.[33]

1. The Original Gospel Hypothesis

Here the fundamental thesis is that all three Synoptic Gospels are derived from an original gospel composed in Hebrew or Aramaic that contained the whole life of Jesus. Thus Gotthold Ephraim Lessing (1729–1784)[34] supposed that the Synoptic Gospels are independent of each other, but all

---

[32] Cf. Helmut, Merkel, *Die Widersprüche zwischen den Evangelien. Ihre polemische und apologetische Behandlung in der Alten Kirche bis zu Augustinus*, WUNT 13 (Tübingen: J. C. B Mohr [Paul Siebeck], 1971). The primary sources are reproduced in Helmut Merkel, *Die Pluralität der Evangelien als theologisches und exegetisches Problem in der Alten Kirche*, TC III (Bern 1978). English translation available in Schaff, Philip, ed. *A Select Library of the Nicene and Post-Nicene Fathers of The Christian Church*. First Series. Volume VI. *Saint Augustine: Sermon on the Mount, Harmony of the Gospels, and Homilies on the Gospels* (Grand Rapids: Wm. B. Eerdmans Publishing Co., 1979).

[33] On the history of the individual hypotheses, cf. especially Walter Schmithals, *Einleitung* 44–233.

[34] Cf. Gotthold E. Lessing, *Thesen aus der Kirchengeschichte* (1776); *Neue Hypothese über die Evangelisten als bloß menschliche Geschichtsschreiber betrachtet* (1778).

developed from an Aramaic 'Gospel of the Nazarenes' that goes back to the apostles. According to Lessing, this original document was mentioned by the Church Fathers by different names, 'Gospel of the Apostles,' 'Gospel of the Hebrews,' 'Gospel of the Nazarenes,' or 'Gospel of Matthew.' Lessing also understood the comment in Papias regarding a Hebrew Gospel of Matthew as referring to the original gospel he postulated. 'In short, Matthew, Mark, and Luke are nothing else than differing and non-differing translations of the so-called Hebrew document of Matthew, which each one made as well as he could.'[35] The differences between the individual Gospels are to be explained from the different forms of the original gospel, so that Mark 'apparently used a less complete copy.'[36]

A comprehensive basis for the original-gospel hypothesis was provided in 1804 by Johann Gottfried Eichhorn (1752–1827), who argued for an Aramaic original gospel that each of the Synoptic evangelists had in a different form. Eichhorn sees the text of this original gospel preserved in the forty-four pericopes common to all the Gospels.[37] Eichhorn supposes the author of this original gospel to have been 'an unknown, but well instructed student of the apostles, who was skilled in writing.'[38] The original gospel contained the major elements of the life of Jesus, beginning with the baptism by John and concluding with the resurrection of Jesus. Alongside these different recensions of the original gospel, the Synoptic evangelists are supposed to have used additional sources, which explains the differences between the first three Gospels.

The original-gospel hypothesis could not establish itself, since it pushed the difficulties of the extant Gospels back into the darkness of a literature that has been lost. However, the insight that the Gospels presuppose a lengthy literary process of development was a progressive step forward.

2. The Diēgēsis ('Fragments') Hypothesis (cf. διήγησις, Luke 1.1, 'narrative,' 'account').

The theory advocated by F. D. E. Schleiermacher (1768–1834), among others, construes the Gospels as the final stage of a process of the collection of individual narratives. Soon after the death of Jesus, among the early Christians stories and speeches from the life of Jesus were told, collected, written down, and circulated. Luke 1.1–4 in particular appears to confirm

---

[35] Gotthold E. Lessing, *Neue Hypothese*, § 50; cited according to Lessing, *Gesammelte Werke* III, ed. K. Wölfel (Frankfurt 1967).

[36] *Ibid.* §49.

[37] Cf. Johann G. Eichhorn, *Einleitung in das Neue Testament* (Leipzig: Weidmann, 1820²) 1.161–167.

[38] *Ibid.* 177.

this process, since Luke is 'neither an independent author . . . nor does he have at his disposal several documents in circulation that deal with the whole life of Jesus . . . but is from beginning to end only a collector and organizer of already existing narratives, which he incorporates unchanged into his own writing.'[39] Luke found both the passion story and the travel narrative already in existence, his own contribution consisting primarily in his well-considered selection of materials. This hypothesis appropriately brings into focus the role that the collection of individual units of tradition played in the formation of the Gospels, but at the same time it is unable to provide a convincing explanation for the extensive agreement in the order of pericopes.

3. The Oral Tradition Hypothesis

If Eichhorn had supposed the source of the Synoptic Gospels to be different editions of a written original gospel, Johann Gottfried Herder (1744–1803) postulated an oral original gospel as the root of the first three Gospels. For him the Gospels are the result of a process of proclamation for which orality was the natural medium. 'A law is written; a message of good news is proclaimed.'[40] There was an office of 'evangelist,' those who had accompanied the apostles and who continued to proclaim as the oral gospel those stories that they had previously heard from the mouths of the apostles. This primitive oral gospel was oriented to a pattern that had been established by the apostles themselves, which explains the common elements. At the same time, the nature of the extant Gospels makes it clear that the evangelists were also individual authorial personalities. The process that resulted in normative written documents began as churches in various regions wanted to have their own version of the gospel and as heretics falsified the tradition. The differences between the Gospels are explained by Herder on the basis of their respective purposes: 'It was the responsibility of the evangelist to report and narrate for his particular group.'[41] This hypothesis was extended by Johann Carl Ludwig Gieseler (1792–1854),[42] who proposed an oral Aramaic gospel going back to the

---

[39] Friedrich Schleiermacher, 'Ueber die Schriften des Lukas, ein kritischer Versuch' (1817), in *Sämtliche Werke* (Berlin: G. Reimer, 1836) 1. Abt. 2.219; cf. further Friedrich Schleiermacher, 'Einleitung in das neue Testament,' ed. G. Wolde, *Sämtliche Werke* (Berlin: G. Reimer, 1845) 1. Abt. vol 8.

[40] Johann G. Herder, 'Vom Erlöser der Menschen. Nach unsren drei ersten Evangelien . . . Neben einer Regel der Zusammenstimmung unserer Evangelien aus ihrer Entstehung und Ordnung,' 1796, in *Herders sämmtliche Werke*, ed. B. Suphan, Vol. 9 (Hildesheim: G. Olms, 1967 =[Berlin 1880]) 211.

[41] *Ibid.* 217.

[42] Cf. Carl L. Gieseler, *Historisch-kritischer Versuch über die Entstehung und die frühesten Schicksale der schriftlichen Evangelien* (Leipzig: W. Engelmann, 1818).

disciples of Jesus, which was later translated into Greek to meet the needs of the Christian mission, and received its first fixed written form in the Greek language. The oral tradition hypothesis recognized for the first time the considerable role that oral tradition played in the process of the formation of the Gospels, but did not provide a persuasive explanation for the vast number of verbatim agreements.

4. The Utilization Hypothesis

Each of the three theories described above proceed on the assumption that there was no direct literary connection between the Synoptics. In contrast, the utilization hypothesis affirms that there is literary dependence among them. As already mentioned, Augustine already supposed that the Gospels originated in their canonical order, so that the later Gospels presupposed the earlier. Theodor Zahn and Adolf Schlatter are modern advocates of the order Matthew → Mark → Luke, in modified form.

The order Matthew → Luke → Mark was first argued in 1789 by Johann Jakob Griesbach (1745–1812),[43] who supposed that Mark used Matthew and Luke as his sources. The Gospel of Mark is contained almost completely in Matthew and/or Luke, and follows the order of either Matthew or Luke. Mark had both of the larger Gospels before him, and followed either Matthew or Luke depending on the situation of his readers. Griesbach explains the considerable omissions and abbreviations from the intention of Mark, which was from the beginning only to create an excerpt of the two other Gospels.

This thesis was advocated among others by Ferdinand Christian Baur and David Friedrich Strauss (1808–1874), each of whom modified it in his own way. A decisive step forward within the framework of the utilization hypothesis was attained by the philologist Karl Lachmann (1793–1851)[44] who posited that Mark formed the foundation for Matthew and Luke (= the priority of Mark). The point of departure for his thesis was the observation that Matthew and Luke, in the material that each shares with Mark, agree with each other only to the extent that they agree with Mark. In the material they do not share with Mark, each goes his own way. Mark thus forms the middle term for Matthew and Luke. The difference in the order of pericopes is greatest when Matthew is compared with Luke, and the least when Mark is compared with one of the two other Synoptics.

---

[43] Johann J. Griesbach, *Commentatio qua Marci evangelium totum e Matthaei et Lucae commentariis decerptum esse monstratur* (Jena 1789/90) printed in *Commentationes theologicae*, ed. J. C. Velthausen and others (Leipzig, 1794) 1.360ff.

[44] Cf. Karl Lachmann, 'De ordine narrationum in evangeliis synopticis,' ThStKr 8 (1835) 570–590.

From this Lachmann inferred the conclusion that the order of Mark is more original than that of Matthew and Luke, both of whom presuppose Mark. In addition, he theorized that Matthew already possessed a collection of Jesus' sayings into which he inserted the Markan material.

The way for the two-source theory was thus prepared when in 1838, independently of each other, the works of Christian Gottlob Wilke (1788–1854)[45] and Christian Hermann Weisse (1801–1866)[46] appeared. Wilke gave a comprehensive argument for the priority of Mark, showing that Matthew and Luke are similar to each other in the material they share with Mark, while in the material they use independently of Mark they appear more as individual authors. To be sure, Wilke does not attribute the material common to Matthew and Luke, but not in Mark, to a second common source in addition to Mark. He thought Matthew derived it from the Gospel of Luke, but did not explain where Luke received this material. Thus Christian Hermann Weisse can be considered the real founder of the two-source theory, since he not only argued for the priority of Mark (as did Wilke), but also indicated that independently of each other Matthew and Luke used a second source, a lost collection of Jesus' sayings. In addition, both Matthew and Luke had their respective special material (*Sondergut*). It was Heinrich Julius Holtzmann[47] and Paul Wernle who made the two-source theory the generally accepted solution to the Synoptic problem.

3.2.3 *The Two-Source Hypothesis*

The Two-Source Hypothesis regards the Gospel of Mark as the *oldest* Gospel, which served Matthew and Luke as a written source. In addition Matthew and Luke used another *source* which has been lost, but which can be reconstructed from the two extant Gospels (see below 3.3). It consisted primarily of sayings and speeches of Jesus and is called the 'Sayings Source,' abbreviated 'Q' (from German *Quelle*, 'source').[48]

One compelling argument for the priority of Mark is the *order of pericopes* in the Synoptics. From 12.1 on, Matthew clearly follows the

---

[45] Cf. Christian G. Wilke, *Der Urevangelist oder exegetisch kritische Untersuchung über das Verwandtschaftsverhältnis der drei ersten Evangelien* (Dresden und Leipzig, 1838).

[46] Cf. Christian H. Weisse, *Die evangelische Geschichte kritisch und philosophisch betrachtet* (2 vols. Leipzig: Arnold, 1838).

[47] Cf. in addition to his monographs *Die synoptischen Evangelien* and *Einleitung in das Neue Testament* especially Heinrich J. Holtzmann, *Die Synoptiker* (HCI Freiburg, ²1892). The influential *Synopsis of the First Three Gospels* by A. Huck appeared in 1892 as the companion volume to Holtzmann's commentary on the Gospels, and is still a valuable tool.

[48] This terminology was apparently introduced by Johannes Weiss; cf. Frans Neirynck, 'The Symbol Q (Quelle),' in *Evangelica*, BETL 60 (Leuven: Leuven University Press, 1982) 683–689.

Markan order of pericopes when he takes over Markan material. Matthean transformation of the order of Markan pericopes is concentrated in Matt. 8–9. Following the presentation of Jesus as teacher and miracle worker in Matt. 4.23 there follows the Sermon on the Mount (Matt. 5–7) and a cycle of ten miracle stories (Matt. 8–9). Within this new composition Matthew makes five changes in the Markan order: (1). the healing of the leper Matt. 8.1–4/Mark 1.40–45; (2). the healing of Peter's mother-in-law (Matt. 8.14–15/ Mark 1.29–31; (3). the stilling of the storm Matt. 8.23–27/Mark 4.35–41; (4). the healing of the Gadarene demoniac Matt. 8.28–9.1/Mark 5.1–20; (5). the healing of the woman with the flow of blood and the daughter of Jairus Matt. 9.18–26/Mark 5.21–43. Matthew combines the call of the disciples (Mark 3.13–19) and their sending forth (Mark 6.7–11) with other sayings of the Lord into a great missions discourse, in the process of which he relocates some individual sayings (Matt. 5.13b/Mark 9.50; Matt. 10.42/Mark 9.41; Matt. 13.12/Mark 4.25). How persistently Matthew follows the Markan order, despite individual changes and the appropriation of much additional material, is seen in his placing the Sermon on the Mount between Mark 1.21 and 1.22. Matthew places Mark 1.22 (the amazement of the people at Jesus' teaching) at the end of the Sermon on the Mount, so that as in Mark this verse reports the reaction to the first preaching of Jesus. Of 118 Markan sections taken over by Matthew, only 12 are not preserved in the Markan order.[49]

So also Luke makes only a few rearrangements of the Markan order in the first part of his Gospel. Thus he replaces the novelistic story of the death of John the Baptist in Mark 6.14–29 by a summary notice in Luke 3.19–20, in order to separate the figure of John more clearly from the person of Jesus. This results in the baptism of Jesus not being narrated until after the imprisonment of the Baptist is reported (Luke 3.21–22). On the other hand Luke reformulates the story of the rejection of Jesus in Nazareth (Mark 6.1–6) into a scene programmatic for the whole Gospel by developing essential elements of his theology in Jesus' inaugural sermon in 4.16–30. Luke narrates the call of the disciples after Jesus' first activity, and thereby shifts the call of Peter into the foreground (Luke 5.1–11). The summary of Mark 3.7–12/Luke 6.17–19 is placed after the call of the twelve apostles (Luke 6.12–16), in order to preserve a better transition to the Sermon on the Plain. By relocating the story of Jesus' true relatives (Mark 3.31–35) after the Parable of the Sower and its interpretation Luke obtains the appropriate narrative stage setting for the parables discourse,

---

[49] Matthew takes over 118 of the 128 Markan sections. The data is derived from Robert Morgenthaler, *Statistische Synopse* (Zürich: Gotthelf, 1971) 231.

and a first illustration of its message. Alongside these more substantial reordering of Markan pericopes, Luke also relocates a few individual sayings (Luke 12.1/Mark 8.14.15; Luke 14.34/Mark 9.50; Luke 22.39/Mark 14.26). Like Matthew, Luke too follows the order of Markan pericopes in the material he takes over, except for the redactional modifications mentioned above. What would appear at first glance as an outline strongly divergent from Mark's is due to Luke's omission of a larger number of Markan pericopes than is the case with Matthew (Matthew takes over 118 pericopes, Luke only 96),[50] and from the comprehensive body of special materials (*Sondergut*) that Luke has included mainly in the 'Travel Narrative' (Luke 9.51–19.27). In addition, Luke does not fuse his sources together, as does Matthew, but juxtaposes them to each other, so that an observably different presentation of the life of Jesus emerges. In summary one may say that from the perspective of the order of pericopes Mark is the middle term for Matthew and Luke. The lack of agreement in the order of pericopes between Matthew and Luke when they diverge from the Markan order clearly shows that the only judicious explanation for the literary relationship between the first three Gospels is that Mark provided the common source and framework for Matthew and Luke.

A further indication of the priority of Mark is provided by the *linguistic and material improvements* made by both Matthew and Luke. If the agreements between individual pericopes (e.g. Matt. 24.4–8/Mark 13.5–8/Luke 21.8–11) only prove that some kind of literary relationship must exist, the improvements made in style and content speak for the priority of Mark.

In numerous places Matthew and Luke improve Mark's simple and popular Greek. In many instances Matthew smoothes out the Markan text (e.g. Matt. 16.24 avoids Mark's doubled ἀκολουθέω [follow]), introduces his own preferred expressions (cf. βασιλεία τῶν οὐρανῶν [kingdom of heaven] in Matt. 13.11, 31; 19.14, 23), and makes changes in the Markan vocabulary (e.g. μαστιγόω [flog] for δέρω [beat] in Matt. 10.17).[51]

Luke makes considerably more changes in his Markan text. Aramaic words are adopted by him only in translation or not at all (cf. Luke 6.14; 8.54; 22.39, 42, 46; 23.33), simple Markan verbs are replaced with composite verbs (e.g. ἀνακράζω [cry out] for κράζω [cry], Luke 8.28), uses the genitive absolute much more frequently than Mark (cf. Luke 8.4 συνιόντος δὲ ὄχλου πολλοῦ [when a great crowd gathered]), and the dominant paratactic use of καί [and] is frequently replaced by δέ [but] (cf. Luke 6.6–11) as well as by participial constructions and relative clauses (e.g. in 9.11 Luke

---

[50] Robert Morgenthaler, *Statistische Synopse* 232.
[51] On the Matthean editing of Markan material cf. especially Wernle, *Die synoptische Frage* 146ff.

abbreviates the awkward and longwinded expression καὶ εἶδον . . . καὶ ἐπέγνωσαν . . . συνέδραμον . . . καὶ προῆλθον [and they saw . . . and recognized . . . and hurried there . . . and arrived ahead of them] to γνόντες ἠκολούθησαν [when they found out, they followed).[52]

In addition to the improvements in Mark's language made by Matthew and Luke there are numerous changes in the Markan text. Thus Matthew simply omits such troublesome details as the unusual lowering of the lame man through the roof (Mark 2.4) and replaces the words problematic in Jesus' mouth τί με λέγεις ἀγαθόν [why do you call me good] of Mark 10.18 with τί με ἐρωτᾷς περὶ τοῦ ἀγαθοῦ (why do you ask me abut the good) (Matt. 19.17). Luke clarifies the ambiguous subject of Mark 2.15, omits the second description of the afflicted person in the story of the healing of the epileptic (Mark 9.21–24), and ethicizes the saying about taking up the cross with the addition of καθ' ἡμέραν (day by day) (Luke 9.23).

A further argument for the priority of Mark has to do with the quantity of the common material itself. Of the Markan material, only three pericopes (Mark 4.26–29; 7.31–37; 8.22–26) and a few individual sayings (Mark 2.27; 3.20–21; 9.48–49; 14.51–52; 15.44) appear neither in Matthew nor in Luke. The word statistics also speak for the priority of Mark, since from a total of 11,078 words of the text of Mark 8,555 are reproduced by Matthew and 6,737 by Luke.[53]

The Markan texts that do not appear in Matthew or Luke – the Markan special material (Sondergut) – present a problem for the classic Two-Source Hypothesis, since their absence cannot always be attributed to the redactional activity of Matthew or Luke. The omission of the healing miracles in Mark 7.31–37 and 8.22–26 may be clarified by the explanation that for both Matthew and Luke the massive portrayal of Jesus as a certain kind of miracle worker tended to become objectionable. The same grounds may be presumably be introduced for the omission of Mark's report that Jesus' relatives considered him deranged (Mark 3.20–21), and the instructions for driving out a certain kind of demon in Mark 9.29. The comment about the flight of the naked young man at the arrest of Jesus (Mark 14.51–52) and the saying about being salted with fire in Mark 9.49 were perhaps no longer understood by Matthew and Luke.[54] On the other hand, on the assumption that canonical Mark lay before Matthew and Luke, it is difficult to explain why both of them decided to omit the parable of the

---

[52] On Luke's linguistic alterations of Mark cf. Wernle, *Die synoptische Frage* 18ff. and Tim Schramm, *Der Markus-Stoff bei Lukas*, SNTSMS 14 (Cambridge: Cambridge University Press, 1971).

[53] Cf. Morgenthaler, *Statistische Synopse* 89.

[54] Cf. Vielhauer, *Urchristliche Literatur* 273.

seed growing secretly of Mark 4.26–29. There is no clear redactional reason for their joint omission of Mark 2.27, 9.48, and 15.44.

A modification of the usual Two-Source Hypothesis is also required by the absence of Mark 6.45–8.26 between Luke 9.17 and 9.18 – the Lucan 'Great Omission' – as well as by numerous smaller agreements of Matthew and Luke against Mark. No motive may be brought forward for an intentional omission of Mark 6.45–8.26 by Luke. The explanation one repeatedly finds in the literature that Luke intentionally skipped the ministry of Jesus outside Galilee, i.e. in Gentile territory, runs aground on the incorporation of Mark 5.1–20 in Luke 8.26–39.[55] The only explanation left is that Mark 6.45–8.26 had either dropped out of, or had not yet been added to, the copy of Mark available to Luke.

Distributed over the whole extent of the Markan material redacted by Matthew and Luke are found verbatim minor agreements of Matthew and Luke against Mark.[56] This phenomenon is a matter of ca. 700 common alterations, additions (positive agreements) and omissions (negative agreements) distributed over the whole Gospel.

Example: The agreements of Matt. 12.1–8 and Luke 6.1–5 against Mark 2.23–28.[57]

Matt. 12.1 / Luke 6.1: Matthew and Luke omit ὁδὸν ποιεῖν (to make a path) and add respectively καὶ ἐσθίειν (and to eat) and καὶ ἤσθιον (and were eating).

Matt. 12.2 / Luke 6.2: Matthew and Luke replace καί (and) with δέ (but) and write εἶπον (said) instead of ἔλεγον (were saying).

Matt. 12.3 / Luke 6.3: In place of λέγει (says) Matthew and Luke read εἶπεν (said). χρείαν ἔσχεν (has need) is omitted by both.

Matt. 12.4 / Luke 6.4: ἐπὶ Ἀβιαθὰρ ἀρχιερέως (at the time of Abiathar the high priest) is missing in both; the preposition σύν (with) is replaced by μετά, (with), the participle οὖσιν (being) is omitted and μόνοις (alone) and μόνους (alone) are respectively added.

The whole verse Mark 2.27 with the following ὥστε (so) is lacking in Matthew and Luke.

Matt. 12.8 / Luke 6.5: In Matthew and Luke υἱὸς τοῦ ἀνθρώπου (Son of Man) stands at the end of the verse as the subject, and the καί (and) before τοῦ σαββάτου (of the Sabbath) is omitted by both evangelists.

---

[55] Contra Hans Conzelmann, *Theology of Saint Luke* (see below 3.6.1) 49–51.

[56] A catalogue of minor agreements is found in Frans Neirynck, *The Minor Agreements in a Horizontal-Line Synopsis* (Leuven: Leuven University Press, 1991); cf. further Strecker, *Minor Agreements* 221–230.

[57] Cf. Hermann Aichinger, 'Quellenkritische Untersuchung der Perikope vom Ährenausraufen am Sabbat Mk 2,23–28 par,' SNTU 1 (1976) 110–153.

As additional larger text units that speak for the existence of a slightly-revised form of canonical Mark that came to Matthew and Luke, cf. Mark 1.29–31 par; 2.1–12 par; 3.22–27 par; 4.10–12 par; 4.30–32 par;[58] 4.35–41 par;[59] 9.2–10 par.[60]

As examples of single verses cf. Mark 14.65 (Matt. and Luke have as a common addition to Mark the question of the members of the Sanhedrin τίς ἐστιν ὁ παίσας σε; ([who struck you?]); Mark 5.27; Mark 9.19; Mark 14.44–45.

On the basis of the classical Two-Source Hypothesis that Matthew and Mark used our canonical Mark as a source, there is no satisfactory explanation either for most of the Markan special material (especially the omission of Mark 4.26–29) or for the numerous smaller agreements of Matthew and Luke against Mark, since according to this theory there ought to be no agreements that are explainable either as dependence on a common source or from 'coincidental' revisions made independently by the two redactors. The number of minor agreements, and their distribution over the whole Gospel, make it very unlikely that Matthew and Luke so often independently edited the Markan text in the same place and in exactly the same way.[61] The phenomenon that the minor agreements are distributed rather uniformly throughout the text means they can be satisfactorily explained only by a comprehensive model, not merely from case to case. The classical Two-Source Hypothesis is therefore to be supplemented by accepting the fact that Matthew and Luke used not our canonical Mark, but a slightly revised edition that is to be called Deuteromark, since it is later than our canonical Mark.[62] The character of this reworked edition is difficult to determine; it could have been a comprehensive new edition of the Gospel,[63] or a redactional layer.[64] The first possibility could

---

[58] Cf. Franz Kogler, *Das Doppelgleichnis vom Senfkorn und vom Sauerteig in seiner traditions-geschichtlichen Entwicklung*, FzB 59 (Würzburg: Echter, 1988).

[59] Cf. Albert Fuchs, 'Die "Seesturmperikope" Mk 4,35–41par im Wandel der urkirchlichen Verkündigung,' SUNT 15 (1990) 101–133.

[60] Cf. Christoph Niemand, *Studien zu den Minor Agreements der synoptischen Verklärungsperikopen*, EHS.T 352 (Frankfurt: Lang, 1989).

[61] The minor agreements are understood by Frans Neirynck from case to case as independent redactional alterations, 'The Minor Agreements and the Two-Source-Theory' in *Evangelica* 2.3–42.

[62] This is different from the explanation for this phenomenon given by the 'Urmarkus' hypothesis popular at the turn of the twentieth century, namely that Matthew and Luke used an *older* form of Mark than canonical Mark.

[63] As vigorously argued by Albert Fuchs in numerous publications.

[64] As in Georg Strecker – Udo Schnelle, *Einführung in die neutestamentliche Exegese* (Göttingen: Vandenhoeck & Ruprecht, 1989³) 55–56; Ulrich Luz, *Matthäus* (see below 3.5.1) 2. 254, 301 and elsewhere; Andreas Ennulat, *Die Minor Agreements. Ein Diskussionsbeitrag zur Erklärung einer offenen Frage des synoptischen Problems*, Tübingen: J. C. B. Mohr (Paul Siebeck,

only be seriously considered if it were possible to identify a Deuteromarkan theology. A. Fuchs sees this theology as an extending of the ecclesiological elements and a christological centering by Deuteromark. A comprehensive theological differentiation between canonical Mark and Deuteromark cannot be distinguished, however, and Deuteromark should be regarded as a stratum of editorial revision.

The claim for the priority of Mark made by the classical Two-Source Hypothesis is only modified by the theory of a Deuteromark in that an explanation for the greater part of the Markan special material and for the 'minor agreements' can now be given.[65]

3.2.4 The Special Materials of Matthew and Luke

In addition to texts that derive from Mark or Q, both Matthew and Luke contain special materials (*Sondergut*), i.e. pericopes that are *only* present in Matthew or Luke. The Matthean special materials:

1–2	Birth Story
12.5–7,11–12	Sayings about the Sabbath
13.24–30	Parable of the Tares
13.36–43	Interpretation of the Parable of the Tares
13.44–46	Parables of the Hidden Treasure and the Pearl
13.47–50	Parable of the Net
13.51–52	Treasures Old and New
14.28–31	Peter Walks on the Water
16.17–19	Peter the Rock
17.24–27	The Temple Tax
18.10	The Angels of the Little Ones
18.(15) 16–20	Discipline in the Community
18.23–35	Parable of the Unforgiving Servant
19.10–12	Concerning Eunuchs
20.1–16	Parable of the Laborers in the Vineyard
21.14–16	Blind, Lame, and Children in the Temple
21.28–32	Parable of the Two Sons
25.1–13	Parable of the Ten Virgins
25.31–46	The Last Judgment

1990); M. Eugene Boring, 'The Synoptic Problem, "Minor Agreements", and the Beelzebul Pericope,' in *The Four Gospels*, ed. Frans Van Segbroeck et al. (FS F. Neirynck) BETL 100 (Leuven: Leuven University Press, 1992) 587–619.

[65] Contra Fuchs, 'Seesturmperikope' 128, who no longer bases his work on the Two-Source Hypothesis as the model on which the synoptic problem is to be solved, but speaks of a 'three-level theory' (Mark, Deuteromark, then Matthew or Luke).

26.52–53	Words of Jesus at his Arrest
27.3–10	The End of Judas
27.19	Pilate's Wife
27.24–25	Pilate and the People
27.51–53	Miracles at Jesus' Death
27.62–66	Guards at the Tomb
28.2–3	The Angel who Moved the Stone
28.9–10	Jesus Appears to the Women
28.11–15	The Report of the Guard
28.16–20	Jesus Appears to the Eleven on a Mountain in Galilee

The Lucan Special Material:

1–2	Birth Story
3.10–14	John Replies to Questioners
3.23–38	Genealogy
5.1–1	The Miraculous Draft of Fish
7.11–17	The Widow's Son at Nain
7.36–50	The Woman with the Ointment
8.1–3	The Ministering Women
9.51–56	Jesus is Rejected by Samaritans
10.18–20	The Return of the Seventy
10.29–37	The Good Samaritan
10.38–42	Martha and Mary
11.5–8	The Importunate Friend at Midnight
11.27–28	True Blessedness
12.13–21	The Rich Fool
12.35–37	The Returning Master
12.47–48	On Rewarding Servants
12.49	Saying about Fire
12.54–56	Signs of the Time
13.1–9	Repentance or Destruction (Parable of the Barren Fig Tree)
13.10–17	Healing the Crippled Woman on the Sabbath
13.31–33	Warning against Herod
14.1–6	Healing the Man with Dropsy
14.7–14	Teaching on Humility
14.28–33	Conditions of Discipleship
15.8–10	Parable of the Lost Coin
15.11–32	Parable of the Prodigal Son
16.1–12	Parable of the Unjust Steward
16.14–15	The Pharisees Reproved
16.19–31	Parable of the Rich Man and Lazarus
17.7–10	We are Unprofitable Servants

17.11–19	Cleansing of the Ten Lepers
18.1–8	Parable of the Unjust Judge
18.9–14	The Pharisee and the Publican
19.2–10	Zacchaeus
19.41–44	Jesus Weeps over Jerusalem
22.15–18	The Paschal Meal as a Farewell Meal
22.35–38	The Two Swords
23.6–16	Jesus before Herod and Pilate
23.39–43	The Two Thieves
24.13–35	Jesus appears to Two on the Way to Emmaus
24.36–53	Jesus' Appearance, Last Words, and Ascension

No direct information is available concerning the origins of the special materials, but the majority must certainly derive from the oral tradition available to each evangelist. The classification is not certain for a number of texts, which may belong either to Q^{Mt} or Q^{Lk} respectively (see below 3.3.2), or to the special materials of each evangelist.Matt. 5.21–22, 27–28, 33–37 (Expositions of the Law); Matt. 6.2–6, 16–18 (Religious Rules), Matt. 18.15–18 (Congregational Discipline), Matt. 22.11–13 (Parable of the Wedding Garment); Luke 15.8–10 (Parable of the Lost Coin), and Luke 15.11–32 (Parable of the Prodigal Son).

The extensive Lukan special materials exhibit particular thematic emphases (Jesus' partiality for the poor, his critique of riches, Jesus' association with sinners and women, the significance of prayer, the challenge to humility, a positive affirmation of the Samaritans).[66] No information is available on the bearers of the special traditions that came to Luke; only suppositions are possible. The community responsible for these traditions could have been associated with the Jerusalem church.[67] 'It was convinced that Israel can only survive when it once again is concerned about those who have been excluded, when it, like Jesus is filled with compassion and turns to those who cannot help themselves.'[68]

In contrast, the Matthean body of special materials is not a united complex of tradition, is without discernable theological organizing motifs, and is hardly to be assigned to a single circle of tradition bearers.[69]

---

[66] Cf. Hans Klein, *Barmherzigkeit gegenüber den Elenden und Geächteten. Studien zur Botschaft des lukanischen Sonderguts*, BThSt 10 (Neukirchen: Neukirchener Verlag, 1987); Gerd Petzke, *Das Sondergut des Evangeliums nach Lukas* (Zürich: Theologischer Verlag, 1990); Bertram Pittner, *Studien zum lukanischen Sondergut*, EThS 18 (Leipzig,1991); Benhard Heininger, *Metaphorik, Erzählstruktur und szenisch-dramatische Gestaltung in den Sondergutgleichnissen bei Lukas*, NTA 24 (Münster: Aschendorff, 1991).

[67] So Klein, *Barmherzigkeit* 134.

[68] *Ibid.* 130.

[69] On the analysis of the texts cf. Hans Theo Wrege, *Das Sondergut des Matthäus-Evangeliums* (Zürich: Theologischer Verlag, 1991), who, however, assigns to the Matthean special materials

3.2.5 Diagram of the Two-Source Hypothesis

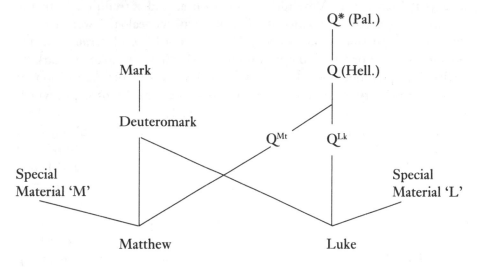

3.2.6 Other Theories of Synoptic Relationships

The Two Source Hypothesis has always been only one model for resolving the problems presented by the phenomena of the Synoptic Gospels. In current research there are four alternative models of particular significance:

1. The *Two-Gospel Hypothesis*. This proposal, advocated especially by W. R. Farmer and his circle,[70] in its general form affirms only that Matthew and Luke were composed before Mark and John. According to Farmer, who disputes the existence of Q, the first Gospel was composed by Matthew on the basis of extensive oral and written traditions. Luke wrote next, drawing his material from Matthew and additional oral and written traditions. Finally Mark formulated his Gospel by drawing extensively from the common elements of Matthew and Luke, also making use of a limited amount of oral and/or written tradition. The following are the main arguments presented for this form of the utilization hypothesis oriented to Griesbach, in which Matthew was the first written Gospel.

---

many texts usually regarded as belonging to Q. Cf. further Hans Klein, 'Judenchristliche Frömmigkeit im Sondergut des Matthäus,' NTS 35 (1989) 466–474, and his *Bewährung im Glauben*, BThSt 20 (Neukirchen: Neukirchener Verlag, 1996). According to Klein the Matthean special material consists mainly of three complexes: in the parables the major theme is the turning of Jesus to the poor and suffering; the sayings about the Law warn against a lax manner of life; and the sayings about Peter and community discipline are central foundational elements of ecclesiology.

[70] The current position of Farmer and his circle, with references to the most recent literature, is best seen in the anthology edited by David L. Dungan, *The Interrelations of the Gospels* 125–230. Cf. in addition *A Synopsis of the Four Gospels. In Greek. Arranged according the Two-Gospel-Hypothesis*, ed. J. B. Orchard (Göttingen: Vandenhoeck & Ruprecht, 1983).

(a) The testimony of Patristic witnesses: According to Eusebius HE 6.14.5–7, Clement of Alexandria handed on an older tradition from the presbyters, according to which the Gospels with genealogies were written first. And Augustine on one occasion (*De Consensu Evangelistarum* 4.10, 11) presupposes the order of composition to be Matthew → Luke → Mark.[71]

(b) The phenomenon of order is clarified by the presupposition of Matthean priority. Mark composes his work as a Third Gospel, in which he was primarily oriented to Matthew, and to a lesser agree to Luke. This is the explanation for the agreements, with the omissions resulting from the theological intentions of Mark, who omitted Jewish tradition and attempted to smooth out the contradictions between Matthew and Luke. Mark did not intend to replace Matthew and Luke, however, but only to supplement them.

(c) Mark's procedure is the result of his historical location. The Gospel of Mark originated in Rome. 'Mark's Gospel is fundamentally a restatement of the Gospels of Matthew and Luke for Roman Christians facing persecution.'[72] The Roman location also explains the nearness to Paul and the orientation to the missionary speeches of Peter in Acts, where the sermons also begin with the appearance of John the Baptist and the sayings of Jesus play no role. 'Using Peter's public speeches as his guide and model Mark sought to produce the kind of vivid narrative message that the Apostle Peter had consistently proclaimed.'[73]

(d) The 'minor agreements' are taken as evidence for the composition of Matthew and Luke prior to Mark, being regarded as the results of Mark's reworking of the texts of Matthew and Luke.

While the Two-Gospel Hypothesis can make quite good sense of individual phenomena of the Synoptic problem, at the same time three fundamental objections must be raised against this theory: (1.) The theory cannot convincingly represent Mark's theological and literary intentions in his reception of the two larger Gospels. Especially the decomposition of the great speech complexes in Matthew such as the Sermon on the Mount (Matt. 5–7) cannot be made plausible. (2.) So also, if Luke used the Gospel of Matthew, the criteria of his decomposition of Matthean text complexes

---

[71] The key text 4.11 reads: Mark 'follows both (i.e. Matthew and Luke). For however much he agrees with Matthew in many things, he agrees just as much with Luke in others. Thereby is shown his solidarity with the Lion and the Calf . . .' (Cf. Rev. 4.6, 7; Augustine had previously identified Mark with the human figure in the vision.) On this analysis, cf. Helmut Merkel, 'Die Überlieferungen der Alten Kirche über das Verhältnis der Evangelien,' in *The Interrelations of the Gospels*, ed. D. L. Dungan, 566–590.

[72] William R. Farmer, 'The Statement of the Hypothesis,' in *The Interrelations of the Gospels*, ed. D. L. Dungan, 155.

[73] *Ibid.*

must be shown. (3.) The extensive verbatim agreements in the sayings tradition present a further problem for the Two-Gospel Hypothesis. On the one hand it must be explained why Luke makes radical changes throughout extensive sections of Matthew's composition, while on the other hand closely follows Matthew in the sections represented by the sayings tradition. In addition, if there were no Q, the extent of the Matthean special material would be remarkable.

2. A very complex *Multiple-Stage Hypothesis* for resolving the Synoptic problem is advocated by M. É. Boismard[74]. He takes over elements of both the Two-Source Hypothesis and the Griesbach Hypothesis. In this view, four written documents form the beginning point of the tradition: the preliminary versions of each of the Synoptics and of Q. At the next stage, two of these documents become the basis of the Gospels of Mark and Matthew ('Intermediate Mark' and 'Intermediate Matthew'). A preliminary version of the Gospel of Luke ('Proto-Luke') was formed at the third level. Proto-Luke incorporates Q material and at the same time is influenced by the preliminary version of Matthew. The Synoptic Gospels receive their final form at the fourth level, in which elements of 'Intermediate Mark' influenced the Gospels of Matthew and Luke, while at the same time Mark is influenced by 'Proto-Luke' and 'Intermediate Matthew.' Mark is thus dependent on preliminary forms of Matthew and Luke (somewhat as in the Griesbach Hypothesis). For their part, Matthew and Luke are supposed to have integrated a preliminary version of Mark, and Q was used by preliminary forms of Matthew and Luke (somewhat as in the Two-Source Hypothesis). 'The Synoptic problem is complex; it may only be resolved by a complex solution.'[75]

The strength of this theory of interwoven networks is its flexibility by which a large number of phenomena can be explained without forcing the data to conform to the theory. On the other hand, there is no other literary evidence for the preliminary forms of the Gospels that must be presupposed, so that the high degree of complexity of the theory moves it into the realm of pure postulation.

3. *Variations of the Utilization Hypothesis.* M. D. Goulder[76] attempts to

---

[74] For the foundational work on this hypothesis, cf. Pierre Benoit and M. É. Boismard, *Synopse des quatre évangiles, en français, Tome II: Commentaire*, by M. É. Boismard with the collaboration of A. Lamouille and P. Sandevoir (Paris 1972). For the current discussion cf. M. É. Boismard, 'Théorie des niveaux multiples,' in *The Interrelations of the Gospels*, ed. D. L. Dungan, 231–288. In addition cf. M. É. Boismard and A. Lamouille, *Synopsis Graeca Quattuor Evangeliorum* (Leuven – Paris, 1986).

[75] M. É. Boismard, 'Théorie des niveaux multiples' 232.

[76] Cf. M. D. Goulder, *Luke. A New Paradigm*, 2 vols. JSNT.S 20 (Sheffield: Sheffield University Press, 1989).

prove that Luke knew and cited from the Gospel of Matthew. In his view, about 90 CE Luke composed his Gospel for the Gentile churches as a combination of Matthew and Mark. The Lucan special materials are 'Lucan development of matter in Matthew.'[77] Goulder rejects the existence of Q. Rather, the texts usually considered Q or Matthean special materials are 'entirely his [sc. Matthew's] elaboration of Mark'.[78]

4. *Variation of the Oral Tradition Hypothesis*: Bo Reicke wanted to explain the agreements between the Synoptic Gospels entirely on the basis of parallels in the traditional material handed on orally.[79] Neither Mark nor Q served Luke or Matthew as a source, but the agreements between them show 'that in Matthew and Luke as also in Mark, the triple tradition derived from a living tradition delivered acoustically.'[80] Parallels within triple tradition contexts are supposed to have been supplemented by material from the double tradition and by singly-attested traditions. Reicke supposes that the earliest Jerusalem church was the point of origin and the center of this formation of traditions, which was historically a very reliable stream of tradition. Peter stayed in Jerusalem in the house of the mother of the evangelist Mark (cf. Acts 12.12), so that very early Mark could have taken over the material that came together under his roof and translated it into Greek.

In all the above cases, a hypothesis that when strictly applied in purely literary terms does not resolve every problem has been replaced by another hypothesis that has even greater difficulties. In particular, the priority of Mark is a fundamental conclusion that is not to be disputed. If Matthew were the oldest Gospel, then Mark would have used his Matthean source in contradictory ways, namely by radically shortening the whole while extensively expanding many individual pericopes. But why should Mark have omitted the Lord's Prayer, the sayings about God's hearing and answering prayer, the sayings about judging, the parable of the faithful and unfaithful servants, and much more, while at the same time expanding the Jairus story to three times its Matthean size and more than doubling the stories of the Gerasene demoniacs and the healing of the epileptic?[81] On the supposition that in addition to Matthew, Mark also knew Luke, the question remains unresolved of why he included in his Gospel neither the extensive Lucan special materials nor the series of pericopes in which

[77] M. D. Goulder, *Luke. A New Paradigm* 1.23.
[78] *Ibid.* 1.22.
[79] Cf. Bo Reicke, 'Die Entstehungsverhältnisse der synoptischen Evangelien', in *ANRW* 25.2 (Berlin: Walter de Gruyter, 1984) 1758–1791; and *The Roots of the Synoptic Gospels* (Philadelphia: Fortress Press, 1986).
[80] Reicke, 'Entstehungsverhältnisse' 1782.
[81] Cf. Robert Morgenthaler, *Statistische Synopse* (see above 3.2.3) 286.

Matthew and Luke agree almost verbatim. The high degree of verbal agreement in the parallel pericopes of Mark, Matthew, and Luke, as well as the demonstrable reworking of Markan language and content by Matthew and Luke speak unambiguously against the supposition that there was no literary contact between the Synoptic Gospels. In addition, at least Luke 1.1–4 explicitly presupposes the use of literary sources!

The point of departure for study of the Synoptic problem must therefore continue to be the Two-Source Hypothesis, even though in individual cases it must be applied less mechanically than in its earliest days. It continues to be the hypothesis that *explains the most phenomena with the least degree of difficulty*.

3.3 The Sayings Source Q

3.3.1 Literature

Reconstructions of the Text.

Schulz, Siegfried. *Griechisch-deutsche Synopse der Q-Überlieferungen*. Zürich: Theologischer Verlag, 1972; Polag, Athanasius. *Fragmenta Q*. Neukirchen-Vluyn: Neukirchener Verlag, 1979; Schenk, Wolfgang. *Synopse zur Redequelle der Evangelien*. Düsseldorf: Patmos, 1981; Kloppenborg, John S. *Q-Parallels*. Sonoma: Polebridge Press, 1988; Neirynck, Frans. *Q-Parallels*. Leuven: Leuven University Press, 1988; Robinson, James M.; Hoffmann, Paul; Kloppenborg, John S., General Editors. *Documenta Q. Reconstructions of Q Through Two Centuries of Gospel Research Excerpted, Sorted, and Evaluated*. Several Volumes. Leuven: Peeters, 1996ff.

Commentaries

Zeller, Dieter. *Kommentar zur Logienquelle*, SKK.NT 21. Stuttgart: Katholisches Bibelwerk, 1984.

Monographs

Harnack, Adolf von. *The Sayings of Jesus. The Second Source of St. Matthew and St. Luke. New Testament Studies II*, tr. J. R. Wilkinson. London: Williams & Norgate, 1908; Tödt, Heinz Eduard. *The Son of Man in the Synoptic Tradition*, tr. D. M. Barton. Philadelphia: Westminster Press, 1965; Lührmann, Dieter. *Die Redaktion der Logienquelle*, WMANT 33. Neukirchen-Vluyn: Neukirchener Verlag, 1969; Schulz, Siegfried. *Q- Die Spruchquelle der Evangelisten*. Zürich: Theologischer Verlag, 1972; Polag, Athanasius. *Die Christologie der Logienquelle*, WMANT 45. Neukirchen-Vluyn: Neukirchener Verlag, 1977; Zeller, Dieter. *Die weisheitlichen Mahnsprüche bei den Synoptikern*, Fzb 17. Würzburg: Echter, 1977; Laufen, Rudolf. *Die Doppelüberlieferungen der Logienquelle und des Markusevangeliums*, BBB 54. Königstein/Bonn: Hanstein, 1980; Hoffmann, Paul. *Studien zur Theologie der Logienquelle*, NTA 8.

Münster: Aschendorff, 1982³; Kloppenborg, John S. *The Formation of Q*. Philadelphia: Fortress Press, 1987; Sato, Migaku. *Q und Prophetie*, WUNT 2.29. Tübingen: J. C. B. Mohr (Paul Siebeck), 1988; Kosch, Daniel. *Die eschatologische Tora des Menschensohnes*, NTOA 12. Göttingen: Vandenhoeck & Ruprecht, 1989; Schüling, Joachim. *Studien zum Verhältnis von Logienquelle und Markusevangelium*, FzB 65. Würzburg: Echter, 1991; Kloppenborg, John S. and Leif Vaage, eds. *Early Christianity, Q and Jesus*, Semeia 55. Atlanta: Scholars Press, 1992; Bergemann, Thomas. *Q auf dem Prüfstand*, FRLANT 158. Göttingen: Vandenhoeck & Ruprecht, 1993; Kloppenborg, John S., ed. *The Shape of Q. Signal Essays on the Sayings Gospel*. Minneapolis: Fortress, 1993; Weiser, Alfons. *Theologie des Neuen Testaments II. Die Theologie der Evangelien*. Stuttgart: Kohlhammer, 1993, 21–43; Catchpole, David R. *The Quest for Q*. Edinburgh: T. & T. Clark, 1993; Piper, R. A., ed. *The Gospel Behind the Gospels. Current Studies on Q*, SupNT 75. Leiden: E. J. Brill, 1995; Tuckett, Christopher M. *Q and the History of Early Christianity*. Peabody: Hendrickson, 1996.

Articles

Bammel, Ernst. 'Das Ende von Q,' in *Verborum Veritatis* (FS G. Stählin), eds. Otto Böcher and Klaus Haacker. Wuppertal: Brockhaus, 1970, 39–50; Robinson, James M. 'LOGOI SOPHON- On the Gattung of Q,' in *Trajectories through Early Christianity*, eds. Helmut Köster and James M. Robinson. Philadelphia: Fortress Press, 1971; Wanke, Joachim. 'Kommentarworte. Älteste Kommentierungen von Herrenworten,' BZ 24 (1980) 208–233; Delobel, Joël, ed. *Logia- The Sayings of Jesus*, BETL 59. Leuven: Leuven University Press, 1982 (important collection of essays); Zeller, Dieter. 'Redaktionsprozesse und wechselnder "Sitz im Leben" beim Q-Material,' in J. Delobel, *Logia* (Leuven: Leuven University Press, 1982) 395–409; Schürmann, Heinz. 'Beobachtungen zum Menschensohn-Titel in der Redequelle,' in *Gottes Reich- Jesu Geschick*, ed. H. Schürmann. Freiburg: Herder, 1983, 153–182; Schürmann, Heinz. 'Das Zeugnis der Redequelle für die Basileia-Verkündigung Jesu,' in *Gottes Reich- Jesu Geschick*, ed. H. Schürmann. Freiburg: Herder, 1983, 65–152; Horn, Friedrich W. 'Christentum und Judentum in der Logienquelle,' EvTh 51 (1991) 344–364; Polag, Athanasius. 'The Theological Center of the Sayings Source' in *The Gospel and the Gospels*, ed. Peter Stuhlmacher. Grand Rapids: Wm. B. Eerdmans, 1991, 97–105; Schürmann, Heinz. 'Zur Kompositionsgeschichte der Redequelle,' in *Der Treue Gottes trauen* (FS G. Schneider), eds. Claus Bussmann and Walter Radl. Freiburg: Herder, 1991, 325–342; Catchpole, David R. 'The Beginning of Q. A Proposal,' NTS 38 (1992) 205–221; Kosch, Daniel. 'Q und Jesus,' BZ 36 (1992) 30–58; Seeley, David. 'Jesus' Death in Q ,' NTS 38 (1992) 222–234; Karrer, Martin. 'Christliche Gemeinde und Israel. Beobachtungen zur Logienquelle,' in *Gottes Recht als Lebensraum* (FS H. J. Boecker), ed. P. Mommer et al. Neukirchen-Vluyn: Neukirchener Verlag, 1993, 145–163.

History of Research

Neirynck, Frans. 'Recent Developments in the Study of Q,' in J. Delobel, *Logia*. 29–75.

3.3.2 *Extent of the Sayings Source*

The following data speak for the existence of Q as a second written source used by Matthew and Luke:

1. In addition to sections parallel to Mark, Matthew and Luke have *common materials* of about 4000 words,[82] marked in part by a high degree of verbal agreement (cf. Matt. 3.7–10/Luke 3.7–9; Matt. 12.43–45/Luke 11.24–26; Matt. 23.37–39/Luke 13.34–35). These agreements include the structure of long periodic sentences and the position of particles and possessive pronouns.[83]

2. Matthew and Luke have *doublets* (a text which an evangelist has twice) and *double traditions* (texts which both evangelists have twice: once in the Markan context, once in materials common only to Matthew and Luke). Both phenomena support the thesis that Matthew and Luke used another common source in addition to Mark.

Examples of doublets:[84] Luke reports the sending out of the disciples twice, in chapters nine and ten. The first time is based on Mark 6.7–13, the second is parallel to Matt. 10. Matthew hands on the traditional saying of the 'Sign of Jonah' both in its Markan context (Matt. 16.4) and as a parallel to Luke (Matt. 12.39). In addition cf. Matt. 19.9 and 5.32 (prohibition of divorce); Matt. 18.8–9 and 5.29–30 (concerning anger). Examples of double traditions: Matt. 13.12/Mark 4.25/Luke 8.18 and Matt. 25.29/Luke 19.26 ('to those who have, more will be given'); Matt. 16.24–25/Mark 8.34–35/Luke 9.23–24 and Matt. 10.38–39/Luke 14.27/17.33 (on taking up the cross).

Since Mark has only one doublet (Mark 9.35b / 10.43–44), Matthew and Luke must have used another source in common.[85]

---

[82] Cf. Robert Morgenthaler, *Statistische Synopse* (see above 3.2.3) 83; Kloppenborg, *Q-Parallels* 209 counts 4464 words in the Matthean material and 4652 in the Lucan.

[83] Bergemann, *Q auf dem Prüfstand* 47–60 makes a high percentage of verbal agreement the sole criterion in assigning texts to Q. Those texts with a lesser degree of verbal agreement usually considered to belong to Q 'may not be assigned to Q, but are to be explained in terms of oral tradition or other sources' (*ibid.* 60). Bergemann carries this approach through in his reconstruction of the Q 'foundational speech' (*Grundrede*, the common source of the Sermon on the Mount/Plain), the nucleus of which manifests a verbal agreement of only 30%. He infers from this: 'The nucleus of the foundational speech was not an integral part of Q. The nucleus of the foundational speech is an independent complex of traditions' (*ibid.* 235). This analysis is based too exclusively on word statistics and pays too little attention to thematic connections and the formative power of redactional work within the Q material (see below 3.3.5./3.3.6). Besides that, the successive history of the process of formation of Q (see below 3.3.5) would lead one to expect in any case that the process of tradition and formation would lead to the incorporation of material with differing degrees of verbal agreement.

[84] A complete list is given in R. Morgenthaler, *Statistische Synopse* 128ff.

[85] Cf. Morgenthaler, *Statistische Synopse* 140.

The contents of Q are as follows:

I. The Beginnings

Matthew		Luke
(3.1–3[4–6]	Appearance of John the Baptist	3.2–4)[86]
3.7–10	Call to Repentance / Children of Abraham	3.7–9
3.11, 12	The Coming One / Baptism in the Spirit	3: (15)16, 17
(3.13, 16, 17	The Baptism of Jesus	3.21, 22)
4.1–11	The Temptation of Jesus	4.1–13

II. Sermon on the Mount/Plain

5.1, 3, 4–5, 6–10	The Beatitudes	6.12, 17, 20, 21
(–	The Woes	6.24–26)
5.44	Love for Enemies	6.27, 28
5.39b–41	Patient Endurance	6.29
5.42	Giving / Loaning	6.30
7.12	The Golden Rule	6.31
5.45–47	Conduct appropriate to Children of God	6.32–35
5.48	Merciful like the Father	6.36
7.1, 2	Judging – Giving – Measure to Others	6.37, 38
15.14	Blind Guides	6.39
10.24, 25	Disciples – Master	6.40
7.3–5	Log – Splinter	6.41, 42
7.16–20	Good and Bad Trees	6.43, 44
12.34b, 35	Treasure of the Heart	6.45
7.21	Those who Say 'Lord Lord'	6.46
7.24–27	On Building Houses	6.47–49
7.28	Conclusion	7.1a

III. The Nobleman of Capernaum

8.5–10, 13	The Nobleman of Capernaum	7.(1b–6a)6b–10

IV. Sayings about John the Baptist

11.2, 3	The Baptist's Question	7.18–20(21)
11.4–6	Response to the Baptist's Question	7.22, 23
11.7–9	Testimony for the Baptist	7.24–26

---

[86] Uncertain texts are in parentheses; Luke preserves the original order of Q better than Matthew. For evidence and rationale, cf. Kloppenborg, *Formation* 69–80.

11.10	Quotation from Malachi 3.1	7.27
11.11	The One who is Greater	7.28
11.16–19	On the Obstinate Children	7.31–35

V. Discipleship and Mission

8.19, 20	Discipleship – 'Foxes'	9.57, 58
8.21, 22	Discipleship – 'Dead Bury their Dead'	9.59–60
(–	Discipleship – 'Looking Back'	9.61, 62)
(–	Selection – Sending	10.1)
9.37, 38	Great Harvest – Few Workers	10.2
10.16a	Like Sheep among Wolves	10.3
10.9–13	Conduct En Route	10.4–7
10.7–15	Conduct in the Town	10.8–12
11.21–23	Woes over the Towns	10.13–15
10.40	The Authority for the Mission	10.16
11.25–27	The Joyful Prayer of Thanksgiving	10.21, 22
13.16, 17	Blessing of the Eye Witnesses	10.23, 24

VI. Prayer

6.9–13	The Lord's Prayer	11.(1)2–4
7.7, 8	Hearing and Answering Prayer	11.9, 10
7.9–11	The Father and the Asking Child	11.11–13

VII. Disputes

9.32–34; 12.22–24	The Charge of Collusion with Beelzebul	11.14, 15(16)
12.25, 26	1. Response: the Kingdom of Satan	11.17, 18
12.27, 28	2. Response: the Kingdom of God	11.19, 20
12.29	On the Stronger One	11.21, 22
12.30	For Jesus / against Jesus	11.23
12.43–45	On Backsliding	11.24–26
12.38, 39	Demand for Signs / Sign of Jonah	11.16, 29
12.40	Interpretation of the Saying	11.30
12.41, 42	Queen of the South and the Ninevites	11.31, 32
5.15; 6.22, 23	Sayings about Light	11.33–35(36)
23.25(26)	Against the Pharisees 1: Dishes	11.39b–41
23.23	Against the Pharisees 2: Tithing	11.42
23.6, 7	Against the Pharisees 3: Seeking Honor	11.43
23.27, 28	Against the Pharisees 4: Tombs	11.44
23.4	Against the Scribes 1: Burdens	11.(45)46
23.29–31	Against the Scribes 2: Tombs of the Prophets	11.47, 48

5.32	Prohibition of Divorce	16.18
18.7	On Anger	17.1(2)
18.21, 22	Forgiveness	17.3, 4
17.20	On Faith	17.(5)6

XI. Eschatological Events

24.26	Against False Messianic Hopes	17.(22)23
24.27	Interpretive Saying: Like Lightning	17.24
24.28	On Carcass and Vultures	17.37b
24.37–39a	As in the Days of Noah	17.26, 27
24.39b	As in the Days of Lot	17.(28, 29)30(31)
24.40, 41	Two Final Destinies	17.34, 35
25.14–30	On the Talents	19.12–27
19.28	Participation in the Final Judgment	22.28–30

In addition to the texts common to Matthew and Luke, there are texts now contained in only one Gospel that possibly belonged to Q (or to Q^{Mt} or Q^{Lk} respectively): Matt. 5.5, 7–9, 19, 21–30, 33–37; 6.2–8, 16–18; 7.6; 10.5–6, 23; 19.10–12; Luke 3.10–14; 7.3–6a, 29–30; 9.61–62; 11.5–8; 12.16–21, 47–48; 15.8–10, 11, 32; 17.7–10[87].

The outline of the contents above shows that the Q source is composed predominantly of sayings material, containing only a few narratives (the temptation of Jesus Matt. 4.1–11 / Luke 4.1–13; the complex of materials about the Baptist Matt. 11.2–11 / Luke 7.18–28). Although Luke 7.21Q and 10.13Q presuppose Jesus' miraculous deeds, only one miracle story (Matt. 8.5–10, 13 / Luke 7.6b–10) and one reference to a healing (Luke 11.14Q) were incorporated into Q. The sayings material is dominated by words of threat and warning, so that even the two long parables Luke 14.16–24Q and Luke 19.12–27Q stand in the service of Q's message of judgment.

Despite considerable difference, Q agrees with the later Synoptic Gospels in having the same general chronological principle by which the material is arranged, beginning with John the Baptist and concluding with the eschatological discourse (see below 3.3.6). In particular the placement of the temptation story shows, in comparison with the Markan outline, that at least a late redactional layer of Q incorporated chronological-biographical elements.[88]

---

[87] On this cf. also Heinz Schürmann, 'Sprachliche Reminiszenzen an abgeänderte oder ausgelassene Bestandteile der Redequelle im Lukas- und Matthäusevangelium,' in *Traditionsgeschichtliche Untersuchungen zu den synoptischen Evangelien.*, ed. Heinz Schürmann (Düsseldorf: Patmos, 1968) 111–125.

[88] Cf. Kloppenborg, *Formation* 262.

3.3.3 Place and Time of Composition

The Sayings Source presumably originated in (north) *Palestine*, since it's theological perspective is directed primarily to Israel.[89] The proclamations of judgment at the beginning and end of the document are directed against Israel (cf. Luke 3.7–9Q; Luke 22.28–30Q), numerous logia are centered on Palestine by their geographical references and the cultural world they assume (cf. only Luke 7.1Q; 10.13–15Q), the bearers of the Q tradition understand themselves to be faithful to the Law (cf. Luke 16.17Q; Luke 11.42Q), and Q polemic is directed against Pharisees (cf. e.g. Luke 11.39b–44Q).

The Sayings Source was composed before the destruction of the temple,[90] since the sayings against Jerusalem and the temple in Luke 13.34–35Q do not presuppose any military events. A more precise determination of the time of composition must remain hypothetical, but a few indications point to the period between *40 and 50 CE*: (1) Bearers of the sayings tradition, which possibly extends all the way back to pre-Easter times, included both wandering preachers of the Jesus movement as well as local congregations.[91] Thus the conditions in which the Sayings Source originated included both continuity with the beginnings and with the developing congregational structures across the region. (2) The Sayings Source presupposes persecution of the young congregations by Palestinian Jews (cf. Luke 6.22–23Q; Luke 11.49–51Q; Luke 12.4–5 Q; 12.11–12Q). About 50 CE Paul mentions in 1 Thess. 2.14–16 a persecution of Christians in Judea that had already taken place. The execution of James the son of Zebedee by Agrippa I (cf. Acts 12.2) occurred around 44 CE. (3) The positive references to Gentiles in Q (cf. Luke 10.13–15Q; Luke 11.29–31Q; Matt. 8.5–13Q; Matt. 5.47Q; Matt. 22.1–10Q) indicate that the Gentile mission had begun,[92] which is probably to be located in the period between 40 and 50 CE.[93]

---

[89] Cf. Gerd Theißen, *The Gospels in Context* (see above 3.1.1) 221–234.

[90] Cf. Jülicher – Fascher, *Einleitung* 339.

[91] Cf. Sato, *Q und Prophetie* 407.

[92] Cf. Lührmann, *Redaktion* 86–88; Thomas Schmeller, *Brechungen*, SBS 136 (Stuttgart: Katholisches Bibelwerk, 1989) 97; Friedrich W. Horn, 'Christentum und Judentum' 363. According to Luke 10.7–8Q Jewish food laws no longer apply to the Q missionaries!

[93] Theißen, *The Gospels in Context* 206–221, sees in the temptation pericope Matt 4.1–11Q a direct reaction to the attempt by Caligula in the year 40 CE to have a statue of himself installed in the Jerusalem temple (cf. Jos. *War* 2.184–203), and dates Q in the 40s. In contrast, Horn, 'Christentum und Judentum' 346 places the main written collection in Greek in the period after 60 CE; cf. the previous argument of Jülicher and Fascher, *Einleitung* 339–340. The final redaction of the document is dated around 70 CE by Paul Hoffmann, 'QR und der Menschensohn,' in *The Four Gospels*, eds. F. Van Segbroeck et al. (FS F. Neirynck), BETL 100 (Leuven: Leuven University Press, 1992) 421–456. For Hoffmann why Q did not continue as an independent document is thus explained by the brief period it existed before being incorporated into Matthew and Luke.

3.3.4 Tradition and Language

The Sayings Source came to Matthew and Luke in *written* form,[94] as indicated by the following observations:[95] (1) The high degree of verbal agreement between Matthew and Luke, which especially in the longer sections where there is almost 100% symmetry in verbal arrangement can no longer be adequately explained by oral tradition. In addition, the extent of verbal agreement between Matthew and Luke in Q pericopes is higher than in the sections they have taken over from Mark.[96] (2) The parallels in the order of pericopes point to written sources. (3) Doublets and double traditions are indications of a process of formation based on written sources.

The divergences between the Matthean and Lucan Q material suggest that each had a different version of Q (Q^{Mt} or Q^{Lk}).[97]

> Example: While nine beatitudes are found in Matt. 5.3–12, there are only four in Luke 6.20–23. In addition, there is considerable difference in vocabulary between the two texts. The woes (Luke 6.24–26) were obviously not read by Matthew in his copy of Q. Since it is very unlikely that Luke composed the woes himself,[98] they must be assigned to Q^{Lk}.[99]

Whether Q was composed in Aramaic or Greek remains a disputed question. The close agreements between Matthew and Luke make it probable that the copies they used were written in Greek. The LXX is used in Luke 4.4, 8, 10–11, 12Q. The acceptance of an original composition in Aramaic is based on the supposed history of the tradition of numerous individual texts (from the historical Jesus through the pre- and post-Easter circle of the disciples), but unambiguous linguistic evidence cannot be provided to support this hypothetical reconstruction.[100] Both the predominately bilingual character of first-century Palestine and the problem of exact retranslations into Aramaic point rather to a Q that was originally composed in Greek, which does not exclude the possibility of individual sayings having had a previous Aramaic form.

---

[94] This consensus of scholarship is rejected by Joachim Jeremias, 'Zur Hypothese einer schriftlichen Logienquelle Q,' in *ABBA* (Göttingen: Vandenhoeck & Ruprecht, 1966) 90–92 and by Hans-Theo Wrege, *Die Überlieferungsgeschichte der Bergpredigt*, WUNT 9 (Tübingen: J. C. B. Mohr [Paul Siebeck] 1968).

[95] Cf. Kloppenborg, *Formation* 42–51.

[96] Cf. Sato, *Q und Prophetie* 16.

[97] Cf. above *ibid.* 47–62.

[98] So e.g. François Bovon, *Lukasevangelium* (see below 3.6.1) 1.298.

[99] Cf. the analysis of Friedrich W. Horn, *Glaube und Handeln in der Theologie des Lukas* (see below 3.6.1) 122–137. A survey of the present state of the discussion is offered by Frans Neirynck, 'Q^{Mt} and Q^{Lk} and the Reconstruction of Q,' in *Evangelica*, BETL 99 (Leuven: Leuven University Press, 1991) 475–480.

[100] Cf. Kloppenborg, *Formation* 51–64 (discussion of all relevant problems!); Schulz, *Q* 27–28.

3.3.5 *The Origin of the Sayings Source*

The process by which the Sayings Source came into being is difficult to determine. That the Q materials came together through a variety of traditional channels is acknowledged on all sides, but the stages of tradition, composition, and redaction that resulted in the completed Sayings Source is vigorously debated. Thus D. Lührmann distinguished older Q-traditions (characterized by a Son of Man Christology and imminent expectation of the parousia) and later materials in which the parousia hope had receded, the Gentile mission was presupposed, and the dominant role was played by wisdom materials.

S. Schulz differentiates between older Palestinian-Jewish Christian Q texts and traditions from a later Hellenistic-Jewish Christian Q community of Syria. In this theory, the oldest Q layer contained sayings from the post-Easter Spirit-inspired enthusiasts (e.g. Beatitudes, Lord's Prayer), the charismatic-eschatological sharpening of the Torah (e.g. the command to love enemies, the prohibition of divorce), and the prophetic message of the near Creator God (e.g. Matt. 6.19–21Q). Schulz's younger stratum contained sayings about the earthly Jesus (e.g. Matt. 4.1–11Q), was concerned with the delay of the parousia (e.g. Matt. 7.13–14 Q) and the judgment of Israel (e.g. Matt. 19.28Q), deals with the acceptance of publicans and sinners (Matt. 18.12–14Q), and included sayings about following Jesus and life in the church (cf. Matt. 10.38Q).

So too A. Polag regards Q as composed of several identifiable strata. The Aramaic 'primary tradition' was rooted in the pre-Easter circle of disciples. Then follows a 'secondary traditional stratum' in which small collections of sayings were already grouped together (e.g. Luke 6.20–21, 27–36Q; 10.4–11, 16Q). The 'primary collection' was then formed redactionally, forming the body of Q in Greek. In the further course of tradition additions were made to this primary collection, which reflected the particular situations of the community's life, especially the polemic against false teachers (cf. e.g. Luke 9.57–62Q; 11.1b–13Q; 16.17Q; 17.1–2Q and others). Polag postulates a fifth developmental stage, a late scribal redaction containing clear christological reflections (cf. e.g. Luke 3.7–9, 16–17 Q; Luke 4.1–13Q; Luke 7.1–10Q).

J. S. Kloppenborg proposes to explain the origins of Q in terms of a three-stratum model. In his view the oldest layer of Q was composed of 'wisdom speeches,' including the nuclear elements of the Sermon on the Plain/Mount and the Missions Discourse, as well as Luke 11.2–4, 9–13 Q; Luke 12.2–12, 22–34 Q; Luke 13.24–14.35 Q, and others.[101] At a later stage

---

[101] Cf. Kloppenborg, *Formation* 171–237.

this complex was combined with, and partly reshaped by, materials that treat the proclamation of judgment against Israel (preaching of the Baptist, the nobleman of Capernaum, the Baptist's question, the Beelzebul controversy, the demand for signs, the Q apocalypse).[102] The third and final stratum was provided by the temptation story,[103] which presents Jesus as a model for one's relationship to God.

A complex model for the origin of Q is presented by H. Schürmann. He understands Q as 'a compositional structure that grew by stages . . . , in which in six thematic speeches of Jesus that are intentionally arranged in a well thought-through order, along with smaller collections of sayings of the Baptist and Jesus.'[104] Schürmann does not speak of 'strata of tradition' but reckons with four 'compositional forms,' which are at the same time 'compositional stages': (1) 'Sayings Pairs.' This type designates combinations of sayings of the Lord in which for example a 'supplementary saying' or 'commentary saying' is added to a 'primary saying.' (2) 'Sayings Groups.' 'Sayings Pairs' are combined into 'Sayings Groups' and provided with 'prefaces' and/or 'epilogues.' (3) 'Structured Compositions.' These are formed by the intentional combination of 'Sayings Groups' so that here we meet the redactional activity that gives Q its 'form and structure.'[105] (4) 'Speech Compositions.' As macro-texts these differing compositional forms gather up Jesus' words and address them to the new post-Easter situation. Most of the 'Speech Compositions' originated prior to the final redaction of Q.

M. Sato distinguishes within his formative model two great redactional blocks that take up previously existing groups and collections of sayings and edit them into literary units. 'Redaction A' comprises the 'John the Baptist complex' (Luke 3.2–7.35Q), 'Redaction B' the 'missions complex' (Luke 9.57–10.24Q). The sayings clusters that follow were added by the 'Redaction C' and attached to the two preceding redactions. According to Sato, characteristic for 'Redaction C' are the pronouncements of judgment against Israel and the motif of divine wisdom. Luke 4.1–13Q; 7.27Q; and 10.22Q are distinguishable from the other Q-materials on formal and/or material grounds and must certainly be regarded as later additions. Sato operates with an open-ended model, for 'Q was not redactionally fixed all at once, but came to its final stage through a long process of collection, additions, redactions and editorial reworkings. The Sayings Source is

---

[102] *Ibid.* 102–170.

[103] Cf. *ibid.* 246–262; for a critique of Kloppenborg's position cf. Dieter Zeller, 'Eine weisheitliche Grundschrift in der Logienquelle?' in *The Four Gospels*, ed. Franz Van Segbroeck et al. (FS F. Neirynck), BETL 100 (Leuven: Leuven University Press, 1992) 389–401.

[104] Schürmann, 'Kompositionsgeschichte' 327.

[105] *Ibid.* 333.

characterized by successive stages of formation.'[106] A description of the origin of Q that attempts to be more precise than this is in Sato's view hardly possible.

There is a relative consensus among Q scholars that Q came into being in a *succession of stages* with beginning- and endpoints that can be determined. The process began with oldest sayings material coalescing into sayings clusters (cf. e.g. Luke 11.52Q; Luke 16.17Q; Luke 9.57–60Q; 11.39–51Q).[107] At the end of this process the addition of the temptation story (Matt. 4.1–11Q) projects Q in the direction of proto-biography. Texts such as Luke 7.27Q and 10.22Q could well have been worked into Q at this late stage.[108] The intermediate formative stage is characterized by the projection and conveyance of smaller units of tradition into more and more complex compositional structures. Sociologically this process is influenced by the separation from Israel and emphasis on the motif of judgment. Thus the introductory and concluding units that are central in the composition of Q manifest a sharp polemic against Israel (cf. Luke 3.7–9, 15–17Q / Luke 17Q; 19.12–27Q; 22.28–30Q). As introit and testamentary conclusion of the Sayings Source, these texts formulate with great sharpness the failure of the Q-mission to Israel and the final break with the (previously) elect people. Rejection of the message and persecution of the messengers, and the resulting judgment on Israel also determine Luke 6.22–23Q; 7.31–35Q; 11.29–32Q; 11.49–51Q; 13.34–35Q; Matt. 22.6Q, and give the theological perspective of the present form of the Sayings Source its theological stamp.[109] The process of Q's origin and development can no longer be reconstructed in detail, but a certain movement cannot fail to be perceived: following a failed mission to Israel there is a turning away from the synagogue and a (partial) turning toward the Gentiles.

The process by which Q originated was influenced by both wisdom material (cf. Luke 7.35Q; 10.21Q; 11.31, 49Q)[110] and prophetic/apocalyptic material.[111] The opposition between these two streams of tradition constructed by Kloppenborg and Sato is only an apparent tension, and has already been overcome in Q (cf. Luke 11.31–32Q: Solomon and Jonah as

---

[106] Sato, *Q und Prophetie* 46.

[107] Cf. Horn, 'Christentum und Judentum' 347–352.

[108] Cf. Sato, *Q und Prophetie* 35–38.

[109] Cf. Horn, 'Christentum und Judentum' 357ff.; a different position is advocated by Karrer, 'Christliche Gemeinde und Israel' 146ff.

[110] On this cf. Walter Grundmann, *Weisheit im Horizont des Reiches Gottes* (Stuttgart 1988) 130–239; Hermann v. Lips, *Weisheitliche Traditionen im Neuen Testament*, WMANT 64 (Neukirchen: Neukirchener Verlag, 1990) 197–227, 267–280.

[111] Cf. Sato, *Q und Prophetie* passim.

witnesses at the judgment; Luke 11.49Q: prophets and apostles as emissaries of Wisdom.)

3.3.6 Structure and Genre of the Sayings Source

The extant form of the Sayings Source is a carefully composed compositional structure.[112] After the portrayal of the beginnings of Jesus' ministry comes the Sermon on the Mount as the programmatic speech. The story of the Nobleman of Capernaum is an unmistakable signal of the inclusion of the Gentiles in the eschatological act of God intended primarily for Israel. To this were joined sayings about John the Baptist and the meaning of discipleship. The very positive statements about the Baptist point to the competing Baptist movement, which is now instructed by its teacher regarding both his own high status and the significance of Jesus. The sayings concerning prayer are to be understood against the background of the two following sections: in the midst of conflicting claims to loyalty, only a vital relationship with God provides the power courageously to confess the Son of Man, which is God's will. Conflict with Israel and the challenge to confess Jesus characterize the current situation of the Q-community. So too the sayings on anxiety and alertness provide an insight into the problems of the community's life. People can let dependence on wealth and anxiety about tomorrow, as well as doubt about the return of the Son of Man, paralyze their faithful response. The penultimate compositional unit is woven together from a great variety of material, before the Sayings Source is brought to an appropriate conclusion by sayings about the eschatological events.

The efforts to classify the form of the Sayings Source as a whole have produced quite different results. Since a passion story and resurrection account is lacking, the Sayings Source cannot be described as a complete Gospel. Thus A. Jülicher designated Q a 'Semi-Gospel.'[113] E. Bammel classifies the Sayings Source as a 'Testament,' pointing to Luke 22.28–30.[114] J. M. Robinson understands Q in analogy to the Coptic Gospel of Thomas as a collection of wisdom sayings, to which he gives the generic designation λόγοι σοφῶν (sayings of the wise).[115] J. S. Kloppenborg adopts this general point of view, seeing Q as a chreia collection.[116] In support of

---

[112] Cf. Schürmann, 'Zeugnis der Redequelle' 76–77.

[113] Cf. Jülicher – Fascher, *Einleitung* 347.

[114] Cf. Bammel, 'Das Ende von Q' 48.

[115] Cf. Robinson, 'LOGOI SOPHON: On the Gattung of Q' 71–113. Translator's note: more recently Robinson and several of his associates insist on referring to Q as a 'Sayings *Gospel*.' (E.g., J. M. Robinson, 'The Sayings Gospel Q,' in *The Four Gospels*, eds., F. Van Segbroeck et al. (FS Frans Neirynck) (Leuven: Leuven University Press, 1992) 1.361–388.

[116] Cf. Kloppenborg, *Formation* 263–345.

this view he can point to a series of parallels in the ancient world, but at the same time his defining Q as a 'wisdom collection'[117] does not do justice to the strong biographical elements of the Sayings Source. It is not the case that this biographical dimension was first introduced by the late addition of the temptation story, which rather strengthened the biographical tendencies already present in Q.[118]

M. Sato classifies the Sayings Source as a kind of 'prophetic book.'[119] The macro-genre is constituted by the numerous small micro-genres, behind which stands a prophetic circle of disciples. According to Sato, the sapiential horizon of numerous sayings is incorporated into the dominant prophetic perspective. To be sure, the Sayings Source does not contain an account of the prophet's call, a central element in the genre 'prophetic book,' and the prophetic nature of Jesus' ministry is not explicitly emphasized.[120] The phenomenon that Q is not a unity from the perspective of tradition criticism, form criticism, or the history of religions leads Schürmann to the conclusion that the 'Sayings Source' is a distinctive literary genre.[121] 'We have here a distinctively new kind of redactional composition which reports the "coming" of Jesus, his "destiny," and his becoming manifest in his word (of the kingdom) and which concludes by announcing his parousia. Since the document has been lost, it received no traditional name, but alongside the passion story and as its counterpart became the second major element that constituted the raw materials for the genus "gospel."'[122] The uniqueness of Q is at once both stronger and weaker than its representation in this thesis, for Schürmann can rightly point to the singularity of the Sayings Source, but this very fact makes it impossible to give it a generic designation.[123] D. Dormeyer describes Q as an 'ideal sayings-biography.'[124] It is generically kin to the narrative 'ideal biography' of Matthew and Luke, and thus could be incorporated by them into the Markan framework.

The biographical and narrative elements of Q, as well as its structure as

---

[117] Cf. Kloppenborg, *Formation* 328.

[118] Against Kloppenborg, *Formation* 326: 'The addition of the temptation narrative to Q is probably not enough to allow us to claim a biographical genre for Q; however its addition is one step in that direction.'

[119] Cf. Sato, *Q und Prophetie* 299 et passim.

[120] Cf. Lührmann, 'Mark and Q' 65, who points to texts such as Luke 7.26/Matt 11.9; Luke 11.31–32/Matt 12.41–42, where the category of 'prophetic' is considered inadequate for portraying the person of Jesus.

[121] Schürmann, 'Das Zeugnis der Redequelle' 65 note 1.

[122] *Ibid.* 77.

[123] Cf. Sato, *Q und Prophetie* 2.

[124] Cf. Detlev Dormeyer, *Das Neue Testament im Rahmen der antiken Literaturgeschichte* (see above 2.3.2) 214–220.

a whole, show that the Sayings Source was a collection of sayings that was developing in the direction of a 'gospel,' and that its integration into the Gospels of Matthew and Luke was consistent with this development. Thus the designation '*Semi-Gospel*' appropriately indicates the place of Q in the history of early Christian theology, even if it does not properly specify its genre in the strict sense.[125] The singularity of Q means that its genre can be indicated only in relation to other genres, which of course means that the determination of the genre of Q as a whole will depend upon 'which stream of tradition within Q one considers of primary importance in characterizing Q as a whole.'[126] The Sayings Source was evolving in the direction of the genre 'gospel,' so that from this perspective it can be considered a 'semi-gospel.'

3.3.7 *The Tradents of the Sayings Tradition*

The circle of tradents that handed on the traditions found in Q was composed of two different types: alongside wandering missionaries there was also an extensive network of settled disciples of Jesus.[127] Indications of *wandering missionaries* are found in texts such as Luke 9.57–62Q; 10.1–12, 16Q; 12.22–31, 33–34Q. In these texts an ethos of homelessness and poverty come to expression, renunciation of violence is proclaimed (Luke 6.27–38Q), and normal binding human relationships lose their significance (Luke 14.26Q; 12.51–53Q).[128] Such a life style does not represent an unparalleled phenomenon within the history of early Christianity, for already Paul (and his inner circle of co-workers) practiced a comparably radical style of personal life and missionary work (cf. 1 Cor. 9.5, 14–15), and the Didache documents this phenomenon as still present at the beginning of the second century (cf. Did 11–13). Finally, it should be noted that impressive parallels are presented by the Cynic movement, whose radical ethos agrees in many points with the Q traditions (cf. Epictetus, *Discourses* 3.22).[129]

Many sayings in Q, however, presuppose the life of a *settled community*, such as the parable of the Mustard Seed and the parable of the Leaven (Luke 13.18–21Q), the prohibition of divorce (Luke 16.18Q), or the saying

---

[125] Cf. Schulz, *Q* 23–25; Georg Strecker, *History of New Testament Literature* (see above 1.2) 130.

[126] Hermann v. Lips, *Weisheitliche Traditionen* (see above 3.3.5) 226.

[127] Cf. Sato, *Q und Prophetie* 375ff.

[128] Cf. Gerd Theißen, 'Wanderradikalismus,' in *Studien zur Soziologie des Urchristentums*, WUNT 19 (Tübingen: J. C. B. Mohr [Paul Siebeck] 1983²) 79–105; critical questions directed against this position are found in Thomas Schmeller, *Brechungen* (see above 3.3.3) 50ff.

[129] On this key text, cf. Margarethe Billerbeck, *Epiktet: Vom Kynismus*, PhAnt 34 (Leiden, 1978).

about the householder and the thief (Luke 12.39–40Q).[130] The wandering missionaries had many settled sympathizers in the local communities[131] who offered them a material basis for their mission and who provided them with lodging (cf. Luke 9.58Q) and support (Luke 10.5–7Q). This indicates a two-fold social stratification in the Q circle. Material poverty continues to be reflected in numerous Q sayings (e.g. Luke 6.20–21Q; 7.22Q; 11.3Q), while at the same time the challenge to decide between God and Mammon (Luke 16.13Q) or heavenly and earthly treasures (Luke 12.33–34Q), as well as the readiness to give unconditionally to others in Luke 6.30Q all infer a community with some economic resources (cf. further Luke 14.15–24Q). The sayings were gathered and preserved in the local settled communities, and this is the probable location of their preliminary editing. The relation between the wandering missionaries and the settled communities need not be thought of in static terms, since a vigorous exchange surely prevailed between the two circles, each of which recruited members from the other.[132] Here too radicality and normality conditioned and supplemented each other.

It may be that the beginnings of the Q circle reach back to pre-Easter times,[133] but it was only after Easter that the formation of the sayings tradition, the wandering mission, and local community structures began in earnest. The wandering missionaries transmitted sayings of the historical Jesus (e.g. Luke 6.20–21Q; 10.4–6Q; 11.20Q; 17.26–27, 30Q), but at the same time functioned as prophets of the Risen One. Prophets emerged as mouthpieces of the exalted Lord, as immediately-inspired spokespersons who delivered intelligible oracles from the risen Jesus, and interpreted the community situation, the Scripture, or sayings of the historical Jesus (cf. e.g. Luke 6.22–23Q; 10.21–22Q; Matt. 12.31–32Q; Matt. 19.28Q).[134] The Q sayings served as parenesis, catechesis, and missionary proclamation; the broad spectrum of the tradition does not permit a more precise description. Many texts in Q are directed both to 'outsiders' and 'insiders.'

---

[130] Cf. further Luke 6.43Q; 6.47–49Q; 7.32Q; 11.11–13Q; 14.42–46Q; 12.58Q; 13.25Q.

[131] Cf. Gerd Theißen, *Sociology of Early Palestinian Christianity*, tr. John Bowden (Philadelphia: Fortress Press) 17–23.

[132] Differently Schmeller, *Brechungen* 93–98, who regards the wandering missionaries as commissioned representatives of the Q community and formulates the results of his analysis as follows: '1. Q is a community document. 2. The Q community sent out missionaries who lived as wandering charismatics. 3. If there were Q sayings created or transmitted exclusively by such wandering charismatics, they can no longer be distinguished. 4. The missionary discourse is community tradition but still comes close to providing a witness for the lifestyle of the wandering charismatics that can be positively evaluated' (96).

[133] Cf. the sketch in Sato, *Q und Prophetie* 375–379.

[134] Cf. the foundational study of M. Eugene Boring, *The Continuing Voice of Jesus* (Louisville: Westminster/ John Knox, 1991) 15–234.

3.3.8 The Sayings Source and the Gospel of Mark

The common material in Q and Mark (cf. Mark 1.2; 1.7–8; 1.12–13; 3.22–26, 27–29; 4.21, 22, 24, 25; 4.30–32; 6.7–13; 8.11, 12; 8.34–35; 8.38; 9.37, 40, 42, 50; 10.10–11; 10.31; 11.22–23; 12.37b–40; 13.9, 11, 33–37) has repeatedly led to the hypothesis of a literary dependence of Mark on Q.[135] But if Mark had known Q, his criteria for selecting the material he used, and especially the sayings he omitted, cannot be explained. The reasons given remain hypothetical (Mark as supplement to the sayings source,[136] Q as supplement to Mark,[137] a critical debate by Mark with the Christology of the sayings source[138]), and fail to make plausible the considerable differences in the literary configuration and the theological orientation between Q and Mark. A direct literary connection between Mark and Q must be regarded as improbable.[139] The text complexes they share point rather to *independent access* of each to old Jesus-traditions, but contacts between the two streams of tradition at the pre-redactional level are not to be excluded.[140]

3.3.9 Basic Theological Ideas of the Sayings Source

The theology of the Sayings Source is derived from its basic conviction that the stance one takes to Jesus and his message is a matter of one's salvation.[141] In Q, neither the promises of salvation nor the threats of judgment are to be separated from the person of the speaker. In Q too, at the beginning of Jesus' proclamation stands the message of salvation, the pronouncements of salvation pregnantly formulated in Luke 6.20–21Q as beatitudes to which no conditions are attached. Jesus pronounces those who have seen and heard to be blessed (Luke 10.23–24Q), announces that

---

[135] Cf. Bernhard Weiß, *Lehrbuch der Einleitung in das Neue Testament* (Berlin, 1897³) 468–469; Wilhelm Bousset, 'Wellhausens Evangelienkritik II,' *ThR* 9 (1906) 44; in recent study cf. especially Wolfgang Schenk, 'Der Einfluß der Logienquelle auf das Markusevangelium,' *ZNW* 70 (1979) 141–165; Walter Schmithals, *Einleitung* 403; in addition the works of Jan Lambrecht (most recently, 'John the Baptist and Jesus in Mark 1.1–15: Markan Redaction of Q,' *NTS* 38 [1992] 357–384). A critical review of the present discussion is provided by Frans Neirynck, 'Recent Developments' 421–433.

[136] Cf. Jan Lambrecht, 'Q-Influence on Mark 8,34–9,1,' in *Logia*, ed. J. Delobel (227–304) 304.

[137] Cf. Schmithals, *Einleitung* 403: 'The Sayings-Source Q was from the beginning composed as a supplement to the Gospel of Mark, which it presupposes.'

[138] Cf. Schenk, 'Einfluß' 162: 'Possibly Mark was concerned to dispose of the Sophia-Christology of the Q redaction.' Cf. also Boring, *Sayings of the Risen Jesus* (see above 3.3.7) 195–203.

[139] Cf. Lauffen, *Doppelüberlieferungen* 59–77; Schüling, *Studien* 215.

[140] Jülicher – Fascher, *Einleitung* 347. 'In any case, the influence of the Markan plan on Q is the more likely.' To be sure, Jülicher assumes that Mark and Q were composed at about the same time.   [141] Cf. Kosch, *Q und Jesus* 44ff.

the time of salvation has dawned, for 'the blind see and the lame walk, lepers are made clean and the deaf hear, the dead are raised, and the poor have good news preached to them' (Luke 7.22Q). The disciples are sent out to offer peace (Luke 10.5–6Q) and to announce the nearness of the kingdom of God to them (Luke 10.9, 11Q). The stance one takes to Jesus and his message is not without consequences, for 'everyone who acknowledges me before others, the Son of Man also will acknowledge before the angels of God; but whoever denies me before others will be denied before the angels of God' (Luke 12.8–9Q). Rejecting the saving message of Jesus results in the threat of judgment. The Q missionaries are sent out sharing the same destiny as their Lord, 'like sheep among wolves' (Luke 10.3Q) subject to persecution by the Jews (Luke 6.22–23Q). Their pronouncements of judgment apply to 'this generation' that rejects the message of Jesus and his messengers (cf. Luke 7.31Q; 11.29Q; 11.30–32Q; 11.50Q). The call to repentance did not affect large numbers of Israel (cf. Luke 10.13–15Q; 15.7Q), who take offense at Jesus (Luke 7.23Q) and demand further legitimization (Luke 11.29–30Q). Thus it will be on the day of the Son of Man as it was in the days of Noah, 'They were eating and drinking, and marrying and being given in marriage, until the day Noah entered the ark, and the flood came and destroyed all of them' (Luke 17.26–27).

Differently than in Mark, Matthew, and Luke, there are no discernible themes that structure the material as a whole and give it a united theological character. 'That which binds the Q collection into a whole . . . is its theological presupposition, namely the conviction of the tradents that Jesus opens to people who encounter him the possibility to decide for God and his kingdom, and to live out this decision in their history. In this event, his own word is an effective force.'[142] This thoroughgoing orientation in Q toward a Jesus who gives *authoritative instruction* could also explain why the passion, death, and resurrection of Jesus are only alluded to indirectly or not expressed at all, and why affirmations of the atoning death of Jesus are entirely absent. The death of Jesus on the cross is presupposed in the Sayings Source (cf. Luke 14.27Q; 13.34–35Q; in addition Luke 6.22–23Q; 6.27–29Q; 11.47–51Q; 12.4Q), but in contrast to other New Testament writings, its saving dimensions are not developed.[143] Q concentrates on the identity of the earthly and the exalted Jesus.[144] It is this identification alone

---

[142] Polag, 'Mitte der Logienquelle' 110.

[143] This does not mean, however, that the Sayings Source was unaware of the salvific significance of Jesus' death. Contra H. E. Tödt, *Son of Man* 251.

[144] Cf. only Luke 7.34Q; 9.58Q; 17.24, 26Q, where the identity of the earthly Jesus with the coming Son of Man is presupposed. On the concept of exaltation involved, cf. Wilhelm Thüsing, *Erhöhungsvorstellung und Parusieerwartung in der ältesten nachösterlichen Christologie*, SBS 42 (Stuttgart: Katholisches Bibelwerk, 1970).

that confers on the words of Jesus their binding quality and forms the basis of the faith of the Q community that Jesus' message has the highest relevance for present and future. The significance of Jesus, according to the testimony of the Sayings Source, is not expressed in kerygmatic formulae, but is rather experienced in the immediate hearing and doing of the words of Jesus. In this conception, Easter is no foreign body, but rather it is precisely through the resurrection of Jesus that his words preserve their continuing significance, also in the time after Easter. It is the Easter event that demands the transmission of the words of the earthly and exalted one, without itself becoming a theme.[145]

3.4 The Gospel of Mark

3.4.1 Literature

Commentaries

Lohmeyer, Ernst. *Das Evangelium des Markus*, KEK 1/2. Göttingen: Vandenhoeck & Ruprecht, 1967[8]; Schweizer, Eduard. *The Good News According to Mark*, tr. Donald H. Madvig, NTD 1. Richmond: John Knox Press, 1970; Klostermann, Erich. *Das Markusevangelium*, HNT 3. Tübingen: J. C. B. Mohr (Paul Siebeck), 1971[5]; Ernst, Josef. *Das Evangelium nach Markus*, RNT. Regensburg: Pustet, 1981; Mann, C. S. *Mark*, AncB 27. Garden City: Doubleday & Co., Inc., 1986; Schmithals, Walter. *Das Evangelium nach Markus*, ÖTK 2.1–2. Gütersloh: Gütersloher Verlagshaus (Gerd Mohn), 1986[2]; Lührmann, Dieter. *Das Markusevangelium*, HNT 3. Tübingen: J. C. B. Mohr (Paul Siebeck), 1987; Gnilka, Joachim. *Das Evangelium nach Markus*, EKK II 1.2. Neukirchen: Neukirchener Verlag, 1986[2], 1989[3]; Grundmann, Walter. *Das Evangelium nach Markus*, ThHK 2. Berlin: Evangelische Verlagsanstalt, 1989[10]; Guelich, Robert. *Mark*, WBC 34A. Dallas: Word Press, 1989; Pesch, Rudolf. *Das Markusevangelium*, HThK II 1.2. Freiburg: Herder, 1989[5], 1991[6]; Gundry, Robert H. *Mark. A Commentary on His Apology for the Cross*. Grand Rapids, Michigan: Wm. B. Eerdmans, 1993.

Monographs

Marxsen, Willi. *Mark the Evangelist*, tr. J. Boyce. Nashville: Abingdon, 1969; Kertelge, Karl. *Die Wunder Jesu im Markusevangelium*, StANT 23. Munich: Kösel, 1970; Kuhn, Heinz-Wolfgang. *Ältere Sammlungen im Markusevangelium*, SUNT 8. Göttingen: Vandenhoeck & Ruprecht, 1970; Wrede, William. *The Messianic Secret*, tr. J. C. G.

---

[145] Other recent attempts at resolving this problem: Sato, *Q und Prophetie* 383, responds to the question of why there is no passion story in Q: 'In no prophetic book of the Old Testament is there a report of the death of the prophet.' Hermann v. Lips, *Weisheitliche Traditionen* (see above 3.3.5) 278, thinks that Q understood Jesus as a rejected messenger of Wisdom, and that the death of Jesus was a pointer to the nearness of the coming kingdom of God, 'without the death of Jesus itself having salvific significance.'

Greig. Cambridge/London: James Clark & Co., 1971; Koch, Dietrich A. *Die Bedeutung der Wundererzählungen für die Christologie des Markusevangeliums*, BZNW 42. Berlin: Walter de Gruyter, 1975; Kelber, Werner H., ed. *The Passion in Mark*. Philadelphia: Fortress Press, 1976; Robinson, James M. *The Problem of History in Mark and Other Marcan Studies*. Philadelphia: Fortress Press, 1982; Breytenbach, Cilliers. *Nachfolge und Zukunftserwartung nach Markus*, AThANT 71. Zürich: Theologischer Verlag, 1984; Dschulnigg, Peter. *Sprache, Redaktion und Intention des Markus-Evangeliums*, SBB 11. Stuttgart: Katholisches Bibelwerk, 1986²; Söding, Thomas. *Glaube bei Markus*, SBB 12. Stuttgart: Katholisches Bibelwerk, 1987²; Schenke, Ludger. *Das Markusevangelium*. Stuttgart: Kohlhammer, 1988; Räisänen, Heikki. *The 'Messianic Secret' in Mark's Gospel*, tr. Christopher Tuckett. Edinburgh: T. & T. Clark, 1990; Fendler, Folkert. *Studien zum Markusevangelium*, GTA 49. Göttingen: Vandenhoeck & Ruprecht, 1991; Scholtissek, Klaus. *Die Vollmacht Jesu*, NTA 25. Münster: Aschendorff, 1992; Weiser, Alfons. *Theologie des Neuen Testaments II* (1993; see above 3.3.1) 44–78; Tolbert, Mary Ann. *Sowing the Gospel. Mark's World in Literary-Critical Perspective*. Minneapolis: Fortress, 1991; Yarbro Collins, Adela. *The Beginning of the Gospel. Probings of Mark in Context*. Minneapolis: Fortress, 1992.

Articles

Hahn, Ferdinand, ed. *Der Erzähler des Evangeliums. Methodische Neuansätze in der Markusforschung*, SBS 118/119. Stuttgart: Katholisches Bibelwerk, 1985 (important collection of essays); Vielhauer, Philipp. 'Erwägungen zur Christologie des Markus-evangeliums,' in *Aufsätze zum Neuen Testament*, TB 31. Munich: Kaiser, 1965; Pesch, Rudolf, ed. *Das Markus-Evangelium*, WdF CDXI. Darmstadt: Wissenschaftliche Buchgesellschaft, 1979 (important collection of essays with contributions by E. Schweizer, G. Strecker, J. Roloff, U. Luz and others); Weber, Reinhard. 'Christologie und "Messiasgeheimnis": ihr Zusammenhang und Stellenwert in den Darstellungs-intentionen des Markus,' EvTh 43 (1983) 108–125; Hengel, Martin. 'The Gospel of Mark: Time of Origin and Situation,' in *Studies in the Gospel of Mark*, tr. John Bowden. Philadelphia: Fortress Press, 1985, 1–30; Lührmann, Dieter. 'Die Pharisäer und die Schriftgelehrten im Markusevangelium,' ZNW 78 (1987) 169–185; Breytenbach, Cilliers, 'Grundzüge markinischer Gottessohn-Christologie,' in *Anfänge der Christologie* (FS F. Hahn), eds. Cilliers Breytenbach and Henning Paulsen. Göttingen: Vandenhoeck & Ruprecht, 1991, 169–184; Hengel, Martin. 'Literary, Theological, and Historical Problems in the Gospel of Mark,' in *The Gospel and the Gospels*. ed. Peter Stuhlmacher (see above 3.1.1) 209–251.

Histories of Research

Pokorný, Petr. 'Das Markus-Evangelium: Literarische und theologische Einleitung mit Forschungsbericht,' in *ANRW* 25.3. Berlin: Walter de Gruyter, 1984, 1969–2035.

3.4.2 *Author*

The author of the oldest Gospel does not give his name; it is the title that first attaches the name 'Mark' to the document. About 130 CE Papias of Hierapolis[146] reports concerning Mark, 'Mark was the interpreter (ἑρμηνευτής) of Peter and wrote down accurately everything that he remembered of the words and deeds of the Lord. It was not, however, in order (οὐ μέντοι τάξει τὰ ὑπὸ τοῦ κυρίου ἢ λεχθέντα ἢ πραχθέντα). For he had neither heard the Lord nor followed him. But later, as I said, he followed Peter, who adjusted his instructions to the needs [of his hearers], but with no intention of providing a connected presentation of the Lord's sayings. Thus Mark did nothing wrong (οὐδὲν ἥμαρτεν Μάρκος) by writing down some things as he remembered them. For he was careful not to omit anything of what he had heard, nor to repeat anything false' (Eusebius HE 3.39.15).

Papias traces this tradition back to the presbyter John, claiming it was delivered to him by followers of the elders whom he had asked about traditions from the apostles (cf. Eusebius HE 3.39.4). Papias offers a twofold defense of Mark: (1) the lack of order in Mark is not a grievous defect. (2) Mark was not an eyewitness of the life of Jesus, but the basis of his Gospel was the oral instruction of Peter, and this is what gives it authenticity and trustworthiness. The first objection may have grown out of a comparison with other Gospels (especially Matthew). Is the Mark–Peter connection a reliable historical tradition,[147] or an apologetic note?[148] The Papias tradition with its tracing of the Gospel of Mark only indirectly to Peter makes clear that the name of Mark as the author of the Gospel was firmly anchored in the tradition from the very beginning. Only in this way can the remarkable state of affairs be accounted for in which a Gospel is ascribed to an early Christian theologian who did not belong to the circle of the original disciples or apostles. But who was this Mark? One immediately thinks of the missionary John Mark firmly connected to the Pauline tradition, as indicated by Phlm. 24 [Col. 4.10]; 2 Tim. 4.11; Acts 12.12, 25; 15.37, 39. A direct connection between this tradition and the Papias notice cannot be discerned. A possible intermediate link might however be present in 1 Peter 5.13, where the author of 1 Peter says 'Your sister church in Babylon, chosen together with you, sends you greetings; and so

---

[146] On Papias and his work, cf. Vielhauer, *Urchristliche Literatur*, 757–765; Ulrich H. J. Körtner, *Papias von Hierapolis*, FRLANT 133 (Göttingen: Vandenhoeck & Ruprecht, 1983).

[147] So for example Hengel, 'Literary, Theological and Historical Problems in the Gospel of Mark' 232ff.

[148] So for example Kurt Niederwimmer, 'Johannes Markus und die Frage nach dem Verfasser des zweiten Evangeliums,' ZNW 58 (1967) 172–188; Vielhauer, *Urchristliche Literatur* 260.

does my son Mark.' It may be that the names 'Mark' and 'Silvanus/ Silas' (cf. 1 Thess. 1.1; 2 Cor. 1.19; 2 Thess. 1.1; 1 Peter 5.12) have penetrated from the Pauline into the Petrine tradition.[149] In that case, the Mark–Peter connection made by Papias could have originated from his awareness of 1 Peter 5.13. Thus a decision cannot yet be made concerning the historical trustworthiness of this tradition, since no distinctive Petrine theology can be discerned behind the Gospel of Mark, nor does Peter play a role in it beyond that already given him in the pre-Markan tradition. No one would suppose that the figure of Peter stands behind the distinctive theology of the Gospel of Mark, if there were no Papias tradition! Nor can a recognizable connection between Pauline theology and the Gospel of Mark be determined. The second Gospel is thus the work of a Christian by the name of Mark, who is otherwise unknown to us.[150]

Was Mark a Jew by birth? In favor of this view would be the correct use of numerous Aramaic (or Hebrew) words in the Gospel.[151] On the other hand, Mark's mother tongue seems to be Greek, for the characteristics of the Markan language do not point to Semitic influence, but correspond to the style of Hellenistic folk literature and the literary Koine.[152] Since Mark demonstrably writes for a Gentile church (cf. 3.4.4), he can be described as a Greek-speaking Gentile Christian who also has a command of Aramaic, probably a native of Syria who grew to adulthood there.[153]

3.4.3 Place and Time of Composition

Mark wrote his Gospel for Greek speaking readers and hearers, as is indicated by the regular translation of Hebrew or Aramaic expressions (cf. e.g. Mark 3.17; 5.41; 7.11, 34; 9.43; 14.36; 15.22, 34). So too, the explanation of Jewish ritual prescriptions in Mark 7.3–4, 14.12, and 15.42 suggests that

---

[149] Cf. Ulrich H. J. Körtner, 'Markus der Mitarbeiter des Petrus,' ZNW 71 (1980) 160–173.

[150] Among those who make the case for John Mark of Jerusalem as author of the Gospel are Jülicher and Fascher, *Einleitung* 296–297; Hengel, 'Literary, Theological and Historical Problems in the Gospel of Mark' 229ff.; Bo Reicke, *Roots of the Synoptic Gospels* (see above 3.2.6) 165; this possibility is considered by Rudolf Pesch, *Markusevangelium* 1.474. A Christian named Mark, otherwise unknown to us, is regarded as the author by e.g. Kümmel, *Introduction* 97; Vielhauer, *Urchristliche Literatur* 346; Schenke, *Markusevangelium* 29–30.

[151] Cf. H. P. Rüger, 'Die lexikalischen Aramaismen im Markusevangelium,' in *Markus-Philologie*, ed. Hubert Cancik (see above 3.1.1) 73–84.

[152] Evidence in Marius Reiser, *Syntax und Stil des Markusevangeliums*, WUNT 2.11 (Tübingen: J. C. B. Mohr [Paul Siebeck] 1984).

[153] If Mark 7.31 can be meaningfully integrated into the Markan composition technique (on this cf. F. G. Lang, 'Über Sidon mitten ins Gebiet der Dekapolis,' *Geographie und Theologie in Markus 7,31*, ZDPV 94 (1978) 145–160, then this text cannot be the basis of denying to Mark any knowledge of the geography of Palestine and neighboring areas. To be sure, Mark 5.1ff. remains problematic in that it presupposes Gerasa to lie in the immediate vicinity of the Galilean sea.

the Markan community was outside Palestine. The numerous Latinisms also catch the eye: *modius* (4.21), *legio* (5.9, 15), *speculator* (6.37), *denarius* (6.37), *pugnus* (7.3), *sextarius* (7.4), *quadrans* (12.42), *flagellare* (15.15), *praetorium* (15.16), *centurio* (15.39, 44–45).[154] In addition, in Mark 12.42 the Greek τὸ λεπτόν ('penny') is translated into the Roman monetary system. Rome is thus often regarded as the place of composition,[155] especially since the Mark/Peter connection can also be seen as pointing to a Roman origin. Against Rome as the place of composition, it must be noted that the Latinisms come from the military or economic world, and thus are not necessarily indications of a connection with the center of the Empire. In addition, the problems of the Roman church reflected in Paul's letter to them ca. fourteen years earlier play no role in the Gospel of Mark (νόμος is completely lacking in Mark!), which would have to mean that Mark was written in Rome for a community outside Rome! Thus Antioch,[156] Syria in general,[157] Galilee,[158] and the Decapolis[159] have been suggested as settings for the writing of Mark, or the attempt to locate its place of origin has been abandoned as fruitless.[160] But Asia Minor also deserves consideration, for this could have been the setting for the Peter/Mark tradition (1 Pet. 5.13; Papias of Hierapolis). Further, the Markan church consisted almost entirely of Gentile Christians, which might also point to Asia Minor.

The Gospel of Mark was written either shortly before or shortly after 70 CE.[161] The precise dating is dependent on the interpretation of Mark 13.2, 14. Both verses, in their present macrocontext, refer to the destruction of

---

[154] On the more extensive possible influence of Latin, cf. Dschulnigg, *Sprache* 277–278.

[155] So e. g. Grundmann, *Markusevangelium* 25–26; Ralph P. Martin, *Mark: Evangelist and Theologian* (Exeter: Paternoster Press, 1972) 52–70; Pesch, *Markusevangelium* 1.13; Hengel, 'The Gospel of Mark' 30; Dschulnigg, *Sprache* 276–280, 620; Pokorný, *Markus-Evangelium* 2021.

[156] Cf. Schmithals, *Markusevangelium* 1.49; Koester, *Introduction* 2.166.

[157] Cf. e.g. Kümmel, *Introduction* 119; Vielhauer, *Urchristliche Literatur* 347; Lührmann, *Markusevangelium* 7; Schenke, *Markusevangelium* 47; Gerd Theißen, *The Gospels in Context* (see above 3.1.1) 235–258 (the southern part of Syria). Hengel, 'The Gospel of Mark' 28–29, considers the lack of geographical clarity in the expression Συροφοινίκισσα ('Syro-Phoenician') (7.26) to speak against a Syrian origin.

[158] Cf. Marxsen, *Introduction* 143.

[159] Cf. Siegfried Schulz, *Die Stunde der Botschaft* (Bielefeld: Luther, 1982³) 9.

[160] Cf. Gnilka, *Markusevangelium* 1.34: the Gospel of Mark was written to Gentile Christians of the West. Guelich, *Mark* xxix–xxxi, considers both the question of authorship and provenance to be unsolvable, but that neither is in fact relevant for understanding the Gospel.

[161] On the question of whether the Qumran fragment 7Q5 supports the early dating of Mark, as argued by Carsten P. Thiede, *Die älteste Evangelienhandschrift? Das Markus-Fragment von Qumran und die Anfänge der schriftlichen Überlieferung des Neuen Testaments* (Wuppertal: TVG, 1986); cf. the critique of H. U. Rosenbaum, 'Cave 7Q5! Gegen die erneute Inanspruchnahme des Qumran-Fragments 7Q5 als Bruchstück der ältesten Evangelien-Handschrift,' *BZ* 31 (1987) 189–205.

the temple by the Romans in 70 CE.[162] The disputed point, of course, is whether these verses already look back on the destruction of Jerusalem or whether they are real prophecies that announce the disaster that is about to befall the city. M. Hengel votes for a dating of Mark prior to 70 CE: 'It presumably originated in the politically explosive time after the murder of Nero and Galba but before the renewal of the Jewish war by Titus, i.e. sometime between the winter of 68/69 CE and the winter of 69/70 CE. The destruction of the temple is not yet presupposed; rather, the author anticipates the advent of the antichrist (as Nero redivivus) in the holy place, and the breaking in of the final, most severe stage of the Messianic woes before the parousia.'[163] To be sure, Hengel's interpretation does not distinguish between the source that has been edited into Mark 13 and the Markan redaction, but identifies Mark 13.2, 14 with the time in which the whole Gospel was composed. Both verses, however, are probably pre-Markan tradition[164] and cannot be used as evidence that the Gospel itself was written prior to 70 CE. 'While the standpoint of the author of the source was situated before v. 14, that of the author of the Gospel must be located after vv. 14–20 (22).'[165] From the viewpoint of the evangelist, Mark 13.2, 14 are *vaticinia ex eventu*, and the Gospel of Mark was probably written after the destruction of the temple early in the 70s (cf. also Mark 12.9; 15.38).[166]

3.4.4 Intended Readership

Mark wrote his Gospel for a predominantly Gentile Christian church.[167] This may be inferred from the explanations of Jewish customs already

---

[162] G. Zuntz, 'Wann wurde das Evangelium Marci geschrieben?' in *Markus-Philologie*, ed. Hubert Cancik (see above 3.1.1) 47–71, refers Mark 13.14 to Caligula's attempt to install a statue of himself in the Jerusalem temple (cf. Philo, *LegGai* 197–337; Jos, *Bell* 2. 184–203; *Ant* 18. 256–309), and on this basis dates the whole Gospel in the year 40 CE. Theissen, *The Gospels in Context* (see above 3.1.1) 125–165, also interprets the 'desolating sacrilege' in terms of the Caligula crisis and places the origin of the traditional apocalypse now contained in Mark 13 in the year 40 CE. Theissen dates Mark itself, however, shortly after 70 CE (cf. *ibid.* 258 note 59, 272) and considers 13.14 to be older tradition taken up by the evangelist.

[163] Hengel, 'The Gospel of Mark' 28. The composition of Mark (shortly) before 70 CE is argued, for a variety of reasons, by Marxsen, *Introduction* 143 (written between 67–69 in Palestine); Lohse, *Formation* 138; Dschulnigg, *Sprache* 620; Schenke, *Markusevangelium* 39; Guelich, *Mark* xxxii.

[164] Evidence in Egon Brandenburger, *Markus 13 und die Apokalyptik*, FRLANT 134 (Göttingen: Vandenhoeck & Ruprecht, 1984) 49–54, 81ff.

[165] *Ibid.* 81.

[166] The Gospel is dated in the period (shortly) after 70 CE also by Vielhauer, *Urchristliche Literatur* 347; Gnilka, *Markusevangelium* 1.34; Pesch, *Markusevangelium* 1.14; Theißen, *The Gospels in Context* (see above 3.1.1) 272; Schweizer, *Theological Introduction* 122. The time of composition was 'around 70 AD' according to Kümmel, *Introduction* 98; Wikenhauser – Schmid, *Introduction* 221; Lührmann, *Markusevangelium* 6.

[167] Cf. Schenke, *Markusevangelium* 32ff.

mentioned, and from the translations of Semitic expressions. The lack of the term νόμος (law) and the incorporation of legal material show clearly that in the Markan church the law was no longer relevant in terms of cultic regulations, but only as the moral law (cf. Mark 10.1–12, 17–27; 12.28–34).[168] The double commandment of love constitutes the conclusion, goal, and high point of the debates and discussions between Jesus and the Jews concerning the Law. The Markan church is carrying on a Gentile mission, for Gentiles are explicitly included in the acts and preaching of Jesus in the Gospel. Jesus' preaching in Galilee was already extended to Gentiles (Mark 1–6) and resulted in Jesus' mighty deeds being known among Gentiles (Mark 5.1–20; cf. v. 20). Jesus' activity among Gentiles then begins with the programmatic annulment of Jewish ritual prescriptions (Mark 7.1–23).[169] The healing of a Gentile woman (Mark 7.24–30), of a person impaired in both hearing and speaking (Mark 7.21–37), and the feeding of the 4000 (Mark 8.1–10) must be understood as illustrations of the fundamental annulment of the basic 'clean-unclean' distinction in Mark 7.1–23. Following the Markan order of the text, the acclamation in Mark 7.37 was spoken by Gentiles. If the feeding of the 5000 forms the conclusion of Jesus' work among the Jews, then the feeding of the 4000 represents the conclusion of his work among the Gentiles. The eucharistic overtones of Mark 8.6 indicate, in the Markan perspective, that Jesus once had table fellowship with Gentiles, and now continues this in the eucharist. While the majority of the Jews harden their hearts against faith in Jesus, the Gentiles open their lives to the Son of God, Jesus Christ. The handing over of the prerogatives of the Jews in the history of salvation to the Gentile nations (cf. Mark 12.9), and the worldwide proclamation of the gospel among all nations (cf. Mark 13.10; 14.9) are from this perspective quite consistent. Finally, it is the Roman centurion at the crucifixion, a Gentile, who is the first person on the internal level of the story who confesses Jesus to be the Son of God (15.39). The Markan portrayal of the disciples also shows elements of the author's missionary theology.[170] The disciples function as paradigms; just as they followed Jesus and were sent forth by him (Mark 6b–13), so now the Markan church is to be ready for mission in word and deed. The experiences of the missionary activity of the Markan church have influenced the materials in 4.1–9, 10–12, 13–20.

---

[168] Cf. here Hans Hübner, *Das Gesetz in der synoptischen Tradition* (Göttingen: Vandenhoeck & Ruprecht, 1986²) 213–226; Ulrich Luz (– Rudolf Smend), *Gesetz* (Stuttgart: Kohlhammer, 1981) 116–119; Heikki Sariola, *Markus und das Gesetz*, AASF, Diss. Hum. Litt. 56 Helsinki 1990).

[169] For Mark, note especially 7.19c: καθαρίζων πάντα τὰ βρώματα ('Thus he declared all foods clean').

[170] Cf. here Zenji Kato, *Die Völkermission im Markusevangelium*, EHS.T 252 (Frankfurt: Lang, 1986).

To be sure, the Markan church was not composed exclusively of Gentiles, for the issue of clean and unclean points to the presence of Jewish Christians within the community (Mark 7). The adoption of the authoritative decision of Jesus (Mark 7.15) in Mark 7.18ff. indicates the Markan solution to the problem: he votes for a new praxis in which Gentile and Jewish Christians live together based on the authority of Jesus. Table fellowship in the Christian community includes both Gentile and Jewish Christians (Mark 2.15–16; 7.24ff.). In the Christian community there are new fasts (2.19–20), and observance of the Sabbath is oriented to human need (2.23–28; 3.1–6).

There are no recognizable sharp ethical conflicts within the community, the ethical instructions in Mark 10.1–45 and 12.13–17 being normal parenesis. The advent of Christian charismatics and prophets poses problems for Mark (13.6), since they obviously announce dates and locations for the parousia of Christ (cf. Mark 13.21). The evangelist describes them explicitly as ψευδόχριστοι (false Messiahs) and ψευδοπροφῆται (false prophets) (Mark 13.22), and explicitly warns against their activities (Mark 13.5–6, 21b, 23). Possible conflicts with their surroundings are indicated by statements about persecutions by Gentile and Jewish authorities in 13.9, 13. In addition, the references to distress and persecution in Mark 4.17; 10.30; 13.19 could be a reflection of repressions in their immediate Gentile and Jewish surroundings. Thus Mark explicitly demands from his community a comprehensive readiness to suffer (8.34–38).

3.4.5 Outline, Structure, Form

1.1–8.26	Part One: Jesus' Ministry within and outside Galilee
1.1–6.56	The Preaching of the Gospel in Galilee
1.1–13	John the Baptist; the Baptism of Jesus
1.14–45	The Preaching of Jesus
2.1–3.6	Conflict Stories
3.7–35	Healings; Call of the Disciples; Jesus' Relatives
4.1–34	Parables
4.35–5.43	Miracle Stories
6.1–56	Completion of the Galilean Ministry
7.1–8.26	The Ministry of Jesus among the Gentiles
7.1–7.23	Clean and Unclean
7.24–37	Healings among the Gentiles
8.1–9	Feeding the 4000 as Completion of the Journey through Gentile Territory
8.10–26	The Return to Galilee

8.27–10.52	Part Two: Jesus' Way to the Passion
8.27–9.1	Peter's Confession; 1st Passion Prediction; Call to Suffering Discipleship
9.2–50	Transfiguration; Miracles; 2nd Passion Prediction; Instruction
10.1–52	Way to Jerusalem; Instruction; 3rd Passion Prediction; Miracles

11.1–16.8	Part Three: Jesus in Jerusalem
11.1–25	Entry into Jerusalem; Cleansing the Temple
11.27–12.44	Conflict Stories; Didactic Stories
13.1–37	Eschatological Discourse
14.1–15.47	The Passion of Jesus
16.1–8	The Empty Tomb
(16.9–20)	Secondary Conclusion: Appearances of the Risen One; Sending forth the Disciples

The structure of the Gospel of Mark is the direct expression of the theological intention of the evangelist. Mark understands himself to be obligated to his central theological conviction also in the manner in which he has composed the Gospel: the resurrected Jesus Christ is no other than the earthly, crucified Jesus of Nazareth. For Mark, the way and the message of the earthly Jesus are transparent to the crucified and risen one. In terms of literary analysis, this can be seen on several levels. The basic compositional and theological framework of the whole Gospel is provided by Mark 1.9–11; 9.7; 15.39 (cf. 3.1.3 and 3.4.9), in which the central title 'Son of God' simultaneously affirms Jesus' divinity and his destiny of suffering and death. The reader of the Gospel knows from the very beginning that the way of Jesus leads from baptism to the cross, and that an adequate and appropriate understanding of the person of Jesus can only be attained from the post-Easter perspective of the cross and resurrection. So too, the manner in which the narrative order of the Gospel converges stands in the service of the theological affirmation of the Gospel. For Jesus' ministry in Galilee already has the Jerusalem goal in view. Both Mark 2.6, 7 and 2.18–22 already point forward to the suffering of Jesus. Already in 3.6 the sentence of death is passed on Jesus, and his opponents from Jerusalem already dispute with him in 3.22 and 7.1. So too the death of John the Baptist already points to Jesus' death. The three passion predictions (Mark 8.31; 9.31; 10.32–34) point the way of Jesus to the cross, as do the notices of his death sentence in Mark 11.18 and 12.12 prior to the beginning of the passion story proper.

The final point to be made in this regard is that basic theological structure and the way the narrative order converges also corresponds to the *threefold* division of the Gospel.[171] The first major section of the Gospel portrays Jesus' ministry in Galilee and beyond (Mark 1.1–8.26). The universal orientation of Markan theology is reflected in the ministry of Jesus among Gentiles in Mark 7.24–8.9,[172] for which Mark 7.1–23 presents the theological foundation. The first major section concludes with the return of Jesus to Galilee, so that the way of Jesus to Jerusalem and the passion is formed by Part Two, 8.27–10.52. The redactional ἐν τῇ ὁδῷ (on the road) in 8.27 and 10.52 is a clear indication that the evangelist himself understands this section as a discrete unit. The content of 8.27–10.52 is also distinctive by the concentration of key christological terms it contains (cf. especially the confession of Peter, the sayings about suffering discipleship, the transfiguration story, and the passion predictions. The triumphal entry into Jerusalem (Mark 11.1ff.) opens Part Three, which concludes with 16.1–8 in the critical received text. The predictions of appearances of the resurrected one in 14.28 and 16.7 draw the readers' view back to Galilee, and at the same time make clear that for Mark 'Galilee' and 'Jerusalem' have theological overtones. Galilee is the place of the eschatological revelation of God, Jerusalem on the other hand is the place of continuing hostility to Jesus. With this reversal of Jewish understandings of the saving event Mark again emphasizes the transition of salvation from Jews to Gentiles (cf. Mark 12.1–12).

3.4.6 Literary Integrity

Mark 16.9–20 are not present in Vaticanus and Sinaiticus,[173] which means that the oldest preserved version of the Gospel of Mark ends with 16.1–8. It is disputed whether the Gospel always concluded with 16.8 or the original conclusion has been lost. There have been several attempts to reconstruct the original Markan conclusion from other traditions that have been preserved (e.g. Matt. 28.16–17; Mark 16.15–20),[174] but without con-

---

[171] Cf. e.g. Vielhauer, *Urchristliche Literatur* 331–332. A survey of older proposals for the structure of the Gospel is offered by Rudolf Pesch, *Naherwartungen* (Düsseldorf: Patmos, 1968) 50–53. In recent times a two part structure has been argued for by e.g. Dietrich A. Koch, 'Inhaltliche Gliederung und geographischer Aufriß im Markusevangelium,' NTS 29 (1983) 145–166 (Introduction 1.1–13; Part One 1.14–8.26; Part Two 8.27–16.8) and Schenke, *Markusevangelium* 62–74 (Introduction 1.1–13; Part One 1.14–10.52; Part Two 11.1–16.8). A five-part division of the Gospel is proposed by F. G. Lang, 'Kompositionsanalyse des Markusevangeliums,' ZThK 74 (1977) (1–24) 12–13.

[172] On the Markan route of Jesus' journey, cf. especially F. G. Lang, *Geographie und Theologie in Mk 7,31* (see above 3.4.2) 154ff.

[173] For details on the textual tradition, cf. Kurt Aland, 'Der Schluss des Markusevangeliums,' in *Neutestamentliche Entwürfe*, TB 63 (Munich: Kaiser, 1979) 246–283.

[174] So Eta Linnemann, 'Der (wiedergefundene) Markusschluß,' ZThK 66 (1969) 255–287; response by Kurt Aland, 'Der wiedergefundene Markusschluß?' ZThK 67 (1970) 3–13.

vincing results. Did Mark then end his Gospel with the sentence, 'and they said nothing to anyone, for they were afraid?' Mark could have intentionally omitted stories of the appearance of the resurrected Jesus in order to guard against a *theologia gloria* in which Jesus' suffering and death on the cross were understood only as a temporary phase in his passage to glory.[175] The silence of the women and the suppression of appearance stories would then take the place of the commands to silence in the framework of the Markan messianic secret. This or similarly subtle interpretations, however, are due to historical-critical exegesis in the twentieth century, but it must remain questionable whether such an understanding would have come within the horizon of the Markan community. Mark himself,[176] by the predictions of the appearances of the resurrected Jesus in Galilee (14.28; 16.7), creates the expectation that such appearances will be narrated. The possibility must therefore be seriously considered that the original Markan conclusion has in fact been lost.

3.4.7 Traditions, Sources

In the composition of his Gospel Mark reworks older traditions. Thus the Markan passion story (14.1–16.8) has as its basis a comprehensive tradition,[177] which possibly had been edited already at the pre-Markan stage, and included at least Jesus' prayer in Gethsemane, his arrest, trial, sentencing, crucifixion, and burial, as well as the narrative of the discovery of the empty tomb.[178] R. Pesch not only counts Mark 14–16 as belonging to the pre-Markan passion narrative, but also includes 8.27–33; 9.2–13, 30–35; 10.1, 32–34, 46–52; 11.1–23, 27–33; 12.1–12, 35–37, 41–44, 13.1–2.[179] But these texts surely are derived from Markan redaction or pre-Markan tradition that was not an integral part of a passion story.[180] The

---

[175] So for example Andreas Lindemann, 'Die Osterbotschaft des Markus,' NTS 26 (1979/80) 298–317.

[176] The redactional character of Mark 14.28 and 16.7 can hardly be disputed. Cf. e.g. Gnilka, *Markusevangelium* 2. 252, 338; Lührmann, *Markusevangelium* 242, 270. One can infer, of course, from the significance of what is *not* said that Mark intentionally ended his Gospel with 16.8 as does J. J. Magness, *Sense and Absence. Structure and Suspension in the Ending of Mark's Gospel* (Atlanta: Scholars Press, 1986).

[177] A survey of research is offered by T. A. Mohr, *Markus- und Johannespassion*, AThANT 70 (Zürich: Theologischer Verlag, 1982) 15–35; for an analysis cf. recently Gerd Theißen, *The Gospels in Context* (see above 3.1.1) 166–199.

[178] Cf. Gnilka, *Markusevangelium* 2.349.

[179] Cf. Pesch, *Markusevangelium* 2.1–27. The other extreme is advocated by Ernst, *Markusevangelium* 395–396, who reckons only Mark 15.20b–47 and 16.1–8 as belonging to the pre-Markan passion narrative.

[180] For a critique of Pesch, cf. especially Frans Neirynck, 'L'évangile de Marc. Àpropos de R. Pesch, Das Markusevangelium (1977, 1979),' in F. Neirynck, *Evangelica*, BETL 60 (Leuven: Leuven University Press, 1982) 491–556.

commands to silence in Mark 8.30 and 9.9, for example, are clearly redactional (see below 3.4.9), and it was Mark who developed the second and third passion predictions from an early form found in 8.31, and who then made the three passion predictions into a basic structural element of the second major part of his Gospel.[181]

Mark incorporated both oral and written traditions into the eschatological discourse in chapter thirteen of his Gospel. Mark 13.7–8, 14–20, 24–27 probably belonged to a written source, while 1b, 2, 9b–13, 21–23, 30–36 derive from oral tradition.[182] A collection of conflict stories is the basis of 2.1–3.6. It is disputed whether this collection was first edited into one unit by Mark[183] or goes back to pre-Markan tradition,[184] and how extensive it was at the pre-Markan level.[185] All the texts in 2.1–3.6 have a comparable Sitz im Leben, reflecting conflict situations between Christians and Jews and/or Gentile Christians and Jewish Christians, and may have already been gathered into one collection on the pre-Markan level.[186] Also Mark 3.1–6[187] belongs to this collection, for the Pharisees of 2.24 are the subject of 3.2, and Jesus' question in 3.4 refers to 2.24, as well as the temporal reference ἐν τοῖς σάββασιν (on the Sabbath) in 2.23 being presupposed in 3.1. Additional pre-Markan collections are found in Mark 4.1–34 (parables)[188] and in Mark 10, where the evangelist has edited a catechetical collection on the theme marriage (10.1–12), possessions

---

[181] Cf. Georg Strecker, 'Die Leidens- und Auferstehungsaussagen im Markusevangelium (Mk 8,31; 9,31; 10,32–34),' in *Eschaton und Historie*, ed. G. Strecker (Göttingen: Vandenhoeck & Ruprecht, 1979) 52–75.

[182] So the analysis of Brandenburger, *Markus 13* 166–167 (includes a defense of his view against other options in the literature). Cf. further Ferdinand Hahn, 'Die Rede von der Parusie des Menschensohnes Markus 13,' in *Jesus und der Menschensohn* (FS A. Vögtle) (Freiburg: Herder, 1975) 240–266; Theißen, *The Gospel in Context* (see above 3.1.1) 125–165.

[183] So e.g. Koch, *Wundererzählungen* 33–34; J. Kiilunen, *Die Vollmacht im Widerstreit* (AASF Diss. Hum. Litt. 40, Helsinki 1985) 249–266; W. Weiss, *'Eine neue Lehre in Vollmacht'*, BZNW 52 (Berlin: Walter de Gruyter, 1989) 20–31.

[184] Foundational Martin Albertz, *Die synoptischen Streitgespräche* (Berlin, 1921); Kuhn, *Sammlungen*. For history of research cf. W. Weiss, *Lehre* 20–31.

[185] Albertz, *Streitgespräche* 5–16: Mark 2.1–3.6; Kuhn, *Sammlungen* 53–98: 2.1–28; Pesch, *Markusevangelium* 1.149–151: 2.15–3.6; Gnilka, *Markusevangelium* 1.131–132: 2.15–28; Lührmann, *Markusevangelium* 15, 56: 2.15–3.5.

[186] For detailed evidence, cf. Kuhn, *Sammlungen* 86–87.

[187] Mark 3.6 may have been pre-Markan material reedited by the evangelist. The alternative, that it is 'traditional,' (so e. g. Jürgen Roloff, *Das Kerygma und der irdischen Jesus* [Göttingen: Vandenhoeck & Ruprecht, 1973²] 64; Pesch, *Markusevangelium* 1. 188) or 'redactional' (so e.g. Gnilka, *Markusevangelium* 1.126; Lührmann, *Markusevangelium* 67) does not fit here, for on the one hand v. 2b calls for a reaction of the opponents, and on the other hand 3.6 becomes a central element in the structure of the Gospel as a whole.

[188] Cf. here (with some difference in details of the analysis) Kuhn, *Sammlungen* 99–146; Pesch, *Markusevangelium* 1.225ff.; Gnilka, *Markusevangelium* 1.191–192; Hans-Joseph Klauck, *Allegorie und Allegorese in synoptischen Gleichnistexten*, NTA 13 (Münster: Aschendorff, 1986²) 185–259.

(10.17–31), and striving after rank (10.35–45).[189] Whether the evangelist incorporated a collection of miracle stories in 4.35–6.52 is disputed.[190] Alongside these larger collections of tradition, Mark integrated several smaller narrative complexes into his Gospel.

3.4.8 History-of-religions Standpoint

In his influential essay on Markan Christology, Ph. Vielhauer advocates the thesis that Mark structured his Gospel in analogy to the ancient Egyptian enthronement ritual. 'The baptism corresponds to the "apotheosis" . . . The transfiguration corresponds to the "presentation" . . . The crucifixion corresponds to the actual enthronization . . .'[191] 'By using the enthronization ritual both to bind together the disparate material of the Jesus tradition and to divide it into segments, the evangelist interprets the story of Jesus from baptism to the crucifixion as the process of his enthronement by which Jesus is installed as the eschatological king, the Cosmocrator in Heaven.'[192] Vielhauer's thesis cannot be sustained in this form, since it is debatable whether such a three-stage royal ritual ever existed in ancient Egypt in such fixed form.[193] In addition, the central christological title for Mark, υἱὸς θεοῦ (Son of God), can be derived from Wisdom of Solomon 2.13, 18, where the suffering righteous man appears as παῖς θεοῦ (child of God) and υἱὸς θεοῦ (Son of God).[194]

T. J. Weeden sees the Markan church involved in a situation of acute conflict.[195] While the evangelist is engaged in strengthening his persecuted community by Jesus' call to suffering discipleship, missionaries had arrived who advocated a θεῖος ἀνήρ ('divine man') Christology. Weeden identifies the opponents with the 'false prophets' of Mark 13.21–22, who according to Mark 13.6, 21 presented themselves with charismatic displays as mediums of the exalted Lord. The opponents' theology appealed to the original disciples of Jesus for their justification, so that the dispute between Jesus and his disciples in the Gospel is transparent to the conflict between

---

[189] On this cf. Kuhn, *Sammlungen* 146–191; Pesch, *Markusevangelium* 2.127–130; Gnilka, *Markusevangelium* 2.105.

[190] Cf. the discussion of the problems in Kuhn, *Sammlungen* 191–213.

[191] Vielhauer, 'Christologie des Markusevangeliums' 213; cf. also Vielhauer, *Urchristliche Literatur* 344.

[192] Vielhauer, 'Christologie des Markusevangeliums' 213.

[193] On this cf. Gerhard Friedrich, 'Die formale Struktur von Mt 28,18–20,' ZThK 80 (1983) (137–183) 137–151, who refers to more recent Egyptological research in which the theses of E. Norden on the ancient Egyptian kingship ritual on which Vielhauer depends are no longer supported.

[194] Cf. Lührmann, *Markusevangelium* 38

[195] Cf. Theodore J. Weeden, *Mark – Traditions in Conflict* (Fortress Press: Philadelphia 1971).

Mark and his opponents. Mark is supposed to have taken up essential traditions of his opponents (miracle stories, parables), re-edited them, and brought them into service to his own theological conception.

A related idea is advocated by R. P. Martin.[196] In his view Mark is engaged in debate with docetic heretical teachers, who similarly to Paul's opponents in Corinth denied the suffering of Jesus. In contrast to them, in the situation of persecution Mark calls for taking up one's cross in discipleship to the suffering Son of Man.

These and other attempts to understand the theology of Mark as a result of debates between rival groups in the Markan community must be evaluated rather skeptically. A difficulty is already posed by the attempt to reconstruct the standpoint of the supposed opponents in terms of the history of religions and the history of theology, since the Gospel of Mark makes no statements about them, and since the analogies to Paul remain very hypothetical. In addition, the motif of the disciples' failure to understand cannot be referred to a group of opponents within the church (cf. Mark 4.10–12; 14.28; 16.7).

3.4.9 Basic Theological Ideas

The Gospel of Mark as a narrative of the 'way' of Jesus Christ from baptism to cross is a call to suffering discipleship of Jesus Christ. Mark wants to lead his community to an appropriate understanding of the person and work of Jesus Christ and to a replication of the 'way' of Jesus in their own lives. For Mark, understanding the faith and living the faith belong inseparably together. In the communication of this insight, the disciples in Mark play a central role.[197] They are called by Jesus himself (Mark 1.16–20; 3.13–18), and already during his lifetime are authorized to continue his work (6.6b–13). The sending forth of the disciples to teach and perform acts of ministry is of great significance for the Markan community, for therein they recognize the source of their own mission, which thereby appears as a legitimate continuation of the ministry of Jesus. The disciples are the connecting link between the time of Jesus and the contemporary Markan community.[198] In his portrayal of them Mark clarifies for his own church who Jesus Christ is and what discipleship to him means.

---

[196] Cf. Ralph P. Martin, *Mark: Evangelist and Theologian* (see above 3.4.3).

[197] Cf. on the Markan understanding of discipleship Ernest Best, *Following Jesus. Discipleship in the Gospel of Mark*, JSNT.S 4 (Sheffield: Sheffield University Press, 1981); R. Busemann, *Die Jüngergemeinde nach Markus 10*, BBB 57 (Königstein – Bonn, 1983); C. Clifton Black, *The Disciples according to Mark*, JSNT.S 27 (Sheffield: Sheffield University Press, 1989).

[198] On this cf. Hans-Joseph Klauck, 'Die erzählerische Rolle der Jünger im Markusevangelium. Eine narrative Analyse,' NT 24 (1982) 1–26.

The Markan *secrecy theory* facilitates the understanding of the identity of Jesus Christ. In the Gospel of Mark the hiddenness of the identity of Jesus as the saving figure is found in different forms, which in their various ways are all intended to be understood within the framework of an overarching christological secrecy theory:

(1) The *recognition of the Messiah by the demons* and the *commands to silence* directed to them: In Mark 1.25; 1.34; 3.12 are found commands to silence directed to demons who have made a declaration about the person Jesus Christ that is in fact correct (Mark 1.24: ἅγιος τοῦ θεοῦ [Holy One of God]; Mark 3.11: υἱὸς τοῦ θεοῦ [Son of God]).[199] Even if the command to silence in Mark 1.25 can be understood as an element in the exorcistic ritual within the framework of the traditional constituents of an exorcism story, the two commands to silence to the demons in the summaries of miracle working activity in Mark 1.32–34 and 3.7–12 must be regarded as unambiguously redactional.[200] Mark wants thereby to make it clear that the attempt to understand the identity of Jesus on the basis of his miracles is not sufficient for an adequate understanding of what it means to call him 'Son of God.' Jesus cannot be considered Son of God on the basis of miracles alone.

(2) The *hidden performance* of Jesus' miracles: Jesus prohibited their being publicized, but this prohibition was violated. In Mark 5.43a and 7.36a, in the context of a miraculous healing Jesus forbids those present or the healed one himself to make the miraculous event public. This directive is disobeyed in Mark 7.36b, just as the precise order given in the traditional story in Mark 1.44 is violated in Mark 1.45.[201] The intention of the prohibition of publicizing the miracles is to prevent Jesus from being defined purely on the basis of his miracles, and from being usurped by them. The mystery of Jesus' identity is not yet disclosed by his miraculous deeds. At the same time, the violations of Jesus' prohibition show that his becoming known as a miracle worker is something that cannot be prevented (cf. also Mark 7.24!). Mark does not regard this state of affairs negatively; he merely wants to refuse the claim by the miracle stories to determine the identity of the person of Jesus in any absolute

---

[199] In Mark 5.8 in place of the command to silence the evangelist places a command for the demons to come out, as a reaction to the demons' recognition of him in 5.7. A command to silence would have been out of place here, since in the traditional story adopted by the evangelist an interchange between Jesus and the demons was a given element of the narrative.

[200] For an analysis, cf. Gnilka, *Markusevangelium* 1.76–77, 85–86, 133. Bernd Kollmann, 'Jesu Schweigegebote an die Dämonen,' ZNW 82 (1991) 267–273, considers the command to silence in 1.25 also to be redactional.

[201] On the redactional character of Mark 1.45; 5.43a; 7.36 cf. Gnilka, *Markusevangelium* 1.91, 211, 296.

sense. At the level of the internal logic of the text, most of the commands to silence and prohibitions to publicize the miraculous make no sense; they point rather to an overarching christological understanding.

(3) The *disciples' lack of understanding*: Prior to Mark 8.27 the disciples' lack of understanding is directed to Jesus' teaching (4.13; 7.18) and his person (4.40–41; 6.52). The picture is different after 8.27: both the private instruction of the disciples and their continued misunderstanding appear in a more intensified form. If the disciples in Mark 8.17, 21 are portrayed as still dull and having their hearts hardened, a transition is made at the point of Peter's confession in Mark 8.29. A different level in the perception of the disciples has been reached, for from this point on they are aware of Jesus' identity as the Messiah. But the command to silence of Mark 8.30 and the reaction of Peter to the first prediction of the passion (8.31) show that the disciples in Mark 8.27–33 have just as little understanding of the mystery of suffering inherent in Jesus' person as before, as is also the case in Mark 9.5–6, 30–32; 10.32–34. With the motif of the disciples' lack of understanding Mark also clarifies to a certain extent, from the negative side, how the person of Jesus may *not* be understood. A full understanding of the person of Jesus can not be limited to his honor and glory and exclude the role of suffering. Rather, both belong to a full understanding of the identity of Jesus.

(4) *Commands to silence* directed to the *disciples*: The two commands to silence directed to the disciples in Mark 8.30 and 9.9 are of great significance for the Markan secrecy theory. By the command to silence in 8.30 Mark makes clear[202] that the confession made by Peter does not in itself provide a full and complete understanding of the person of Jesus. This is shown by the first passion prediction that immediately follows (8.31), and by the reaction of Peter. The fundamental significance of Mark 9.9 for the Markan secrecy theory was recognized already by W. Wrede.[203] Mark limits the applicability of the commands to silence to the time prior to Jesus' resurrection, at which time the secret of Jesus' identity will be dis-

---

[202] Contra Pesch, *Markusevangelium* 2.33, 39, Mark 8.30 is to be considered redactional. The reasons: (1) ἐπιτιμάω (rebuke) is a favorite word of Mark (cf. Mark 3.12; 8.32, 33; 9.25; 10.13, 48); (2) the purpose clause introduced with ἵνα (in order that) corresponds to Markan style (cf. Mark 3.9, 12; 5.43; 6.12; 7.36; 9.9, 18; 13.34); (3) μηδείς (no one) or μηδέ (not even) is a recurring element in the Markan commands to silence (cf. Mark 5.43; 7.36; 8.26; 9.9); (4) with the plural αὐτοῖς (to them) all the disciples are placed under the command to silence, although only Peter had spoken the confessional statement; (5) in terms of both form and content Mark 8.30 conforms to the other Markan commands to silence (cf. Mark 1.34; 3.12; 5.43; 7.36; 8.26; 9.9). Mark 8.30 is considered redactional by, among others, Schweizer, *Mark* 173; Gnilka, *Markusevangelium* 2.10; Weber, *Christologie und 'Messiasgeheimnis'* 118; Lührmann, *Markusevangelium* 143.

[203] Cf. Wrede, *Messianic Secret* 67–68.

closed.[204] A full understanding of who Jesus is cannot be perceived prior to the cross and resurrection of Jesus Christ.

The following items stand in an *indirect connection* with the Markan secrecy theory: the separation of those who are healed from the general public (cf. Mark 5.37, 40; 7.33; 8.23); the reduction of the circle of disciples (cf. Mark 5.37; 13.3); the withdrawal of Jesus (cf. Mark 1.35, 45; 3.7, 9; 6.31–32, 46; 7.24), and topological motifs such as οἶκος, οἰκία (house) (cf. Mark 7.17; 9.28, 33; 10.10), πλοῖον, πλοιάριον (boat) (cf. Mark 3.9; 6.32, 54; 8.13ff.), ὄρος (mountain) (cf. Mark 3.13; 6.46; 9.2, 9; 13.3), ἔρημος τόπος (desert place) (cf. Mark 1.35, 45; 6.31–32).

The core of the *parable theory* (Mark 4.10–12) goes back to pre-Markan tradition, and is not a direct element in the Markan secrecy theory. The secrecy theory in Mark is not an apologetic device for explaining Jewish unbelief and also implies no intentional 'hardening.' Rather, it is intended to lead to the right understanding of the person of Jesus. This is the reason the evangelist presents a considerable correction of the parable theory in 4.13b and constructs an indirect connection to the secrecy theory by means of the motif of the disciples misunderstanding.[205]

The individual elements of the Markan secrecy theory did not originate from any historical interest, but they are directed to the readers and are intended to lead them to a fuller understanding of the person of Jesus Christ. At the same time, the secrecy theory makes it possible for the evangelist Mark to fuse the pre-Markan traditions of Jesus as the miracle worker and the passion traditions into a new unity within the framework of the new literary genre 'Gospel.' Mark 9.9 also makes clear that the secrecy theory must be understood as a form of the Markan *theology of the cross.* An

---

[204] Räisänen, *The Messianic Secret in Mark's Gospel* 186–192, 247–248; Pesch, *Markusevangelium* 2.39, 77, consider Mark 9.9 to be traditional. The agreements in form and content between 9.9 and the clearly redactional commands to silence in 5.43 and 7.36 speak against this view.

5.43: καὶ διεστείλατο αὐτοῖς . . .   ἵνα μηδεὶς γνοῖ τοῦτο
(And he commanded them that no one should know this.)

7.36: καὶ διεστείλατο αὐτοῖς . . .   ἵνα μηδενὶ λέγωσιν
(And he commanded them that they tell no one . . .)

9.9: καὶ . . . διεστείλατο αὐτοῖς . . .   ἵνα μηδενὶ . . . διηγήσωνται
(And he commanded them to tell no one . . .)

In addition, neither the theme of the resurrection nor a designation for a time when the command to silence will no longer apply can be derived from the internal narrative logic of Mark 9.2–8. Finally, it should be noted that the disciples' lack of understanding in 9.10 and the end of the time when the command to silence applies in 9.9 are related very closely, suggesting that both originated in the Markan redaction. Cf. among others, Schweizer, *Mark* 184; Gnilka, *Markusevangelium* 2.40; Lührmann, *Markusevangelium* 157.

[205] On the relation of Mark 4.33 to the Markan theory of the parables, cf. Gnilka, *Markusevangelium* 1.190–191.

essential element of this theology of the cross is formed by the revelations of the divine sonship of Jesus[206] in Mark 1.11; 9.7; 15.39. While previously only God and the demons know the true identity of Jesus, in 15.39 the centurion beneath the cross becomes the first human being to make a proper confession of the person of Jesus (see above 3.1.3). Additional elements of the Markan theology of the cross are provided by the three passion predictions (Mark 8.31; 9.31; 10.32–34) and the words about suffering discipleship in Mark 8.34–9.1. For Mark, discipleship of Jesus Christ means taking up the cross. Jesus himself has walked this path in advance and opened it to those who believe in him.

3.4.10 Tendencies of Recent Research

Since the groundbreaking study of William Wrede, the 'Messianic secret' has stood at the center of Markan research. Wrede did not trace the Messianic secret back to the evangelist Mark himself,[207] but saw in it the work of the post-Easter Christian community prior to Mark.[208] In Wrede's view the Messianic secret originated from the necessity of harmonizing the unmessianic life of Jesus and the faith of the post-Easter community. 'There is thus hardly any other possibility than that the view of the secret originated in a moment in which one did not yet know of a Messianic claim made by Jesus during his earthly life, and that means in a moment when the resurrection was understood as the beginning of Jesus' Messiahship.'[209] In the course of further research, neither the thesis of originally unmessianic Jesus tradition nor the idea of a pre-Markan origin of the Messianic secret has been sustained. Thus Hans-Jürgen Ebeling interpreted the Messianic secret as the unified organizing principle of the Markan proclamation,[210] and with the advent of the redaction critical way of posing the issue after the Second World War the insight generally prevailed that both the essential individual elements of the Messianic secret and its theological intention are to be attributed to the evangelist Mark himself. This is still essentially the general consensus of scholarship, for which the works

---

[206] On the christological titles in Mark cf. Rudolf Schnackenburg, *Jesus in the Gospels: A Biblical Christology* (Louisville: Westminster/ John Knox, 1995) 45–73.

[207] Cf. Wrede, *Messianic Secret* 145: 'Is the idea of the messianic secret an invention of Mark's? The notion seems quite impossible.'

[208] Cf. *ibid.*: 'But what is its (sc. the idea of the Messianic secret) origin? We have to do with an idea which must have dominated fairly large circles, even if not what one would necessarily call very large circles.' But Wrede also repeatedly emphasizes Mark's contribution to the form of the Messianic secret now present in our text.

[209] *Ibid.* 227.

[210] Cf. Hans J. Ebeling, *Das Messiasgeheimnis und die Botschaft des Marcus-Evangeliums*, BZNW 19 (Berlin: Walter de Gruyter, 1939).

of E. Schweizer[211] and the commentary on Mark by J. Gnilka[212] can be regarded as representative, though weighty questions have recently been raised against it. H. Räisänen separates the 'parable theory' completely from the Messianic secret[213] and answers the question whether Mark has a unified secrecy theory with an absolute negative. 'Of the motifs which were closely linked by Wrede the silencing commands addressed to the demons and those directed to the disciples belong closely together. One may say that these two motifs constitute the "Messianic secret" proper.'[214] None of the other elements have any direct significance for the Markan 'Messianic secret.' To be sure, Räisänen understands Mark to be a thinker with his own theological ideas, 'but any sort of satisfactory unified and comprehensive picture of his theology can hardly be attained without violent and artificial manipulation from the interpreter. So we will have to be satisfied to see the oldest evangelist as more of a tradent and less of a theologian or hermeneut than recent scholarship has generally supposed.'[215]

The commentary on Mark by R. Pesch makes a similar argument. He too sees in Mark a somewhat conservative redactor, and considers the thesis of a Markan Messianic secret to be unsustainable. 'Mark has no recognizable independent christological conception; the Christology of his Gospel is essentially determined by the Christology of his sources, which he fuses together into an overall picture of Jesus Christ (1.1) by placing them together and mixing them up in his overall composition.'[216] Like Räisänen,[217] Pesch also sees the central command to silence in Mark 9.9 (as well as Mark 8.30) to be tradition rather than redaction, with neither being elements in a comprehensive Messianic secret.[218] In contrast, R. Weber

---

[211] In addition to his commentary on Mark, cf. especially Eduard Schweizer, 'The Question of the Messianic Secret in Mark,' in *The Messianic Secret*, ed. Christopher Tuckett (Philadelphia: Fortress Press, 1983) 65–74; and 'Die theologische Leistung des Markus' in *Beiträge zur Theologie des Neuen Testaments*, ed. Eduard Schweizer (Zürich, 1970) 21–42.

[212] Cf. Gnilka, *Markusevangelium* 1.167–170 (Excursus, 'Das Messiasgeheimnis').

[213] Cf. Heikki Räisänen, *Die Parabeltheorie im Markusevangelium* (Helsinki 1973); Räisänen, *The 'Messianic Secret'* 76–143.

[214] Räisänen, *'The Messianic Secret'* 242.

[215] *Ibid.* 251. In *The 'Messianic Secret'* 254, Räisänen formulates the goal of the Messianic secret as follows: '. . . Mark tries to reject the claims of people like the bearers of Q-tradition who appealed to the authority of the historical Jesus. Mark defends (unjustifiably at the historical level) his Hellenistic viewpoint by showing that the disputed points go back to Jesus himself.' The Messianic secret is 'a historicizing subsidiary idea which Mark uses to carry on an actual debate' (*ibid.* 257–258).

[216] Pesch, *Markusevangelium* 2.41.

[217] Cf. Räisänen, *The 'Messianic Secret'* 242–243; but cf. also his statement in *The 'Messianic Secret'* 187: '9,9 may be taken as Markan.' To be sure, in Räisänen's view this changes nothing in regard to the interpretation of this verse, which in any case is not for him the key to the secrecy theory.

[218] Cf. Pesch, *Markusevangelium* 2.39. A similar argument to that of Räisänen and Pesch is made by Ernst, *Markusevangelium*, 240–245 and in 'Das sog. Messiasgeheimnis – kein

rightly insists on the fundamental significance and unified nature of the Markan secrecy theory.[219] The gist of what it affirms is that 'although Jesus was Son of God before the cross and resurrection, he still cannot be adequately understood apart from these events.'[220]

There is a clear tendency in recent Markan interpretation no longer to interpret Mark only from the point of view that the Messianic secret was a central element of his theology. Other aspects of Markan theology have stepped to the foreground. Th. Söding has worked out the Markan understanding of faith. 'Mark develops an understanding of faith that, while it is complex and tensive, by precisely this means is also theologically profiled. He understands faith as made possible by Jesus the Son of God (understood as both the earthly Jesus and resurrected Lord), as the response required by God's kingdom activity, which in substance becomes an unreserved trust in God that determines one's whole life, a faith that in its orientation to Jesus Christ is a tension-filled unity of faith as affirming the Christian confession and faith as personal trust.'[221]

The fundamental connection between discipleship and future expectation is emphasized by C. Breytenbach. The discipleship stories preserve their paradigmatic significance also in the time after Easter. In the knowledge of Jesus' resurrection the disciples bind themselves 'unreservedly to the Gospel that represents him . . . The Markan understanding of discipleship is thoroughly oriented to the future. The christological perspective toward the past is constantly supplemented by a prospective view toward the future. It is the crucified one himself who is expected as the coming Son of Man. It is by this means that the future expectation is bound to the idea of the powerful breaking in of the kingdom of God, hidden for the present but certain to come in the future (Mark 8.38; 9.1; 13.26–27), and it is from this expectation that discipleship receives its motivating power.'[222] K. Scholtissek points to the significance of the ἐξουσία-concept (redactional in Mark 1.22, 27; 2.10; 3.15; 6.7; 11.28, 29, 33; 13.34) for Markan Christology. In his view the ἐξουσία (authority) of the earthly Jesus is 'the expression of the Messianic sending of the Son of God to proclaim and to mediate the nearness of the kingdom of God.'[223]

"Hauptschlüssel" zum Markusevangelium,' in *Theologie im Werden*, ed. J. Hainz (Paderborn: Schöningh 1992) 21–56.

[219] In addition to the essay named in 3.4.1, cf. R. Weber, *Christologie und Messiasgeheimnis im Markusevangelium*, Diss. theol., Marburg 1978; for a comprehensive critique of Räisänen cf. further Fendler, *Studien* 105–146.

[220] Weber, *Christologie und 'Messiasgeheimnis'* 125.

[221] Söding, *Glaube bei Markus* 552.

[222] Breytenbach, *Nachfolge und Zukunftserwartung* 338.

[223] Scholtissek, *Die Vollmacht Jesu* 293.

A further important point on which recent investigations of the Gospel of Mark have been concentrated is that of the narrative structure of the Gospel (literary criticism).[224] From this perspective the focus of attention is on the narrative as a whole in synchronic perspective. The narrator of the Gospel, his narrative world, as well as the implied reader and/or historical hearer-readers are included in this perspective, as well as the plot and point of view, i.e. the manner in which the story is presented to the reader. The third-person narrative style, the omniscient narrator, the space/time plane(s) of the story, the appearance of characters, scenes, and events, transitions and structure of scenes, psychological elements in the narration, and comprehensive narrative structures are investigated. 'Was Mark collector, redactor, or narrator? . . . In my opinion it can be shown that Mark presents the story of Jesus to us as he saw it, and for this reason I would like to call him a narrating author. It is certainly the case that he was more than a collector.'[225] With care D. Lührmann integrates new ways of posing the questions into his exposition. Certainly Mark takes up previously-existing traditions, but the Gospel is 'not to be regarded as merely the adding together of pre-formed texts, but as a new formulation of the tradition that leads to a new work.'[226]

3.5 The Gospel of Matthew

3.5.1 Literature

Commentaries

Lohmeyer, Ernst (H.W. Schmauch). *Das Evangelium nach Matthäus*, KEK (Sonderband). Göttingen: Vandenhoeck & Ruprecht, 1967[4]; Klostermann, Erich. *Das Matthäus-Evangelium*, HNT 4. Tübingen: J. C. B. Mohr (Paul Siebeck), 1971[4]; Schweizer, Eduard. *The Good News According to Matthew*, tr. David E. Green. Atlanta: John Knox, 1975; Sand, Alexander. *Das Evangelium nach Matthäus*, RNT. Regensburg: Pustet, 1986; Gnilka, Joachim. *Das Matthäusevangelium*, HThK I 1,2. Freiburg: Herder, 1988[2]; 1988; Schnackenburg, Rudolf. *Matthäusevangelium*, NEB 1/2. Würzburg: Echter, 1991[2]; 1987; Grundmann, Walter. *Das Evangelium nach*

---

[224] Cf. among others Werner Kelber, *Mark's Story of Jesus* (Philadelphia: Fortress Press, 1979); Jack D. Kingsbury, *The Christology of Mark's Gospel* (Minneapolis: Fortress Press, 1983); *Conflict in Mark* (Minneapolis: Fortress Press, 1989); B.M.F. van Iersel, *Reading Mark* (Edinburgh: T. & T. Clark, 1989); Robert M. Fowler, *Let the Reader Understand. Reader-Response Criticism and the Gospel of Mark* (Philadelphia: Fortress Press, 1991).

[225] Willem S. Vorster, 'Markus – Sammler, Redaktor, Autor oder Erzähler?,' in *Der Erzähler des Evangeliums*, ed. Ferdinand Hahn, SBS 118–119 (Stuttgart: Katholisches Bibelwerk, 1985) 35–36.

[226] Lührmann, *Markusevangelium* 15.

Matthäus, ThHK 1. Berlin: Evangelische Verlagsanstalt, 1992[7]; Luz, Ulrich. *Das Evangelium nach Matthäus*, EKK I/1,2. Neukirchen: Neukirchener Verlag, 1992[3]; 1990. (Vol. 1 tr. Wilhelm C. Linns, *Matthew. A Commentary* [Minneapolis: Augsburg, 1989]); Luck, Ulrich. *Das Evangelium nach Matthäus*, ZBK 1. Zürich: Theologischer Verlag, 1993; Boring, M. Eugene. *The Gospel of Matthew*, NIB 8. Nashville: Abingdon Press, 1994; Hagner, Donald. *Matthew*, WBC 33AB. Dallas: Word, 1993, 1995); Davies, W.D. - Allison, Dale C. *A Critical and Exegetical Commentary on Matthew*, ICC. Edinburgh: T. & T. Clark, 1988; II 1991; III 1997.

Monographs

Hummel, Reinhart. *Die Auseinandersetzung zwischen Kirche und Judentum im Matthäusevangelium*, BEvTh 33. Munich: Kaiser, 1966; Bornkamm, Günther; Barth, Gerhard; Held, Heinz Joachim. *Tradition and Interpretation in Matthew*, tr. Percy Scott. Philadelphia: Westminster, 1967; Trilling, Wolfgang. *Das wahre Israel*, StANT 10 (= EThSt 7). Munich: Kösel, 1967[3]; Walker, Rolf. *Die Heilsgeschichte im ersten Evangelium*, FRLANT 91. Göttingen: Vandenhoeck & Ruprecht, 1967; Stendahl, Krister. *The School of St. Matthew*. Philadelphia: Fortress Press, 1968[2]; Strecker, Georg. *Der Weg der Gerechtigkeit*, FRLANT 82. Göttingen: Vandenhoeck & Ruprecht, 1971[3]; Sand, Alexander. *Das Gesetz und die Propheten*, BU 11. Regensburg: Pustet, 1974; Schweizer, Eduard. *Matthäus und seine Gemeinde*, SBS 71. Stuttgart: Katholisches Bibelwerk, 1974; Broer, Ingo. *Freiheit vom Gesetz und Radikalisierung des Gesetzes*, SBS 98. Stuttgart: Katholisches Bibelwerk, 1980; Frankemölle, Hubert. *Jahwebund und Kirche Christi*, NTA 10. Münster: Aschendorff, 1984[2]; Kingsbury, Jack D. *Matthew as Story*. Philadelphia: Fortress Press, 1988[2]; Strecker, Georg. *The Sermon on the Mount*, tr. O. C. Dean, Jr. Nashville: Abingdon, 1988; Kingsbury, Jack D. *Matthew: Structure, Christology, Kingdom*. Minneapolis: Fortress Press, 1989[2]; Balch, David L., ed. *Social History of the Matthean Community*. Minneapolis: Fortress Press, 1991 (important collection of essays); Stanton, Graham N. *A Gospel for a New People: Studies in Matthew*. Edinburgh: T. & T. Clark, 1992; Wong, K. Ch. *Interkulturelle Theologie und multikulturelle Gemeinde im Matthäusevangelium*, NTOA 22. Göttingen: Vandenhoeck & Ruprecht, 1992; Luz, Ulrich. *The Theology of the Gospel of Matthew*. tr. J. Bradford Robinson (Cambridge: University Press, 1995); Weiser, Alfons. *Theologie des Neuen Testaments II* (1993; see above 3.3.1) 79–116; Saldarini, Anthony J. *Matthew's Christian-Jewish Community*. Chicago: Univ. of Chicago Press, 1994; Betz, Hans D. *The Sermon on the Mount*, Hermeneia. Minneapolis: Fortress Press, 1995; Bauer, David R., and Powell, Mark Allan, eds. *Treasures New and Old: Contributions to Matthean Studies*. Atlanta: Scholars Press, 1966.

Articles

Stegemann, Hartmut. 'Die des Uria', in *Tradition und Glaube* (FS K. G. Kuhn), ed. Gert Jeremias et. al. Göttingen: Vandenhoeck & Ruprecht, 1971, 246–276; Luz, Ulrich. 'Die Erfüllung des Gesetzes bei Matthäus,' ZThK 75 (1978) 398–435; Lange, Joachim, ed. *Das Matthäus-Evangelium*, WdF 525. Darmstadt: Wissenschaftliche Buchgesellschaft, 1980 (important collection of essays with contributions by G.

Bornkamm, E. Schweizer, G. Strecker, U. Luz and others); Bornkamm, Günther. 'The Authority to 'Bind' and 'Loose' in the Church in Matthew's Gospel,' in *The Interpretation of Matthew*, ed. Graham Stanton. Philadelphia: Fortress Press, 1983, 85–97; Schenke, Ludger, ed. *Studien zum Matthäusevangelium* (FS W. Pesch). SBS, Stuttgart: Katholisches Bibelwerk, 1988; Oberlinner, Lorenz- Fiedler, Peter, eds. *Salz der Erde- Licht der Welt. Exegetische Studien zum Matthäusevangelium* (FS A. Vögtle). Stuttgart: Katholisches Bibelwerk, 1991; Roloff, Jürgen. 'Das Kirchenverständnis des Matthäus im Spiegel seiner Gleichnisse,' NTS 38 (1992) 337–356.

Histories of Research

Stanton, Graham. 'The Origin and Purpose of Matthew's Gospel,' *ANRW* 25.3. Berlin: Walter de Gruyter, 1985, 1889–1951; Sand, Alexander. *Das Matthäus-Evangelium*. EdF 275, Darmstadt: Wissenschaftliche Buchgesellschaft, 1991.

3.5.2 Author

The following statement about authorship was reported by Papias on the basis of the 'tradition of the elders' available to him: 'Then Matthew put together [or 'wrote'] the sayings [λόγια] in the Hebrew dialect [διάλεκτος] and each one translated [ἡρμήνευσεν, 'interpreted'?] them as he was able.'[227] The antiquity of this tradition ascribing the Gospel to the apostle Matthew is confirmed by Gospel of the Ebionites fragment 4,[228] and by the titles of the Gospels, which are to be dated around the beginning of the second century. The comment by Papias provides no basis for firm historical conclusions, however, for there is no compelling evidence for an earlier Hebrew version of Matthew, and in Papias the statement about Matthew is the conclusion of a discussion about Matthew and Mark. Two observations speak against the identification[229] of the author with the disciple Matthew (cf. Matt. 10.3; Mark 3.18; Luke 6.15; Acts 1.13): (1) It is very unlikely that an eyewitness of the ministry of Jesus would have used the work of the non-eyewitness Mark as the basis for his own work.[230]

---

[227] Eusebius, HE 3.39.16. Josef Kürzinger, *Papias von Hierapolis und die Evangelien des Neuen Testaments*, Eichstätter Materialien 4 (Regensburg: Pustet, 1983) 103, translates: 'Now Matthew brought the words (about the Lord) in Hebrew style into a literary form. Each one dealt with them as best he could.' Kürzinger refers διάλεκτος (dialect) not to the Aramaic language, but to the Greek of Matthew's composition.

[228] Gospel of the Ebionites fragment 4 = Epiph, Haer 30,13.2–33. Cf. Ph. Vielhauer and G. Strecker, 'Jewish-Christian Gospels,' in *New Testament Apocrypha*, ed. Wilhelm Schneemelcher, ed.W. McL. Wilson (Louisville, Kentucky: Westminster/John Knox Press, 1991) 170.

[229] As argued, for instance, by Bo Reicke, *Roots* (see above 3.2.6) 160 and R. H. Gundry, *Matthew. A Commentary on his Literary and Theological Art* (Grand Rapids: Wm. B. Eerdmans, 1982) 620.

[230] Cf. Luz, *Matthew* 1.94.

(2) The change of names from Mark's Levi (Mark 2.14/ Matt. 9.9) clearly reflects a secondary process that is hardly the work of an eyewitness. A parallel to this practice is found, however, in Matt. 27.56, where the unknown Salome from Mark 15.40 is replaced by the mother of the sons of Zebedee (cf. also Matt. 20.20). The disciple Matthew probably did play an important role in the church from which the Gospel of Matthew comes, which explains the change of names in Matt. 9.9 and the addition ὁ τελώνης (the tax collector) in Matt. 10.3. The theological intention of this laying claim to the testimony of an eyewitness is clear: the evangelist connects his church to one of the Lord's original disciples, a member of the circle of the Twelve, and thus to the earthly Jesus himself, the one whose teaching is presented in the Gospel and whom the church is called to obey.[231] Matthew 13.52 and 23.34 indicate that the author functioned in his community as a *teacher*.[232] The author's use of Scripture and the somewhat catechetically organized ethical instructions are indications of his educational background.[233] Matthew orients his Gospel both to the community as a whole and to other teachers in the community, who like himself have the responsibility of mediating both 'old' and 'new.'

Whether Matthew was a Jewish[234] or Gentile[235] Christian is still a disputed point among scholars. The Gospel provides data that support each possibility. The following observations speak for a *Jewish-Christian standpoint* of Matthew:

(a) The fundamental affirmation of the Law (cf. Matt. 5.17–20; 23.3a, 23b).

(b) The sustained reference to the Old Testament and the emphatic application of the idea of fulfillment (cf. e.g. Matt. 1.22–23; 2.5–6, 15, 17–18; 3.3; 4.4–16; 8.17 and others).

---

[231] Cf. Luz, *Matthäusevangelium* 2.42.

[232] Cf. Stendahl, *School* 20 (Matthew as a 'handbook issued by a school'); Strecker, *Weg der Gerechtigkeit* 39 (Christian scribe); Schmithals, 'Evangelien' *TRE* 10 (1982) 619 (leader of a catechetical school); Luz, *Matthew* 1.78, 94. (Matthew as a teacher, not the head of a 'school,' but as the creative exponent of his church); Gnilka, *Matthäusevangelium* 2.516, 532, who distinguishes between the church and the 'Matthean school' in the sense of a teaching office within the community); Martin Hengel, ThR 52 (1987), 342–43 note 28 ('something like the head of a Christian school').

[233] Luz rightly emphasizes 'He probably was not a scribe in the sense of a rabbinically trained exegete; the characteristics for this are lacking' (*Matthew* 1.94. Luz stresses the author's developed feeling for the Greek language and his synagogue education.)

[234] So for example Schweizer, *Theological Introduction* 128; Luz, *Matthew* 1.79–80; Gnilka, *Matthäusevangelium* 2.515–16; Roloff, 'Kirchenverständnis' 339.

[235] Cf. e.g. Poul Nepper-Christensen, *Das Matthäusevangelium. Ein judenchristliches Evangelium?* (AThD 1. Århus 1954) 202–208; Trilling, *Israel* 215; Strecker, *Weg der Gerechtigkeit* 15–35; Walker, *Heilsgeschichte* passim; John P. Meier, *Law and History in Matthew's Gospel*, AB 71 (Rome: Pontifical Biblical Institute, 1976) 14–21.

(c) The fundamental limitation of Jesus' mission to Israel (cf. Matt. 10.5–6; 15.24).

(d) The Matthean community still keeps the Sabbath (cf. Matt. 24.20).

(e) The Matthean community still lives within the jurisdiction of Judaism (cf. Matt. 17.24–27; 23.1–3).

(f) The Moses typology in Matt. 2.13ff.; 4.1–2; 5.1, and the five great discourses in the Gospel present Jesus as having an affinity to Moses.

(g) The language, structure, reception of the Scripture, argumentation, and history of the influence of the Gospel of Matthew point to a Jewish Christian as its author.

Over against the interpretation of Matthew as a Jewish Christian document stand statements in the text that point to a *Gentile Christian standpoint* of the author:

(a) The Gospel's offer of salvation to all clearly points to a Gentile mission that has been underway for some time (cf. Matt. 28.18–20; 8.11–12; 10.18; 12.18, 21; 13.38a; 21.43–45; 22.1–14; 24.14; 25.32; 26.13).

(b) The nullification of ritual laws (cf. Matt. 15.11, 20b; 23.25–26).

(c) The Matthean critique of the Law. Especially in the Antitheses of the Sermon on the Mount (Matt. 5.21–48) Jesus places his own authority higher than that of Moses, for which there is no parallel in ancient Judaism.

(d) Matthew presents a thoroughgoing polemic against Pharisaic casuistry (cf. Matt. 5.20; 6.1ff.; 9.9ff.; 12.1ff., 9ff.; 15.1ff.; 19.1ff.; 23.1ff.).

(e) Matthew avoids Aramaisms (cf. Mark 1.13/ Matt. 4.2; Mark 5.41/ Matt. 9.25; Mark 7.34/ Matt. 15.30; Mark 7.11/ Matt. 15.5).

(f) The Matthean community understands its life to be at some distance from that of the synagogue (cf. Matt. 23.34b ἐν ταῖς συναγωγαῖς ὑμῶν [in your synagogues]; Matt. 7.29b καὶ οὐχ ὡς οἱ γραμματεῖς αὐτῶν [and not as their scribes]).

(g) Ritual prescriptions for the Sabbath have lost their significance (cf. Matt. 12.1–8).

(h) The rejection of Israel, i.e. that Israel has lost its distinct place in the history of salvation, has been accepted by Matthew as reality for some time (cf. Matt. 21.43; 22.9; 8.11–12; 21.39ff.; 27.25; 28.15).

The tension between these two lists is best understood to mean that the evangelist Matthew is the advocate of a *liberal Hellenistic Diaspora Jewish Christianity* that had been engaged in the Gentile mission for some time.[236] The lack of any reference to the debate over circumcision in Matthew

---

[236] For this understanding cf. e.g. Stegemann, 'Die des Uria' 271, who states 'that the Jewish components of Matthean theology were from the beginning Hellenistic-Jewish . . .'.

points in the same direction, for in the earlier conservative Palestinian Judaism the relaxing of the practice of circumcision was regarded as contempt for the Torah, while in broad circles of Hellenistic Diaspora Judaism circumcision was not considered an important issue.[237] The history of the influence of the Gospel of Matthew in the early church also suggests a kind of Judaism that was open to accepting Gentiles. Thus the rigid historical classifications such as 'Jewish Christian' or 'Gentile Christian' probably had not reflected the reality of the Matthean community and the self understanding of the evangelist for some time (see below 3.5.9).

3.5.3 Place and Time of Composition

The comprehensive Jewish-Christian traditions, Matthew 4.24 (καὶ ἀπῆλθεν ἡ ἀκοὴ αὐτοῦ εἰς ὅλον τὴν Συρίαν [and his fame spread into all Syria]) and the attestation in the Didache (cf. Did 7.1, 8; 10.5, 16) and Ignatius of Antioch (cf. IgnSm. 1.1/Matt. 3.15; IgnPhld. 3.1/Matt. 15.13)[238] suggest *Syria* as the place where Matthew was written.[239] The Gospel offers no evidence for a more precise location (Antioch in Syria,[240] Damascus,[241] Sidon or Tyre,[242] the Syrian interior[243]).

Matthew presupposes the destruction of the temple (cf. Matt. 22.7; 21.41; 23.38). The *terminus ad quem* is provided by the knowledge of the Gospel by Ignatius (around 110 CE). The Gospel of Matthew was therefore probably written *around 90 CE*.[244]

---

[237] Stegemann *ibid.* 273.

[238] On this cf. Wolf-Dietrich Köhler, *Die Rezeption des Matthäusevangeliums in der Zeit vor Irenäus*, WUNT 2.24 (Tübingen: J. C. B. Mohr [Paul Siebeck], 1987) 19–56, 73–96.

[239] There is a broad scholarly consensus on this. Cf. only Strecker, *Weg der Gerechtigkeit* 37; Luz, *Matthew* 1.91; Gnilka, *Matthäusevangelium* 2.514; Luck, *Matthäusevangelium* 15.

[240] So for example Schweizer, *Matthäus und seine Gemeinde* 138–139; J. Zumstein, 'Antioche sur l'Oronte et l'Évangile selon Matthieu', SNTU 5 (1980) 122–138; John P. Meier, 'Antioch,' in *Antioch and Rome*, eds. Raymond E. Brown and John P. Meier (New York: Paulist Press, 1983) 11–86; Luz, *Matthew* 1.91 (a likely possibility); Schnackenburg, *Matthäusevangelium* 1. 8–9.

[241] Cf. Gnilka, *Matthäusevangelium* 2.515.

[242] Cf. G. D. Kilpatrick, *The Origins of the Gospel according to St. Matthew* (Oxford: Oxford University Press, 1946) 134.

[243] Cf. Gerd Theißen, *The Gospels in Context* (see above 3.1.1) 272–273.

[244] Cf. also Strecker, *Weg der Gerechtigkeit* 35–36 (90–95); Gnilka, *Matthäusevangelium* 2.520 (around 80); Schnackenburg, *Matthäusevangelium* 9 (85–90); Luz, *Matthew* 1.93 (composed not long after 80); differently Robert Gundry, *Matthew* (see above 3.5.2) 599–609, who argues for 65–67 as the time of composition.

3.5.4 Intended Readership

The situation of the Matthean community is essentially defined by its break with Israel,[245] which had led to repressions and persecutions of Matthean Christians (cf. Matt. 10.17–18; 23.34).[246] The distance from and dispute with Israel[247] is seen on the linguistic plane, e.g. in the stereotypical usage of 'their' or 'your' synagogues (cf. Matt. 4.23; 9.35; 10.17; 12.9; 13.54; 23.34, as well as 6.2, 5 and 23.6) and the 'scribes and Pharisees' (cf. Matt. 5.20; 12.38; 15.1; 23.2, 13, 15, 23, 25, 27, 29). Matthew exposes and surpasses the 'hypocritical' acts of the Pharisees and scribes (cf. e.g. Matt. 6.1–18; 23.1–36) by the doing of the 'better' righteousness (Matt. 5.20) and the full accomplishment of the original will of God (cf. e.g. Matt. 5.21–48; 6.9, 10b; 12.50; 15.4; 18.14; 19.3–9; 21.31), which is the presupposition for entrance into the kingdom of heaven (cf. Matt. 23.13). Israel's rejection has been reality for the Matthean community for a long time (cf. Matt. 8.11–12; 21.43; 22.9), and the Gentile mission is its self-evident practice (cf. alongside Matt. 28.18–20 especially Matt. 12.21; 13.38a; 24.14; 26.13). The prominent placement of the mission command as the hermeneutical and theological key for the whole Gospel (see below 3.5.9) shows that the community was not in the process of opening a new phase of its life by beginning a mission to the Gentiles,[248] but had systematically carried on a Gentile mission for a long time. This is suggested not only by the numerous affirmations of the universal offer of salvation, but also by the history of early Christian theology. The Gentile mission documented in pre-Pauline, Pauline, pre-Markan, and pre-Lukan texts makes it appear very unlikely that the Matthean community did not take this step until forty or fifty years later.

---

[245] Cf. Luz, *Matthew* 1.88; Klaus Pantle-Schieber, 'Anmerkungen zur Auseinandersetzung von ἐκκλησία und Judentum im Matthäusevangelium,' ZNW 80 (1989) 145–162; Jürgen Roloff, *Die Kirche im Neuen Testament*, GNT 10. Göttingen: Vandenhoeck & Ruprecht, 1993, 146–154. According to Roloff, the internal situation of the Matthean community is characterized by two conflicts: (1) Matthew had to debate with a strict Jewish Christian group that could imagine a Gentile mission 'only with the condition of a full adoption of the Torah' (147); (2) The nucleus of the community had developed from the circle of radical wandering charismatics, whose ethos was shared only to a limited extent by the settled members of the church, the 'little ones' (Matt 10.42; 11.11; 18.6, 14).

[246] Thus the addition of καὶ τοῖς ἔθνεσιν in Matt 10.18 shows clearly that for the Evangelist the dispute already lies some time back in the past and he has integrated it into his universal conception. Cf. Strecker, *Weg der Gerechtigkeit* 30.

[247] Contra Günter Bornkamm, 'End-Expectation and Church in Matthew,' in *Tradition and Interpretation in Matthew*, eds. Bornkamm – Barth – Held 39 ('Matthew's Gospel confirms throughout that the congregation which it represented had not yet separated from Judaism,' and Hummel, *Auseinandersetzung* 29, 31, 159–160, who assume a continuing nominal membership in the synagogue coupled with an internal feeling of independence from it.

[248] This is affirmed for example by Luz, *Matthew* 1.82–87.

The repeated challenge to do the will of God (cf. Matt. 7.21; 12.50; 21.31) signals a fundamental problem of the Matthean community: abiding in the sphere of God's gracious act, without growing weary in faith and love. Matthew directs a wide range of parenetic materials against the problem of 'little faith' (cf. Matt. 6.30; 14.31; further 8.26; 16.8; 17.20), placing the emphasis on the doing of the whole Torah (cf. Matt. 5.17–19) or on 'righteousness' (cf. Matt. 3.15; 5.6, 10, 20; 6.1, 33; 21.32), on being 'perfect' (cf. Matt. 5.48; 19.21) and on the 'fruits' of faith (cf. Matt. 3.10; 7.16–20; 12.33; 13.8; 21.18–22, 33–46). With the challenge to put faith into courageous action and to remain steadfast in faith, Matthew combines an orientation to the Last Judgment (cf. Matt. 3.10; 5.29; 7.16ff.; 10.15; 18.21–35; 19.30; 23.33, 35–36; 24.42 and elsewhere). It is hardly a coincidence that only in Matthew are found portrayals of the Last Judgment that serve as the motivation for the parenesis (cf. Matt. 7.21ff.; 13.36ff.; 25.31ff.). The community exists in the present as a *corpus permixtum*, in which both righteous and unrighteous live together (cf. Matt. 13.36–43), so that it is precisely for this reason that the evangelist issues calls to wakefulness (cf. Matt. 24.42; 25.13) – but at the same time the promise applies, 'But the one who endures to the end will be saved' (24.13).

In 7.25 and 24.11 the evangelist warns the community against ψευδο-προφῆται (false prophets). The theological profile of these opponents remains unclear; they are often categorized as 'Hellenistic antinomians' on the basis of Matt. 5.17–20; 7.12–27; 11.12–13; 24.10–13.[249] Matthew accuses them of ἀνομία (lawlessness) (cf. Matt. 7.23; 24.12), who produce bad fruits (cf. Matt. 7.16–20), and who do not do the will of God (Matt. 7.21). Obviously these opponents undermine the comprehensive ethical conception of Matthew (cf. Matt. 24.12) and thereby endanger the unity of the community.

The Matthean community knows no institutionalized offices (cf. Matt. 23.8–12), but has within it prophets (cf. Matt. 10.41; 23.34, as well as 5.12 and 10.20), scribes (cf. Matt. 13.52; 23.34, as well as 8.19) and charismatics (cf. 10.8). Peter has a special position within the community.[250] He appears as the 'first' apostle (Matt. 10.2), speaker for the circle of disciples (Matt. 15.15; 18.21), and his conduct in Matt. 14.28–31 is presented as an instructive example for the right relation between faith and doubt. The 'rock

---

[249] Foundational is Gerhard Barth, 'Matthew's Understanding of the Law,' in *Tradition and Interpretation in Matthew*, eds. Bornkamm – Barth – Held 58–164; cf. further Eduard Schweizer, 'Gesetz und Enthusiasmus bei Matthäus' in *Das Matthäus-Evangelium*, ed. J. Lange 350–376. A catalogue of the variety of proposed solutions (Zealots, Pharisees, Essenes, strict Jewish Christians, Paulinists) is found in Luz, *Matthew* 1.441–442, who categorizes the false prophets as 'partisans of Mark.'

[250] On this cf. Luz, *Mattäusevangelium* 2.467–471; Roloff, *Kirche* 162–165.

saying' of Matt. 16.18 presents him as founder of the church, to whom alone the authority to bind and loose is given (Matt. 16.19). But in Matt. 18.18 this authority is also possessed by the community as a whole, which means that Peter is presented as an exemplar of all the disciples: what is said about him in regard to understanding, authority, strength of faith or lack of it may be applied by the community to itself. If the present form of the Gospel of Matthew reflects the way of the church from its Jewish-Christian beginnings to its practice of the universal mission to the Gentiles, then this only corresponds to the course of Peter's own life, who as the first witness of the Easter event (cf. 1 Cor. 15.5) opened himself to a more liberal form of Judaism (cf. Gal. 2.11ff.) and then finally himself carried on a mission to Gentiles (cf. 1 Cor. 9.5). It is possible that these remarkable agreements between the life of Peter and the life of the Matthean community are the basis for Peter's authority within it.

3.5.5 Outline, Structure, Form

1.1–2.23	Prehistory
3.1–4.11	John the Baptist; Baptism and Temptation of Jesus
4.12–25	Beginning of Jesus' Public Ministry
5.1–7.29	Sermon on the Mount
8.1–9.34	Miracles
9.35–11.1	Missionary Discourse
11.2–12.50	Healings and Conflicts
13.1–52	Parables
13.53–17.27	Journeys in Galilee
18.1–35	Speech on Church Discipline as Conclusion of the Galilean Ministry
19.1–20.34	On the Way to Jerusalem
21.1–25.46	Jesus' Ministry in Jerusalem
26.1–28.20	Passion, Resurrection and Appearances

The Gospel of Matthew does not have a clear structural plan for the whole Gospel that may be easily recognized.[251] Thus scholars have proposed very different outlines, two of which are of particular significance: (1) The division of the Gospel into five 'books' by B. W. Bacon was very influential.[252] Bacon combines narrative complexes with the five Matthean speeches, so that five blocks of material result (chs. 3–7; chs. 8–10; 11.1–13.52; 13.53–

---

[251] On the composition of the Gospel as a whole cf. especially Luz, *Matthew* 1.33–36 and Kingsbury, *Matthew: Structure, Christology, Kingdom* 1–39.

[252] Cf. Benjamin W. Bacon, 'The "Five Books" of Matthew against the Jews,' in *Studies in Matthew* (New York: H. Holt and Company, 1930).

18.35; chs. 19–25), with chs. 1–2 forming the introduction and chs. 26–28 the conclusion. (2) Matt. 4.17 and 16.21 are often taken as structural signals.[253] This results in two major parts, in principle oriented to the Markan outline: Matt. 4.17–16.20, Jesus' ministry in and around Galilee, and Matt. 16.21–25.46, Jesus' way to Jerusalem. To these two major sections a long introduction and the passion story are then added. Then in most reconstructions the high point of the first major part is formed by the confession of Peter at Caesarea Philippi (Matt. 16.13–20). The turning point of the narrative of the way of Jesus is marked by 16.21, signaled by the passion prediction.

Matthew adopts the new literary genre 'gospel' and despite considerable deviations, orients his presentation of the Christ event to the Markan model.[254] Noticeable elements in comparison to Mark are the expansions at the beginning and end of the Gospel. The Matthean prehistory (1.1–2.23) presents a christologically motivated introduction to the public ministry of Jesus. At the same time the account of salvation history is lengthened at the beginning by adding the genealogy (1.1–17) and birth story (1.18–25). At the end of the Gospel Matthew goes beyond Mark by telling stories about Jesus' tomb and stories of his appearance that testify to the resurrection faith (cf. Matt. 27.62–66, the guards at the tomb, and 28.9–10, the appearance to the women). Matthew's presentation reaches its climax in the appearance of the Resurrected One to his disciples and in the missionary command (Matt. 28.16–20).[255]

Despite the considerable expansions and modifications of individual elements of the tradition, Matthew essentially follows the Gospel of Mark (see above 3.2.3), so that his work too is characterized by a basic narrative structure. Matthew places the Sermon on the Mount between Mark 1.21 and 1.22, so that the amazement of the crowds at the teaching of Jesus is now, as in Mark, the reaction to Jesus' first sermon (cf. Matt. 7.28–29). By the almost identical formulation of Matt. 4.23 and 9.35 the Sermon on the Mount and the cycle of miracle stories of chapters 8 and 9 are bound together into a literary unit. Jesus is presented as Messiah in word and deed.[256] The heavy-handed changes in the Markan order in the material

---

[253] Cf. e.g. Lohmeyer, *Matthäusevangelium* 7–10; Schnackenburg, *Matthäusevangelium* 1.5–7.

[254] Contra Frankemölle, *Jahwebund* 331–400, who wants to understand the Gospel of Matthew as a work of kerygmatic history in dependence on Old Testament models, especially Deuteronomy.

[255] On the broad framework of the story of Jesus in Matthew cf. Schnackenburg, *Jesus in the Gospels* (see above 3.4.9) 75–94.

[256] Cf. Julius Schniewind, *Das Evangelium nach Matthäus*, NTD 1 (Göttingen: Vandenhoeck & Ruprecht, 1984[13]) 36: 'The Messiah of word, who preaches, is pictured in chapters 5–7, just as the Messiah of deed, who heals, is portrayed in chapters 8–9.'

used in chapters 8–9 are explained by the theological intentions of the evangelist: Matthew is here narrating the founding legends of the church of Jews and Gentiles and the resulting split that occurred in Israel.[257] From chapter 12 on, Matthew follows Mark closely, with the exception of the speeches. Jesus' ministry in Jerusalem (chs. 21–25) and the passion story (chs. 26–28) are clearly distinguished literary units.

The outline of chs. 12–20 is difficult to discern, but in any case weighty theological central points are provided by the speeches in chapters 13 and 18. The evangelist has composed the five great speeches from previously existing traditions. The Sermon on the Mount (chs. 5–7), the missionary discourse (ch. 10), the parables (ch. 13), the instruction on church discipline (ch. 18) and the eschatological discourse (chs. 24–25) are all concluded with the expression 'and it happened, when Jesus had completed these words . . . ' (7.28; 11.1; 13.53; 19.1; 26.1) and thus related to each other. Smaller speech units are found in 11.7–19 (on John the Baptist), 11.20–30 (woes and praise), 12.22–37 (Beelzebul speech), 15.1–20 (clean and unclean). Matthew loves the principle of round numbers: alongside the five great speech complexes are three pre-Matthean antitheses (Matt. 5.21–22, 27–28, 33–37) and three Matthean antitheses (Matt. 5.31–32, 38ff., 43ff.), the triad alms, prayer and fasting in 6.1–8, seven beatitudes (5.3–9, a pre-Matthean composition), seven petitions in the Lord's Prayer (6.9–13), seven parables (13.1–52), seven woes (23.1–36), and ten miracles of Jesus (8.1–9.34).

As additional examples of Matthew's narrative technique we may name:[258] (1) preliminary intimations that cannot be understood from the immediate context but lead one more deeply into the narrative where they become clear later (cf. Matt. 1.5–6; 2.3, 23; 3.15; 4.15) (2) key concepts with which complex theological ideas are summarized (e.g. δικαιοσύνη, πατήρ, ἀκολουθέω, κρίσις [righteousness, Father, following, judgment]); (3) repetitions (cf. e.g. the formula of 'weeping and gnashing of teeth' in 8.12; 13.42, 50; 22.13; 24.51; 25.30); inclusions (cf. e.g. the Immanuel motif in 1.23 and 28.20).

To the distinctive linguistic elements of Matthew[259] belong his favorite words and expressions such as βασιλεία τῶν οὐρανῶν (kingdom of heaven)

---

[257] On this cf. Christoph Burger, 'Jesu Taten nach Matthäus 8 und 9,' ZThK 70 (1973) 272–287; Ulrich Luz, 'Die Wundergeschichten von Mt 8–9,' in *Tradition and Interpretation in the New Testament* (FS E. E. Ellis), eds. Gerald Hawthorne and Otto Betz (Grand Rapids: Wm. B. Eerdmans – Tübingen: J. C. B. Mohr [Paul Siebeck], 1987) 149–165.

[258] Cf. Luz, *Jesusgeschichte des Matthäus* 12–17.

[259] Cf. Wolfgang Schenk, *Die Sprache des Matthäus* (Göttingen: Vandenhoeck & Ruprecht, 1987); Luz, *Matthew* 1.49–72.

(Matt. 32/Mark 0/Luke 0), ἀναχωρέω (depart) (Matt. 10/Mark 1/Luke 0); νόμος καὶ προφῆται (the law and the prophets) (Matt. 4/Mark 0/Luke 1); μαθητής (disciple) (Matt. 72/Mark 46/Luke 37); λέγω δὲ ὑμῖν (but I say to you) (Matt. 7/Mark 0/Luke 4); θέλημα θεοῦ or πατρός [will of God or the Father]) (Matt. 6/ Mark 1/ Luke 1); δικαιοσύνη (righteousness) (Matt. 7/Mark 0/Luke 1); δίκαιος (righteous) (Matt. 17/Mark 2/Luke 11); γραμματεῖς / Φαρισαῖοι (scribes/Pharisees) (Matt. 11/Mark 3/Luke 5); ὁ δὲ ἀποκριθεὶς εἶπεν (he answered and said) (Matt. 18/Mark 2/Luke 0).

3.5.6 Literary Integrity

The literary integrity of the Gospel of Matthew is undisputed.

3.5.7 Traditions, Sources

Matthew's primary source was an edition of the Gospel of Mark that had been slightly revised from the form now preserved as canonical Mark (see above 3.2.3 on Deuteromark). This judgment is based on those texts that agree with Luke against canonical Mark, but which cannot be explained as Matthean redaction.

Matthew integrates the copy of Q available to him into the outline of his Gospel as a whole. He mostly incorporates the Q material as blocks into the course of the life of Jesus as this was already given by the Q source itself, the Gospel of Mark, and his own special materials.[260] Thus the great speeches of Jesus are connected to the narratives of Jesus' deeds by the stereotyped concluding verse. In the Sermon on the Mount Jesus appears as the teacher of the 'better righteousness.' Matthew adopts the strong ethical impulse from Q with its emphasis on active doing of the will of God (cf. e.g. Matt. 7.21, 24–27) while at the same time relativizing orthopraxy (cf. Matt. 7.22), and with Q emphasizes the indicative of salvation (cf. Matt. 5.3–15). In the portrayal of Jesus' mighty deeds in chapters 8–9 the Q material now emphasizes the process of separation between Israel and the disciples (cf. Matt. 8.11–12; 9.32–34). Matthew often elaborates the ethic of discipleship and mission by the addition of Q materials (cf. e.g. Matt. 9.37–38; 10.7–8, 39–40). The evangelist emphasizes the privileged place of the disciples in 13.16–17, as the eschatological blessing is pronounced on them that is later addressed to Peter (cf. Matt. 16.17–19) and the whole community (cf. Matt. 18.18). In the discourse on church life in

---

[260] For a detailed analysis, cf. Eduard Schweizer, 'Aufnahme und Gestaltung von Q bei Matthäus,' in *Salz der Erde – Licht der Welt*, eds. Lorenz Oberlinner and P. Fiedler (FS A. Vögtle) SBS. Stuttgart: Katholisches Bibelwerk, 111–130.

Matthew 18 the evangelist adopts Q material and develops it into a challenge to be willing to forgive (cf. Matt. 18.15, 21–22). Matthew amplifies the growing conflict with the scribes and Pharisees especially in chapter 23 by using extensive Q materials (cf. Matt. 23.4, 6–7, 13, 23, 25–27, 29–32, 34–36). The evangelist also composes a considerable part of the eschatological discourse at the end of the Gospel from Q sayings (cf. Matt. 25.[10–12], 14–30; perhaps also 31–46). The portrayal of Jesus in the Gospel of Matthew as an authoritative teacher is also essentially due to material from Q.

Whether Matthew's *'reflection citations'* (or 'fulfillment citations') constitute an additional connected source continues to be a disputed point. The 'reflection citations' are located, with their respective redactional introductions, in Matt. 1.23; 2.6, 15, 18, 23; 4.15–16; 8.17; 12.18–21; (13.14–15); 13.35; 21.5; 27.9–10 (cf. also Matt. 26.54, 56).[261] In them the hermeneutical pattern 'promise/ fulfillment' is articulated in a way that particularly corresponds to the Matthean understanding of salvation history. The introductory formulae manifest common features: following the idea of fulfillment comes the reference to the biblical passage which sometimes includes the name of the prophet (Isaiah, Jeremiah). Several quotations display a mixed form of the text that includes all known forms of the Old Testament text.[262] While G. Strecker accepts the view that Matthew is here reworking a Christian testimonia collection,[263] W. Rothfuchs understands the reflection citations to be the evangelist's editing of oral church tradition.[264] U. Luz supposes that the reflection citations had been transmitted to the evangelist in written form, already connected to the narratives that follow them.[265] It must be considered unlikely that the formation of the reflection citations goes back to Matthew himself, since the demonstrably redactional elements in them are so small.[266] If we can be relatively confident that the form of the reflection citations themselves is pre-Matthean, still the location of the quotations in the Gospel seems rather to

---

[261] For analysis, cf. especially Strecker, *Weg der Gerechtigkeit* 49–84; Wilhelm Rothfuchs, *Die Erfüllungszitate des Matthäus-Evangeliums*, BWANT 88 (Stuttgart: Kohlhammer, 1969); Luz, *Matthew* 1.156–164.

[262] For a detailed treatment, cf. especially Stendahl, *School* 39–142.

[263] Cf. Strecker, *Weg der Gerechtigkeit* 83: 'From all this it follows that Matthew in the reflection citations used a source, namely a collection of prophetic predictions transmitted to him in written form.'

[264] Cf. Rothfuchs, *Erfüllungszitate* 89: 'The *hapax legomena* found here and there suggest that a written source of the prophetic words was used by the evangelist. Nonetheless, the Matthean peculiarities that are found repeatedly in the citations demand the conclusion that the evangelist edited the source.'

[265] Cf. Luz, *Matthew* 1.161.

[266] Cf. Luz, *Matthew* 1.160 note 26.

be the intentional redactional work of the evangelist, so that the use of a testimonia collection seems the most likely possibility.

3.5.8 Basic Theological Ideas

The appearance of the Risen One, his inthronization as Lord of all and the missionary command in Matt. 28.16–20 not only form the conclusion of the Gospel of Matthew, they are the goal to which the whole Gospel moves and constitute the perspective from which it is to be read.[267] Matthew 28.16–20 is therefore the *theological* and *hermeneutical key* to a proper understanding of the work as a whole.[268]

> Matt. 28.16–20 contains some traditional elements, but its present form represents the redactional work of the evangelist. Thus vv. 16–17 are to be regarded as Matthean constructions in both form and content.[269] V. 18a is also redactional (προσέρχομαι [approach] 52x in Matthew; for ἐλάλησεν αὐτοῖς λέγων [he spoke to them saying] cf.13.3; 14.27; 23.1), while echoes of pre-Matthean motifs can be heard in 18b (e.g. the pairing of οὐρανός/γῆ [heaven/earth]). V. 19 again shows clear traces of the evangelist's work (πορεύομαι [go] in 9.13; 10.7; 18.12; 21.6 and elsewhere; μαθητεύω [become a disciple] redactional in 13.52; 27.57), while on the other hand the baptismal formula in v. 19b reflects the baptismal practice of the community. V. 20 contains several of Matthew's linguistic characteristics (e.g. τηρέω [keep], διδάσκω [teach]; on συντέλεια τοῦ αἰῶνος [end of the age] cf. 13.39, 49; 24.3). The promise of v. 20b takes up Matthew 18.20, and may therefore also go back to the evangelist (cf. also 1.23 Emmanuel).

At the center of Matthew 28.16–20 stands the idea of the universal lordship of Jesus, expressed in the inthronization of v. 18b, the fourfold πᾶς in vv. 18b, 19a, 20ab and in the promise of his constant presence with the church until the end of the age in v. 20b. The presentation of Jesus in the first Gospel is oriented throughout to this confession of faith contemporary with the Matthean community. If Jesus has been given universal ἐξουσία

---

[267] To the point, Otto Michel, 'Der Abschluß des Matthäusevangeliums,' in *Das Matthäus-Evangelium*, ed. J. Lange. 125: 'It is only with the presupposition of Matt 28.18–20 that the Gospel as a whole is written (cf. Matt 28.19 with 10.5ff.; 15.24; Matt. 28.20 with 1.23 and the return to the baptism of 3.1). The conclusion returns in a certain way to the beginning and teaches us to understand the whole Gospel, the story of Jesus, from its ending, i.e. in the post-Easter perspective. *Matt 28:18–20 is the key to understanding the whole book.*'

[268] For the foundational analysis cf. Günter Bornkamm, 'Der Auferstandene und der Irdische. Mt 28,16–20,' in *Zeit und Geschichte* (FS R. Bultmann), ed. Erich Dinkler (Tübingen: J.C. B. Mohr [Paul Siebeck], 1964) 171–191.

[269] Cf. Strecker, *Weg der Gerechtigkeit* 208ff.

(authority) by the resurrection, then corresponding affirmations of the ἐξουσία of the earthly Jesus are given (cf. Matt. 11.27) – in each case it is God who gives ἐξουσία to the Son. It is not the ἐξουσία itself, but the area in which it is exercised, from which restrictions are now removed. For Matthew, the demand made by the Risen One and that of the earthly Jesus correspond to each other. The Emmanuel motif (cf. Matt. 1.23; 28.20) opens the story of the earthly Jesus in the Godward direction, while at the same time the abiding presence of the Risen One is bound to the earthly Jesus. Jesus is presented as the one true Teacher, whose commands are valid not only for the disciples but for the whole world. The authority of the Risen One now empowers the disciples, which means also the present Matthean community, to carry on mission work among the Gentiles, to spread Jesus' teaching as binding authoritative instruction, and thereby to be the church of Jesus Christ. The Great Commission thus binds together central themes of Matthean theology that determine the Gospel through-out.

The way of Jesus appears in the First Gospel from the very beginning as the *way of God* to the *Gentiles*. The earlier mission to the synagogues had been unsuccessful (cf. Matt. 23.34; 10.17), and had for a long time been simply a matter of past history, for now the whole world is the mission field of the Matthean community. If Jesus Christ in 1.1 appears as the 'son of Abraham' and the genealogy begins with Abraham in 1.2, even this is already a universal perspective at the beginning, for God can raise up children to Abraham from the stones (cf. Matt. 3.9). The women mentioned in 1.3–6 of the genealogy (Tamar, Ruth, Rahab, and the wife of Uriah) are all non-Jews, thus bringing another universalistic perspective to expression.[270] The four Gentile women at the beginning correspond to 'all nations' at the end. In Matthew's understanding, it was not only after Jesus had been rejected by Israel, but from the very beginning God's saving act had included the Gentiles. In 2.1ff. Gentiles bow in worship to Jesus, while the Jewish king attempts to kill the child. After the preaching of judgment against Israel by John the Baptist (cf. Matt. 3.1–12) and the Sermon on the Mount, Jesus performs acts of healing on outsiders to Jewish society (Matt. 8.1–4, a leper; 8.5–13, a Gentile; 8.14–15, a woman). As founding legends of the Matthean community, Matthew 8–9 signals the standpoint of the evangelist. He lives in a church composed of Jewish Christians and Gentile Christians, for whom a Gentile is the first example and model of faith (cf. Matt. 8.10). In the narrative of the centurion of Capernaum the Matthean

---

[270] Cf. H. Stegemann, 'Die des Uria' 266ff.; on the other hand Luz, *Matthew* 1.94, speaks only of a 'universalistic undertone.'

community recognizes its own story. The centurion accepts the pre-
eminent ranking of Israel in the history of salvation (Matt. 8.8), but while
Israel becomes subject to God's judgment, he becomes the firstborn of the
Gentile Christians (Matt. 8.11–12).[271] Matt. 10.17–18 presupposes that the
disciples preach the Gospel to Gentiles as well as to Jews.[272] Matt. 12.21
and 13.38a also point to the universal mission to all nations, while in
12.18–21 the Gentile mission is grounded in the text of the Old Testament
(Isa. 42.1–4).[273] It is only consistent with the preaching of the gospel to all
nations (cf. also Matt. 24;14; 26.13) that at the last judgment all nations
appear before the throne of the Son of Man (cf. Matt. 25.31–46).

In the Gospel of Matthew Jesus' teaching is presented as the binding
exposition of the *will of God*, for the Risen One proclaims the binding force
of the words of the earthly Jesus (Matt. 28.20a). For Matthew the will of
God manifest in the Old Testament reaches its goal in Jesus, a perspective
articulated with particular clarity by the reflection citations. The evangelist
understands the advent and preaching of Jesus to be not the abrogation of
the law, but its fulfillment (cf. Matt. 5.17–20). But in what sense does Jesus
fulfill the law? By no means merely by repeating the formulations of the
Old Testament law, but rather as presenting its authoritative interpretation, as shown by the antitheses. The correspondence between 5.20 and
5.48 shows that the antitheses are examples of the 'better righteousness'
demanded by the evangelist. In the first antithesis (5.21–26) Jesus radical-
izes the Torah's commandment against murder. So too, from the Jewish
perspective the second antithesis on adultery (5.27–30) represents the
radicalization of a prohibition in the Torah. In contrast, the third antithesis
on divorce (5.31–32) involves a nullification of a command of Torah (cf.
Deut. 24.1, 3). The ἐξουσία (authority) of Jesus makes it possible for him
to set aside a valid command of Torah in order to bring the true will of God
into force. So too the absolute prohibition of oaths in 5.33–37 breaks the
framework of Old Testament and Jewish thought and is grounded solely in
the authority of Jesus. As he had already done for the absolute prohibition
of divorce, Matthew makes this command practicable for his community,
without thereby demolishing the original intention of Jesus' preaching. By
rejecting completely the basic Old Testament law of retaliation in Matt.
5.38–42 and by advocating the absolute law of love for the enemy in Matt.
5.43–48, the preacher of the Sermon on the Mount abandons completely

---

[271] Luz, *Matthäusevangelium* 2.16 minimizes the significance of this text when he says the
centurion of Capernaum was for Matthew 'a marginal figure who gives a perspective on the
future.'

[272] Cf. Gnilka, *Matthäusevangelium* 1.376–377.

[273] Cf. Walker, *Heilsgeschichte* 78–79.

the thinking of his time[274] and emphasizes that the true will of God lies only in unlimited love and perfect justice.

The antitheses show how Matthew understands the fulfilling of the law by Jesus: validity and binding force are not located in the Old Testament tradition, but solely in the authority of Jesus. That is why for Matthew radicalizing the Torah and abrogation of the Torah are not opposites, because both can be grounded and held together only by the authority of Jesus. Not the Old Testament law as such, but only the *authoritative interpretation* of the Old Testament by Jesus is binding on the Matthean community. It is thus not the case that Jesus' authority simply sets aside a wrong interpretation of the Torah, but Jesus claims to set forth the original intention of God's law, sometimes by rejecting the letter of the Torah.

It is already made clear by the antitheses that the love commandment is the center of the Matthean understanding of the law. The better righteousness and perfection demanded by Jesus (Matt. 5.20, 48) are identical with each other and with the Golden Rule in Matt. 7.12. They attain concrete form in deeds of mercy (cf. Hos 6.6 in Matt. 9.13; 12.7; cf. also 23.23c) and in the unqualified love of God and neighbor (cf. Matt. 19.19; 22.34–40), which again finds its highest expression in love for the enemy. For Matthew obedience to the law does not consist in the observation of many individual prescriptions, commandments and rules, but in the practice of love and justice in everyday life. The love commandment as the summary of the Matthean understanding of the law receives its binding force only through the One who by his authority lets the true will of God again be heard. The Matthean understanding of the law must therefore be attained from a point of view in which Christology is central.

The distinctive element in the Matthean *ethic* is the demand to do the will of God. To believe in Jesus means at the same time to do his will. Just as Jesus himself understands his ministry as the fulfillment of all righteousness (Matt. 3.15), so also is δικαιοσύνη (righteousness) the central content of Matthean ethics (Matt. 5.6, 10, 20; 6.1, 33; 21.32). The 'better' righteousness appears as the presupposition for entrance into the kingdom of heaven (5.20), and is manifested in an ethical conduct that is set forth programatically and as a binding commandment in the antitheses. The goal and standard of the 'better' righteousness is 'perfection' (5.48).[275] The

---

[274] For history-of-religions parallels cf. John Piper, *Love your Enemies* (SNTSMS 38) (Cambridge: Cambridge University Press, 1979).

[275] According to Strecker, *Weg der Gerechtigkeit* 149–158, δικαιοσύνη (righteousness) in Matthew consistently describes the ethical conduct of the disciples, their doing of right. Differently e.g. Martin Johannes Fiedler, '"Gerechtigkeit" im Matthäus-Evangelium,' TheolVers 8 (1977) 63–75; Heinz Giesen, *Christliches Handeln. Eine redaktionskritische Untersuchung zum*

disciples are therefore called to let their ethic be directed by Jesus' teaching and acting with authority. Just as Jesus himself in Gethsemane fulfills the third petition of the Lord's prayer (Matt. 26.42/6.10), the church must also surrender itself to the will of God. The continuing validity of the Old Testament alongside the new commandment is no contradiction for Matthew, but they attain their unity in the authority of Jesus Christ. However, Matthew's strong emphasis on the ethical imperative by no means suggests that he neglects the indicative of God's saving act (cf. Matt. 5.1–12; 28.19, 20: baptism as the ground of the saving relationship with God stands before 'teaching';[276] Matt. 7.7–12: prayer is the foundation that makes possible the 'better' righteousness).[277] Rather, characteristic for Matthew is the weaving together of indicative and imperative, with the emphasis on the imperative, so that one can speak of a certain kind of imperative, namely an 'indicative imperative' (cf. e.g. Matt. 11.28–30).[278]

A central element of the ethical motivation in Matthew is formed by the concept of reward and punishment (reward: cf. Matt. 5.12, 19; 6.1, 19–21; 10.41–42; 18.1–5; 19.17, 28; 20.16, 23; 25.14ff.; punishment: cf. Matt. 5.22; 7.1, 21; 13.49–50; 22.13; 24.51; 25.30) and the concept of God bound up with this.[279] Jesus will return as Son of Man, the eschatological judge (Matt. 7.22–23; 13.30, 41; 16.27; 24.29–31; 25.31), and only in the future judgment of the world will the separation between 'called' and 'chosen' be accomplished (cf. Matt. 24.42–51). Then people will be judged on the basis of what they have done, with some pronounced to be 'righteous' and some thrown into the 'eternal fire' (cf. Matt. 13.36–43, 47–50). The *deeds* of faith will be the decisive criterion for each individual in the last judgment (cf. Matt. 16.27: κατὰ τὴν πρᾶξιν αὐτοῦ ['according to his or her works']). Thus for Matthew the important thing is not necessarily the nearness of the eschatological judgment, but its reality.[280] According to the parable of the wedding feast (Matt. 22.1–14) there are many who are called, both good and bad are invited, but only those who have a 'wedding garment,' i.e. those who can show good works, are numbered among the 'chosen' and not rejected by the King. By means of such pictures of the Last Judgment Matthew speaks to his community of its unqualified responsibility. At the

---

δικαιοσύνη-*Begriff im Matthäus-Evangelium*, EHS.T 181 (Frankfurt: Lang, 1982), according to whom 'righteousness' in Matthew also includes the righteousness of God (esp. Matt 6.33).

[276] Cf. Gerhard Friedrich, 'Die formale Struktur von Mt 28,18–20' (see above 3.4.8) 182–183; cf. further Paul Nepper-Christensen, 'Die Taufe im Matthäusevangelium,' NTS 31 (1985) 189–207.

[277] Cf. Grundmann, *Matthäusevangelium* 223–224.

[278] Cf. Strecker, *Weg der Gerechtigkeit* 171: 'As in the message of Jesus, the imperative is identical with the indicative; the "gift" of the kingdom is at the same time the "demand".'

[279] Cf. Daniel Marguerat, *Le Jugement dans l'Évangile de Matthieu* (Geneva: Fides 1981).

[280] Cf. Siegfried Schulz, *Ethik des Neuen Testaments* (see above 2.4.9) 455.

same time, with his story of the Last Judgment in 25.31–46 he avoids all calculation of one's own goodness, for good and evil deeds are not recognized at the time, and the decision of the final Judge is unanticipated.

It is precisely as a *corpus permixtum* that the Matthean church is a *missionary church*. It knows itself to be borne along by the promise of the Risen One to be with his church (cf. Matt. 18.20; 28.20). Now after Easter, the disciples are to call others to discipleship and to launch out into a universal mission. In the Gospel of Matthew, the disciples always represent the church.[281] Their portrayal is transparent to the present time of the Matthean community (cf. e.g. Matt. 18.1–35). For Matthew, to be a Christian means to be a disciple; discipleship is realized in following Jesus (cf. Matt. 8.23; 9.19, 37ff.; 12.49–50; 19.16–26; 27–28). The historical Jesus' call to discipleship now corresponds to responsive obedience to the will of the exalted Jesus Christ as developed in the Gospel of Matthew. Discipleship involves troubles and distress (cf. Matt. 8.23ff.), and demands a willingness to suffer (cf. Matt. 10.17ff.), the strength required to be lowly (cf. Matt. 18.ff.), to serve (cf. Matt. 20.20ff.) and to perform deeds of mercy and love (cf. Matt. 25.31–46).

3.5.9 Tendencies of Recent Research

At the center of research on the Gospel of Matthew stands the question of the theological intention of the evangelist. How is the Gospel as a whole related to the divergent tendencies that appear in individual texts? The author is understood to be a Gentile Christian by, among others, W. Trilling, G. Strecker, R. Walker, and J. P. Meier. W. Trilling claims Matthean theology supports his position.'The final redactor of the Gospel of Matthew thinks decisively in Gentile Christian universal terms.'[282] So too G. Strecker argues that the standpoint of Matthean theology can only be understood by making a strict separation between tradition and redaction. Strecker points out that no Jewish Christian positions are found in the characteristics of the strictly redactional layer of the Gospel; these positions are restricted to the traditions the author has edited into his composition. In this view Matthew already represents a progressive position in the history of early Christian theology, for his portrayal of Jesus is marked by a historicization of the traditional material, an ethicizing of the kerygma, and by an institutionalizing of earlier traditions.[283] 'The non-

---

[281] On the Matthean understanding of discipleship cf. Ulrich Luz, 'Die Jünger im Matthäusevangelium,' in *Das Matthäusevangelium.*, ed. J. Lange, 377–414.

[282] Trilling, *Das wahre Israel* 215.

[283] Cf. Georg Strecker, 'Das Geschichtsverständnis des Matthäus,' in *Das Matthäus-Evangelium*, ed. J. Lange, 326–349.

Jewish, Hellenistic elements of the redaction suggest that the author should be assigned to Gentile Christianity.'[284] The Gentile Christian perspective of Matthew is also emphasized by R. Walker, since 'the Gospel of Matthew considers "Israel" to be a phenomenon of salvation history that already lies in the past and affirms the new stage of salvation history as the calling of the Gentiles.'[285] G. Bornkamm resolves the tensive combination of particularistic and universalistic tendencies in Matthew in a different manner. For him, the Jewish accents of the Gospel of Matthew reflect the milieu in which Matthew wrote. But as the exponent of a Jewish Christian community Matthew is also in the situation of placing before the church its new assignments such as the Gentile mission.

Along with R. Hummel and E. Schweizer, U. Luz interprets the Gospel of Matthew as a Jewish Christian document.[286] Luz supports his claim by pointing to the rootedness of the evangelist in Jewish literature and the Jewish thought world, the Matthean understanding of the Torah and his appeal to the Old Testament, as well as the history of the influence of the Gospel of Matthew in later Jewish Christian circles. He rejects the postulation of an opposition between tradition and redaction in an exclusive sense, and emphasizes that the evangelist may not be portrayed as alienated from his traditions. Luz seeks to resolve the tensions within the Gospel with the thesis 'that the Gospel comes from a situation in which the Jewish–Christian community stood at a turning point.'[287] After the catastrophe of the first Jewish war the Matthean community began to open itself up to the Gentile mission, and the evangelist is a somewhat reserved advocate of this new openness.

So too J. Gnilka sees in Matthew a Jewish Christian whose church is in the painful process of separating from the synagogue. 'Still, the connection with the synagogue is not yet fully broken. The juristic authority of the synagogue was for the community, for many of its members, still a reality that it must still take very seriously.'[288] J. Roloff likewise understands the Gospel of Matthew as a Jewish Christian book. The Matthean community had, however, already separated from the synagogue and was engaged in the Gentile mission.[289] H. Frankemölle places the Jewish Christian Matthew in the stream influenced by the historical thinking of the Old Testament (Deuteronomy, Chronicles).'From the point of view of form criticism, Matthew should be seen as one who, using the sayings collection

---

[284] Strecker, *Weg der Gerechtigkeit* 34.

[285] Walker, *Heilsgeschichte* 145.

[286] cf. Luz, *Matthew* 1.80ff.

[287] *Ibid.* 84.

[288] Gnilka, *Matthäusevangelium* 2.534.

[289] Cf. Jürgen Roloff, *Kirche* (see above 3.5.4) 146–147.

in Q and the "Gospel" of Mark as sources, attempted to formulate the story of Jesus' ministry and the existence of his church within the horizon of Old Testament covenant theology into a New Testament theology of history for the changed situation brought about by the fall of Jerusalem.'[290]

The alternative between tradition and redaction in the works of Trilling and Strecker cannot be maintained in this form, for the evangelist took up even the most strict Jewish traditions into his Gospel, and they too influence his own thinking. On the other hand, the clear indications of a Gentile Christian perspective of the evangelist pointed out by contemporary Matthean exegesis are sometimes too quickly passed over in favor of the attempt to locate Matthew entirely within Judaism or Jewish Christianity. Finally, it must be asked whether the distinction between Gentile Christianity and Jewish Christianity can still have a heuristic function at all for the appropriate understanding of the Gospel of Matthew. Matthew fuses particularistic-Jewish Christian traditions with universalistic-Gentile Christian texts, and precisely the combination of both streams must be regarded as his work.[291]

Within the literary-critical analysis of Matthew's narrative (e.g. J. D. Kingsbury), it is the debate with Israel and its leaders that has mostly been considered the dominant factor in determining the content and compositional line of the plot. 'Matthew has constructed his story of Jesus according to an "internal principle." He has narrated it as the story of the conflict between Jesus and Israel.'[292]

In recent years the exegesis of the Sermon on the Mount has returned to the center of Matthean studies. A disputed item is the literary genesis of this text block. While H. D. Betz holds the Sermon on the Mount to be a pre-Matthean Jewish Christian composition, most exegetes continue to regard it as a Matthean composition containing traditional elements. The theme of the Sermon is also identified very differently. While G. Strecker focuses on Matt. 5.17 as the theme and central element of the Sermon, U. Luz considers the Lord's Prayer as the true center of the first great speech of Jesus.[293] To whom does the Sermon apply? Is it addressed to everyone, does it apply within the Christian church, or can only an exclusive group

---

[290] Frankemölle, *Jahwebund* 394–395.

[291] This constructive work of Matthew is not seen properly by Schnackenburg, *Jesus in the Gospels* (see above. 3.4.9) 89 when he states: 'Thus Matthew has left standing side by side the sending to Israel by the historical Jesus and the commission of the resurrected One to go to all nations.' On the other hand, the view of Wong, *Interkulturelle Theologie* 125–154 advances the argument when he proposes that we understand the combination of 'Gentile Christian' and 'Jewish Christian' texts in terms of the equality that Matthew affirms between Gentile Christians and Jewish Christians who live alongside and with each other in the Matthean church.

[292] Luz, *Jesusgeschichte des Matthäus* 78.

[293] Cf. Luz, *Matthew* 1.388.

or the individual Christian fulfill the radical demands of the Sermon on the Mount?[294] The issue of whether the commands of the Sermon can actually be fulfilled continues to be vigorously debated. For Matthew, the ethical radicalism of the Sermon on the Mount expresses the higher righteousness that characterizes the Christian community composed of Jews and Gentiles. But can these ethical demands, thought of as timeless imperatives, really be fulfilled by anyone? It may be that the question of whether anyone can in fact live up to the radical challenge of the Sermon is the wrong question, for it would lead to legalism and a manner of life intended neither by Jesus nor by Matthew. Thus the suggestion of J. Eckert is helpful in leading beyond this impasse, namely to understand the radicalism of the Sermon on the Mount as an appeal to understand oneself as completely open to the will of God in view of the near approach of the kingdom of God, and precisely thereby to make possible a truly human life.[295]

3.6 The Gospel of Luke

3.6.1 *Literature*

Commentaries

Klostermann, Erich. *Das Lukas-Evangelium*, HNT 5. Tübingen: J. C. B. Mohr (Paul Siebeck), 1975³; Ernst, Josef. *Das Evangelium nach Lukas*, RNT. Regensburg: Pustet, 1977; Schmithals, Walter. *Das Evangelium nach Lukas*, ZBK 3.1. Zürich: Theologischer Verlag, 1980; Schneider, Gerhard. *Das Evangelium nach Lukas*, ÖTK 3,1.2. Gütersloh: Gütersloher Verlagshaus (Gerd Mohn), 1984²; Fitzmyer, Joseph A. *The Gospel According to St. Luke*, AncB 28.28A. Garden City: Doubleday & Co., 1981, 1985; Schweizer, Eduard. *The Good News According to Luke*, tr. David E. Green. NTD 3. Atlanta: John Knox Press, 1984; Wiefel, Wolfgang. *Das Evangelium nach Lukas*, ThHK 3. Berlin: Evangelische Verlagsanstalt, 1988; Bovon, François. *Das Evangelium nach Lukas*, EKK III/1.2. Neukirchen: Neukirchener Verlag, 1989, 1996 (=1.1–14.35); Nolland, John. *Luke*, WBC 35A. Waco: Word, 1989 (= 1.1–9.20); Schürmann, Heinz. *Das Lukasevangelium*, HThK III 1.2/1. Freiburg: Herder, 1984³, 1993 (=1.1–11.54).

Monographs

Conzelmann, Hans. *The Theology of St. Luke*, tr. Geoffrey Buswell. New York: Harper & Brothers, 1960; Robinson, William C. *The Way of the Lord* (privately published), 1962; Flender, Helmut. *St. Luke: Theologian of Redemptive History*, tr. Reginald and Ilse Fuller. Philadelphia: Fortress, 1967; Lohfink, Gerhard. *Die Himmelfahrt Jesu*,

---

[294] On this cf. Gerhard Lohfink, 'Wem gilt die Bergpredigt?,' ThQ 163 (1983) 264–284.
[295] Cf. Jost Eckert, 'Wesen und Funktion der Radikalismen in der Botschaft Jesu,' MThZ 24 (1973) 301–325.

StANT 26. Munich: Kösel, 1971; Schram, Tim. *Der Markus-Stoff bei Lukas*, SNTSMS 14. Cambridge: Cambridge University Press, 1971; März, Claus P. *Das Wort Gottes bei Lukas*, EThSt 11. Leipzig: St. Benno, 1974; Lohfink, Gerhard. *Die Sammlung Israels*, StANT 39. Munich: Kösel, 1975; Busse, Ulrich. *Die Wunder des Propheten Jesus*, FzB 24. Würzburg: Echter, 1977; Grässer, Erich. *Das Problem der Parusieverzögerung in den synoptischen Evangelien und in der Apostelgeschichte*, BZNW 22. Berlin: Walter de Gruyter, 1977³; Jeremias, Joachim. *Die Sprache des Lukasevangeliums*, KEK Sonderband. Göttingen: Vandenhoeck & Ruprecht, 1980; Nützel, J. M. *Jesus als Offenbarer nach den lukanischen Schriften*, FzB 39. Würzburg: Echter, 1980; Taeger, Jens W. *Der Mensch und sein Heil*, StNT 14. Gütersloh: Gütersloher Verlagshaus (Gerd Mohn), 1982; Horn, Friedrich W. *Glaube und Handeln in der Theologie des Lukas*, GTA 26. Göttingen: Vandenhoeck & Ruprecht, 1986²; Klinghardt, Matthias. *Gesetz und Volk Gottes*, WUNT 2.32. Tübingen: J. C. B. Mohr (Paul Siebeck), 1988; Nebe, Gottfried. *Prophetische Züge im Bilde Jesu bei Lukas*, BWANT 27. Stuttgart: Kohlhammer, 1989; Schottroff, Luise and Wolfgang Stegemann, *Jesus von Nazareth – Hoffnung der Armen*. Stuttgart: Kohlhammer, 1990³; Stegemann, Wolfgang. *Zwischen Synagoge und Obrigkeit. Zur historischen Situation der lukanischen Christen*, FRLANT 152. Göttingen: Vandenhoeck & Ruprecht, 1991; Korn, M. *Die Geschichte Jesu in veränderter Zeit*, WUNT 2.51. Tübingen: J. C. B. Mohr (Paul Siebeck), 1993; Morgenthaler, Robert. *Lukas und Quintilian: Rhetorik als Erzählkunst*. Zürich: Theologischer Verlag, 1993; Weiser, Alfons. *Theologie des Neuen Testaments II* (see above 3.3.1) 117–152; Tannehill, Robert C. *The Narrative Unity of Luke-Acts*, 2 vols. Minneapolis: Fortress, 1991, 1994.

Articles

Osten-Sacken, Peter v. d. 'Zur Christologie des lukanischen Reiseberichtes,' EvTh 33 (1973) 476–496; Braumann, G., ed. *Das Lukas-Evangelium*. WdF 280. Darmstadt: Wissenschaftliche Buchgesellschaft, 1974 (important collection of essays by H. Conzelmann, E. Lohse, E. Haenchen, W. G. Kümmel, G. Klein and others); Merk, Otto. 'Das Reich Gottes in den lukanischen Schriften,' in *Jesus und Paulus* (FS W. G. Kümmel) eds. E. Earle Ellis and Erich Grässer. Göttingen: Vandenhoeck & Ruprecht, 1978², 201–220; Schweizer, Eduard. 'Zur Frage der Quellenbenutzung durch Lukas,' in *Neues Testament und Christologie im Werden*. Göttingen: Vandenhoeck & Ruprecht, 1982, 33–85; Bovon, Francois. *Lukas in neuer Sicht*. Neukirchen-Vluyn: Neukirchener Verlag, 1985 (collection of essays); Schneider, Gerhard. *Lukas, Theologe der Heilsgeschichte*, BBB 59. Bonn: Hanstein, 1985 (collection of essays); Bussmann, Claus and Radl, Walter, eds. *Der Treue Gottes trauen* (FS G. Schneider). Freiburg: Herder, 1991.

Histories of Research

Rese, Martin. 'Das Lukas-Evangelium. Ein Forschungsbericht,' *ANRW* II 25. Berlin: Walter de Gruyter, 1985, 2258–2328; Bovon, François. *Luke the Theologian. 33 years of Research*, tr. Ken McKinney. Allison Park, Pa: Pickwick Press, 1987; Radl, Walter. *Das Lukas-Evangelium*, EdF 261. Darmstadt: Wissenschaftliche Buchgesellschaft, 1988.

3.6.2 *Author*

The author of the Third Gospel is unknown. The first person to name Luke the traveling companion of Paul as the author was Irenaeus of Lyon, about 180 CE: 'Now Luke, the traveling companion of Paul, wrote down the gospel as proclaimed by him [Paul]'(*Against Heresies* 3.1.1; cf. Eusebius, *HE* 5.8.3).[296] Irenaeus (*Against Heresies* 3.14.1) documents this ascription by referring to the 'we-passages' of Acts (16.10–17; 20.5–15; 21.1–18; 27.1–28.16), in which 'Luke' appears as a close coworker with Paul (cf. further Col. 4.14: Λουκᾶς ὁ ἰατρὸς ὁ ἀγαπητός [Luke the beloved physician]; Phlm. 24; 2 Tim. 4.11). The Muratorian Canon (ca. 200 CE) reports concerning the Gospel of Luke: 'Luke the physician, after the ascension of Christ, after Paul had taken him along as a learned person, wrote in his own name according to his [Paul's] perspective.'[297] Justin Martyr (ca. 150 CE) probably knew the Gospel of Luke, as suggested by a series of allusions in his text (cf. e.g. Justin, *Apology* 1.50.12 with Luke 24.44–45; Acts 1.8).[298] The Church Fathers (especially Tertullian, *Against Marcion* 4) report that Marcion about 140 CE composed his 'Gospel' by omissions and modifications of the Gospel of Luke. Obviously the 'Gospel' created by Marcion is evidence that the Gospel of Luke already existed,[299] but this says nothing about its authorship.[300] No comments on Luke from Papias have been preserved, though the Armenian translation of the *Commentary on the Apocalypse* by Andrew of Caesarea (ca 600 CE) contains a fragment in which Papias cites Luke 10.18.[301] From this data we can surmise that the tradition attributing the authorship of the Third Gospel to Luke the traveling companion of Paul was circulating quite some time before 150 CE.[302]

About the origin of this tradition we can only conjecture. The most

---

[296] On the question of a possible (Roman) source used by Irenaeus for this tradition, cf. Claus-J. Thornton, *Der Zeuge des Zeugen* (see below 4.1) 10–39.

[297] Cited according to Helmut Merkel, *Die Pluralität der Evangelien* (see above 3.2.2) 11.

[298] On this cf. Ernst Haenchen, *The Acts of the Apostles* (see below 4.1) 8–9; Jürgen Wehnert, *Wir-Passagen* (see below 4.1) 56–57.

[299] On the 'Gospel of Luke' in Marcion, cf. especially Adolf v. Harnack, *Marcion* (see below 5.5.3) 52ff.

[300] The 'Anti-Marcionite Prologues' to the Gospels report concerning Luke: 'Luke was a Syrian of Antioch, a physician by profession, a disciple of the apostles, and later a follower of Paul until his martyrdom. He served the Lord without distraction, without a wife, and without children. He died at the age of eighty-four in Boeotia, full of the Holy Spirit.' Jürgen Regull, *Die antimarcionitischen Evangelienprologe* (Freiburg: Herder, 1969), has shown that these prologues have no common origin, are not directed against Marcion, and were written in the fourth century CE at the earliest.

[301] Cf. Folker Siegert, 'Unbeachtete Papiaszitate bei armenischen Schriftstellern,' NTS 27 (1981) (605–614) 606.

[302] Cf. Wehnert, *Wir-Passagen* (see below 4.1) 59–60; Thornton, *Der Zeuge des Zeugen* (see below 4.1) 69.

likely hypothesis continues to be that the name 'Luke' attached to the two volume work 'To Theophilus' is due to a combination of statements in Acts and the Pauline and Deuteropauline letters.[303] The reference to the name 'Luke' in Phlm. 24, Col. 4.14, and 2 Tim. 4.11 is not yet connected with the authorship of the Third Gospel, so that the tradition most likely presupposes these three letters as already existing. It is clear from the second half of Acts that the author had extensive information about the life of Paul up to the time of his imprisonment in Rome. The letter of 2 Timothy, according to its own claim written in Rome (cf. 2 Tim. 1.17), begins precisely where Acts ends (cf. Acts 28.30–31). According to 2 Tim. 4.11 Luke is the last of Paul's faithful coworkers, which sets him apart from the other coworkers and predestines him to be named as the author of the two volume work 'To Theophilus.'[304]

The possible origin of the ancient church tradition does not yet decide the issue of its historical value, however. Was in fact the author of the Gospel of Luke and the Book of Acts a companion of the apostle Paul? A comparison of the Lucan and Pauline theologies shows that this question is to be answered negatively.[305] Central elements of the theology of Paul are missing from his portrayal in Acts (only an echo of the Pauline doctrine of justification is found, in Acts 13.38; cf. also the universal statements in Acts 1.8 and 28.28, and the emphasis on faith or grace in Acts 15.11). The author's own theology is quite different from Paul's.[306] Thus one must

---

[303] Cf. most recently the arguments of Wehnert, *Wir-Passagen* (see below 4.1) 60–66.

[304] The significance of 2 Timothy 4.11 is polemically devalued by Thornton, *Der Zeuge des Zeugen* (see below 4.1) 79: 'Can we really take seriously the possibility that the Third Gospel and Acts remained anonymous until the beginning of the second century, at which time someone on completely arbitrary grounds decided to enhance the importance of Luke, previously a marginal companion of Paul, and that again about two decades later his name was claimed for the Third Gospel and Acts?' Against this must be said: If Luke and Acts were written ca. 90 CE, 2 Timothy around 100 CE, and the tradition of Lucan authorship at the beginning of the second century CE, then this is a compact chronological series with little gaps to be filled in!

[305] Cf. for this understanding Schneider, *Lukasevangelium* 1.32–33; Wiefel, *Lukasevangelium* 4; Bovon, *Lukasevangelium* 1.22–24; Schweizer, *Luke* 6. The question of authorship is left open by Fitzmyer, *Luke* 1.53. On the other hand, Martin Hengel argues for the physician and companion of Paul (from Acts 16.10ff.), *Acts and the History of Earliest Christianity* (see above 2.1) 66; Thornton, *Der Zeuge des Zeugen* (see below 4.1) 341 *et passim*. Peter Stuhlmacher, *Biblische Theologie des Neuen Testaments* I (see above 2) 1.227–228, equates Λούκιος in Acts 13.1 and Rom. 16.21 with Λουκᾶς and infers 'that Luke was a converted Jew of the Diaspora and a Christian teacher in Antioch, who became acquainted with Paul and accompanied Paul on part of his missionary journeys' (*ibid.* 228).

[306] On this cf. the balanced presentation by Gerhard Schneider, *Apostelgeschichte* 1.112–118 (see below 4.1); on the major theological themes in the Lucan picture of Paul cf. especially Gottfried Schille, *Das älteste Paulus-Bild* (see below 5) 17–33. Of basic importance are also the differences between the Pauline and Lucan anthropologies. Taeger, *Der Mensch und sein Heil* 222, provides a fitting formulation of the Lucan view: 'God wants to save human beings; the preachers declare how they become participants in this salvation—but for all intents and purposes, the decisive step must be taken by human beings themselves (and they are capable of doing this).'

agree with Ph. Vielhauer: 'the author of Acts in his Christology is pre-Pauline, in his natural theology, concept of the law, and eschatology is post-Pauline. He presents no specifically Pauline idea.'[307]

In addition, Luke is not correctly informed about important details in the missionary work of Paul. For example, Acts speaks of five trips to Jerusalem by Paul, while the Pauline letters clearly presuppose only three. Furthermore, the differing portrayals of the people with whom Paul deals (Acts 15.2–21: James as the mediator between conservative Pharisees on the one side and Peter, Paul, and Barnabas on the other side; Gal. 2.9: on the one side Paul and Barnabas, on the other side James, Peter, and John) and the decisions of the apostolic conference (compare Gal. 2.10 with Acts 15.22–29) indicate that the author was not a personal associate of Paul's (compare in addition Acts 16.1–3 with Gal. 2.3–4). Luke restricts the title 'apostle' to the twelve (with the exception of the conventional use of the term in 14.4, 14, taken from tradition), while for Paul himself the acknowledgment of his apostolic office was basic to his self understanding (1 Cor. 9.1ff.) and his missionary work (1 Cor. 15.9–10, Gal. 2.8). Also, the picture of Paul as θεῖος ἀνήρ ('divine man') given by Acts (13.6–12; 14.8–18; 20.7–12) does not fit well historically. According to Acts, the Petrine mission to Gentiles precedes that of Paul (cf. Acts 10.1–11.18), which contradicts Gal. 2.1–10), where Paul must defend his mission to Gentiles against the 'three pillars,' which thus means against Peter. In Acts 17.22–31 the Stoic doctrine of the kinship of humanity with the deity is placed in Paul's mouth,[308] which has no parallel in the undisputed Pauline letters. One must then proceed on the basis that Luke knew traditions about Paul's missionary work, but was not a personal associate with Paul during these missionary journeys. He is not interested in the person or theology of Paul, but in his role in the early Christian missionary history. Finally, the ancient church's traditions about Lucan authorship themselves indicate that their identification of the author may all be inferred from the New Testament itself.

The unknown author of the Third Gospel, whom we shall continue to call 'Luke,' presents himself in Luke 1.1–4 as a theologian and historian who has a literary education, and who above all is interested in convincing his readers of the trustworthiness of the tradition of Christian teaching.

Hengel, *Acts and the History of Earliest Christianity* 66 attempts to avoid the problem by the supposition that 'At a later stage he [sc. Luke] evidently had no more opportunity of getting information about the apostle through his own works.'

[307] Ph. Vielhauer, 'Paulinism' (see below 4.1) 48.

[308] On this cf. Max Pohlenz, 'Paulus und die Stoa,' in *Das Paulusbild in der neueren deutschen Forschung* ed. Karl H. Rengstorf (see above 2) 522–564.

Luke's Hellenistic education does not permit any inferences regarding his origin or whether he was a Jewish or Gentile Christian. That he was a Jewish Christian is suggested by his familiarity with the LXX, his interest in Scripture, Law, and Prophets, the supreme importance of Jerusalem, the portrayals of synagogue worship in Luke 4.16–30 and Acts 13.14–41, and the Jewish milieu of numerous individual traditions. On the other hand, Luke avoids Semitic concepts, shows no interest in the debate about cultic issues, his intended readership seems to be among Gentile Christians, and his soteriology is characterized by a receding of the doctrine of atonement. We must therefore regard Luke as a *Gentile Christian* who lived in contact with the Diaspora synagogue and who consciously integrated Jewish Christian traditions into his composition.

3.6.3 Place and Time of Composition

The time when Luke composed his two volumes may be determined only approximately. Luke used Mark and Q as sources. He looked back on the destruction of Jerusalem (Luke 21.24) and the death of Paul (Acts 20.25, 38; 21.13). Luke writes from the perspective of the third Christian generation, which is already interested in a presentation of the epochs of salvation history. From this data we may date the Gospel of Luke in the period *around 90 CE.*[309]

Determination of the place of composition is problematic, for none of the suggested places, Aegea,[310] Antioch,[311] Ephesus, Macedonia, Achaia, Caesarea,[312] and Asia Minor[313] has any convincing evidence in its favor. Possibly the movement from Jerusalem to Rome that dominates the perspective of Acts points to the capital city of the empire as the place of composition (cf. Acts 1.8, where 'to the ends of the earth' means Rome [cf. Psalms of Solomon 8.15], as well as Acts 19.21, where Paul intends to go to Jerusalem, but after that 'must' see Rome). Furthermore, the agreements between 1 Clement 5, 42 and Luke's writings (the picture of Paul, the understanding of church offices) are an indication of *Rome.*[314]

---

[309] Cf. for this understanding Wiefel, *Lukasevangelium* 5; Bovon, *Lukasevangelium* 1.23; Fitzmyer, *Luke* 1.57; Schneider, *Lukasevangelium* 1.34; Eckhard Plümacher, *Lukas als griechischer Historiker* (see below 4.1) 238; Gerd Theißen, *The Gospels in Context* (see below 3.1.1) 271–281 (Luke and Matthew were written 80–90 CE).

[310] Cf. Hans Conzelmann, 'Der geschichtliche Ort der lukanischen Schriften im Urchristentum,' in *Das Lukas-Evangelium*, ed. G. Braumann, 244–245.

[311] Considered by Schneider, *Lukasevangelium* 1.34; *Apostelgeschichte* 1.121 (see below 4.1).

[312] Cf. e.g. Hans Klein, 'Zur Frage nach dem Abfassungsort der Lukasschriften,' EvTh 32 (1972) 467–477.

[313] Cf. e.g. Schmithals, *Einleitung* 367.

[314] Cf. also Bovon, *Lukasevangelium* 1.23; Jürgen Roloff, *Apostelgeschichte* (see below 4.1) 5;

3.6.4 Intended Readership

Luke writes for a predominately Gentile Christian community, for he clearly presupposes the Gentile mission in which freedom from the Law is proclaimed (cf. Acts 10; 28.28). In addition, for him the displacement of Israel from its favored place in the history of salvation is already a reality (cf. Luke 21.21, 22, 24; Acts 28.25–27). He is aware of his obligation to the tradition of Greco-Roman history writing (cf. Luke 1.1–4), but is not always correctly informed about Palestinian geography (cf. Luke 17.11; 9.10, 12; 4.29),[315] and avoids Semitic concepts and expressions (cf. Luke 22.40; 23.33) or replaces them with Greek ones (cf. e.g. Luke 18.41/Mark 10.51: κύριε [Lord] instead of ῥαββουνί [rabbouni], Luke 9.33/Mark 9.5: ἐπιστάτης [master] instead of ῥαββί [rabbi]; Luke 22.42/Mark 14.36: πατήρ [father] instead of αββα ὁ πατήρ [Abba, father]; Luke 6.15/Mark 3.18: ζηλωτής [Zealot] instead of Κανανα῀ιος [Canaanean]). Luke omits Markan pericopes and possibly also texts from the Q source in which Palestinian features dominate and that were obviously no longer of relevance for the Lucan community (cf. Mark 7.1–23; Mark 7.24–30; 7.31–37; 8.1–10; 8.11–13; 8.14–21; 8.22–26; in addition Matthew 5.19a; 21–48; 6.1–8, 16–18). So too the thoroughgoing use of the LXX[316] and using 'Judea' to refer to Palestine (Luke 1.5; 4.44; 6.17; 7.17; 23.5; Acts 2.9; 10.37) indicate that Luke is writing for a predominately Gentile Christian community outside Palestine.[317]

The situation of the Lucan community is earmarked by that set of problems that were characteristic of the third generation of early Christianity about the turn of the century.

(1.) The fading of the hope for the parousia. The expectation of the first and second generation that the parousia would happen immediately had become a problem for Luke and his church as time continued to

---

Theißen, *The Gospels in Context* 254–258 (Luke looks at Palestine from a western perspective); Korn, *Die Geschichte Jesu in veränderter Zeit* 12 n. 25. The question is considered unsolvable by e.g. Vielhauer, *Urchristliche Literatur* 407; Fitzmyer, *Luke* 1.57.

[315] On this cf. C. C. McCown, 'Geographie der Evangelien. Fiktion, Tatsache und Wahrheit,' in *Das Lukas-Evangelium*, ed. G. Braumann, 13–42. In contrast, Martin Hengel emphasizes that Luke had personal knowledge of 'some towns of the coastal area, the road from Jerusalem to Caesarea and the way in which the temple area and the Roman barracks were connected' ('Luke the Historian and the Geography of Palestine in the Acts of the Apostles,' in *Between Jesus and Paul*, tr. John Bowden (London: SCM Press, 1983) 127.

[316] On this cf. Traugott Holtz, *Untersuchungen über die alttestamentlichen Zitate bei Lukas*, TU 104 (Berlin: Akademie Verlag, 1968).

[317] Wiefel, *Lukasevangelium* 4, describes the Gentile Christian Luke as 'evangelist of the Greeks.' Of course one must reckon with an influential Jewish Christian minority in the Lucan church; cf. Matthias Klinghardt, *Gesetz und Volk Gottes*, *passim*, who, however, emphasizes the Jewish Christian elements, in the theology of Luke too strongly.

progress.[318] Luke rejects the speculations that derived from an unbroken expectation of the nearness of the parousia (cf. Luke 17.20–21; 19.11; 21.8; Acts 1.6–8). He replaces the summary of Jesus' preaching in Mark 1.15 with the inaugural sermon of Jesus in Nazareth (cf. especially Luke 4.21), corrects the saying about the near expectation of the parousia of Mark 9.1 (cf. Luke 9.27), and adjusts the parable of the pounds (Luke 19.12–27) by adding the introduction of 19.11. This does not mean that Luke has abandoned the hope of the parousia,[319] but he combines the uncertain time of the Lord's arrival (Luke 12.40; 17.24, 26–30; Acts 1.7) with a call to patient endurance (cf. Luke 8.15) and watchfulness (Luke 12.35ff.; 21.34, 36). So too, the words about the nearness of the kingdom of God (cf. Luke 10.9, 11) show that Luke has not fundamentally renounced the near expectation, but precisely in view of sluggishness and the community's danger of defection has connected the proclamation of Christ's advent and the coming judgment with ethical admonitions.

(2.) Wealth and Poverty in the Community.[320] By the turn of the century people of prominence and wealth belonged to the circle of the Christian community (cf. Acts 17.4; 18.8), so that the proper use of wealth and property became a central problem of the Lucan ethic (cf. Luke 3.11; Acts 2.45; 4.34–37). Wealthy members were self-righteous and greedy (cf. Luke 12.13–15; 16.14–15) and despised the poor (cf. Luke 18.9). By their striving after wealth they were in danger of falling away from the faith (cf. Luke 8.14; 9.25). Over against these negative phenomena in his community, the evangelist pictures the earliest church as a voluntary community of mutual love. They gave up their possessions to those in need (Acts 2.45; 4.34), and held their private property in common (Acts 4.32). By portraying the church as a voluntary community of mutual love, the evangelist makes the connection with the challenge of Jesus summarized in Acts 20.35, 'It is more blessed to give than to receive.' In the thematic blocks Luke 12.13–34 and 16.1–31, Jesus shows the inherent problematic of wealth in that life does not find its meaning in possessions (cf. Luke 12.15) and that the profit

---

[318] On this theme cf. Grässer, *Problem der Parusieverzögerung*, and especially Gerhard Schneider, *Parusiegleichnisse im Lukas-Evangelium*, SBS 74 (Stuttgart: Katholisches Bibelwerk, 1975).

[319] Contra Ernst Haenchen, *Acts* (see below 4.1) 95–96; Conzelmann, *Theology of St. Luke* 121; cf. Gerhard Schneider, *Apostelgeschichte* (see below 4.1) 142.

[320] In addition to Horn, *Glaube und Handeln in der Theologie des Lukas*, cf. especially Johannes Degenhardt, *Lukas – Evangelist der Armen* (Stuttgart: Katholisches Bibelwerk, 1965); Martin Hengel, *Property and Riches in the Early Church*, tr. John Bowden (Philadelphia: Fortress, 1974); Walter Schmithals, 'Lukas – Evangelist der Armen,' ThViat XII (1973/74) 153–167; Louise Schottroff and Wolfgang Stegemann, *Jesus von Nazareth*; Hans-Joseph Klauck, 'Gütergemeinschaft in der klassischen Antike, in Qumran und im Neuen Testament,' in *Gemeinde – Amt – Sakrament* (Würzburg: Echter, 1989) 69–100.

motive and greed for money are against the will of God (cf. Luke 12.15; 16.14). So too the stories of the disputes among the disciples (Luke 9.46–48; 22.24–27) and of the Great Banquet (Luke 14.7–24), critique the attitude of rich Christians. The call to discipleship and abandoning one's possessions are so closely interrelated (cf. Luke 5.11, 28; 8.3; 9.3; 10.4; 18.28) that the Lucan Jesus can say programatically: 'So therefore, none of you can become my disciple if you do not give up all your possessions' (Luke 14.33). Jesus connects his demand for distancing oneself from possessions with the readiness to give alms (cf. Luke 12.21, 33–34; 16.9, 27–31).[321] Thus the call to discipleship directed to the rich ruler (Luke 18.18–23) is bound to the demand to sell all (πάντα is only in the Lucan version of the story, 18.22!) and give to the poor. 'Indeed, it is easier for a camel to go through the eye of a needle than for someone who is rich to enter the kingdom of God' (Luke 18.25). At the same time, Luke holds fast to the conviction that such giving is a voluntary act (cf. Acts 5.4) according to the resources of each individual (cf. Acts 11.29). The Ebionite traditions (Luke 1.46–55; 6.20–26; 16.19–26) that originally proclaimed a divine reversal of relationships between rich and poor in the transcendent world to come, become for Luke a challenge to human repentance in the present.

Luke directs his parenesis primarily to the rich people in his community and calls them to distance themselves from wealth in view of the danger of falling away from the faith. He cannot be onesidedly described either as 'evangelist of the rich' or as 'evangelist of the poor,' but is 'evangelist of the church.'[322] His goal is not uncompromising criticism of the rich, but the realization of the community of mutual love between rich and poor in the church, which presupposes the willingness of the rich to give alms. Christian existence is not directed toward the acquisition of wealth and excess, but is realized in the willingness to love and serve the neighbor. In this the renunciation of wealth by Jesus' disciples in the Gospel and the earliest church in Acts serve as Luke's models; the same unreserved discipleship and a community that lives by mutual love is also to find its appropriate form in Luke's own church.

(3.) *The Relation of State and Church.*[323] Luke pictures the encounters

---

[321] Horn, *Glaube und Handeln in der Theologie des Lukas* 231 *et passim* sees in the parenesis about almsgiving directed to the rich Luke's own conception of social ethics. In contrast, Schottroff and Stegemann, *Jesus von Nazareth* 150 speak of the equalization of goods within the community as Luke's social goal.

[322] Cf. Horn, *Glaube und Handeln in der Theologie des Lukas* 243.

[323] In addition to Stegemann, *Zwischen Synagoge und Obrigkeit*, cf. especially Gerhard Schneider, *Verleugnung, Verspottung und Verhör Jesu nach Lukas 22, 54–71*, StANT 22 (Munich: Kösel, 1969); Walter Radl, *Paulus und Jesus im lukanischen Doppelwerk. Untersuchungen zu Parallelmotiven im Lukasevangelium und in der Apostelgeschichte*, EHS.T 49 (Bern – Frankfurt: Lang, 1975).

between Jesus and the representatives of the state in view of the situation of the church in the Roman empire of his own time. Thus the Jews become simply the persecutors of Jesus or the Christians (Mark 15.16–20 is elaborated by Luke; cf. also Acts 13.50; 17.5–7, 13; 21.17ff.). The Roman procurator three times affirms Jesus' innocence (cf. Luke 23.4, 14–15, 22) and pleads for his release (cf. Luke 23.16, 20, 22), so that the Jews alone appear to be guilty of Jesus' death. Paul is portrayed as an upright Roman citizen (cf. Acts 25.8), whose rights as a citizen are acknowledged by the government courts (Acts 16.37ff.; 22.25ff.). Roman citizenship finally delivers him from the clutches of the Jews (cf. Acts 23.10, 27) and keeps him in Roman protective custody (Acts 28.30–31). The Romans place themselves between Christians and their Jewish attackers, and protect them (Acts 19.23–40; 23.29; 25.25; 26.31). Luke obviously wants to preserve his Christian community's freedom in the eyes of the state, which it needs for the practice of its life, worship, and mission. Luke meets potential attacks from the state by showing that Christians are loyal to government authorities and pose no danger to the empire. Of course, this does not prevent him from also transmitting critical words (cf. Luke 3.19; 13.32–33) and from having Peter say that Christians must obey God rather than human beings (Acts 5.29).

Alongside the above issues, which are obligatory in any discussion of problems in the Lucan church, there also appear to have been disputes with false teachers (cf. Acts 20.29, 30) – even though a more precise designation of their 'heresy' is not possible.[324] Luke combats the error with an appeal to the tradition and the continuity of orthodox doctrine (Acts 20.27, 28). Luke does not presuppose a situation of acute persecution;[325] rather, his challenge to courageous confession (cf. Luke 12.1–12)[326] is in view of local repression and harassment (cf. Acts 13.45, 50; 14.2, 5, 19; 16.19ff.; 17.5–6, 13; 18.12, 17; 19.9, 23–40), and the potential danger of the community in the high-voltage field between synagogue and Roman courts.

3.6.5 Outline, Structure, Form

---

[324] Jürgen Roloff, *Apostelgeschichte* (see below 4.1) 5 supposes they were Gnostics, as does Charles Talbert, *Luke and the Gnostics* (Nashville: Abingdon, 1996).

[325] For a critique of this theory advocated especially by Schmithals, cf. Horn, *Glaube und Handeln in der Theologie des Lukas* 216–220.

[326] For analysis, cf. Stegemann, *Zwischen Synagoge und Obrigkeit* 40–90.

The Gospel of Luke[327] is distinguished from the other Gospels by the Preface of Luke 1.1–4, by which Luke programatically determines the purpose of his Gospel writing.[328] The following prehistory is characterized by the paralleling of John the Baptist and Jesus.[329] Another literary opening section is found in Luke 3.1–4.13, in which the evangelist first presents John the Baptist as the one who prepares the way (Luke 3.1–20), then Jesus is introduced and tested (Luke 3.21–4.13). The brief Galilean section in 4.14–9.50 is again programatically introduced by Jesus' sermon in Nazareth (Luke 4.16–30), which marks the beginning of the public ministry of Jesus.[330] The greatest insertion in Mark's outline is formed by the *Travel Narrative* (Luke 9.51–19.27),[331] which Luke has composed entirely by integrating Q traditions into his own special materials, before he again takes up the Markan outline at 18.15. The goal and orientation point for the Lucan portrayal of the life of Jesus is Jerusalem (cf. within the Travel Narrative especially Luke 13.22; 17.11), where he works especially in the temple (Luke 19.29–21.38). Luke understands the time of suffering as the path to glory (cf. Luke 24.26), so passion and Easter form for him an indissoluble unity. The Easter stories all happen on one day and find their conclusion and climax in the ascension of Jesus. The decisive elements of Luke's narrative technique are his refinement of the episodic style of his traditions and the composition of longer textual units, framed and interpreted by introductory and concluding statements (cf. e.g. Luke 4.16–30). Features of Luke's compositional technique are addenda, supplements and narrative variations.[332] It is hardly accidental that key narratives are placed in the center of each volume (cf. Luke 15.11–32; Acts 15.1–35).

---

[327] On the problems of the evangelist's composition, cf. especially Conzelmann, *Theology of St. Luke* 18–94.

[328] Cf. here especially Günter Klein, 'Lukas 1,1–4 als theologisches Programm,' in *Das Lukas-Evangelium*, ed. G. Braumann, 170–203.

[329] For analysis cf. most recently Korn, *Die Geschichte Jesu in veränderter Zeit* 33–55.

[330] Cf. Korn, *Geschichte Jesu* 56–85, who sees in Jesus' inaugural sermon the opening scene for the whole of Luke's two volume composition.

[331] The extent of the travel narrative is understood differently by others: *9.51–19.28* (cf. Gerhard Sellin, 'Komposition, Quellen und Funktion des lukanischen Reiseberichtes [Lk 9,51–19,28],' NT 20 [1978] 100–135); *9:51–19:44* cf. Peter v. d. Osten-Sacken, 'Christologie' 476 n. 2; Korn, *Geschichte Jesu* 87.

[332] Cf. Anton Dauer, *Beobachtungen zur literarischen Arbeitstechnik des Lukas*, BBB 79 (Frankfurt: Lang, 1990).

Luke also, though he arranges the Jesus traditions that came to him into a somewhat biographical presentation, is still oriented to the Gospel of Mark. The unusual expansion of Mark's journey to Jerusalem is determined especially by the additional material that Luke had to integrate into the Markan outline. Nevertheless, Luke is unique among the evangelists when he introduces his Gospel with a prologue that makes clear both his theological intent and his literary ambitions as an author. Luke's authorial methods are characterized by editing the traditions that came to him into a more history-like and biography-like form as well as its reformation into more rhetorical configurations.[333] As a historian, Luke is concerned with completeness, accuracy, and reliability, in accord with the traditions of ancient historiography. Thus πράγματα ('acts') and διήγησις ('narrative') were terms used by historians at the time of Luke,[334] and the synchronisms and dates of Luke 1.5; 2.1, 2; 3.1, 2; Acts 11.28 and Acts 18.12 identify Luke as a historian. Furthermore, Luke's tendency to divide salvation history into definite periods, each having its own importance, is not without contemporary parallels, for especially the historical monographs of Sallust manifest a comparable structure.[335] It therefore seems possible to describe the two volumes of Luke-Acts as *historical monographs*, without violating the character of the Lucan presentation of the life of Jesus as a Gospel.[336] The widely disseminated genre of historical monograph made it possible for Luke to make a comprehensive presentation of the impact of the life of Jesus within its individual epochs.

3.6.6 Literary Integrity

The literary integrity of the Gospel of Luke is undisputed.

3.6.7 Traditions, Sources

The extensive Lucan special materials have repeatedly raised the question whether, in addition to Mark and his copy of the Sayings Source, Luke also had a third source (S^{Lk} or L)[337] that he edited into his composition. Thus

---

[333] On this cf. most recently Manfred Diefenbach, *Die Komposition des Lukasevangeliums unter Berücksichtigung antiker Rhetorikelemente*, FTS 43 (Frankfurt: Knecht, 1993).

[334] Documentation in E. Plümacher, *EWNT* 1.779–780.

[335] Cf. Eduard Plümacher, 'Neues Testament und hellenistische Form. Zur literarischen Gattung der lukanischen Schriften,' TheolViat 14 (1977/78) 109–123.

[336] *Ibid.* 116–117.

[337] On the history of this issue, cf. Kendrick Grobel, *Formgeschichte und synoptische Quellenanalyse*, FRLANT 53 (Göttingen: Vandenhoeck & Ruprecht, 1937) 67ff.; Schmithals, *Einleitung* 329–332.

B. Weiss[338] regarded S[Lk] as an independent written source that must be understood as a parallel source to Q and represents the Jerusalem church. W. Bussmann also postulated a specific source for the Lucan special materials, but he emphasized the difficulties involved in reconstructing the wording of this source. Bussmann regarded Luke, the physician and traveling companion of Paul, as the author of this source.[339] The thesis of B. H. Streeter,[340] that Luke himself composed a 'Proto-Luke' from Q and L, was influential for a while: 'Luke himself may have been the person who originally combined Q and L, and then, at some subsequent date, produced an enlarged edition of his earlier work by incorporating large extracts from Mark and prefixing an account of the Infancy . . . Proto-Luke appears to be a document independent of Mark and approximately of the same date.'[341] Thus in this view the present Gospel of Luke is an expanded second edition of Proto-Luke with the Marcan material inserted. J. Jeremias[342] and F. Rehkopf[343] adopted a modified form of the Proto-Luke hypothesis in which the third evangelist integrated Marcan material into a Lucan special source (Luke [1.1–2.52] 3.1–4.30; 6.12–16, 20–49; 7.1–8.3; 9.51–18.14; 19.1–28; 22.14–24.53).

Further research has failed to establish a third source used by Luke, for the linguistic evidence of such an independent source is lacking. There are linguistic differences within the special materials, and the whole bears the marks of Luke's own editorial work. Finally, both the disparity of the materials and the lack of an internal principle of order speak against the existence of an independent source for Luke's special materials.[344]

---

[338] Cf. Bernhard Weiß, *Die Quellen des Lukasevangeliums* (Stuttgart & Berlin, 1907).

[339] Cf. Walter Bussmann, *Synoptische Studien* III (Halle, 1931); Emanuel Hirsch, *Frühgeschichte des Evangeliums* II (Tübingen: J. C. B. Mohr [Paul Siebeck], 1941) 171ff., traces the Lucan special material back to a 'Gospel' (= Luke II) that was written about the same time as Q.

[340] Cf. B.H. Streeter, *The Four Gospels* (see above 3.2.1) 199–222. The hypothesis was extended by Vincent Taylor, *Behind the Third Gospel. A Study of the Proto-Luke Hypothesis* (Oxford: Oxford University Press, 1926).

[341] Streeter, *The Four Gospels* 200.

[342] Cf. Joachim Jeremias, *The Eucharistic Words of Jesus* 96–100.

[343] Cf. Friedrich Rehkopf, *Die lukanische Sonderquelle*, WUNT 5 (Tübingen: J. C. B. Mohr [Paul Siebeck], 1959).

[344] For debate with older theories cf. Kümmel, *Introduction* 131ff. In more recent discussion, especially Eduard Schweizer argues for a third independent source used by Luke ('Zur Frage der Quellenbenutzung durch Lukas' 83–85). His principal arguments are '1. Analogies to the sections for which we have an external control in Mark and Q; 2. the statement in the foreword about "many" predecessors; 3. linguistic characteristics . . .; 4. items of content such as the focus on women and the poor, but also the emphasis on pure grace; 5. changes in order in comparison with Mark, especially in the passion story; 6. agreements with John, sometimes also with Matthew against Mark, especially in the passion story and Easter story; 7. tensions that point to several layers of tradition . . .' (*ibid.* 84–85).

3.6.8 Basic Theological Ideas

An appropriate representation of Luke's theology must begin with the historical, literary, and hermeneutical claims emphasized by the author himself in Luke 1.1–4. His work is characterized by historical and theological substance, for Luke wants to produce a solid foundation for the instruction of neophytes. He writes a history of salvation that begins with the birth of John the Baptist and concludes with the preaching of the kingdom of God in the capital city of the empire, openly and unhindered by the Romans.

An *interest in salvation history* is already indicated by the author's intentional paralleling of the birth of John the Baptist and the birth of Jesus (Luke 1.5–2.21). By the synchronisms of Luke 2.1 and 3.1–2 Luke connects the story of Jesus with the history of his times, understanding the advent of Jesus as the decisive event not only in sacred history, but in the secular history of the world. As a special segment within the history of God's dealings with humanity, Luke characterizes the ministry of Jesus with the comment that Satan withdrew after he had unsuccessfully tempted Jesus (Luke 4.13), not to reappear until Judas' betrayal of Jesus (Luke 22.3). In view of Luke's theological interest expressed in the way he has put the story together, the time of Jesus is therefore properly designated by Hans Conzelmann's phrase as a '*Satan-free time*.'[345] So too the inaugural sermon in Nazareth (Luke 4.16–30) spotlights the unique character of the advent of Jesus: he is *the* bearer of the Spirit (Luke 4.18), and in him the promise of the Scripture is fulfilled (Luke 4.21).[346]

After the ministry of Jesus in Galilee, Luke 9.51 forms a clearly recognizable beginning of a new literary unit, as Jesus turns toward Jerusalem as the place of the passion and resurrection. Luke expands Jesus' trip from Galilee to Jerusalem in Mark 10 to make it an extensive travel narrative that comprises more than a third of the Gospel (Luke 9.51–19.27). The concept of a definite Lucan section designated 'travel narrative' is fitting, since after Luke 9.51 the journey motif appears repeatedly (9.52–53, 56–57; 10.38; 13.22, 33; 14.25; 17.11; 19.1, 11). Luke builds some of his basic theological affirmations into the composition of this literary unit, as already indicated in 9.51 by the expression συμπληροῦσθαι τὰς ἡμέρας τῆς ἀναλήμψεως αὐτοῦ (when the days drew near for him to be taken up). A line of salvation history is prepared for by the use of συμπληρόω and elaborated by the plural τὰς ἡμέρας (the days), which refers to the death, resurrection, and

---

[345] Cf. Conzelmann, *Theology of St. Luke* 156.
[346] On this cf. Ulrich Busse, *Das Nazareth-Manifest Jesu*, SBS 91 (Stuttgart: Katholisches Bibelwerk, 1978).

ascension of Jesus.[347] The perspective of the travel narrative therefore
includes not only Jesus' way to suffering in Jerusalem, but also embraces
his resurrection and ascension. In the travel narrative Jesus himself
instructs the church and thereby enables it to live according to his will in
the time of his absence. There is thus an indissoluble connection in the
travel narrative between statements that begin with a christological point,
but have an ecclesiological-ethical point in view as their final goal. The
church is addressed as that community that must answer to its Lord at the
parousia. Within this parenesis, a central role is played by the right use of
possessions (see above 3.6.4) and the appropriate understanding of Jesus'
return, as shown in an exemplary fashion by the Parable of the Pounds
(Luke 19.11–27).

Luke 16.16, found within the travel narrative, is a key text for Lucan
theology. Hans Conzelmann votes for understanding ἀπὸ τότε (from then)
in an exclusive sense, which he can support by the use of μεχρὶ 'Ιωάννου
(until John) in v. 16a.[348] The epoch of the Law and Prophets extends up to
and including John the Baptist, but with the advent of Jesus a new period,
the '*midst of time*,' begins. But the following can be said in favor of understanding 16.16 in an inclusive sense that embraces the ministry of John:
(1) Through the synchronism of Luke 3.1–2 the Baptist is placed at the
beginning of (i.e. within) the decisive time of salvation.[349] (2) Luke 3.18
describes the preaching of John the Baptist as 'good news' ('gospel') in that
he proclaims the coming Messiah (3.16–17). (3) According to Acts 1.21–22
the decisive epoch in the history of salvation begins with the advent of John
the Baptist. (4) The paralleling of the birth stories of John and Jesus show
that from Luke's perspective they do not belong to two different epochs
of salvation history. Thus Luke 16.16 cannot be used as evidence for a
precise determination of Lucan divisions of salvation history.

If Jesus' ministry in Jerusalem, his death on the cross and his resurrection form the conclusion of the 'time of Jesus,' then once again the precise
delineation of a third epoch in the history of salvation within Luke-Acts,
the 'time of the church,' becomes somewhat uncertain. For Hans
Conzelmann the '*time of the church*' begins with the pouring out of the
Spirit on Pentecost.[350] In this delineation, the problematic element is where
to locate the ascension of Jesus. Luke 24.47 had already pointed to the
further course of the world mission (cf. Acts 1.8), and Luke 24.49 looked

---

[347] On this cf. Horn, *Glaube und Handeln in der Theologie des Lukas* 260–268.

[348] Cf. Conzelmann, *Theology of St. Luke* 23 *et passim*.

[349] The preaching of the kingdom of God then begins with the Baptist; cf. W. G. Kümmel,
'"Das Gesetz und die Propheten gehen bis Johannes",' in *Das Lukas-Evangelium* ed. G.
Braumann, 398–415.

[350] Cf. Conzelmann, *Theology of St. Luke* 213.

forward to the conferring of the Spirit (cf. Acts 1.4–5, 8). Since the ascension occurs before the eyes of the apostles (Luke 24.51; Acts 1.9–11), it legitimates them as eyewitnesses, a decisive act for the following portrayal of the ministry of the apostles. The ascension thus maintains the continuity between the 'time of Jesus' and the 'time of the church,' a continuity symbolized and embodied by the apostles. A rigid separation between the 'time of Jesus' and the 'time of the church' is not possible; it is rather the case that Jesus' ascension enables the existence of the church in the world. The 'time of Jesus' is for Luke the central time of salvation, from which the church goes forth and to which it must always refer back.[351]

In any case, there is one central theme of Lucan ecclesiology that resists being pressed into a segmented outline of various periods: the continuity between Israel and the church. For Luke, the church is a work of God (cf. Luke 1.54, 68, 72; 2.34; Acts 5.35–39; 13.40–41; 15.16–18; 20.28), a part of a long development that does not first begin with the advent of Jesus or the mission of the apostles. Thus Stephen's speech makes clear that Israel had always resisted the will of God (cf. Acts 7.51) and that already in the time of the Old Testament there was a history of 'gathering-in and separation in Israel.'[352] At the same time, the Lucan prehistory (Luke 1.5–2.40) emphasizes that in Israel there were always pious and righteous people who waited in expectation of the redemption of Israel. Luke also uses the figure of John the Baptist to show the continuity between Israel and the church (cf. Acts 13.23, 24). Jesus is aware of his own mission as the gathering of the children of Israel, which finds its realization in the community of disciples. The fact that the group of disciples remains in Jerusalem through Easter and Pentecost explicitly illustrates the continuity of the true Israel intended by Luke. While the unbelieving part of Israel rejects Jesus, the Gentiles are called to salvation (Acts 10–11) and thus become a part of Israel. The primary witness to the continuity of salvation history within the new epoch of early Christian mission that manifests the turn from the Jews to the Gentiles is the converted Jew Paul, who becomes a missionary to the Gentiles. In Luke-Acts the church is portrayed as the true Israel. It corresponds to the eternal will of God, is obtained by the blood of Jesus and knows itself to be led by the Holy Spirit (Acts 20.27–28).

With his conception of salvation history, Luke provides his church with an orientation in time and history that became necessary with the delay of

---

[351] Cf. Jürgen Roloff, *Kirche* (see above 3.5.4) 191: 'the church, inasmuch as it has developed through the witnesses of the messengers of Jesus, stands in continuity with the story of Jesus that has been determined by God's own act.'

[352] Lohfink, *Die Sammlung Israels* 93.

the parousia of Jesus. Luke resolutely thought through the problem of the delay, without thereby completely abandoning the near expectation (see above 3.6.4). It is rather the case that precisely his holding fast to the near expectation called for reflection on the continuation of history. It is not the expectation of the parousia, but only setting dates for it that Luke rejects! Orientation to a changed historical situation is of service to Luke as he consciously thinks through the relation of state and church (see above 3.6.4). Luke sees such reflection as unavoidable, since the church must and will continue to exist in a continuing world.

In any case, the Lucan conception of the *apostleship of the Twelve*[353] must be seen against the background of the new understanding of time and history he develops. For Luke the Twelve Apostles are witnesses of the time of beginnings (cf. Luke 1.1–2; Acts 1.8, 21–22; 2.14, 37). They are at one and the same time the foundation for the church's tradition and prototypes of later church offices. The selection of Matthias (cf. Acts 1.21–26) illustrates the foundational significance of the circle of the Twelve for the continuity between the time of Jesus and the time of the church. The apostolic commission of the Twelve Apostles begins with the first Pentecost, as the promised Holy Spirit is sent upon them by Jesus himself (cf. Acts 1.8; 2.1ff.). Luke pictures the work of the Twelve as carried further by Paul. The 'Apostolic Council' (Acts 15.22–29; 16.4) brings the time of the Twelve Apostles to a conclusion, which also allows Luke to underscore that the office of the Twelve is unique and unrepeatable.

The manner in which Luke portrays the work of the *Holy Spirit* is also integrated into his theological understanding of salvation history as a whole. Basic to this understanding is Jesus' own possession of the Spirit, which is prophesied in Luke 1.35 and manifested in his baptism (cf. Luke 3.22). Jesus himself then baptizes with the Holy Spirit and fire (cf. Luke 3.16; Acts 1.5; 11.16). The Spirit leads Jesus into the wilderness (Luke 4.1) and then back to Nazareth (cf. Luke 4.14), where Jesus makes the central affirmation: 'The Spirit of the Lord is upon me, because he has anointed me' (Luke 4.18a). Pentecost is thus for Luke the fulfillment of the baptism in the Holy Spirit that will be given by Jesus, as already announced by the Baptist (cf. Luke 3.16; Acts 1.5; 2.4). Jesus himself says to his disciples before his ascension that he will send the Spirit to them (cf. Luke 24.49). According to Acts 1.6–8 the Holy Spirit will be the decisive equipment for the witnesses of Christ in the time of the Lord's absence. The Spirit is given to Christians in baptism (cf. Acts 2.38), and the true acting subject

---

[353] Cf. the differing conceptions of Günter Klein, *Die Zwölf Apostel*, FRLANT 77 (Göttingen: Vandenhoeck & Ruprecht, 1961); Jürgen Roloff, *Apostolat – Verkündigung – Kirche* (Gütersloh: Gütersloher Verlagshaus [Gerd Mohn], 1965) 169–235.

in the story of the church's mission as it unfolds in Acts is the Holy Spirit (cf. Acts 8.29, 39; 11.12; 16.7–8). The Spirit not only repeatedly intervenes in the course of saving history (cf. also Luke 1.41–43, 67–69; 10.21; 12.12), but also effects important decisions and changes of track in the church's journey through history, such as the agreement at the Apostolic Council (cf. Acts 15.28) and the induction of presbyters into their ecclesiastical office (Acts 20.28). The Spirit thus continues the ministry of Jesus within the church, and maintains the continuity of the saving acts of God in history.

For Luke the understanding of the work of the Holy Spirit is directly connected with his understanding of the proclamation of the kingdom of God. Luke binds the presence of the kingdom of God to the person of Jesus (Luke 4.43; 11.20; 17.20–21). The kingdom of God is the content of the preaching of Jesus (Luke 4.43; 8.1; 9.11; 16.16b; Acts 1.3), of the disciples (Luke 9.2, 60; Acts 8.12), and of Paul (Acts 14.22; 20.25; 28.23, 31). 'In that the Resurrected One who is still present speaks of the kingdom of God (Acts 1.3), but denies that this kingdom will be established soon and instead points to the promise of the Spirit and the carrying out of the world mission (Acts 1.6–8), Luke also connects for the church the kingdom of God and the presence of salvation in Jesus.'[354] In the preaching of the kingdom of God as it is led by the Spirit, Luke thus places before the eyes of his community the proclamation of the kingdom of God as its central and continuing task, as explicitly illustrated by Paul's preaching of the kingdom of God in Rome in the closing scene of Acts (Acts 28.23, 31).

3.6.9 Tendencies of Recent Research

The discussion concerning the theological organization of Luke-Acts continues to be determined by the theses of Hans Conzelmann, according to which Luke overcame the problem of the delay of the parousia by constructing an outline of salvation history. 'Luke grasped the fact that the expectation of the near parousia is something that cannot be handed on by tradition. That he composes intentionally is seen from the fact that the near expectation does not simply disappear, but is replaced by a picture of salvation history.'[355] Luke's outline of salvation history is divided into three chronological epochs [356] in which God's plan for humanity from creation to parousia of Christ is realized: (1) The time of Israel as the time of the Law

---

[354] Merk, *Das Reich Gottes* 211.

[355] Conzelmann, *Outline of the Theology of the New Testament* (see above 2) 150.

[356] The essential points of Conzelmann's interpretation were anticipated by Heinrich v. Baer, *Der Heilige Geist in den Lukasschriften*, BWANT 39 (Stuttgart: Kohlhammer, 1926).

and the Prophets (Luke 16.16). (2) The time of Jesus as the midst of time [the German title of Conzelmann's book was *Die Mitte der Zeit* = 'the midst of time'] (Luke 4.14–22.2). (3) The time of the church as the time of the Spirit (Acts 2.1ff.). So also Conzelmann believed that the ministry of Jesus may be subdivided into three stages, the 'Messianic consciousness' of Jesus (cf. Luke 3.21–9.17), the 'passion consciousness' of Jesus (cf. Luke 9.18–19.27), and the 'royal consciousness' of Jesus (cf. Luke 19.28–23.56). To be sure, some sort of periodization within Luke-Acts is undeniable, and Luke does resolutely think through the meaning of God's salvation as it occurs within the process of world history. On the other hand, more recent exegesis has found problems with Conzelmann's exact delineation of salvation history epochs, since Luke 16.16 cannot be understood in an exclusive sense, and Jesus' ascension forms the connecting link between the time of Jesus and the time of the church (see above).

In contrast to Conzelmann, G. Schneider emphasizes that a division of the history of salvation into two parts is constitutive for Luke's delineation, namely 'that Luke connects the time of Jesus most closely with the time of the church (from the perspective of the proclamation of the kingdom of God), placing both over against the time of the Law and the Prophets (Luke 16.16).'[357] Nor does Schneider evaluate the idea of salvation history as Luke's substitute for the near expectation of the parousia he has abandoned. 'Rather, the orientation to salvation history serves to point out the continuity of the proclamation from the prophets to Jesus and from Jesus through his apostolic witnesses until it reaches Paul, the real missionary to the Gentiles.'[358] Overcoming the problem of the delay of the parousia is not the central focus of the Lucan writing of history, for Luke does not abandon the near expectation, and his concept of salvation history is much more than a substitute for an idea he has given up. It provides Luke's church with the necessary orientation in time and the assurance of continuity within God's redemptive plan. Therefore the charge of 'early catholicism' against Luke made by E. Käsemann, Ph. Vielhauer, and S. Schulz is not adequate to grasp properly what Luke's theology is really about.[359] Luke does not provide a substitute for something else, but he does

---

[357] Gerhard Schneider, *Apostelgeschichte* I (see below 4.1) 136–137; cf. also Jürgen Roloff, 'Die Paulusdarstellung des Lukas,' (see below 4.1) 528 note 53; Alfons Weiser, *Apostelgeschichte* I (see below 4.1) 31–32. For Korn, *Die Geschichte Jesu in veränderter Zeit* 272, 'the life of Jesus is the "midst of time" in the material sense. It divides history into the time of expectation and the time of fulfillment. Jesus' ministry, along with the mission of the church in his name, forms the eschatological time of salvation qualified by the proclamation of the gospel (Luke 16.16).'

[358] Schneider, *Apostelgeschichte* 1.137.

[359] Regarding this discussion cf. especially W. G. Kümmel, 'Lukas in der Anklage der heutigen Theologie,' in *Das Lukas-Evangelium* ed. G. Braumann 416–436.

interpret the idea of the parousia in terms of his concept of the history of salvation. It would be better to say that Lukan ecclesiology is oriented to the idea of the handing on of tradition, though not to apostolic succession.[360] Rather, in Acts 20.17–38 the appointment and installation of officers is bound to the Spirit (v. 28). Luke shows no great interest in the subject of church offices and officers; he merely projects the organizational structure of the church in his own time and place, the presbytery, back into the time of Paul (Acts 14.23). Nor can the Lucan understanding of ethics be properly grasped under the heading of 'early catholicism.' Luke knows (as does Paul in 2 Cor. 9.6–7) the connection between doing good and heavenly reward (e.g. Luke 6.35, 38; 12.33–34; 16.9; Acts 10.31), and the motif of future judgment obviously belongs to the motivation of parenesis. Precisely here, there can be no talk of a 'de-eschatologizing' in order to make room for a periodizing of salvation history.

The prophetic features in Luke's picture of Jesus have been pointed out by G. Nebe (Luke 4.16–30; 7.16, 39; 9.7–8, 19; 24.19–21). The concept of 'prophet' gave Luke 'an excellent opportunity to portray Jesus within the larger context of titular Christology, providing him a broad range of motifs and materials, as well as words, deeds, and destiny.'[361] While for W. Schmithals it is necessary to understand Luke-Acts within the context of a persecution situation,[362] for W. Stegemann the concrete historical situation of the Lucan church is not determined by persecutions from the synagogue or the government authorities. 'In fact, it makes more sense to understand the relations between Lucan Christianity and the Diaspora synagogues to be rather distant. This then might have led to tensions, just as there may have been tensions between Luke's church and the Gentile public, from which forensic conflicts might have developed. Thus one might speak of a certain danger from the government measures against the church, but not of persecution in the real sense.'[363]

[360] This aspect is emphasized by Schürmann, *Lukasevangelium* 1.3, according to which Luke is a man of the church 'who also wants to serve it with his literary work, more precisely, by using his literary work to secure the tradition of the church.'

[361] Nebe, *Prophetische Züge* 207.

[362] Cf. only Walter Schmithals, *Acts* (see below 4.1) 11ff.

[363] Stegemann, *Zwischen Synagoge und Obrigkeit* 268.

4

The Acts of The Apostles

4.1 Literature

Commentaries

Haenchen, Ernst. *The Acts of the Apostles*. Philadelphia: Westminster, 1971; Bauernfeind, Otto. *Kommentar und Studien zur Apostelgeschichte*, WUNT 22. Tübingen: J. C. B. Mohr (Paul Siebeck), 1980; Schneider, Gerhard. *Die Apostelgeschichte*, HThK V 1.2. Freiburg: Herder, 1980, 1982; Schmithals, Walter. *Die Apostelgeschichte des Lukas*, ZBK 3.2. Zürich: Theologischer Verlag, 1982; Pesch, Rudolf. *Die Apostelgeschichte*, EKK V/1.2. Neukirchen: Neukirchener Verlag, 1986; Conzelmann, Hans. *Acts of the Apostles*, tr. James Limburg et al. Philadelphia: Fortress, 1987; Roloff, Jürgen. *Die Apostelgeschichte*, NTD 5. Göttingen: Vandenhoeck & Ruprecht, 1988²; Lüdemann, Gerd. *Early Christianity according to the Tradition in Acts*. Minneapolis: Fortress, 1989; Weiser, Alfons. *Die Apostelgeschichte*, ÖTK 5/1.2. Gütersloh: Gütersloher Verlagshaus (Gerd Mohn), 1989², 1985; Schille, Gottfried. *Die Apostelgeschichte des Lukas*, ThHK 5. Berlin: Evangelische Verlagsanstalt, 1990³; Barrett, Charles K. *A Critical and Exegetical Commentary on Acts*, ICC. Edinburgh: T. & T. Clark, 1994 (= chaps. 1–14).

Monographs

Jackson, F.J.F. and Lake, K. eds. *The Beginnings of Christianity* I–V. London: Macmillan, 1920–1933; Burchard, Christoph. *Der dreizehnte Zeuge*, FRLANT 103. Göttingen: Vandenhoeck & Ruprecht, 1970; Löning, Karl. *Die Saulustradition in der Apostelgeschichte*, NTA NF 9. Münster: Aschendorff, 1971; Plümacher, Eckhard. *Lukas als hellenistischer Schriftsteller*, SUNT 9. Göttingen: Vandenhoeck & Ruprecht, 1972; Stolle, Volker. *Der Zeuge als Angeklagter*, BWANT 102. Stuttgart: Kohlhammer, 1973; Wilckens, Ulrich. *Die Missionsreden der Apostelgeschichte*, WMANT 5. Neukirchen-Vluyn: Neukirchener Verlag, 1974³; Maddox, Robert. *The Purpose of Luke-Acts*. Edinburgh: T. & T. Clark, 1982; Hemer, Colin J. *The Book of Acts in the Setting of Hellenistic History*, WUNT 49. Tübingen: J. C. B. Mohr (Paul Siebeck), 1989; Wehnert, Jürgen. *Die Wir-Passagen der Apostelgeschichte*, GTA 40. Göttingen: Vandenhoeck & Ruprecht, 1989; Thornton, Claus-Jürgen. *Der Zeuge des Zeugen. Lukas als Historiker der Paulusreisen*, WUNT 56. Tübingen: J. C. B. Mohr (Paul Siebeck), 1991; Parsons, Mikeal C. and Tyson, J. B. eds. *Cadbury, Knox, and Talbert. American Contributions to the Study of Acts*. Atlanta: Scholars Press, 1992; Tyson, Joseph B. *Images of Judaism in Luke-Acts*. Columbia: Univ. of South Carolina Press, 1992; Lentz,

J. C. *Luke's Portrait of Paul*, SNTSMS 77. Cambridge: Cambridge Univ. Press, 1993; Parsons, Mikeal C. and Richard I. Pervo. *Rethinking the Unity of Luke and Acts*. Minneapolis: Fortress Press, 1993.

Articles

Dibelius, Martin. *Studies in the Acts of the Apostles*, ed. Heinrich Greeven. London: SCM Press, 1956 (fundamental collection of essays); Vielhauer, Philipp. 'On the Paulinism of Acts,' in *Studies in Luke-Acts*, eds. Leander Keck and J. Louis Martyn. Nashville: Abingdon Press, 1966, 33–50 (important collection of essays); Plümacher, Eckhard, 'Lukas als griechischer Historiker,' PRE.S 14 (1974), cols. 235–264; Plümacher, Eckhard. 'Apostelgeschichte,' *TRE* 3 (1978) 483–528; Kremer, Jacob, ed. *Les Actes des Apôtres*. BETL XLVIII. Leuven: Leuven University Press, 1979 (important collection of essays); Roloff, Jürgen. 'Die Paulusdarstellung des Lukas,' EvTh 39 (1979) 510–531; Weiser, Alfons. 'Das "Apostelkonzil" (Apg 15,1–35): Ereignis, Überlieferung, lukanische Deutung,' BZ 28 (1984) 145–167.

History of Research

Plümacher, Eckhard. 'Acta-Forschung 1974–1982,' ThR 48 (1983) 1–56; 49 (1984) 105–169.

4.2 Author

The way in which the original dedication in Luke 1.3 is taken up again in Acts 1.1, as well as the extensive linguistic and theological agreements and cross-references between the Gospel of Luke and the Acts indicate that both works derive from the same author (on Luke, see above 3.6.2). The title πράξεις ἀποστόλων (acts of apostles) is documented since Irenaeus (*Against Heretics* 3.13.3). It is probably not original, for it is not the acts of the apostles, but the divine action in the missionary history of early Christianity that stands center stage in the narrative of the second volume of Luke's two-volume work.

4.3 Place and Time of Composition

As is the case with the Gospel of Luke, so also with Acts, it is the problems of the third Christian generation that are reflected (cf. Acts 20.18–35). The concept of the third generation that sees itself in conscious continuity to the period of beginnings and thereby understands its place in the present is also presupposed in the Pastoral Letters and elaborated in 1 Clement 42.[1]

---

[1] Cf. here Gottfried Schille, *Frei zu neuen Aufgaben. Beiträge zum Verständnis der dritten urchristlichen Generation* (Berlin: Evangelische Verlagsanstalt, 1986).

This is a clear indication that Acts also belongs in the period near the end of the first Christian century. If Luke is placed around 90 CE, then Acts is probably a little later, between 90 and 100 CE.[2]

The geographical data in Acts suggest some place in the Aegean or Rome as the place of composition. Paul's work takes place essentially in the Aegean area, and God's plan for salvation history leads him to Europe. H. Conzelmann infers from these observations: 'Now the Aegean and Rome are not necessarily mutually exclusive alternatives. For example, the author could have grown up in the Aegean and later moved to Rome.'[3] The arguments already introduced in 3.6.3. above speak for *Rome*: (1) The Lukan presentation of the spread of the Gospel finds its goal in Rome (cf. Acts 1.8; 19.21). (2) There are agreements between the Lukan two-volume work and 1 Clement 5 and 42 on both the picture of Paul and the understanding of church polity.

4.4　Intended Readership

There is no reason to suppose that the situation was any different for the Lucan community when Acts was composed than that pictured for the Gospel in 3.6.4.

4.5　Outline, Structure, Form

1.1–14	Foreword (dedication; ascension)
1.15–8.3	The apostles as witnesses of the gospel in Jerusalem; Acts 6.1ff.: a turning point in the life of the community
8.4–11.18	Proclamation of the gospel in Samaria and the coastal areas; Acts 9.32ff.: the Gentile mission comes in view
11.19–15.35	The Antiochene mission; Acts 15.1–33: the Apostolic Council as the end of the earliest period of the church
15.36–19.20	The mission of Paul in Asia Minor and Greece
19.21–21.17	Paul on the way to Jerusalem (and Rome)
21.18–26.32	Paul's arrest and trial
27.1–28.31	Paul's journey to Rome; his work in Rome

In Acts 1.8 Luke formulates the program for his whole presentation:

---

[2] Cf. also Roloff, *Apostelgeschichte* 5; Schille, *Apostelgeschichte* 41; Schneider, *Apostelgeschichte* 1.121; Weiser, *Apostelgeschichte* 1.40–41, 80–90; Schmithals, *Apostelgeschichte* 17. 90–110; a late date is advocated by Koester, *Introduction* 2.310.: not later than 135.

[3] Conzelmann, 'Der geschichtliche Ort der lukanischen Schriften' (see above 3.6.3) 245.

'But you will receive power when the Holy Spirit has come upon you; and you will be my witnesses in Jerusalem, in all Judea and Samaria, and to the ends of the earth.' The spread of the gospel under the guidance of the Holy Spirit is obviously presented by Luke in a geographical perspective. After the foreword of Acts 1.1–14, 1.15–8.3 pictures the proclamation and witness of the apostles in the earliest church of Jerusalem. A new development within the earliest church is formed when the Hellenists step forth in Acts 6.1ff., since the gospel is carried by them beyond its point of origin in Jerusalem to Judea, Samaria, and the surrounding areas. This mission is pictured in Acts 8.4–11.18. A first section within this unit is marked off by Acts 9.31, where the growth of the church in these areas under the guidance of the Holy Spirit is summarized. After 9.32, the Gentile mission comes in view, which is programmatically founded by the baptism of Cornelius by Peter, and the accounting for this given by Peter. The Antiochene mission (Acts 11.19–15.35) forms a clear unit, the central point of which is formed by the missionary work of Paul and Barnabas.

The Apostolic Council in Acts 15.1–33 can be seen as the midpoint of Acts in terms of both its literary composition and its subject matter. Here the earliest period of the church, led by Jerusalem, comes to an end, and the time of the law-free Gentile mission represented by Paul begins. From Acts 15.35 onward, Luke concentrates the spotlight exclusively on Paul. An extensive description of the mission in Asia Minor is given, which was a fundamental event for the further development of the church. A further turning point is formed by Acts 19.21, in which Paul, under the guidance of the Holy Spirit, resolves to go to Jerusalem and then to Rome. The orientation of the whole work on the axis 'from Jerusalem to Rome' is here programatically formulated. As Acts 19.21–21.27 presents the journey of the apostle to Jerusalem, so Acts 21.18–26.32 follows his arrest and trial. The conclusion of the work is formed by the apostle's journey to Rome and his unhindered missionary activity in the capital of the world (Acts 27.1–28.31). With Paul, the gospel of the kingdom of God (Acts 28.31) has extended to the 'end of the earth,' i.e. to Rome.

Suggestions about how the work as a whole is to be outlined extend from a two-part scheme (I: 1.1–11.18; II: 11.19–28.31)[4] through a three-part scheme (Introduction 1.1–26; I: 2.1–5.42; II: 6.1–15.35; III: 15.36–28.31)[5] to a five-part scheme (Prolog 1.1–26; I: 2.1–5.42; II: 6.1–9.31; III: 9.32–15.35; IV: 15.36–19.20; V: 19.21–28.31).[6] The main themes of Acts

---

[4] Cf. Schille, *Apostelgeschichte* viii–ix. Also Plümacher, 'Apostelgeschichte' 486, votes for a two-part outline, but places the dividing point at Acts 15.33.

[5] Cf. Schneider, *Apostelgeschichte* 1.66; somewhat differently Weiser, *Apostelgeschichte* 1.27–28: a) 2.1–8.3; b) 8.4–15.35; c) 15.36–28.31.   [6] Cf. Roloff, *Apostelgeschichte* 13–14.

(earliest church, Hellenists, pre-Pauline and Pauline mission, Paul on the way to Rome) are somewhat collapsed into each other in the presentation, so that a consistent and exact principle governing the outline cannot be discerned; thus the difficulties of making a precise outline.

Luke writes an elevated Koine Greek, but sections of Acts with clear echoes of the Septuagint style are also found (cf. Acts 2.14–36; 3.12–26; 4.9–12; 5.29–32; 20.18–35) as well as texts in which the elevated Hellenistic style approaches the style of the classical period (Acts 17.22–31; 26.2–27). This phenomenon of stylistic imitation has parallels in Hellenistic historiography. The goal of such an imitation was to give a particular character to the personalities or historical epochs pictured by the author.[7]

The narrative style of Acts is characterized by great liveliness. Luke does not present his theological insights in the form of abstract propositions, but communicates them by vivid scenes intended to bring the readers to their own understanding of what is intended. The story of Pentecost (Acts 2), the narrative of the centurion Cornelius (Acts 10.1–11.18), the Areopagus speech in Athens (Acts 17.16–33), and the speech of Paul at Miletus (Acts 20.17–38) are stamped with this narrative style. But the narrative art of Luke is also seen in smaller units, so that for example in Acts 7.58 he brings Saul, persecutor of the Christians, into the scene as a witness to the martyrdom of Stephen. We may regard as additional techniques of the Lucan narrative style the abrupt new beginnings such as 10.1ff. and 18.12, and the intentional repetitions that emphasize an important event, such as the conversion of Paul in Acts 9.1–22; 22.3–21 and 26.9–20. A further compositional technique of Luke is illustrated by the summary notices and reports in which the steady growth of the church is reported (cf. Acts 1.14; 6.7; 9.31 and 2.42–47; 4.32–35; 5.12–16).

There is a noticeable change in the narrative rhythm within the story as a whole. On the one hand, the events in Jerusalem (Acts 2–5) are presented very broadly and extensively. From this rather static description of the state of affairs in the earliest Jerusalem church, Luke then changes in chapters 6–15 to a brisk series of different scenes that take place in very different locations. So too the portrayal of the Pauline mission in Asia Minor and Greece (Acts 15.36–19.20) evokes the impression that the apostle is constantly underway. The dynamic proclamation of the gospel is thus embodied in the person of Paul.[8] In the last major section of Acts (19.21–28.31) we find yet another narrative rhythm, dominated by the

---

[7] Cf. Plümacher, 'Apostelgeschichte,' 489–491, 501ff.

[8] On the 'dramatic episode' style of Acts, cf. Plümacher, *Lukas als hellenistischer Schriftsteller* 80–136.

detailed portrayal of the encounter of Paul with his Jewish opponents and Roman authorities. Luke thereby joins together a series of individual scenes, in order to communicate to the reader that the break between church and Judaism is identified with the journey of Paul from Jerusalem to Rome, and that this is a development willed by God.

On the macro-level, Acts may be designated a *'historical monograph,'*[9] a genre that was especially appropriate for developing a portrayal of history divided into epochs.

4.6 The Text of Acts

The textual tradition of Acts represents a special problem in New Testament text criticism,[10] since the 'Western' text (main witnesses: D 05, G 67,[11] $\mathfrak{P}^{38}$, $\mathfrak{P}^{48}$, sy^hmg)[12] is about 8.5% longer than the 'Alexandrian' text (main witnesses. ℵ, B, A, $\mathfrak{P}^{45}$, $\mathfrak{P}^{53}$). The Western text is characterized by stylistic and linguistic smoothness (cf. e.g. Acts 12.4–5), clarifications and precision (cf. e.g. Acts 12.1, 3, 4–5, 7, 10; 16.10–11; 18.2; 19.9; 20.15; 21.1), the resolution of real or supposed tensions (cf. e.g. Acts 3.11; 10.25; 12.22; 14.6–7; 14.18–19; 15.34; 16.30, 35, 39; 20.4) as well as changes in the content. A striking example is provided by the prescriptions of the Apostolic Decree in Acts 15.20, 29. While the 'Egyptian' text form understands it as ritual prescriptions, the 'Western' text interprets them in an ethical sense by the omission of 'whatever has been strangled' and the addition of the 'Golden Rule.' In Acts 13.27–28 the guilt of the Jews for Jesus' death is emphasized (for additional theological interpretations cf. 11.28; 14.25; 16.35; 18.27; 28.31).[13]

---

[9] Cf. Conzelmann, *Acts* xi; Plümacher, 'Die Apostelgeschichte als historische Monographie,' in *Les Actes des Apôtres*, ed. Jacob Kremer, 457–466; Schneider, *Apostelgeschichte* 1.123; Weiser, *Apostelgeschichte* 1.31. Other determinations of the genre: 'biography of philosophers' (cf. Charles H. Talbert, *Literary Patterns, Theological Themes and the Genre of Luke-Acts*, SBLMS 20 [Missoula: Scholars Press, 1974] 125–140); 'apostolic romance' (Koester, *Introduction* 2.51).

[10] A good introduction to the problem is given by Bruce M. Metzger, *A Textual Commentary on the Greek New Testament* (London – New York 1975) 259–272.

[11] Cf. here *Apostelgeschichte 1,1–15,3 im mittelägyptischen Dialekt des Koptischen (Codex Glazier)*, ed. Hans M. Schenke, TU 137 (Berlin: Akademie Verlag, 1991). Schenke evaluates the Codex Glazier as a second important witness to the 'D-Text.'

[12] Cf. further $\mathfrak{P}^{29}$, $\mathfrak{P}^{69}$, 0171. The term 'Western' text in the modern discussion goes back to F. J. Hort (1828–1892). The peculiarities of this form of the text were first recognized in the MSS of the (Latin) west of the ancient church; hence it was dubbed the 'Western' text. In contrast, Kurt and Barbara Aland, *The Text of the New Testament: An Introduction to the Critical Editions and to the Theory and Practice of Modern Textual Criticism* (see above 1.3) 63ff., prefer to speak of the 'D-Text.'

[13] On this cf. especially Eldon J. Epp, *The Theological Tendency of Codex Bezae Cantabrigiensis in Acts*, SNTSMS 3 (Cambridge: Cambridge University Press, 1966).

Numerous speculations have been offered regarding the origin of the 'Western' text. Thus F. Blass reckoned with two editions of Acts composed by Luke himself, with the older one being reflected in the 'Western' text.[14] This thesis was taken up by Th. Zahn[15] and recently argued anew by M. É. Boismard and A. Lamouille.[16] To be sure, most text critics and exegetes regard the 'Western' text of Acts as an intentional reworking undertaken with the goal of smoothing out the style, making more precise the content, and removing perceived tensions in the original text.[17] The 'Western' text probably did not originate in the western part of the Roman empire, but in Syria. In Syria 'and only there do we find several versions independent of each other that presuppose the "Western" form of the text . . . Therefore I would like to accept the view that the "Western" primary redaction originated in Syria, and in fact somewhere east of Antioch, where, on the one hand, Greek was still a living language, and on the other hand Syriac was near enough to explain the sudden and intensive expansion in the Syriac-speaking areas.'[18] The 'Western' text cannot be understood as a united and consistent entity. It originated in Syria, with its early formation reaching back into the second century and its primary redaction falling in the first half of the third century. Tangible evidence for this form of the text first appears in the Greek manuscripts of the second half of the third century. The papyri show no trace of it before the beginning of the third century.[19] Therefore the readings of the 'Western' text, like those of all other manuscripts, can only be introduced as evidence for the correctness in individual cases. For the most part, the readings of the 'Western' text are secondary, but their originality might be considered in e.g. Acts 12.10; 19.1; 20.15; 27.5.

---

[14] Cf. Friedrich Blaß, 'Die zweifache Textüberlieferung in der Apostelgeschichte,' ThStKr 67 (1894) 86–119.

[15] Cf. Theodor Zahn, *Die Urausgabe der Apostelgeschichte des Lukas*, FGNK 9 (Leipzig 1916).

[16] Cf. M.É Boismard and A. Lamouille, *Le Texte Occidental des Actes des Apôtres. Reconstruction et réhabilitation* I–II, Synthèse 17 (Paris: J. Gabalda, 1984)

[17] For an exemplary treatment, cf. Barbara Aland, 'Entstehung, Charakter und Herkunft des sogenannten westlichen Textes. Untersucht an der Apostelgeschichte,' EThL 62 (1986) 5–65.

[18] *Ibid*. 63. On the Acts-text of Irenaeus cf. *ibid*. 43–56. The summary: 'The text of Acts used by Irenaeus was an early manuscript of the paraphrasing type. We know this type from other MSS that have no necessary direct connection with the text used by Irenaeus. They merely derive from a similar free, paraphrasing form of the text. . . . That these MSS derive from a milieu that shared the same mentality as the text used by Irenaeus can be seen throughout, but the relationship cannot be seen either in the simple category of Vorlage and copy or in the category of text type and individual members of the type' (*ibid*. 53).

[19] Cf. Kurt Aland, 'Alter und Entstehung des D-Textes im Neuen Testament. Betrachtungen zu P69 und 0171,' *Miscellània Papirològica Ramon Roca-Puig en el seu vuitantè Aniversari* (Barcelona 1987) 37–61.

4.7 Traditions, Sources

A central focus of research on Acts continues to be the issue of whether Luke used and edited extensive sources for his second document, as he did for the first. The point of departure for recent discussion has been the source analysis of Adolf von Harnack,[20] who proposed a three-source theory for Acts: alongside a source A from Jerusalem or Caesarea (3.1–5.16; 8.5–40; 9.31–11.18; 12.1–23) and a Source B of less historical value (2.1–47; 5.17–42), he reckoned with an 'Antioch Source' (Source C) comprised of Acts 6.1–8.4; 11.19–30; 12.25–15.35. Especially his proposal of an *'Antioch Source'* as the basis of Acts 6–15 found considerable support and is still a significant theory today. It is advocated, for example, by R. Bultmann,[21] M. Hengel,[22] R. Jewett,[23] F. Hahn ('report' of the Antioch church),[24] R. Pesch,[25] and (cautiously) G. Schneider.[26] To be sure, against the hypothesis of an 'Antioch Source' is the fact that the 'Antiochene' character proposed as a criterion of source analysis has not been convincingly delineated, there is no criterion proposed for which there are external controls, and thus the extent of the proposed source has always been differently assessed.[27] A coherent 'Antioch Source' can thus not really be proven.[28] There can be no doubt, however, that in the first part of Acts Luke reworks both large complexes of traditional material and individual traditional elements. This traditional material probably included legends about Peter that already lay before Luke in written form (cf. the pre-Lucan traditions in Acts 3.1–10; 9.32–35; 10.1–11.18; 12.1–17).[29] Moreover, Luke took over written lists of names (cf. Acts 1.13; 6.5; 13.1; 20.4), reports from the church life in Jerusalem and Antioch (e.g. Acts

---

[20] Cf. the trilogy on Acts by Adolf von Harnack, *Luke the Physician: The Author of the Third Gospel and the Acts of the Apostles.* NY: Putnam, 1907; *The Acts of the Apostles.* NY: Putnam, 1901; *The Date of the Acts and the Synoptic Gospels.* NY: Putnam, 1911.

[21] Cf. Rudolf Bultmann, 'Zur Frage nach den Quellen der Apostelgeschichte,' in *Exegetica*, ed. Erich Dinkler (Tübingen: J. C. B. Mohr [Paul Siebeck], 1967) 412–423.

[22] Cf. Hengel, *Acts and the History of Earliest Christianity* (see above 2.1) 65.

[23] Cf. Robert Jewett, *A Chronology of Paul's Life* (see above 2.1) 10ff.; Jewett, *ibid.* 10, wants to see the 'Antioch Source' as standing behind 'approximately' the following texts: 6.1–8.4; 9.1–30; 11.19–30; 12.25–14.23; 15.35ff.

[24] Cf. Ferdinand Hahn, 'Zum Problem der antiochenischen Quelle in der Apostelgeschichte,' in *Rudolf Bultmanns Werk und Wirkung*, ed. B. Jaspert (Darmstadt: Wissenschaftliche Buchgesellschaft, 1984) 316–331.

[25] Cf. Pesch, *Apostelgeschichte* 1.48.

[26] Cf. Schneider, *Apostelgeschichte* 1.103.

[27] Cf. Plümacher, 'Apostelgeschichte' 493.

[28] Cf. for example Dibelius, *Studies* 104; Conzelmann, *Acts* xxxvii–xxxviii; Vielhauer, *Urchristliche Literatur* 386; Plümacher, 'Apostelgeschichte' 493; Weiser, *Apostelgeschichte* 1.37.

[29] Cf. Roloff, *Apostelgeschichte* 10, 68; Schneider, *Apostelgeschichte* 1.103.

4.36, 37; 6.1–6; 11.20, 26), traditional miracle stories (cf. Acts 5.1–11; 9.36–43; 14.8–18), traditions about the persecution of apostles (cf. Acts 4–5; 6–7; 12) and legends of their missionary work (cf. Acts 8.26–40; 9.1–19; 22.3–16; 26.12–18).[30]

The textual data of the second half of Acts also indicates a use of sources ('*we*'-source; '*itinerary*'). The phenomenon of the 'we passages' (Acts 16.10–17; 20.5–15; 21.1–18; 27.1–28.16)[31] which begin and end without transitions, is accounted for by three different theories that partially overlap, each of which is to be taken seriously as a possible explanation.[32]

(1) Luke, the companion of Paul and author of Acts, here brings his own experience and perspective on the events directly into the narrative.[33] Even if one disregards the difficulties of authorship involved in this theory (cf. 3.6.2), why a Luke who took his traditions very seriously (cf. Luke 1.3–4) would introduce his eyewitness testimony only for minor details but not for the decisive stations of early Christian missionary history still remains unexplained.

(2) The 'we passages' are elements of a source. This view advocated especially in the nineteenth century purely on the grounds of literary analysis (among others, by F. D. E. Schleiermacher, W. M. L. de Wette)[34] was taken up by Martin Dibelius (adopting the work of E. Norden)[35] from the perspective of form criticism. Dibelius both extended the theory and at the same time decisively modified it.[36] In Acts 13.1–14.28 and 15.35–21.18

---

[30] Of course there is considerable variation in the delineation of these individual narrative units based on form criticism and tradition. Cf. the lists in Roloff, *Apostelgeschichte* 10; Weiser 1.37; Schille, *Apostelgeschichte* 18–24.

[31] On the text-critical reconstruction and exact determination of the 'we passages,' cf. Wehnert, *Wir-Passagen* 5–46.

[32] For the history of research, cf. *ibid.* 47–124.

[33] This explanatory paradigm has been adopted by, among others, E. Earl Ellis, *The Gospel of Luke*, CeB (London: Oliphant, 1974²) 40–54; Johannes Munck, *The Acts of the Apostles*, AB 31 (Garden City: Doubleday & Co., 1967) xxix–xxxv; Robert Jewett, *Chronology* (see above 2.1) 12–17 (with reservations!); Martin Hengel, *Acts and the History of Early Christianity* (see above 2.1) 65–66; Thornton, *Der Zeuge des Zeugen* 192ff. and elsewhere. Thornton does not understand the 'we passages' as evidence from an eyewitness. 'Luke is concerned about only one thing: it was not the missionary ambition of Paul or an incidental decision made about travel routes that brought the gospel to Europe, but God himself initiated this step. Luke is a witness of this. But this is not a matter of testimony in the sense of a historical eyewitness, but the testimony of faith that the experienced past events are directed by God' (*ibid.* 364). Thornton, 341, suggests the following solution to the problem of eyewitness testimony: 'Luke the companion of Paul could have participated in the three trips that he narrates in the we-style; in chapters 16 and 20–21 and perhaps also in chapters 27–28 he could possibly have used sources that either he himself or another participant in the journey had drawn up.'

[34] An extensive history of research is provided by Wehnert, *Wir-Passagen* 66–103.

[35] Cf. Eduard Norden, *Agnostos Theos* (Darmstadt: Wissenschaftliche Buchgesellschaft, 1974⁶ [=1913]) 313–327.

[36] Dibelius, although repeatedly opposing a purely source-critical analysis, nevertheless considers decisions about sources to be constitutive: 'In a writer who assimilated his material so well,

Luke reworked a list of stations visited on Paul's missionary journeys that can be identified as traditional on the basis of formal characteristics (noting insignificant stations, 'comments upon the Apostles' reception, their hosts, their activities, and the results'[37]). To be sure, Dibelius distinguishes from this 'itinerary' the report of the journey to Rome in Acts 27.1–28.16, which was originally based on a secular story.[38] Dibelius sees the *Sitz im Leben* of the 'itinerary' in the missionary practice of Paul. Luke obviously had before him 'a list of stations [which] might well have been used on such journeys for the practical reason that, if the journey was made on another occasion, the route and the same hosts might be found again.'[39] Dibelius never gave a conclusive answer to the question of how the 'we sections' and the 'itinerary' were related to each other.[40] Possibly Luke himself inserted the 'we passages.'[41]

In contrast to this, according to W. Bindemann the 'we passages' manifest common formal elements among themselves, while showing differences from Luke's picture of history, and have their own ideological profile, so that we must speak here of a distinct source. This source consisted of 'a number of smaller, individually distinct, but already complex units, that had been joined together by notes on the itinerary.'[42]

(3) The first person plural in the sections under consideration were inserted by the evangelist Luke himself.[43] Since the 'we reports' mostly belong to the sea voyages, Luke could have adopted the use of the first person plural used in the stories of ocean voyages in contemporary literature. With this 'we' he then lifts up the claim to be an experienced world traveler, which again was a topos of contemporary historiographical

---

it is not very probable that a source (identified word by word as in the Old Testament) should be discernible within the text; moreover the "we-passages" resemble the "they-passages" both in vocabulary and in style. It must certainly be assumed that Luke had available as a source for Paul's journeys an itinerary of the stations on the journey' (Dibelius, *Studies* 104).

[37] Dibelius, *Studies* 104.

[38] Cf. *ibid.* 204–205.

[39] *Ibid.* 199.

[40] Cf. *ibid.* 73 note 27: 'I shall not deal with the questions as to whether the itinerary was the work of the same author and whether the 'we' was already in the text of this source or added when the Acts was written, since the answers to these questions do not affect my examination.'

[41] Cf. *ibid.* 104–105.

[42] Walter Bindemann, 'Verkündigter Verkündiger. Das Paulusbild der Wir-Stücke in der Apostelgeschichte: seine Aufnahme und Bearbeitung durch Lukas,' ThLZ 114 (1989) (705–720) 710.

[43] Cf. especially Schille, *Apostelgeschichte* 337: 'At any rate, the assumption of a we-source is mistaken: the "we" appears almost always in sections that are understandable as redactional work, and must therefore be attributed to Lucan reworking. . . . If the "we" is supposed to point to Silas and Timothy, then it would simply come too late. Rather, Luke wanted "to emphasize the significance of the moment" (F. Overbeck).'

practice.[44] One must still ask whether Luke really used the 'we' that suggests eyewitness testimony only as a purely literary convention, especially since not all 'we passages' belong to sections portraying sea voyages (cf. Acts 16.12–17; 20.7–8; 21.8–18). J. Wehnert also traces the 'we' in these passages back to Luke himself, but suggests a new paradigm for their explanation. He sees the transition from the third person singular of Daniel 1–6 to the first person singular of Daniel 7.2 as a structural parallel to Acts 16.8ff., and classifies the 'we' as a stylistic means in the tradition of Hellenistic Judaism. By means of this stylistic device Luke reworks traditional material that probably goes back to Paul's companion Silas. To be sure, this is not a matter of sources or travel diary, but 'If Silas (one of the eyewitnesses mentioned by Luke in Luke 1.2) was in fact one of Luke's sources of information, then we should think of oral communication that was adopted and included in Acts after having been extensively reworked into Luke's own linguistic form.'[45] Because Luke had no 'I' speaker at his disposal, he made use of the information derived from a companion of Paul and emphasized it with the 'we' form.

Probably Luke himself formulated the first person plural in most of the 'we passages.' He could have taken it from Acts 27–28[46] and pressed it into the service of his composition elsewhere. In the present form of the text, the 'we passages' especially emphasize the transition to Europe and journeys to Jerusalem and Rome. 'There is thus an extremely plausible reason why the author of the volume wanted to highlight these sections of his sources: they are to serve as sources validated by eyewitnesses.'[47] Independently of how the first person plural is evaluated, the 'we passages' are mostly regarded as elements of an itinerary that Luke had at his disposal for Paul's journeys through Asia Minor, Macedonia and Greece as far as Corinth.[48]

---

[44] Cf. Conzelmann, *Acts* 215, 221; Plümacher, 'Apostelgeschichte' 514; Vernon K. Robbins, 'The We-Passages in Acts and Ancient Sea Voyages,' BR 20 (1975) 5–18. Conzelmann, *Acts* xxxiv–xl; Plümacher, 'Apostelgeschichte' 494–95, regard the hypothesis of an itinerary very skeptically, understanding the text primarily in terms of the Lucan reworking of individual traditions.

[45] Wehnert, *Wir-Passagen* 189. Wehnert's thesis presents two problems: (1) Silas is mentioned for the last time in Acts 18.5. Where does the information in Acts 20–21, 27–28 come from? (2) Wehnert is not able to offer exact parallels for the use of the first person plural in the texts under consideration.

[46] Cf. Weiser, *Apostelgeschichte* 2.391.

[47] Schneider, *Apostelgeschichte* 1.94–95.

[48] In recent exegetical studies an itinerary has been argued for, with different reasons in different cases, by Roloff, *Apostelgeschichte* 239; Schneider, *Apostelgeschichte* 1.91; Weiser, *Apostelgeschichte* 2.387–392 (with an extensive argument!); Lüdemann, *Early Christianity according to the Traditions in Acts* 22. E. Haenchen, *Acts* 85ff. reckons with traditions from the travel diary of a member of the offering delegation for the 'we passages' in Acts 20.5–21.18 (see *ibid.* 582). From Acts 16.10 onward Luke is supposed to have made use of a 'much used itinerary'

The itinerary that derived from the circle of Paul's associates obviously included brief notes about travel routes and particular events on the journeys. Luke reworked the nucleus of this itinerary in Acts 15.36–19.40. When one proceeds beyond this consensus, there are naturally very different estimates of the precise extent of the itinerary. While for M. Dibelius it formed the basis of the Pauline journeys in Acts 16.4–21.18, J. Roloff limits the itinerary to Acts 16–19 and distinguishes from it a 'report from the offering delegation'[49] in Acts 20–21. A firm decision cannot be made here, but it is clear that Luke inserts both individual items of tradition as well as larger units assembled by himself into a preexisting framework. This outline of travel notes and lists of stations was probably composed of the following texts:[50] Acts 16.6–8, 11–12a; 17.1, 10–11b, 15a, 17, 34; 18.1–3, 7–8, 11, 18, 19a, 21b, 22–23; 19.1, 9b. 10a; 20.1b–6, 13–15; 21.1–4a, 7–9, 15–16. Whether the itinerary used in Acts 16–19 (20–21) is the continuation of the source used in chapters 13–14, or whether the portrayal of the Pauline mission in Acts 13–14 goes back to an independent missionary report of the Antioch church, is a question that can hardly be decided.[51] Similarly disputed is the basis in tradition for the reports about the arrest and trial of Paul in Acts 21.27–26.32. While, following M. Dibelius,[52] it is often assumed that Luke himself worked up individual traditions from Pauline tradition into a total picture,[53] others reckon with a comprehensive pre-Lucan report, the basic structure of which is still visible in Acts 21.27–36; 22.24–29; 23.12–24.23, 26–27; 25.1–12.[54]

The basis for the story of Paul's sea voyage to Rome in Acts 27.1–28.16 was probably provided by a secular story composed in the 'we' style, that was edited by Luke by the insertion of references to Paul (Acts 27.3b, 9–11, 21–26, 31, 33–36, 43a; 28.2–10).[55] Without these verses, a tightly structured narrative emerges in Acts 27.1–2, 3a; 4–8, 12–20, 27–30, 32, 37–42, 43b–44; 28.1, 11–12. Moreover, then tensions within the text are resolved, for a smooth flow of the narrative occurs only when v. 12 directly follows v. 8 and v. 27 follows on v. 20. Another possibility is suggested by J. Roloff,

(*ibid.* 490). For recent criticism of the itinerary hypothesis cf. especially J. Wehnert, *Wir-Passagen* 106–108 (persuasive form critical parallels for an itinerary are lacking); Thornton, *Der Zeuge des Zeugen* 273–274.

[49] Cf. Roloff, *Apostelgeschichte* 239.

[50] Cf. Weiser, *Apostelgeschichte* 2.388.

[51] So Roloff, *Apostelgeschichte* 10; contra Schneider, *Apostelgeschichte* 2.195.

[52] Cf. Dibelius, *Studies in the Acts* 7–8.

[53] Cf. e.g. Plümacher, 'Apostelgeschichte' 500; Schneider, *Apostelgeschichte* 1.102; Weiser, *Apostelgeschichte* 2.390

[54] Cf. here Stolle, *Der Zeuge als Angeklagter* 260–267; Roloff, *Apostelgeschichte* 316; Lüdemann, *Early Christianity according to the Traditions in Acts* 22.

[55] Cf. on this the persuasive analysis of Weiser, *Apostelgeschichte* 2.390ff., 656ff.

who proposes that a report of the experiences of Aristarchus the companion of Paul comprising Acts 27.1–9a, 12–20, 27–30, 32, 38–44; 28.1,
11–13, 14b, 16b formed the textual basis for chapters 27–28.[56] Luke then
reworked this source in the 'we' style, adding the scenes featuring Paul.
Against this proposal, however, is that Luke would then have been the first
to make Paul the central figure in the story. But it is precisely if the basic
elements of this account go back to a report from one of Paul's companions
that it would remain unexplained why Paul was not the central character
from the very beginning.

A special problem is posed by the question of the basis in tradition for the
twenty-four *Acts speeches*, that comprise almost a third of Acts (speeches of
Peter: 1.16–25; 2.14–39; 3.12–26; 4.8b–12; 5.29–32; 10.34–43; 11.5–17;
15.7–11; speeches of Paul: 13.16–41; 14.15–17; 17.22–31; 20.18–35;
22.1–21; 24.10–21; 26.2–27; 27.21–26.28.17–20; speech of Stephen: 7.2–53;
additional speeches: 5.35–39 (Gamaliel); 15.13–21 (James); 19.25–27
(Demetrius); 19.35–40 (city official of Ephesus); 24.2–8 (Tertullus); 25.24–
27 (Festus). Although it has repeatedly been asserted that the basic content
of the Acts speeches are reliable reports,[57] research has rightly generally
come to the conclusion that they cannot be understood as authentic
accounts of speeches that were actually given. This is seen, for example, in
the tensions between the speeches and their immediate contexts, for which
Paul's Areopagus speech is the classic example: while according to Acts
17.16 Paul was distressed by the abundance of idols he saw when he arrived
in Athens, in Acts 17.22 he praises the Athenians because of their piety. In
Paul's speech before the elders of Ephesus (Acts 20.18–35) in vv. 20–21, 27,
33–34 Paul vehemently defends his work without any objections having
previously being raised against it. It is not the immediate context, but the
function within the framework of Acts as a whole, that lets the significance
of the speeches be recognized. Their intention is not to report a particular
historical event, but to communicate to the reader insight into the supra-
historical significance of the particular historical moment,[58] which corresponds to the function of speeches in ancient historical writings. To be sure,
the lack of clear criteria for distinguishing traditional material from redaction within Acts makes the identification of pre-Lucan units more difficult;
still, it is likely that in the composition of the speeches Luke made use of
traditional material in varying degrees from case to case.[59] So also the

---

[56] Cf. Roloff, *Apostelgeschichte* 359; a similar argument had already been made by Haenchen,
Acts 85; in addition cf. Lüdemann, *Early Christianity according to the Traditions in Acts* 260, who
likewise reckons with a report of his own experiences from Aristarchus.

[57] Cf. e.g. M. B. Dudley, 'The Speeches in Acts,' EvQ 50 (1978) 147–155.

[58] Dibelius, *Studies in Acts* 127.

[59] On this cf. Ferdinand Hahn, 'Das Problem alter christologischer Überlieferungen in der

missionary speeches form a special group within the Acts speeches (cf. Acts 2.14–39; 3.12–26; 4.8b–12; 5.29–32; 10.34–43; 13.16–41), and basically may be attributed to Lucan redaction.[60] The missionary speeches stand at turning points in the history of the early church, and themselves trigger the following events (compare, for example, Acts 2.14–39 with 2.41–42).

In the second book of his two-volume work, Luke took up both a comprehensive source document (an 'itinerary' of Paul's journeys) and individual units of tradition of varying lengths that had come to him in oral or written form. All such traditions were worked over by Luke redaction-ally and integrated into the context of his total work. The place of origin of these traditions cannot be located with certainty, but we may assume that Luke had before him traditions from various churches, legends about various figures, reports about individual missionaries and delegates of various congregations. We can no longer determine how Luke came into possession of this body of material. Possibly it was the Third Evangelist, who as a Hellenistic historian gained his material 'by inquiring of travelers, from his own trips, and by information gleaned from letters and from third parties generated his own material from the most varied sources of authority.'[61]

4.8 Basic Theological Ideas

One can speak of an independent theology of Acts only in a qualified way,[62] even though Luke does make clear theological emphases in the second volume of his composition. He understands his preceding Gospel writing as a representation of 'what Jesus did and taught' (Acts 1.1). The choice of the apostles and the gift of the Spirit now bind together the time of Jesus and the works of the apostles (cf. Acts 1.2). The charge to carry out the Spirit-empowered witnessing in Jerusalem, all Judea, Samaria, to the

Apostelgeschichte unter besonderer Berücksichtigung von Act 3,19–21,' in *Les Actes des Apôtres*, ed. Jacob Kremer, 129–154. A positive view of the possibility of excavating old tradition from the speeches is also found in Roloff, *Apostelgeschichte* 49–51; in addition cf. Weiser, *Apostelgeschichte* 1.99–100. A skeptical view is argued by Schmithals, *Apostelgeschichte* 16, 33, 35–36.

[60] On this cf. Wilckens, *Missionsreden* 200ff. (Luke had recourse to the traditions of the Deuteronomistic preaching of repentance mediated by Hellenistic Judaism); in addition cf. Weiser, *Apostelgeschichte* 1.100; M. Korn, *Die Geschichte Jesu in veränderter Zeit* (see above 3.6.1) 214–225.

[61] Plümacher, 'Apostelgeschichte' 500; cf. also Haenchen, *Acts* 86 (Luke had 'various possibilities of collecting the required material').

[62] Korn, *Die Geschichte Jesu in veränderter Zeit* (see above 3.6.1) 270, sees the relationship between Luke's two volumes as follows: 'Between Luke and Acts there is an irreversible connection that corresponds to cause and effect or argument and inference.'

end of the world (Acts 1.8) is the final word of the departing Lord to his apostles, and Acts is nothing other than the fulfillment of this command of Jesus by the witnesses.[63] Thus for Luke there is a close connection between the problematic of the parousia and the work of the apostles in history. The question of the date of the parousia (Acts 1.6) is explicitly rejected (1.7), with the question of the parousia being answered by the command to preach the gospel and to be Christ's witnesses (1.8). At the same time, Acts 1.11 holds fast to the promise of the parousia, but the witnesses of the ascension will not be the witnesses of the parousia. As Luke presents the way of the Spirit-led witnesses of Christ in the world, so at the same time he gives an answer to the delay of the parousia. The faithfulness of God to his promises is seen precisely in the ministry of witness given by the apostles. 'Thus in place of the expectation of the nearness of the end as it had been expressed in the traditional Jesus material, Luke recommends a constant readiness in view of the coming end.'[64] Nonetheless, in Acts too the expectation of the parousia continues to be a constitutive element of Lucan eschatology, as shown by Acts 1.11; 3.21; 10.42; 17.31. To be sure, Luke's perspective on salvation history contributes to overcoming the problem posed by the delay of the parousia. But the parousia still forms the end of the time of the church and thus the goal of God's saving acts in history.

Luke's scheme of salvation history is thus much more than a substitute for disappointed hopes for a near parousia. This theology emphasizes not only the faithfulness of God to his promises and pictures the working of the Holy Spirit in history, but also answers the question central for the Lucan community of whether the Gentile church was in any sense a part of the people of God. The question in Acts 1.6b about the restoration of the kingdom to Israel already deals with God's faithfulness to Israel. Luke responds to this problematic by representing in Acts the working of God through the Holy Spirit that leads to the formation of the church of Jews and Gentiles as the true Israel. The apostles as guarantors of the tradition legitimize not only the proclamation of the church but also the opening of the earliest Christian congregations to the whole world. Already the baptism of the Ethiopian official in Acts 8.26–40 and the threefold presentation of the conversion of Paul (Acts 9.1–22; 22.3–21; 26.9–20) serves this goal. The Cornelius story (Acts 10.1–11.18) is an extensive reflection on the inclusion of Gentiles in the universal saving plan of God. God himself reveals both to Cornelius and to Peter that the Gentiles too share in the

---

[63] On the fundamental idea of the continuity of salvation history in Luke, cf. Pesch, *Apostelgeschichte* 1.51.

[64] Schneider, *Apostelgeschichte* 1.142.

saving act of Christ. The gift of the Spirit that also comes on the Gentiles (Acts 10.44) is the fulfillment of the Jesus' promise in Acts 1.5 and, like the Pentecost event in Jerusalem, introduces a new, decisive step in the saving plan of God. The reference back to the saying of the resurrected Jesus in Acts 11.16 (cf. 1.5) makes clear that in the Lucan perspective the pouring out of the Spirit on the Gentiles corresponds both to God's will for universal salvation and to the promise of the risen Christ. So also the Jewish Christians in Jerusalem receive this new insight with joy, and accept that it is God's will that Gentiles too are to receive salvation (cf. Acts 11.18). Not the church, but Judaism is placed in the wrong by the break between synagogue and Gentile Christianity. In Paul's preaching, salvation is always offered to the Jews (cf. Acts 13.45–48; 18.5–7; 28.17–28), but Israel does not accept this salvation, so that the Gentiles occupy the place of Israel as the elect people of God (Acts 15.14).

For Luke, however, the primary witness of the continuity of salvation history that still exists within the major turn in early Christian missionary history from the Jews to the Gentiles is the converted Jew *Paul*.[65] He comes on the stage almost unnoticed as an 'extra' in Acts 7.58, only to become the real hero of the book.[66] For Luke, he is not one of the apostles that form the foundation of witnesses to the faith, but is *the* representative of the second Christian generation. The theological goal of the Lucan picture of Paul jells in the last third of Acts (19.1–28.31), where the way of Paul from Jerusalem to Rome is traced. In this process the polarity that develops between Jerusalem and Rome is of fundamental significance. Jerusalem appears in Luke at first as the place of salvation for Israel. Here the earliest Christian community lives as the true Israel in an ideal fellowship (Acts 2.42–47; 4.32–35), so that Jerusalem represents the continuity between Israel and the church.[67] But at the same time Jerusalem is the place where Israel's leaders, and through them also the people of Israel, increasingly harden themselves against the Christian message. Just as the apostles and the earliest church are subject to continual persecutions (cf. Acts 4.1–22; 6.8–15; 7.54–60; 8.1), so Paul too becomes a suffering witness to the faith (cf. Acts 21.27–22.21; 23.1–11; 12–22). By rejecting the testimony of the Twelve, the earliest church, and Paul, instead of the place of salvation (*Heil*) Jerusalem becomes the place of danger and disaster (*Unheil*).

---

[65] On the Lucan picture of Paul, cf. alongside Christoph Burchard, Jürgen Roloff and Gottfried Schille, in *Das älteste Paulusbild* (see below 5) 9–52, especially Karl Löning, 'Paulinismus in der Apostelgeschichte,' in *Paulus in den neutestamentlichen Spätschriften*, ed. Karl Kertelge. QD 89 (Freiburg: Herder, 1981) 202–234 and Maddox, *Luke-Acts* 66–90.

[66] On the analysis of the biographical Pauline texts in Acts cf. especially Burchard, *Der dreizehnte Zeuge*, passim.

[67] Cf. Gerhard Lohfink, *Sammlung Israels* (see above 3.6.1) 93–99.

Luke makes clear, however, that God has not bound the church as the true Israel to Jerusalem. A new *Lebensraum* was created by the Gentile mission itself, represented by Rome the world capital. The crucial turn in salvation history from Jews to Gentiles corresponds in Luke's perspective to the turn from Jerusalem to Rome. Luke thus traces a development at the end of which stands the Gentile church at the end of the first century – and thus pictures the situation of his own church. In view of the ultimate break with Israel, Paul legitimizes the church of Gentile and Jewish Christians. 'For Luke's church, Paul has become the figure with whom they can identify, in whose story they come to understand the transformation that has come about in the dramatic turns of their own history.'[68]

Luke also uses Paul as the example to demonstrate 'that Christian preaching does not impinge upon the power of the Empire.'[69] It is not the Roman state that persecutes Paul, but the Jews (cf. Acts 13.50; 17.5–7, 13; 21.27ff.). They proceed against Paul with illegal measures (cf. Acts 23.12–15; 25.3), or appeal to the state against him (cf. Acts 18.12ff.; 24.1ff.; 25.5), but when they do they are always rebuffed. In Luke's view, the state must indeed take measures against sacrilege and crime, but it is not the business of the state to interfere in disputed religious issues (cf. Acts 18.12–17). Thus neither Gallio (Acts 18.15) nor Festus (Acts 25.18, 25) finds any grounds on which to charge Paul. According to Roman law Paul was innocent and should have been released (cf. Acts 25.25; 26.31–32), and only corruption and refusal by the Roman authorities compelled him to appeal to Caesar (cf. Acts 24.26–27; 25.9).

The Lucan picture of Paul is the real theological center of Acts. Paul functions as the representative of the second Christian generation, to whom the Lucan church owes its own faith. Paul should by no means be degraded in contrast to the Twelve, for he is the 'thirteenth witness' called by the Lord himself (cf. Acts 22.15; 26.16).

4.9 Tendencies of Recent Research

There is once again a renewed interest in the issue of the historical value of Acts. While exegesis oriented to a purely redaction-critical method (E. Haenchen, H. Conzelmann, Ph. Vielhauer) tended to have a rather low estimate of the historical value of Acts, more recently especially J. Roloff and M. Hengel have emphasized that Luke preserved numerous old and historically reliable traditions in Acts. M. Hengel insists that, 'We only do

---

[68] Roloff, 'Paulusdarstellung' 520.
[69] Conzelmann, *Acts* xlvii.

justice to the significance of Luke as the first theological "historian" of Christianity if we take his work seriously as a source,'[70] and J. Roloff also warns against 'placing the source question too quickly on the shelves.'[71] The establishing of extensive sources or reconstructable units of tradition is once again valued positively, despite the skeptical positions of G. Schille and W. Schmithals; the question of what traditional basis Luke had for his portrayal of Paul is in the center of this discussion. Extreme positions ('Luke as eyewitness of the Pauline mission' – 'Luke as novelist') are losing ground, and being replaced with an interest in the extent and manner of the traditions edited by Luke. Today it is hardly disputed that Luke the historian and author was strongly influenced by the conventions of Hellenistic historiography, as emphasized repeatedly by E. Plümacher. To be sure, J. Wehnert insists that the concentration on Luke the 'Hellenistic author' must be extended 'in the direction of Luke the homo religiosus, especially regarding his religious connections (and therefore also his literary connections) to Hellenistic Judaism.'[72]

There is thus an undeniable tendency in recent studies to reevaluate both the historical and theological achievement of Luke. The goal of Luke's historical composition is no longer seen primarily in overcoming the problem of the delay of the parousia. Rather, according to such scholars as G. Schneider, J. Roloff, and A. Weiser, Luke was concerned to clarify for the third Christian generation their standpoint in salvation history and thus also the continuity of their church's Christian witness with the testimony of the prophets, Jesus, and the eyewitnesses, and thus ultimately to show the faithfulness of God to his promises. In this regard the decisively important element is Luke's portrait of Paul, which is seen by J. Roloff and others as the real center of Acts.[73]

---

[70] Hengel, *Acts and the History of Earliest Christianity* (see above 2.1) 60.

[71] Roloff, *Apostelgeschichte* 9.

[72] Wehnert, *Wir-Passagen* 199.

[73] Cf. also Peter Lampe and Ulrich Luz, 'Post-Pauline Christianity and Pagan Society,' in *Christian Beginnings*, ed. Jürgen Becker; tr. Annemarie S. Kidder and Reinhard Kraus (Louisville: Westminster/John Knox, 1993) for whom Acts is 'the acts of Paul with a detailed introduction.'

5

The Deuteropauline Letters

*Literature on the continuing influence of Paul (*Wirkungsgeschichte*)*

Müller, Ulrich B. *Zur frühchristlichen Theologiegeschichte*. Gütersloh: Gütersloher Verlagshaus (Gerd Mohn), 1976; Dassmann, Ernst. *Der Stachel im Fleisch. Paulus in der frühchristlichen Literatur bis Irenäus*. Münster: Aschendorff, 1979; Lindemann, Andreas. *Paulus im ältesten Christentum*, BHTh 58. Tübingen: J. C. B. Mohr (Paul Siebeck), 1979; Schille, Gottfried. *Das älteste Paulusbild*. Berlin: Evangelische Verlagsanstalt, 1979; Strecker, Georg. 'Paulus in nachpaulinischer Zeit,' in *Eschaton und Historie*, ed. G. Strecker. Göttingen: Vandenhoeck & Ruprecht, 1979, 311–319; Kertelge, Karl. *Paulus in den ntl. Spätschriften*, QD 89. ed. K. Kertelge. Freiburg: Herder, 1981; Müller, Peter. *Anfänge der Paulusschule*, AThANT 74. Zürich: Theologischer Verlag, 1988.

5.1 Pseudepigraphy as a Historical and Theological Phenomenon

Balz, Hans. 'Anonymität und Pseudepigraphie im Urchristentum,' ZThK 66 (1969) 403–436; Speyer, Wolfgang. *Die literarische Fälschung im heidnischen und christlichen Altertum*, HAW 1.2. Munich: Beck, 1971; Hengel, Martin. 'Anonymität, Pseudepigraphie und "Literarische Fälschung" in der jüdisch-hellenistischen Literatur,' in *Pseudepigrapha* I., ed. K. v. Fritz. Geneva, 1972, 231–308; Brox, Norbert. *Falsche Verfasserangaben*, SBS 79. Stuttgart: Katholisches Bibelwerk, 1975; Brox, Norbert. *Pseudepigraphie in der heidnischen und jüdisch-christlichen Antike*. WdF. ed. N. Brox. Darmstadt: Wissenschaftliche Buchgesellschaft, 1977; Fischer, Karl Martin. 'Anmerkungen zur Pseudepigraphie im Neuen Testament,' NTS 23 (1977) 76–81; Pokorný, Petr. 'Das theologische Problem der neutestamentlichen Pseudepigraphie,' EvTh 44 (1984) 486–496; Meade, David G. *Pseudonymity and Canon*. Grand Rapids: Wm. B. Eerdmans, 1986; Wolter, Michael. 'Die anonymen Schriften des Neuen Testaments,' ZNW 79 (1988) 1–16.

Of the twenty-seven documents in the New Testament, only the authentic letters of Paul were composed under the author's own name. The Apocalypse and 2–3 John also include a designation of the original author (cf. Rev. 1.1, 4, 9; 2 John 1; 3 John 1), but here, in contrast to the authentic letters of Paul, it is unclear who stands behind the seer John of

Revelation and the πρεσβύτερος of 2–3 John. Seven documents of the New Testament were composed anonymously, with the purported authors' names being added subsequently in the course of the tradition (Matthew, Mark, Luke, Acts, John, Hebrews, 1 John). The remaining books of the New Testament must be designated as pseudepigraphical, i.e., they were originally circulated under the names of authors who had not actually written them.[1]

Within the context of ancient literature, New Testament pseudepigraphy does not represent anything unusual. Numerous examples of pseudepigraphical writings are found in both Greco-Roman and Jewish literature. Numerous writings were ascribed to figures from mythical pre-history such as Orpheus and to historical persons such as the physician Hippocrates from Cos.[2] So too in philosophical literature the composition of documents under a false literary name was common, with numerous inauthentic writings published under the names of Plato, Aristotle and Pythagoras. The high point of pseudepigraphical composition in Greek literature is found in the realm of epistolary literature.[3] Letters, including sometimes an extensive correspondence, were ascribed to practically every great figure in Greek intellectual history (e.g., Euripides, Democritus, Socrates, Plato, and Alexander the Great).

Numerous books of the Old Testament were handed on anonymously or under the names of pseudepigraphical authors. Thus within the Pentateuch the whole legal tradition was attributed to Moses, who received on Sinai the final and unchangeable will of God. Deuteronomy, which presents itself as the direct word of Moses (cf. Deut 1.1), must be seen as the center and high point of this development. So also prophetic books were re-edited and expanded (cf. Deutero-Isaiah, Trito-Isaiah).[4] On the basis of 1 Kings 5.9–14, Solomon was regarded as the archtypical bearer of the Wisdom tradition,[5] so that to him were ascribed not only the book of Proverbs, the Song of Solomon, Ecclesiastes, and the Wisdom of Solomon, but also the book of the Psalms of Solomon composed in Pharisaic circles of first century Judaism, and the Odes of Solomon among later Christians (2 cent. CE). Here one can clearly recognize the tendency to authorize particular literary genres and kinds of material by attributing them to famous personalities.

---

[1] For explication of the term and concept, cf. Speyer, *Die literarische Fälschung* 13–44; Brox, *Falsche Verfasserangaben* 11–15.

[2] On pseudepigraphy among Greeks and Romans, cf. especially W. Speyer, *ibid.* 111–149.

[3] On this point cf. J. Sykutris, 'Epistolographie,' PRE.S 5 (1931) 185–220; Lewis R. Donelson, *Pseudepigraphy* (see below 5.5.1) 23–42.

[4] On this point cf. Meade, *Pseudonymity* 17–43.

[5] On pseudepigraphy in Jewish wisdom literature cf. Meade, *ibid.* 44–72.

A high point of pseudepigraphy was reached in Jewish apocalyptic.[6] Especially in the second and third centuries before Christ numerous writings were composed in the name of the great prophetic figures of the past. The stream of Old Testament tradition had been essentially closed, so that apocalyptic groups had to legitimize their writings by attributing them to religious heroes of the past. Thus to Enoch, who according to Genesis 5.24 had been taken to heaven without dying, a comprehensive body of material was ascribed, the most important documents of which are Ethiopic and Slavic books of Enoch.[7] Books were attributed to Moses (Assumption of Moses) and to the Patriarchs (Testaments of the Twelve Patriarchs). Later figures such as Baruch, disciple of Jeremiah (Apocalypses of Baruch) and Ezra (e.g. 4 Ezra) were regarded as authorities that could not be challenged, and documents were attributed to them in order to gain a hearing for the concerns of the groups that composed them. Jewish pseudepigrapha also appeared under the names of non-Jewish authors, such as the collection of Sibylline Oracles (2 cent. BCE–1 cent. CE) or the Letter of Aristeas (2 cent. BCE).

The existence of Greek and Jewish pseudepigrapha shows that New Testament pseudepigraphy is not to be seen as a special case. Even though it is true that the motives that led to the production of pseudepigraphical literature are varied in detail and hardly comparable,[8] it is nonetheless the case that non-Christian and Christian pseudepigrapha share the common concern to legitimize their writings by attributing them to bearers of authority in their respective contexts. This general tendency of pseudepigraphy and the parallels from the perspective of the historical study of religions are not adequate, however, to explain the distinctive nature of New Testament pseudepigraphy.

New Testament pseudepigraphy has clear temporal boundaries, with most of the pseudepigraphical writings having been composed between 60 and 100 CE, the authentic letters of Paul forming the early boundary and the authentic letters of Ignatius the later. Within the history of early Christianity, this is the period of radical change and new orientation. The first generation of witnesses had died, an organizational structure for the whole church did not yet exist, congregational offices were in the process of being formed, the church was becoming fully aware of the problem of the delay of the parousia, the first extensive persecutions of the church

---

[6] Cf. *ibid.* 73–85. On the introductory issues of the apocryphal and pseudepigraphical writings cf. Leonhard Rost, *Einleitung in die alttestamentlichen Apokryphen und Pseudepigraphen einschließlich der großen Qumran-Handschriften* (Heidelberg: Quelle u. Meyer, 1985³).

[7] On the Enoch literature cf. Meade, *Pseudonymity* 91–102.

[8] Cf. Speyer, *Die literarische Fälschung* 131ff., 218ff.; Brox, *Falsche Verfasserangaben* 49–67.

were occurring, and finally in this period both the painful separation from Judaism and internal disputes with false teachers within the church's own ranks were taking place. In addition we may surmise from 2 Thess. 2.2 that opponents of what came to be mainstream Christianity were claiming Paul's authority by pseudepigraphical writings. In this situation of new orientation and the reinterpretations necessarily associated with it, for many groups in early Christianity pseudepigraphy was obviously the most effective means by which to exercise influence on the way things were developing.[9] Since there were no longer any individuals who possessed an authoritative standing in the church as a whole, the authors of pseudepigraphical documents reached back to authoritative figures in the past in order adequately to express their goals for the changing church situation of their own time and place. Both pseudepigraphy and anonymity were literary means of exerting influence and discovering appropriate solutions in the problems and conflicts of the last third of the first century CE. In addition, for the Deuteropauline writings the existence of a Pauline school (see above 2.2.2) was of great importance, since the authors of Colossians, Ephesians, 2 Thessalonians and the Pastorals obviously understand themselves to be disciples of Paul who want to communicate the heritage of their teacher in their own times. In this manner the person of the apostle received a legitimizing and normative significance. In the Deuteropaulines the mimesis that Paul himself had called for (cf. 1 Cor. 4.16) received an embodiment on the literary plane. New Testament pseudepigraphy was thus related to a very particular historical situation, and must be seen as a successful attempt of the third Christian generation's struggle to overcome its central problems. The goal of New Testament pseudepigraphy consisted not only in establishing the continuity of apostolic tradition in the time after the death of the apostles. Rather, the authority of the apostle was above all to be brought to bear in new words and language for the present. By appealing to the origins of the tradition, the authors grounded their claim to the binding authority of their new interpretations directed to the new problems that had arisen in the present. The secondary attribution to authors of the past thus always testifies to the significance of the primary authors!

When it comes to details, the authors of the New Testament pseudepigrapha make use of very different means. While for example Hebrews only

---

[9] Cf. Fischer, 'Anmerkungen zur Pseudepigraphie' 79ff. Wolter, 'Die anonymen Schriften' 15, emphasizes the separation from Judaism as a supplementary factor that called for a new conception of the idea of tradition. Now Jesus 'himself became the founder of a new tradition and the guarantor of a new identity, both of which were ultimately sanctioned by God himself' (*ibid.* 16).

gives hints in 13.23 that it wants to be understood as having been written by Paul, the Pastorals present a completely developed fictional picture of Paul. So also the epistolary beginnings and conclusions imitate the Pauline style with their data about addressees, their greetings, naming of particular names, and sharing of personal information (cf. 1 Tim. 1.1–2; 6.21; 2 Tim. 1.1–3; 4.19–22; Titus 1.1–4; 3.12–15). Moreover, the author gives a detailed picture of the current situation of Paul (cf. 1 Tim. 1.20; 2 Tim. 4.13), and even provides Paul's reflections in view of his approaching death (cf. 2 Tim. 4.6–8, 17–18). The New Testament authors of pseudepigraphical writings use in differing degrees and intensity the elements of stylistic imitation, the fictive portrayal of the situation with chronological data or descriptions of historical circumstances and the picturing of the personal situation of the authoritative figure portrayed as the author. These are stylistic means adopted in order to confer the required emphasis on the person adopted as authority (e.g. Paul or Peter). The stylistic means chosen by the author are affected by the situation in which the pseudepigraphical document is to have an effect. When for example in 1 Tim. 5.23 Paul advises Timothy to drink a little wine for the sake of his stomach, then this Pauline instruction is also directed against the rigorous ascetic movement opposed by the author in 1 Tim. 4.3–9 (cf. also Col. 2.16!).

A theological evaluation of the phenomenon of pseudepigraphy may not have as its starting point the ethical categories of deceit or fraud,[10] but must take into consideration the internal connection between the historical situation and the phenomenon of New Testament pseudepigraphy. In the last third of the first century, the literary form of pseudepigraphy was the most effective means of addressing and resolving the problems that had newly arisen as the authors of the pseudepigraphical documents interpreted them from the point of view of the past authorities they claimed to represent. The ethical category of 'fraud' is therefore inappropriate as a way of grasping the phenomenon of pseudepigraphy. It is better to speak of 'adopted authorial designations' in which the apostolic authority steps forward as guarantor for the validity of what is said.[11] New Testament pseudepigrapha must be seen as the theologically legitimate and ecclesiologically necessary attempt to preserve the apostolic tradition in a changed situation, at the same time giving the necessary response to new situations and questions. This is why the characteristic perspective of the pseudepigraphical writings is that of the whole church, for they originated out of a sense of ecumenical responsibility.

---

[10] Cf. Brox, *Falsche Verfasserangaben* 81ff.
[11] Cf. Brox, *ibid.* 105, who emphasizes 'the motive of participation in the precedence of the past.'

5.2 The Letter to the Colossians

5.2.1 Literature

Commentaries

Dibelius, Martin (Heinrich Greeven). *An die Kolosser, Epheser, an Philemon*, HNT 12. Tübingen: J. C. B. Mohr (Paul Siebeck), 1953³, 1–53; Lohse, Eduard. *Colossians and Philemon*, Hermeneia. Philadelphia: Fortress Press, 1971; Ernst, Josef. *Der Brief an die Philipper, an Philemon, an die Kolosser, an die Epheser*, RNT. Regensburg: Friedrich Pustet, 1974; Conzelmann, Hans. *Die kleineren Briefe des Apostels Paulus*, NTD 8. Göttingen: Vandenhoeck & Ruprecht, 1976, 176–202; Gnilka, Joachim. *Der Kolosserbrief*, HThK 10.1. Freiburg: Herder, 1980; O'Brien, Peter. *Colossians*, WBC 44. Dallas: Word Books, 1982; Schweizer, Eduard. *The Letter to the Colossians*. Minneapolis: Augsburg, 1982; Lindemann, Andreas. *Der Kolosserbrief*, ZBK 10. Zürich: Theologischer Verlag, 1983; Pokorný, Petr. *Der Brief des Paulus an die Kolosser*, ThHK 10.1. Berlin: Evangelische Verlagsanstalt, 1987; Wolter, Michael. *Der Brief an die Kolosser*, ÖTK 12. Gütersloh: Gütersloher Verlagshaus (Gerd Mohn), 1993.

Monographs

Käsemann, Ernst. *Leib und Leib Christi*, BHTh 9. Tübingen: J. C. B. Mohr (Paul Siebeck), 1933; Percy, Ernst. *Die Probleme der Kolosser- und Epheserbriefe*, SVSL. Lund: Gleerup, 1946; Lähnemann, Johannes. *Der Kolosserbrief. Komposition, Situation und Argumentation*, StNT 3. Gütersloh: Gütersloher Verlagshaus (Gerd Mohn), 1971; Bujard, Walter. *Stilanalytische Untersuchungen zum Kolosserbrief als Beitrag zur Methodik von Sprachvergleichen*, SUNT 11. Göttingen: Vandenhoeck & Ruprecht, 1973; Ludwig, Helga. *Der Verfasser des Kolosserbriefes. Ein Schüler des Paulus*. Diss. theol., Göttingen, 1974; Zeilinger, Franz. *Der Erstgeborene der Schöpfung*. Wien: Herder, 1974; Burger, Christoph. *Schöpfung und Versöhnung*, WMANT 46. Neukirchen-Vluyn: Neukirchener Verlag, 1975; Lona, Horacio E. *Die Eschatologie im Kolosser- und Epheserbrief*, FzB 48. Würzburg: Echter Verlag, 1984; Sappington, Thomas J. *Revelation and Redemption at Colossae*, JSNT. MS 53. Sheffield: Sheffield Academic Press, 1991.

Articles

Bornkamm, Günther. 'The Heresy of Colossians,' in *Conflict at Colossae*, eds. Fred O. Francis and W. A. Meeks. Missoula: SBL, 1973, 123–145; Grässer, Erich. 'Kolosser 3,1–4 als Beispiel einer Interpretation secundum homines recipientes,' in *Text und Situation*, ed. Erich Grässer. Gütersloh: Gütersloher Verlagshaus (Gerd Mohn), 1973, 123–151; Lohse, Eduard. 'Christologie und Ethik im Kolosserbrief,' in *Die Einheit des Neuen Testaments*, ed. Eduard Lohse. Göttingen: Vandenhoeck & Ruprecht, 1973, 249–261; Stegemann, Ekkehard. 'Alt und neu bei Paulus und in den Deuteropaulinen (Kol-Eph),' EvTh 37 (1977) 508–536; Lindemann, Andreas. 'Die Gemeinde von Kolossä,' WuD 16 (1981) 111–134; Merklein, Helmut. 'Paulinische Theologie in der Rezeption des Kolosser- und Epheserbriefes,' in *Paulus in den neutestamentlichen Spätschriften* (1981), ed. Karl Kertelge (see above 5) 25–69; Ernst, Josef. 'Kolosserbrief,' *TRE* 19 (1989) 370–376; Lohse, Eduard. 'Christusherrschaft und Kirche,' in

Die Einheit des Neuen Testaments , ed. E. Lohse. Göttingen: Vandenhoeck & Ruprecht, 1973, 262–275.

Histories of Research

Schweizer, Eduard. 'Zur neueren Forschung am Kolosserbrief,' in *Neues Testament und Christologie im Werden* ed. Eduard Schweizer. Göttingen: Vandenhoeck & Ruprecht, 1982, 122–149; Schenk, Wolfgang. 'Der Kolosserbrief in der neueren Forschung (1945–1985),' *ANRW* 25. 4. Berlin: Walter de Gruyter, 1987, 3327–3364.

5.2.2 Author

According to Col. 1.1 the authors of the Letter to the Colossians are the apostle Paul and Timothy his coworker. The addressees are sometimes addressed in the first person plural (cf. Col. 1.3, 9, 28), but in Col. 1.24; 2.1; 4.7, 18 only the apostle Paul speaks, so that the letter appears as his writing and is supposed to stand under apostolic authority. The greeting written with his own hand in Col. 4.18 underscores this claim. Colossians' own statements about its authorship were fundamentally questioned for the first time by E. Th. Mayerhoff in 1838.[12] Then F. C. Baur sees Colossians as the writing of a Pauline disciple from the Gnostic epoch of the second century.[13] H. J. Holtzmann adopts a middle course when he peels away the later layer to discover an original letter of Paul as its nucleus, which was then reworked in a Gnostic manner by the author of Ephesians.[14] Today most exegetes regard Colossians as a pseudepigraphical letter.[15] But acceptance of Pauline authorship still continues to play an important role in critical research.[16] Eduard Schweizer[17] and W. H.

---

[12] Cf. Ernst Th. Mayerhoff. *Der Brief an die Colosser mit vornehmlicher Berücksichtigung der drei Pastoralbriefe kritisch geprüft* (Berlin 1838).

[13] Cf. Ferdinand C. Baur, *Paul, The Apostle of Jesus Christ*, tr. A. Menzies (London: Williams and Norgate, 1875) 8–9.

[14] Cf. Heinrich J. Holtzmann, *Kritik der Epheser- und Kolosserbriefe auf Grund einer Analyse ihres Verwandtschaftsverhältnisses* (Leipzig: Wilhelm Engelmann, 1872); a brief summary is found in his *Einleitung* (1886²) 295ff.

[15] Cf. among others Bornkamm, 'Heresy' 138 note 1; Conzelmann, *Kolosserbrief* 176–177; Lohse, *Colossians and Philemon* 84–91, 177–183; Gnilka, *Kolosserbrief* 19ff.; Lindemann, *Kolosserbrief* 9–11; Pokorný, *Kolosserbrief* 2–4; Wolter, *Kolosserbrief* 31.

[16] Among those who consider Colossians to be by Paul are Dibelius, *Kolosserbrief* 53; Ernst Lohmeyer, *Die Briefe an die Kolosser und an Philemon*, KEK IX/2 (Göttingen: Vandenhoeck & Ruprecht, 1953⁹) 12; Jülicher – Fascher, *Einleitung* 134; Percy, *Probleme* 66, 136 and often; Kümmel, *Introduction* 340–346 (cf. however his cautious correction [for Colossians and 2 Thessalonians], 'L'exégèse scientifique au XXᵉ siècle: le Nouveau Testament,' in *Le monde contemporain et la Bible*, eds. C. Savart and J. N. Aletti, BiToTe (Paris 1985) (473–515) 483–484; Ernst, 'Kolosserbrief' 373.

[17] Cf. Schweizer, *Colossians* 24–26. An extensive supporting argument is found in Eduard Schweizer, 'Der Kolosserbrief – weder paulinisch noch nachpaulinisch?' in *Neues Testament und Christologie im Werden* (see above 5.2.1) 150–163.

Ollrog[18] advocate a secretary hypothesis in which Timothy was the author of the letter. J. Lähnemann[19] considers it possible that Epaphras (cf. Phlm. 23; Col. 1.7; 4.12) could have been the author of the letter.

The advocates of the authenticity of Colossians explain the undoubtedly distinctive features of the letter as the result of its challenge to a heresy within the community. The completely new situation of the church called for a different formulation of the Pauline theology. In contrast, those who challenge the genuineness of the letter point to the peculiarities of the language and style of Colossians.[20]

Thus 37 hapax legomena for the New Testament are found in Colossians,[21] e.g., ἀρεσκεία (pleasing 1.10); ὁρατός (visible 1.16); πρωτεύω (be supreme 1.18); εἰρηνοποιέω (make peace 1.20); στερέωμα (firmness 2.5); φιλοσοφία (philosophy 2.8); θεότης (deity 2.9); νεομηνία (new moon 2.16); ἐμβατεύω (dwell on 2.18); δογματίζω (submit to rules 2.20); ἐθελοθρησκία (self-imposed worship 2.23); πλησμονή (restraining 2.23); αἰσχρολογία (filthy language 3.8); Σκύθης (Scythian 3.11); μομφή (grievance 3.13); παρηγορία (comfort 4.11). An additional 28 words are found elsewhere in the New Testament, but not in the undisputed letters of Paul. Fifteen words that appear in Ephesians and Colossians are found elsewhere in the New Testament, but not in the undisputed letters of Paul.[22] On the other hand, a whole series of central Pauline terms are missing from Colossians, e.g., ἀποκάλυψις (revelation), δικαιοσύνη (righteousness), δικαιόω (justify), ἐλευθερία (freedom), ἐλευθερόω (set free), ἐπαγγελία (promise), καυχάομαι (boast), καύχημα (boasting), κοινωνία (fellowship), νόμος (law), πιστεύω (believe), σῴζω (save), σωτηρία (salvation).[23]

These data are of course significant only in a qualified manner, since numerous hapax legomena are found either in traditional material (Col. 1.15–20) or in the dispute with false teachers (Col. 2.6–23), in either case being already provided for the author by the tradition or the situation. Moreover, the undisputed Pauline letters also manifest numerous hapax legomena, and 1 Thessalonians also lacks many of the Pauline terms that became common in the later letters.

Colossians also has a characteristic literary style. Thus the recipients are

[18] Cf. Ollrog, *Paulus und seine Mitarbeiter* (see above 2.2.2) 219–232.
[19] Cf. Lähnemann, *Kolosserbrief* 181–182 note 82.
[20] Cf. Bujard, *Stilanalytische Untersuchungen passim*; Lohse, *Colossians and Philemon* 84–91; Ludwig, *Der Verfasser des Kolosserbriefes* 8–51; Schenk, 'Kolosserbrief' 3328–3338.
[21] Statistics according to *Vollständige Konkordanz zum griechischen Neuen Testament*, Bd. II: *Spezialübersichten*, ed. K. Aland (Berlin: Walter de Gruyter, 1978) 2.456. English translations are generally as in the NRSV, though several words are of disputed meaning.
[22] Cf. the complete list in Lohse, *Colossians and Philemon* 85–86.
[23] Cf. *ibid.* 86–87.

not addressed with the typical 'brothers and sisters.' Conjunctions and transitional particles common to Paul are missing from Colossians (e.g., μᾶλλον [rather], οὐδέ [neither], εἴ τις [if any one], εἴπερ [if indeed], οὐ μόνον δέ - ἀλλὰ καί [not only but also], οὐκέτι [no longer]), as are inferential particles (διό [therefore], διότι [because], ἄρα [then], ἄρα οὖν [so then]), while a heaping up of genitive connections (cf. Col. 1.5, 13, 27; 2.2, 11) and the use of the preposition ἐν (in) are characteristic. A plerophoric style is characteristic of the letter as a whole (cf. e.g., Col. 1.3–11). The individual units are strung together rather loosely, so that a clear connection between the series of infinitives, relative clauses, and participial constructions is often not possible. The train of thought is often associative, so that in several places the line of argument is not so connected and compelling as in the undisputed Pauline letters. There is not a single question in Colossians! However, linguistic and stylistic peculiarities alone are not sufficient to settle the question of authorship. Their importance is first seen in connection with the distinctive features characteristic of Colossians' content and theology.

1. Christology: The significance of the saving work of Jesus Christ for the whole cosmos stands at the center of the Christology of Colossians. Christ is the first-born before every creature, in him all was created and through him all continues to exist (cf. Col. 1.15–17). As lord and mediator of creation he rules over every created being, visible and invisible. Christ is the head of all the forces of the universe (Col. 2.10) and triumphs over all cosmic powers (Col. 2.15). In him the universe has its continuing existence, and he assigns all the powers within it their proper role. The community already participates in the present in this reign of Christ. Through his death he reconciles the believers with God (Col. 1.22) and erases the charges against them (Col. 2.14). Now Christ can also be proclaimed to the Gentiles as lord of the cosmos (Col. 1.27). Col. 3.11d is a pregnant expression of the Christology of the letter: τὰ πάντα καὶ ἐν πᾶσιν Χριστός (Christ is all, and is in all).

> The cosmic Christology of Colossians, which is characterized by thinking about the spheres and locations where power is exercised, can connect with statements of the undisputed Pauline letters in which the cosmic lordship of Christ is also proclaimed (cf. 1 Cor. 8.6; Phil. 2.9–11; 3.21). The author of Colossians, however, goes far beyond these traditional statements in that he makes the cosmic dimension the foundation and center of his Christology. Moreover, in elaborating his Christology he makes use of traditions that are not genuinely Pauline. It is rather the case that he takes the hymn of Colossians 1.15–20 as the basis and point of departure for the Christology of his whole letter.

2. Eschatology: The eschatology of Colossians[24] is structured on its Christology, and has a cosmic orientation as its point of departure.[25] Through baptism believers die with Christ and are already risen with him (Col. 2.12, 13; 3.1), so that other powers can no longer rule over them. The powers belong to the realm of the 'below,' while Christians are oriented to the 'above,' where Christ is (cf. Col. 3.1–2). The full participation of the believer in the death and resurrection of Jesus Christ is indicated by the σύν-expressions in Col. 2.12, 13; 3.1. Here, in contrast to Rom. 6.3–4, the past tense is also used with reference to the eschatological events.[26] Characteristic for Paul, however, is the eschatological reservation that the new being in Christ appropriated in the Spirit (cf. 2 Cor. 1.22; 5.5; Rom. 8.23) is not demonstrable within the categories of this world, but will first be revealed at the eschaton (in addition to Rom. 6.3–4, cf. especially 1 Cor. 13.12; 2 Cor. 4.7, 5.7; 1 Cor. 15.46). Pauline eschatology is characterized by the dialectic of 'already' and 'not yet.' Paul never speaks of a resurrection for Christians that has already happened, so that here one must see a decisive difference between the eschatology of Colossians and Paul's own eschatology. To be sure, Colossians also builds in precautions against an enthusiastic leap over the realities of the present,[27] while at the same time doing away with the eschatological reservation in the sense of the undisputed Pauline letters.[28] Another distinctive feature is seen in the ἐλπίς concept. 'Hope' appears in Col. 1.5, 23, 27 as the transcendent objective reality of salvation already prepared. 'Hope' no longer means the view with which the believer looks toward the future (cf. Rom. 8.24), but rather the reality of salvation that stands ready in heaven for the believer, and it is this objective reality that is called 'hope.'

3. Ecclesiology: The central concept of Colossians' ecclesiology is that of the σῶμα Χριστοῦ (body of Christ).[29] While it is used by Paul in parenetic

---

[24] A comprehensive discussion of all questions is found in Lona, *Eschatologie* 83–240 (Colossians is located on the same line as Paul, but pursues a different point of departure for developing its thought).

[25] Cf. Nikolaus Walter, '"Hellenistische Eschatologie" im Neuen Testament,' in *Glaube und Eschatologie* (FS W. G. Kümmel), eds. Erich Grässer and Otto Merk (Tübingen: J. C. B. Mohr [Paul Siebeck], 1985) (335–356) 344ff. It is clear that in Colossians spatial metaphors are dominant, e.g. 'hidden/revealed,' 'below/above.'

[26] Continuity and discontinuity between Rom. 6 and Col 3.1–4 are carefully analyzed by Grässer, 'Kolosser 3,1–4' 129ff.; Peter Müller, *Anfänge der Paulusschule* (see above 5) 87–134.

[27] Cf. διὰ τῆς πίστεως (through faith) in Col 2.12, κέκρυπται (is hidden) in Col 3.3; the parousia of Christ as a datum of the revelation of Christ's glory in Col 3.4.

[28] Cf. Merklein, 'Rezeption' 43ff.; contra Günter Klein, 'Eschatologie,' *TRE* 10 (1982) 286–287.

[29] Comparative material from the history of religions is presented by Eduard Schweizer, 'σῶμα,' *TDNT* VII, 1024–1094; for Colossians cf. *ibid.* 1074–1077.

contexts (cf. esp. 1 Cor. 12; Rom. 12),[30] in Colossians it receives a cosmo-logical meaning. The church is the universal sphere of salvation made possible by and ruled over by Jesus Christ (cf. Col. 1.18, 24; 2.17, 19; 3.15). While in Paul's letters Christ himself is described as the body of the church (cf.1 Cor. 12.12–13; Rom. 12.4–5), in Col. 1.18 Christ appears as head of the body (contrast 1 Cor. 12.21). The author of Colossians thereby abandons Paul's picture oriented to the concrete situation of the church and takes over the cosmological concept of the worldwide body of the church of which Christ is the head. Colossians does not develop the Pauline conception further, but takes up the idea mediated by Hellenistic Judaism (cf. 5.3.8):[31] the concept of a deity that rules throughout the whole extent of the universe (cf. e.g., Philo, Migr 220; Fug 108–113). Christ created the universe, reconciled it, and as head of the body exercises his lordship over it in the present.

4. The function of the apostle: While the content of Paul's preaching was the gospel of Jesus Christ, in Colossians the central message appears as the μυστήριον τοῦ Χριστοῦ (mystery of Christ) or θεοῦ (God) (cf. Col. 1.26, 27; 2.2; 4.3).[32] Behind this mystery stands the church presently being formed and built up, which, from another point of view, owes its existence to the preaching of the apostle. This is why the person and suffering of the apostle is also included within the content of the mystery (cf. Col. 1.24–29). As a minister to the body of Christ Paul reveals to the community the mystery of the divine will, so that his person is no longer separable from the content of the gospel. Although not present in body, he is still present with the community in spirit (Col. 2.5), the community which is now to proclaim Christ as the apostle himself proclaimed him (Col. 2.6). All other preaching is regarded as merely human teaching (Col. 2.8), not as apostolic tradition. The gospel is no longer defined only by its content, Jesus Christ, but essentially by the preaching of the apostle.

5. The concept of faith: While in Paul πίστις means the gift of a new relation to God and a new self-understanding, the author of Colossians uses πίστις in Col. 1.23; 2.5, 7 in connection with the concept of standing firm. The expressions of staying, standing fast, and of being firmly grounded points to the fact that πίστις in Colossians includes the idea of holding fast to tradition. This is another instance in which the idea of tradition has exercised a formative power on Colossians.

---

[30] For Paul cf. here Ernst Käsemann, 'The Theological Problem Presented by the Motif of the Body of Christ' in *Perspectives on Paul* tr. Margaret Kohl (Philadelphia: Fortress Press, 1971) 102–121; Udo Schnelle, *Gerechtigkeit und Christusgegenwart* (see above 2.4.10) 139–143, 243–245; on the ecclesiology of Colossians cf. Jürgen Roloff, *Kirche* (see above 3.5.4) 223–231.

[31] Merklein, 'Rezeption' 63, calls this process the 'Paulinization' of traditional material.

[32] Cf. Merklein, 'Rezeption' 28ff.

6. Pneumatology: There is a notable decline in pneumatology in Colossians, with πνεῦμα occurring only in Col. 1.8 and 2.5. While in Paul pneumatology is a dynamic element that permeates his theology and Christology, in Colossians it is only a marginal theme, for here it has spatial and static dimensions that dominate Christology and eschatology. Also the figure of the apostle Paul and the idea of tradition connected with it no longer permit rudimentary spiritual experiences (cf. in contrast 1 Thess. 5.19; 1 Cor. 14.1).

The distinctive linguistic and stylistic features, taken with the characteristic elements of content and theology, permit only one conclusion, namely that it was not Paul himself, but a *student of the apostle* who composed the letter. This connection with the Pauline school is also indicated by the author's knowledge of Paul's letters and his familiarity with Pauline theology. Thus the author adopted the formal structure of the Pauline letter prescript: Col. 1.1 agrees verbatim with 2 Cor. 1.1; Col. 1.2 is quite similar to 2 Cor. 1.2. The parallels in the lists of greetings in Philemon and Colossians show that the author of Colossians also knew this letter (cf. Phlm. 2/Col. 4.17; Phlm. 10/Col. 4.9; Phlm. 23/Col. 4.12; Phlm. 24/Col. 4.10).[33] Also the macrostructure of Colossians is oriented to that of the undisputed Pauline letters, for the bipartite structure comprising a predominately didactic and a primarily ethical section is already found in Galatians and Romans. To be noted here is the conception of Colossians as a prison letter (cf. Col. 4.3, 10, 18) and the proximity to Phil. 1.7, 13, 17, which in any case presuppose a knowledge of Paul's letters. Familiarity with Pauline theology is seen also in Col. 2.12, where ideas in part comparable to Rom. 6.4 are found. Moreover, a certain similarity exists between Col. 2.20 and Gal. 4.3, 9 (στοιχεῖα τοῦ κόσμου [basic principles of the world]), and also the use of the triad πίστις, ἀγάπη, ἐλπίς (faith, love, hope) in Col. 1.4–5 points to Pauline influence (cf. 1 Thess. 1.3; 5.8; 1 Cor 13.13; Gal. 5.5–6; further Phlm. 5; 1 Thess. 3.6).[34] The adoption of stylistic forms and content from Paul's letters not only serves the author as a means of pseudepigraphy,[35] but he claims Pauline authorship in order to legitimize and establish his position as the alternative to that of his opponents.

Can the author of Colossians be identified more precisely? The suggestion repeatedly made that Timothy was the author can neither be proven

---

[33] Cf. Lohse, *Colossians and Philemon* 175–176.

[34] Cf. Thomas Söding, *Die Trias Glaube, Hoffnung, Liebe bei Paulus* (see above 2.5.9) 177ff.

[35] Andreas Lindemann, *Paulus im ältesten Christentum* (see above 5) 114–122, emphasizes that on the one hand, Colossians clearly attaches itself to the Pauline heritage, but that on the other hand the only direct literary contacts are with Philemon.

nor refuted. The existence of other pseudepigraphical Pauline letters points, however, to a vigorous literary activity within the Pauline school, so that the assumption of an unknown disciple of Paul as the author of Colossians is the more probable hypothesis.

5.2.3 *Place and Time of Composition*

The Letter to the Colossians contains no information about its place of composition. Paul is in prison (Col. 4.3, 10, 18), but this picture is derived from the pseudepigraphical fiction. The cities of Colossae (Col. 1.2), Laodicea (Col. 2.1; 4.13, 15, 16) and Hierapolis (Col. 4.13) are mentioned, so that one may assume that the letter was written in their immediate neighborhood, or more likely in Ephesus,[36] the probable location of the Pauline school. In any case, Colossians originated in the area of *southwest Asia Minor*.[37] The author of the letter obviously had at his disposal personal knowledge of Paul's coworkers, since the Tychicus mentioned in Col. 4.7 appears again in the list of delegates that accompanied the collection in Acts 20.4, and the possibility of a literary connection between the two documents is to be excluded. The information about the missionary who founded the church, Epaphras (Col. 1.7; 4.12), is also to be regarded as appropriate, since the congregations addressed knew the history of their own church. So too the false teaching opposed by the letter manifests a certain similarity to the dispute in Galatia, so that the apostle is pictured as continuing the struggle against falsifications of his gospel. Of the Deuteropauline writings, Colossians is closest to Paul himself, and was probably written around 70 CE.[38]

5.2.4 *Intended Readership*

The beginnings of the city of Colossae (Κολοσσαί) are shrouded in darkness,[39] but already in the fifth century BCE it was regarded as an important city of Phrygia (cf. Herodotus 7.30.1). Colossae was propitiously located on a great business route that led from Ephesus to Tarsus in Cilicia. The importance of Colossae declined with the flowering of Laodicea, which was located in the immediate vicinity and in the first century was experiencing

---

[36] Lohse, *Colossians and Philemon*, 181 note 12; Gnilka, *Kolosserbrief* 22; Pokorný, *Kolosserbrief* 15.

[37] Cf. Lindemann, *Kolosserbrief* 11.

[38] Cf. Gnilka, *Kolosserbrief* 23; Pokorný, *Kolosserbrief* 15; Lindemann, *Kolosserbrief* 11 (between 70 and 80); Lohse, *Colossians and Philemon*, 182 note 17 (around 80); Wolter, *Kolosserbrief* 31 (between 70 and 80).

[39] On this point cf. Lohse, *Colossians and Philemon* 2; Gnilka, *Kolosserbrief* 1–4.

an economic boom (cf. Strabo 12.8.13, 16). Tacitus reports that Laodicea was demolished by an earthquake in 60/61 CE (*Annals* 14.27.1), and in the fifth century CE Orosius writes that Laodicea, Hierapolis, and Colossae were destroyed by an earthquake (*Against the Pagans* 7.7.12). To what extent the earthquake of 60/61 CE also hit Colossae, and whether Orosius refers to the same event as Tacitus, must remain open questions. While Laodicea was rebuilt by its inhabitants from their own resources (Tacitus, *Annals* 14.27.1), the fate of Colossae is unclear.[40] Whether a Christian community still existed in Colossae after 61 CE can neither be affirmed nor denied with certainty. To be sure, the letter is addressed to the church in Colossae, but from the very beginning was composed with a wider circle of readers and hearers in view. That can be seen from Col. 4.16: 'And when this letter has been read among you, have it read also in the church of the Laodiceans; and see that you read also the letter from Laodicea.' The references to Laodicea (cf. Col. 2.1; 4.13, 15, 16) and Hierapolis (cf. Col. 4.13) suggest that Colossians was directed to all congregations in which the false teaching might gain some influence.[41]

The congregations addressed were composed primarily of Gentile Christians (cf. Col. 1.27; 2.13). At the same time, one must reckon with a strong Jewish Christian influence (cf. Col. 4.11b!), for the population of these cities contained numerous Jews, whose ancestors had been settled there by Antiochus III (cf. Josephus, *Ant* 12.147–153). So too the references to circumcision in Col. 2.11 and Sabbath keeping in Col. 2.16 point to Jewish Christians. The churches had been founded not by Paul himself (cf. Col. 2.1), but by Epaphras, who had originally evangelized the communities (Col. 1.7) and had continued to wrestle in prayer (Col. 4.12–13) in behalf of the churches in Colossae, Laodicea and Hierapolis. The churches are explicitly reassured that they have held fast to the faith delivered to them and have maintained their love for all the saints (cf. Col. 1.3–8). But now deceptive speech (Col. 2.4) and a new 'philosophy' (cf. Col. 2.8) threaten to lead the congregations away from the teaching they have received. Colossians steps out against this φιλοσοφία (philosophy), and at the same time strengthens the churches in their apostolic faith.

---

[40] Wolter, *Kolosserbrief* 35, on the basis of inscriptions, emphasizes that Colossae was still a significant city after the earthquake.

[41] Lindemann, *Kolosserbrief* 12–13, even speaks of Colossae as a 'fictitious address,' since the author of Colossians really had the church at Laodicea in his mind's eye as he wrote.

5.2.5 Outline, Structure, Form

1.1–2	Prescript	— Introduction
1.3–14	Thanksgiving and intercession	

1.15–2.23	PART ONE	
1.15–20	The Christ hymn	
1.21–23	Application of the hymn to the church	
1.24–2.5	The office of the apostle	
2.6–23	Dispute with false teachers	— Body
3.1–4.6	PART TWO	
3.1–4	Transition	
3.5–17	Catalogue of virtues and vices	
3.18–4.1	Household code	
4.2–6	General admonitions	

4.7–9	Apostolic parousia	
4.10–17	Greetings	— Conclusion
4.18	Final farewell (Eschatokoll)	

Colossians manifests a clear structure that begins with an introductory section (prescript, thanksgiving) followed by the body of the letter consisting of a didactic and a parenetic section.[42] The epistolary conclusion, like the preceding elements, is also dependent on the formal structure of the authentic Pauline letters. A comparison with Galatians and Romans shows that the author of Colossians was familiar with the Pauline letter form and consciously adopted it. Within the doctrinal main section the hymn in Col. 1.15–20 forms the basis for the whole theological argumentation. The explicit debate with the false teaching follows in Col. 2.6–23, within which 2.12–13 gives a pregnant summary of the author's position. The section 3.1–4 assumes a double function in that the main ideas of the preceding unit are both summarized and given an ethical interpretation.

The division of Colossians into two major parts, one more didactic and the other more ethical, is confirmed by the use of ἐν Χριστῷ (in Christ) and ἐν

---

[42] Cf. Lohse, *Colossians and Philemon* 3; Conzelmann, *Kolosserbrief* 176; Schweizer, *Colossians* 15–16; Lindemann, *Kolosserbrief* 14. Gnilka, *Kolosserbrief* 8, votes for an outline with three main parts (1.9–29; 2.1–19; 2.20–4.6), while Pokorný, *Kolosserbrief* 19–22 opts for a four-part outline (1.3–23; 1.24–2.5; 2.6–23; 3.1–4.6). George E. Cannon, *The Use of Traditional Materials in Colossians* (Macon: Mercer University Press, 1983) 136–166, arrives at the following structure: Salutation 1.1–2; Thanksgiving 1.3–23; Letter Body 1.24–4.1; Letter Closing 4.10–18.

κυρίῳ (in the Lord). The use of both formulae by Paul shows clearly that ἐν Χριστῷ has an affinity with didactic affirmations and ἐν κυρίῳ is more related to parenetic statements.[43] Here too the author of Colossians follows the Pauline pattern, for ἐν Χριστῷ is found exclusively in the didactic part of the letter (1.2, 4, 28), while ἐν κυρίῳ occurs only in the parenetic section (3.18, 20; 4.7, 17).

The letter is directed to all the churches in the Lycus valley threatened by the false teaching, so that Colossians can be described as a 'circular letter.'

5.2.6 Literary Integrity

In all the research on Colossians, its literary integrity has remained uncontested.

5.2.7 Traditions, Sources

Like Paul himself, so also the author of Colossians develops essential parts of his theology from previous traditional elements. Central for the Christology of the letter is the *Christ hymn* in Col. 1.15–20.[44]

The traditional hymn begins at v. 15, where a sudden change of style can be detected. While Col. 1.3–14 manifests the stylistic traits typical of the letter as a whole (participial construction, loosely appended infinitives, heaping up of synonyms, piling up of genitive constructions, repetitions), these are lacking in 1.15–20.[45] In addition, there are linguistic peculiarities: ὁρατός (visible [1.16]), πρωτεύω (be supreme [1.18]), and εἰρηνοποιέω (make peace [1.20]) are hapax legomena in the New Testament. In the authentic Pauline letters neither θρόνοι (thrones) nor ἀρχαί (rules) are found (1.16). Paul himself speaks of the blood of Christ only in conjunction with traditional material (cf. Rom. 3.25; 1 Cor. 10.16; 11.25, 27), and the expression αἷμα τοῦ σταυροῦ αὐτοῦ ([blood of his cross] 1.20) is unparalleled in Paul's own writings.

---

[43] Cf. Fritz Neugebauer, *In Christus* (Göttingen: Vandenhoeck & Ruprecht, 1961) 65–149.

[44] In addition to the commentaries on Colossians 1.15–20 cf. especially Harald Hegermann, *Die Vorstellung vom Schöpfungsmittler im hellenistischen Judentum und Urchristentum*, TU 82 (Berlin: Akademie Verlag, 1961) 89–93; Burger, *Schöpfung* 3–53; Reinhard Deichgräber, *Gotteshymnus und Christushymnus in der frühen Christenheit*, SUNT 5 (Göttingen: Vandenhoeck & Ruprecht, 1967) 143–155; Klaus Wengst, *Christologische Formeln und Lieder des Urchristentums*, StNT 7 (Gütersloh: Gütersloher Verlagshaus [Gerd Mohn] 1972) 170–179; F. Zeilinger, *Der Erstgeborene der Schöpfung* 179–205; Jürgen Habermann, *Präexistenzaussagen* (see above 2.9.7) 225–266.

[45] Cf. Ludwig, *Der Verfasser des Kolosserbriefes* 32ff.

In outlining the hymn one should begin with the paralleling of ὅς ἐστιν (who is) in 1.15 and 1.18b, which suggests a two-part structure. Moreover, πρωτότοκος πάσης κτίσεως (firstborn of all creation) in 1.15 corresponds to πρωτότοκος ἐκ τῶν νεκρῶν (firstborn from the dead) in 1.18b. Then each relative clause is followed by a causative ὅτι (1.16, 19). Both 1.17 and 1.18a are added on by means of a καὶ αὐτός (and he), 1.20 by καὶ δι' αὐτοῦ (and through him).

The hymn is divided into two strophes not only by its form, but also by its content. Just as the first strophe (1.15–18a) speaks of the cosmological significance of the Christ event, so in the second strophe the focus is on the soteriological dimension (1.18b–20). The epexegetical genitive τῆς ἐκκλησίας (the church) joined to ἡ κεφαλὴ τοῦ σώματος (the head of the body) in 1.18a disturbs this structure, since it introduces the soteriological-ecclesiological aspect of the second strophe into the first strophe. In addition, this interpretative phrase corresponds to the understanding of the church as the body of Christ as developed by the author of Colossians himself in e.g., Col. 1.24. An additional interpretative element is seen in the doubled prepositional phrase διὰ τοῦ αἵματος τοῦ σταυροῦ αὐτοῦ (through the blood of his cross) [δι' αὐτοῦ (through him)] (1.20). The reference to the crucifixion must be seen as an addition by the author of Colossians himself, who thereby binds the cosmic dimension of the Christ event to the cross and thus to history.[46] Parallels to the hymn in Phil. 2 are undeniable, since in each case the traditional piece is connected to its context by interpretative additions. From the point of view of the history of religion, the hymn is related to ideas in Hellenistic Judaism in which the things predicated of Christ in the hymn are said of divine wisdom.[47] The author makes this Christ hymn, which probably originated in Asia Minor, the starting point of his argument, since he is writing to a church in which hymnic traditions were of great importance (cf. Col. 3.16b).

The author of Colossians makes use of a traditional form in the catalogue of virtues and vices in 3.5–17.[48] The text manifests a clear structure in which each of its two parts begins with clauses constructed in parallel form (cf. Col. 3.5, 12). Two vice catalogues are found in the first section (3.5–11), a virtue catalogue in the second (3.13–14). The conclusion of this

---

[46] Cf. *ibid.* 79.

[47] On this point cf. the data in Lohse, *Colossians and Philemon* 41–612; Sappington, *Revelation and Redemption* 172–176.

[48] In addition to the commentaries, cf. especially Siegfried Wibbing, *Die Tugend- und Lasterkataloge im Neuen Testament und ihre Traditionsgeschichte unter besonderer Berücksichtigung der Qumran-Texte*, BZNW 25 (Berlin: Walter de Gruyter, 1959); Eduard Schweizer, 'Gottesgerechtigkeit und Lasterkataloge bei Paulus (inkl. Kol und Eph),' in *Rechtfertigung* (FS E. Käsemann), eds. J. Friedrich et al. (Tübingen: J. C. B. Mohr [Paul Siebeck], 1976) 453–477.

section is formed by the wish for peace and other blessings for the community (3.15–17). The two vice catalogues in 3.5 and 3.8, just like the virtue catalogue in 3.12, consist of five asyndetic members in series (cf. for Paul Rom. 1.29–31; 2 Cor. 12.20, 21; Gal. 5.19–21, 22, 23). In 3.11 the author takes over a tradition found in slightly different form also in Gal. 3.28 and 1 Cor. 12.13.

The household code (*Haustafel*) in Col. 3.18–4.1 is thoroughly traditional; it manifests no specific stylistic traits of Colossians and also stands out from its context in both form and content. The members of the Christian household are addressed in three pairs (women/men; children/fathers; slaves/masters), in which one can recognize a line that descends from the closest relationship (wife and husband) to the relation of slave and master. In each case the weaker member of the pair is presented first, both members are referred to each other in the mutual admonition, and in each case the order is address/admonition/rationale. There are no household codes in the undisputed Pauline letters, but a close parallel is found in Eph. 5.22–6.9.

5.2.8 History-of-religions Standpoint

From the point of view of the history of religion, how should the heresy against which Colossians struggles be classified? The essential elements of the false teaching are implied in the letter itself: (1) The demands of the opponents included circumcision for Gentile Christians (cf. Col. 2.11). (2) Additional characteristics of the false teaching included ascetic prescriptions concerning food and commandments about festivals (cf. Col. 2.16–17, 21–22, 23b). Possibly sexual abstinence was also required (Col. 2.21a). (3) A central article of the opponents' doctrine was the paying of religious respect to the 'elements [elemental spirits] of the universe' (cf. Col. 2.8, 15, 20). (4) The worship of angels (cf. Col. 2.18) also belonged to the φιλοσοφία (philosophy) (cf. Col. 2.8) in Colossae. Additional elements of the false teaching may also be inferred from the author's polemic. He offers a defense against assertions set forth by the false teachers (Col. 2.20–21), and describes the doctrine of the opponents as [merely] 'an appearance of wisdom' and as being 'puffed up in the flesh' (cf. Col. 2.18, 23). Obviously the opponents, who had been schooled in rhetoric (Col. 2.4) set forth norms to be observed by means of which the Christians in Colossae were to be freed from the power of the elemental spirits (cf. Col. 2.14).

Since the Colossian philosophy represents a very complex structure from the point of view of the history of religion, it is not surprising that a number of different theories have arisen to explain its origins.[49] The most important interpretative models (partly overlapping) are: (1) the influence of Qumran Essenes (W. D. Davies);[50] (2) Hellenistic gnosticism with a Jewish background (E. Lohmeyer);[51] (3) syncretistic mystery cults (M. Dibelius);[52] (4) gnosticizing Judaism (G. Bornkamm);[53] (5) syncretistic Judaism (E. Lohse, J. Gnilka);[54] (6) a syncretistic doctrine under the strong influence of neopythagoreanism (E. Schweizer);[55] (7) a syncretistic conglomeration of Phrygian nature religion, Iranian mythology concerning the elemental spirits of the universe, and a Hellenized Judaism (J. Lähnemann);[56] (8) Jewish-gnostic syncretism (A. Lindemann);[57] (9) the influence of gnosticism (P. Pokorný);[58] (10) ascetic-mystic piety in the context of Jewish apocalyptic (T. J. Sappington);[59] and (11) Hellenistic-Jewish revelatory wisdom (M. Wolter).[60]

The point of departure for a determination of the classification of the Colossian philosophy within the categories of Hellenistic religion must be the Jewish elements. In Galatia too the demand for circumcision (Gal. 5.2, 6), observation of a particular calendar (Gal. 4.10), and the στοιχεῖα τοῦ κόσμου ('elements' or 'elemental spirits of the universe') (Gal. 4.3, 9) were among the elements of the false teaching (see above 2.7.8). In contrast to the Judaizing doctrine in Galatia, the issue of the Law plays no role in Colossae (νόμος is entirely lacking!), and the Old Testament is taken as a basis for the argument neither by the author of Colossians nor by his opponents (there is no citation from the Old Testament!). In addition, clear syncretistic elements of the opponents' philosophy are present. Differently than in Galatia, the expression στοιχεῖα τοῦ κόσμου does not point to the connection between fulfilling the Law and the ordering of the calendar, but to the realm of Hellenistic philosophy.

---

[49] John J. Gunther, *Paul's Opponents* (see above 2.6.8) 34, lists 44 different suggestions with regard to Colossians alone!

[50] Cf. W. D. Davies, 'Paul and the Dead Sea Scrolls: Flesh and Spirit,' in *The Scrolls and the New Testament*, ed. Krister Stendahl (New York: Harper and Brothers, 1957) 166–168.

[51] Cf. Lohmeyer, *Kolosserbrief* 3–8.

[52] Cf. Dibelius, *Kolosserbrief* 35–36.

[53] Cf. Bornkamm, 'Heresy' 130–131; in addition Hans M. Schenke, 'Der Widerstreit gnostischer und kirchlicher Christologie im Spiegel des Kolosserbriefes,' *ZThK* 61 (1964) 391–403; Hans F. Weiss, 'Gnostische Motive und antignostische Polemik im Kolosser- und Epheserbrief,' in *Gnosis und Neues Testament*, ed. Karl-W. Tröger (Berlin: Evangelische Verlagsanstalt, 1973) (311–324) 313–314.

[54] Cf. Lohse, *Colossians and Philemon* 127–131; Gnilka, *Kolosserbrier* 163–170.

[55] Cf. E. Schweizer, *Colossians* 125–134.

[56] Cf. Lähnemann, *Kolosserbrief* 82–100.

[57] Cf. Lindemann, *Kolosserbrief* 81–86.

[58] Cf. Pokorný, *Kolosserbrief* 95–101.

[59] Cf. Sappington, *Revelation and Redemption* 170 and often.

[60] Cf. Wolter, *Kolosserbrief* 162.

The powerful elements earth, water, air, fire (and the ether), which constitute the universe and assure its harmony, were described as στοιχεῖα.[61] As the constitutive elements of the cosmos, they influenced the destiny of human beings at the same time as they were mythologized and portrayed as beloved spirits. Speculations about the elements of the world, connected with adoration of angels and observance of a specific calendar are found in the ideas of syncretistic streams of Hellenistic Judaism.[62] Notable parallels are also found in neopythagorean writings.[63] In each case there is the clear tendency to present the powers and elements as worthy of worship by incorporating them into the cosmic order.

The juxtaposition of the στοιχεῖα τοῦ κόσμου with Christ in Col. 2.8 indicates that in the philosophy of the opponents the στοιχεῖα τοῦ κόσμου were thought of as personal beings. They appear as powers that want to exercise lordship over human beings (cf. Col. 2.10, 15). Probably the Colossians both worshipped and feared the elemental spirits, so that along

---

[61] For documentation cf. Gerhard Delling, στοιχεῖον, *TDNT* 7.666–687; Josef Blinzler, *Lexikalisches zu dem Terminus τὰ στοιχεῖα τοῦ κόσμου bei Paulus*, AB 18 (Rome: Pontifical Biblical Institute, 1963) 429–443; Eduard Schweizer, 'Slaves of the Elements and Worshipers of Angels: Gal. 4.3, 9 and Col 2.8, 18, 20,' *JBL* 107 (1988) 455–468 (see above 2.7.8); Lohse, *Colossians and Philemon* 96–98; Eduard Schweizer, 'Altes und Neues zu den "Elementen der Welt" in Kol 2,20; Gal. 4,3.9', in *Wissenschaft und Kirche* (FS E. Lohse), eds. Kurt Aland and Siegfried Meurer (Bielefeld, 1989) 111–118; Dietrich Rusam, 'Neue Belege zu den στοιχεῖα τοῦ κόσμου (Gal. 4,3.9; Kol 2,8.20),' *ZNW* 83 (1992) 119–125; Wolter, *Kolosserbrief* 122–124.

[62] For his derivation of the false teaching from Hellenistic Judaism, Lohse, *Colossians and Philemon* 97–98, can point especially to the connection between the worship of the powers, calendar observance (Col 2.16), and the worship of angels (Col 2.18). Rusam, 'Neue Belege,' 125, infers from his analysis of the data that by στοιχεῖα τοῦ κόσμου clearly the four physical elements of fire, water, earth, and air are to be understood: 'The assumption of E. Lohse and H. Schlier, that στοιχεῖα τοῦ κόσμου refers to "beloved spirits" is lacking any lexical basis, since there is not a single instance of the words being used in this sense.' This judgment is probably appropriate with regard to the purely lexical data, but does not yet explain the specific application in Colossians in which, e.g., the στοιχεῖα τοῦ κόσμου are juxtaposed to Χριστός (Christ) in Col 2.8, which is difficult to understand unless there had been a personal component in the conception of the στοιχεῖα.

[63] E. Schweizer points repeatedly to a text by Alexander Polyhistor from the first century BCE that manifests a series of parallels to the philosophy in Colossae. According to it, from the primal monad there originated 'the visible bodies including the elements fire, water, earth and air, that continued to be in dynamic movement. From them originated the spherical enlivened and immaterial cosmos. Within this was included the earth at its center, spherical in shape and inhabited all around . . . The ether surrounding the earth was unshakable, unhealthy, with everything in it mortal, but above it was the sphere in which everything continued in motion, pure and healthy, and everything in it was immortal and therefore divine . . . Hermes was the pater familias of the souls, since he is the one who led the souls out of the bodies, from earth and sea, and he leads the pure ones to the highest (element or orbit), while the impure were . . . imprisoned in unbreakable chains from the Furies . . . Sanctification happens through purifications and baths . . . and they abstained from edible animal flesh, gray mullet, blacktail fish, eggs, poultry, beans, and other things that are also proscribed for those who participate in the initiatory acts in the temple' (cited from E. Schweizer, 'Altes und Neues zu den "Elementen der Welt"' 113–114).

with ascetic practices, circumcision, humility and the worship of angels appear as means by which to come to terms with the supposed demands of the elemental spirits. The Colossian heresy was put into practice as a kind of mystery cult, for the expressions ἃ ἑόρακεν ἐμβατεύων ('dwelling on visions' – translation disputed) in Col. 2.18 (cf. Apuleius, *Metamorphoses* XI 23.5ff.) and ἐθελοθρησκία in Col. 2.23 point to an initial ceremony similar to that of the mystery cults, with circumcision functioning as a rite of initiation.[64]

The Colossian philosophy represents a confluence of elements from Hellenistic Judaism, contemporary neopythagorean philosophy and the mystery cults, so that from the point of view of the history of religion a monocausal explanation seems to be impossible. The opponents of the author of Colossians obviously practiced their doctrine and cult within the church. They did not understand themselves to be heretics, but saw in their philosophy a legitimate form of expression of the Christian faith.

5.2.9 Basic Theological Ideas

The Letter to the Colossians develops its theology in debate with the opposing philosophy. As the opponents proclaim a connection between Christian faith and service to the cosmic powers and rulers, so the author of Colossians opposes this doctrine with *solus Christus*.[65] For the false teachers, Christ alone does not suffice for participation in the fullness of salvation. In opposition to the worldly anxiety and the uncertainty of the church, the author of Colossians emphasizes the full presence of salvation in Jesus Christ. The hymn grounds the christocentrism of the letter, and thus already stands in the service of its polemic against the false teaching (cf. the allusion to Col. 1.19 in 2.9, and the reflection of 1.16b–17 in 2.10). The christocentric position of the author comes pregnantly to expression in Col. 2.6–23 in the repeated use of ἐν αὐτῷ (in him) (2.6, 7, 9, 10, 15), ἐν ᾧ (in whom) (2.11, 12), and σύν (with) phrases (2.12, 13, 20). Through baptism (Col. 2.12), the Colossians already live in the all-encompassing realm of Christ's lordship.[66] As people who have been baptized, they are

---

[64] Cf. Lohse, *Colossians and Philemon* 126–127.

[65] This is fittingly stated by Hartmut Löwe, 'Bekenntnis, Apostelamt und Kirche im Kolosserbrief,' in *Kirche* (FS G. Bornkamm), eds. Dieter Lührmann and Georg Strecker (Tübingen: J. C. B. Mohr [Paul Siebeck], 1980) 310: 'Over against the *traditiones humanae* proclaimed as divine, the author of the letter places the *traditio divina* of Jesus Christ contained in the baptismal confession (2.6).' A concentrated summary statement of the theology of Colossians is found in Lindemann, *Kolosserbrief* 86–89.

[66] According to Pokorný, *Kolosserbrief* 22, the theology of Colossians is concentrated in the thesis statement of 2.12–13: 'This thesis distinguishes Colossians and Ephesians from the other Pauline letters and at the same time forms the backbone of their theological argument.'

risen with Christ, who rules over all powers, and they should orient their existence by this new reality (cf. Col. 3.1–4). The present participation of believers in salvation is as comprehensive as the lordship of Christ over all cosmic powers and rulers. The cosmic lordship of Christ makes the opponents' demand for circumcision, ascetic practices, humility, and worship of angels pointless. Believers are already reconciled (Col. 1.20, 22) and circumcised (Col. 2.11), they already participate in the victory of Jesus Christ and must therefore no longer serve other powers (cf. Col. 2.15, 18, 20, 23). No other practices or rituals are necessary in order to participate fully in salvation. By using the terms φιλοσοφία (philosophy), παράδοσις (tradition) and στοιχεῖα τοῦ κόσμου (elemental spirits of the universe), the author takes over the vocabulary of the false teachers in order to juxtapose them to his own judgments. Thus φιλοσοφία appears as κενὴ ἀπάτη (empty deceit) and παράδοσις as τῶν ἀνθρώπων (tradition, from human beings) and οὐ κατὰ Χριστόν (not according to Christ). All wisdom is contained in Christ (Col. 1.28; 2.3; 3.16); there are no other sources of wisdom alongside Christ, so that the opponents are obviously placing on display only an appearance of wisdom (Col. 2.23).

In the same manner and to the same extent, Christology, cosmology, and realized eschatology must be understood as responses to the challenge of the opponents' teaching. Thus the spatial categories that dominate Colossians' world of thought must to a considerable part be attributed to the opponents, but the author of the letter himself tends strongly to thinking in terms of space (rather than temporal categories). Nonetheless, he is not merely the advocate of an enthusiastic theology dominated by the idea of transcendent salvation already present. To be sure, the Colossians already participate in a salvation that cannot be lost, but this is a matter of faith (Col. 2.12). Their resurrected life is a matter of objective reality, but not a public, observable reality, for it is hidden with Christ in God (cf. Col. 3.3) and thereby withdrawn from human verification. Futuristic affirmations of the Christian hope clearly recede into the background in favor of the spatial world of thought, but at the same time they are integrated into the spatially-oriented way of thinking and to be understood within this context.[67] Their fundamental significance for the theology of Colossians is seen in the way in which affirmations of the future saving act of God at the parousia of Christ are still maintained (cf. Col. 3.4, 24). These futuristic affirmations are also constitutive for the letter's parenesis, for while Christians already participate in salvation, they do not yet live in

---

[67] Cf. Horacio E. Lona, *Eschatologie* (see above 5.2.1) 234: 'The temporal aspect is not eliminated in Colossians, but integrated into a christological concept.'

the heavenly realm 'above.' Rather, they are to orient their lives to the future revelation of salvation and live by that hope. The usual parenesis is dominant also in Colossians, with no conflict apparent in the field of ethics (cf. 3.5–17; 3.18–4.1). As early Christianity's first pseudepigraphical writing, Colossians thus documents the transition to a more developed and expanded Pauline understanding. The person of the apostle, and the regard in which he is held, are adopted in order to oppose developments that place the work of the apostle in danger.[68]

5.2.10 Tendencies of Recent Research

There appears to be a developing consensus on the issue of authorship, with only a few exegetes continuing to regard Colossians as an authentic letter of Paul. To be sure, the secretary hypothesis, especially as advocated by Eduard Schweizer, continues to be important. If there can be no doubt that opposition to the false teaching at work within the church is the real goal of the letter, how to understand the heresy itself with regard to its context in the history of religion continues to be a disputed point. In the most recent discussion three interpretative models have emerged as especially significant: the philosophy in Colossae appears as the product of a syncretistically oriented Hellenistic Judaism (E. Lohse, J. Gnilka), neo-pythagorean influence is regarded as determinative (E. Schweizer), or strong influences of a syncretistic gnosticism are assumed (P. Pokorný).

It is to be expected that there would continue to be disagreements as to the exact wording of the original hymn in Col. 1.15–20. While the expressions τῆς ἐκκλησίας (the church) in 1.18 and διὰ τοῦ αἵματος τοῦ σταυροῦ αὐτοῦ (through the blood of his cross) in 1.20 are regarded by the majority of exegetes as redactional additions to the original hymn, there is no consensus regarding what additional modifications to the hymn are included in its present form.

In recent years the focus of study has concentrated on Colossians' reception of Paul (H. Merklein, A. Lindemann, E. Dassmann [see above 5]). Both the composition of the letter and the content of its line of argument indicate that the author was thoroughly acquainted with Pauline theology, and thus that he belonged to the Pauline school. In this process a decisive role is attributed to Paul (cf. Col. 1.25), for the person of Paul himself now belongs to the Pauline gospel that is to be proclaimed. The letter thus makes the claim to be fundamentally oriented both to the person of the

---

[68] Cf. Vielhauer, *Urchristliche Literatur* 202–203, according to whom Colossians also prepares the way for the speculative Christology of Ephesians and the orthodox ecclesiasticism of the Pastorals.

apostle and to his theology. The content of the letter is not a matter of an actual development of Pauline theology, but rather the author of Colossians primarily takes traditions of Hellenistic Jewish Christianity and connects them to Paul. This 'Paulinization' of traditional materials is intended to secure the identity of the gospel. It also opens 'innovative perspectives, in that – as they are executed all the more intensively – they go beyond Paul and in Ephesians the adopted cosmic Christology is finally built up into the concept of an ecclesiological Christology.'[69]

5.3 The Letter to the Ephesians

5.3.1 Literature

Commentaries

Dibelius, Martin (Heinrich Greeven). *An die Kolosser, Epheser, an Philemon*, HNT 12. Tübingen: J. C. B. Mohr (Paul Siebeck), 1953³, 54–100; Gnilka, Joachim. *Der Epheserbrief*, HThK 10.2. Freiburg: Herder, 1982³; Schnackenburg, Rudolf. *Ephesians*, EKK 10, tr. Helen Heron. Edinburgh: T. & T. Clark, 1991; Mußner, Franz. *Der Brief an die Epheser*, ÖTK 10. Gütersloh: Gütersloher Verlagshaus (Gerd Mohn), 1982; Conzelmann, Hans. *Die kleineren Briefe des Apostels Paulus*, NTD 8. Göttingen: Vandenhoeck & Ruprecht, 1976, 86–124; Ernst, Josef. *Der Brief an die Philipper, an Philemon, an die Kolosser, an die Epheser*, RNT. Regensburg: Friedrich Pustet, 1974; Lindemann, Andreas. *Der Epheserbrief*, ZBK 8. Zürich: Theologischer Verlag, 1985; Barth, Markus. *Ephesians*. AncB 34. 34A. Garden City: Doubleday & Co., 1974; Schlier, Heinrich. *Der Brief an die Epheser*. Düsseldorf: Patmos Verlag, 1971⁷; Pokorný, Petr. *Der Brief des Paulus an die Epheser*, ThHK 10.2. Leipzig: Evangelische Verlagsanstalt, 1992.

Monographs

Schlier, Heinrich. *Christus und die Kirche im Epheserbrief*, BHTh 6. Tübingen: J. C. B. Mohr (Paul Siebeck), 1930; Mußner, Franz. *Christus, das All und die Kirche*, TThSt 5. Trier: Paulinus-Verlag, 1968²; Pokorný, Petr. *Der Epheserbrief und die Gnosis*. Berlin: Evangelische Verlagsanstalt, 1965; Ernst, Josef. *Pleroma und Pleroma Christi*, BU 5. Regensburg: Friedrich Pustet, 1970; Fischer, Karl Martin. *Tendenz und Absicht des Epheserbriefes*. Göttingen: Vandenhoeck & Ruprecht, 1973; Merklein, Helmut. *Das kirchliche Amt nach dem Epheserbrief*, StANT 33. Munich: Kösel, 1973; Lindemann, Andreas. *Die Aufhebung der Zeit*, StNT 12. Gütersloh: Gütersloher Verlagshaus (Gerd Mohn), 1975; Arnold, Clinton E. *Ephesians: Power and Magic*, SNTSMS 63. Cambridge: Cambridge University Press, 1989; Lona, Horacio E. *Die Eschatologie im Kolosser und Epheserbrief* (see above 5. 2. 1).

---

[69] Merklein, 'Rezeption' 63.

Articles

Colpe, Carsten. 'Zur Leib-Christi-Vorstellung im Epheserbrief,' in *Judentum-Christentum- Kirche* (FS J. Jeremias), ed. Walter Eltester BZNW 26. Berlin: Walter de Gruyter, 1960, 172–187; Kuhn, Karl G. 'Der Epheserbrief im Lichte der Qumrantexte,' NTS 7 (1960/61) 334–346; Käsemann, Ernst. 'Das Interpretationsproblem des Epheserbriefes,' in *Exegetische Versuche und Besinnungen II*, ed. E. Käsemann. Göttingen: Vandenhoeck & Ruprecht, 1970³, 253–261; Lindemann, Andreas. 'Bemerkungen zu den Adressaten und zum Anlaß des Epheserbriefes,' ZNW 67 (1976) 235–251; Mußner, Franz. 'Epheserbrief,' *TRE* 9 (1982) 743–753; Luz, Ulrich. 'Überlegungen zum Epheserbrief und seiner Paränese,' in *Vom Urchristentum zu Jesus* (FS J. Gnilka), eds. Hubert Frankemölle and Karl Kertelge. Freiburg: Herder, 1989, 376–396.

History of Research

Merkel, Helmut. 'Der Epheserbrief in der neueren Diskussion,' *ANRW* 25. 4. Berlin: Walter de Gruyter, 1987, 3156–3246.

5.3.2 Author

The Letter to the Ephesians presents itself as a letter of the apostle Paul composed while he was in prison (cf. Eph. 1.1; 6.21). Against this claim stand weighty arguments that point to a *deuteropauline* authorship.

(1) Ephesians manifests linguistic peculiarities. Thus there are 35 words not found elsewhere in the New Testament,[70] the most significant of which are: ἑνότης (unity) (Eph. 4.3.13), κοσμοκράτωρ (cosmic power) (Eph. 6.12), μεσότοιχον (dividing wall) (Eph. 2.14) and πολιτεία (citizenship) (Eph. 2.12). For deciding this issue, special importance should be attached to expressions that do not occur at all in the undisputed Pauline letters, but which are characteristic of the theology of Ephesians:[71] εὐλογία πνευματική (spiritual blessing) (Eph. 1.3); καταβολὴ κόσμου (foundation of the world) (Eph. 1.4); ἄφεσις τῶν παραπτωμάτων (forgiveness of trespasses) (Eph. 1.7); μυστήριον τοῦ θελήματος αὐτοῦ (mystery of his will) (Eph. 1.9); ὁ λόγος τῆς ἀληθείας (the word of truth) (Eph. 1.13); ὁ πατὴρ τῆς δόξης (the father of glory) (Eph. 1.17); αἰὼν τοῦ κόσμου τούτου (ruler of this world) (Eph. 2.2); ἡ πρόθεσις τῶν αἰώνων (the eternal purpose) (Eph. 3.11); τὸ πνεῦμα τοῦ νοός (the spirit of your minds) (Eph. 4.23); μιμηταὶ τοῦ θεοῦ (imitators of God) (Eph. 5.1); βασιλεία τοῦ Χριστοῦ καὶ τοῦ θεοῦ (kingdom of Christ and God) (Eph. 5.5). Like Colossians, so also Ephesians shows a preference for extra-long sentences

---

[70] Statistics according to Kurt Aland, *Vollständige Konkordanz* (see above 5.2.2) 456.
[71] Cf. Gnilka, *Epheserbrief* 16–17.

(cf. Eph. 1.3–14) and the stringing together of similar words (cf. Eph. 1.19; 6.10). Also to be noted is the extensive use of adnominal genitive constructions (cf. Eph. 1.6, 10, 18, 19 and often).[72]

(2) Constitutive for Ephesians is the way in which it reflects back on the apostle Paul, the anamnesis of his person and his theology. Thus Ephesians 3.1ff. already reflects the Gentile apostolate of Paul from the perspective of its role in salvation history. Paul appears alongside the holy apostles and prophets as the receiver of God's revelation that leads to the universal church of Jews and Gentiles. Not a trace is left of the debates concerning Paul's apostleship (cf. 1 Cor. 9.1ff.) and of the severe conflicts between Jewish Christians and Gentile Christians. Paul no longer contends for his position, but it is already honored for its role in the history of the church.[73]

(3) The list of church officials in Eph. 4.11–12 points to a church structure that has been radically changed in comparison to the churches of Paul's own time.[74] While 'apostles' and 'prophets' also appear in 1 Cor. 12.28, the title of 'evangelist' is missing from Paul. 'Teachers' are listed third in 1 Cor. 12.28, but appear in Eph. 4.11 after apostles, prophets, evangelists and pastors. Charismatic offices such as miracle workers, those with gifts of healing, and speakers in tongues are missing from Ephesians. Ephesians presupposes a pattern of ministry in which prophets and evangelists were probably wandering preachers, while pastors and teachers were responsible for preaching, direction, and instruction in the local congregations. The apostolic office is not thought of as actually still functioning, but is regarded in terms of its theological significance: the apostles are the foundation of the church (Eph. 2.20), to whom the mystery event of the Christ was revealed (cf. Eph. 3.5).[75]

(4) Ephesians obviously uses Colossians as a literary source (see below 5.3.7).

(5) The theology of Ephesians is, on the one hand, significantly different from that of the undisputed Pauline letters,[76] while, on the other hand, there are extensive agreements with the theology of Colossians. In its Christology the dominant idea is that of the cosmic rule of Christ: the Risen One is enthroned at the right hand of God (Eph. 1.20), to whom God

---

[72] On this point cf. most recently Gerhard Sellin, 'Über einige ungewöhnliche Genitive im Epheserbrief,' ZNW 83 (1992) 85–107.

[73] Cf. Merklein, 'Rezeption' (see above 5.2.1) 32–33.

[74] For an analysis cf. Merklein, *Das kirchliche Amt* 57–117.

[75] On the doctrine of church offices in Ephesians and its relation to Paul, cf. Merklein, *ibid.* 235–383.

[76] Schnackenburg, *Ephesians* 26ff., speaks here of a 'change of perspectives.'

the Creator has subjected everything (Eph. 1.22a), and he now reigns over the universe by the power of his transcendent life (Eph. 1.23). In no other New Testament document does ecclesiology receive such a prominent place as in Ephesians.[77] As in Paul, the church has its origin in the sacrifice of Jesus Christ on the cross (Eph. 2.13, 14, 16). At the same time, however, Paul's dynamic conception of the church as the body of Christ has been transformed via its use in Colossians into the spatial-static concept of Christ as the head and the church as his body. Corresponding to Ephesians' worldview,[78] present eschatology is dominant (cf. Eph. 2.5, 6, 8, 19; 3.12). The doctrine of justification no longer has a polemical ring, being included within the framework of statements about baptism (cf. Eph. 2.5, 8–10).[79]

(6) According to Acts 19.9–10 the apostle worked more than two years in Ephesus. He was thus both known to the church and acquainted with circumstances in Ephesus. In contrast to this, Eph. 1.15 and 3.2 give the impression that apostle and church did not know each other at all. Moreover, the whole document makes a very impersonal impression, so that e.g., there is not a single greeting to members of the church in Ephesians. Finally, the place designation ἐν Ἐφέσῳ (Eph. 1.1) cannot be regarded as original (see below 5.3.4).

The overwhelming majority of exegetes consider Ephesians to be a deuteropauline writing, e.g., Martin Dibelius, Werner Georg Kümmel, Willi Marxsen, H. M. Schenke, Karl Martin Fischer, Phillipp Vielhauer, A. Wikenhauser, J. Schmid, Hans Conzelmann, J. Ernst, Joachim Gnilka, Franz Mußner, Rudolf Schnackenburg, Andreas Lindemann and Petr Pokorný[80]. A secretary-hypothesis is presently advocated especially by A. van Roon.[81] The more prominent advocates of the authenticity of the letter

---

[77] Cf. Schnackenburg, *Ephesians* 293–310 ('The Church in the Epistle to the Ephesians'); Jürgen Roloff, *Kirche* (see above 3.5.4) 231–232, speaks of a Copernican revolution: 'In the authentic letters of Paul, the Christ event always stands in the center and the church is seen in its relation to this, while in this deuteropauline writing the church is the point of departure, and the Christ event is interpreted in its light.'

[78] On the worldview of Ephesians, cf. Lindemann, *Epheserbrief* 121–123.

[79] Cf. Mußner, *Epheserbrief* 28.

[80] Cf. Dibelius, *Epheserbrief* 83–84; Kümmel, *Introduction* 361; Marxsen, *Introduction* 196–198; Schenke and Fischer, *Einleitung* 1.181–186; Vielhauer, *Urchristliche Literatur* 207–212; Wikenhauser and Schmid, *Einleitung* 488–489; Conzelmann, *Epheserbrief* 86; Ernst, *Epheserbrief* 258–262; Gnilka, *Epheserbrief* 13; Mußner, *Epheserbrief* 33; Schnackenburg, *Ephesians* 24–25; Lindemann, *Epheserbrief* 9–12; Pokorný, *Epheserbrief* 40–42.

[81] Cf. A. van Roon, *The Authenticity of Ephesians*, NT.S 39 (Leiden: E. J. Brill, 1974) 207–208 and passim. The real author of Ephesians, however, remains for van Roon the apostle Paul; cf. *ibid.* 440: '. . . that it is not only plausible but even probable that Paul was the author of Eph.'

are Heinrich Schlier, F. F. Bruce and Marcus Barth.[82] While Schlier in 1930 still considered Ephesians to be deuteropauline,[83] in his commentary he regards Ephesians as a Pauline writing.[84] He explains the peculiarities of Ephesians from the situation of the aged Paul as a prisoner in Rome. Paul had now come to a new internal understanding of the saving event, to a deeper insight into its meaning. This appeal to Paul's age is not convincing, because the sum total of the differences between the Pauline writings and Ephesians is too great.

We can say little about the person of the actual author: he belonged to the Pauline school and was a Hellenistic Jewish Christian,[85] as indicated by texts such as Eph. 1.3–14; 2.20–22; 3.20–21; 6.13–17. He set before himself the goal of saving the unity of the church of Jewish and Gentile Christians in Asia Minor, a unity that was threatened.

5.3.3 *Place and Time of Composition*

The exact location where Ephesians was composed can no longer be determined, but the extensive familiarity with Colossians points to *Asia Minor*.[86] Arguments for a more precise location (e.g., Ephesus)[87] are worthy of consideration. The determination of the period within which Ephesians was written is limited by Colossians as the earlier limit and the letters of Ignatius as the later (cf. Eph. 5.27 and *IgnPol.* 5.1; Eph. 2.20–22 with *IgnEph.* 9.1).[88] Given these presuppositions, the most probable date for Ephesians is between *80 and 90* CE.[89]

---

[82] Cf. Barth, *Ephesians* 1.36–50.

[83] Cf. Schlier, *Christus und die Kirche* 39 note 1.

[84] Cf. Schlier, *Epheserbrief* 22–28. But Schlier finally again had doubts about the Pauline origin; cf. Schnackenburg, *Ephesians* 24 note 16.

[85] Cf. Gnilka, *Epheserbrief* 18; Schnackenburg, *Ephesians* 35–36.

[86] Cf. Kümmel, *Introduction* 366; Schenke and Fischer, *Einleitung* 1.187; Schnackenburg, *Ephesians* 36–37 (unknown author from a church in the Lycus valley); Lindemann, *Epheserbrief* 12.

[87] Among those who vote for Ephesus are Ernst, *Epheserbrief* 263; Mußner, *Epheserbrief* 36; Gnilka, *Epheserbrief* 20; Pokorný, *Epheserbrief* 42.

[88] On IgnEph 12.2 ('Paul . . .makes mention of you in every letter') cf. Andreas Lindemann, *Paulus im ältesten Christentum* (see above 5) 84–85.

[89] Cf. Schenke and Fischer, *Einleitung* 1.187; Mußner, *Epheserbrief* 36; Schnackenburg, *Ephesians* 33; Pokorný, *Epheserbrief* 43. Vielhauer, *Urchristliche Literatur* 215, argues for the turn from the first to second century CE as the time of composition; Gnilka, *Epheserbrief* 20, for the beginning of the 90s of the first century.

5.3.4 *Intended Readership*

The destination of the letter as indicated by the words ἐν Ἐφέσῳ (in Ephesians) is lacking in 𝔓⁴⁶, B*, ℵ*, 1739, 424 and in Origen. It is probable that Marcion also did not read this phrase in his text of 'Ephesians,' (cf. Tertullian, *Adv Marc* 5.11.12), and described the document as a letter to Laodicea. The external text critical evidence thus speaks against the originality of ἐν Ἐφέσῳ. The internal evidence points in the same direction. If the letter itself contained no specific designation of the place to which it was written, then one can readily imagine that a later supplement was made to make it conform to the formal scheme of the authentic Pauline letters and Colossians. Ephesus would easily suggest itself, since Paul had worked in this city for a long time, and he might well have written a letter to this church. At the same time, it is difficult to suggest a plausible reason why an original ἐν Ἐφέσῳ would have been struck from the text, so that the phrase is to be considered secondary according to the rules of text criticism.[90]

From the point of view of grammar and style, how is the text to be understood without this phrase? The lack of a location after the substantival participle of εἰμί remains unusual,[91] but still the text τοῖς ἁγίοις τοῖς οὖσιν καὶ πιστοῖς ('to the holy and faithful ones') is syntactically quite possible as an address of two members: 'to the saints and believers . . . '.[92] A different explanatory model has been suggested by Ernest Best:[93] the original address of the circular letter read τοῖς ἁγίοις καὶ πιστοῖς ἐν Χριστῷ Ἰησοῦ. This was followed by a later insertion 'Ephesus,' to make the geographical location more precise, which then caused τοῖς ἁγίοις (to the saints) to be expanded to πρὸς τοὺς ἁγίους τοὺς ὄντας ἐν Ἐφέσῳ (to the saints who are in Ephesus). 'Some scribes however remembered that the original letter had no geographical reference and so when they copied it they simply omitted the reference to Ephesus, thus creating the text of Vaticanus.'[94] In view of the manuscript tradition, this suggestion too remains, of course, only a speculation.

To be sure, the reception of the Letter to the Colossians (see below

---

[90] Cf. Dibelius, *Epheserbrief* 56–57; Schnackenburg, *Ephesians* 39–42. Gnilka, *Epheserbrief* 5–7; Lindemann, 'Anlaß des Epheserbriefes' 238–239, argue for the originality of ἐν Ἐφέσῳ as a fictive address.

[91] Moreover, in 𝔓⁴⁶ the article τοῖς is missing before οὖσιν.

[92] So Dibelius, *Epheserbrief* 56–57; Schnackenburg, *Ephesians* 40–41, who translates τοῖς οὖσιν as an idiomatic expression meaning 'there, at that time.'

[93] Cf. Ernest Best, 'Ephesians 1.1 Again,' in *Paul and Paulism* (FS C.K. Barrett), eds. Morna D. Hooker and Stephen G. Wilson (London: SPCK, 1982) 273–279. Older theories are reviewed by Schnackenburg, *Ephesians* 40–41.

[94] Best, 'Ephesians 1.1 Again' 278.

5.3.7) makes it clear that Ephesians was directed to Christians in the province of Asia. 'Since Ephesus was the capital of the province of Asia and was a Pauline center (*sedes Pauli*), one must presuppose that the most important group that the Letter to the Ephesians would in fact reach was the church in Ephesus.'[95]

The situation of the churches addressed is obviously characterized by tensions between Jewish Christians and Gentile Christians. The readers of the letter are directly addressed in 2.11, 3.1 and 4.17 as Gentile Christians, and their relation to Jewish Christians is both the sole content of the instruction in Eph. 2.11–22, and one of the major themes of the letter as a whole. Ephesians outlines the concept of a church of Gentile and Jewish Christians that together form the one body of Christ. The author is thereby reacting to a parallel development in the churches of Asia Minor: Jewish Christians already represent a minority and Gentile Christians no longer regard them as equal partners.[96] Against this, Ephesians attempts 'to prevent a decision that makes being a Christian impossible for the Jew as a Jew.'[97]

The religio-cultural situation in Ephesus was determined by local cults, mystery religions, and the all-overriding presence of the Artemis cult with its variety of practices (including magic).[98] The prominent emphasis on the power of God or Christ in Eph. 1.15–23; 3.14–19, 20–21; 6.10–20 is probably to be understood against the background of this religious environment and points to the religious insecurities of many new members of the community. Ephesians proclaims to them: God's power stands over the demonic principalities and powers, the lords of darkness and the spiritual forces of evil in the heavenly places (cf. Eph. 6.12).[99]

5.3.5 *Outline, Structure, Form*

1.1–2	Prescript	
1.3–14	1st thanksgiving	— Introduction
1.15–23	2nd thanksgiving	

---

[95] Pokorný, *Epheserbrief* 37.

[96] Cf. Fischer, *Tendenz und Absicht* 79–94.

[97] *Ibid.* 93.

[98] On the Artemis cult cf. Winfried Elliger, *Ephesos* (see above 2.2.2) 113–136; Arnold, *Power and Magic* 20ff. On the debate between Christianity and the Artemis cult, cf. especially Richard Oster, 'The Ephesian Artemis as an Opponent of Early Christianity,' JAC 19 (1976) 24–44. Cf. further Peter Lampe, 'Acta 19 im Spiegel der ephesischen Inschriften,' BZ 36 (1992) 59–76; G. H. R. Horsley, 'The Inscriptions of Ephesos and the New Testament,' NT 34 (1992) 105–168.

[99] Cf. Arnold, *Power and Magic* 122.

2.1–3.21	PART ONE	
2.1–10	The believers' 'once' and 'now'	
2.11–22	The church of Jews and Gentiles	
3.1–13	The apostle as minister of the mystery of revelation	
3.14–21	Intercession and doxology	— Body
4.1–6.9	PART TWO	
4.1–16	Admonition to realize the unity of the body of Christ	
4.17–24	The old and new humanity	
4.25–5.20	Individual admonitions	
5.21–6.9	The household code [Haustafel]	

6.10–20	Concluding parenesis	
6.21–22	Recommendation of Tychicus	— Conclusion
6.23–24	Final farewell [Eschatokoll]	

In its macrostructure Ephesians agrees with Colossians and several of the authentic Pauline letters: two major sections, a didactic unit followed by a parenetic one. At the same time there are also significant differences. One notable feature is the doubled proemium at the letter's beginning, with only the second leading into the real theme of the letter (cf. Eph. 1.15–23). While the first major section of Colossians is only adopted selectively by Ephesians (the exceptions being Col. 1.1–2, 2.15–29), Ephesians makes extensive use of the parenesis in Colossians 3.5–4.6. The letter concludes with an almost complete absence of greetings, travel plans, or personal reports. This underscores the timeless character of Ephesians, which is no occasional writing, but can be described as a circular letter to the Pauline churches in Asia Minor. Other classifications include 'didactic theological writing,'[100] 'wisdom speech,'[101] 'meditation,'[102] 'liturgical homily,'[103] 'theological tractate'[104] 'epistolary prayer.'[105]

---

[100] Cf. Mußner, 'Epheserbrief' 743.

[101] Cf. Schlier, *Epheserbrief* 21.

[102] Cf. Marxsen, *Introduction* 198.

[103] Cf. Gnilka, *Epheserbrief* 33.

[104] Cf. Andreas Lindemann, *Paulus im ältesten Christentum* (see above 5) 41; Georg Strecker, *History of New Testament Literature* (see above 2.1) 48–49.

[105] Cf. Luz, 'Überlegungen zum Epheserbrief' 386.

5.3.6 Literary Integrity

The literary integrity of Ephesians is uncontested. The possibility of glosses should, however, be considered in Eph. 2.5b and 2.8–9. The notable elements here are the direct shift from the first person plural to the second person plural and the independence of the content from the context in both sections.[106]

5.3.7 Traditions, Sources

The author of Ephesians obviously used Colossians as a direct source, as can be seen from the numerous agreements between the two letters.[107]

(1) *Contacts in macrostructure*: Ephesians and Colossians not only have in common the bipartite structure of a didactic and a parenetic part, but agreements are found also in the prescript and the conclusion. Only in Colossians and Ephesians are the recipients addressed as ἅγιοι and πιστοὶ ἐν Χριστῷ ᾿Ιησοῦ (holy and faithful in Christ Jesus). The concluding words of each letter that speak of the sending of Tychicus (Eph. 6.21–22/ Col. 4.7–8) are practically identical. One can also perceive clear agreements in the requests for prayer in Eph. 6.18–10/Col. 4.2–3. Finally, the structure of the sections Eph. 5.19–6.9/ Col. 3.16–4.1 is strikingly similar: the comparable instructions for worship (Eph. 5.19–20/Col. 3.16–17) is in each case followed by the household code. Instructions on the relations of wives to husbands, children to fathers and slaves to masters are treated in the same order, and these are the only two cases where these three groups appears in just this way.

(2) *Contacts in language and themes*: Eph. 1.6–7/Col. 1.13–14; Eph. 1.10/Col. 1.20 ; Eph. 1.13/Col. 1.5; Eph. 1.15–16/Col. 1.3–4; Eph. 1.20/ Col. 2.12; 3.1; Eph. 2.1–6/Col. 2.12–13; Eph. 3.3–5/Col. 1.26; Eph. 3.1–13/Col. 1.23–28; Eph. 4.22–24/Col. 3.9–10. To be noted in addition is the fact that in the ethical section comparable virtues (Eph. 4.2–3/Col. 3.12–14; Eph. 4.32/Col. 3.12–13) and vices (Eph. 4.19/Col. 3.1; Eph. 4.31/Col. 3.8) appear.

(3) *Agreements in brief expressions*: ἀμώμους κατενώπιον αὐτοῦ (blameless before him) (cf. Eph. 1.4/Col. 1.22); πλοῦτος τῆς δόξης (glorious riches) (cf. Eph. 1.18; 3.16/Col. 1.27). So also there is a comparable

---

[106] On this point cf. Hans Hübner, 'Glossen in Epheser 2,' in *Vom Urchristentum zu Jesus* (FS J. Gnilka), eds. Hubert Frankemölle and Karl Kertelge (Freiburg: Herder, 1989) 392–406.

[107] Cf. the tabulations in Dibelius, *Epheserbrief* 83–85; C. Leslie Mitton, *The Epistle to the Ephesians* (Oxford: Clarendon Press, 1951) 280–318; Gnilka, *Epheserbrief* 7–13; Lindemann, *Aufhebung der Zeit* 44–48; Schnackenburg, *Ephesians* 30–33; Pokorný, *Epheserbrief* 3–5; Schenke and Fischer, *Einleitung* 1.181–186.

formulation of the way the powers are described in Eph. 1.21/Col. 1.16 and in the theme of circumcision in Eph. 2.11/Col. 2.11.

(4) *Agreements in terminology with difference in the ideas concerned*: Eph. 4.16/Col. 2.19; Eph. 1.9; 3.5, 9ff./Col. 1.26; 2.2; 4.3; Eph. 2.16/ Col. 1.20, 22; Eph. 3.2/Col. 1.25.

The author of Ephesians did not use Colossians in a schematic way. Rather, he adopted only those ideas that he could make serviceable to his own concerns. In addition to Colossians, the author of Ephesians also probably used the Corinthian letters (cf. Eph. 1.22a/1 Cor. 15.27; Eph. 1.3–4/2 Cor. 1.3–5; Eph. 6.19–20/2 Cor. 5.19–20) and Romans (Eph. 4.1–16/Rom. 12).[108]

The author of Ephesians integrated early Christian liturgical traditions into his composition. Such elements of tradition may possibly be seen in Eph. 1.3–14; 1.20–23; 2.4–10; 2.14–18; 2.19–22; 5.14. The existence, delimitation, and reconstruction of such traditional units is naturally vigorously debated, with a certain consensus manifest only for Eph. 2.4–10 and 5.14ab, which are rightly seen as baptismal tradition.[109] The ethical part of the letter is strongly influenced by parenetic traditions principally from Hellenistic Judaism (via Hellenistic Jewish Christianity) (cf. Eph. 4.17–19; 4.22–24; 5.3–6; 5.22–6.9; 6.11–17).

5.3.8 History-of-religions Standpoint

Ephesians exhibits a complex background from the point of view of the history of religion. Concepts such as πλήρωμα (fulness) (Eph. 1.10, 23; 3.19; 4.13), ἄνθρωπος (humanity) (cf. Eph. 2.15; 3.5, 16; 4.8, 14, 24; 5.31; 6.7), τέλειος ἀνήρ (mature human being) (Eph. 4.13), μεσότοιχον τοῦ φραγμοῦ (dividing wall) (Eph. 2.14) need explanation, just as is the case with such imagery as the church as the body of Christ (cf. Eph. 1.22–23; 2.14c; 2.21; 4.3–4; 4.12, 15; 5.23), as the bride of Christ (cf. 5.21–23), as the fulness of Christ (cf. Eph. 1.23; 3.19; 4.10, 13), and the body of Christ as a heavenly building (Eph. 2.20–22). The present eschatology of Ephesians (cf. Eph. 1.20–23; 2.6–8; 5.14) could be elements of a gnostic understanding of human existence. Finally, in contrast to Colossians, Ephesians is not directed against a particular false teaching, which makes even more difficult the determination of the standpoint of the author as he

---

[108] Cf. Gnilka, *Epheserbrief* 22; Andreas Lindemann, *Paulus im ältesten Christentum* (see above 5) 122–130 (literary contacts only with 1 Corinthians); Pokorný, *Epheserbrief* 15–21 (Ephesians rooted in the Pauline school tradition).

[109] For history of research and the methodological problems involved, cf. H. Merkel, 'Epheserbrief' 3222–3237.

both adopts the religious influences of his environment and distinguishes himself from them.

Under these circumstances the assessment of Ephesians in terms of the history of religion has resulted in quite different evaluations. Among those who see the influence of gnosticism are H. Schlier, E. Käsemann, P. Pokorný, H. Conzelmann, A. Lindemann and, in a modified form, K. M. Fischer.[110] An Old Testament and Jewish background (Qumran) is assumed by K. G. Kuhn and F. Mußner.[111] Ephesians is seen as standing in the line of tradition deriving from Hellenistic Judaism by H. Hegermann, C. Colpe, E. Schweizer, J. Gnilka und R. Schnackenburg.[112]

Comparable ideas to those in Ephesians are found in the literature of both Hellenistic Judaism and gnosticism. However, parallels from Hellenistic Judaism, in contrast to those from gnosticism, have a dimension that is in principle to be preferred to those from gnosticism, namely that of temporal priority. Thus the cosmic dimensions of the concept of the 'body of Christ' by no means necessarily point to gnosticism. In Philo too the cosmos appears as a body, whose head is the Logos (cf. Fug, 108–113, QuaestEx. 2.117). The cosmos is described as τέλειος ἄνθρωπος (mature human being) (*Migr.* 220; cf. Eph. 4.13), as a 'gigantic human form' (*RerDivHer.* 155), as the 'most perfectly fulfilled living being' (*SpecLeg.* 1.210–211), and as 'son of God' (*SpecLeg.* 1.96). Philo also has the imagery of the divine energy that permeates the universe, comparable to the πλήρωμα concept (fulness) of Ephesians and also associated with the image of the macro-anthropos (*VitMos.* 2.132–133; *QuaestEx.* 2.68; 120; *QuaestGen.* 4.130).[113] The concept of the church as a building in Eph. 2.20–22 has contacts with an image widespread in ancient Judaism. In particular, the Qumran community understood itself as the building, temple, dwelling place of God (cf. 1QS 5.5; 8.7, 8; 1QH 6.26–27; 7.8–9 and often).[114] It is not, however, a matter of direct dependence. Despite all the differences, Ephesians is still oriented to Paul, for whom Christ is the only

---

[110] Cf. Schlier, *Christus und die Kirche* 74–75; Ernst Käsemann, *Leib und Leib Christi* (see above 5.2.1) 145 and often; Pokorný, *Epheserbrief und Gnosis* 82ff. (with more hesitation in *Epheserbrief* 22–24); Conzelmann, *Epheserbrief* 87; Lindemann, *Epheserbrief* 121; Fischer, *Tendenz und Absicht* 173–200.

[111] Cf. Kuhn, 'Der Epheserbrief im Lichte der Qumrantexte' 334–346; Franz Mußner, 'Beiträge aus Qumran zum Verständnis des Epheserbriefes,' in *Neutestamentliche Aufsätze* (FS J. Schmid) (Regensburg: Pustet, 1963) 185–198.

[112] Cf. Harald Hegermann, 'Zur Ableitung der Leib-Christi-Vorstellung im Epheserbrief,' ThLZ 85 (1960) 839–842; Colpe, 'Leib-Christi-Vorstellung im Epheserbrief' 178ff.; Eduard Schweizer, 'Die Kirche als Leib Christi in den paulinischen Antilegomena,' in *Neotestamentica*, ed. E. Schweizer (Zürich: Zwingli Verlag, 1963) 293–316; Gnilka, *Epheserbrief* 33–45; Schnackenburg, *Ephesians* 36.

[113] Cf. Harald Hegermann, *Vorstellung vom Schöpfungsmittler* (see above 5.2.7) 58ff., 106ff.

[114] Cf. Mußner, *Epheserbrief* 89ff.

foundation for the church (1 Cor. 3.11) and the community itself the building (1 Cor. 3.9), the Spirit-filled temple of God (1 Cor. 3.16–17). The idea
of the growth of the body (Eph. 2.21–22; 4.12, 15–16) goes back to Col.
2.19. As the foundation and head of the building, Christ is also the goal of
its growth, because he fills the building with his δύναμις (power). The
image of the church as the bride of Christ (Eph. 5.21–33) in any case does
not point to gnostic influences,[115] but is adapted from Old Testament
imagery (cf. Hos. 1–3; Ezek. 16; Jer. 2.2; Isa. 62.5). Moreover, in 2 Cor.
11.2 Paul sees himself as the attendant to the bride who has arranged the
engagement of the church to Christ. An ecclesiological extension of Col.
1.19; 2.9–10 is seen when the church is spoken of as the fullness of the one
who fills all things (cf. especially Eph. 1.22–23). The views of the Stoics,
Philo, or gnosticism cannot explain what is distinctive in the pleroma concept in Ephesians: the church is the sphere in which the fullness of Christ
that encompasses the universe is in fact effective and powerful.

Neither does the breaking down of the dividing wall and the creation of
the new humanity in Eph. 2.14–16 point to a gnostic background. Rather,
it is the Torah that is here seen as the 'dividing wall' (2.15a; cf. Arist. 139!),
whose divisive effects in the one church of Jews and Gentiles have been
overcome.[116]

The descent and ascent of the redeemer in Eph. 4.9–10 do seem to lead
into the proximity of gnostic ideas. There are, however, considerable
differences, for the whole line of argument is indebted to the christological
adaptation of Ps. 68.19 in Eph. 4.8, in which again it is the image of the
ascent of the redeemer derived from the early Christian faith in the
resurrection that stands at the beginning (Eph. 4.8–9). It was only then
developed into the familiar series 'descent/ascent' from the postulated
gnostic myth.

It is not parallels from Jewish or pagan streams of tradition that are
determinative for the theology of Ephesians, but above all the Letter to the
Colossians, which sets the tone for and determines the shape of Ephesians.
This fact already excludes a monocausal location of Ephesians in the context of the history of religion. Influences of earlier (Christian) gnosticism
of course cannot be excluded, but parallels from Hellenistic Judaism and
the adoption of Pauline and deuteropauline (Colossians) ideas are sufficient
to explain the theology of Ephesians.

---

[115] Differently Fischer, *Tendenz und Absicht* 176–200, who thinks that Ephesians here has a
positive perspective on gnostic ideas, and adopts them.

[116] Cf. Mußner, *Epheserbrief* 75ff.; Schnackenburg, *Ephesians* 112–116. In contrast,
Lindemann, *Epheserbrief* 47ff., supposes that in 2.14–16 the author of Ephesians 'adopted a (non-
Christian) gnostic text' (*ibid.* 49).

5.3.9 Basic Theological Ideas

The Christology of the Letter to the Ephesians is expressed in terms of a *spatial view of the world*.[117] God, the creator of all that is, and Jesus Christ are enthroned over all in the heavenly realm, while the space between heaven and earth is ruled by aeons, angels, and demonic powers, and the world of human beings and the dead constitutes the lowest realm. At the same time, Jesus Christ fills all reality, which Ephesians bring pregnantly to expression with the phrase τὰ πάντα (cf. 1.10, 11, 23; 3.9; 4.10, 15).

Within the framework of this picture of the world the author of Ephesians develops his Christology of exaltation and lordship. The resurrected Christ sits at the right hand of God (Eph. 1.20; cf. 4.8, 10a). God has placed all things under his feet, corresponding to his eternal counsel (Eph. 1.10, 22a), and he fills the universe with the fullness of his life (Eph. 1.23; 4.10b). Christ is the head of the church, towering above all things (cf. Eph. 1.22b; 5.23), who has included the church in his cosmic status. As the σῶμα Χριστοῦ (body of Christ) the church is the realm of salvation opened up by Christ, and permeated and ruled by him (cf. Eph. 1.22–23; 2.16; 4.15–16). Just as there is no church without Christ, so there is no Christ without the church. God reveals his wisdom to the powers through the church (Eph. 3.10), and in Eph. 3.21 the church is even the object of a doxology. To be sure, the ecclesiology of Ephesians cannot be understood in the sense of an *'ecclesia triumphans;'* for the author of Ephesians it is rather a matter of the *ecclesiological relevance of the gospel*. It is true, on the one hand, that the church is already that which it should and shall be, but on the other hand its essential being is yet to be revealed. That is indicated in the metaphor of growth and is made concrete in the way in which Ephesians portrays the relationship of Jewish Christians and Gentile Christians. By Christ's own deed of reconciliation the opposition between Jews and Gentiles was abolished (cf. Eph. 2.11–13 and 2.19–20); the Law as the boundary between the two realms has lost its divisive significance. Christ is the redeemer of the church (cf. Eph. 5.23), so that in Ephesians ecclesiology must be understood as a function of soteriology.

Closely associated with ecclesiology is the concept of tradition filled in by the figure of Paul. The grace made known through Paul has torn down the wall of separation between Jews and Gentiles (cf. Eph. 3.3, 6) and makes possible the one universal church, whose dimensions are reflected on and developed. Christ is the cornerstone of the church that is built on the foundation of the apostles and prophets (Eph. 2.20). Thus the apostolic

---

[117] Cf. the outline in Lindemann, *Epheserbrief* 122.

tradition, guaranteed by Paul, appears as the norm for the connection to Christ.

In Ephesians the perfect tense is consistently transferred to the eschatological realities: just as Christ has already attained the victory (cf. Eph. 1.20–23), so the elect church already finds itself in the present sphere of salvation (cf. Eph. 1.5, 9, 11, 19; 2.10; 3.11). In baptism, believers are already saved by grace (Eph. 2.5, 6, 8), risen and set in the heavenly places (Eph. 2.6). As fellow citizens with the saints and members of the household of God (Eph. 2.19) they already share completely in the redemption through Christ's blood (cf. Eph. 1.7). The clear shift in comparison with Paul's own eschatology is seen in the way temporal categories recede and spatial ones come to the fore. The tension between present and future loses its importance, so that now the contrast between above and below becomes dominant. The spatially oriented theology of Colossians, the hymnic traditions (prayers: Eph. 1.3–23; 3.14–19; 6.18–20; doxology: Eph. 3.14–19) and the experience of the presence of salvation in the sacraments leads in Ephesians to a theology in which it is not the future that determines the present, but the present that determines the future. What is to be in the future is already fully revealed in the present. In this conception of things the problem of the delay of the parousia no longer arises. This present eschatology of Ephesians does not, however, simply abolish the importance of time and history in general. Ephesians does not advocate a timeless ontology of the church. Thus the baptized are challenged to resist the oppressive powers 'on the evil day' (Eph. 6.13). The coming judgment is a motivation for parenesis (Eph. 6.8), idolaters will not inherit the kingdom of God (Eph. 5.5), for the wrath of God is coming on the disobedient (Eph. 5.6). So too the coming aeon stands under the lordship of Christ (Eph. 1.21b). Ephesians reminds Christians of their hope (Eph. 1.18; 4.4) and speaks of the day of redemption (Eph. 4.30) for which they are sealed. Believers are to redeem the present time (Eph. 5.16) for it is the final time. As for Paul (2 Cor. 1.21, 5.5; Rom. 8.23) so too for Ephesians the Spirit is the deposit paid on future redemption (Eph. 1.13–14; 4.30). As the body of Christ, the church is subject to a process of growth and maturity (cf. Eph. 2.21–22; 3.19; 4.13, 16) that includes a perspective on the future.

In Ephesians a persistent ethical interest is articulated, and the extensive parenetic sections of Colossians are taken over (cf. Col. 3.5–4.6) by the author. To the foundational ethical instructions in Eph. 4.1–16 is added a sharp critique of the pagan manner of life (cf. Eph. 4.17–5.20). This way of life is the result of abandoning God, for as the pagans stand before God they find themselves in the situation of alienation (Eph. 4.18). In contrast the Christians follow the teaching of their Lord (Eph. 4.20–21) in which they are instructed. This doctrine of Christ agrees with the interpretation of the Christian faith as it appears in Ephesians.

5.3.10 *Tendencies of Recent Research*

The pseudepigraphical character of Ephesians and its literary dependence on Colossians are widely acknowledged. At the center of recent discussion stands the question of the particular situation to which Ephesians was directed. A. Lindemann proceeds on the basis that Ephesians is not related to any particular history or situation. He wishes to confirm the dehistoricization of the thought of Ephesians especially with regard to its eschatology which in his view almost completely eliminates the future dimension. He considers this to be the influence of gnosticism, which he believes influenced not only Ephesians' eschatology but the theology of the letter as a whole. 'For Ephesians, time and history are "in Christ" – that means for this theology: in the church – abolished. From such a present every future is cancelled.'[118] In contrast to this F. Mußner and H. E. Lona emphasize that in Ephesians the importance of time and history is by no means abolished, that rather here the future appears as an 'epiphany of the present.'[119] K.-M. Fischer imbeds Ephesians in a very concrete historical situation. Ephesians is combatting the introduction of an episcopal church structure, so that 'for him the apostles and prophets continue to be the only foundation of the church, as they have ever been.'[120] Documentation for this thesis is provided by Eph. 4.11, which makes no distinction between present offices (evangelists, pastors and teachers) and offices of the past (apostles and prophets). 'Exegetically there is thus only one possibility: for Ephesians the apostles and prophets continue to be the essential church officers, to which he emphatically holds fast.'[121] Alongside the question of church offices, Fischer's analysis regards the other issue that shapes the thought of Ephesians to be the relation of Jewish Christians and Gentile Christians. Against the background of an increasingly sharp anti-Judaism among Gentile Christians, Ephesians advocates the equality of the Jewish Christian inheritance within the one body of Christ. 'The thesis of Ephesians is clear and unambiguous: Israel is God's people and has its

---

[118] Lindemann, *Aufhebung der Zeit* 248.

[119] Cf. Mußner, *Epheserbrief* 28–30; Horacio E. Lona, *Eschatologie* (see above 5.2.1) 241ff. Lona speaks of an 'ecclesiological eschatology' in Ephesians. 'The presence and futurity of salvation is spoken of only in connection with the reality of the church' (*ibid.* 442). Moreover, Eph 1.13–14; 4.30 show 'that the emphasis on the presence of salvation does not stand in contrast to the future fulfillment of salvation' (*ibid.* 427).

[120] Fischer, *Tendenz und Absicht* 33.

[121] *Ibid.* 38.

covenant promises; the Gentiles have nothing. That is its point of departure. But since the unimaginable miracle has happened, that Christ has broken down the wall between Gentiles and Jews, the Law with its commandments, he has provided the Gentiles access to God in the one church (2.11ff.).'[122] So here too Ephesians stands against the tendencies that were beginning to permeate the church in Asia Minor. F. Mußner interprets Ephesians as directed to a completely different front. He derives the head and body ecclesiology from the political philosophy of the time. Since in these texts (e.g. in the fable of Menenius Agrippa) the subject is the undivided lordship of the emperor (= head) over the Roman Empire (= body), Ephesians' body Christology presents an opposing picture. The claim to the cosmic rule of Jesus Christ stands here intentionally in contrast to the Caesar cult. 'It appears that especially the Christianity of Asia Minor had a predeliction for understanding the presence of salvation, in particular with regard to Christology, more precisely the Christus Pantocrator. This Christology appears to have been intentionally directed against the Caesar cult that flourished especially in Asia Minor.'[123] So too H. E. Lona sees a social relevance to the concept of the church as the body of Christ: 'The universal dimension of the church corresponds to the cosmopolitan openness of the citizens of the Roman Empire.'[124]

The location of Ephesians in the context of the history of religion remains disputed. While Andreas Lindemann, Karl-Martin Fischer and Petr Pokorný in very different ways continue to reckon with gnostic influence, a growing number see the views that come to expression in Ephesians as rooted in the Old Testament and/or Hellenistic Judaism (Mußner, Schnackenburg, Gnilka).

The focal point of interest has returned in recent years to Ephesians' picture of Paul. H. Merklein emphasizes the normative function of Paul for the letter's understanding of tradition. The apostles and prophets form the foundation and norm for what is Christian, that now is dependent no longer on the deceitful trickery of human beings (Eph. 4.14). Because the apostle is the ambassador of the mystery of the gospel (Eph. 6.20), this mystery can appropriately be proclaimed by him alone. The recourse to Paul and the pseudepigraphical character of Ephesians associated with it thus necessarily results from the picture of Paul mediated in the letter.

---

[122] *Ibid.* 80.
[123] Mußner, 'Epheserbrief' 747.
[124] Lona, *Eschatologie* 444.

5.4 The Second Letter to the Thessalonians

5.4.1 Literature

Commentaries

Dibelius, Martin. *An die Thessalonicher I–II. An die Philipper*, HNT 11. Tübingen: J. C. B. Mohr (Paul Siebeck), 1937³, 39–58; Dobschütz, Ernst v. *Die Thessalonicherbriefe*, KEK 10. Göttingen: Vandenhoeck & Ruprecht, 1909 (= 1974); Friedrich, Gerhard. *Die Briefe an die Galater, Epheser, Philipper, Kolosser, Thessalonicher und Philemon*, NTD 8. Göttingen: Vandenhoeck & Ruprecht, 1976, 252–276; Trilling, Wolfgang. *Der zweite Brief an die Thessalonicher*, EKK 14. Neukirchen: Neukirchener Verlag, 1980; Bruce, F. F. *1 & 2 Thessalonians*, WBC 45. Dallas: Word Books, 1982; Marxsen, Willi. *Der zweite Thessalonicherbrief*, ZBK 11. 2. Zürich: Theologischer Verlag, 1982; Marshall, I. Howard. *1 & 2 Thessalonians*, NCeB. London: Grand Rapids: Wm. B. Eerdmans, 1983; Wanamaker, C. A. *The Epistles to the Thessalonians*, NIGTC. Grand Rapids: Eerdmans, 1990.

Monographs

Wrede, William. *Die Echtheit des zweiten Thessalonicherbriefes*. Leipzig: Hinrichs, 1903. Trilling, Wolfgang. *Untersuchungen zum zweiten Thessalonicherbrief*, EThSt 27. Leipzig: St. Benno, 1972; Jewett, Robert. *The Thessalonian Correspondence* (see above 2. 4. 1); Holland, Glen S. *The Tradition That You Have Received from Us: 2 Thessalonians in the Pauline Tradition*, HUTh 24. Tübingen: J. C. B. Mohr (Paul Siebeck), 1988; Hughes, Frank W. *Early Christian Rhetoric and 2 Thessalonians*, JSNT. S 30. Sheffield: Sheffield Academic Press, 1989; Donfried Karl P. 'The theology of 2 Thessalonians,' in *The Theology of the Shorter Pauline Letters* (see above 2. 4. 1) 81–113.

Articles

Braun, Herbert. 'Zur nachpaulinischen Herkunft des zweiten Thessalonicherbriefes,' in *Gesammelte Studien zum NT und seiner Umwelt*, ed. H. Braun. Tübingen: J. C. B. Mohr (Paul Siebeck) 1962, 205–209; Lindemann, Andreas. 'Zum Abfassungszweck des zweiten Thessalonicherbriefes,' ZNW 68 (1977) 35–47; Bailey, John A. 'Who wrote II Thessalonians?' NTS 25 (1978/79) 131–145; Trilling, Wolfgang. 'Literarische Paulusimitation im 2. Thessalonicherbrief,' in *Paulus in den ntl. Spätschriften*, ed. Karl Kertelge (see above 5) 146–156; Collins, Raymond F. *The Thessalonian Correspondence*, BETL 87, ed. R. F. Collins. Leuven: Leuven University Press, 1990, 373–515 (important articles on 2 Thess.!).

History of Research

Trilling, Wolfgang. 'Die beiden Briefe des Apostels Paulus an die Thessalonicher,' *ANRW* 25. 4. Berlin: Walter de Gruyter, 1987, 3365–3403.

5.4.2 *Author*

The Pauline authorship of 2 Thessalonians has been disputed since the beginning of the nineteenth century.[125] Ferdinand Christian Baur adopted the objections that had already been made (literary dependence on 1 Thessalonians, unpauline ideas and expressions, weighty differences in eschatology), and on the basis of their lack of independent content declared both Thessalonian letters to be inauthentic.[126] The discussion was placed on a new basis by William Wrede, who in his 1903 study of the authenticity of 2 Thessalonians made the literary relationship between the two letters into the key to the question of authorship. Wrede presented an extremely detailed argument that is today still convincing evidence that the author of 2 Thessalonians used 1 Thessalonians as a literary model and source. The literary dependence of 2 Thessalonians on 1 Thessalonians continues to be a primary argument for the *pseudepigraphical* character of 2 Thessalonians (see below 5.4.7).

A fundamental difference exists between the eschatological instructions in 1 Thess. 4.13–18; 5.1–11 and 2 Thess. 2.1–12; 1.5–10.[127] The eschatology of 1 Thessalonians is characterized by the immediate expectation of the imminent parousia, which forms the central element of all Paul's eschatological affirmations through the writing of Philippians (cf. Phil. 4.5b). In 2 Thess. 2.2 the author turns against the motto ἐνέστηκεν ἡ ἡμέρα τοῦ κυρίου (the day of the Lord is at hand/already here) and outlines a schedule of the final events that cannot be harmonized with the portrayal in 1 Thessalonians. In 1 Thess. 4.13–18 the spotlight is on the coming of the Lord and the taking up of all Christians into the clouds. The goal of the eschatological event is expressed as σὺν κυρίῳ εἶναι (to be with the Lord) (1 Thess. 4.17).

A completely different course of events is presented by 2 Thess. 2.1–12. Before the parousia of Christ, the ἄνθρωπος τῆς ἀνομίας (man of lawlessness) must first appear (2 Thess. 2.3), who will put himself in God's place as the counterpart and opponent of God (2 Thess. 2.4). The full epiphany of this opponent has not of course yet occurred (2 Thess. 2.6–7), but nonetheless he is already at work in the present and misleads the unbelievers. The adversary will remain (see below 5.4.8), until Christ destroys him at the parousia, and those who have persisted in unbelief will be judged. Both the problem of the delay of the parousia (2 Thess. 2.6–7) and the advent of an eschatological adversary distinguish 2 Thess. 2.1–2

---

[125] For the history of research, cf. Trilling, *Untersuchungen* 11–45.

[126] Cf. Ferdinand C. Baur, *Paul, the Apostle of Jesus Christ* (see above 5.2.2.) 2.94, 341ff.

[127] Cf. on this point Peter Müller, *Anfänge der Paulusschule* (see above 5) 20–67.

fundamentally from 1 Thess. 4.13–18; 5.1–11. While 1 Thess. 5.1 explicitly rejects calculations of the time of the parousia, in 2 Thess. 2.1–12 we have a schedule of eschatological events that not only permits, but requires such observations and calculations (cf. v. 5!). While in Paul the appearance of the Resurrected One stands at the center (cf. 1 Thess. 4.16; 1 Cor. 15.23), the spotlight in 2 Thess. 2.8 is on the destruction of the antichrist. While the tension between 'already' and 'not yet' is typical for Pauline eschatology, for 2 Thess. the characteristic structure of the argument is 'not now – but in the future.'

Although the author of the second letter made use of 1 Thessalonians, there are still peculiarities in language and style.[128] That there are seventeen expressions in 2 Thessalonians that occur nowhere else in the New Testament is very revealing.[129] In contrast to the undisputed Pauline letters, 2 Thessalonians lacks antithetical formulations, passages in the style of the diatribe, and (with the exception of 2 Thess. 2.5) real questions. Differently from the lively, sometimes abrupt argument of Paul's letters, 2 Thessalonians appears as a didactic composition with a narrowly limited theme. The manner of expression is flavored by 42 words and expressions repeated twice or more.[130] In summary it may be said: "The use of words, stylistic peculiarities and the train of thought must be seen together. Typical ideas, words, and expressions point to a more developed situation in doctrine and forms of Christian life than is seen in 1 Thessalonians and all the other undisputed Pauline letters.'[131] Among those who consider 2 Thessalonians to be deuteropauline are Alfred Jülicher and Erich Fascher, Herbert Braun, Wolfgang Trilling, Eduard Lohse, Willi Marxsen, Philipp Vielhauer, Helmut Koester, Andreas Lindemann, G. S. Holland, Frank W. Hughes and Peter Müller.[132] The following regard the letter as written by Paul: Erich v. Dobschütz, Martin Dibelius, Beda Rigaux, Werner Georg Kümmel and F. F. Bruce.[133] Walter Schmithals also considers the

---

[128] Cf. Trilling, *Untersuchungen* 46–66.

[129] *Ibid.* 49.

[130] *Ibid.* 62.

[131] *Ibid.* 66.

[132] Cf. Jülicher and Fascher, *Einleitung* 67; Herbert Braun, 'Zur nachpaulinischen Herkunft des zweiten Thessalonicherbriefe' 205–209; Trilling, *2 Thessalonicherbrief* 27–28; Lohse, *Formation* 86–87; Marxsen, *2 Thessalonicherbrief* 9ff.; Vielhauer, *Urchristliche Literatur* 99; Koester, *Introduction* 2.242; Andreas Lindemann, *Paulus im ältesten Christentum* (see above 5) 130ff.; Holland, *2 Thessalonians in the Pauline Tradition* 129; Hughes, *Early Christian Rhetoric* 95; Peter Müller, *Anfänge der Paulusschule* (see above 5) 5–13.

[133] Cf. Von Dobschütz, *Thessalonicherbriefe* 32–47; Dibelius, *2 Thessalonicherbrief* 40–41; Beda Rigaux, *Les Épîtres aux Thessaloniciens*, EtB. (Paris – Gembloux: J. Gabalda, 1956) 112–152; Kümmel, *Introduction* 260–262 (but cf. 5.5.2 note 16!); Bruce, *1–2 Thessalonians* xxxii–xxxiii, 141–142: the authors are Paulus, Silvanus and Timothy, but the content of the whole is considered to be from Paul.

letter to be genuine, but connects this conclusion with hypotheses concerning both Thessalonian letters pertaining to their literary integrity (see above 2.4.6) and the presumed history of religion context (see below 5.4.8). Robert Jewett votes for the authenticity of 2 Thessalonians, but at the same time notes that the letter 'must be placed in a category of "probably Pauline".'[134] Whether the unknown author of 2 Thessalonians belonged to the Pauline school in the narrow sense must remain an open question,[135] since there is no passage that can be considered a creative adoption or development of Pauline theology.

5.4.3 *Place and Time of Composition*

The external attestation of 2 Thessalonians (Marcion, *PolyPhil* 11.3–4[?][136]) does not make an exact dating possible. In terms of internal criteria, the problem of the delay of the parousia points to the *end of the first century* CE, with a comparable theme being found in 2 Pet. 3.1–13.[137] An early dating, but with the presupposition of the pseudepigraphical character of the document, is advocated by Otto Merk.[138] According to this view, the letter would have been written as a contemporizing of the message of 1 Thessalonians still in the lifetime of the apostle Paul, or very soon after his death.

The advocates of the authenticity of 2 Thessalonians mostly date the letter in the immediate proximity of 1 Thessalonians. Thus W. G. Kümmel supposes that Paul wrote 2 Thessalonians 'a few weeks after he had written I Thess., when the first letter was still fresh in his mind.'[139] The letter will then have been composed in 50 or 51 CE, from Corinth.[140] Of course, with this presupposition it can hardly be explained why Paul deviates so strongly from 1 Thess. 4.13–18 in the portrayal of the eschatological events and does not go into the problem of those who have died before the parousia. Those who contest the authenticity of 2 Thessalonians cannot, in the nature of the case, precisely name a place of

---

[134] Jewett, *Thessalonian Correspondence* 17.

[135] Trilling, *2 Thessalonicherbrief* 27, expresses the opinion that the author did not belong to the Pauline school.

[136] According to Lindemann, 'Abfassungszweck' 42; Trilling, *2 Thessalonicherbrief* 27–28, there is probably no citation from 2 Thessalonians in Polycarp.

[137] 2 Thessalonians is dated in the last years of the first century by e.g., Trilling, *2 Thessalonicherbrief* 28; Marxsen, *Introduction* 44; Bailey, 'Who wrote II Thessalonians?' 143; Andreas Lindemann, *Paulus im ältesten Christentum* (see above 5) 133.

[138] Cf. Ernst Würthwein and Otto Merk. *Verantwortung* (Stuttgart: Kohlhammer, 1982) 153.

[139] Kümmel, *Introduction* 268; similarly Bruce, *1–2 Thessalonians* xxxv.

[140] Bruce also votes for Corinth, *ibid.*

composition, though Asia Minor or Macedonia are the places most frequently named.

5.4.4 Intended Readership

The questions addressed in 2 Thessalonians are not the problems of a specific local situation, but issues that extend beyond the congregation.[141] The reference to persecutions in 2 Thess. 1.4–5 tells us little about the church's situation, since both their initiators and their extent remain in the dark and may possibly even be a literary reflection of the distress and persecution of 1 Thess. 1.6–7; 2.14–16; 3.3ff. The central problem of the churches addressed and the occasion of the letter appears in 2 Thess. 2.2: a prophetic announcement that the day of the parousia was already present had obviously caused confusion and uncertainty in the church. The advocates of this realized eschatology appeal to the insight given by the Spirit, to the word of the apostle, and to a (real or purported) letter of Paul (cf. 2 Thess. 2.2, 15). This affirmation that the eschatological events are already present and the reality of the Christian community in a time that continues to go on and on cannot be harmonized without some sort of contradiction that calls for a leap from the real present into some sort of eschatological fanaticism. For the writer of the letter, the old aeon continues to be with us. The day of the Lord's return is not yet here, it cannot even have dawned, for in the old aeon God's adversary continues to rule. The problematic of the delay of the parousia is to be mitigated by an outline of the eschatological events that portrays the character of the present as the continuing time in which the antichrist is at work and places the time in which the lordship of Christ will be ultimately revealed in the future.

In 2 Thess. 3.6–12 the author mentions members of the church who live disorderly, idle lives, do not work and engage in useless activities. The general nature of the statement and the parallels in 1 Thess. 5.13–14/2 Thess. 3.6, 10 permit us to assume that the background of this statement is formed by abuses occasioned and evoked by the motto of 2 Thess. 2.2.

---

[141] Cf. Trilling, *2 Thessalonicherbrief* 27.

5.4.5 Outline, Structure, Form

1.1–2	Prescript	— Introduction
1.3–12	Thanksgiving	

2.1–12	The parousia after the appearance of the antichrist	
2.13–3.5	Thanksgiving for the election of the church; admonition and intercession	— Body
3.6–15	Particular instructions	

3.16	Benediction	— Conclusion
3.17, 18	Final farewell [Eschatokoll]	

2 Thessalonians has a simple structure: the introduction is followed by the body, which has three thematic units, of which only 2 Thess. 2.1–12 has no parallel in 1 Thessalonians.[142] The writing closes with a conclusion that is literarily dependent on Paul. The new beginning with εὐχαριστέω (I give thanks) in 2 Thess. 2.13, oriented to the similar structure and terminology in 1 Thess. 2.13, is striking.[143]

In accord with its structure and content, 2 Thessalonians can be described as a general monitory and didactic composition.

5.4.6 Literary Integrity

The literary unity of 2 Thessalonians is practically uncontested.[144]

5.4.7 Traditions, Sources

1 Thessalonians served 2 Thessalonians as *model and source*. This is clear from both the parallels in the overall structure of both letters as well as from the numerous agreements in wording.[145]

---

[142] On this point cf. Maarten J. J. Menken, 'The Structure of 2 Thessalonians,' in Collins, *Thessalonian Correspondence* 373–382. Menken divides 2 Thessalonians into three approximately equal sections (apart from the introduction and conclusion): 1.3–12; 2.1–17; 3.1–16. For him the τὸ λοιπόν (remainder) of 2 Thess. 3.1 signals the beginning of the final parenesis.

[143] On this point cf. Schnider and Stenger (see above 2.3.2) 46–47.

[144] On the theses of Schmithals, see above 2.4.6.

[145] Cf. the survey in Wrede, *Echtheit* 3–36; Marxsen, *2 Thessalonicherbrief* 15–41.

(a) Agreements in structure

Prescript

1 Thess. 1.1	2 Thess. 1.1–2

First thanksgiving

1 Thess. 1.2–3	2 Thess. 1.3
1 Thess. 1.6–7	2 Thess. 1.4
1 Thess. 1, 2, 3, 4 (parts!)	2 Thess. 1.11

Second thanksgiving

1 Thess. 2.13	2 Thess. 2.13

Transition to parenesis

1 Thess. 3.11, 13	2 Thess. 2.16, 17

Requests and admonitions

1 Thess. 4.1	2 Thess. 3.1
1 Thess. 4.1	2 Thess. 3.6
1 Thess. 4.10–12	2 Thess. 3.10–12

The disorderly in the congregation

1 Thess. 5.14	2 Thess. 3.6, 7, 11

Conclusion

1 Thess. 5.23	2 Thess. 3.16
1 Thess. 5.28	2 Thess. 3.18

The comparison reveals remarkable agreements. Especially important are the parallels in the prescripts and conclusions, the second thanksgiving in each case, and the prayer request as the transition to parenesis. The parallels cannot be explained as merely coincidental, but point to literary dependence.

(b) Agreements in wording

Three central text complexes demonstrate the literary relationship of dependence.

Prescript

1 Thessalonians 1.1	2 Thessalonians 1.1, 2
Παῦλος καὶ Σιλουανὸς καὶ Τιμόθεος τῇ ἐκκλησίᾳ Θεσσαλονικέων ἐν θεῷ πατρὶ καὶ κυρίῳ Ἰησοῦ Χριστῷ, χάρις ὑμῖν καὶ εἰρήνη.	Παῦλος καὶ Σιλουανὸς καὶ Τιμόθεος τῇ ἐκκλησίᾳ Θεσσαλονικέων ἐν θεῷ πατρὶ καὶ κυρίῳ Ἰησοῦ Χριστῷ, χάρις ὑμῖν καὶ εἰρήνη . . .
(Paul, Silvanus, and Timothy, To the church of the Thessalonians in	(Paul, Silvanus, and Timothy, To the church of the Thessalonians in

God the Father and the Lord Jesus
Christ: Grace to you and peace.)

God our Father and the Lord Jesus
Christ . . .
Grace to you and peace from God
our Father and the Lord Jesus Christ
. . .)

Transition to parenesis

1 Thessalonians 3.11
Αὐτὸς δὲ ὁ θεὸς καὶ πατὴρ ἡμῶν
καὶ ὁ κύριος ἡμῶν Ἰησοῦς . . .

(Now may our God and Father
himself and our Lord Jesus direct
our way to you.)

2 Thessalonians 2.16
Αὐτὸς δὲ ὁ κύριος ἡμῶν Ἰησοῦς
Χριστὸς καὶ ὁ θεὸς ὁ πατὴρ ἡμῶν,
. . .

(Now may our Lord Jesus Christ
himself and God our Father, who
loved us and through grace gave us
eternal comfort and good hope, . . .)

Conclusion

1 Thessalonians 5.23
Αὐτὸς δὲ ὁ θεὸς τῆς εἰρήνης
(May the God of peace himself
sanctify you entirely; and may your
spirit and soul and body be kept
sound and blameless at the coming
of our Lord Jesus Christ.)

2 Thessalonians 3.16
Αὐτὸς δὲ ὁ κύριος τῆς εἰρήνης
(Now may the Lord of peace himself
give you peace at all times in all ways.
The Lord be with all of you.)

1 Thessalonians 5.28
ἡ χάρις τοῦ κυρίου ἡμῶν Ἰησοῦ
Χριστοῦ μεθ' ὑμῶν
(The grace of our Lord Jesus Christ
be with you.)

2 Thessalonians 3.18
ἡ χάρις τοῦ κυρίου ἡμῶν Ἰησοῦ
Χριστοῦ μετὰ πάντων ὑμῶν
(The grace of our Lord Jesus Christ
be with all of you.)

The author of 2 Thessalonians uses 1 Thessalonians in a twofold way as
a literary model and source: on the macro-level he structures his composition on the model of the first letter. Alongside this almost mechanical
dependence is the selective adoption of particular motifs. Thus in 1.5–10
the author of 2 Thessalonians departs from 1 Thessalonians to formulate a
section on the judgment to take place at the parousia, in order then in 1.11
again to take up themes from 1 Thess. 1.2–4. So also 2 Thess. 2.1–12 has
no counterpart in 1 Thessalonians, but in 2 Thess. 2.13 the author resumes
following his source at 1 Thess. 2.13. Only the hypothesis of the literary
dependence of 2 Thessalonians on 1 Thessalonians can adequately explain
these agreements.

5.4.8 History-of-religions Standpoint

Scholars continue to debate the setting in the history of religion of the eschatological view opposed in 2 Thessalonians: ἐνέστηκεν ἡ ἡμέρα τοῦ κυρίου (2 Thess. 2.2). Walter Schmithals derives this motto from gnostic circles, in which he understands it to refer to a spiritualizing or reinterpretation of traditional church eschatology.[146] By receiving special knowledge, the resurrection is understood to have happened already, the future day of the Lord is already here. The gnostic texts Schmithals brings forward in support of this (e.g. Irenaeus, *Haer* 1.25.5; 3.31.2; *GosThom* 51) do in fact speak of a resurrection of Christians that has already occurred, but they are all later texts than 2 Thessalonians. Moreover, 2 Thess. 2.1–12 contains no references to a gnostic false teaching,[147] but points instead to enthusiastic prophetic phenomena (cf. Mark 13.22; Mt 7.15; 24.23–24). Thus the linguistic and imagery world of 2 Thess. 2.2–3 shows clear marks of apocalyptic influence (cf. ἀποκαλύπτω [reveal] in v. 3; an intentional antithesis to the appearance of Christ in 1.7; on σαλεύω [shake] cf. Isa. 13.10; Ezek. 32.7–8; Joel 2.10; 4.15–16; 1 Enoch 102.2; Mark 13.25par, on θροέομαι [be alarmed] cf. the Synoptic apocalypse Mark 13.7; Matt. 24.6, on ἀποστασία [falling away, apostasy] cf. 1 Enoch. 93.9; Jub. 23.16ff.). Probably in their declaring that the day of the Lord was already present the early Christian prophets appealed to their gift of the Spirit and to a letter of Paul (2 Thess. 2.2), which can only refer to 1 Thessalonians.[148] In that passage Paul counted on still being alive when the Lord returned, which he expected very soon. It is possible that early Christian prophets adopted this statement of Paul, and after Paul's death concluded that what Paul had expected to live to see must in fact have already occurred. These prophets would have thought of their eschatological ideas as the consistent development of Paul's own thought, while at the same time abolishing the distinction between 'already' and 'not yet' that was fundamental for Paul. This is why the author of 2 Thessalonians consistently opposes this teaching in the name of Paul, even though he himself makes use of unpauline ideas in order to do so.

In 2 Thess. 2.6–7 the author of the letter speaks of a power that restrains the revelation of the antichrist. To the κατέχων ('restrainer') is attributed the function of delaying the appearance of God's final opponent until a specific point in time. Here 2 Thessalonians utilizes a tradition that

---

[146] Cf. Walter Schmithals, 'Die historische Situation der Thessalonicherbriefe' (see above 2.4.6) 146ff.

[147] For debate with the theses of Walter Schmithals, cf. Trilling, *Untersuchungen* 125ff.

[148] Cf. Trilling, *2 Thessalonicherbrief*, 76–77; Marxsen, *2 Thessalonicherbrief*, 80.

originally probably derived from Hab. 2.3:[149] 'For there is still a vision for the appointed time; it speaks of the end, and does not lie. If it seems to tarry, wait for it; it will surely come, it will not delay.' By using the apocalyptic motif of the κατέχων ('restrainer') the letter writer emphasizes that God will bring about the promised end, even if it is delayed. The events of the end time are subject to the will of God and will unfold according to his plan. It is not necessary to decide whether the power that restrains is personal or an impersonal world power (the Roman Empire),[150] for finally it is God himself who hinders the appearance of the antichrist until the determined point in time. Of course there cannot be any direct identification of the κατέχων ('restrainer') and God (cf. 2 Thess. 2.7b), but this is still the logical consequence of the line of argument. The delay of the parousia corresponds to the will of God, and is itself the restraining power.[151]

5.4.9 Basic Theological Ideas

The central concern of the letter is expressed in the didactic eschatological discourse of 2 Thess. 2.1–12. The author places his own portrayal of the eschatological events over against an enthusiastic present eschatology appealing to 1 Thess. 4.13–5.11. By taking up prophetic-apocalyptic motifs (cf. Dan. 11.36ff.; Isa. 11.4), the author names the coming apostasy, the advent of the Man of Sin and his work as stages of the final events. They will precede the parousia of Christ, so that the church can now judge for itself whether the eschatological outline of events that are filled with struggle corresponds to reality. The revelation of the eschatological Adversary has not yet occurred, so the parousia of Christ can neither have already happened nor be imminent. At the same time, the church knows that the Evil One is already at work in the present and that it is God alone who still restrains his full public manifestation. The present effective activity of the Evil One qualifies the present as the time of decision for the future. Thus the parousia of Christ is connected with the last judgment (cf. 2 Thess. 2.10b–12; 1.3–12). While unbelievers will be judged, the church that is presently enduring distress can be encouraged by the prospect of the salvation to come in the future.

The parenesis of 2 Thessalonians is formally oriented to that of 1 Thessalonians, while its content is determined by the comprehensive

---

[149] On this point cf. August Strobel, *Untersuchungen zum eschatologischen Verzögerungsproblem*, NT.S 2 (Leiden: E.J. Brill, 1961) 98–116.

[150] On particular issues and the history of exegesis, cf. Trilling *2 Thessalonicherbrief* 94–105.

[151] Cf. *ibid.* 92.

reference back to the apostle Paul. The teaching mediated from the apostle to the church serves as its ethical norm (cf. 2 Thess. 2.15; 3.6, 14). In addition, Paul appears as the model that the community is called to follow (2 Thess. 3.7–9). The apostle admonishes the community (παραγ-γέλλω [command] in 2 Thess. 3.4, 6, 10, 12). God's election corresponds to holiness of life (2 Thess. 2.13). They are to avoid those in the church who are idle, in order to move them to insight and repentance (cf. 2 Thess. 3.6–12).

The whole argumentation of 2 Thessalonians is based on the person of the apostle himself. The calling of the community is inseparably bound up with the Pauline gospel (2 Thess. 2.14). The church withstands false teachers by holding fast to the teaching of the apostle (2 Thess. 2.5, 6; cf. 1.10b), and – as is the case with the apostle himself – gives no room for evil people (cf. 2 Thess. 3.6–8). Alongside his authoritative word, the apostle's own manner of life (cf. 2 Thess. 3.8) should help the church to orient itself amidst the confusions of the present and to hold fast to the apostolic proclamation.

This orientation to Paul cannot, to be sure, obscure the fact that 2 Thessalonians, in contrast to Colossians and Ephesians, has not productively developed Pauline theology further in a changed situation.[152] There is not a single echo of Paul's doctrine of justification, and the concept of πίστις (faith) is used in a predominately formal (cf. 2 Thess. 1.3, 4, 11; 3.2) or neutral sense (cf. 2 Thess. 2.11–12). Obviously the letter pursues only the one goal of correcting a misinterpretation of the eschatology of 1 Thessalonians.

5.4.10 Tendencies of Recent Research

There is an extensive consensus in recent exegesis on the pseudepigraphical character of 2 Thessalonians. Given this presupposition, there remains some discussion about the correct dating of the letter, for arguments can be presented for both the composition of the letter during the lifetime of the Paul or shortly after his death (Otto Merk) as well as for a distance of several decades from 1 Thessalonians. The issue of the real intention of 2 Thessalonians stands at the center of this discussion. Did the author want only to suppress a false interpretation of 1 Thess. 4.13–5.11, or to replace 1 Thessalonians as a whole? Following A. Hilgenfeld[153] and H. J. Holtzmann,[154] A. Lindemann argues that 2 Thessalonians was conceived as

---

[152] Cf. Andreas Lindemann, *Paulus im ältesten Christentum* (see above 5) 132–133.

[153] Cf. Adolf Hilgenfeld, 'Die beiden Briefe an die Thessalonicher,' ZWTh 5 (1862) 225–264.

[154] Cf. Heinrich J. Holtzmann, 'Zum zweiten Thessalonicherbrief,' ZNW 2 (1901) 97–108.

a refutation of and replacement for 1 Thessalonians. In particular, the expression ὡς δι᾽ ἡμῶν (as though from us) in 2 Thess. 2.2 and the mark of authenticity in 2 Thess. 3.17 indicates to Lindemann that 2 Thessalonians wants to discredit 1 Thessalonians as inauthentic. '"Paul" explains in "his" letter to the Thessalonians (not in a "second Thessalonians") that a particular eschatological view has been imposed upon him, has by no means actually been advocated by him, but that those who are upsetting the church "through Spirit and word" are relying on a falsified letter. The author now presents the correct eschatological παράδοσις (tradition) in this letter "to the Thessalonians".'[155] According to this hypothesis, also adopted by W. Marxsen[156] and F. Laub,[157] 2 Thessalonians would have to be understood as written to oppose what the author considered to be a forgery. The author would have then attempted to suppress the purported 'first' letter to the Thessalonians by his own pseudepigraphical writing.

There are, of course, weighty arguments against this hypothesis: could it really have been possible to describe 1 Thessalonians as a forgery ca. forty years after its composition? The strong dependence on 1 Thessalonians suggests rather that the author of 2 Thessalonians was convinced of the authenticity of the letter that lay before him. He would then have had to have presented 1 Thessalonians as a forgery against his own better knowledge. This is an action with which a New Testament author ought not to be charged! The authority of the apostle claimed in the whole of 2 Thessalonians does not serve to correct Paul by 'Paul,' but to defend the eschatological statements of 1 Thessalonians from a false interpretation. The apostle himself would have been among those who would not share the eschatological views of the author's opponents, so that under these circumstances the author of 2 Thessalonians can rightly claim the authority of Paul, without however setting forth authentic Pauline eschatology himself.

5.5 The Pastoral Letters

The designation 'Pastoral Letters' for 1 Timothy, 2 Timothy, and Titus was probably coined in the eighteenth century by the Halle exegete P. Anton,[158] who thereby appropriately expressed the intention of all three

---

[155] Lindemann, 'Abfassungszweck' 39.
[156] Cf. Marxsen, *2 Thessalonicherbrief* 33ff.
[157] Cf. Franz Laub, 'Paulinische Autorität in nachpaulinischer Zeit,' in Collins, *The Thessalonian Correspondence* 403–417.
[158] Cf. Paul Anton, *Exegetische Abhandlung der Paulinischen Pastoral-Briefe* (Halle I 1753. II 1755).

letters: their concern for the founding and formation of the ecclesiastiacal pastoral offices. This designation, to be sure, fits 2 Timothy in only a restricted sense, but nonetheless in modern times the three letters are always regarded as a unity. All three letters are directed to individuals; they are not personal letters, however, but are written with an authoritative claim. The directions for the proper practice of the pastoral office have the character of general rules to be applied to the office as such. Moreover, the Pastorals are generally in agreement on the church situation and theological world of thought they presuppose. The element that unites them is the consistent demand for the readers to mark a clear line between orthodoxy and heresy and to keep themselves separate from heretics, the positive counterpart of which is to hold fast to the person of the apostle Paul and the tradition guaranteed through him. The threat to the Pauline identity of the churches addressed is met by the author of the Pastorals with the concept of a personal and material continuity oriented to the model of Paul himself and attaining concrete form in particular instructions.

5.5.1 Literature

Commentaries

Dibelius, Martin and Conzelmann, Hans. *The Pastoral Epistles*, Hermeneia. Philadelphia: Fortress, 1972; Hasler, Victor. *Die Briefe an Timotheus und Titus*, ZBK 12. Zürich: Theologischer Verlag, 1978; Roloff, Jürgen. *Der Erste Brief an Timotheus*, EKK XV. Neukirchen: Neukirchener Verlag, 1988; Brox, Norbert. *Die Pastoralbriefe*, RNT VII/2. Regensburg: Pustet, 1989[5]; Merkel, Helmut. *Die Pastoralbriefe*, NTD 9/1. Göttingen: Vandenhoeck & Ruprecht, 1991; Holtz, Gottfried. *Die Pastoralbriefe*, ThHK 13. Berlin: Evangelische Verlagsanstalt, 1992[5]; Oberlinner, Lorenz. *Die Pastoralbriefe* (Erster Timotheusbrief), HThK X I/2.1. Freiburg: Herder, 1994; Bassler, Jouette M. *1 Timothy, 2 Timothy, Titus*, Abingdon New Testament Commentaries. Nashville: Abingdon, 1996.

Monographs

Campenhausen, Hans v. *Apostolic Authority and Spiritual Power in the First Three Centuries*. Philadelphia: Fortress Press, 1969; Trummer, Peter. *Die Paulustradition der Pastoralbriefe*, BET 8. Frankfurt: Lang, 1978; Lips, Hermann v. *Glaube- Gemeinde-Amt. Zum Verständnis der Ordination in den Pastoralbriefen*, FRLANT 122. Göttingen: Vandenhoeck & Ruprecht, 1979; Donelson, Lewis R. *Pseudepigraphy and Ethical Argument in the Pastoral Epistles*, HUNT 22. Tübingen: J. C. B. Mohr (Paul Siebeck), 1986; Wolter, Michael. *Die Pastoralbriefe als Paulustradition*, FRLANT 146. Göttingen: Vandenhoeck & Ruprecht, 1988; Schlarb, Egbert. *Die gesunde Lehre. Häresie und Wahrheit im Spiegel der Pastoralbriefe*, MThSt 28, Marburg: Elwert, 1990.

Articles

Hegermann, Harald. 'Der geschichtliche Ort der Pastoralbriefe,' *TheolVers* II, Berlin 1970, 47–64; Haufe, Günter. 'Gnostische Irrlehre und ihre Abwehr in den Pastoral-briefen,' in *Gnosis und Neues Testament*, ed. Karl W. Tröger. Berlin: Evangelische Verlagsanstalt, 1973, 325–339; Stenger, Werner. 'Timotheus und Titus als literarische Gestalten,' Kairos 16 (1974) 252–267; Merk, Otto. 'Glaube und Tat in den Pastoral-briefen,' ZNW 66 (1975) 91–102; Roloff, Jürgen. 'Amt/Ämter/Amtsverständnis,' *TRE* 2 (1978) 509–533; Oberlinner, Lorenz. 'Die "Epiphaneia" des Heilswillens Gottes in Christus Jesus. Zur Grundstruktur der Christologie der Pastoralbriefe,' ZNW 71 (1980) 192–213; Lohfink, Gerhard. 'Paulinische Theologie in den Pastoral-briefen,' in *Paulus in den ntl. Spätschriften*, ed. Karl Kertelge (see above 5) 70–121; Trummer, Peter, 'Corpus Paulinum – Corpus Pastorale,' in *Paulus in den ntl. Spätschriften*, ed. Karl Kertelge (see above 5) 122–145; Kretschmar, Georg. 'Der paulinische Glaube in den Pastoralbriefen,' in *Der Glaube im Neuen Testament* (FS H. Binder), eds. Ferdinand Hahn and Hans Klein, BThSt 7. Neukirchen-Vluyn: Neukirchener Verlag, 1982, 113–140; Roloff, Jürgen. 'Pfeiler und Fundament der Wahrheit. Erwägungen zum Kirchenverständnis der Pastoralbriefe,' in *Glaube und Eschatologie* (FS W. G. Kümmel), eds. Erich Grässer and Otto Merk. Tübingen: J. C. B. Mohr (Paul Siebeck), 1985, 229–247; Zmijewski, Josef. 'Die Pastoralbriefe als pseudepigraphische Schriften,' in *Das Neue Testament. Quelle christlicher Theologie und Glaubenspraxis*, ed. J. Zmijewski. Stuttgart: Kohlhammer, 1986, 197–219; Reiser, Marius. 'Bürgerliches Christentum in den Pastoralbriefen?' Bib 74 (1993) 27–44.

5.5.2 *Author*

After important preliminary works by F. D. E. Schleiermacher[159] and J. G. Eichhorn,[160] critical work on the Pauline authorship of the Pastoral letters began in a thoroughly comprehensive way with F. C. Baur.[161] He set the historical standpoint of the Pastorals in the debate with Gnosticism in the second century. H. J. Holtzmann then gave an extensive foundation for the pseudepigraphical character of the Pastorals in his 1880 commentary.[162]

The following can be presented as substantive arguments *against* the Pauline authorship of the Pastorals:[163]

(1) The historical situation presupposed in the Pastoral Epistles cannot

---

[159] Cf. Friedrich D. E. Schleiermacher, *Ueber den sogenannten ersten Brief des Paulos an den Timotheos* (Berlin 1807).

[160] Cf. Johann G. Eichhorn, *Einleitung in das NT* III/1 (Leipzig: Weidmann, 1812) 315–328.

[161] Cf. F. C. Baur, *Paul: His Life and Works* (see above 5.2.2) 2.98: 'The more carefully and impartially these writings are examined, criticaly and exegetically, the less it will be possible to doubt their late origin.'

[162] Cf. Heinrich J. Holtzmann, *Die Pastoralbriefe, kritisch und exegetisch behandelt* (Leipzig: Engelmann, 1880).

[163] On this point cf. finally Roloff, *1 Timotheus* 21–39; Merkel, *Pastoralbriefe* 5–16.

be harmonized either with the data of Acts or with that of the authentic Pauline letters. According to 1 Tim. 1.3 Timothy is residing in Ephesus, while Paul, having left from there, journeys toward Macedonia. The apostle intends to return to Ephesus soon (1 Tim. 3.14; 4.13). The apostle is thus pictured as free to do what he will; there are no indications of imprisonment in the letter. According to Acts 19.22 it was not Paul who traveled to Macedonia while Timothy remained in Ephesus, but the opposite: Timothy is sent ahead to Macedonia while the apostle remained in Ephesus. Timothy is then the 'co-author' of 2 Corinthians written in Macedonia, and in Acts 20.4 is listed among the delegation sent with the collection when Paul went to Jerusalem. There are also matters of content that do not fit the purported situation of the letter. Timothy had for years been a close coworker with Paul, yet according to 1 Tim. 1.3 he is expressly warned once again before Paul's departure to struggle against the heretics. What function would the letter have had in view of the brief absence of Paul (1 Tim. 3.14; 4.13)? What themes and problems are addressed with which Timothy would not have long since been familiar from his long years of service as a co-worker in the Pauline mission?

If Paul writes 1 Timothy and Titus while engaged in his missionary activity, in 2 Timothy he is presented as a suffering prisoner (2 Tim. 1.8, 12, 16; 2.9) who is near to death (2 Tim. 4.6, 8). In view of this situation, why does he ask Timothy to bring with him the cloak and books he had left in Troas (cf. 2 Tim. 4.13)? According to 2 Tim. 1.15; 4.10–11, 16, all Paul's co-workers except Luke have abandoned him, while in 2 Tim. 4.21 Paul sends greetings from four co-workers and 'all the brothers!' According to 2 Tim. 4.20, Trophimus has been left behind in Miletus sick; in Acts 21.29 he accompanies Paul to Jerusalem. Finally, there is no explanation for why Timothy should be ashamed of Paul's imprisonment (cf. 2 Tim. 1.8).

Paul cannot be considered a candidate for the authorship of Titus, since the mission on Crete and Paul's spending the winter in Nicopolis (Titus 3.12) is found neither in the authentic Pauline letters nor in Acts. Crete is mentioned only in Acts 27.7–8 as a station for the prisoner Paul on the trip to Rome. A tension exists between the wish expressed in Titus 3.12, that Titus should come to Paul as quickly as possible, and Titus 1.5, where he receives the assignment to travel through the cities of Crete and appoint elders in every town.

(2) The Pastorals reflect the problems of the third Christian generation. Thus church organization is more advanced than in the days of Paul. The house church of Paul's day no longer provides the dominant organizational structure, but the model of the ancient household provides the basis for

organizing the church of a particular location (cf. 1 Tim. 3.15; 2 Tim. 2.20–21 Titus 1.7). Bishops, presbyters, and deacons are installed in their offices for an extended period by the laying on of hands of other ecclesiastical authorities, and they have the right of support by the church (cf. 1 Tim. 1.18; 3.1–7, 8–13; 4.14; 5.17–22; 2 Tim. 1.6; 2.1–2; Titus 1.5–9. The charismatic-functional church structure of Paul (cf. 1 Cor. 12.4–11, 28–29; Rom. 12.3–8) is replaced by a system of office holders. As prominent personalities they attract some public interest, and they must conduct themselves in a way that is appropriate to such a position (cf. 1 Tim. 3.7, 10; 5.8, 14; 6.11ff.; Titus 2.5, 8). The apostolic tradition of the faith is of fundamental importance, appearing as 'sound doctrine' (1 Tim. 1.10). Church officials make their confession of this traditional faith before witnesses, as they are inducted into office (cf. 1 Tim. 6.12–13; cf. further 4.6). The debate with Judaism is no longer important; the church's reflection is rather focused on the position of the Christian community in a non-Christian pagan environment. The maxim that is to be applied here: Christians should respect the authorities and live inconspicuously in piety and propriety (cf. 1 Tim. 2.2).

(3) The Pastorals manifest numerous exceptional linguistic features.[164] The large number of *hapax legomena* is striking: 66 in 1 Timothy, 60 in 2 Timothy, and 32 in Titus.[165] The Pastorals also have a distinctive vocabulary in comparison to the other Pauline letters. 'The Pastoral Epistles . . . with their total of 3484 words would normally have a distinctive vocabulary somewhere between that of 2 Corinthians and Galatians, i. e. around 130 distinctive words. In fact, however, they have 335 words not found elsewhere in Paul, a good 50 more than Romans, which is twice as long! That is a number, of course, which speaks very strongly against the authenticity of the Pastoral Epistles.'[166] Characteristic terms for the theology of the Pastorals are: ἀγάπη (love), ἅγνος (holy), αἰών (age), ἀλήθεια (truth), διδασκαλία (teaching), διδάσκω (teach), δικαιοσύνη (righteousness), δόξα (glory), εἰρήνη (peace), ἐπίγνωσις (knowledge), ἐπιφάνεια (epiphany), εὐσέβεια (godliness), καθαρός (pure), κακός (bad), καλός (good), λόγος (word), μανθάνω (learn), μῦθος (myth), πίστις (faith), πνεῦμα (spirit), συνείδησις (conscience), σῴζω (save), σωτήρ (savior), ὑγιαίνω (be healthy).

(4) The Pastorals manifest considerable differences from the theology

---

[164] On this cf. the foundational and still valuable study of Holtzmann, *Pastoralbriefe* 84–118.
[165] Word statistics according to *Vollständige Konkordanz*, ed. Kurt Aland (see above 5.2.2) 456–457.
[166] Robert Morgenthaler, *Statistik des neutestamentlichen Wortschatzes* (Zürich: Gotthelf, 1982³) 38.

of the undisputed Pauline letters. Lacking are concepts such as the 'righteousness of God,' 'freedom,' 'cross,' 'son of God,' and 'body of Christ.' A reflection of the specific Pauline doctrine of justification is found only in Titus 3.4–7; the antithesis 'flesh/ spirit' does not occur at all. In addition, there are shifts in the manner in which the same subjects are treated. While in Paul 'faith' is the means by which salvation is appropriated, in 1 Timothy the dominant meaning is the content of faith as doctrine to be believed.[167] The central concept διδασκαλία (didaskalia = teaching) occurs fifteen times in the Pastorals, but only six times in the remainder of the New Testament. Thus 'faith' appears as 'believing the right thing over against heresy' (cf. 1 Tim. 1.19; 4.1, 6; 6.21; 2 Tim. 2.18; 3.8) and is regarded as the characteristic stance of Christian existence. The 'churchiness' of the Pastorals' concept of faith is seen finally in the motif of Christian education as the process by which one comes to faith. Timothy is reminded of the sincere faith of his mother and grandmother (cf. 2 Tim. 1.5). It is even said of the ancestors of Paul himself that they served God with a pure conscience (cf. 2 Tim. 1.3). 'Faith' can be named in a series with other virtues such as 'good conscience' (1 Tim. 1.5, 19; 3.9), 'love, holiness, and modesty' (1 Tim. 2.15), 'purity' (1 Tim. 4.12), 'righteousness, godliness, endurance, and gentleness' (1 Tim. 6.11) (cf. further 2 Tim. 1.13; 2.22; 3.10–11; Titus 2.2). In the Pastorals the parousia of Christ becomes an epiphany, a manifestation that will arrive at the proper time (cf. 1 Tim. 6.14; 2 Tim. 4.1, 8; Titus 2.13) while at the same time suggesting an indefinitely distant future. The image of women conveyed by the Pastorals, in contrast to Paul's letters, is not a model that assumes collegial participation and partnership, but is characterized by exhortations to subordination (cf. 1 Tim. 2.9–15; 5.14).

The overwhelming majority of exegetes regard the Pastorals as pseudepigraphical writings, including for example M. Dibelius (and H. Conzelmann), A. Jülicher and E. Fascher, W. G. Kümmel, N. Brox, Ph. Vielhauer, J. Roloff, and H. Merkel.[168] On the other hand, their authenticity has been defended for example by Th. Zahn, A. Schlatter, W. Michaelis, B. Reicke[169] and J. van Bruggen.[170]

---

[167] On this point cf. Kretschmar, *Glaube* 113ff.

[168] Cf. Dibelius, *The Pastoral Epistles* 1–5; Jülicher and Fascher, *Einleitung* 165ff.; Kümmel, *Introduction* 370ff.; N. Brox, *Pastoralbriefe* 22ff.; Ph. Vielhauer, *Urchristliche Literatur* 225; Roloff, *1 Timotheusbrief* 23–29; Merkel, *Pastoralbriefe* 6–9.

[169] Cf. Bo Reicke, 'Chronologie der Pastoralbriefe,' ThLZ 101 (1976) 81–94.

[170] Cf. Theodor Zahn, *Introduction* (see above 2.9.3) 2.1–33; Adolf Schlatter, *Der Glaube im Neuen Testament* (Stuttgart 1927⁴) 405ff.; Wilhelm Michaelis, *Einleitung in das Neue Testament*, (Bern 1961³), 238–259; Jakob van Bruggen, *Die geschichtliche Einordnung der Pastoralbriefe* (Wuppertal: TVG, 1981) *passim*.

If the direct authorship of the Pastorals by Paul must be virtually excluded, the possibility of an indirect authorship remains. Here the secretary hypothesis hold the most important place,[171] according to which the Pastorals were composed independently by one of the apostle's colleagues on the basis of instruction and materials from him (advocated by O. Roller, J. Jeremias, G. Holtz, J. N. D. Kelly, C. F. D. Moule).[172] But the difficulties that stand against Pauline authorship are not resolved by this theory. The Pastorals know of no collaborative authorship, and in 1 Timothy and Titus there is no indication that these writings were composed only at Paul's behest rather than by Paul himself. The apostles own linguistic features are also found in letters we know were dictated to a secretary (cf. Rom. 16.22), so the problem of the linguistic peculiarities of the Pastorals is not set aside by the secretary hypothesis.

The author of the Pastorals was an unknown member of the Pauline school who wrote and circulated the letters 'in the course of a new edition of the previous corpus' of the Pauline letters.[173] A connection is suggested between the first collections of Pauline letters and the Pastorals, because the Pastorals probably 'originated at the same time and were presented to the public in the form of a three-member letter corpus.'[174] The Pastorals are intended to overcome an internal crisis in the church caused by false teaching, to implement appropriate official structures in circumstances that had changed and to secure the continuing influence of the apostle Paul in the whole church. The author made use of the elevated common language of his own time and oriented his composition to Greek and Hellenistic-Jewish traditions and forms (see below 5.5.5). He quotes sayings from poetry (cf. Titus 1.12) and makes use of philosophical concepts (cf. 1 Tim. 6.6: αὐτάρκεια [self-sufficiency]). The author was probably an educated Hellenistic (Jewish) Christian who lived in a city of Asia Minor and had in view the churches of his own area.

---

[171] For additional theories that are no longer current (the fragmentary hypothesis, the identification of the author of the Pastorals with one of the personalities of the early church otherwise known) cf. Roloff, *1 Timotheusbrief* 32–36.

[172] Cf. Otto Roller, *Das Formular der paulinischen Briefe* (see above 2.3.2) 16ff.; Joachim Jeremias, *Die Briefe an Timotheus und Titus*, NTD 9 (Göttingen: Vandenhoeck & Ruprecht, 1975¹¹) 8; Holtz, *Pastoralbriefe* 13–16; J. N. D. Kelly, *A Commentary on the Pastoral Epistles*, BNTC (London: Black, 1963) 34; C. F. D. Moule, *The Birth of the New Testament* (London: Black, 1962) 220–221.

[173] Trummer, 'Corpus Paulinum – Corpus Pastorale' 133.

[174] Roloff, *1 Timotheusbrief* 43.

5.5.3 *Place and Time of Composition*

The Letters to Timothy[175] are concerned with the church situation in *Ephesus* and so probably originated there.[176] Thus Timothy appears as the advocate of Pauline theology in Ephesus (cf. 1 Tim. 1.1–3), and even 2 Timothy, which claims to be written in Rome (cf. 2 Tim. 1.17; 1.5; 2.9), presupposes the activity of Timothy in Ephesus (cf. 2 Tim. 1.18; 4.19). Rev. 2.1–6 documents for the end of the first century CE the existence of a large Christian community in Ephesus, and as the location of the Pauline school the city possessed prominence and importance. So too the internal connection between the first collection of Paul's letters and the composition of the Pastorals points to Ephesus.[177]

The following reasons may be given for dating the composition of the Pastorals around *100 CE*:[178] (1) The tradition about Paul's own life and person is still drawn from the living tradition of the church. (2) The structure of church offices in the Pastorals is different from the church order presupposed in Ignatius and Polycarp for the time between 110 CE and 130 CE.[179] (3) The Pastorals belong within the process of the formation of the Pauline corpus. (4) The early form of a Christian gnosticism, the type of false teaching opposed by the Pastorals, points to the period around 100 CE.

Is the occurrence of the term ἀντιθέσεις (antitheses) in 1 Tim. 6.20 an allusion to the 'Antitheses' of Marcion?[180] This (no longer extant) work was something like an 'Introduction to the New Testament,' and was written around 140 CE.[181] In that case the Pastorals would have to be dated in this period and regarded as anti-Marcion polemic. Against this, of course, is the obviously positive reception of the Old Testament among the false teachers opposed by the Pastorals (cf. 1 Tim. 5.5, 8), a state of affairs that cannot be harmonized with Marcion's curt rejection of the Old Testament. Moreover,

---

[175] Titus has nothing to say about the conditions under which it was written, but there can be no doubt that it belongs in immediate proximity to the letters to Timothy.

[176] Cf. Roloff, *1 Timotheusbrief* 42; Hegermann, *Ort* 61–62; Brox, *Pastoralbriefe* 58 (Asia Minor); Vielhauer, *Urchristliche Literatur* 237 (Asia Minor/Ephesus); Ernst Dassmann, *Stachel im Fleisch* (see above 5) 172 (Asia Minor). Andreas Lindemann, *Paulus im ältesten Christentum* (see above 5) 149 and Merkel, *Pastoralbriefe* 13, vote for Rome.

[177] Cf. Excursus 2: The Collection of the Pauline Letters and the Formation of the Canon.

[178] The Pastorals are also dated around 100 CE by Brox, *Pastoralbriefe* 58; Roloff, *1 Timotheusbrief* 45–46; Merkel, *Pastoralbriefe* 10; Hegermann, *Ort* 47; Lindemann, *Paulus im ältesten Christentum* 47.

[179] In Pol Phil 4.1 there is an echo of 1 Tim 6.7, 10, but that it is actually a quotation cannot be proven.

[180] Among those who follow F. C. Baur in this are Walter Bauer, *Earliest Christianity* (Philadelphia: Fortress Press, 1971); Vielhauer, *Urchristliche Literatur* 237.

[181] Cf. A. v. Harnack, *Marcion: the Gospel of the Alien God*, tr. John E. Steely (Durham, NC: Labyrinth Press, 1990) 26 (the 'Antitheses' were written between 139 and 144 CE).

the Pastorals were obviously accepted by later Marcionites into their collection of Pauline letters.[182] The term ἀντιθέσεις is obviously an intentional anti-formulation by the author of the Pastorals himself, who sets his παραθήκη over against the deviating position of the false teachers.[183]

1 Timothy stands as the leading member of the group of Pastorals, for the comprehensive introduction of himself in 1 Tim. 1.12–17 introduces not only 1 Timothy, but the Pastorals as a whole. Whereas in 1 Tim. 3.14 and 4.13 the imminent arrival of the apostle is announced, Titus already no longer speaks of this, and 2 Timothy explicitly presupposes the continuing absence of the apostle. As the last word of the apostle before his death, 2 Timothy appears to be virtually Paul's last will and testament (cf. 2 Tim. 4.1–8) and forms the conclusion of the collection of Paul's letters.

5.5.4 *Intended Readership*

1 Timothy is addressed to Paul's closest co-worker, who appears in 1 Thess. 1.1, 1 Cor. 1.1, 2 Cor. 1.1, Phil. 1.1 and Phlm. 1.1 as co-sender of the letter. *Timothy* was probably converted by Paul (cf. 1 Cor. 4.17; differently Acts 16.1)[184] and took the place of Barnabas in the Pauline missionary program. The apostle valued him very highly (cf. 1 Cor. 4.17; 1 Thess. 3.2–3; Phil. 2.20–22; Rom. 16.21), and in 1 Cor. 16.10 Paul says of him: 'He is doing the work of the Lord just as I am.' Timothy was known in the Pauline churches as an important co-worker with the apostle, so that the choice of his name as the fictive addressee lay near to hand.

The Gentile Christian *Titus* belonged to the earliest group of Pauline co-workers and went with him to the Apostolic Council in Jerusalem (Gal. 2.3). There is no reference to Titus from the time of the Apostolic Council to the final phase of gathering the collection. After the Jerusalem conference, he does not appear again until 2 Corinthians within the context of organizing the collection, where he is the decisive person in resolving the conflict between Paul and the Corinthian church (cf. 2 Cor. 2.13; 7.6, 13, 14; 8.6, 16, 23; 12.18).

Although the Pauline missionary congregations in western Asia Minor are addressed only indirectly, they are the real conversation partners of the author of the Pastorals. Timothy and Titus appear already in the Pauline

---

[182] Cf. *ibid.* 170*f.

[183] Cf. Egbert Schlarb, 'Miszelle zu 1 Tim 6, 20,' ZNW 77 (1986) 276–281.

[184] Paul's circumcision of Timothy after he had become a Christian (as in Acts 16.3) must be considered improbable historically, since it contradicts the theology and practice of Paul as reported in Galatians 2.3.

letters as the apostle's representatives, who implement his instructions in critical congregational situations (cf. for Timothy 1 Cor. 4.16, 17; 16.10–11; 1 Thess. 3.2–3; Phil. 2.19, 23; for Titus 2 Cor. 2.13; 7.14ff.; 8.23). The Pastorals contain nothing less than the apostle's instructions that are now mediated to the congregations by the ideal type of post-apostolic office holders (Timothy/Titus). In the letters it is the absent Paul himself whose voice is heard, but whose physical presence is possibly going to be delayed according to 1 Tim. 3.15. Nevertheless, through the Pastorals Paul succeeds in addressing his churches, and is present in the current crisis.

The congregations to which the Pastorals are addressed are composed of Gentile Christians, but also contain a considerable number of Jewish Christians.[185] Thus liturgical forms from Hellenistic Jewish Christianity are found in 1 Tim. 1.17; 6.15–16. The comparison of the false teachers with Jannes and Jambres in 2 Tim. 3.8 can be understood only against the background of Jewish legends[186] about these men who are not mentioned in the Old Testament, just as the office of elders presupposed in the churches derives from Jewish tradition (see below 5.5.9).

The churches are characterized by social stratification. Christian house-holders are mentioned several times (cf. 1 Tim. 3.4–5, 12; 5.4, 8; 2 Tim. 1.16; 4.19; cf. further 1 Tim. 5.13; 2 Tim. 3.6; Titus 1.11); large houses with expensive furnishings were obviously not unusual (cf. 2 Tim. 2.20). The Christian household serves as a model for the congregation's under-standing of itself, with the ecclesiology of the Pastorals oriented to the metaphor of the household (cf. 1 Tim. 3.4, 15).[187] So too the references to women's jewelry (cf. 1 Tim. 2.9), slaves of Christian masters (1 Tim. 6.2), warnings against striving after profit and the love of money (cf. 1 Tim. 6.6–10; 2 Tim. 3.2; Titus 1.7), the separate instructions directed to the rich in 1 Tim. 6.17–20, show that members of the upper economic class belonged to the congregations to which the Pastorals were directed.[188]

The congregations have substantial financial means at their disposal, for the elders are paid (as is surely the case for the bishops, the primary officers, as well)[189] (cf. 1 Tim. 5.17–18; 3.1). There was also a church budget for taking care of widows (cf. 1 Tim. 5.16). The misuse of this arrangement (cf. 1 Tim. 5.14–15) is indirect testimony that the welfare system did its job well. In addition to the wealthy who obviously domi-

---

[185] Cf. Merkel, *Pastoralbriefe* 12.
[186] On this cf. Strack-Billerbeck, *Kommentar* 3.660–664.
[187] On the οἶκος concept of the Pastorals, cf. especially Schlarb, *Gesunde Lehre* 314–356.
[188] Cf. Peter Dschulnigg, 'Warnung vor Reichtum und Ermahnung der Reichen,' BZ 37 (1993) 60–77.
[189] Cf. Roloff, *1 Timotheusbrief* 308–309.

nated the congregational life, the Pastorals mention slaves (cf. 1 Tim. 6.1; Titus 2.9–10) and widows (cf. 1 Tim. 5.3ff.), handworkers (cf. 2 Tim. 4.14) and lawyers (cf. Titus 3.13) and call for helping the poor (cf. 1 Tim. 5.10). The community had early Christian teachers at work in it (cf. 1 Tim. 1.3, 7; 4.1; 6.3; 2 Tim. 4.3; Titus 1.11), some of whom had precipitated a crisis by their partially successful agitation. By adhering to what was considered respectable good conduct in the eyes of outsiders, the church attempted to anticipate criticism and ward it off in advance. It prays for the government authorities and leads a blameless life (cf. 1 Tim. 2.2; Titus 3.1). The author of the Pastorals is just as concerned for the public regard of the church leaders (cf. 1 Tim. 3.1–13) as he is concerned for those who occupy differing social status to live together in the church (cf. Titus 2.1–10).

How did the Pastorals attain authority in Asia Minor almost forty years after the death of Paul? As letters to private individuals they could have emerged from the private sphere and become public only very late. According to Heb. 13.23 Timothy was released from Roman imprisonment and continued his missionary work. This and similar personal traditions about Timothy (and Titus) opened up a not inconsiderable temporal leeway, if the Pastorals were not composed and published until after the (real or supposed) deaths of their (fictive) addressees.

5.5.5 *Outline, Structure, Form*

In a form-critical analysis of the Pastorals, it is better to treat 1 Timothy and Titus together and 2 Timothy separately. 2 Timothy lacks official instructions to the church, congregational offices are not mentioned, and interest in legal categories is minimal.[190] In contrast, apostolic instructions to the churches and the elements of later church structure (e.g., regulations for church officials, rules concerning widows, codes pertaining to different groups in the church) in 1 Timothy/Titus have led to the classification of both letters as 'manuals of church order.'[191] This formal classification does not of course explain the constitutive epistolary elements of 1 Timothy/Titus and does not fit the specific communications situation they presuppose. 1 Timothy/Titus are concerned with *official epistolary*

---

[190] Cf. the listing of the differences between 1 Timothy/Titus and 2 Timothy in Wolter, *Pastoralbriefe als Paulustradition* 143–154.

[191] Cf. M. Dibelius, *Geschichte der urchristlichen Literatur* 48ff.; Hans W. Bartsch, *Die Anfänge urchristlicher Rechtsbildungen*, ThF 34 (Hamburg 1965) 160ff.; Kümmel, *Introduction* 384; Wikenhauser and Schmid, *Einleitung* 536; Schenke and Fischer, *Einleitung* I. 222ff.; Koester, *Introduction* 2.301.

instructions directed to individuals who for their part have responsibility for church offices and are themselves authorized to issue directives.[192] As in the letter of Ignatius to Polycarp (written ca. 110 CE), instructions to individuals are mixed with community parenesis. Additional literary parallels are provided by instructions from rulers to high officials (*Mandata principis* [cf. e.g., the exchange of letters between Pliny the Younger and the emperor Trajan] and Hellenistic royal letters.)[193]

Outline of 1 Timothy

1.1–2	Prescript	Introduction
1.3–20	Timothy's assignment: to combat false doctrine	
2.1–3.16	PART ONE	
2.1–7	Prayer for all people	
2.8–15	Men and women at prayer	
3.1–13	Qualifications for bishops and deacons	
3.14–16	Concluding statement	Body
4.1–6.2	PART TWO	
4.1–11	Opposition to false teaching	
4.12–5.2	The church leader as model	
5.3–13	The status and enrollment of widows	
5.17–25	The office of presbyters [elders]	
6.1–2	Christian slaves	
6.3–19	Concluding parenesis	Conclusion
6.20, 21	Concluding admonition and blessing	

The beginning of the letter remains on the sender-receiver plane and has a legitimizing function; Paul communicates to Timothy the mandate for the assignment he is to carry out. In the body of the letter the church is drawn into the communication process. Its prayer for all people corresponds to the universality of the divine saving will. Following the instruction on prayer come regulations for the external order of worship (1 Tim. 2.8–15). In the center of Part One stands the list of qualifications for bearers of church office presented as a table of duties. While in Part One

---

[192] Cf. Wolter, *Pastoralbriefe als Paulustradition* 196; Roloff, *1 Timotheusbrief* 48–49; Merkel, *Pastoralbriefe* 11.

[193] Cf. the analysis of all relevant texts in Wolter, *Pastoralbriefe als Paulustradition* 161–177.

the instructions pertain directly to the church, in Part Two Timothy communicates to the church the instructions received from Paul (cf. 1 Tim. 4.11!). Conduct over against the false teachers and duties within the congregation mutually condition each other, for only the unrestricted authority of the leader of the church can successfully resist the false teaching (cf. 1 Tim. 4.7). The rules for taking care of widows are directed to a reorganization of social procedures already in existence. It is also clear that problems in the church existed in connection with the council of presbyters [elders], problems that are now to be overcome by the bishop. The conclusion takes up the note already sounded in the introduction in that once again Timothy is reminded of his mandate (cf. 6.12–16). Brief concluding admonitions and a blessing form the conclusion.

Outline of Titus

1.1–4	Prescript	Introduction
1.5–16	Church order	
1.5–6	Presbyters [elders]	
1.7–9	The bishop	
1.10–16	False teachers	
2.1–15	Instructions to various groups	
2.1	Heading	Body
2.2	Old men	
2.3–5	Old and young women	
2.6–8	Young men	
2.9–10	Slaves	
2.11–15	Basis of Christian ethical conduct	
3.1–11	Further admonitions	
3.12–14	Concluding instructions	Conclusion
3.15	Greetings and blessing	

The prescript is oriented to that of Romans, followed by instructions for the way presbyters and bishops should live. Titus 1.10–16 makes combatting false teaching into a central task of church leadership. The defense against heretics is followed by a positive presentation of the life of the church (2.1–10). Each of the various groups is challenged to live a blameless life, which has its theological basis in the prospect of the appearance of the savior, Jesus Christ (Titus 2.11–15). The appended general instructions conclude with a rule of church discipline (Titus 3.10–11). The letter's conclusion takes up elements from 1 Corinthians and Romans.

While 1 Timothy and Titus can be understood as epistolary directions to church officials who are themselves charged with the responsibility of instruction, a different communication situation is reflected in 2 Timothy. Here the community fades into the background and the sole concern is the relation between the apostle and his disciple. As in no other deuteropauline letter, in 2 Timothy the material continuity of the tradition is thought of in terms of personal continuity. In 2 Timothy this constellation also serves, however, to encourage the community toward a continuing orientation to Paul, so that this writing can be described as a testamentary admonitory discourse. The *testamentary character* of 2 Timothy is seen in comparison with Acts 20.17–35 (Paul's farewell speech at Miletus): the departing apostle predicts the advent of false teachers (Acts 20.29–30/2 Tim. 3.1–5a, 6–7; 4.3–4) and insists on strict separation from them (Acts 20.28/2 Tim. 3.5b; 4.5). He emphasizes his own exemplary conduct (Acts 20.18–21, 27, 35/2 Tim. 4.7) and has in view his imminent death (Acts 20.23/2 Tim. 4.6).

Outline of 2 Timothy

1.1–2	Prescript	Introduction
1.3–5	Proemium	
1.6–2.13	PART ONE	
1.6–14	Epistolary self commendation	
1.15–18	Reports on Paul's imprisonment	
2.1–13	The apostle as a model of suffering	
2.14–4.8	PART TWO	Body
2.14–26	Personal ethical approvedness	
3.1–9	False teaching	
3.10–17	Timothy's apostolic succession	
4.1–8	The testament of Paul	
4.9–18	The situation of Paul	
4.19–21	Greetings	Conclusion
4.22	Blessing	

The introduction is consistently oriented to the formula of the undisputed Pauline letters and, differently from 1 Timothy/Titus, the prescript is followed by a thanksgiving. With the following epistolary self-commendation, the author likewise stands in the tradition of the authentic Pauline letters. The apostle's example also determines the section about suffering discipleship in 2.1–13. The central sections of Part Two make it clear that the value and legitimacy of the office holder proves itself in the way he deals with false teaching. To the negative picture of the heretics is juxtaposed the model of Timothy (3.10–17). Final instructions, virtually Paul's last will and testament, conclude the body of the letter. Detailed personal traditions bring the letter to an end.

5.5.6 Literary Integrity

The literary integrity of the Pastoral letters is uncontested.

5.5.7 Traditions, Sources

The Pastorals obviously presuppose a small collection of Paul's letters.[194] In particular, 1 Corinthians and Romans serve as sources for 1 Timothy. Thus 1 Tim. 1.2 reflects 1 Cor. 4.17; 1 Tim. 1.8–10a reflects Rom. 3.21, 28; 7.12; 1 Tim. 1.12–13 reflects 1 Cor. 7.25; 1 Tim. 1.20 reflects 1 Cor. 5.5; 1 Tim. 2.6–7 reflects Rom. 9.1; 1 Tim. 2.11–15 reflects 1 Cor. 14.33b–36; 1 Tim. 5.18 reflects 1 Cor. 9.8–14 and 1 Tim. 6.4–5 reflects Rom. 1.28–30. In addition, in 1 Tim. 3.15b there is an allusion to 2 Cor. 6.16; in 1 Tim. 1.12–13 to Phil. 4.13, and in 1 Tim. 4.6–10 to Col. 1.24–29. In contrast, however, it cannot be shown that Acts is used in 1 Timothy.[195]

1 Timothy adopted numerous elements from the common tradition of the church. Among these are the rules for church officials in 1 Tim. 3.1–13 and 5.17, the statements about the organized group of widows in 1 Tim. 5.3–10 and concerning slaves in 1 Tim. 6.1–2. The detailed regulations for church discipline in 1 Tim. 5.19–21 also derive from church tradition. This traditional material does not in itself form a coherent unit, so that the assumption of a manual of church order as a possible source for 1 Timothy must be considered improbable (as for the Pastorals as a whole). In addition to legal traditions, other traditional elements in 1 Timothy are kerygmatic formulae (1 Tim. 2.5–6), a Christ hymn (1 Tim. 3.16) and fragments of an ordination parenesis (1 Tim. 6.13–14). Titus 3.3–7 contains a reference to Gal. 4.3–7. The procedure for installation of elders [presbyters] and bishops in Titus 1.5–9 and the regulations for various

---

[194] Cf. on this point Andreas Lindemann, *Paulus im ältesten Christentum* (see above 5) 134–149.
[195] Cf. Roloff, *1 Timotheusbrief* 40.

groups within the congregation in Titus 2.1–10 also derive from pre-formed church tradition.

2 Timothy is oriented to Rom. 1.8–15; clear lines of connection may be discerned between 2 Tim. 1.7/Rom. 8.15; 2 Tim. 1.8/Rom. 1.16; 2 Tim. 2.8/Rom. 1.3; 2 Tim. 2.4–6/1 Cor. 9.7 and 2 Tim. 2.11–13/Rom. 6.3–4. The anamnesis of Paul in 2 Timothy is certainly based in part on personal traditions handed on in the churches (cf. 2 Tim. 1.3; 4.16–18).

In the Pastorals, the knowledge and use of Pauline letters and the incorporation of living traditions from the church are complementary processes, not mutually exclusive alternatives. This overlapping must be seen as characteristic for the way the Pauline tradition worked at the end of the first century CE.

5.5.8 History-of-religion Standpoint

The Pastorals combat a false teaching at work within the churches that has combined elements of a very different sort. Thus the opposed teachers claim to provide γνῶσις (knowledge) (1 Tim. 6.20–21; cf. also 1 Tim. 4.3; 2 Tim. 3.7; Titus 1.16). The ascetic demands to abstain from marriage and from certain foods also point in the direction of an early form of Christian gnosticism (cf. 1 Tim. 4.3; *Testimony of Truth* [NHC IX/3.29.20ff.]; Irenaeus, *Against Heresies* I 1.24.2; 28.1.4). Gnostic parallels are also found to the opponents' claim that the resurrection has already happened (2 Tim. 2.18; cf. *Treatise on Resurrection* [NHC I/4 49.15–16]; *Gospel of Philip* [NHC II/3 104.15–19; 121.1–8]). 'Myths and endless genealogies' also characterize the false teaching according to 1 Tim. 1.4; 4.7; 2 Tim. 4.4; Titus 1.14; 3.9. Numerous mythological speculations are likewise found in gnostic texts.

The false teaching is also characterized by Jewish elements. Thus the opponents claim to be teachers of the Law (1 Tim. 1.7; cf. Titus 1.9). According to Titus 1.10 the seductive teachers come from the circumcision group; in Titus 1.14 the mythological speculations are called Ἰουδαϊκοὶ μύθοι (Jewish myths). It is probably not the case that the opposed teaching penetrated the community from outside, since its advocates obviously appear in congregational gatherings (cf. 2 Tim. 2.16, 25; 3.8; Titus 1.9; 3.9). They had considerable success within the churches, as whole households accepted their teaching. Many devotees of the new doctrine were found among the wealthy women (cf. 2 Tim. 3.6). The naming of names in 1 Tim. 1.20; 2 Tim. 2.17; 4.14 also indicate that the false teaching was sponsored by elements within the church.

From the point of view of the history of religion, the doctrine of the oppo-nents[196] is mostly classified as a form of Jewish Christian gnosticism.[197] In this thesis the Jewish elements are considered a constitutive part of the false teaching, with a Jewish origin of gnosticism as such often a presupposition of this view. To be sure, this assumption is very disputed, for central elements of Jewish faith (strict monotheism, God as creator, positive valua-tion of creation) are very difficult to combine with the basic anti-creation orientation of gnostic systems. Moreover, if the Jewish elements are only classified as marginal phenomena, the suggestion easily emerges that we have here an early form of Christian gnosticism.[198] The ascetic tendencies within the opposed teaching have supported the assumption that the false teaching opposed by the Pastorals is to be attributed to encratite wandering prophets.[199] The appeal to γνῶσις (knowledge or 'gnosis'), the preoccupa-tion with myths and endless genealogies cannot however be integrated into this explanatory model.[200]

From the perspective of the history of religion, the doctrine opposed by the Pastoral letters must thus be described as *an early form of Christian gnosticism* that has incorporated some Jewish elements without having its basic content determined by them. Obviously the opponents advocate a massive realized eschatology in which salvation is understood as already present, probably derived from their interpretation of baptism and the possession of the Spirit associated with it. The ascetic tendencies of the opposing doctrine indicate that it understood the present world as the place of imprisonment, from which the gnostics sought to free entrapped souls by means of the redeeming knowledge of God. Both the creator and the creation are evaluated negatively, for the goal of the opposing doctrine was to overcome the hostile material world. In contrast, 1 Tim. 4.4–5 empha-sizes God's good work of creation, none of which is to be rejected. The mission of the false teachers was accomplished primarily in small house churches (2 Tim. 3.6ff.), which corresponds to the esoteric character of gnostic teaching. In terms of both chronology and content, the opposing

---

[196] A survey of research is presented by John J. Gunther, *St. Paul's Opponents* (see above 2.6.8) 4–5, who enumerates seventeen different categories into which the opponents have been placed. For the history of research cf. also Schlarb, *Gesunde Lehre* 73–82.

[197] Cf. Dibelius, *Pastorals* 65–67; Kümmel, *Introduction* 378–380; Walter Schmithals, *Gnosis und Neues Testament* (see above 2.6.8) 93–94; Brox, *Pastoralbriefe* 33ff.; G. Haufe, 'Gnostische Irrlehre' 332–333; Schenke and Fischer, *Einleitung* 219–220.

[198] Cf. Roloff, *1 Timotheusbrief* 228–239; Wolter, *Pastoralbriefe als Paulustradition* 265–266; Merkel, *Pastoralbriefe* 10, 13.

[199] Cf. Kretschmar, *Glaube*, 117, 138; Ulrich B. Müller, *Zur frühchristlichen Theologiegeschichte* (see above 5) 58ff. (Müller considers there to have been two groups opposed by the Pastorals: 1. Encratite wandering Jewish Christian prophets; 2. Pauline enthusiasts).

[200] For critique cf. Wolter, *Pastoralbriefe als Paulustradition* 261–264.

teaching stands closest to the statements of Revelation about false teachings in the churches of Asia Minor (cf. Rev. 2.6, 14, 15, 20, 24).

5.5.9 Basic Theological Ideas

Basic to the theology of the Pastorals is their reflexive movement back to Paul as apostle and teacher of the church. Paul is the apostle of Jesus Christ authorized by the will of God, *the* minister of the gospel (cf. 1 Tim. 1.1; 2.7; Titus 1.1; 2 Tim. 1.1; 1.11). The Pauline apostolate is valid for all nations and peoples (cf. 1 Tim. 2.7; 2 Tim. 4.17), to whom Paul proclaims the gospel with which he has been entrusted (1 Tim. 1.11; 2.6–7; 2 Tim. 1.10–11, 12; Titus 1.3). The gospel appears in the Pastorals as παραθήκη (deposit), as the most precious treasure of the church (cf. 1 Tim. 6.20–21; 2 Tim. 1.12, 14). In the gospel the saving event is proclaimed, and it is the apostolic ministry now to preserve and maintain this gospel by didactic proclamation.

As proclaimer of the gospel and guarantor of the tradition, Paul appears in the Pastorals as teacher as well as apostle. Paul the teacher instructs the churches in sound doctrine (cf. Titus 2.1). Within this teaching the gospel itself is included (cf. Titus 2.11–14), while at the same time the term παραθήκη (deposit) describes the totality of what is delivered to the churches as proclamation and ethical instruction. While the errorists with their false teaching split the churches, Timothy and Titus and thus the churches addressed through them are to hold fast to the original teaching and to the Scriptures (cf. 1 Tim. 1.3–7; 6.3–5; 2 Tim. 3.10–12, 15–16; Titus 1.10–2.15). The author of the Pastorals refuses to let the churches have anything to do with the false teaching – not discussion, but distance is commanded (cf. 1 Tim. 6.20; 2 Tim. 2.14, 16, 23; 3.5; Titus 3.9–11). Extensive sections of the Pastorals read like official directives (cf., e.g., 1 Tim. 2.1, 8, 12; 3.2, 7; Titus 2.1, 15; 2 Tim. 1.13–14; 2.1, 14, 22–23; 3.10) that when obeyed will serve to combat the false teaching.

As the prototypical believer Paul is at the same time the model for the churches (cf. 1 Tim. 1.15–16). In doctrine, in manner of life, in faith, and in suffering, the churches are to follow the example of Paul (cf. 2 Tim. 3.10–11; 1.13). Just as on the internal level of the text Paul serves as model for Timothy, so Timothy is to serve as a model for the churches (cf. 1 Tim. 4.12; 2 Tim. 3.10–11; cf. further Titus 2.7). Timothy and Titus are the apostles' own children in the faith (cf. 1 Tim. 1.2, 18; 2 Tim. 1.2; 2.1; Titus 1.4), so that Paul as model is made present in the church through those who exercise the ministerial office. Taken as a whole, the Pastorals present a thoroughly powerful picture of Paul, who as preacher, teacher, counselor and church organizer intervenes and fights for his churches. Paul is equally apostle, ecclesiastical authority, and the ideal Christian. The author of the Pastorals did not have to establish this superior position of Paul in the churches to which he writes, but rather writes in the context of a living Pauline tradition.

Closely associated in the Pastorals with the person of Paul are statements about the *offices of church leadership*.[201] It is the connection with the past figure of Paul that gives authority to official ministers in the church. The ministry of the gospel entrusted to Paul by God (cf. 1 Tim. 1.12) is now, in the absence of Paul, exercised by Timothy and Titus as prototypes of church leaders. Just as Paul was obligated in everything for the truth of the gospel, so also the church leaders now have the responsibility to preserve the tradition legitimated by the Pauline message (cf. 1 Tim. 6.20; 2 Tim. 1.2, 14).

In the process of representing this, the author of the Pastorals had the task of combining and reinterpreting two types of church structure that already existed in the churches before him.[202] The Pastorals contain statements about the office of elders [presbyters] (1 Tim. 5.17–18, 19; Titus 1.5–6) as well as lists of duties and qualifications for bishops and deacons (1 Tim. 3.2–13; Titus 1.7–9). The combination of the offices of elders [presbyters] and bishops/deacons is documented several times in the literature at the end of the first century CE (cf. Acts 14.23; 20.17; 1 Pet. 5.1–5; 1 Clem. 40–44). The office of elder that originated in Jewish tradition[203] requires age and maturity of the individual as decisive qualifications for leadership. This office is not found in the undisputed letters of Paul, since for him age itself is not a charismatic gift, and he considers all the functions and ministries of church leadership to represent the authority of the Spirit (cf. 1 Cor. 12.28–31).[204] Philippians, from the last phase of Paul's work, documents the ministry of the ἐπίσκοπος (bishop) and διάκονος

---

[201] On this point cf. Roloff, *1 Timotheusbrief* 169–189; Merkel, *Pastoralbriefe* 90–93.

[202] According to Roloff, *1 Timotheusbrief* 170, the author is not introducing any new offices, but he is concerned 'to integrate the already existing offices and ministries into a unified structure as far as possible and by giving them a new and deeper interpretation to restructure them so that they can better meet the tasks and challenges of the situation of his church.' In contrast, according to H. Merkel, *Pastoralbriefe* 13, the tensions that exist within the different statements about church offices in the Pastorals can be explained 'most simply by assuming that the office of elder was already known in the churches, while the author of the letters wants to introduce the model of bishops/deacons.'

[203] On this point cf. the Jerusalem inscription from the period 70 BCE reproduced by Adolf Deissmann, *Light from the Ancient East* (see above 2.3.1) 439–441; cf. in addition Acts 1.30; 14.23; 15.2, 4, 22–23; James 5.14.

[204] On the radical decrease in the number of statements about the Spirit in the Pastorals, cf. Wolter, *Pastoralbriefe als Paulustradition* 41ff.

(deacon) (Phil. 1.1). At first serving as leaders of the house churches, the *episkopoi* often had a variety of responsibilities in the individual congregations.

So too the διάκονοι exercised a number of different functions, including assignments within the framework of eucharistic worship and the church's ministry to the poor (cf. Mark 10.43–44; 2 Cor. 3.6; 4.1; 5.18). The parallel existence of these two forms of church structure in the Pastorals raises the question of which one the Pastor himself is pushing forward. A fusion of both types of organization was obviously not his goal, since only in Titus 1.5–9 do both forms of church order simply stand alongside each other without really being connected. It is rather the case that the author of the Pastorals favors a structure of bishops and deacons.[205] According to 1 Tim. 3.1 the office of the bishop is a good thing toward which one should aspire. The bishop is no longer merely responsible for one house church, but is the leader of the whole church in any given locale, surrounded by deacons and responsible elders. The new form of the bishop's office and the gradual takeover of the presbytery is illustrated by the ordination of Timothy in 1 Tim. 4.14. To be sure, the elders lay their hands on Timothy (according to 2 Tim. 1.6 Timothy was ordained by Paul), but he is ordained to be ἐπίσκοπος (bishop) of the whole local church.[206] It was not only the advent of false teaching that accelerated the establishment of a functionally efficient leadership office, since the ἐπίσκοπος (bishop) is to be responsible for the whole church in his area (cf. 1 Tim. 5.1–22). The church as a holy edifice established on God's authority, in which the saving truth that appeared in Jesus Christ and which alone is able to save is present (cf. 1 Tim. 3.15–16; 2 Tim. 2.19–21) must define itself over against false teaching. It is not legal categories, however, that define the essential nature of the episcopal office, since it is primarily a spiritual office, for it is the competence to teach that qualifies the leader of the church (1 Tim. 3.2; Titus 1.9). The bishop is addressed as the householder of God (Titus 1.7–9) who holds firm to right doctrine and withstands the opponents. As the apostle led his churches by the gospel, so now disciples of the apostle, equipped with Paul's own instructions, step forth in this role (cf. 1 Tim. 4.11, 13, 16; 2 Tim. 1.13; 2.24; 3.10, 14–17; Titus 2.1). Even in the apostle's absence, the gospel he proclaimed and his untiring ministry to the churches remain

---

[205] Cf. Roloff, *1 Timotheusbrief* 175.

[206] Cf. v. Lips, *Glaube – Gemeinde – Amt* 279: 'The significance of ordination as authorization and equipment of the office holder has as its goal on the one hand their official function and authority in the church, and on the other hand the preservation of tradition by inserting them into the continuity represented by the office.'

as the norm for the ministry of the apostle's students, to whom in turn the present church leaders are to orient themselves. As Scriptures filled with God's Spirit (cf. 2 Tim. 3.16), the Pastorals also make the claim to formulate for the churches comprehensively and definitively the binding will of the apostle Paul.

The Pastorals propagate a piety and style of life characterized by a circumspect and virtuous life of faith, works of love, endurance, modesty, hospitality and charity (cf. 1 Tim. 2.2; 4.7, 12; 6.6–11, 17–19; 2 Tim. 1.7; 2.22; 3.10; Titus 1.8; 2.1–2, 6, 11–13; 3.4–7). The author of the Pastorals thereby orients himself to the conventional norms of his time, and has the social integration of his churches as a goal (cf. 1 Tim. 2.2). The bishop must have a good reputation among non-Christians as well as among insiders (1 Tim. 3.7); women are not permitted to teach (1 Tim. 2.12) and slaves are to respect their masters (1 Tim. 6.1) and be obedient to them (Titus 2.9). For the churches of the Pastorals, there was obviously no contradiction between harking back to the apostle Paul as authority and model and at the same time adapting to pagan ethical norms, since both were presuppositions for the identity and stability of the churches. The false teachers nonetheless attempted to give the churches a new identity that on the one hand placed the basic appeal to Paul in question and on the other propagated a separation from the world. Then the existence of the churches would have been threatened both by social isolation and breaking away from their tradition.

The author of the Pastorals, in his particular historical situation also adopted genuine elements of Pauline theology. Titus 3.3–7 and 2 Tim. 1.8–10 precisely reproduce the substance of the Pauline doctrine of justification: God justifies human beings by grace alone, without works of the Law (cf. Gal. 2.16; Rom. 3.21ff.). The link between baptism and justification in Titus 3.5 is also found in 1 Cor. 6.11 and Rom. 6. The Pastorals predominant imperative is firmly anchored in the indicative in Titus 3.3–7. So too the dominant image of Paul in the three letters as model for church officers and for the whole church adopts a motif of the authentic Pauline letters, where the apostle repeatedly commends himself as a model for his churches (cf. 1 Thess. 1.6–7; 1 Cor. 4.16–17; 11.1; Gal. 4.12; Phil. 3.17; 4.9). In contrast, however, a clear theological deficit is revealed in the pneumatology of the Pastorals. The paucity of statements in which the term 'Spirit' appears is already significant. To be sure, the πνεῦμα (Spirit) is not simply restricted to those who hold ministerial office (cf. Titus 3.5), but still they are clearly the primary bearers of the Spirit (cf. 2 Tim. 1.6, 14; 1 Tim. 4.14). Ordination as both spiritual and legal-institutional act has as its goal both the authority of the office holder and the preservation of tradition.[207] Eschatological statements also recede, the parousia of the Lord will occur at the 'right time' (1 Tim. 6.15). This requires that the church have a continuing, sure foundation – sound doctrine (compare 2 Tim. 4.1 with 4.2–3). The eschatology of the Pastorals is not characterized by the undetermined future, but only by that which is permanent.

5.5.10 Tendencies of Recent Research

The Pastorals are frequently measured against the standard of Pauline theology and are evaluated as the product of a retrogressive theological development. Thus while S. Schulz accepts the necessity that the Pastorals were conditioned by their times, he does not accept the adequacy of the theological content of the Pastorals. 'After all, if one looks at the continuing effects of these theses of an early catholic understanding of office, apostolic succession and tradition, of the ideal of Christian brotherhood and a pious life . . . , then precisely for the sake of Paul one will not want to reproduce this early catholic development, but must countermand it.'[208] In the most recent study, however, it is no longer wholesale criticism that is the dominant note, but the concern to understand that the Pastorals want to come to terms with the particular historical situation and the theological leadership of Paul. In this process the central issue is the intention involved in the reception of Paul. J. Roloff emphasizes that the author by no means practices a rigid principle of tradition, 'but an interpretation of what has been received in a way that both appropriates it and applies it to new situations. From the conviction that it is in the historical form of the word of Paul that the church encounters the gospel, and that this word alone is the authority from which it can expect authentic direction and leadership, practical consequences are drawn here, in that a model for dealing with this apostolic word is developed. Thereby the development is initiated which, although already prepared for in several respects within the authentic Pauline letters, it was still by no means self-evident: the word of the apostle becomes an object of church proclamation.'[209] M. Wolter points to the Pauline imprint that had been stamped on the churches to which the Pastorals are directed. 'For the author of the Pastorals, and originally also for their churches, Paul was more than an authority; he was an indispensable element of their Christian identity.'[210] The Pastorals attempt to solve

---

[207] Cf. v. Lips, *Glaube – Gemeinde – Amt* 277ff.
[208] Siegfried Schulz, *Die Mitte der Schrift* (Stuttgart: Kohlhammer 1976) 109.
[209] Roloff, *1 Timotheusbrief* 377–378.
[210] Wolter, *Pastoralbriefe als Paulustradition* 270.

a problem that presents itself to every Christian community, 'namely that of the continuing orientation to its normative beginnings in view of a changed historical situation already given to the community and the threat of losing its identity. This threat is made the sharper by foreign options for understanding its identity that come from outside.'[211] In the context of this interpretation the Pastorals' doctrine of church offices loses its controversial theological explosiveness, for the bishop's office that is in process of formation is an essential instrument in securing the identity of the community, an instrument that is both historically necessary and theologically legitimate. Moreover, the ecclesiology of the Pastorals is not outlined on the basis of their concept of tradition and church office. 'For the Pastorals too the central determining factor for the view of the church is the Christ event.'[212]

So also the ethics of the Pastorals cannot simply be labeled wholesale as 'middle class,' since 'several times the Pastorals offer, precisely where one least expects it, only the development of ideas and tendencies that began with Paul himself.'[213]

The proximity of the Pastorals to genuine Pauline theology has received differing evaluations. H. Merkel sees the letters as completely in line with Paul, and considers that 'the theological basis of the Pastorals is the doctrine of justification.'[214] In contrast, J. Roloff detects in the Pastorals a substantial reduction of the Pauline doctrine of justification, for 'the force fields within which the doctrine of justification stands in Paul, with sin, law, and the works of the law on the one side, and Christ, grace, and faith on the other side, are no longer perceived' by the Pastorals.[215] In the judgment of N. Brox the Pastorals offer 'not so much an independent, original theology as instructions for a practical Christianity.'[216] Against the frequent affirmation of the Pastorals' lack of theological competence L. R. Donelson sets forth their tightly woven and reflective line of argument. They know that they are obligated to abide by Aristotelian logic,[217] and are oriented primarily to ethics. 'Given the theological fact that Jesus is not accessible and that the Spirit keeps relatively quiet, these letters suggest that the ordained and educated clergy can provide a version of Christianity that is reasonable and moral.'[218]

---

[211] *Ibid.*
[212] Roloff, *1 Timotheusbrief* 216.
[213] Reiser, 'Bürgerliches Christentum?' 43.
[214] Merkel, *Pastoralbriefe* 14.
[215] Roloff, *1 Timotheusbrief* 380.
[216] Brox, *Pastoralbriefe* 50.
[217] Cf. Donelson, *Pseudepigraphy* 67–113.
[218] *Ibid* 201.

Excursus 2: The Collection of the Pauline Letters and the Formation of the Canon

Literature

Collection of the Pauline Letters

Harnack, Adolf v. *Die Briefsammlung des Apostels Paulus und die anderen vorkonstanti-nischen christlichen Briefsammlungen.* Leipzig: Hinrichs, 1926; Mitton, C. L. *The Formation of the Pauline Corpus of Letters.* London 1955; Schmithals, Walter. 'Zur Abfassung und ältesten Sammlung der paulinischen Hauptbriefe,' ZNW 51 (1960) 225–245; Lietzmann, Hans. 'Einführung in die Textgeschichte der Paulusbriefe,' in *An die Römer*, ed. Hans Lietzmann (1971) (see above 2.8.1) 1–18; Gamble, Harry. 'The Redaction of the Pauline Letters and the Formation of the Pauline Corpus,' JBL 94 (1975) 403–418; Aland, Kurt. 'Die Entstehung des Corpus Paulinum,' in *Neutestamentliche Entwürfe*, TB 63, Munich: Kaiser, 1979, 302–350; Sand, Alexander. 'Überlieferung und Sammlung der Paulusbriefe,' in *Paulus in den neutestamentlichen Spätschriften*, ed. Karl Kertelge (1981) (see above 5) 11–24; Trobisch, David. *Die Entstehung der Paulusbriefsammlung*, NTOA 10. Göttingen: Vandenhoeck & Ruprecht, 1989; Trobisch, David. *Paul's Letter Collection: Tracing the Origins.* Minneapolis: Fortress Press, 1994

History of the New Testament Canon

Harnack, Adolf v. *Das Neue Testament um das Jahr 200.* Freiburg: J. C. B. Mohr (Paul Siebeck), 1889; Jülicher, A. (Fascher, E.), *Einleitung,* 451–558; Leipoldt, Johannes. *Geschichte des neutestamentlichen Kanons I.II.* Leipzig: Hinrichs, 1907, 1908; Lietzmann, Hans. 'Wie wurden die Bücher des neuen Testaments heilige Schrift?,' in *Kleine Schriften II*, ed. Kurt Aland, TU 68. Berlin: Akademie Verlag, 1958 (= 1907) 15–98; Käsemann, Ernst, ed. *Das Neue Testament als Kanon.* Göttingen: Vandenhoeck & Ruprecht, 1970; Campenhausen, Hans v. *The Formation of the Christian Bible.* Philadelphia: Fortress Press, 1972; Ohlig, Karl Heinz. *Die theologische Begründung des neutestamentlichen Kanons in der Alten Kirche.* Düsseldorf: Patmos, 1972; Sand, Alexander. *Kanon. Von den Anfängen bis zum Fragmentum Muratorianum*, HDG I 3a(1). Freiburg: Herder, 1974; Kümmel, W. G. *Introduction* (1975) 475–513; Schneemelcher, Wilhelm. 'Bibel III,' TRE 6 (1980) 22–48; Lührmann, Dieter. 'Gal. 2, 9 und die katholischen Briefe. Bemerkungen zum Kanon und zur regula fidei,' ZNW 72 (1981) 65–87; Merk, Otto. 'Bibelkanon 2,' EKL 1 (1986) 470–474; Metzger, Bruce M. *The Canon of the New Testament.* Oxford: Clarendon, 1987; Ritter, Adolf M. 'Die Entstehung des neutestamentlichen Kanons: Selbstdurchsetzung oder autoritative Entscheidung?' in *Kanon und Zensur*, eds. A. and J. Assmann. Munich: Wilhelm Fink, 1987, 93–99; Stuhlhofer, F. *Der Gebrauch der Bibel von Jesus bis Euseb. Eine statistische Untersuchung zur Kanonsgeschichte.* Wuppertal: Brockhaus, 1988; Paulsen, Henning. 'Sola scriptura und das Kanonproblem,' in *Sola scriptura*, eds. H. H. Schmid and J. Mehlhausen. Gütersloh: Gütersloher Verlagshaus (Gerd Mohn), 1991, 61–78; Schneemelcher, Wilhelm. 'General Introduction,' in *New Testament Apocrypha I* (1991) (see above 3.5.2) 9–75; Söding, Thomas. 'Erweis des Geistes und der Kraft. Der theologische Anspruch der paulinischen Evangeliumsverkündigung und die Anfänge der neutestamentlichen Kanons-Bildung,' Cath (M) 47 (1993) 184–209; Zahn, Theodor. *Geschichte des Neutestamentlichen Kanons I.II.* Leipzig-Erlangen: A. Deichert, 1888, 1892.

From the very beginning, the letters of Paul were read aloud in the gathered congregation (cf. 1 Thess. 5.27, Rom. 16.16), and the addressees could look at the original copy (cf. Gal. 6.11). The apostle himself counted on his letters being shared with other congregations, as indicated by the plural ταῖς ἐκκλησίαις τῆς Γαλατίας (the churches of Galatia) in Gal. 1.2 and the prescript in 2 Cor. 1.1b 'Corinth and all the saints in Achaia'. The exchange of Pauline letters among the individual congregations is confirmed by Col. 4.16. The authour of 2 Thessalonians reckons with the possibility of 'counterfeit' Pauline letters (2.2; 3.17), which presupposes the circulation of several letters among the churches under the name of Paul. Finally, 2 Peter documents the awareness and existence of numerous Pauline letters, when it remarks on the 'things difficult to understand' of which Paul speaks in all his letters.

These few New Testament statements about the way Paul's letters were treated in earliest Christianity already testify to the high regard in which they were held. Paul's letters were written from the needs of some actual occasion, but they were still much more than mere incidental writings. When Paul was absent, his letters took the apostle's place, for after all they contained the Pauline gospel and the ethical instructions necessary for life within the Christian community. It is by no means the case that in the churches they were filed away,[219] since with the exception of Ephesus the apostle did not remain very long at any one place, so that already during his lifetime his letters attained lasting significance. According to 2 Cor. 10.10–11, the persuasive power of Paul's letters was praised even by his opponents, so we cannot suppose that they were quickly forgotten.

After the death of the apostle, his co-workers and students became the bearers of a deutero-Paulinism that attempted to preserve the Pauline heritage in a new situation in church history. This deutero-Paulinism presupposed an enduring importance for the person of Paul and for his letters, so that it also assumed a key function in the collection of Paul's letters.[220]

[219] Contra H. M. Schenke and K. M. Fischer, *Einleitung* 1.239: 'They [sc. the Pauline letters] were read forth to the addressees, had their intended effect, more or less, or not at all, and then disappeared in the pigeonholes of the people who were in charge of them.'

[220] The thesis of David Trobisch, *Paulusbriefsammlung* 119–120 must be regarded as problematic, namely that Paul himself laid the foundation for the collection of his letters: 'On a trip to Jerusalem he met once again with a delegation from Ephesus. He gives them a copy of Romans, to which he appends a list of personal greetings and final wishes, along with a copy of

This is already confirmed by Colossians, which knows the Corinthian letters, Philemon, Romans, Galatians, and Philippians.[221] Ephesians as a reworking and expansion of Colossians appears also to refer to 1 Corinthians, Romans, and Galatians. 2 Thessalonians is oriented completely to a single authentic Pauline letter. The Pastoral corpus is of particular significance, their author adopting material from 1–2 Corinthians, Romans, Philippians, Colossians, and probably from Philemon. While Ephesians and 2 Thessalonians obviously are related more to single documents, it is probable that the Pastoral corpus already knew a collection of Pauline writings. When in 2 Tim. 3.16 the Pastorals are described as inspired Scripture, this points to a process of collection and selection within developing early Christian literature. Thus the assumption of P. Trummers is appropriate: 'As Pauline Pseudepigrapha, the Pastorals could only have been written and circulated in the course of a new edition of the previous corpus of Pauline letters. Despite the presence of credulity and the partly uncritical procedure of early Christian groups, a different origin would still have had to face a very perceptive critique and rejection.'[222] The Pauline corpus that was in process of growth was obviously supplemented by the Pastorals. The author of the Pastorals could thereby draw a living oral Pauline tradition alongside the authentic letters of Paul.

Deuteropaulinism testifies to an origin of the Pauline Corpus in *successive stages*. At first small local collections were formed,[223] which were then formed into larger units, a process in which the supplementation of the Pauline corpus by the Pastorals served as a catalyst. So too glosses such as 1 Cor. 14.33b–36, 2 Cor. 6.14–7.1; Rom. 7.25b; 16.25–27 point to a process of collection and to some extent of re-editing of the Pauline letters. There is no need to postulate some external event that provoked the collection of Paul's letters (e.g. by Marcion);[224] it was rather a natural process that began after the death of the apostle. The apostle's co-workers and the churches that stood in the Pauline tradition collected his letters in order to orient

---

2 Corinthians. Without being aware of it, he thereby laid the foundation for a collection out of which the Pauline Corpus would grow in stages: the most widely read collection of letters in world literature' (*ibid.* 130). Trobisch's assumptions proceed on the basis of a recension of the documents by the author himself, according to which Paul himself is responsible for the final redactional form of his letters (which consisted of small 'letters;' on 2 Corinthians cf. *ibid.* 123–128). He thus makes a thoroughly disputed structure of literary critical hypotheses (cf. Excursus 1 and the section 2.6.6 above) the basis for a string of historical suppositions!

[221] Cf. Eduard Lohse, *Colossians and Philemon* (see above 5.2.1) 181–82.

[222] Peter Trummer, 'Corpus Paulinum – Corpus Pastorale' (see above 5.5.1) 133.

[223] Cf. Walter Bauer, *Orthodoxy and Heresy* (see above 5.5.3) 221; Aland, *Corpus Paulinum* 335ff.

[224] Contra Campenhausen, *The Formation of the Christian Bible* 176–177: 'Marcion's Bible, however, now posed unavoidably the further question of the place and status of the Pauline letters.'

themselves theologically to him. Moreover, the Pauline letters make a truth claim which leads directly to their collection and normative function (cf. 1 Thess. 1.5; 2.13; 1 Cor. 2.4; 3.11; Rom. 1.16; 10.14–17).[225]

Only hypothetical statements may be ventured as to the contents of the first small collections, but 1–2 Corinthians, Romans, Galatians, Philippians, and Philemon were probably included from the very beginning. The previous missionary territory of Paul in Asia Minor also certainly played a decisive role in the collection of the Pauline letters. Thus Ephesus has often been supposed to have been the location of the first collection of Paul's letters.[226] There are a number of indications that point in this direction: (1) The church at Ephesus, as the location of the Pauline school, certainly had several Pauline letters at its disposal. (2) The assignment of the originally nameless Ephesians to the church in Ephesus confirms the great importance of this center of early Christian mission and theology. (3) Colossians and the Pastorals were probably written in Ephesus, which underscores the importance of this church for the deuteropauline movement. Finally, in this multi-cultural city letter collections of various famous authors of antiquity were known,[227] and Acts 19.19 testifies to the existence of book production in Ephesus. But the first collections of some Pauline books were also made in other churches,[228] thus for example in Rome,[229] where 1 Corinthians was known alongside Romans, and where possibly also Hebrews was for the first time included in a Pauline collection. These smaller collections of Pauline letters that stood at the beginning of the process probably overlapped somewhat, and then were included in successive 'primitive collections' and then in larger collections. This process of forming larger collections began about the turn of the century.[230]

Of the extra-canonical writings, 1 Clement, written about 96 CE in Rome, presupposes the existence of 1–2 Corinthians and Romans (cf. 1 Clem. 47.1–3).[231] The prescript and conclusion of the letter (1 Clem. 65.2) are clearly oriented to Pauline letter formulae; cf. additionally 1 Clem.

---

[225] Cf. Söding, 'Erweis des Geistes und der Kraft' 208.

[226] Cf. Edgar J. Goodspeed, *The Formation of the New Testament* (Chicago: University of Chicago Press, 1927²) 28; Mitton, *Formation* 44–49, 75–76; now especially Trobisch, *Paulusbriefsammlung* 113–117.

[227] On ancient letter collections, cf. Trobisch, *Paulusbriefsammlung* 84–104.

[228] For Corinth as the beginning point of the Pauline letter collection, cf. Theodor Zahn, *Geschichte des Neutestamentlichen Kanons* I/2, 836–837; Adolf v. Harnack, *Briefsammlung* 8–10; Schmithals, 'Zur Abfassung und ältesten Sammlung' 243–244.

[229] Lietzmann, *Einführung* 3 argues for Rome.

[230] The 'primitive collections' were probably made between 80 and 90 CE; cf. Aland, *Corpus Paulinum* 336.

[231] Cf. Andreas Lindemann, *Paulus im ältesten Christentum* (see above 5) 177–199.

3.3/1 Cor. 4.10; 1 Clem. 24/1 Cor. 15; 1 Clem. 32.2/ Rom. 9.5; 1 Clem. 35.5–6/ Rom. 1.29–32. On the other hand, there is no evidence of the reception of additional Pauline letters. Probably 1 Clement presupposes Hebrews (compare Heb. 1.3–13 with 1 Clem. 36.2–5),[232] in which case it must remain an open question as to whether Clement considers it Pauline. The letters of Ignatius, all written in Asia Minor around 110 CE within a brief period of time, show that Ignatius at least (cf. IgnEph. 12.2!) knew 1 Corinthians (cf. IgnEph. 16.1/1 Cor. 6.9–10; IgnEph. 18.1/1 Cor. 1.18, 20, 23; IgnRom. 5.1/1 Cor. 4.4) and Romans (IgnEph. 8.2/Rom. 8.5, 8–9).[233] So also Polycarp of Smryna used several letters of Paul, including Philippians (cf. Polycarp/Phil. 3.2; 11.3), 1 Corinthians (cf. Phil. 3.2–3/ 1 Cor. 13.13; Phil. 5.3/ 1 Cor. 6.9–10; Phil. 11.2/ 1 Cor. 6.2), 2 Corinthians (cf. Phil. 6.2b/ 2 Cor. 5.10), Galatians (cf. Phil. 3.3/ Gal. 6.2) and 1 Timothy (cf. Phil. 4.1/ 1 Tim. 6.10a).[234] Moreover, Polycarp formed a collection of Ignatius' letters, probably in analogy to a collection of Paul's letters that already existed (cf. Polycarp, Phil.).[235]

Further developments in the second century show that both the smaller as well as the larger collections of Paul's letters were not at the earliest stages unified, consistent collections. Thus Marcion, on dogmatic grounds, placed Galatians as the first item in his collection, since it was fundamental to his theology: Galatians, 1–2 Corinthians, Romans, 1–2 Thessalonians, Laodiceans [= Ephesians], Colossians, Philemon, Philippians). The other letters Marcion arranged according to their length, counting 1–2 Corinthians and 1–2 Thessalonians as one unit in each case.[236] The enumeration of the Pauline letters in the Muratorian Canon that originated ca. 200 CE probably follows a particular manuscript and presents the order: 1–2 Corinthians, Ephesians, Philippians, Colossians, Galatians, 1–2 Thessalonians, Romans, Philemon, Titus, 1–2 Timothy. In 𝔓[46] (ca. 200 CE), the arrangement appears to be according to length: Romans, Hebrews, 1–2 Corinthians, Ephesians, Galatians, Philippians, Colossians, 1(–2) Thessalonians (the text breaks off here).[237]

No generally accepted principle of order can be detected in the earliest canonical lists. They seem to confirm the assumption that the Pauline

---

[232] Cf. Kurt Aland, 'Methodische Bemerkungen zum Corpus Paulinum bei den Kirchenvätern des zweiten Jahrhunderts,' in *Kerygma und Logos* (FS C. Andresen), ed. A. M. Ritter (Göttingen: Vandenhoeck & Ruprecht, 1979) (29–48) 33ff.

[233] Cf. Lindemann, *Paulus im ältesten Christentum* (see above 5) 199–221.

[234] Cf. *ibid.* 221–232.

[235] Cf. Lietzmann, *Einführung* 3.

[236] On the 'Bible' of Marcion, cf. Adolf v. Harnack, *Marcion* (see above 5.5.3) 35ff.

[237] On this manuscript cf. Trobisch, *Paulusbriefsammlung* 26–28. The unusual position of Hebrews (shorter than 1 Corinthians) may be related to the tradition current in Rome.

corpus was formed from smaller collections, to which probably belonged 1–2 Corinthians, Galatians, Romans, Hebrews, Ephesians, Philippians and 1–2 Thessalonians. As the tradition developed additional writings were added, and an ordering according to length and a distinction between letters to churches and to individual persons begins to be recognizable, without already being a recognized principle.

The *tradition of dominical sayings* and the Christian interpretations of the *Old Testament* (LXX/MT)[238] form the point of departure for the formation of early Christian tradition. At the beginning of the process of the formation of the canon stand the *collections of Pauline letters*.[239] With them the tradition attains for the first time a form that can be interpreted. It initiates a process of reception that in differing ways is also to be presupposed with other writings of early Christian literature. This process attains its first discernable contours in the *Apostolic Fathers*. They cite the Old Testament (LXX) as γραφή (scripture), as something that is simply to be assumed, and adopt along with Paul's letters, in a different way, the traditions from and about Jesus. Echoes of the Synoptic tradition are found in 1 Clement, Didache, Ignatius, Barnabas, Hermas, Polycarp, and 2 Clement. Highest authority was attributed to the words of Jesus, even

---

[238] Ritter, *Entstehung des Kanons* 93–94, rightly emphasizes that important theologians of the ancient church also were always concerned with the Hebrew text of the Bible (Origen, Lucian of Antioch, Jerome). On the Old Testament canon cf. Gunther Wanke, 'Bibel I' *TRE* 6 (1980) 1–8. The Old Testament canon was not fixed at the 'synod' of Jamnia, but developed out of a lengthy process that even by ca. 100 CE was not yet firm on the inclusion of marginal books (cf. Günther Stemberger, 'Jabne und der Kanon,' JBTh 3 [1988] 163–174; further H. Peter Rüger, 'Das Werden des christlichen Alten Testaments,' JBTh 3 (1988) 175–189). At the same time, one must note that near the end of the first century CE Josephus, *Apion* 1.38–41 and 4 Ezra 14.44–47 indicate that a biblical canon of 22 (24) documents may be presupposed as obvious.

[239] In my opinion this is based on reasons of chronology and the observation that a process of reception first begins with the Pauline letters; cf. Edgar J. Goodspeed, 'The Editio princeps of Paul,' JBL 64 (1945) 193–204; Mitton, *Formation* 58ff.; Lindemann, *Paulus im ältesten Christentum* 33–35; Ferdinand Hahn, 'Die Heilige Schrift als älteste christliche Tradition und als Kanon,' in *Exegetische Beiträge zum ökumenischen Gespräch*, ed. F. Hahn (Göttingen: Vandenhoeck & Ruprecht, 1986) 34; Stuhlhofer, *Gebrauch der Bibel* 108–112; Söding, 'Erweis des Geistes und der Kraft' 206. The fact of the matter is that this position is also advocated by Theodor Zahn, *Grundriß der Geschichte des Neutestamentlichen Kanons* (Wuppertal 1985³) (= Leipzig: A. Deichert, 1904²) 35–41 when he deals first with the Pauline letters in his discussion of the oldest traces of the New Testament canon.

In contrast, Bruce M. Metzger, *The Canon of the New Testament* 257–262, evaluates the frequency with which the Gospels are cited as evidence that the Gospels attained canonical status first. Of course, in early Christianity and the ancient church the Jesus tradition was considered clearly superior to the Paul tradition on theological grounds. But this evaluation cannot be simply transferred to the historical question of the process of the formation of the canon! The Gospels, as collections of dominical sayings, first attained recognizable authority in the middle of the second century, a process that had clearly begun earlier for the Pauline letters (contra Th. Zahn, *Grundriss* 41, who claims that already between 80 and 110 CE the fourfold Gospel had attained canonical status).

though we cannot perceive that canonical status was already attributed to the Gospels themselves. 1 Clement nowhere refers to a written Gospel.[240] Contacts with the Synoptics (cf. 1 Clem. 13.2; 46.8) go back to oral tradition.

The Didache means by 'the gospel' (8.2; 11.3; 15.3, 4) the Gospel of Matthew;[241] thus the Didache, which originated about 110 CE,[242] documents the emerging authority of the one great Gospel. Ignatius too knows the Synoptic tradition, but whether he had the Gospel of Matthew in written form is disputed.[243] Ignatius speaks several times of the 'gospel,' (IgnPhld. 5.1.2; 8.2;[244] 9.2; IgnSm. 5.1; 7.2) without thereby referring to a fixed literary document. A knowledge of Matthew and Luke by Polycarp is to be supposed (cf. Phil. 2.3; 7.2), but neither document functions for him as 'Holy Scripture.' Whether the author of Barnabas (ca. 130 CE) knew the Gospel of Matthew is uncertain (but cf. Barn 4.14); for him the Old Testament is *the* Scripture. References to the Synoptic tradition are found in Hermas (cf. Sim. 9.20.1–2; Mand. 4.1.1; 4.9.8; Vis. 2.6). In Rome ca. 140 CE the author certainly knew Gospels, but does not cite them as authority.[245]

In 2 Clement a larger number of logia of Synoptic types are found (cf. 2 Clem 2.4; 3.2; 4.2; 6.1, 2; 8.5; 9.11; 13.4), which are in part introduced with quotation formulae. Alongside these are found quotations of unknown origin; cf. 2 Clem. 4.5; 5.2–4; 12.2; 13.2. These data and the introductory formula in 2 Clem. 8.5 (λέγει γὰρ ὁ κύριος ἐν τῷ εὐαγγελίῳ [for the Lord says in the Gospel]) suggest that the author of 2 Clement used, in addition to the Old Testament, an apocryphal gospel that has not come down to us.[246] There is a clearly recognizable tendency in 2 Clement to trace the authority of the Lord back to written documents. Papias occupies a special position in this regard, exhibiting an explicit interest in the transmission of early Christian traditions (cf. Eusebius, HE 3.39.4) and in the circumstances in which the Gospels of Mark and Matthew were written (see

---

[240] Cf. on this point Andreas Lindemann, *Die Clemensbriefe*, HNT 17 (Tübingen: J. C. B. Mohr [Paul Siebeck], 1992) 18.

[241] Cf. on this point Klaus Wengst, *Schriften des Urchristentums* (see above 3.1.4) 2.24–32.

[242] Cf. Kurt Niederwimmer, *Die Didache*, KAV 1 (Göttingen: Vandenhoeck & Ruprecht, 1989) 79.

[243] On this point cf. Helmut Koester, *Synoptische Überlieferung bei den Apostolischen Vätern* TU 65 (Berlin: Akademie Verlag, 1957) 24–61; Henning Paulsen, *Studien zur Theologie des Ignatius von Antiochien*, FKDG 29 (Göttingen: Vandenhoeck & Ruprecht, 1978) 37–39.

[244] By 'documents' in this passage Ignatius probably means the writings of the Old Testament. Cf. Walter Bauer and Henning Paulsen, *Die Briefe des Ignatius von Antiochia und der Polykarpbrief* (see above 2.9.6) 86.

[245] Cf. Koester, *Synoptische Überlieferung* 242–256.

[246] Cf. here Klaus Wengst, *Schriften des Urchristentums* (see above 3.1.4) 2.217–224; Lindemann, *Die Clemensbriefe* 192–195.

above 3.4.2 and 3.5.2). At the same time, Papias appears to give priority to the still living oral tradition, the written Gospels still receiving no authoritative position with him.[247]

This picture gradually changes in the middle of the second century. Justin (died ca. 165 CE) explains to his readers that the 'memoirs' (ἀπομνημονεύματα) of the apostles are called 'Gospels' (Apol. 66.3), and in Sunday worship 'the memoirs of the apostles or the writings of the prophets' are read (Apol. 67.3). The authors of the 'memoirs' are the apostles and those who followed them (Dial. 103.8). Justin not only knows all four Gospels but presupposes that they are regularly read in Christian worship.[248] The gospel-harmony, the *Diatessaron* (διὰ τεσσάρων = through the four [Gospels]) of Tatian, who had been converted by Justin,[249] likewise documents the knowledge and authority of the four Gospels, while at the same time letting us see how freely they were still used in relation to the oral tradition during the second half of the second century CE. It is not possible to distinguish canonical and apocryphal Gospels before Irenaeus; we can only speak of Gospels that later became either canonical or non-canonical.

With *Irenaeus* (died ca. 200 CE) the foundational phase of the process of canon formation achieves a first major turning point.[250] Concerning the composition of the four Gospels he writes: 'Matthew also issued a written Gospel among the Hebrews in their own dialect, while Peter and Paul were preaching at Rome and laying the foundations of the Church. After their death, Mark, the disciple and interpreter of Peter, did also hand down to us in writing what had been preached by Peter. Luke also, the companion of Paul, recorded in a book the Gospel preached by him. Afterwards, John, the disciple of the Lord, who also had leaned on his breast, did himself publish a Gospel during his residence at Ephesus in Asia.'[251] In addition, for Irenaeus the book of Acts and thirteen letters of Paul (Philemon is not quoted) are considered Scripture.[252] Of the Catholic Epistles Irenaeus

---

[247] Cf. Schneemelcher, 'Bibel' 31–32.

[248] Justin also refers to Revelation; Paul's letters are not named, but probably presupposed. On Justin cf. v. Campenhausen, *The Formation of the Christian Bible* 88–102; Eric F. Osborn, *Justin Martyr*, BHTh 47 (Tübingen: J. C. B. Mohr [Paul Siebeck], 1973).

[249] On his person and work, cf. Martin Elze, *Tatian und seine Theologie*, FKDG 9 (Göttingen: Vandenhoeck & Ruprecht, 1960); cf. in addition Robert M. Grant, 'Tatian and his Bible,' *Studia Patristica* 5, ed. Kurt Aland and Frank L. Cross, TU 63 (Berlin: Akademie Verlag, 1957) 297–306.

[250] Cf. v. Campenhausen, *The Formation of the Christian Bible* 181ff.; Schneemelcher, 'General Introduction' 26. On the reception of New Testament writings in Irenaeus, cf. Josef Hoh, *Die Lehre des Hl. Irenäus über das Neue Testament*, NTA VII/4.5 (Münster: Aschendorff, 1919).

[251] Irenaeus, *Against Heresies* 3.1.1 = Eusebius, HE 5.8.2–4.

[252] Cf. the texts in Erwin Preuschen, *Analecta* II (Tübingen: J.C.B. Mohr [Paul Siebeck], 1910²) 12–17.

mentions 1 Peter and 1–2 John. He is acquainted with Revelation, and Hermas is presented as γραφή (scripture) (*Against Heresies* 4.20.2). According to Eusebius (HE 5.26) Irenaeus also knew the Letter to the Hebrews. The fourfold Gospel was for Irenaeus already a given quantity. He explicitly defends it, e.g. by claiming that the four living creatures in Rev. 4.9 symbolize the four Evangelists (*Against Heresies* 3.11.8). Around 180 CE there thus existed (at least for southern France) a tripartite New Testament, only the third part of which was still open. Irenaeus considers the documents he regards as normative (preeminently the four Gospels) to be the deposit of the one gospel, the gospel preached and handed on by the apostles, the gospel that was faithfully preserved in the apostolic churches of the bishops and presbyters standing in the succession.[253] Irenaeus did not reflect on the canon, but presupposes the canonical principle. As a criterion of adequate theology in the debate with gnostics, he makes use of the rule of truth (κανών τῆς ἀληθείας, cf. *Against Heresies* 1.9.4; 2.27.1; 2.28.1; 3.2.1; 3.11.1; 3.12.6; 3.15.1). It contains the doctrine of Jesus Christ in the form of assured apostolic tradition, which is received in baptism and repeated in the confessions of faith.[254] Over against the omissions and falsifications of the gnostics Irenaeus sets the clear teaching of the church. It is clear to him 'that the truth proclaimed by the church is trustworthy, and that the theories of these men are but a tissue of falsehoods' (*Against Heresies* 1.9.5).

Evidence for the development at the end of the second century CE of a bipartite canon consisting of the Old and New Testaments also comes from the letter of the churches of Vienne and Lyon to the brothers and sisters in the faith in Asia Minor, a letter that cites Revelation as γραφή (Scripture) (cf. Eusebius, HE 5.1.58). The apologist Athenagoras (ca. 180 CE) quotes in his writings from the Old Testament, Matthew, Mark, and John as well as some of the letters of Paul, without, however, specifically naming them. Around 180 CE Melito of Sardis gives a catalogue of the books in the Old Testament canon (cf. Eusebius, HE 4.26.14: τὰ τῆς παλαιᾶς διαθήκης βιβλία [the books of the Old Covenant]), which allows us to suppose 'that he may well have given similar attention to ascertaining authentic New Testament documents.'[255] In 192 CE an unknown anti-Montanist author emphasized that no one should add to or take away from 'the word of the gospel of the New Testament' (τῷ τῆς τοῦ εὐαγγελίου καινῆς διαθήκης λόγῳ) (cf. Eusebius, HE 5.16). This is the first time that the expression

---

[253] These criteria are often described as 'catholic norms:' regula fidei, canon, office. On this cf. Karlmann Beyschlag, *Grundriß der Dogmengeschichte* (see above 2.5.8) 1.165–189.

[254] Cf. J. N. D. Kelly, *Early Christian Creeds* (New York: Longmans, Green, 1950) 80–86.

[255] Metzger, *The Canon of the New Testament* 123.

καινή διαθήκη is found in connection with a body of Christian literature.[256] The author presupposes a relatively fixed and normative collection of books, to which no changes can be made. Tertullian (born ca. 160 CE) quotes all the New Testament writings with the exception of James, 2 Peter, 2–3 John, and ascribes Hebrews to Barnabas.[257] Tertullian consistently presupposes the bipartite Bible of the Old and New Testaments. In Clement of Alexandria (died before 215 CE) quotations are found from all the New Testament books except Philemon, James, 2 Peter, and 2–3 John. He regards Hebrews as a Pauline letter (cf. Eusebius, HE 6.14.2–4).[258] Clement also cites from the Gospel of the Egyptians and the Gospel of the Hebrews, but distinguishes them from the 'Four Gospels.'[259] The way in which Clement receives ancient authors and documents later considered to be heretical shows that for him the boundaries of the canon were still open.

Toward the end of the second century it is clear that lists of the authoritative writings of Christianity were being made. The oldest extant such list, the Muratorian Canon that probably originated in Rome, is especially important.[260] The four Gospels are presented first,[261] then follow Acts and thirteen letters of Paul. At the end of this list of letters the author mentions two counterfeit Pauline letters (Laodiceans, Alexandrians). Then follow Jude and two letters of John, with a surprising item, the Wisdom of Solomon written 'by friends of Solomon in his honor.' Only two apocalypses are mentioned, that of Peter and the Revelation of John, with Hermas being numbered merely among the writings for private reading at home. The conclusion is formed by listing books of gnostic heretical teaching, which are specifically rejected.

Around 200 CE we have a clear picture: the four Gospels, Acts, and the thirteen letters of Paul are regarded as 'Holy Scripture.' The status of individual writings among the Catholic Epistles is still open, with Hebrews and Revelation being especially disputed. The criteria for the formation of the canon were *apostolicity*, *regula fidei*, and *use and acknowledgment in all churches.*

---

[256] Cf. W. C. van Unnik, ''Η καινή διαθήκη – A Problem in the Early History of the Canon,' in *Sparsa Collecta* 2, NT.S 30 (Leiden: E. J. Brill, 1980) 157–171.

[257] Texts in Preuschen, *Analecta* 2.24–26.

[258] Clement claimed Paul wrote Hebrews in the Hebrew language, and Luke then translated it into Greek.

[259] Texts in Preuschen, *Analecta* 2.18–24.

[260] The text is reprinted in Schneemelcher, 'General Introduction' 34–36. On the Muratorian Canon see especially von Campenhausen, *Formation of the Christian Bible* 243–262.

[261] Although the text is fragmentary, there is a consensus among scholars that line 1 refers to the Gospel of Mark and that Matthew was previously listed. Cf. Metzger, *Canon of the New Testament* 195.

What importance may be attached to gnosticism, Marcion, and the Montanists for the decisive phase of canon formation in the second century? *Gnostic Christians* developed their systems to a considerable degree by their arbitrary interpretation of the Old Testament and later by interpreting books that were accepted into the New Testament canon.[262] Both Basilides and Carpocrates as well as Valentinus and his disciples were all exegetes. The first exposition of a New Testament book was the commentary on John by Heracleon, the disciple of Valentinus (second half of the second century).[263] In addition to these, gnostic groups created and used numerous apocryphal writings.[264] This compelled the church to determine and secure the normative tradition.

The middle of the second century was a very important period for the formation of the canon. *Marcion* (ca. 85–160 CE) played a key role as the first person to define a collection of authoritative early Christian writings.[265] An edited version of the Gospel of Luke and an edition of ten Pauline letters freed of their purportedly Judaistic interpolations formed the 'canon' for his church. Marcion coordinated his 'Antitheses' to this 'Bible,' providing a work that gave the reasons for his exegetical and systematic decisions (see above 5.5.3). The contrast between law and gospel was connected by Marcion with the idea of two gods, the creator God who rules by law, and the 'alien' God who in the gospel deals with us in a merciful and compassionate manner. While the Old Testament sets forth the creator God, the Apostolikon and Gospel, when purified from its erroneous additions, proclaims the good and righteous God who has appeared in Jesus Christ.

According to A. v. Harnack, Marcion is 'the creator of the Christian Holy Scriptures.'[266] With the canon, something new emerges quite precipitously into the history of Christian theology.[267] H. v. Campenhausen adopted this position: 'The idea and the reality of a Christian Bible were the works of Marcion, and the Church which rejected his work, so far from

---

[262] On this cf. Georg Heinrici, *Die valentinianische Gnosis und die heilige Schrift* (Berlin: Wiegandt u. Greben, 1871); Carola Barth, *Die Interpretation des Neuen Testaments in der Valentinianischen Gnosis* (Leipzig: Hinrichs, 1911); Metzger, *Canon of the New Testament* 75–90.

[263] Cf. Elaine Pagels, *The Johannine Gospel in Gnostic Exegesis: Heracleon's Commentary on John* (New York: Abingdon, 1973) 57.

[264] Cf. the survey in Henri Charles Puech, 'Other Gnostic Gospels and Related Documents,' in *New Testament Apocrypha* I, ed. W. Schneemelcher (see above 3.5.2.) 354–414 (important Nag Hammadi texts also printed there).

[265] Alongside the foundational study of v. Harnack, *Marcion* (see above 5.5.3), cf. also v. Campenhausen, *The Formation of the Christian Bible* 148–165; Lindemann, *Paulus im ältesten Christentum* (see above 5) 378–395; Barbara Aland, 'Marcion/Marcioniten,' *TRE* 22 (1991) 89–101; Metzger, *Canon of the New Testament* 90–99.

[266] Harnack, *Marcion* (see above 5.5.3) 151.

[267] Cf. Adolf v. Harnack, *History of Dogma* (London, Williams & Norgate, 1896) 1.378, 387.

being ahead of him in this field, from a formal point of view simply followed his example.'[268] It is true, of course, that prior to Marcion there was no normative establishment of canonical Scripture, but the Gospels and especially the letters of Paul had for a long time been firm elements of Christian tradition, being read in the worship service and cited as authorities. Marcion's adoption of the Pauline corpus shows the high regard in which these writings were already held in the middle of the second century.[269] Marcion's revising of the text and the reaction that this occasioned can only be explained if it be accepted that there was already an awareness of the extent and form of normative tradition. The fundamentally dualistic conception of Marcion and his rejection of the Old Testament could not continue without reaction, while at the same time being embedded in the comprehensive process of early Christian and ancient church formation of tradition and the determination of its authentic form. It is therefore to be supposed that Marcion did not first begin the process of canon formation, but as a part of this process himself accelerated it by his actions.[270]

Montanism was a prophetic movement that broke out in Phrygia in 172 (or 157) CE,[271] whose advocates claimed to communicate current revelations from the Holy Spirit. The goal of the Montanists was a reform of church life (marriage, fasts, penance, martyrdom). The Montanists are important for the formation of the canon in two ways: (1) The phenomenon of current eschatological prophecy raised the question of the relation of present revelation to the tradition that had been handed on. (2) The Montanists produced many new writings themselves (cf. Eusebius HE 6.20.3: καινὰς γραφάς, new writings/Scriptures) and themselves adopted above all the Gospel and Revelation of John. They thereby evoked a vigorous debate concerning the legitimacy of these two writings (Alogoi, Gaius)[272] and thus made the issue of identifying the normative tradition even more intense. Montanism was not 'the factor which brought about the concentration of the Canon into a "New Testament",'[273] but like Marcion did accelerate the process of canon formation.

---

[268] Campenhausen, *Formation of the Christian Bible* 148.

[269] Cf. Lindemann, *Paulus im ältesten Christentum* (see above 5) 381. Lindemann points out in addition that there can be no talk of a 'silence' of Paul in the course of the second century (Hermas, Justin, Hegesippus), though this view is often stated.

[270] Cf. Kümmel, *Introduction* 487–488; Schneemelcher, 'Bibel' 37; Merk, 'Bibelkanon' 472; Ritter, 'Entstehung des Kanons' 96; Metzger, *Canon of the New Testament* 99.

[271] For an introduction cf. W. H. C. Frend, 'Montanismus,' *TRE* 23 (1993) 271–279; on the history of the canon cf. Henning Paulsen, 'Die Bedeutung des Montanismus für die Herausbildung des Kanons,' VigChr 32 (1978) 19–52; Metzger, *Canon of the New Testament* 99–110.

[272] Cf. S. G. Hall, 'Aloger,' *TRE* 2 (1978) 290–295.

[273] So v. Campenhausen, *Formation of the Christian Bible* 22.

The consolidation of the canon in the third century and its authoritative conclusion in the fourth century were definitively influenced by the territorial history of the respective regions of the church. Through his extensive travels, Origen (ca. 185–254 CE) became an important witness to the history of the canon not only in the *Greek-speaking East*,[274] but in other parts of the Empire as well. He was the first to establish which documents had attained authority throughout the church as a whole (cf. Eusebius, HE 6.25). He distinguished three classes: (1) ὁμολογούμενα, i.e., generally acknowledged writings (the four Gospels, Acts, thirteen letters of Paul, 1 Peter, 1 John, Revelation); (2) ἀμφιβαλλόμενα, i.e., writings about which there was some doubt (2 Peter, 2–3 John, Hebrews,[275] James, and Jude); (3) ψευδῆ, i.e., falsifications, writings composed by heretics (Gospel of Thomas, Gospel of the Egyptians, Gospel of Matthias, Gospel of Basilides).

In his own writings Origen wavers as to the precise boundaries of the canon. In the East, especially Revelation remained on the 'disputed' list. About the middle of the third century Bishop Dionysius of Alexandria concluded that it could not have been written by the apostle John and attributed it to an unknown John (cf. Eusebius, HE 7.25). This judgment had a lasting effect, so that Eusebius (ca. 264–340 CE) still commented in his *Ecclesiastical History* (begun before 300 CE) that one could include Revelation in the list of *homologumena* 'if one is so inclined' (HE 3.25.2). The books that without doubt belong in this category are the four Gospels, Acts, fourteen letters of Paul (including Hebrews[276]), 1 Peter and 1 John. The second category is comprised of writings acknowledged in several areas of the church, but not in others (ἀντιλεγόμενα [disputed]): James, Jude, 2 Peter, 2–3 John. In the category of rejected, false (νόθα) books he lists Hermas, Barnabas, Didache, Acts of Paul, Apocalypse of Peter, Gospel of the Hebrews and also the Revelation of John (HE 3.25.4).

The twofold naming of Revelation, listing it in two categories, shows that in some particular cases a consensus had not been attained even at this late date, for Cyril of Jerusalem, Gregory Nazianus, and Amphilochius of Iconium also rejected Revelation. This is confirmed by the Codex Claramonanus (D^P, 6th century), where a list of biblical books in Latin, originally composed in Greek, is included between Philemon and

---

[274] Cf. on this point Metzger, *Canon of the New Testament* 135–141.

[275] Origin considers the theology of Hebrews to be Pauline, but not its style and form of expression. According to his information, Clement of Rome or Luke could have written the letter. He can accept it if churches declare this document to be Pauline, but at the same time comments, 'But who actually wrote this letter, surely God only knows' (Eusebius, HE 6.25.14: τίς δὲ ὁ γράψας τὴν ἐπιστολήν, τὸ μὲν ἀληθὲς θεὸς οἶδεν.)

[276] But cf. Eusebius, HE 3.3.4; 38.1–3, where he reviews divergent opinions.

Hebrews. The list was probably originally composed around 300 CE.[277]
Here, 'canonical' books are the four Gospels, the letters of Paul,[278] the
seven Catholic Epistles and Revelation, while Hebrews is missing. The list
also includes Barnabas, Hermas, the Acts of Paul and the Apocalypse of
Peter. Particularly in the East the number of Catholic Epistles was disputed for a long time (cf. Eusebius). It is not until the thirty-ninth festal
letter of Athanasius, Easter 367 CE, that we can see the seven Catholic
Epistles having been firmly established.[279] The following twenty-seven
writings are set forth without qualification as the 'springs of salvation': the
four Gospels, Acts, seven Catholic Epistles, fourteen letters of Paul
(including Hebrews), Revelation. Athanasius adds to this list: 'These are
the springs of salvation, in order that he who is thirsty may fully refresh
himself with the words contained in them. In them alone is the true
doctrine of piety proclaimed. Let no one add anything to them or take
anything away from them . . . '.[280] Nonetheless, the status of Revelation
remained a topic of dispute in the Greek church for centuries. Thus the
Stichometry of Nicephoros from the ninth century still does not include
Revelation in the canon.

In the *Latin West* the development toward a closing of the canon took
place more quickly. To be sure, the canonical status of individual Catholic
Epistles and especially of Hebrews as a Pauline letter remained debatable
for a long time. Thus Gaius does not include Hebrews in the Pauline
letters,[281] and the Muratorian Canon also ignores it. Cyprian (died 258 CE)
documents the four Gospels, Acts, thirteen letters of Paul, 1 Peter, 1 John,
Revelation, but not James, 2 Peter, 2–3 John and Hebrews. In a North
African canon (Mommsen Canon, from ca. 360 CE) James, Jude, and
Hebrews are missing.[282] So too Ambrosiaster (ca. 370 CE) and Pelagius (ca.
360–418 CE) do not list Hebrews among the letters of Paul. It was first
under the influence of the canon of Athanasius and the influence of Jerome
(347–420 CE) that the canon with twenty-seven books became normative.

---

[277] Cf. on this point Theodor Zahn, *Geschichte des Neutestamentlichen Kanons* II/1, 157–172;
differently Jülicher (- Fascher), *Einleitung* 525.

[278] Philippians, 1–2 Thessalonians are missing, probably as an oversight.

[279] Dieter Lührmann supposes that the sevenfold structure must be seen as an ordering
principle related to Galatians 2.9 at least from the time of the Muratorian Canon: 'The meaning
of expanding the epistolary section of the New Testament beyond the Pauline Corpus by precisely these Catholic Epistles is then to place alongside the letters of Paul those of the three
"principal apostles" in order to document a common testimony of the apostles for church
doctrine' (Lührmann, 'Gal. 2,9 und die katholischen Briefe' 72).

[280] Text according to Schneemelcher, 'General Introduction' 50.

[281] Cf. Eusebius HE 6.20.3, where Eusebius explicitly comments: 'Still today it is not considered a writing of the apostle by some Romans.'

[282] Text in Preuschen, *Analecta* 36–40.

The Decretum Gelasianum[283] contains a canonical list that probably goes back to a Roman synod in 382 CE. It includes the twenty-seven books of the Athanasian canon, though in a different order. The synod of Hippo Regius (393 CE) and the synod of Carthage (397 CE) included Hebrews in the canon, but clearly distinguished it from the Pauline letters. Only after a further synod in 419 CE was Hebrews explicitly included among the Pauline letters.[284] Since the turn from the fourth century to the fifth, in the Latin church the canon has been closed and accepted.

A special development occurred in the areas of the church where the *Syrian language* was spoken.[285] Tatian's *Diatessaron* was considered authoritative in many churches until the fifth century. Alongside it, the letters of Paul (including Hebrews, but without Philemon) and Acts were used, with the Catholic Epistles and Revelation missing. In addition Ephraem (ca. 306–373) knew the document called 'Third Letter to the Corinthians' and considered it canonical. The oldest Syrian translations of the four Gospels, Acts, and the fourteen letters of Paul were made around 300 CE (*Vetus Syra*). The most widely used Syriac version of the Bible, the Peshitta (first half of the fifth century), was adjusted to coincide with the Greek canon. 3 Corinthians was no longer listed, and alongside the four Gospels, Acts, and fourteen Pauline letters (including Hebrews) there now appears also the three large Catholic Epistles (James, 1 Peter, 1 John), but 2–3 John, 2 Peter, Jude, and Revelation are still missing. The Syrian canon thus consisted of twenty-two books. For the Nestorian church of east Syria this continued to be the canon. In the Monophysite church of west Syria in 508 CE the Peshitta, under the authorization of Bishop Philoxenus of Mabbug, was revised (the adoption of 2–3 John, 2 Peter, Jude, Revelation). Nonetheless, the authority of James, 2 Peter, Jude, 2–3 John and Revelation remained in dispute for a long time.

The process of the formation of the New Testament canon was essentially carried on and determined by the *churches* in which the individual writings possessed authority. Authoritative sessions of individuals, movements, or synods[286] did not call for the assembling of holy scriptures; it was a matter of internal consistency and necessity: the Old Testament as the canon that already existed, and the internal claim made by the Pauline letters and the Gospels themselves, as well as the ever increasing distance

---

[283] Text in Schneemelcher, 'General Introduction' 38–40.

[284] On the chequered reception history of Hebrews, cf. Stuhlhofer, *Gebrauch der Bibel* 105–108.

[285] On this point cf. Metzger, *Canon of the New Testament* 218–223.

[286] The word κανών in the sense of 'list of authoritative writings' appears for the first time in Canon 59 of the provincial synod of Laodicea (ca. 360 CE). Cf. Zahn, *Grundriß* 1–11; Metzger, *Canon of the New Testament* 289–293.

from the original events, all demanded a reception of witnesses normative
for Christian faith. Marcion, the Montanists and the formation of the
imperial church in the fourth century merely accelerated this development.
The formation of the canon thus belongs within the process of the necessary and consistent self-definition of the church.

As a process of gathering, the formation of the canon was at the same
time a process of selection. The ancient church thereby withstood both the
temptation toward a reductionism (Marcion, Tatian) as well as the danger
of an inflation (gnosticism) of normative writings.[287] With the canon of
twenty-seven documents the church held fast to a plurality, without
making pluralism into a program.

---

[287] On the writings with temporary or local canonicity cf. Metzger, *Canon of the New
Testament* 186–189 (e.g. Gospel of the Hebrews, Gospel of the Egyptians, Gospel of Peter; Acts
of Paul, Acts of John, and Acts of Peter; the Third Letter of Paul to the Corinthians, the Epistle
to the Laodiceans, the Apocalypse of Peter, the Apocalypse of Paul).

6

The Letter to the Hebrews

6.1 Literature

Commentaries

Windisch, Hans. *Der Herbräerbrief*, HNT 14. Tübingen: J. C. B. Mohr (Paul Siebeck), 1931²; Braun, Herbert. *An die Hebräer*, HNT 14. Tübingen: J. C. B. Mohr (Paul Siebeck), 1984; Hegermann, Harald. *Der Brief an die Hebräer*, ThHK 16. Berlin: Evangelische Verlagsanstalt 1988; Attridge, Harry W. *The Epistle to the Hebrews*, Hermeneia. Philadelphia: Fortress Press, 1989; Bruce, F. F. *The Epistle to the Hebrews*, NIC. Grand Rapids: Eerdmans, 1990²; Lane, William L. *Hebrews*, WBC 47. Waco: Word, 1991; Strobel, August. *Der Brief an die Hebräer*, NTD 9. Göttingen: Vandenhoeck & Ruprecht, 1991⁴; Weiß, Hans Friedrich. *Der Brief an die Hebräer*, KEK 13. Göttingen: Vandenhoeck & Ruprecht, 1991; Grässer, Erich. *An die Hebräer*, EKK XVII/1.2.3. Neukirchen: Neukirchener Verlag, 1990, 1993, 1997.

Monographs

Schierse, Franz-Josef. *Verheißung und Heilsvollendung. Zur theologischen Grundfrage des Hebräerbriefes*, MThS 9. Munich: Zink, 1955; Grässer, Erich. *Der Glaube im Hebräerbrief*, MThSt 2. Marburg: Elwert, 1965; Theißen, Gerd. *Untersuchungen zum Hebräerbrief*, StNT 2. Gütersloh: Gütersloher Verlagshaus (Gerd Mohn), 1969; Hofius, Otfried. *Katapausis*, WUNT 11. Tübingen: J. C. B. Mohr (Paul Siebeck), 1970; Zimmermann, Heinrich. *Das Bekenntnis der Hoffnung*, BBB 47. Bonn: Hanstein, 1977; Laub, Franz. *Bekenntnis und Auslegung*, BU 15. Regensburg: Pustet, 1980; Loader, William R.G. *Sohn und Hoherpriester*, WMANT 53. Neukirchen-Vluyn: Neukirchener Verlag, 1981; Peterson, David. *Hebrews and Perfection*, SNTSMS 47 Cambridge: Cambridge University Press, 1982; Käsemann, Ernst. *The Wandering People of God*. Minneapolis: Augsburg, 1984; Rissi, Mathias. *Die Theologie des Hebräerbriefes*, WUNT 41. Tübingen: J. C. B. Mohr (Paul Siebeck), 1987; Vanhoye, Albert. *Structure and Message of the Epistle to the Hebrews*. Rome: Pontifical Biblical Institute, 1989; Hurst, Larry D. *The Epistle to the Hebrews. Its Background of Thought*, SNTSMS 65. Cambridge: Cambridge University Press, 1990.

Articles

Braun, Herbert. 'Die Gewinnung der Gewißheit in dem Hebräerbrief,' ThLZ 96 (1971) 321–330; Grässer, Erich. 'Zur Christologie des Hebräerbriefes' in (FS H.

Braun) Tübingen: J. C. B. Mohr (Paul Siebeck) 1973, 195–206; Vanhoye, Albert.
'Hebräerbrief,' *TRE* 14 (1985) 494–505; Laub, Franz. '"Schaut auf Jesus" (Hebr. 3,1).
Die Bedeutung des irdischen Jesus für den Glauben nach dem Hebräerbrief,' in *Vom
Urchristentum zu Jesus* (FS J. Gnilka), eds. Hubert Frankemölle and Karl Kertelge.
Freiburg: Herder, 1989, 417–432; Roloff, Jürgen. 'Der mitleidende Hohepriester,' in
Exegetische Verantwortung in der Kirche. Göttingen: Vandenhoeck & Ruprecht, 1990,
144–167; Hegermann, Harald. 'Christologie im Hebräerbrief,' in *Anfänge der
Christologie* (FS F. Hahn), ed. Cilliers Breytenbach and Henning Paulsen. Göttingen:
Vandenhoeck & Ruprecht, 1991, 337–351; Laub, Franz. '"Ein für allemal
hineingegangen in das Allerheiligste"' (Hebr 9,12). Zum Verständnis des
Kreuzestodes im Hebräerbrief,' BZ 35 (1991) 65–85; Söding, Thomas. 'Zuversicht
und Geduld im Schauen auf Jesus. Zum Glaubensbegriff des Hebräerbriefes,' ZNW
82 (1991) 214–241; Grässer, Erich. 'Aufbruch und Verheißung,' in *Aufsätze zum
Hebräerbrief,* eds. Martin Evang and Otto Merk, BZNW 65. Berlin: Walter de
Gruyter, 1992 (important collection); Backhaus, Knut. 'Der Hebräerbrief und die
Paulus-Schule,' BZ 37 (1993) 183–208.

History of Research / Bibliographies

Feld, Helmut. *Der Hebräerbrief,* EdF 228. Darmstadt: Wissenschaftliche Buchgesellschaft, 1985; Grässer, Erich. ThR 30 (1964) 138–236; ThR 56 (1991) 113–139.

6.2 Author

The authorship question is one of the great riddles of Hebrews. The
letter itself provides no information at all about the author, although it may
be the case that Heb. 13.23–24 is supposed to suggest Pauline authorship:
'I want you to know that our brother Timothy has been set free; and if he
comes in time, he will be with me when I see you. Greet all your leaders
and all the saints. Those from Italy send you greetings.' These comments
are quite unexpected in view of the preceding content of the letter, so that
the epistolary conclusion Heb. 13.22–25 oriented to the Pauline letter form
could have been added secondarily, possibly by the editor of a collection of
Pauline letters.[1] On the other hand, if the letter's conclusion is considered
original, the only positive indication that could be based on it is that the
author of Hebrews wants his writing to be understood within the context
of Pauline theology. In view of this situation with regard to the tradition,
it is no surprise that in the course of the history of the letter's interpretation it has been attributed to a large number of personalities in early

---

[1] Cf. Grässer, *Hebräerbrief* 22. One might adduce in support of this thesis the fact that in the
oldest textual attestation 𝔓⁴⁶ (ca. 200 CE) Hebrews is found immediately following Romans. On
the varied history of Hebrews in the process of the formation of the canon cf. above Excursus 2:
'The Collection of the Pauline Letters and the Formation of the Canon.'

Christianity. The spectrum reaches from Paul to Mary the Lord's mother.[2] Most recent exegetes have been satisfied to state that Hebrews was written by an unknown author.[3] All agree that the author was familiar with the cultural tradition of Hellenistic Judaism, that he had a comprehensive knowledge of the Old Testament and its hermeneutical tradition in Hellenistic Judaism, and that he was highly skilled in rhetorical ability. As a teacher of the church (cf. Heb. 6.1–2, as well as 5.12; 13.9) who at the same time is himself a hearer (cf. Heb. 1.2; 2.1, 3), he attempts to awaken a fresh confidence in the faith by a comprehensive new interpretation of the Christ kerygma. A. Strobel considers Apollos possibly to be the author of Hebrews.[4] In his person are united a Hellenistic-Alexandrian education and personal contact with the apostle Paul. So also H. Hegermann places the author in immediate proximity to Paul, a companion of Paul who had a Hellenistic Jewish education.[5] In contrast, E. Grässer regards the semi-pseudonymous character of Hebrews as no accident. 'On theological grounds Hebrews was from the outset composed as an anonymous document.'[6] The issue of authorship is not important for a theological understanding of the writing, since the theologically significant content of Hebrews speaks for itself.

6.3 Place and Time of Composition

Hebrews 13.23–24 probably represents a claim that the document was written in Italy (Rome).[7] Additional evidence for a *Roman*[8] origin is the possible reflection of Heb. 1.3–4 in 1 Clement 36.2–5, especially since a church tradition available to both authors may stand behind both texts,[9]

---

[2] On this point cf. the data in Grässer, *Hebräerbrief* 1.19–21.

[3] This view is advocated, with individual variations in their line of argument, by Braun, *Hebräerbrief* 3; Bruce, *Hebrews* 20; Attridge, *Hebrews* 6; F. Laub, *Hebräerbrief*, SKK 14 (Stuttgart: Katholisches Bibelwerk, 1988) 17; Claus Peter März, *Hebräerbrief*, NEB 16 (Würzburg: Echter, 1990²) 18–20; Grässer, *Hebräerbrief* 1.19–22; Weiß, *Hebräerbrief* 61.

[4] Cf. Strobel, *Hebräerbrief* 12.

[5] Cf. Hegermann, *Hebräerbrief* 9–10.

[6] Grässer, *Hebräerbrief* 1.22.

[7] The expression 'those from Italy send you greetings' in Heb 13.24 can be interpreted in two ways: (1) those who write from Italy (so e.g., Strobel, *Hebräerbrief* 185); (2) those who originally came from Italy but are now elsewhere send greetings back to Italy (so e.g., Hegermann, *Hebräerbrief* 287).

[8] Among those who argue for Rome as the place of composition are Bruce, *Hebrews* 14; Laub, *Hebräerbrief* 18; Vielhauer, *Urchristliche Literatur* 251; Grässer, *Hebräerbrief* 1.22. Strobel, *Hebräerbrief* 13, speaks in general of Italy as the provenance of Hebrews. Braun, *Hebräerbrief* 2; Hegermann, *Hebräerbrief* 11; Weiß, *Hebräerbrief* 76 argue that a probable location for the writing of Hebrews cannot be determined.

[9] Cf. Hegermann, *Hebräerbrief* 33; Grässer, *Hebräerbrief* 1.22.

and the description of the congregational leaders as ἡγούμενοι (leaders) in
Heb. 13.7, 17, 24 and 1 Clem. 1.3. However, certainty cannot be attained
on this point. The claim of Hebrews to have been written in Rome can also
be understood as evidence for a different point of origin, perhaps in the
eastern part of the Empire.[10] So also, the time when Hebrews was written
can be inferred only hypothetically. The lack of any reference to the
temple's destruction (but cf. Heb. 8.13) is often regarded as an argument
for dating it before 70 CE.[11] But of course Hebrews is not oriented to the
temple, but to the tabernacle (cf. Heb. 9.1–7; NRSV translates 'tent' in
NT), and its argument is made independently of historical presuppositions.[12] Hebrews already looks back on the beginnings of the Jesus tradition
and utilizes a reflective understanding of Christian tradition (cf. Heb. 2.3;
13.7). The church has already had to endure a persecution (cf. Heb.
10.32–34), so that the probable time of composition may be placed between
80 and 90 CE.[13] From the point of view of tradition history, the proximity
to 1 Clement confirms the location of Hebrews in the history of early
Christian theology at the *end of the first century* CE.[14]

6.4 Intended Readership

What sort of situation among the addressees occasioned the author of
Hebrews[15] to write a λόγος τῆς παρακλήσεως (word of exhortation) (Heb.
13.22)? In response to the message of salvation the Christian community
addressed had become 'sluggish' and 'dull in understanding' (cf. Heb. 5.11;
6.11–12). Attendance at the common worship services is being neglected
(cf. Heb. 10.25), and the church must start all over again with the funda-
mentals of the faith (cf. Heb. 5.12–6.2). Apostasy from the faith and the
problems associated with the possibility of a second repentance are themes
currently alive in the church's discussions (cf. Heb. 6.4–6; 10.26–29;
12.16–17; in addition 3.12 and 12.25).[16] Whoever denies the faith has

---

[10] As argued by Kurt Aland, *Corpus Paulinum bei den Kirchenvätern* (see above Excursus 2)
43–44.
[11] Cf. Bruce, *Hebräerbrief* 22 (before 70 CE); Strobel, *Hebräerbrief* 11 (ca. 60).
[12] Cf. Grässer, *Hebräerbrief* 1.25.
[13] Cf. Vielhauer, *Urchristliche Literatur* 251; Laub, *Hebräerbrief* 19; Hegermann, *Hebräerbrief*
11; Grässer, *Hebräerbrief* 1.25; Weiß, *Hebräerbrief* 77.
[14] For Kurt Aland, *Corpus Paulinum bei den Kirchenvätern* 44, the reception of Hebrews in 1
Clement is the decisive argument for his thesis that Hebrews belongs in the time around 70 CE.
[15] The superscripted title Πρὸς Ἑβραίους is rightly today generally regarded as secondary.
Cf. Grässer, *Hebräerbrief* 1.41–45. Hebrews is often considered to be addressed to a church group
in Rome; so most recently Backhaus, 'Hebräerbrief und die Paulus-Schule' 196ff.
[16] For an analysis of the texts cf. Ingrid Goldhahn-Müller, *Die Grenze der Gemeinde*, GTA 39
(Göttingen: Vandenhoeck & Ruprecht, 1989) 75–114.

trampled the Son of God underfoot and profaned the blood of the covenant (Heb. 10.29). Like the generation of Israelites in the wilderness, the community to which Hebrews is directed stands in the danger of despising the grace of God (cf. Heb. 3.7–4.13; 12.15). However, if they stand steadfast in faith and obedience in view of the promise, in contrast to the wilderness generation they shall indeed enter into the promised eschatological rest. The community must not abandon the confidence of faith (cf. Heb. 10.35); drooping hands and weak knees must be strengthened (cf. Heb. 12.12), so that Jesus' death on the cross does not become a mockery (cf. Heb. 6.6). The community needs ὑπομονή (patient endurance) (Heb. 10.36; cf. 3.14; 6.11–12; 11.1; 12.1). They must hold fast to the confession (cf. Heb. 3.1; 4.14; 10.23) and overcome their weariness in the faith. Since the community is in danger of a slackening of faith even to the point of apostasy, Hebrews is dominated by the tone of exhortation and warning (cf. Heb. 2.2–3; 3.13; 6.4–8; 10.24–25; 12.5, 25–29; 13.9, 17, 22). Obviously the author of Hebrews attempts to overcome the church's fatigue, drowsiness, dwindling knowledge, lack of courage and feeling of lostness by his exposition of the confession of faith.

According to Heb. 6.1–2 the addressees have separated themselves 'from dead works' to 'faith in God,' which is mostly seen as an allusion to pagan cults. Hebrews 3.12 warns against a 'falling away from the living God,' and the Jew/Gentile contrast plays no dominating role in Hebrews, so that the addressees are often seen as Gentile Christians.[17] They cannot be described, however, as a purely Gentile community. If the author intends to attain his goal of *strengthening and renewing their faith*, then the hearers must not only have been familiar with the Old Testament and the Jewish cultus, but also the subtle exegetical argumentation of Hebrews (e.g., Heb. 7) must have been understandable to them. According to Heb. 8.10, which takes up and interprets Jer 31.33 (LXX), the new covenant is made with the house of Israel, so that the community to which Hebrews is addressed could scarcely have consisted only of Gentile Christians. In Heb. 13.9, 10 conflicts in the community on the clean/unclean issue become visible (cf. Heb. 9.14), and possibly the author is alluding to Jewish or Jewish-Christian heresies. The church is probably composed of both Gentile Christians and Hellenistic Jewish Christians,[18] for whose faith the references to the Old Testament and its Jewish-Hellenistic exegetical tradition obviously were of great importance. In contrast, anyone who considers the

---

[17] Cf. e.g., Windisch, *Hebräerbrief* 127; Kümmel, *Introduction* 398–401; Hegermann, *Hebräerbrief* 10; Weiß, *Hebräerbrief* 72ff.

[18] Strobel, *Hebräerbrief* 10, speaks of a congregation of Jewish-Christian Hellenistic hearers; Rissi, *Theologie* 11–12, 23–24, of a particular group of Jewish Christians.

question of the previous religious background of the members of the community to be irrelevant[19] underestimates the presuppositions that would be necessary among the addressees for receiving the theology of Hebrews. Particularly if the letter intends to overcome doubt and to communicate confidence, both an understanding and an affirmation of the refined argumentation of Hebrews must be possible.

6.5 Outline, Structure, Form

I. Part One 1.1–4.13

1.1–4	The eschatological speaking of the Father in the Son
1.5–14	The testimony of the Scriptures about the Son
2.1–4	Admonition: Hearing and obeying the word
2.5–18	The Son and the sons
3.1–6	Admonition: look to Jesus the High Priest
3.7–4.11	Entrance into God's rest through faith
4.12–13	Admonition: God's word judges

II. Part Two 4.14–10.31

4.14–16	Introductory admonition
5.1–10	Jesus, the appointed High Priest who shares our own feelings
5.11–6.20	Admonition: challenge to knowledge and assurance of faith
7.1–28	A High Priest according to the order of Melchizedek
8.1–13	The new covenant
9.1–28	The new heavenly cultic worship
10.1–18	The sacrifice of Jesus made once for all
10.19–31	Admonition: challenge to confidence in the faith

III. Part Three 10.32–13.25

10.32–39	Holding on to the faith during sufferings
11.1–40	The example of earlier witnesses of faith
12.1–29	Holding on to the faith
13.1–19	Concluding parenesis
13.20–21	Benediction
13.22–25	Admonition: apostolic parousia; greetings; final farewell (Eschatokoll)

---

[19] Cf. Vanhoye, 'Hebräerbrief' 497; Grässer, *Hebräerbrief* 1.24.

Scholars have often divided the letter corpus between the introduction (Heb. 1.1–4) and the concluding benediction (Heb. 13.20–21) into five sections:[20]

> I.   1.5–2.18
> II.   3.1–5.10
> III. 5.11–10.39
> IV.   11.1–12.13
> V.   12.14–13.19

The exordium Heb. 1.1–4 is followed by a didactic section on the exalted status of Jesus in comparison to the angels, which has as its goal the parenesis in 2.1–4. So also 2.5–18 is directed toward a parenesis (3.1–6). The view of the coming judgment in 4.12–13 concludes the third subsection. At the same time there is a correspondence between the beginning and ending of the first major section, which is framed by two hymnic-liturgical pieces. The content of the first major section may be summarized: God has spoken in the Son.[21]

The second major section begins with the admonition in 4.14–16, a variant form of which is taken up again in 10.19–23. The thematic grounding in 4.14–16 is followed by a section on the nature of Jesus' high priesthood (5.1–10), which leads into a comprehensive admonitory challenge to knowledge and assurance of faith (5.11–6.20). The main didactic section 7.1–10.18 has as its theme the position of Jesus as High Priest (7.1–28), the place and character of his service (8.1–9.28), and his once-for-all sacrifice (10.1–18). Following the preceding pattern an admonition is again added, that from what they already know they should draw the appropriate conclusion: hold fast to the confession and resist the possibility of apostasy. A view of the coming judgment (10.30–31) also concludes the second major part, the theme of which is that Christ is the true High Priest at the right hand of God.

The third major part is also characterized by the framing technique, with the description of the situation of suffering (10.32ff.; 13.7) as the basis for the appeal to stand firm in the faith (10.35; 13.9) and to have patient endurance and confidence (10.36; 13.14). The author refers first to the

---

[20] Cf. especially Albert Vanhoye, *Literarische Struktur und theologische Botschaft des Hebräerbriefes* I, SNTU IV (1979) 119–147; II, SNTU V (1980) 18–49.

[21] On the outline here presented, cf. especially Wolfgang Nauck, 'Zum Aufbau des Hebräerbriefes,' in *Judentum – Urchristentum – Kirche* (FS J. Jeremias) ed. Walter Eltester, BZNW 26 (Berlin: Walter de Gruyter, 1960) 199–206. A similar outline is proposed by Hegermann, *Hebräerbrief* 4–6. Also Grässer, *Hebräerbrief* 1.28–30, chooses a three part outline, though for him the second major part does not begin until Heb 7.1, with 4.14–6.20 described as a 'transitional section.' Weiß, *Hebräerbrief* 47, has the second main part end with Heb 10.18.

addressees own holding fast to the faith (10.32–39), to which he adds the examples of the earlier witnesses to the faith (11.1–40), in order then to point to Jesus himself as the author and perfecter of faith (12.2). The community should orient its present existence to him (12.1–29). The concluding section of the letter begins at 13.1, the form of which is oriented to that of the Pauline letters.[22] The concluding parenesis (13.1–19) is followed by the benediction (13.20–21), a final admonition (13.22), the apostolic parousia (13.23), greetings (13.24), and a concluding benediction as final farewell (Eschatokoll) (13.25). The theme of part three: stand fast in the faith and follow Jesus Christ, the author and perfecter of faith.

The outline of Hebrews corresponds to the author's theological goal. The key to the outline is found in the combination of parenetic sections with didactic sections that affirm the foundations of the faith. They are intentionally placed by the author in an alternating structure in such a manner that they engage and interpret each other.[23] The author wants to help his church to recover its confidence and assurance in faith. His real intention becomes visible when it is recognized that the parenetic sections are the points where the structure of his argument is focused. Hebrews thus manifests a clear structure on both the macro-level (grounding, development, admonition) and in each of the three main parts. Within each major section the author makes use of a variety of literary devices: the framing of thematic units, literary brackets in subsections (cf. Heb. 7.1–10; 7.11–28; 8.3–9.28; 10.1–18), thematic statements that announce the subject to follow (cf. Heb. 1.4; 2.17; 5.10; 7.22; 10.39), change of literary genre (didactic foundational arguments, parenesis). The author also adopts and makes use of elements of literary rhetoric.[24]

Scholarship has made a wide range of judgments with regard to the literary genre of Hebrews as a whole. It is primarily the lack of the formal marks of a letter at the beginning that has led scholars to assign Hebrews to a number of different categories: epistle,[25] sermon,[26] homily,[27] mystery discourse,[28] tract,[29] theological meditation,[30] 'epideictic oration,'[31] book.[32]

[22] Cf. Schnider and Stenger, *Studien* (see above 2.3.2) 73ff.
[23] Cf. Laub, *Bekenntnis und Auslegung* 4–5.   [24] Cf. Grässer, *Hebräerbrief* 15.
[25] Cf. Adolf Deissmann, *Light from the Ancient East* (see above 2.3.1) 243.
[26] Cf. e.g., Otto Michel, *Der Brief an die Hebräer*, KEK 13 (Göttingen: Vandenhoeck & Ruprecht, 1985¹⁴) 4; Wikenhauser and Schmid, *Einleitung* 545; Albert Vanhoye, *Homilie für haltbedürftige Christen, Struktur und Botschaft des Hebräerbriefes* (Regensburg: Pustet, 1981) 11 (Hebrews is the only early Christian sermon preserved in the New Testament).
[27] Andreas Lindemann, *Paulus im ältesten Christentum* (see above 5) 234.
[28] Vielhauer, *Urchristliche Literatur* 242.   [29] Cf. Windisch, *Hebräerbrief* 122.
[30] Rissi, *Theologie* 13.   [31] Attridge, *Hebrews* 14.
[32] Grässer, ThR 56, 138: 'Rather, it [Hebrews] is a book, and in fact the only book of the New Testament that has a single theme: Christ, the true High Priest.'

These formal classifications attempt to do justice to the literary distinctiveness of Hebrews, but at the same time they are imprecise and without real analogies, so that Hebrews is still often described as a 'letter'.[33] As marks of a letter one can point not only to the epistolary conclusion and the direct communication between author and addressees, but also the concrete references to the community situation in Heb. 10.32–34; 12.4; 13.10. The numerous parenetic sections also indicate that the author is aware of the situation of the addressees. 1 John is to be mentioned as a parallel, where also the epistolary beginning is missing and the structure of the whole is characterized by an alternation of theological and parenetic sections. To be sure, the epistolary conclusion does not alter the literary character of Hebrews as a whole, which was not conceived as a letter, but as a well thought through speech. Thus it is best to accept the generic designation that the author himself gave to his work: λόγος τῆς παρακλήσεως (Heb. 13.22). This corresponds to the parenetic orientation of the document, which functions as a *'word of exhortation.'*[34]

6.6 Literary Integrity

Whether the epistolary conclusion Heb. 13.22–25 belonged to the original document is a disputed point. In view of the way the letter begins and the theology of Hebrews, one is surprised to find the epistolary conclusion dependent on the Pauline letter form, which is possibly intended to place Hebrews under the authority of Paul. Does this correspond to the original intention of the author? He reserves the title 'apostle' for Christ himself (3.1), and possibly the anonymous character of Hebrews is intended by the author himself. 'The reason for this is common to the other anonymous documents of early Christianity: Jesus Christ alone is reclaimed as the exclusive personal authority and normative origin of the tradition (2.3). The other reason is closely related: Hebrews regards salvation as given by the Word of God alone, the Word that is not at human disposal, so that the effort to secure its authority by appealing to an apostolic office would be contrary to the essential nature of its theology of the Word.'[35] In this view the epistolary conclusion would be secondary, and against the intention of

---

[33] Cf. Strobel, *Hebräerbrief* 9; Berger, *Formgeschichte des Neuen Testaments* (Heidelberg: Quelle & Meyer, 1984) 366; Hegermann, *Hebräerbrief* 1–2.

[34] Walter G. Übelacker, *Der Hebräerbrief als Appell*, CB.NT 21 (Lund 1989) considers the postscript of Heb 13.22–25 to be original, and describes Hebrews as an 'admonition' [*Mahnwort*] which he classifies within the genre of deliberative speech. Weiss, *Hebräerbrief* 35–41 classifies Hebrews as a 'word of exhortation' composed on the model of the Jewish-Hellenistic homily.

[35] Grässer, *Hebräerbrief* 1.17.

the original author. In favor of the originality of 13.22–25 one can present both the epistolary function of Hebrews as a whole and the individual epistolary elements it contains. 'Accordingly, Hebrews is a letter, an early Christian kerygmatic letter of the same kind as Paul's letters.'[36] If the real epistolary function of Hebrews is rejected, but the epistolary conclusion not considered secondary, the inference of Martin Dibelius is possible: ' . . . the author lets his composition which he had written as a speech (but not a speech that was really intended for oral delivery by himself) modulate at the conclusion into parenesis, reports, and greetings, in order to give it the conventional epistolary conclusion on the analogy of Paul's letters (the reference to Timothy), but did not intend to send it as a real letter.'[37] Or it could be that the author himself did in fact take a speech that was not originally intended for further distribution and provide it with an epistolary conclusion himself, in order to send it as a real letter.

A decision among these possibilities leads inevitably to paradoxical problems. Against the view of a purely fictive epistolary conclusion is the observation that the later editors have not carried through the fiction clearly and completely, for example by adding a prescript resembling the Pauline letters.[38] On the other hand, Hebrews is not easily subsumed under the Pauline letter form. The author probably provided his work with concluding epistolary elements *with a view to its further distribution.* Hebrews 13.22–25 can be understood as an epistolary supplement, a kind of cover letter, which would give particular importance to the instructions for its reception of 13.22.[39] Hebrews is accordingly a 'word of exhortation' that has been sent forth as a letter that is to be read forth in the congregational assemblies. There remains some uncertainty here, however, for just like the content of the λόγος δυσερμήνευτος (word difficult to interpret) (Heb. 5.11), so also its literary form and integrity are difficult to determine.

---

[36] Hegermann, *Hebräerbrief* 2.

[37] Dibelius, *Geschichte der urchristlichen Literatur* 128; similarly Vielhauer, *Urchristliche Literatur* 240–241. According to Weiss, *Hebräerbrief* 38, 13.22–25 is a supplement composed by the author himself.

[38] Cf. Wikenhauser and Schmid, *Einleitung* 545.

[39] Cf. especially the analysis of Übelacker, *Der Hebräerbrief als Appell* 197ff. Attridge, *Hebrews* 405 also votes for the originality of the epistolary conclusion, arguing that the conclusion is an intentional element of the literary and rhetorical composition of the whole document as it had been thought through by the author. According to Backhaus, 'Hebräerbrief und die Paulus-Schule' 194–196, the authentic conclusion Heb 13.22–25 indicates contacts between the author of Hebrews and the Pauline school in Rome.

6.7 Traditions, Sources

The author of Hebrews is in contact with several streams of tradition. In Heb. 3.1; 4.14; 10.23; 13.15 he mentions the early Christian creedal confession, at least one early Christian hymn is cited in (1.3),[40] and the hymnic character of Heb. 5.7–10; 7.1–3, 26 can be pondered.[41] The author makes use of the Old Testament in a way without parallel in the rest of the New Testament. In addition to ca. 35 direct quotations, there are about 80 allusions to Old Testament passages. Quotations are exclusively from the LXX; deviations may be explained by the author's use of differing LXX codices, or by his quoting from memory.[42] The length of individual citations is striking, e.g. Jer. 31.31–34 is quoted in its entirety only in Heb. 8.8–12 in the New Testament, and then taken up again in an abbreviated form in 10.15–18. Parallels can be seen between the author's hermeneutical method and those of ancient Judaism.[43] Thus in Heb. 3.7–4.11 there is a midrash on Ps. 95.7–11, a brief commentary in the pesher style is found for example in Heb. 2.6–9, and allegorical interpretation is present in Heb. 3.6; 13.13. Typology is often used (e.g., Heb. 6.13–20; Melchizedek in Heb. 7) as is the schema of prophecy and fulfillment (e.g., Heb. 1.5, 13; 5.5; 8.8–12), in order to present comprehensively the manner in which the old order of salvation has been surpassed by the saving act of God in Jesus Christ. It is possible that the author of Hebrews could make use of individual programmatic texts or complexes of texts that had already been assembled, either by himself or in his community (cf. Heb. 3.7–4.11[44]; 7.11–25, 28; 8.4, 6–13; 9.9b; 10.1a, 3–10, 14). Proximity to the way the Old Testament was interpreted in Jewish wisdom writings is evident also in the great series of examples of faith in Heb. 11 (cf. e.g., Sir. 44ff.).

Lines of connection may also be seen between Hebrews and early Christian streams of tradition. Thus Heb. 1.1–4 has points of agreement with John 1.1–18; Phil. 2.6–11; Rom. 1.3–4; 1 Cor. 8.6; Col. 1.15ff. Like Paul (cf. Gal. 3; Rom. 4), Heb. 6.13–20 and 11.8–19 also takes up the promise to Abraham. The concept of the sin offering is found in both Rom. 3.25 and Heb. 2.17–18. Hebrews, like Paul (cf. 1 Cor. 11.23–26), knows the

---

[40] In addition to the commentaries, cf. here the analysis of Jürgen Habermann, *Präexistenzaussagen* (see above 2.9.7) 267–299.

[41] Cf. on this point Zimmermann, *Das Bekenntnis der Hoffnung* 44ff. Grässer, *Hebräerbrief* 1.312ff.; Hegermann, *Hebräerbrief*, ad loc., are skeptical about regarding Heb 5.7; 7.1–3, 26 as hymnic fragments.

[42] For analysis cf. Friedrich Schröger, *Der Verfasser des Hebräerbriefes als Schriftausleger*, BU 4, (Regensburg: Pustet, 1968) 35–197, 247–256.

[43] Cf. the extensive listing in Schröger, *ibid.* 256–299.

[44] Cf. Hegermann, *Hebräerbrief* 6.

first covenant/new covenant antithesis. Even though these agreements between Paul and Hebrews from the point of view of the history of traditions point to a common origin from Hellenistic Jewish Christianity, there are still considerable theological differences between Hebrews and Paul.[45] The theme of justification is unimportant for Hebrews, and there are major differences in their understanding of the law as well. On the one hand, there is a certain continuity, for both Paul and Hebrews proceed from the conviction that the law could not provide salvation. The Christ event incontestably reveals the soteriological weakness of the law. But Hebrews' understanding of the law is oriented primarily to the cultic law. For Hebrews the connections between law and sin, law and self-justification, are not really taken up. There are also basic differences in their respective understandings of faith, with Hebrews statements about πίστις (faith) being primarily parenetic. Thus on the one hand Hebrews stands in a stream of tradition with Pauline points of contact, but on the other hand the author cannot be seen as a member of the Pauline school. It is rather the case that Hebrews represents an independent theology.

6.8 History-of-religions Standpoint

Hebrews is a complex composition that is open to various interpretations from the point of view of the history of religion. Three main directions may be identified within scholarly study[46] of the document:

1. The gnostic interpretation: Ernst Käsemann saw the basis of Hebrews' theology in the motif of the wandering people of God.[47] He understands this motif as an independent adoption and interpretation of the gnostic motif of the heavenly ascent of the soul, in which the Primal Man reminds all his scattered fragments of their divine origin and leads them back to their home in the heavenly world. Hebrews 2.11 must be considered the key passage for Käsemann's interpretation,[48] the text that affirms the essential kinship of Son and 'sons' [note the literal translation of the Greek in NRSV margin, 'are all of one'). In this view salvation takes place for the community to which Hebrews is directed as the pilgrimage of the redeemed wandering forth to the divine rest, preceded by Jesus their High Priest. Gerd Theissen refines the gnostic interpretation of Hebrews, in that for him only the συγγένεια (kinship) concept provides a parallel to

---

[45] Cf. Andreas Lindemann, *Paulus im ältesten Christentum* (see above 5) 233–240.
[46] Weiß, *Hebräerbrief* 96–114.
[47] Cf. Ernst Käsemann, *The Wandering People of God* 239–240.
[48] Cf. *ibid.* 145ff.

gnosticism. Christ and his own are related to each other by their common origin and by their common goal: the procession to the heavenly city.[49] So also E. Grässer[50] and F. Laub[51] see a connection with gnostic views in the ontological relationship between the being of the redeemer and that of the redeemed. But of course the concept of preexistent souls is not found in Hebrews, and Heb. 2.11 can also be interpreted in terms of creation theology: the Son and the 'sons' both have their origin in God the creator.[52] The positive statements in Hebrews about the Son as the mediator of creation (cf. Heb. 1.2) fundamentally separate Hebrews from gnosticism, just as is the case with the kind of journey on which the community finds itself: it is the way of faith, of readiness to suffer and endure.

2. The apocalyptic interpretation: O. Michel and O. Hofius set Hebrews primarily against apocalyptic as its proper history-of-religion background. 'Hebrews stands within a Christian tradition that has taken up strong motifs from apocalyptic, but obviously has also reworked Hellenistic-Alexandrian motifs.'[53] The apocalyptic structure of Hebrews is seen in its pairing of promise and fulfillment, within a community that knows that it already possesses the heavenly gifts of the future world to come (Heb. 6.5). In his debate with Käsemann Hofius investigates the κατάπαυσις ([heavenly] rest) motif and comes to the conclusion: 'Hebrews knows nothing of the idea of a wandering pilgrimage journey to heaven or to places already prepared in heaven, but rather shares the apocalyptic expectation that the preexistent heavenly places of salvation will emerge from their present hidden state on the day of consummation.'[54] So also the conception of a curtain before the throne of God (cf. Heb. 6.19–20; 10.19–20), interpreted by Käsemann from within a gnostic context, is understood by Hofius to point to another complex of traditions: 'The idea of a curtain before God's throne has been taken over by the author of Hebrews along with the theologoumenon of the heavenly sanctuary from the Merkabah mysticism of ancient Judaism.'[55] Doubtless lines of connection from Hebrews to Jewish apocalyptic can be drawn, just as they can be drawn to Rabbinic tradition, but they are not adequate to explain the complex location of Hebrews within the context of the history of religion.

---

[49] Cf. Theissen, *Untersuchungen* 123: 'The common origin determines the common goal, and vice versa.'

[50] Cf. Grässer, *Hebräerbrief* 1.135–136.

[51] Cf. Laub, 'Schaut auf Jesus' 427.

[52] Cf. Hegermann, *Hebräerbrief* 75.

[53] Otto Michel, *Hebräerbrief* (see above 6.5) 58.

[54] Hofius, *Katapausis* 150.

[55] Otfried Hofius, *Der Vorhang vor dem Thron Gottes*, WUNT 14, (Tübingen: J. C. B. Mohr [Paul Siebeck], 1972) 95.

3. Jewish-Alexandrian theology: A. Strobel and H. Hegermann see Hebrews as standing in close proximity to the world view and theology of Hellenistic-Alexandrian Judaism, in particular to that of Philo of Alexandria. Numerous parallels can be pointed out between Hebrews and Philo, including cosmology (cf. Heb. 1.1–4 with Philo, *Confusion of Tongues* 145–148; *Sobriety* 1.215), high priestly speculations (cf. Heb. 4.14–5.10 with Philo, *Special Laws* 1.82–97, 228, 230; 2.164; *Sobriety* 1.214–216; *Flight* 106–118; *Life of Moses* 2.109–135), statements about Melchizedek (cf. Heb. 7.1 with Philo, *Allegorical Interpretation* 3.79–82; *Abraham* 235ff.; *Concerning God* 99), and reflections on the nature of faith (cf. Heb. 11 with Philo, *Abraham* 268–270; Her 90–95), as well as a variety of agreements in the way they take up and use individual ideas and concepts.[56] The agreements in the linguistic and thought world of Hebrews and Philo point to a comparable milieu in which similar traditions and religious presuppositions were circulating, namely to Hellenistic Judaism with an Alexandrian cast. The author of Hebrews is not, however, a direct student of Philo's,[57] for the Jewish-Hellenistic wisdom literature also manifests such points of contact (cf. Heb. 1.3 with WisSol 7.26; Heb. 11.1–38 with Sir 44–50, WisSol 10), and the theology of Hebrews is characterized by numerous contacts with streams of early Christian tradition. A monocausal explanation of the setting of Hebrews in the history of religion is thus not possible, but it must be seen in great proximity to the *kind of Hellenistic Judaism theology prominent in Alexandria.*

6.9 Basic Theological Ideas

Hebrews is not directed polemically to outsiders, but parenetically to insiders. It is concerned to restore the self-confidence of its community, for the pillars that support the faith have begun to shake. The basis for the line of argument in Hebrews is the knowledge that the old economy of salvation can no longer be thought of as the saving path. The power of sin that separates from salvation cannot be overcome by the law, for the law is unable to lead to perfection (Heb. 7.18–19a), it is weak and incapable of taking away sins (Heb. 10.1–2, 11). The law does not have the power to

---

[56] In addition to the commentaries of A. Strobel and H. Hegermann, see on this point especially Ronald Williamson, *Philo and the Epistle to the Hebrews*, ALGHJ IV (Leiden: E. J. Brill, 1970), who investigates all relevant parallels.

[57] So Ceglas Spicq, *L'Épître aux Hébreux* I/II (Paris: Gabalda, 1952/53), also considered a possibility by Strobel, *Hebräerbrief* 16, but rightly rejected by Williamson, *Philo and the Epistle to the Hebrews*, passim.

lead human beings to their true destination: free access to God and participation in the holiness and glory of God's own nature. This can only be
done by the Son, who was made like his human brothers and sisters in
every respect, 'so that he might be a merciful and faithful high priest in the
service of God, to make a sacrifice of atonement for the sins of the people'
(Heb. 2.17). Because Jesus himself suffered and was delivered over to the
temptations of sin, but was never overcome by the power of sin, he is the
only one who can really purify from sins (cf. Heb. 1.3; 2.17, 18; 4.15; 5.7,
8). The whole soteriological conception of Hebrews depends on the two
words χωρὶς ἁμαρτίας (without sin) in Heb. 4.15! The sinlessness of Jesus,
however, is not only due to his divine nature, but is also the result of his
struggle and conscious decision (cf. Heb. 12.2–3). Sinlessness is thus the
mark of both the incarnational and epiphanic difference between Jesus and
all other human beings. The person who is lost in the far country away
from God, whose guilty separation from God cannot be overcome by the
law, is saved from sins and led to perfection only by the blood of Jesus
(Heb. 7.11–19; 9.11–12).

The saving act of the Son, in contrast to the old cult is extensively
developed by the author of Hebrews in cultic categories. The superiority
of the new economy of salvation is developed in a series of antitheses: in
terms of the history of revelation, the superiority of the new is seen in
Jesus' superiority to angels. He is prior to and superior to them in every
respect (Heb. 1.5–2.16). While the earthly high priest must also offer
sacrifice for his own sins, the sinless, heavenly high priest accomplishes the
true sacrifice and thus becomes the author of eternal salvation (cf. Heb.
5.1–10; 8.1–6). The salvific order to which the high priest after the order
of Melchizedek belongs is higher than the order that derives from Abraham
and Levi (cf. Heb. 7). Jesus appears as the mediator of a better covenant
(Heb. 8.6), the heavenly sanctuary is superior to the earthly one in every
respect, for Jesus did not enter into a sanctuary made with hands, but into
heaven itself (Heb. 9.23ff.). The community needs to know that the
pioneer (Heb. 2.10) and forerunner (Heb. 6.20) of their salvation has
entered into the heavenly sanctuary and has thus offered the true sacrifice
(cf. Heb. 7.26; 8.1–2; 9.11, 24). Christian believers may follow Jesus in the
confidence that precisely in their own sufferings they attain to salvation
through the sufferings of the Son and they participate in redemption
through him. The confidence of salvation and experience of it in the
present is to overcome the community's paralysis of faith. The community
can orient itself by the faithfulness of the God who speaks in his Son. In
his once-for-all death on the cross (cf. Heb. 7.27; 9.28; 10.10, 12, 14), the
Son steps through the heavenly curtain τοῦτ' ἔστιν τῆς σαρκὸς αὐτοῦ

(that is his flesh, Heb. 10.20) so that he may now intercede for the believers as their advocate (cf. Heb. 9.24; 4.16). Hebrews neither understands the exaltation of Jesus as a superior act that surpasses the cross as the decisive saving act, nor does he speak of an eternal self-sacrifice of the Son, but he successfully managed 'to get his community to understand the Christ event of cross and exaltation in cult-theological terms as the saving action of God that comprehends earth and heaven, time and eternity.'[58]

The concept of the new covenant also serves to bolster the community's assurance of the *reality of salvation*, for Jesus is the mediator of a genuine new covenant, which alone is able to bring redemption (Heb. 9.15; cf. further 7.22; 8.6, 10; 10.16–18, 29; 12.24). It is hardly accidental that the letter closes in Heb. 13.20 by giving assurance that Jesus has inaugurated the eternal covenant through his blood. From the uniqueness and majesty of the sacrifice of Jesus Christ there follows consistently the admonition not to despise the saving work of Jesus by apostasy. There can be no return for those who have fallen away, for apostasy means treading underfoot Jesus' death on the cross (cf. Heb. 6.4–6; 10.26–29; 12.16–17). So too the eschatology of Hebrews is oriented to the affirmation of salvation in the present, the emphasis being on the perfections of salvation. The community has already arrived at the place of salvation (Heb. 12.22–24), has already entered into the 'rest' of God (Heb. 4.3–4, 10), and has access to the true sanctuary (Heb. 10.19–22). When the eschatological reservation occurs (cf. e.g., Heb. 13.14) it refers not to the content of faith and the present status of salvation, but to preserving salvation in the struggles of faith that threaten believers in the immediate situation. Believers already 'share in Christ' (Heb. 3.14a), if they 'only hold our first confidence firm to the end' (Heb. 3.14b).

6.10 Tendencies of Recent Research

It is more and more recognized that the classical introductory issues are insoluble in the case of Hebrews, but that they are ultimately without importance for the theology of the writing.[59] The questions of where and when it was written can be answered only in terms of hypothetical considerations, and the matter of authorship comes down to the relation of Hebrews to the Pauline school. Either the author of Hebrews belongs to the circle of the apostle Paul (so H. Hegermann, A. Strobel), or the ques-

---

[58] Laub, 'Zum Verständnis des Kreuzestodes' 80.

[59] Cf. Grässer, *Hebräerbrief* 1.19: 'No one needs to know who wrote it in order to understand it.'

tion of authorship is irrelevant both historically and theologically, since Hebrews was composed from the beginning as an anonymous writing (so E. Grässer). The literary genre of Hebrews continues to be vigorously debated, while only with regard to the issue of literary integrity is there a clear tendency, namely to return to the view that the present conclusion of the letter was original. The structure of Hebrews is mostly seen as an outline of three or five sections.

The strong influence of Jewish-Alexandrian theology on Hebrews is uncontested. This does not, however, resolve the issue of the religious context of Hebrews, for Jewish-Alexandrian thinking and motifs from Jewish apocalyptic are no more to be considered alternatives than are Jewish-Alexandrian theology and gnosticism. Whether central ideas of the soteriology of Hebrews are regarded as gnostic finally depends on the definition of 'gnosticism' (see below 8.5.8). E. Grässer affirms: 'Jesus is as τελειωθείς (the one having been made perfect, 5.9) at the same time also τελειωτής (the one who makes perfect, 12.2); he is the redeemed redeemer. Having been brought to perfection himself, he becomes to all who obey him the author of eternal salvation.'[60] Grässer, however, leaves open the question of whether this idea is to be evaluated as gnostic.[61] On the other hand, O. Hofius decidedly rejects a gnostic interpretation of Hebrews, and H. Hegermann and A. Strobel see Hebrews as completely within the context of Jewish-Alexandrian theology. An explanatory model that combines more than one view is advocated by H. F. Weiss; the author of Hebrews adopted a plurality of different ways of thinking from the religious world of his time, but subordinated them all to his own pastoral concerns.[62]

In the center of recent investigation stands the question of the theological intention of the author of Hebrews, with the most debated Christological question being the relation of cross and exaltation. In the context of his moderate gnostic interpretation E. Grässer affirms: 'The life of Jesus and the cross retain their character as episodes within a larger story of which Jesus' exaltation remains the real goal.'[63] H. Braun interprets Hebrews within the framework of a dualism that determines his whole approach. Accordingly, faith means 'the basis for disciplined practice in saying "no" to that which is visible in expectation of the coming world that is presently invisible.'[64] The author of Hebrews directs his gaze only to the

---

[60] Grässer, *Hebräerbrief* 1.309.

[61] Cf. *ibid.* 309 note 351.

[62] Cf. Weiss, *Hebräerbrief* 114.

[63] Grässer, 'Hebräer 1,1–4. Ein exegetischer Versuch,' *Text und Situation*, ed. E. Grässer (Gütersloh: Gerd Mohn, 1973) 224.

[64] Braun, 'Die Gewinnung der Gewißheit' 329.

eternal world opened up by Jesus' exaltation. While for E. Grässer and H. Braun cross and exaltation are alternative, mutually exclusive emphases, F. Laub resolutely attempts to understand them as a material unity. Laub opposes a devaluation of the saving aspect of the cross as contrasted with the exaltation and a corresponding view of the continuing saving activity of Christ. He understands the cultic conceptuality of Hebrews to refer to the cross event, an argument in which Heb. 10.19–20 plays a key role. H. Braun interprets the καταπέτασμα (veil) as the dividing wall between the earthly-temporal world and the heavenly world of divine salvation. By his death on the cross Jesus leaves behind his flesh as 'hindering salvation'[65] and leads the way through the veil. O. Hofius[66] adds a διά (through) to Heb. 10.20b, understands τῆς σαρκὸς αὐτοῦ (his flesh) as an explanatory instrumental statement, and refers it to the incarnation, thereby excluding the identification of the fleshly body of Jesus with the veil. In contrast, F. Laub advocates an identification of the καταπέτασμα (veil) and the flesh of Jesus, which corresponds to the wording of Heb. 10.20. The result is that: 'In the προσφέρειν (sacrifice) on the cross there occurred the high priestly εἰσέρχεσθαι (entrance) of Jesus.'[67] The cultic categories of Hebrews are then nothing other than an exposition of the salvific meaning of the cross.

---

[65] Cf. Braun, *Hebräerbrief* 308.
[66] Cf. Otfried Hofius, *Vorhang* (see above 6.8) 8off.
[67] Laub, 'Zum Verständnis des Kreuzestodes' 77.

7

The Catholic Letters

The Letter of James, the Letter of Jude, the two Letters of Peter, and the three Letters of John have been called the 'Catholic Letters' since the time of Eusebius (HE 2.23.25; 6.14.1),[1] because they were considered to be addressed to the Christian community as a whole (ἡ καθολικὴ ἐκκλησία, the catholic church). In the Latin West this basic meaning shifted to 'universally recognized in the church.' In recent scholarship, study of the Johannine letters has no longer been done within the contextual framework of the Catholic Letters, but they are treated separately as writings of the Johannine school (see below 8).

7.1 The Letter of James

7.1.1 Literature

Commentaries

Windisch, Hans (Preisker, Herbert). *Die Katholischen Briefe*, HNT 15. Tübingen: J. C. B. Mohr (Paul Siebeck), 1951³; Dibelius, Martin (Greeven, Heinrich). *James: A Commentary on the Epistle to James*, tr. Michael A. Williams. Hermeneia. Philadelphia: Fortress Press, 1975; Laws, Sophie. *A Commentary on the Epistle of James*, BNTL. London: Black, 1980; Schrage, Wolfgang. *Die Katholischen Briefe*, NTD 10. Göttingen: Vandenhoeck & Ruprecht, 1980²; Mußner, Franz. *Der Jakobusbrief*, HThK XIII 1. Freiburg: Herder, 1981⁴; Davids, P. H. *The Epistle of James*, NIC. Grand Rapids: Wm. B. Eerdmans, 1982; Vouga, François. *L'Épître du Jacques*, CNT II, 13a. Genève: Labor et Fides, 1984; Schnider, Franz. *Der Jakobusbrief*, RNT. Regensburg: Pustet, 1987; Martin, Ralph P. *James*, WBC 48. Waco: Word, 1988; Frankemölle, Hubert. *Der Brief des Jakobus*, ÖTK 17/1–2. Gütersloh: Gütersloher Verlagshaus (Gerd Mohn), 1994.

Monographs

Meyer, Arnold. *Das Rätsel des Jacobusbriefes*, BZNW 10. Gießen: Töpelmann, 1930; Hoppe, Rudolf. *Der theologische Hintergrund des Jakobusbriefes*, FzB 28. Würzburg:

---

[1] On the term and its prior history, cf. Jülicher and Fascher, *Einleitung* 186–189.

Echter, 1977; Popkes, Wiard. *Adressaten, Situation und Form des Jakobusbriefes*, SBS
125/126. Stuttgart: Katholisches Bibelwerk, 1986; Pratscher, Wilhelm. *Der Herrenbruder Jakobus und die Jakobustradition*, FRLANT 139. Göttingen: Vandenhoeck &
Ruprecht, 1987.

Articles

Wuellner, Wilhelm H. 'Der Jakobusbrief im Licht der Rhetorik und Textpragmatik,'
Ling Bibl 43 (1978) 5–66; Aland, Kurt. 'Der Herrenbruder Jakobus und der
Jakobusbrief,' in *Neutestamentliche Entwürfe*, ed. Kurt Aland, TB 63. Munich: Kaiser,
1979, 233–245; Burchard, Christoph. 'Gemeinde in der strohernen Epistel', in *Kirche*
(FS G. Bornkamm), ed. Dieter Lührmann and Georg Strecker. Tübingen: J. C. B.
Mohr (Paul Siebeck) 1980, 315–328; Luck, Ulrich. 'Die Theologie des Jakobusbriefes,'
ZThK 81 (1984) 1–30; Hengel, Martin. 'Jakobus der Herrenbruder – der erste
"Papst"?, in *Glaube und Eschatologie* (FS W.G. Kümmel), eds. Erich Grässer and Otto
Merk. Tübingen: J. C. B. Mohr (Paul Siebeck) 1985, 71–104; Frankemölle, Hubert.
'Gesetz im Jakobusbrief,' in *Das Gesetz im Neuen Testament*, ed. Karl Kertelge, QD
108. Freiburg: Herder, 1986, 175–221; Zmijewski, Josef. 'Christliche Vollkommenheit.
Erwägungen zur Theologie des Jakobusbriefes,' in *Das Neue Testament: Quelle
christlicher Theologie und Glaubenspraxis*, ed. J. Zmijewski. Stuttgart: Katholisches
Bibelwerk, 1986, 293–324; Hengel, Martin. 'Der Jakobusbrief als antipaulinische
Polemik,' in *Tradition and Interpretation in the New Testament* (FS E. E. Ellis), eds.
Gerald F. Hawthorne and Otto Betz. Grand Rapids: Wm. B. Eerdmans/Tübingen:
J. C. B. Mohr (Paul Siebeck) 1987, 248–278; Paulsen, Henning. 'Jakobusbrief,' *TRE*
17 (1987) 488–495; Baasland, Ernst. 'Literarische Form, Thematik und geschichtliche
Einordnung des Jakobusbriefes,' in *ANRW* II, 25.5. Berlin: Walter de Gruyter, 1988,
3646–3684; Karrer, Martin. 'Christus der Herr und die Welt als Stätte der Prüfung,'
KuD 35 (1989) 166–188; Mußner, Franz. 'Die ethische Motivation im Jakobusbrief,'
in *Neues Testament und Ethik* (FS R. Schnackenburg), ed. Helmut Merklein. Freiburg:
Herder, 1989, 416–423; Lautenschlager, Markus. 'Der Gegenstand des Glaubens im
Jakobusbrief,' ZThK 87 (1990) 163–184.

7.1.2 *Author*

In the New Testament five men are named Ἰάκωβος: James the son of
Zebedee (Mark 1.19; 3.17par; Acts 12.2); James the son of Alphaeus (Mark
3.18par); James the brother of Jesus (Mark 6.3par; 1 Cor. 15.7; Gal. 1.19;
2.9, 12; Acts 12.17; 15.13; 21.18; Jude 1); James the younger (Mark
15.40par) and James the father of the apostle Judas (not Judas Iscariot, cf.
Luke 6.16; Acts 1.13). The Letter of James purports to be from a man well
known and respected in early Christianity, so only James son of Zebedee
and James the brother of Jesus can be intended. James son of Zebedee was
executed in 44 CE under Agrippa I (cf. Acts 12.2). He thus could not have
been the (purported) author, since the Letter of James clearly presupposes
a later situation within the history of early Christianity. James the Lord's

brother, who first joined the Christian community after the death and resurrection of Jesus Christ, was not an apostle (cf. Mark 3.21, 31ff.; John 7.5). The influence of James the Lord's brother grew steadily within the earliest church, as seen from the fact that Paul met with him as early as his first visit to Jerusalem (cf. Gal. 1.19). The persecution of the earliest church under Agrippa I and the flight of Peter from Jerusalem (cf. Acts 12.1–17) led to decisive changes in the leadership structure of the Jerusalem church in the years 43–48.[2] In Gal. 2.9 James stands as the first among the 'pillars,' which probably means that he was the leader of the Jerusalem church. The incident in Antioch, with the arrival of the 'certain people from James' (Gal. 2.12), indicates both the strict Jewish-Christian praxis and the extensive claims to church leadership associated with James the Lord's brother. In 62 CE James, along with other unnamed Jewish Christians, was condemned to death by stoning by the High Priest Annas the Younger on the charge of violation of the Torah (cf. Josephus *Ant.* 20.199–203).[3]

How does this information about James the Lord's brother relate to the statements in the Letter of James itself? In addition to the claim in Jas. 1.1, we may list as evidence in favor of James the Lord's brother as author also the numerous Jewish Christian traditions contained in the letter that manifest a striking proximity to the Jesus tradition. Also, one can readily conceive the debate with Paul that stands behind James 2.14–26 as fitting James the Lord's brother. Finally, the strong emphasis on the unity of faith and works points to this strict Jewish Christian James. The good Greek of the letter and the rhetorical schooling of its author[4] can no longer be used as arguments against James the Lord's brother, since we must now assume that Jerusalem and all Palestine in the first century was predominately bilingual.[5]

Nonetheless, there are weighty arguments against James the Lord's brother as author of the Letter of James. Central themes of strict Jewish Christian theology such as circumcision, Sabbath, Israel, purity laws and temple play no role in the letter. James is numbered among the few New Testament writings in which neither Israel nor the Jews are mentioned by name. The reception of Old Testament figures (cf. James 2.21–25; 5.10–11, 17–18) and also the references to the Law in an exclusively ethical context

---

[2] On this point cf. Gerd Lüdemann, *Opposition to Paul in Jewish Christianity* (see above 2.5.8) 35–52.

[3] For analysis of the text cf. Hengel, 'Jakobus der Herrenbruder' 73–75.

[4] On this point cf. Mußner, *Jakobusbrief* 26–33.

[5] On this point cf. H. B. Rosén, 'Die Sprachsituation im römischen Palästina,' in *Die Sprachen im römischen Reich der Kaiserzeit,* eds. G. Neumann and J. Untermann (Köln and Bonn, 1980) 215–239.

were general practices possible anywhere within early Christianity. In contrast to the Antioch incident, the problem of Gentile Christians/Jewish Christians does not appear at all in the Letter of James. The far-reaching differences in soteriology (see below 7.1.9) indicate that the author of the Letter of James cannot be identical with James the Lord's brother, who according to Gal. 2.9 gave the right hand of fellowship to Paul and explicitly acknowledged his proclamation of the gospel among the Gentiles. In 1.1 the author designates himself δοῦλος θεοῦ καὶ κυρίου Ἰησοῦ Χριστοῦ (servant of God and the Lord Jesus Christ), and in 3.1 indicates that he is an early Christian teacher. To be sure, a special position and dignity is associated with the term δοῦλος (servant) in James 1.1, but it remains worthy of note that the author neither introduces himself as the Lord's brother nor claims the title στῦλος (cf. Gal. 2.9). By including himself in the large group of early Christian teachers (cf. Acts 13.1; 1 Cor. 12.28–29), he disclaims the special authority of the Lord's brother or the three 'pillars' of the Jerusalem mother church, which were used in the Antioch conflict. In addition, James 3.1ff. presupposes an attack on the teaching office and a critical situation associated with it, which again does not correspond to the exclusive position of James the Lord's brother in the history of early Christianity.

If James the Lord's brother were the author of the Letter, then it is amazing that in James 5.10–11 it is Job and not Jesus who serves as an example of willingness to suffer. Also, the presupposed church situation and the polemic in James 2.14–26 point to a later time. The social conflicts within the community that become visible are paralleled especially in the writings of Luke, the Pastorals, and in Revelation. They are evidence of a fundamental social change that happened within the Christian community at the end of the first century. More and more wealthy people entered the church, the gulf between rich and poor church members became greater, and the debate between them grew sharper. In any case, the conflict concerning the unity of faith and works points to the post-Pauline period, as in the churches previously belonging to the Pauline mission field the unity of new being and new actions that Paul had considered self-evident came apart. The polemic of James does not fit Paul himelf (see below 7.1.9), so that one must assume either that James the Lord's brother was completely ignorant of Pauline theology or that we are dealing with a debate in post-Pauline times. The deuteropaulines and 2 Peter 3.15–16 document the fact that these debates in fact took place on very different levels and with distinct emphases. If the Letter of James were to have been written by James the Lord's brother, then it is remarkable that there is no reflection of the sharp criticism of Paul by James in the deuteropauline writings. Finally, the history of the canon speaks against James the Lord's brother as author of the Letter of James. Prior to 200 CE there is no solid evidence of the literary use of James.[6] In the Muratorian Canon (ca. 200) James is missing, just as in Tertullian, and Eusebius (HE 2.23, 24b, 25) reports of James: 'This is the story of James. He is supposed to be the author of the first of the so-called "Catholic Letters," but let it be noted that its authenticity is doubted, since not many of the Elders have referred either to it or the so-called "Letter of Jude," which likewise has been counted among the 'Catholic Letters.' Still, we are aware that these two letters, like the others, have been read aloud in most of the churches.' The Letter of James began to be generally accepted only after 200 CE, cited for the first time as Scripture in Origen (*Select Ps* 30.6 [PG 12.1300]). The canonical status of James continued to be disputed, however, and did not attain general acceptance as a canonical document until very late. This would be an extraordinary development if James had really been written by James the brother of the Lord and this had been known in early Christianity.

Theodor Zahn, Gerhard Kittel, and William Michaelis regard James as the oldest New Testament writing.[7] F. Mußner and M. Hengel also still affirm authorship by James the Lord's brother. Mußner thinks that James was written at the high point of the debate initiated by Paul on the relation of faith and works. He states this qualification, however: 'Perhaps the linguistic and stylistic clothing of the letter derives from a Greek-speaking coworker; this assumption still has nothing to do with a "secretary hypothesis."'[8] Likewise M. Hengel understands James as anti-Pauline polemic. 'The author stands so close to his physical brother that he does not find it necessary constantly to appeal to his authority or to quote him.'[9] A modified form of the hypothesis that the letter is authentic is found in W. Popkes: 'The Letter of James could thus in a certain sense be properly understood as a document of the Lord's brother, even though the final form of it was written later.'[10] In this view the preaching of James provided the basic elements of the Letter, but they were later supplemented, made relevant to changing times, and published by students of James the Lord's brother.

---

[6] On this point cf. Max Meinertz, *Der Jakobusbrief und sein Verfasser in Schrift und Überlieferung*, BSt (F) X 1–3 (Freiburg: Herder, 1905) 55–130; Mußner, *Jakobusbrief* 33–47; Frankemölle, *Jakobusbrief* 94–101.

[7] Cf. Theodor Zahn, *Introduction* I (see above 2.9.3) 73–151; Gerhard Kittel, 'Der geschichtliche Ort des Jakobusbriefe,' ZNW 41 (1942) 71–105; Michaelis, *Einleitung* (see above 5.5.2) 280–282; cf. further Adolf Schlatter, *Der Brief des Jakobus* (Stuttgart: Calwer, 1985³ [=1932]) 7ff.

[8] Mußner, *Jakobusbrief* 8.

[9] Hengel, 'Jakobusbrief' 264.

[10] Popkes, *Adressaten, Situation und Form* 188.

The majority of exegetes, however, rightly consider James to be a *pseud-epigraphical* writing, written by an unknown Hellenistic Jewish Christian, who had a thorough Greek education.[11]

7.1.3 Place and Time of Composition

The provenence of the Letter of James may be determined only very hypothetically. Suggestions range from Jerusalem,[12] Syria,[13] Rome,[14] Alexandria,[15] Egypt,[16] to despairing of making any statement at all.[17] There is much to be said for *Alexandria*, for the imagery of James' thought world (cf. the references of ocean/water in James 1.6; 3.7, 12; 5.7, 18 and the ships of James 3.4), as well as the global business connections in James 4.13ff. suggest a large eastern harbor city. In addition, Alexandria was a center of Jewish-hellenistic wisdom literature.

While the advocates of the authenticity of James date the letter early,[18] on the presupposition of the pseudepigraphical character of the letter one must think in terms of the *end of the first century CE*.[19] That would also fit not only the letter's place in early Christian theological history (rich/poor conflict; disputed interpretation of Paul), but also the possible reception of James 1.1 in Jude 1 (see below 7.3.2).[20]

---

[11] Among those who hold this interpretation are Dibelius, 'Jakobusbrief' 23–35; Windisch, *Jakobusbrief* 3–4; Aland, 'Der Herrenbruder Jakobus' passim; Kümmel, *Introduction* 413–414; Schrage, *Jakobusbrief* 10–11; Vouga, *Jacques* 18; Andreas Lindemann, *Paulus im ältesten Christentum* (see above 5) 241; Lüdemann, *Opposition to Paul in Jewish Christianity* (see above 2.5.8) 140; Laws, *James* 38ff.; Hoppe, *Hintergrund* 148; Schnider, *Jakobusbrief* 16–19; Pratscher, *Jakobus* 209–213; Paulsen, 'Jakobusbrief' 492; Frankemölle, *Jakobusbrief* 45–54.
[12] Cf. e.g., Mußner, *Jakobusbrief* 23 (of course presupposing the authenticity of James!).
[13] Cf. Bent Noack, 'Jakobus wider die Reichen,' StTh 18 (1964) 10–24; Schenke and Fischer, *Einleitung* II 240.
[14] Cf. Laws, *James* 26.
[15] Cf. Schnider, *Jakobusbrief* 18.
[16] Cf. Paulsen, 'Jakobusbrief' 492.
[17] Cf. Vielhauer, *Urchristliche Literatur* 580; Schrage, *Jakobusbrief* 12–13; Frankemölle, *Jakobusbrief*, 60–61.
[18] Cf. e.g. Zahn, *Introduction* I 92–93: ca. 50 CE; Michaelis, *Einleitung* (see above 5.5.2) 282: '. . . shortly after the middle of the fifth decade. . .'; Mußner, *Jakobusbrief* 19: around 60 CE; Hengel, 'Der Jakobusbrief' 259: between 58–62 CE
[19] Cf. e.g., Schnider, *Jakobusbrief* 18: between 80 and 100; Paulsen, 'Jakobusbrief' 492: between 70 and 100; Frankemölle, *Jakobusbrief* 60: last quarter of the first or beginning of the second century.
[20] On 1 Peter and 1 Clement; only traditional echoes are still present in Hermas, cf. Schnider, *Jakobusbrief* 19; Paulsen, 'Jakobusbrief' 492.

7.1.4 Intended Readership

The Letter of James is addressed to the 'twelve tribes in the Dispersion,' i.e. to whole body of Christians outside Palestine (cf. 1 Pet. 1.1).[21] The situation of the churches addressed is characterized by social tensions. Care for needy people is not working (James 1.27; 2.15–16), rich and poor are not treated equally (James 2.1ff.). Jealousy, quarreling, and fighting prevail (James 3.13ff.; 4.1ff., 11–12; 5.9). In the worship services, the rich are given preferential treatment, and the poor are put off with nice words (James 2.16). The rich trust in themselves rather than God (James 4.13–17), large landowners exploit their workers (James 5.1–6). And finally, the Christian congregations are exposed to various local repressions (cf. James 2.6).[22]

The numerous statements in James about rich and poor are by no means the expression of a piety that has spiritualized poverty,[23] but rather this theme must correspond to an experienced reality in the churches addressed by James with the intention of changing the conduct of Christian people.[24] Furthermore, the tensions recognizable in James fit into the pattern of the social history of post-Pauline Christianity.[25] Here a development continues that had already begun in the time of Paul: the integration of people who represent various strata of society with their different economic and social standing. It was already the case in Paul's mission churches that the membership was not composed of a homogeneous social group, but rather included people from all strata. In the post-Pauline time the conflicts obviously sharpened, as more and more wealthy people joined the Christian communities and the gaps between the various groups widened. Thus the Pastorals urge the virtue of contentment (cf. 1 Tim. 6.6–8), and explicitly warn against the consequences of greed for money (cf. 1 Tim. 6.9–10). It is hardly accidental that 1 Timothy concludes with an admonition to the rich (1 Tim. 6.17–19). So too the author of Luke-Acts, with his warnings against riches (see above 3.5.4), clearly indicates that riches and property had become a problem in his church. The Letter to the Hebrews warns against the love of money (Heb. 13.5) and a drifting away from the faith (Heb. 2.1–3). Inertia and sluggishness are to be overcome by works of love (Heb. 6.10–12). Finally, the Revelation of John explicitly documents the

---

[21] Cf. Hengel, 'Der Jakobusbrief' 248.

[22] On this cf. Schnider, *Jakobusbrief* 248.

[23] Contra Dibelius, *James* 39–45.

[24] Cf. Schnider, *Jakobusbrief* 57–58; Frankemölle, *Jakobusbrief* 57–62, 251–259.

[25] On this point cf. Lampe and Luz, 'Post-Pauline Christianity and Pagan Society,' in *Christian Beginnings*, ed. Jürgen Becker and tr. Annemarie S. Kidder and Reinhard Krauss (Louisville: Westminster/John Knox, 1993) 242–280.

sharp critique of Jewish Christian circles against wealth (cf. Rev. 3.17–19; 18.10ff., 15ff. 23–24.)

The sociological picture of the churches to which James is addressed can thus be integrated into the whole development of post-Pauline Hellenistic Christianity, which was characterized by far-reaching changes in social structure and the dissolution of the connection between faith and action.

7.1.5 *Outline, Structure, Form*

1.1	Prescript
1.2–18	The Danger of Temptations
1.19–27	Hearing and Doing the Word
2.1–13	Faith in Jesus and Fulfilling the Law
2.14–26	Justification by Works and Faith
3.1–12	Responsibility for the Word
3.13–18	The Essence of Wisdom
4.1–12	Against Fighting and Slander
4.13–17	Time Is in God's Hands
5.1–6	Against the Antisocial Rich
5.7–11	Admonition to Wait Patiently for the Parousia
5.12	On Swearing
5.13–18	The Power of Prayer
5.19–20	Responsibility for Straying Brothers and Sisters

The prescript of James 1.1 is the only clear indication that the document is a letter. The author uses the Greek form of the prescript that combines the third person sender, the addressees, and the greeting into one sentence (cf. as parallel Acts 15.23; 23.26). The minimal epistolary elements and the apparent lack of thematic connections within several extensive passages lead Dibelius to the conclusion that the document is a didactic writing composed by combining series of proverbs and brief treatments of various subjects.[26] According to Dibelius, missing contextual connections and absence of reference to particular situations are characteristic not only for most sections of James, but for parenesis in general.[27] But links in the chain of thought are in fact not missing from James![28] Thus James 1.2–18 is con-

---

[26] Cf. Dibelius, *James* 1–11.

[27] Cf. *ibid.* 2: 'the entire document lacks continuity in thought.'

[28] Cf. here, for example, the analysis of Wuellner, 'Jakobusbrief' 37ff., who confirms a clear line of thought. Baasland, 'Literarische Form' 3564–3661, in view of the document's literary arrangement and style emphasizes the strong influence of Hellenistic genres and school rhetoric. Frankemölle, *Jakobusbrief* 71–73, 152–180, stresses the formal and material unity of James, thereby placing special importance on the correspondence between Jas 1.2–18 (prologue/exordium) and 5.7–20 (epilogue/peroratio). In the body of the letter (cf. Jas 1.19–27; 2.1–13; 2.14–26;

nected by the motif of temptation, the transition to James 1.19–27 is made by the direct address ἀδελφοί (brothers and sisters), and the content of 1.19–27 is a development of the indicative statements about the 'perfect gift from above' and the 'word of truth' of James 1.17–18. The form of James as a whole is influenced by that of traditional proverbial wisdom, where individual proverbs are strung together by common keywords and interpreted by the author. In chapters 2 and 3 of James, there are longer sections that are more tightly composed. Here the address ἀδελφοί μου in James 2.1, 14; 3.1 is a characteristic formal connecting element, while the content is a matter of diatribe-like parenetic treatments drawn together by an integrating theme. Since the goal of the parenesis in James 2.1–3.12 is a good life actualized by wisdom, 3.13–18 responds to the appropriate question of the source of this wisdom. In the immediate context James 4.1–12 represents a new subject, but in the macrotext this section returns to the theme of temptations in 1.2–18. The admonitions in James 4.13–17 and the prophetic indictment in James 5.1–6 do stand out from their context and represent independent traditions. The author of James introduces 5.7–20 with the typical address ἀδελφοί, while from the point of view of form criticism this section belongs to traditional proverbial parenesis.

Each of the diatribe sections is a tightly composed unity, but at the same time are closely related thematically to their individual contexts. The author attains this at the formal level by his personal address ἀδελφοί (brothers and sisters) (cf. James 1.2, 16, 19; 2.1, 5, 14; 3.1, 10, 12; 4.11; 5.7, 9, 10, 12, 19); this persistent character of direct address must be seen as the principal distinctive formal characteristic of James. But there are also several lines of connection that bind the letter together at the level of its content. The whole writing is permeated by the question of that faith appropriate to wisdom, a faith that is actualized in the unity of being and doing. The keyword πίστις (faith) connects James 1.2–18 and 2.14–26. So also the adjective τέλειος (perfect) binds James 1.2–18 to 1.19–27; 3.1–12. The idea of σοφία ἄνωθεν (wisdom from above) binds James 1.2–18 with 3.13–18. The one who receives and preserves the 'perfect gift of wisdom from above' is the τέλειος ἀνήρ (perfect person) of James 3.2 and the wise person of James 3.13.

Very different designations have been given as the literary genre of James: they range from 'parenesis,'[29] 'parenetic teaching,'[30] 'handbook of

---

3.1–12; 3.13–18; 4.1–12; 4.13–5.6) the semantic network is distinguished by functional oppositions.

[29] Cf. Dibelius, *James* 3; Schrage, *Jakobusbrief* 6.

[30] Cf. Windisch, *Jakobusbrief* 3; Mußner, *Jakobusbrief* 24.

Christian ethics,'[31] 'a tract with a parenetic purpose,'[32] through 'journalistic instruction book,'[33] 'Diaspora letter,'[34] 'protreptic wisdom speech,'[35] 'circular letter,'[36] to 'instructions for neophytes in the framework of a baptismal catechism.'[37] If, in addition to the epistolary elements (James 1.1), one notes the consistent character of address, the catechetical form of tradition associated with the numerous imperatives, James could be well described as a *sapiential letter of admonition and instruction*.

7.1.6 Literary Integrity

The literary integrity of the Letter of James is uncontested.

7.1.7 Traditions, Sources

In earlier studies it was often supposed that a Jewish document had been adopted as a basic source (*Grundschrift*) and reedited to produce our present Letter of James. Thus F. Spitta considered James to have been originally a Jewish composition, the original version of which had been written in the first century BCE. A Christian redactor is then supposed to have attributed it to James the Lord's brother, and added the name 'Jesus' in 1.1 and 2.1.[38] As a variation of this thesis, A. Meyer regarded the *Grundschrift* of James as a Hellenistic Jewish pseudepigraphon from the first half of the first century CE. The central element of this writing was an allegory of the patriarchs based on Jewish onomastic.[39] The document was then Christianized about 80/90, especially by adding the name of Jesus Christ.[40] But since there are no indications of a secondary Christianizing of the document, this thesis rightly found no following in later exegesis.[41]

There can be no doubt, however, that the author of James did take over wisdom traditions current in his church. Thus in James 3.3–12 there is a unified treatment of the power of the tongue, and James 1.2–18; 3.13–18;

---

[31] Cf. Eduard Lohse, 'Glaube und Werke – zur Theologie des Jakobusbriefes,' in *Die Einheit des Neuen Testaments*, ed. E. Lohse (Göttingen: Vandenhoeck & Ruprecht, 1973) 301.

[32] Cf. Georg Strecker, *Literaturgeschichte* (see above 1.2) 72.

[33] Cf. Wuellner, *Jakobusbrief* 65.

[34] Cf. Schnider, *Jakobusbrief* 13; similarly Paulsen, 'Jakobusbrief' 489.

[35] Cf. Baasland, 'Literarische Form' 3654.

[36] Cf. Frankemölle, *Jakobusbrief* 66.

[37] Cf. Popkes, *Adressaten, Situation und Form* 176ff.

[38] Cf. Friedrich Spitta, 'Der Brief des Jakobus,' in *Zur Geschichte und Literatur des Urchristentums* II/1, ed. F. Spitta (Göttingen: Vandenhoeck & Ruprecht, 1896) 1–239.

[39] Cf. A. Meyer, *Rätsel* 240–305.

[40] Cf. *ibid.* 305–307.

[41] Exceptions: Jülicher and Fascher, *Einleitung*, 211–212; Windisch, *Jakobusbrief* 3–4; Rudolf Bultmann, *Theology* (see above 2) 2.162–163.

5.1–6, 13–18 are composed primarily of traditional proverbial wisdom that have been collected, newly arranged, and edited by the author with only minor additions.

There are numerous common elements between James and the Synoptic tradition of Jesus' words.[42] In particular, there are close contacts with the Sermon on the Mount (Plain): James 1.2–4/Matt. 5.48par (perfection), James 1.5/Matt. 7.7par (asking for wisdom), James 1.22–23/Matt. 7.24–26par (doers of the word and not merely hearers), James 2.5/Matt. 5.3par (the kingdom of God for the poor [in spirit]), James 2.13/Matt. 5.7 (the reward of mercy), James 3.18/Matt. 5.9 (the promise to those who make peace), James 4.13–15/ Matt. 6.34 (plans for the future), James 5.1/Lk 6.24 (woes against the rich), James 5.2/Matt. 6.20par (moths devour riches), James 5.10/Matt. 5.12par (prophets as models of suffering), James 5.12/Matt. 5.33–37 (prohibition of oaths). The agreements between James and the Sermon on the Mount range over true piety, mercy, the right understanding of the law, and doing the will of God. They are not to be explained either as literary dependence or as the transmission of Jesus traditions by James the Lord's brother.[43] Rather, both James and the Sermon on the Mount are embedded in a common stream of tradition that is indebted to a kind of Jewish Christianity with a strong sapiential element. Central to the theology of this circle stands the idea of ethical perfection through the fulfilling of the Law, a perfection made possible by the divine gift of wisdom.

7.1.8 History-of-religions Standpoint

The Letter of James is rooted in the thought world of *Hellenistic Jewish wisdom*. Numerous motifs and formulations are reminiscent of Jesus ben Sirach and the Wisdom of Solomon (cf. James 1.2 with Sir. 2.1ff.; James 1.19 with Sir. 5.11; James 3.13–18 with Wis. 7.22–30).[44] Many of the *hapax legomena* of James come from the wisdom literature of the LXX.[45] The Letter of James must be regarded as the New Testament document most influenced by Jewish wisdom theology.

---

[42] For analysis of the text cf. Hoppe, *Hintergrund* 123–145; Popkes, *Adressaten, Situation und Form* 156–176.

[43] So Hengel, 'Jakobusbrief' 251, who assigns the traditional words of Jesus found in James to a very early layer of tradition.

[44] For detailed evidence cf. Hoppe, *Hintergrund*, passim; Ulrick Luck, 'Weisheit und Leiden,' ThLZ 92 (1967) 253–258. Frankemölle, *Jakobusbrief* 85: 'The Letter of James presents itself as a rereading of Jesus ben Sirach.'

[45] On this point cf. B. R. Halson, 'Epistle of James: "Christian Wisdom?"' *StEv* 4 (1968) 308–314.

7.1.9 Basic Theological Ideas

The beginning point and center of the thought of James is the idea of wisdom 'from above' (cf. James 1.17; 3.15, 17), which is given to Christians in baptism as the saving word of truth (cf. James 1.17; 3.15, 17), and places them in the situation of living by the will of God revealed in the law. The wisdom 'from above' is the gift of God that renews human beings and for the first time enables them really to express their faith in deeds and thus to stand before God as righteous persons. This basic theocentric-sapiential concept corresponds to an anthropology that has as its goal the unity and perfection of human being (cf. James 1.2–4, 3.2, 13–18).[46] The split in human nature (cf. δίψυχος in James 1.8; 4.8) is to be overcome, for James has in view a person who has become whole again, a person united with himself or herself as a being in whom word and deed are one. The fragmentation of human life is expressed in doubt (James 1.6), in the disjunction of word and deed (James 1.22–27), in the misuse of the tongue (James 3.3–12), in love for the world (James 4.4ff.), in disdain for the will of God (James 2.1–13; 5.1ff.), in constant conflicts and disputes (James 4.1ff.) and in the confusion of 'yes' and 'no' (James 5.12). This fragmentation of human life goes back to evil desire (cf. James 1.14–15; 4.1–2); it brings forth sin and leads to death (James 1.15). External conflicts are thus the result of an internal conflict. Many members of the church strive after social prestige, and are inconsiderate in their dealings with brothers and sisters of the Christian community. It is not the wisdom 'from above,' but 'earthly' wisdom that shapes the lives of fragmented people (cf. James 3.15). According to James, the Christian overcomes this split in his or her human nature by faith, identified with the gift of wisdom. Both faith and wisdom are manifest in one's works, i.e. deeds that are oriented to the 'royal law' (James 2.8) and the 'perfect law of liberty' (James 1.25; 2.12). Since for James the love command is the goal and center of the Law (cf. James 2.8), there is an organic unity between the divinely given wisdom, faith, and works. It is only the wisdom from above and thus only faith makes it possible to attain perfection by fulfilling the law, the command of love, and thus the unity of faith and works.[47]

For James, there is no more a conflict between faith and law than there is between faith and works, for in each case they are simply two sides of the same coin. If for James the law summed up in the love command is the

---

[46] Cf. Hubert Frankemölle, 'Gespalten oder ganz. Zur Pragmatik der theologischen Anthropologie des Jakobusbriefes,' in *Kommunikation und Solidarität*, eds. H. U. von Brachel and N. Mette (Freiburg–Münster 1985) 160–178; and *Jakobusbrief* 305–320; Popkes, *Adressaten, Situation und Form* 191ff.

[47] Cf. Luck, 'Theologie des Jakobusbriefes' 10–15.

standard for the Christian life, it is also the case that judgment will be according to the standard of the law (cf. James 2.12–13; 3.1; 4.12; 5.1, 9). In this James proceeds on the basis of the equality of all the commandments (cf. ὅλον τὸν νόμον in James 2.10). The love of God, love of neighbor, and the keeping of [all] the commandments appear to James to be a perfect unity. The will of God, revealed in its wholeness in the law, overcomes the imperfect, partial, fragmented life of Christians. Consistent with this, James's theology of the law leads to a social ethic, and even to the beginnings of an ethic for the economic sphere, since the demand of the love command is unlimited in its application to all areas of life. The differences between James and Paul are obvious: while for Paul sin is a supra-personal power that perverts the law into its own service and betrays human striving (cf. Rom. 7.7ff.), for James sin can be overcome by keeping the whole law (James 2.10; 4.17; 5.19–20). As a result, for James there is no conflict between faith and works, though he does presuppose such a conflict in the understanding of his conversation partner.

Is Paul this conversation partner? Since the contrast 'faith and works' is documented nowhere prior to Paul,[48] we must suppose that James is referring to Paul in some way. In addition, James 2.10 appears to refer to Gal. 5.3 (ὅλον τὸν νόμον), and the allusion to Rom. 3.28 in James 2.24 is obvious. Finally, there are also points of contact in the Abraham theme (cf. Rom. 4.2; James 2.21), and the citation from Gen. 15.6 deviates from the LXX text in the same way in both Rom. 4.3 and James 2.23: Ἀβραάμ (Abraham) instead of Ἀβράμ (Abram), and the placing of δέ (but) after ἐπίστευσεν (he believed).[49] The polemic in James 2.14–26 does not, of course, actually hit Paul himself, since for Paul there is no faith without works (cf. only Rom. 1.5; 13.8–10; Gal. 5.6). It could be that James consciously rejected or intentionally misunderstood the Pauline position. Possibly he did not know Romans or Galatians directly himself, but only by indirect literary connections unknown to us. Or he argues against Christians who practice a faith without works and appeal to Paul as their justification. 2 Thessalonians 2.2 and 2 Tim. 2.18 document the existence of a mood of eschatological exaltation within the post-Pauline missionary churches of Asia Minor and Greece which could have led to a neglect of works and would correspond to the position opposed by James. If one takes this view, it is not necessary also to impute to James a complete misunderstanding of Pauline theology or a malicious description of Pauline thought.

James emphasizes the natural and *indissoluble unity* of faith and action. In

---

[48] Cf. Hengel, 'Jakobusbrief' 254.

[49] Cf. Andreas Lindemann, *Paulus im ältesten Christentum* (see above 5) 244–251; Gerd Lüdemann, *Opposition to Paul in Jewish Christianity* (see above 2.5.8) 143–146.

James 2.22 the position of the author becomes visible: faith and works function together, so that faith proceeds to its completed work. This completed faith attains justification before God. This cooperation of faith and works in James need not be conceived as synergism, for in James 2.22 faith consistently remains the subject, having the primacy over works. James is concerned with faith that justifies, faith that brings forth works, is preserved in works, is made complete in works. This perfection is the goal of faith, and works are in the service of this goal. In baptism, God himself implants the word of truth in human beings (cf. James 1.18, 21), the word that is nothing other than the perfect law of liberty (James 1.25). The unity of hearing and doing thus has its source in the will of God, and corresponds to the perfection that has been opened up to the Christian as a real possibility.

As a theocentric document, James develops its theology as an anthropology and as ethics. The name of Jesus Christ appears only twice (James 1.1; 2.1), but the stance and content of this text still confers a special emphasis on Christology. If θεοῦ (of God) in James 1.1 is to be taken as also referring to Jesus, then we would have here a theological confession unique in the New Testament.[50] Also in James 2.1, numerous predicates are ascribed to Jesus, who appears as 'Lord' and 'anointed of glory.' For James, Jesus is included in the glory of God, 'he is the Lord, who in the glory of God determines the faith and works of Christians.'[51] The extraordinary predications in James 1.1, 2.1 and the references to the κύριος (Lord) Jesus in James 5.7, 8, 15 underscore the fundamental significance of Christology for the theology of James.

7.1.10 Tendencies of Recent Research

The question of authorship continues to be a controversial item in the discussion. While F. Mußner, M. Hengel and W. Popkes hold James the Lord's brother to be directly or indirectly the author (on differing grounds), the majority of exegetes regard James as a pseudepigraphical document.

The pervasive wisdom background of James has been confirmed once again by the work of R. Hoppe and U. Luck. According to Hoppe, the Letter of James possesses a united theological conception: 'In faith the hidden wisdom of God communicates the eschatological promise to human beings; in faith human beings must grasp and realize anew the wisdom they

---

[50] So M. Karrer, 'Christus der Herr' 169.
[51] *Ibid.* 173.

have thus received.'[52] In dependence on A. Schlatter, U. Luck sees the Letter of James as determined by a central issue: 'It is concerned with life, and it is wisdom that leads to life.'[53] If it is by sapiential thought that the theology of James is determined, then the possible antithesis to Paul loses its significance for interpreting the letter. The theology of James has its own conceptual presuppositions, and they are not merely developed in opposition to Paul. James is interpreted in this manner by, among others, H. Windisch, E. Lohse, U. Luck, H. Frankemölle, R. Heiligenthal und E. Baasland[54]. H. Frankemölle is even of the opinion: 'In the whole letter James develops no doctrine of the Law; nowhere does Law become the real theme; where it does emerge, it does not form the main topic, but stands rather in a subordinate function to it.'[55]

In contrast, many scholars continue to see James as fighting on an anti-Pauline front. According to A. Lindemann the author of James 'wanted to confront and disprove the Pauline theology, and that with its own means.'[56] M. Hengel describes James 'as a model example of early Christian polemic,'[57] i.e. polemic against Paul. This polemic, in the view of M. Dibelius, W. G. Kümmel, Ph. Vielhauer, W. Schrage and F. Schnider, is not against Paul directly, but against his hyper-Pauline disciples.[58]

In dependence on M. Dibelius James' statements dealing with social ethics are often regarded as pure parenesis without any particular historical background. The examples are considered to be artificially constructed, the admonitions are only elements of a rhetorically effective diatribe style. In contrast, W. Popkes attempts to determine more precisely the ecclesiastical and social-historical situation of the church addressed. 'The Letter of James was not written as an analysis of a situation from the perspective of a somewhat aloof spectator, but as a critical intervention in actual historical events.'[59] The congregations within the framework of post-Pauline Hellenistic Christianity find themselves in a phase of radical upheaval, with

---

[52] Hoppe, *Hintergrund* 147.

[53] Luck, 'Theologie des Jacobusbriefes' 6.

[54] Cf. Windisch, *Jakobusbrief*, 20–21; Eduard Lohse, 'Glaube und Werke' (see above 7.1.5) 290–291; Luck, 'Theologie des Jakobusbriefes' 27–28; Hubert Frankemölle, 'Gesetz' 196ff.; R. Heiligenthal, *Werke als Zeichen*, WUNT 2.9 (Tübingen: J.C.B. Mohr [Paul Siebeck], 1983) 49–52; Baasland, 'Literarische Form' 3678–3679.

[55] Frankemölle, 'Gesetz' 202.

[56] Andreas Lindemann, *Paulus im ältesten Christentum* (see above 5) 249.

[57] Hengel, 'Jakobusbrief' 253; cf. previously Hans Lietzmann, *A History of the Early Church*, I, *The Beginnings of the Christian Church*, tr. B. L. Woolf (Cleveland and New York: Word Publishing Co., 1963) 202–203, according to whom James is a 'definite and conscious polemic against the teaching of Paul.'

[58] Cf. Dibelius, *Jakobusbrief* 220–221; Kümmel, *Introduction* 414–416; Vielhauer, *Urchristliche Literatur*, 573; Schrage, *Jakobusbrief* 35; Schnider, *Jakobusbrief* 77.

[59] Popkes, *Adressaten, Situation und Form* 121.

more and more wealthy people joining the church, a situation that leads to social and theological misunderstandings and conflicts. As instruction for neophytes, the Letter of James attempts in this situation to preserve the unity of faith and works. So also for F. Schnider and H. Frankemölle, the situations described in James have an actual historical background in the communities addressed. F. Mußner, however, holds fast to the view that the cases mentioned in the letter are literary constructions that correspond to rhetorical formations, so that one should not too quickly reconstruct by inference from them concrete circumstances in the churches addressed.[60]

The fundamental significance of ethics and anthropology for the thought of the Letter of James is emphasized by U. Luck, F. Mußner, W. Popkes, and H. Frankemölle. James is directed to people who have become a danger to themselves, people who are in the anxious situation of testing which they may either pass or fail. Temptation and sin are generated by people's own evil desire that leads to human fragmentation of the individual Christian and finally also to misleading the church. Anger, unrighteousness, pride, and impatience are the result. The author of James wants to overcome this fragmentation of Christian existence; he is concerned with the wholeness and perfection of the Christian. The reference point is not, however, individual Christian, but the Christian community. Nevertheless, within this point of view ethics and anthropology are not separated from theology proper: 'The Letter of James is a theocentric writing with a thoroughly thought-through theological conception that is unique to the New Testament. James, like the Jewish wisdom teachers, makes this theocentric basis the foundation for the instruction he gives his readers for a successful life – living successfully with oneself and with one's fellow Christians despite all ambivalences and conflicts.'[61]

7.2 The First Letter of Peter

7.2.1 *Literature*

Commentaries

Windisch, Hans (Preisker, Herbert). *Die Katholischen Briefe*, HNT 15. Tübingen: J. C. B. Mohr (Paul Siebeck), 1951³; Reicke, Bo. *The Epistles of James, Peter, Jude*, AnCB 37. Garden City: Doubleday, 1964; Schelkle, Karl H. *Die Petrusbriefe, Der Judasbrief*, HThK XIII 2. Freiburg: Herder, 1970³; Schweizer, Eduard. *Der Erste Petrusbrief*, ZBK

---

[60] Cf. Mußner, 'Die ethische Motivation im Jakobusbrief' 421.
[61] Frankemölle, *Jakobusbrief* 16.

15. Zürich: Theologischer Verlag, 1973³; Schrage, Wolfgang. *Die Katholischen Briefe*, NTD 10. Göttingen: Vandenhoeck & Ruprecht, 1985¹³; Brox, Norbert. *Der erste Petrusbrief*, EKK 21. Neukirchen: Neukirchener Verlag, 1986²; Michaels, J. Ramsey. *First Peter*, WBC 49. Waco: Word, 1988; Davids, Peter H. *First Peter*, NIC. Grand Rapids: Wm. B. Eerdmans, 1990; Knoch, Otto. *Der Erste und Zweite Petrusbrief, Der Judasbrief*, RNT 8. Regensburg: Pustet, 1990; Goppelt, Leonhard. *A Commentary on 1 Peter*, tr. John E. Alsup. Grand Rapids: Wm. B. Eerdmans, 1993; Boring, M. Eugene. *1 Peter*, Abingdon New Testament Commentaries. Nashville: Abingdon Press, 1998.

Monographs

Goldstein, H. *Paulinische Gemeinde im ersten Petrusbrief*, SBS 80. Stuttgart: Katholisches Bibelwerk, 1975; Millauer, H. *Leiden als Gnade*, EHS XXIII 56. Frankfurt: Lang, 1976; Elliott, John H. *A Home for the Homeless. A Sociological Exegesis of 1 Peter, Its Situation and Strategy*. Philadelphia: Fortress, 1996²; Schröger, Friedrich. *Gemeinde im 1.Petrusbrief*. Passau: Universitäts-Verlag, 1981; Reichert, Angelika. *Eine urchristliche praeparatio ad martyrium*, BET 22. Frankfurt: Lang, 1989; Schutter, William L. *Hermeneutic and Composition in 1 Peter*, WUNT 2.30. Tübingen: J. C. B. Mohr (Paul Siebeck), 1989; Prostmeier, F.R. *Handlungsmodelle im ersten Petrusbrief*, FzB 63. Würzburg: Echter, 1990; Feldmeier, Reinhard. *Die Christen als Fremde*, WUNT 64. Tübingen: J. C. B. Mohr (Paul Siebeck), 1992.

Articles

Bornemann, Wilhelm. 'Der erste Petrusbrief—eine Taufrede des Silvanus?,' ZNW 19 (1919/20) 143–165; Hunzinger, Claus Huno. 'Babylon als Deckname für Rom und die Datierung des 1 Petrusbriefes,' in *Gottes Wort und Gottes Land* (FS H. W. Hertzberg), ed. Henning Reventlow. Göttingen: Vandenhoeck & Ruprecht, 1965, 67–77; Bultmann, Rudolf. 'Bekenntnis- und Liedfragmente im ersten Petrusbrief,' in *Exegetica*, ed. Erich Dinkler. Tübingen: J. C. B. Mohr (Paul Siebeck), 1967, 285–297; Goppelt, Leonhard. 'Prinzipien neutestamentlicher Sozialethik nach dem 1.Petrusbrief,' in *Neues Testament und Geschichte* (FS O. Cullmann), ed. Bo Reicke et al. Zürich-Tübingen: J. C. B. Mohr (Paul Siebeck), 1972, 285–296; Delling, Gerhard. 'Der Bezug der christlichen Existenz auf das Heilshandeln Gottes nach dem ersten Petrusbrief,' in *Neues Testament und christliche Existenz* (FS H. Braun), ed. Hans D. Betz et al. Tübingen: J. C. B. Mohr (Paul Siebeck), 1973, 95–113; Lohse, Eduard. 'Paränese und Kerygma im 1.Petrusbrief,' in *Die Einheit des NT*, ed. Eduard Lohse. Göttingen: Vandenhoeck & Ruprecht, 1973, 307–328; Wolff, Christian. 'Christ und Welt im 1 Petrusbrief,' ThLZ 100 (1975) 333–342; Bauer, Johannes B. 'Der erste Petrusbrief und die Verfolgung unter Domitian,' in *Die Kirche des Anfangs* (FS H. Schürmann), ed. Rudolf Schnackenburg et al. Leipzig: St. Benno (1977) 513–527; Marxsen, Willi. 'Der Mitälteste und Zeuge der Leiden Christi,' in *Theologia Crucis – Signum Crucis* (FS E. Dinkler), eds. Carl Andresen and Günter Klein. Tübingen: J. C. B. Mohr (Paul Siebeck), 1979, 377–393; Neugebauer, Fritz. 'Zur Deutung und Bedeutung des 1 Petrusbriefes,' NTS 26 (1980) 61–86; Karrer, Martin. 'Petrus im paulinischen Gemeindekreis,' ZNW 80 (1989) 210–231; Schweizer, Eduard. 'Zur Christologie des ersten Petrusbriefes,' in *Anfänge der Christologie* (FS F. Hahn), eds.

Cilliers Breytenbach and Henning Paulsen. Göttingen: Vandenhoeck & Ruprecht, 1991, 369–381.

7.2.2 *Author*

From the very beginning the ancient church accepted the First Letter of Peter as a writing by the apostle Peter. The high regard in which the letter was held is documented already in 2 Peter (cf. 2 Pet. 3.1), written ca. 110 CE. Also Polycarp (PolPhil. 8.1, cf. also 1.3; 10.2) and Papias (Eusebius HE 3.39.17) presuppose 1 Peter. On the other hand, it is worthy of note that 1 Peter is not mentioned in the Muratorian Canon. Peter is first explicitly mentioned as the author of the letter in Irenaeus *Against Heresies* 4.9.2; 16.5; 5.7.2.

A number of considerations, however, speak strongly against Petrine authorship: (1) 1 Peter is written in a sophisticated Greek style.[62] But the predominantly bilingual character of Palestine and the later missionary activity of Peter in Greek-speaking areas (1 Cor. 9.5; 1.12) allow the possibility that Peter was proficient in Greek as well as in his native Aramaic. However, the style of 1 Peter corresponds not to the oral, but to the literary Koine, which points clearly to Greek as the author's native tongue.[63] Furthermore, the tradition in the ancient church associated with the Gospel of Mark (see above 3.4.2) presupposes that Peter had not mastered the Greek language. (2) In 1 Pet. 1.1 the author describes himself as ἀπόστολος (apostle), but in 1 Pet. 5.1 as συμπρεσβύτερος (fellow elder). One who was a member of the original circle of Twelve, an apostle, the one to whom the risen Jesus first appeared, need hardly have resorted to this title that appeared late in the development of early Christian ecclesiology. It should be noted that the letter gives no personal information about its purported author. Thus references to the passion of Jesus come into view only as elements of early Christian tradition (cf. 1 Pet. 2.22–25); the primary testimony of an eyewitness is nowhere found in the letter.[64] (3) The numerous points of contact between 1 Peter and the letters of Paul (see below 7.2.7) show that the author of 1 Peter takes up the tradition of the churches of Asia Minor, but does not write as an eyewitness of the life of Jesus and the missionary history of early Christianity. Thus an awareness of the problematic associated with the incident in Antioch (Gal. 2.11–14) is entirely missing from the letter. (4) The author of 1 Peter cites the Old Testament primarily from the LXX (exception: Prov 10.12 in 1 Pet. 4.8).

---

[62] Cf. e.g., the 55 hapax legomena (as enumerated by Kurt Aland, *Vollständige Konkordanz* [see above 5.2.2] 458), which in part originated in the contemporary elevated Greek style.

[63] Cf. Schelkle, *1 Petrusbrief* 13; Goppelt, *1 Peter* 24–25, 38–39; Brox, *1 Petrusbrief* 45.

[64] Cf. Brox, *1 Petrusbrief* 45.

(5) The spread of Christianity presupposed in Asia Minor and the ecumenical perspective in 1 Pet. 5.9b, 13 likewise point to a later phase in early Christian missionary history.[65]

The critical approach to Petrine authorship began in earnest in the nineteenth century,[66] and in recent exegesis 1 Peter is mostly regarded as a pseudepigraphical writing.[67] The authenticity of the letter is defended by G. Wohlenberg, E. G. Selwyn, J. Michl and B. Schwank.[68] A 'secretary hypothesis' is advocated by K. H. Schelkle and F. Neugebauer.[69] Silvanus (cf. 1 Pet. 5.12) not only delivered the letter, but he wrote it in the name of Peter, at Peter's own direction.[70] If Silvanus is identical with Silas the companion of Paul (cf. Acts 15.22–32), this would explain the similarity to Pauline theology. Of course this hypothesis still does not answer the objections mentioned above (especially points 2 and 5), and other questions remain: why does Silas encode his own authorship? Why does the personality of Peter recede so strongly into the background? Finally, 2 Peter knows nothing of a co-authorship by Silvanus, but ascribes 1 Peter to Peter himself (cf. 2 Pet. 3.1).[71]

1 Peter is thus a *pseudepigraphical* writing, permeated and shaped by early Christian traditions that were attributed to Peter and Silvanus by the circle of early Christian tradents in which they were handed on.[72]

7.2.3 Place and Time of Composition

1 Peter contains no direct information about its place of origin. However, both the list of addressees in 1 Pet. 1.1 and the adoption of material that has been shaped in the Pauline tradition point to *Asia Minor* as a possible

---

[65] Cf. Brox, *1 Petrusbrief* 46–47; Goppelt, *1 Peter* 46.

[66] Cf. especially H. H. Cludius, *Uransichten des Christenthums nebst Untersuchungen über einige Bücher des neuen Testaments* (Altona 1808).

[67] Cf. only Rudolf Knopf, *Die Briefe Petri und Judä*, KEK 12 (Göttingen: Vandenhoeck & Ruprecht, 1912[7]) 24–25; Windisch, *1 Petrusbrief* 51; Schrage, *1 Petrusbrief* 64–65; Goppelt, *1 Peter* 48–53; Brox, *1 Petrusbrief* 43–47; Feldmeier, *Christen als Fremde* 197. Elliott, *A Home for the Homeless* 270ff., argues that behind 1 Peter there stands a 'Petrine group' in Rome that produced the letter (similarly Knoch, *1 Petrusbrief* 143–147; and 'Gab es eine Petrusschule in Rom?' SNTU 16 [1991] 105–126). However, neither in 1 Peter nor in any other New Testament document is there compelling evidence for a 'Petrine group.'

[68] Cf. Gustav Wohlenberg, *Der erste und zweite Petrusbrief und der Judasbrief*, KNT XV (Leipzig: Deichert, 1915[12]) xxi; E. G. Selwyn, *The First Epistle of St. Peter* (London: Macmillan, 1947[2]) 59–60; J. Michl, *1 Petrusbrief*, RNT 8.2 (Regensburg: Pustet, 1968[2]) 101; B. Schwank, *Der erste Brief des Apostels Petrus*, Geistliche Schriftlesung 20 (Düsseldorf: Patmos, 1963) 7–11.

[69] Cf. Schelkle, *1 Petrusbrief* 14–15, 134; Neugebauer, 'Deutung und Bedeutung' 69.

[70] The phrase γράφειν διά τινος ('to write through someone') usually refers to the bearer of the letter, not to its author; cf. IgnRom. 10.1; IgnPhld. 11.2; IgnSm. 12.1.

[71] For a thorough critique of the 'secretary hypothesis' cf. already Windisch, *1 Petrusbrief* 80–81.

[72] On this point cf. the reflections of Goppelt, *1 Peter* 369–371.

setting for its composition.[73] Moreover, the specific admonitions and encouragement offered by 1 Peter presuppose that the author knew the actual situation of the churches in Asia Minor very well. On the other hand, the letter presents itself as having been sent from Rome, as indicated by the expression ἀσπάζεται ὑμᾶς ἡ ἐν Βαβυλῶνι συνεκλεκτή (your sister [church] in Babylon sends you greetings) in 1 Peter 5.13. After 70 CE Babylon was used as a code name for Rome (cf. Rev. 14.8; 16.19; 17.5; 18.2, 20, 21),[74] a clear signal for the initiated reader. In addition, the fact that the Petrine-Pauline tradition was located in Rome (cf. 1 Clem. 5.4; IgnRom. 4.3) and the points of contact between 1 Peter and 1 Clement[75] are other indications that the world capital was the point of origin for 1 Peter.[76] For all that, 'Babylon' in 1 Pet. 5.13 still documents only 'that 1 Peter wants to present itself as having been written in Rome, and does not necessarily prove that it was in fact written there.'[77] In a pseudepigraphical writing, the location as well as the author can be fictive. And finally, why would the author use a pseudepigraphical name, if the letter were in fact written in Rome? While a firm decision is not possible, it seems to me that the list of addressees speaks more for Asia Minor than for Rome as the place of origin. In addition, the history of the reception of 1 Peter needs to be considered: it was first known in the East (cf. Polycarp Phil. 1.3; 2.1–2; 5.3, 7.2, 8.1–2, 10.2; Papias), where the description of Babylon as Rome also originated.[78]

The writing of the (pseudepigraphical) 1 Peter is mostly placed in the periods 65–80[79] or 70–100 CE.[80] The following arguments may be presented

---

[73] The following are among the scholars who vote for Asia Minor: Knopf, *1 Petrusbrief* (see above 7.2.2) 25; Hunzinger, 'Babylon' 77; Bauer, 'Der erste Petrusbrief' 524–525; Vielhauer, *Urchristliche Literatur* 588; Marxsen, *Introduction* 236–237; Andreas Lindemann, *Paulus im ältesten Christentum* (see above 5) 253; Reichert, *Urchristliche praeparatio* 525ff.

[74] Cf. further SibOr 5.143; 5.159; syrBar 11.1; 67.7; 4Esdr 3.1, 28, 31.

[75] Cf. the list in Schröger, *Gemeinde im 1 Petrusbrief* 219–222.

[76] The following are among those who adopt this point of view: Bauer, *Orthodoxy and Heresy in Earliest Christianity* (see above 5.5.3), 110–111, 220–221 (a manifesto of the Roman church to the Christians of Asia Minor); Kümmel, *Introduction* 425; Schrage, *1 Petrusbrief* 63–64; Goppelt, *1 Peter*, 48; Brox, *1 Petrusbrief* 42–43 (with hesitation); Schröger, *Gemeinde im 1.Petrusbrief* 212; Prostmeier, *Handlungsmodelle* 123–126.

[77] Brox, *1 Petrusbrief* 42.

[78] Cf. Hunzinger, 'Babylon' 77. Carsten P. Thiede, 'Babylon, der andere Ort: Anmerkungen zu 1 Petr 5,13 und Apg 12,17,' in *Das Petrusbild in der neueren Forschung*, ed. C. P. Thiede (Wuppertal, 1987) 221–229, can, of course, document that 'Babylon' was used as a symbol for luxury, wealth, and an indulgent life prior to 70 CE, but this does not correspond to the use of 'Babylon' in 1 Peter 5.13.

[79] Cf. Goppelt, *1 Peter* 47. Knoch, *1 Petrusbrief* 21.

[80] Thus, tendentiously, Schrage, *1 Petrusbrief* 64 (the last decades of the first century CE); Elliott, *A Home for the Homeless* 87 (between 73 and 92 CE); Brox, *1 Petrusbrief* 41; Schelkle, *1 Petrusbrief* 7–11 (without committing himself to it).

for a narrowing of this period and dating the letter to *around 90 CE*:[81]
(1) While the conflict situations portrayed in the parenetic sections dealing
with suffering certainly do not presuppose a planned and comprehensive
official persecution of Christians, they still clearly go beyond mere local
acts of discrimination. This points to the general period of disputes
near the end of Domitian's rule (93–96 CE).[82] (2) 1 Peter presupposes that
Christianity has spread through Asia Minor (especially Pontus and
Bithynia), as confirmed by Pliny's *Letters* 10.96.6–7 for 90 CE.[83] (3) In 1
Peter the line of demarcation does not run between Jewish Christians
and Gentile Christians, Israel and Church, but between the Christians
and their pagan environment, which points to a later phase of mission
history.[84] (4) 1 Peter belongs to the history of the effects [*Wirkungsgeschichte*] of Pauline theology (see below 7.2.7). (5) 'Babylon' as code word
for the totalitarian claim of the Roman state is not documented until after
70 CE.[85]

7.2.4 Intended Readership

The letter is addressed to 'the elect foreigners of the dispersion of Pontus,
Galatia, Cappadocia, Asia and Bithynia' (1 Pet. 1.1). As was the case in the
Jewish Diaspora, Christians lived in these areas as a scattered minority
group. The names Pontus, Galatia, Cappadocia, Asia and Bithynia do not
refer to geographical regions of Asia Minor, but to Roman provinces.[86]
Understood as provinces, the names comprise adjoining regions that
include almost all of Asia Minor, while if taken to designate geographical
areas the omission of regions that contained Christian communities such as
Phrygia, Pisidia and Lycaonia would be without explanation. So also the
(fictive Roman) perspective of the author suggests that the reference is to
current political designations.

The churches addressed consist mostly of Gentile Christians, as indicated by the repeated reference to their earlier futile way of life (1 Pet. 1.14,
18; 2.25; 4.3), their call to become part of the people of God (1 Pet. 2.10),

---

[81] Cf. for this understanding Knopf, *1 Petrusbrief* (see above 7.2.2) 24–25; Windisch, *1
Petrusbrief* 81; Jülicher and Fascher, *Einleitung* 196–197; Bauer, *Der erste Petrusbrief* 522ff.; Karl
Martin Fischer, *Das Urchristentum* (Berlin: Evangelische Verlagsanstalt, 1985) 174; Prostmeier,
Handlungsmodelle 71; Feldmeier, *Christen als Fremde* 199 (between 81 and 90).

[82] See below 7.2.4.

[83] Cf. Adolf v. Harnack, *The Mission and Expansion of Christianity in the First Three Centuries*
(see above) 2.330–332.

[84] Cf. Prostmeier, *Handlungsmodelle* 39ff.

[85] Hunzinger, 'Babylon' 67ff.

[86] Cf. e.g., Schelkle, *1 Petrusbrief* 27–28; Brox, *1 Petrusbrief* 25–26; for the missionary history
of Asia Minor cf. Harnack, *Mission and Expansion* (see above 7.2.3) 2.326–337.

and descendants of Abraham and Sarah (1 Pet. 3.6).[87] In addition, the husbands of the Christian women addressed in 1 Pet. 3.1 are explicitly described as Gentiles. Slaves also belong to the congregations (1 Pet. 2.18ff.), but, in contrast to Col. 4.1 and Eph. 6.9, there is no reference to their masters. Possibly there were no Christian slaveholders within the purview of the author. The instructions in the social-ethical catalogue of duties in 1 Pet. 2.13–17, 18, 25; 3.1–6.7, like the command for the 'younger' to be subordinate, do not point to actual conflict within the community, but are to be considered elements of customary parenesis.[88] 1 Peter reveals that the churches had both charismatic ministries (1 Pet. 4.10–11) and presbyterial leadership (1 Pet. 5.1–4). A group of elders served as leaders of local congregations that also included charismatic ministries.[89]

A decisive factor for determining the circumstances of the addressees of 1 Peter is the interpretation of the *conflict situation* presupposed by the parenetic sections dealing with suffering. The importance of this theme is signalized already by the vocabulary statistics: of 42 instances of πάσχω (suffer) in the New Testament, 12 are found in 1 Peter! Is it a matter of the sufferings that Christians in Asia Minor endured due to local harassments, or must we presuppose that already more comprehensive and organized actions against the Christian movement were being undertaken? The textual data do not present a homogeneous picture. In 1 Pet. 2.21–25; 3.18; 4.1, the sufferings of Christians are related to the sufferings of Christ: the readiness of Christians to suffer is based on the suffering of Christ as a model. Suffering appears as a constitutive element of Christian existence as such, the natural result of believers living as foreigners in this world (1 Pet. 1.6–7; 5.10). The connection of πάσχω (suffer) with λύπη (sorrow) (1 Pet. 2.19), ὑπομένω (endure) (1 Pet. 2.20), λοιδορέω (insult) (1 Pet. 2.23), δικαιοσύνη (righteousness) (1 Pet. 3.14), ἀγαθοποιέω/κακοποιέω (do good/do evil) (1 Pet. 3.17; 4.15, 19) and ἀλλοτριεπίσκοπος ('mischief maker') (1 Pet. 4.15) points to the realm of social discrimination. Christians are obviously witnessing to their faith, and their ethos sets them apart from their environment (cf. 1 Pet. 2.11–18; 3.1–4.7, 16), and thereby provoke unjust sanctions against them. However, a few passages in 1 Peter cannot be explained merely as reflections of social tensions. According to 1 Pet. 4.15–16 Christians are brought before the courts merely because they are Christians (ὡς Χριστιανός, as a Christian), just as is the case with murderers, thieves, and other criminals. A fiery ordeal is taking place

---

[87] Cf. most recently Prostmeier, *Handlungsmodelle* 38ff.
[88] But cf. 1 Clement 44.3–6 in relation to 1 Peter 5.5!
[89] Cf. on this point Schröger, *Gemeinde im 1. Petrusbrief* 110–124.

among them (cf. 1 Pet. 4.12); they are to resist the devil, and this suffering is being experienced by all Christians throughout the world (1 Pet. 5.8–9). In these texts the persecution clearly has a different perspective and quality, being more than a matter of local harassment.[90] This points to the later period of Domitian's administration, who propagated the Caesar cult especially in the provinces of Greece and Asia Minor.[91] It is still not a matter of comprehensive measures directly organized by the state, but of actions supported by local authorities that lead to discrimination against and persecution of Christians. This would include court actions in which the primary charge was not directly related to the Caesar cult,[92] but Christians were charged with hatred of the human race, hostility to the government, godlessness, superstition, cultic immorality, and damage to the economy – as already indicated in Acts and later documented by Tacitus, *Annals* 15.44, Pliny, *Letters* 10.96.[93]

The situation presupposed in 1 Peter is parallel in two central points to the questions discussed in the correspondence between Pliny the Younger (ca. 111–113 CE the imperial legate of Bithynia and Pontus) and the emperor Trajan (98–117 CE):[94] (1) Christians were arrested because of the name alone (*nomen ipsum*) (1 Pet. 4.16; Pliny, *Letter* 10.96.2). (2) The state did not search out Christians (Pliny, *Letter* 10.97.2), but they were obviously charged by (anonymous) accusers (Pliny, *Letter* 10.96.2, 5, 6). This corresponds to the situation of slander and defamation documented throughout 1 Peter (e.g., 1 Pet. 2.12; 3.14; 4.4c, 12–13, 16). Pliny's question to the emperor presupposes that there was already in place a judicial practice against Christians (in part arbitrary and therefore in need of reform), and he explicitly indicates that twenty years previously – therefore in the days of Domitian – some apostates had renounced their Christian faith (Pliny, *Letter* 10.96.6). In addition, persecution of Christians in the later period of Domitian's reign is documented in 1 Clem. 1.1; Rev. 2.12–13; 13.11–18.

---

[90] Cf. Reichert, *Urchristliche Praeparatio* 74–75; contra Brox, *1 Petrusbrief* 30: 'The letter can be adequately understood from this "everyday situation" of the early church.'

[91] Cf. on this point especially Fischer, *Das Urchristentum* (see above 7.2.3) 168–172.

[92] For Goppelt, *1 Peter* 43–45 the demand to offer sacrifice before the images of the gods or the Caesar (not evident in 1 Peter) is the principal argument for the thesis that 1 Peter is to be dated in the time before Domitian. But then, why should 1 Peter mention this item, which was merely a technique used in examination (cf. Reichert, *Urchristliche Praeparatio* 78–79)? Moreover, in 1 Peter 2.13 there may be an allusion to the Caesar cult: the emperor is presented as a human institution, and is thus subordinated to the κύριος Ἰησοῦς Χριστός (the Lord Jesus Christ).

[93] Cf. on this point Feldmeier, *Christen als Fremde* 105–132.

[94] Cf. Bauer, 'Der erste Petrusbrief' 518ff.; Reichert, *Urchristliche Praeparatio* 76ff.

The persecutions of Christians in Rome under Nero in 64 CE (Tacitus, *Annals* 15.44.2–5) do not constitute the historical background for the parenesis about suffering in 1 Peter,[95] for they were limited to the local situation. There is no documentation for persecutions of Christians in Asia Minor during this early period, just as there is none for the reign of Vespasian (69–79) and Titus (79–81).[96]

7.2.5 Outline, Structure, Form

1.1–2	Prescript	
1.3–9	Thanksgiving	— Introduction
1.10–12	Epistolary Self Commendation	
1.13–2.10	The New Life of those Reborn	
2.11–3.12	Christians in the Structures of the World	— Body
3.13–4.11	Readiness to Suffer Affliction	
4.12–19	Endurance in Persecution	
5.1–11	Concluding Parenesis	
5.12	The Bearer of the Letter	— Conclusion
5.13	Greetings	
5.14	Final Farewell (Eschatokoll)	

1 Peter contains all the conventional epistolary elements. The prescript is dependent on the Pauline formula (cf. 1 Cor. 1.1–3; 2 Cor. 1.1–2). The name of the sender Πέτρος (Peter) is followed by the title ἀπόστολος Ἰησοῦ Χριστοῦ (apostle of Jesus Christ). Parallels to the adscription 1 Pet. 1.1b are found in OT-Jewish literature (cf. 2 Macc. 1.1–9; 1.10–2.18; syrBar 78.1–86.3; cf. in addition Dan. 3.31; 6.26). The blessing of 1 Peter 1.2[97] obviously belongs to the form of the Diaspora letter (cf. R. Gamaliel, bSanh 11b: 'To our brothers, the inhabitants of the Babylonian Diaspora and to our brothers in Media and the whole Diaspora of Israel wherever it may be: may your peace increase').[98] Following the prescript comes the

---

[95] Contra Schelkle, *1 Petrusbrief* 10, who reckons with the possibility of some connection.

[96] This speaks against the assumption of Goppelt, *1 Peter* 43, that the situation presupposed in 1 Peter was 'possible throughout the Empire from the time of Nero.' If being a Christian was already a criminal act during the period favored by Goppelt for dating the letter, 65–80 CE, it would be very difficult to explain the conduct of Pliny 40 years later.

[97] On χάρις καὶ εἰρήνη (grace and peace) cf. 1 Thess. 1.1b; 1 Cor. 1.3; 2 Cor. 1.2; Gal. 1.3; Rom. 1.7; Phil 1.2; Phlm 3.

[98] Cf. Schnider and Stenger, *Studien* (see above 2.3.2) 34.

eulogy of 1 Pet. 1.3–9 (cf. 2 Cor. 1.3; Eph. 1.3), concluded by the eschatological climax of v. 9. While the eulogy has the addressees in view, the place
of the epistolary self commendation is filled by referring to the Old
Testament prophets and the apostolic preachers of the gospel.

The body of the letter begins with the imperative of 1 Pet. 1.13. The
structure of the main section of the letter is clear: from the new life of the
Christian grounded in baptism the author derives a visible witness before
the world manifest in the believers' actions and in willingness to suffer. In
1 Pet. 5.1 the concluding parenesis begins with οὖν (therefore) and
παρακαλῶ (I exhort), which is concluded by the blessing of 1 Pet.
5.10–11. The bearer of the letter is commended in 1 Pet. 5.12a (cf. Acts
15.23; IgnRom. 10.1; IgnPhld. 11.2; IgnSm. 12.1; und Polycarp 14.1), and
in 1 Pet. 5.12b the author once again characterizes his writing as a word of
exhortation (cf. Heb. 13.22). The real postscript of the letter is formed by
the greetings of 1 Peter 5.13 (cf. Rom. 16.16b; 1 Cor. 16.19, 20a; 2 Cor.
13.12b) and the final farewell (Eschatokoll) in 1 Pet. 5.14 (on the final
greeting cf. Rom. 16.16a; 1 Cor. 16.20b; 2 Cor. 13.12a; on the concluding
peace blessing cf. Rom. 15.33; 1 Cor. 16.23; 2 Cor. 13.13; Gal. 6.18).

The absence of the usual characteristics of correspondence in the body
of the document has repeatedly led to doubts as to whether 1 Peter is
really a letter.[99] This peculiarity is explained from the mixture of pragmatic
purpose and literary form.[100] The author of 1 Peter wants to warn,
encourage, and strengthen the Christians of Asia Minor (cf. 1 Pet. 5.12b).
In the process of doing this he cannot go into the problems of individual
congregations, but chooses exemplary traditions and genres appropriate to
the whole range of congregations addressed. From the point of view of
form criticism, 1 Peter should therefore be considered a 'circular letter.'[101]

7.2.6 Literary Integrity

In older studies, the unity of 1 Peter was frequently questioned from the
perspectives of both literary criticism and form criticism.[102] The thesis
first posed by R. Perdelwitz in 1911, that 1 Pet. 1.3–4.11 was a baptismal

---

[99] Cf. Adolf Deissmann, *Light from the Ancient East* (see above 2.3.1) 242–243 ('the letter-like
touches are merely decorative'); M. Dibelius, *A Fresh Approach to the New Testament* 186–188;
most recently Brox, *1 Petrusbrief* 23 ('a fictive composition in the form of a circular letter').

[100] On this point cf. Reichert, *Urchristliche Praeparatio* 96–143; Prostmeier, *Handlungsmodelle*
119–121; Feldmeier, *Christen als Fremde* 133–174.

[101] Cf. Goppelt, *1 Peter* 23; David E. Aune, *Literary Environment* (see above 2.3.1) 221–222;
Reichert, *Urchristliche Praeparatio* 102; Prostmeier, *Handlungsmodelle* 120 ('an encyclical');
Strecker, *History of New Testament Literature* (see above 1.2) 48.

[102] For a history of research on this point, cf. Reichert, *Urchristliche Praeparatio* 27–72.

homily, found many followers. According to this hypothesis, to this originally independent text brief sections of admonition and encouragement
were added at 1.1–2 and 4.12–5.14 to form our present document. As
evidence for this view Perdelwitz pointed to the different situations presupposed: as 1 Peter 1.3–4.11 only points to the possibility of coming
suffering, 4.12–5.14 presupposes that suffering is already present.[103] H.
Windisch thus explains the present form of our document as an expansion
of the original homily into a letter.[104] The author took up the baptismal
homily in 1 Peter 1.3–4.11 – possibly his own previous composition – and
expanded it by adding admonitions to produce the form of 1 Peter known
to us.

This explanatory model was modified by H. Preisker. He proceeds from
the insight of form criticism 'that the document is composed of independent units, strung together without transitions, each of which has
distinctive stylistic elements.'[105] The inference from this observation: in 1
Pet. 1.3–4–11 an early Christian baptismal service found its literary
fixation, which was concluded by a worship service including the whole
congregation (1 Pet. 4.12–5.11). The baptismal act itself occurred between
1 Pet. 1.21 and 1.22, but remained unmentioned because of the arcane
nature of the service of baptism. Accordingly, in 1 Peter we have 'the oldest document of an early Christian worship service.'[106]

According to W. Marxsen 1 Peter originated in three phases: the originally independent text 1 Pet. 1.3–4.11 was at first edited by the same author
to fit to some contemporary situation (1 Pet. 4.12–5.11), to which the
(secondary) epistolary framework 1 Pet. 1.1–2 and 5.12–14 were then
added (either by the same author or by someone else).[107]

In contrast to all this, in favor of the literary and compositional unity of
1 Peter are the numerous connections between 1 Pet. 1.3–4.11 and
4.12–5.11. The theme of suffering is handled in both sections with the
same model of argumentation:[108] (a) Suffering as testing (compare 1 Pet.
1.6–7 with 4.12); (b) the suffering of Christians is related to Jesus' suffering
(cf. 1 Pet. 2.18ff.; 2.21; 4.1 with 4.13); (c) suffering goes back to the
will of God (cf. 1 Pet. 1.6; 3.17 with 4.19); (d) suffering and future glory
(cf. 1 Pet. 1.7 with 4.13; 5.4). So also the consistent admonition and

---

[103] The thesis of Perdelwitz has most recently been adopted by Vielhauer, *Urchristliche
Literatur* 585.
[104] Cf. Windisch (Preisker), *1 Petrusbrief* 76–77, 82.
[105] *Ibid.* 157.
[106] *Ibid.*
[107] Cf. Marxsen, 'Zeuge' 384ff.
[108] Cf. Reichert, *Urchristliche Praeparatio* 37–39.

encouragement toward humility binds together both blocks of text (cf. 1 Peter 3.8; 4.7 with 5.6, 8).

A completely new, unexpected perspective on the addressees that stands in tension with 1 Pet. 1.3–4.11 cannot be demonstrated for 4.12–5.11.[109] To be sure, a dramatic increase in more extensive sufferings comes into view, but as in the previous section these are related to the suffering of Christ. The theme 'hope in suffering' permeates all of 1 Peter. Finally, the allusions to baptism in 1 Pet. 1.3; 2.3; 3.21 do not permit any literary-critical conclusions. They make statements about the old and new being of Christians, without presupposing on the temporal plane of the congregation external to the text that a baptismal service had just taken place.

7.2.7 *Traditions, Sources*

The author of 1 Peter took up traditions into his writing that had already received a distinct form in the life of the church. Thus for example 1 Pet. 1.18–21; 2.21–25, and 3.18–22 give the impression of having been taken over from liturgical tradition. There are, however, different judgments on the extent and form-critical classification of these texts.

The section 1 Pet. 1.18–21 is not a stylistic unity (vv. 18, 19, and 21 are elevated prose; v. 20 is rhythmic parallelism), but several features of this text when viewed from the perspective of tradition history indicate that the elements of this passage are taken from church tradition (v. 18: reference to Isa. 52.3; v. 19: Christ as the Passover lamb [cf. 1 Cor. 5.7; John 1.29; 19.36]; v. 20 once/now schema [cf. Rom. 16.25–26; Col. 1.26; Eph. 3.5, 9; 2 Tim. 1.9–10]; v. 21: resurrection formula [cf. 2 Cor. 4.14; Gal. 1.1; Rom. 8.11]). A self-contained unit of tradition of tradition is found in 1 Pet. 2.21–25.[110] V. 21b is distinguished from the other traditional material in both its content as well as its form (the participial style is found only here). There follows in the source four relative clauses, three of which begin with ὅς (who) and one with οὗ (whose). V. 25 is a pictorial interpretation of the text in a prosaic style and probably comes from the author of the letter. Possibly not only vv. 21b and 25, but also v. 23c[111] and v. 24b[112] are additions by the author. The reconstructed source has a clear structure, is oriented to the LXX of Isa. 53, and from the point of view of form criticism

---

[109] Cf. *ibid.* 46–59, with detailed analysis.

[110] In addition to the standard commentaries, cf. especially Bultmann, 'Bekenntnis und Liedfragmente' 295–297; R. Deichgräber, *Gotteshymnus und Christushymnus* (see above 5.2.7) 140–143; Klaus Wengst, *Christologische Formeln* (see above 5.2.7) 83–85.

[111] Cf. Bultmann, 'Bekenntnis- und Liedfragmente' 296.

[112] So Deichgräber, *Gotteshymnus und Christushymnus* (see above 5.2.7) 141.

can be classified as a hymn to Christ. The author of 1 Peter interprets the purely soteriological affirmations of the source in a parenetic sense, by making Christ an example for the Christian believer. Also in 1 Pet. 3.18–22 we have a reworking of traditional material, even though we cannot reconstruct the original unedited source.[113]

The instructions in 1 Pet. 2.11–3.7 obviously stand in the tradition of the tables of household duties (*Haustafel*) and instructions for the various classes of a stratified society that were current in the ancient world and early Christianity.[114] 1 Peter manifests several differences in contrast to the typical features of the early Christian *Haustafel* (see above 5.2.7). (1) Directions for the conduct of Christians in relation to governmental authorities is a new feature. (2) The situation of a non-Christian household (οἶκος) is included. (3) The polarity of the instructions is developed, with one exception (men/women). (4) In directions to individual groups of the household imperatives are replaced by participles. The description 'table of duties for households or classes of people' for 1 Pet. 2.11–3.7 is not appropriate for the special structure of this section, for not only social classes are addressed (cf. 1 Pet. 2.13–17), and within the *Haustafel* schema the charge to masters, fathers, and children is missing. A more appropriate designation would seem to be 'catalogue of social ethical duties.'[115]

1 Peter stands within the sphere of influence of Pauline and/or post-Pauline theology.[116] Indications that point to this context are first the geographical data of 1 Pet. 1.1–2, the strong dependence on the Pauline letter formula, and the co-opting of Paul's fellow workers Silvanus (cf. 1 Thess. 1.1; 2 Cor. 1.19; 2 Thess. 1.1; Acts 15.22, 27, 32, 40; 16.19–25, 29; 17.4, 10, 14–15; 18.5) and Mark (cf. Phlm. 24; Col. 4.10; 2 Tim. 4.11; Acts 12.12, 25; 13.5, 13; 15.37, 39). The theology of 1 Peter is also influenced by central elements of Pauline theology: χάρις (grace) (1 Pet. 1.2, 10, 13; 2.19–20; 4.10; 5.10, 12), δικαιοσύνη (righteousness) (1 Pet. 2.24; 3.14), ἀποκάλυψις (revelation) (1 Pet. 1.7, 13; 4.13), ἐλευθερία (freedom) (1 Pet. 2.16; cf. Gal. 5.13), καλέω (call) in the sense of the effective call to salvation (1 Pet. 1.15; 2.9, 21; 3.9; 5.10), election (1 Peter 1,1; 2). The ἐν Χριστῷ (in Christ) concept central to Paul's theology is found outside the

---

[113] Cf. Goppelt, *1 Peter* 247–275.

[114] For a comprehensive analysis cf. most recently Prostmeier, *Handlungsmodelle* 141–448.

[115] Cf. Strecker, *History of New Testament Literature* (see above 1.2) 81: 'instruction in social-ethical duties.'

[116] Cf. the listing and (critical) evaluation of the parallels in Schröger, *Gemeinde im 1. Petrusbrief* 212–216, 223–228; Goppelt, *1 Peter* 28–30; Brox, *1 Petrusbrief* 47–51; Lindemann, *Paulus im ältesten Christentum* (see above 5) 252–261; Eduard Schweizer, 'Markus, Begleiter des Petrus?' in *The Four Gospels* (FS F. Neirynck), ed. F. Van Segbroeck et al. (see above 3.1.4) 753–763.

Pauline corpus only in 1 Pet. 3.16; 5.10, 14! Finally, numerous points of contact are present between the parenetic material of 1 Peter and Pauline parenesis, most noticeable of which are the extensive agreements between 1 Pet. 2.13–17 and Rom. 13.1–7. To be sure, important themes of Pauline theology are also missing from 1 Peter (e.g., a developed doctrine of justification and the problematic of the Law associated with it), but this is also true to different degrees of the Deuteropauline writings. It is not the case that 1 Peter is determined by a sharply-defined Pauline theology, but it is undeniable that Pauline theology has influenced the tradition in which the author stands.

7.2.8 History-of-religions Standpoint

The idea of Christ's preaching to the πνεύματα (spirits) in prison (1 Peter 3.19) is unique in the New Testament.[117] Who are the πνεύματα, fallen angels or dead human beings? Numerous parallels from the history of religions can be found for the angelological interpretation.[118] The statements about the fall of angels in Gen. 6.1–4 were developed into an extensive mythology in Jewish apocalyptic thought.[119] In this context, the angels were disobedient to God (cf. 1 Enoch 21.6) and misled human beings into great evil. This is the reason that God chained them and banished them to a prison in the underworld (cf. 1 Enoch 18.14; 21.10). These angels were also responsible for the evil circumstances before the flood (1 Enoch 10.1–22; 67.1–7; 106.13–18; Jub. 5.1–11). God sent Enoch to them, to announce to them that they could expect no mercy and no peace (cf. 1 Enoch 16.4). 2 Peter 2.4 and Jude 6 document that this myth circulated in early Christianity.

To be sure, this myth may not be transferred intact to 1 Pet. 3.19.[120] In the New Testament, κηρύσσω (preach) always refers to the proclamation of salvation, so that Christ did not confirm their rejection to the πνεύματα in prison, but would have announced their deliverance. This would be a clear contradiction, however, to the Jewish traditions and their reception

---

[117] For a comprehensive analysis, cf. Reichert, *Urchristliche Praeparatio* 213–247.

[118] This view is advocated by, among others, Hermann Gunkel, *1 Petrusbrief*, SNT III (Göttingen: Vandenhoeck & Ruprecht, 1917³) 281–282; Knopf, *1 Petrusbrief* (see above 7.2.2) 149–152; Schelkle, *1 Petrusbrief* 106–107.

[119] The data is listed in H. J. Vogels, *Christi Abstieg ins Totenreich und das Läuterungsgericht an die Toten*, FThSt 102 (Freiburg: Herder 1976) 74–86; cf. in addition Friedrich Spitta, *Christi Predigt an die Geister* (Göttingen: Vandenhoeck & Ruprecht, 1890); Bo Reicke, *The Disobedient Spirits and Christian Baptism*, ASNU 13 (Copenhagen, 1946).

[120] On the difficulties of the angelological interpretation, cf. especially Reichert, *Urchristliche Praeparatio* 231–237.

in 2 Peter 2.4, 9; Jude 6–7, 13–15! Therefore the anthropological interpretation of 1 Pet. 3.19 is to be preferred. The πνεύματα are not fallen
angels, but the 'souls of the unrepentant contemporaries of Noah's time.'[121]
Πνεῦμα as a term for post-mortem existence is frequently documented,[122]
and 1 Pet. 4.6 explicitly emphasizes the proclamation of the gospel to the
dead. The author of 1 Peter underscores the universality of the message of
salvation, beginning with the saving work of God appropriated in the act
of baptism, and then developing the water motif, extending the range of
the saving act to include the unrepentant generation of Noah.

7.2.9 Basic Theological Ideas

The prescript 1 Pet. 1.1 provides a hermeneutical foundation for the
letter as a whole. By addressing the churches as 'elect exiles of the
Dispersion' (παρεπίδημος [exile] in the New Testament only 1 Pet. 1.1;
2.11; Heb. 11.13) the author already makes clear his understanding of
Christian existence: the world is not the homeland of Christians, who will
never be able to find security and peace here.[123] Christians live as a
scattered community in a foreign land, even when they remain in the locale
where they were born and grew up. This understanding of Christian
existence is not merely another example of hostility to the world found in
various areas of ancient culture, but has an objective ground in reality:
Christians have been reborn 'to a living hope through the resurrection of
Jesus Christ from the dead' (1 Pet. 1.3). The resurrection of Jesus Christ
from the dead delivered the believers from the human existence determined by the nothingness of a world that is passing away. Jesus ransomed
them by his suffering unto death (1 Pet. 1.18), he has healed them (1 Pet.
2.24) and saved them (1 Pet. 4.18). They have been placed in a new life
situation, so that their life is now determined by the joyful hope of the
parousia.

The locus of this revolutionary event is baptism (cf. 1 Pet. 1.3, 18, 23;
3.21);[124] it is here that the central turning point in the life of the Christian
has taken place (cf. also John 3.5; Titus 3.5).[125] According to 1 Peter, the

---

[121] Goppelt, *1 Peter* 258–259. For the anthropological interpretation cf. also Gerhard
Friedrich, 'κηρύσσω,' *TDNT* 3.707–708; Eduard Schweizer, 'πνεῦμα,' *TDNT* 6.447–448;
Vogels, *Christi Abstieg ins Totenreich* 86; Reichert, *Urchristliche Praeparatio* 247.

[122] Cf. Hebrews 12.23; for Jewish and pagan examples, cf. Reichert, *Urchristliche Praeparatio*
239–243.

[123] Cf. Schröger, *Gemeinde im 1. Petrusbrief* 234: 'The church is revealed as that people that
are strangers in this world but at home in heaven.'

[124] On this point cf. Knoch, *1 Petrusbrief* 105–106.

[125] On baptism in 1 Peter cf. especially Schröger, *Gemeinde im 1. Petrusbrief* 31–54.

Christian life is the life that proceeds from baptism. Placed by baptism into the time between Easter and the parousia, the baptized Christian is not taken out of the world and its troubles, but is enabled to overcome them. Thus, origin of the new life of Christians cannot be proven in this-worldly categories (cf. 1 Pet. 1.3b; 5.10), but at the same time its reality and its results cannot be disputed.[126] 1 Peter thinks of the theological identity and the social position of those who have been baptized in a similar manner.

The *newness of Christian existence* attains visible form in its testimony to the world. Christians live their lives in holiness (1 Pet. 1.14–15; 2.1–2) and the love appropriate to brothers and sisters in the family of God (1 Pet. 1.22). They keep themselves from the desires of the flesh (1 Pet. 2.11–12), avoid the evil practices of their environment (1 Pet. 4.3) and lead a righteous life (1 Pet. 4.1–2). Because their new existence brings with it a new and different style of life, believers are exposed to the abuse of their neighbors (cf. 1 Pet. 3.17). The different lifestyle of Christians alienates the Gentiles (1 Pet. 4.4) and evokes aggressive responses. Although Christians are called to a just and right way of life within the context of the given social institutions, they still must suffer because of their relation to God. This suffering is thankworthy (NRSV 'credit'; literally χάρις, 'grace') in God's eyes, but suffering that is the result of actual sins is not (1 Pet. 2.19; 3.14; 2.20). Christians are called to suffer, for Jesus Christ too suffered unjustly (1 Pet. 2.21–25). The goal of the social-ethical instructions of 1 Peter is the integration of the Christian communities into their social context while at the same time preserving their Christian identity. By presenting a comprehensive interpretation of the present situation of suffering and a way of coping with it, these directions go beyond the realm of the actions as such, and are set forth as applied kerygma.

Suffering, however, not only appears as a result of the new conduct of Christians in society, but is a constitutive element of Christian existence as such, in which God's will is encountered (1 Pet. 4.19). Suffering is for the testing of faith (1 Pet. 1.6; 4.12): whoever suffers unjustly in the present world already experiences the future judgment of God. But those who are disobedient to the gospel of God will shortly find themselves before God's judgment (1 Pet. 4.16–19). Just as for Christ, so also for Christians, suffering is the way to glory (1 Pet. 1.11; 4.13; 5.1). The Christians must wait and hope for eschatological σωτηρία (salvation) (1 Pet. 1.5, 9, 10; 2;2) that will free them from the troubles that appear just

---

[126] Cf. Feldmeier, *Christen als Fremde* 192: 'It is precisely because Christians are foreigners that a distinctive way of life is expected from them.'

before the End.[127] The sufferings of the present also contains a parenetic dimension, for 'whoever has suffered in the flesh has finished with sin' (1 Pet. 4.1b). The theology of 1 Peter is fundamentally characterized by the connection between the suffering of Christ and the sufferings of Christians. The righteous suffers for the unrighteous (1 Pet. 3.18) so that they too can now be called righteous (1 Pet. 4.18).

7.2.10 *Tendencies of Recent Research*

The consensus among recent exegetes is that 1 Peter is a pseudepigraphical writing. On the other hand, the situation of the churches presupposed by the letter remains a disputed point. Most scholars reject the view that there is direct reference to persecution of Christians under Domitian (Goppelt, Brox). The Christians of 1 Peter are not faced with a worldwide persecution, but must contend with local repressions. All that was required was the moral-political charge of '*superstitio*'[128] to provoke pogroms and social discrimination. 'The confrontation is accordingly not the result of an intentionally formulated claim to universality and integration made by Christianity in competition with the Roman state, but the social and political consequences of the situation as a whole, determined by their differing self-understandings and diverging perspectives on what constitutes the basis of an integrated society.'[129] Whether this sociological explanatory paradigm does justice to the whole textual witness of 1 Peter may be doubted, as by J. B. Bauer, K. M. Fischer, and A. Reichert. A mediating position is taken by R. Feldmeier, who argues that the social conflict, and the resulting political conflict, have the same cause: 'It is grounded in the exclusive religious commitment of the Christians, which at the same time generates a social and ethical system that engages in competition with the accepted religious, social and political structure.'[130]

The relation of 1 Peter to the Pauline tradition also continues to be a disputed point. K. M. Fischer decidedly evaluates 1 Peter as a writing of the Pauline school, and even thinks it may have originally been written in Paul's name.[131] The first word of 1.1 would then have been not Π/ΕΤΡ/ΟΣ but Π/ΑΥΛ/ΟΣ! A. Lindemann is more cautious: '1 Peter turns out to be a witness of a Christianity not fundamentally oriented to Paul, but

---

[127] Schweizer, 'Christologie' 372, speaks of a 'future-oriented center of gravity' in 1 Peter.

[128] On this point cf. Dieter Lührmann, 'SUPERSTITIO – die Beurteilung des frühen Christentums durch die Römer,' ThZ 42 (1986) 193–213.

[129] Prostmeier, *Handlungsmodelle* 59–60.

[130] Feldmeier, *Christen als Fremde* 124.

[131] Cf. Schenke and Fischer, *Einleitung* I, 199–203.

influenced by Pauline tradition, perhaps even directly influenced by Pauline letters.'[132] So too Goppelt makes the qualified statement that 1 Peter was influenced by Paul, but was not determined by him.[133] F. Schröger goes a step further, and insists that we should 'stop talking about the "Paulinism" of 1 Peter.'[134] Elliott sees behind 1 Peter a Petrine circle with an independent Petrine tradition independent of Paul.[135]

While the genre of 1 Peter is assessed differently ('writing of encouragement and admonition;' 'letter;' 'fictive circular letter'), there is currently considerable agreement in rejecting models from literary criticism as explanations for the present form of 1 Peter. So too the adoption of liturgical traditions by the author of 1 Peter is mostly affirmed only with hesitation. Recently Reichert has argued that in 1 Pet. 1.20; 3.18d–e, 19, 22b–c there is a post-Pauline hymn in the tradition of Christian perfectionism that has been critically reinterpreted by the author of 1 Peter.

Recently increased significance has been attributed to models of interpretation derived from the sociology of literature, models that have as their starting point the interdependence between historical situation and literary form. Thus according to F. R. Prostmeier, the compositional distinctiveness of 1 Peter consists 'in its characteristic combination of world structures and worldly competence with the model of Christ, in the form of "table"-like monitory instruction.'[136] The pragmatic goal of these monitory instructions is the readiness to offer a Christian witness in the everyday life of the world. 'The Christ-model is both binding norm and the condition of its realization, the standard for the practice of those ethical contents that are simply given with the structures of the world.'[137] In 1 Peter secular models of action are bound to a soteriological-eschatological concept that is oriented to the exemplary fulfillment of the will of God by Jesus Christ.

---

[132] Andreas Lindemann, *Paulus im ältesten Christentum* (see above 5) 260; cf. also Reichert, *Urchristliche Praeparatio* 515–557, who argues for a Pauline or post-Pauline influence on 1 Peter.

[133] Cf. Goppelt, *1 Peter* 30.

[134] Schröger, *Gemeinde im 1. Petrusbrief* 227.

[135] Cf. Elliott, *A Home for the Homeless* 270ff.; cf. further Karrer, 'Petrus im paulinischen Gemeindekreis' 222ff., who does not regard the connection between 1 Peter and the Pauline tradition as very close.

[136] Prostmeier, *Handlungsmodelle* 480.

[137] *Ibid.* 512.

7.3 The Letter of Jude

7.3.1 *Literature*

Commentaries

Windisch, Hans (Preisker, Herbert). *Die Katholischen Briefe*, HNT 15. Tübingen: J. C. B. Mohr (Paul Siebeck), 1951³; Grundmann, Walter. *Der Brief des Judas und der Zweite Brief des Petrus*, ThHK 15. Berlin: Evangelische Verlagsanstalt, 1979²; Schrage, Wolfgang. *Die Katholischen Briefe*, NTD 10. Göttingen: Vandenhoeck & Ruprecht, 1980²; Bauckham, Richard J. *Jude, 2 Peter*, WBC 50. Dallas: Word, 1983; Fuchs, Erich and Reymond, Pierre. *La deuxième Épître de Saint Pierre; L'Épître de Saint Jude*, CNT 13b. Paris: Delachaux et Niestlé, 1988²; Schelkle, Karl H. *Die Petrusbriefe, der Judasbrief*, HThK XIII 2. Freiburg: Herder, 1988⁶; Knoch, Otto. *Der Erste Petrusbrief, Der Zweite Petrusbrief, Der Judasbrief*, RNT. Regensburg: Pustet, 1990; Paulsen, Henning. *Der Zweite Petrusbrief und der Judasbrief*, KEK XII/2. Göttingen: Vandenhoeck & Ruprecht, 1992; Vögtle, Anton. *Der Judasbrief, Der Zweite Petrusbrief*, EKK XXII. Neukirchen: Neukirchener Verlag, 1994.

Monographs

Spitta, Friedrich. *Der zweite Brief des Petrus und der Brief des Judas. Eine geschichtliche Untersuchung*. Halle: Waisenhaus, 1885; Maier, Friedrich. *Der Judasbrief*, BSt X/1–2. Freiburg: Herder, 1906; Werdermann, H. *Die Irrlehrer des Judas- und des 2. Petrus-briefes*, BFChTh XVII 6. Gütersloh: C. Bertelsmann, 1913; Watson, Duane F. *Invention, Arrangement and Style. Rhetorical Criticism of Jude and 2 Peter*, SBLDS 104. Atlanta: Scholars Press, 1988; Bauckham, Richard J. *Jude and the Relatives of Jesus in the Early Church*. Edinburgh: T. & T. Clark, 1990; Heiligenthal, Roman. *Zwischen Henoch und Paulus. Studien zum theologiegeschichtlichen Ort des Judasbriefes*, TANZ 6. Heidelberg: Francke, 1992.

Articles

Ellis, E. Earl. 'Prophecy and Hermeneutic in Jude,' in *Prophecy and Hermeneutic in Early Christianity*, ed. E. Earl Ellis, WUNT 18. Tübingen: J. C. B. Mohr (Paul Siebeck), 1978, 221–238; Hahn, Ferdinand. 'Randbemerkungen zum Judasbrief,' ThZ 37 (1981) 209–218; Gunther, John J. 'The Alexandrian Epistle of Jude,' NTS 30 (1984) 549–562; Sellin, Gerhard. 'Die Häretiker des Judasbriefes,' ZNW 77 (1986) 206–225; Paulsen, Henning. 'Judasbrief,' *TRE* 17 (1988) 307–310; Joubert, S. J. 'Language, Ideology and the Social Context of the Letter of Jude,' Neotestamentica 24 (1990) 335–349; Charles, J. D. 'Literary Artifice in the Epistle of Jude,' ZNW 82 (1991) 106–124.

Histories of Research

Heiligenthal, Roman. 'Der Judasbrief,' ThR 51 (1986) 117–129; Bauckham, Richard J. 'The Letter of Jude: An Account of Research,' in *ANRW* 25.2. Berlin: Walter de Gruyter (1988) 3791–3826.

7.3.2 *Author*

Four possibilities have been proposed: (1) Jude, brother of Jesus (cf. Matt. 13.55; Mark 6.3);[138] (2) Jude, one of the twelve apostles (cf. Luke 6.16; Acts 1.13); (3) the Judas Barsabbas[139] mentioned in Acts 15.22, 27, 32; (4) an unknown author who composed Jude as a pseudonymous writing.

According to its own claim, the Letter of Jude intends to present itself as written by Jude the Lord's brother, which is signaled clearly by the reference to James the brother of Jesus in Jude 1.[140] The missionary activity of the Lord's brothers is documented in 1 Cor. 9.5, and Jude could be a witness to this work. Especially the Jewish Christian thought world of Jude appears to make its attribution to the brother of Jesus as a possibility.[141] After all, why should a later author lay claim to the name 'Jude' in so vague a form?[142] The following arguments, however, speak against authorship by Jude the Lord's brother: (a) Why does the author not directly describe himself as the brother of Jesus, but rather as the brother of James? (b) The term ἀδελφός (brother) is ambiguous, often being used in the New Testament in the sense of 'co-worker' (cf. e.g. Col. 1.1). (c) The concept of tradition in Jude 3, 20, the dispute between orthodoxy and heresy and the topos of the advent of false teachers as a sign of the last days (cf. 1 Tim. 4.1–3; 2 Tim. 4.3–4; 1 Joh. 2.18; 4.1–3; Did 16.3) point to the post-apostolic period. (d) In Jude 17–18 the author himself indicates that he belongs to the later period of early Christianity that already looks back on the epoch of the apostles as the time when the foundations of the faith were laid.

Jude is thus very likely a *pseudepigraphical* writing[143] in which an unknown Jewish Christian claims the authority of Jude the Lord's brother in a contemporary controversy.

---

[138] Cf. also Hegesippus in Eusebius HE 3.19.1–20.6.

[139] So Ellis, *Prophecy* 221–230.

[140] Vgl. Paulsen, 'Judasbrief' 44. The reference to James and the lack of a distinguishing surname speak against possibilities 2. and 3.

[141] Cf. Bauckham, *Jude* 16.

[142] Cf. Ellis, *Prophecy* 226–227.

[143] Among those who hold this interpretation are Knopf, *Judasbrief* (see above 7.2.2) 206–207; Jülicher and Fascher, *Einleitung* 213–214; Kümmel, *Introduction* 427–428; Vielhauer, *Urchristliche Literatur* 593–594; Heiligenthal, *Zwischen Henoch und Paulus* 24; Paulsen, 'Judasbrief' 44–45. The possibility that Jude was written by the brother of Jesus is advocated by Schelkle, *Judasbrief* 140–143; Grundmann, *Judasbrief* 15; Knoch, *Judasbrief* 159–162, thinks of the author as having originated from the circle of Jude (and James) the 'brothers of the Lord.'

7.3.3 Place and Time of Composition

The content of Jude allows the place of origin to be determined only in a very qualified manner. The suggestions are accordingly numerous: Palestine/Syria, Alexandria, Asia Minor. The attribution to Jude the brother of the Lord and the Jewish Christian thought world are proposed as evidence for Palestine/Syria.[144] Against this is the situation of the churches addressed (see below 7.3.4) and the minimal reception of the Letter of Jude in the Syrian region.[145] The history of Jude's influence (cf. Clem. Alex, *Strom* 3.2.11; *Paed* 3.8.44) and the possible reference to the Letter of James suggest Alexandria as the place of origin.[146] Of course, our knowledge of Christianity in Alexandria at the end of the first century CE is so limited that such an attribution must be designated as purely hypothetical. Asia Minor as the place of origin[147] is suggested by the agreements between Jude's and Colossians' doctrine of angels and the similarities to the Pastorals (see below 7.3.8). In addition, Jude can be understood as a witness to the influence of Pauline theology (cf. Jude 19, 20, 24–25). The early reception of Jude by 2 Peter also suggests *Asia Minor*.

The letter is usually dated in the period between 80 and 120 CE.[148] This assumption can be made more precise: at what time would claiming the pseudonym 'Jude' be meaningful and still possible? Here the last two decades of the first century come into consideration, a period in which most of the pseudepigraphical literature in the New Testament originated and apocalyptic ideas were adopted in multiple ways. The Letter of Jude thus probably was written *between 80 and 100 CE*.[149]

7.3.4 Intended Readership

In view of the letter's domination by the polemic against the author's opponents, the profile of Jude's church can only be seen in broad outline. The occasion of the letter's composition is a current danger posed to the faith of the church(es) addressed (Jude 3). Godless people (in the view of the author) have infiltrated the church and deny the κύριος Ἰησοῦς Χριστός (Lord Jesus Christ) (Jude 4). The polemic against the author's opponents

---

[144] Cf. R. Knopf, *Judasbrief* (see above 7.2.2) 209; Schelkle, *Judasbrief* 138; Grundmann, *Judasbrief* 15 (written in Galilee/Syria; its influence extended even to the area of Asia Minor); Hahn, 'Randbemerkungen' 216 (Palestine).

[145] Cf. J.S. Siker, 'The Canonical Status of the Catholic Epistles in the Syriac New Testament,' JThS 38 (1987) 311–340.

[146] Cf. Gunther, 'Epistle;' Paulsen, *Judasbrief* 45.

[147] Among those who argue for Asia Minor is Heiligenthal, *Zwischen Henoch und Paulus* 165

[148] So e.g., Hahn, 'Randbemerkungen' 215 (90–120 CE); Paulsen, *Judasbrief* 45.

[149] Cf. Knopf, *Judasbrief* 208; Kümmel, *Introduction* 429; Koester, *Introduction* 2. 246–247.

is permeated with traditional motifs, so it can hardly be decided whether the opponents are wandering missionary preachers or members of the local congregation(s).[150] Their participation in the 'love feasts' of the congregation (Jude 12) speaks for the latter possibility (cf. further Jude 19, 22, 23). In view of the danger posed by the heresy, Jude attempts to strengthen his church's sense of its own identity. Already the manner in which he addresses his community as 'called' (Jude 1) and 'saints' (Jude 3) serves to distinguish them from the false teachers, whose false doctrine and immoral conduct will lead to destruction (cf. Jude 4, 7–11). In contrast, the church is characterized by holiness and spotlessness. It lives in an excited eschatological expectation: the eschatological rejection of false doctrine (cf. Jude 4, 11, 13, 15) stands over against their salvation to eternal life (Jude 21). The bearers of such a consciousness were probably a Jewish Christian community in which apocalyptic speculations and Enoch traditions were alive.[151] In Jude 22, 23 instructions are given the community for their association with deviant groups: to the Lord's mercy to the church (Jude 21) there corresponds the mercy the church is to show to those who are wavering, a mercy that is to snatch them out of the coming fiery judgment.[152]

7.3.5 *Outline, Structure, Form*

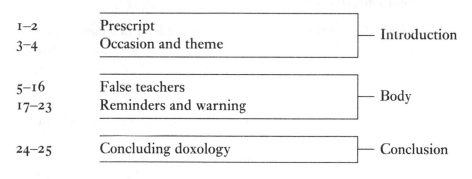

1–2	Prescript	— Introduction
3–4	Occasion and theme	
5–16	False teachers	— Body
17–23	Reminders and warning	
24–25	Concluding doxology	— Conclusion

The prescript stands in the tradition of the Pauline/ Deuteropauline letters (cf. Phil. 1.1; Rom. 1.1–2; 1 Cor. 1.1–2); the blessing prayer of Jude 2 is especially reminiscent of 1 Tim. 1.2; 2 Tim. 1.2; Titus 1.4.[153] As an announcement of the theme, Jude 3–4 has a transition function, manifesting a perceptible correspondence to Jude 17–23. Within the main body of

---

[150] Cf. Paulsen, *Judasbrief* 55.
[151] Cf. Heiligenthal, *Zwischen Henoch und Paulus* 89–94, who goes beyond this general description to describe the tradition-bearing circles in Jude's church as Jewish Christian Pharisees.
[152] On Jude 23b cf. Paulsen, *Judasbrief* 85.
[153] Cf. Paulsen, *Judasbrief* 52–53.

the letter, a referential section (Jude 5–16) may be distinguished from an appellative section (Jude 17–23).[154] While the referential section reveals the nature and destiny of the false teachers, the appellative section Jude 17–23 appeals by the direct address ὑμεῖς δέ, ἀγαπητοί (but you, beloved) (Jude 17, 20) to the experience and judgment of the community. The concluding doxology again manifests a clear similarity to the Pauline letter form (cf. Rom. 16.25–27).[155]

The form critical classification of Jude is disputed. Suggestions range from 'tract for a particular situation,'[156] 'anti-heretical leaflet,'[157] 'open letter,'[158] 'midrash,'[159] to a real letter.[160] In favor of regarding Jude as a real letter, in addition to the prescript and concluding doxology, is especially the claim of the author to place himself in the tradition of the *apostolic letter*.[161] Moreover, Jude is not a writing unaffected by its particular situation, for the incorporation of the forms of traditional polemic does not speak against the goal of the letter to influence a concrete situation.

7.3.6 Literary Integrity

The literary integrity of the Letter of Jude is uncontested.

7.3.7 Traditions, Sources

The argumentation of the Letter of Jude is imbedded in a comprehensive and complex network of traditions.[162] The Old Testament is taken up in numerous references and allusions.[163] There is a remarkable use of the traditions of ancient Judaism that in its density is unique in the New Testament. The series of examples in Jude 5–7 develops the connection between a misguided life and divine judgment and has parallels in Sir

---

[154] Cf. Heiligenthal, *Zwischen Henoch und Paulus* 17–21.

[155] For other proposed outlines cf. Bauckham, 'The Letter of Jude' 3800–3804; Heiligenthal, *Zwischen Henoch und Paulus* 14–16.

[156] Cf. Dibelius, *Fresh Approach* 205–207.

[157] Cf. Schelkle, *Judasbrief* 137.

[158] Cf. Grundmann, *Judasbrief* 17.

[159] Cf. Ellis, *Prophecy* 220–226.

[160] So recently again Bauckham, *Jude* 3; Heiligenthal, *Zwischen Henoch und Paulus* 14ff.; Paulsen, *Judasbrief* 41–42.

[161] Cf. F. Vouga, 'Apostolische Briefe als "scriptura". Die Rezeption des Paulus in den katholischen Briefen,' in *Sola Scriptura*, eds. H.H. Schmid and J. Mehlhausen (Gütersloh: Gerd Mohn, 1991) 194–210.

[162] On this point see, in addition to the commentaries of Bauckham and Paulsen, especially Heiligenthal, *Zwischen Henoch und Paulus*, passim.

[163] On the language of Jude (14 hapax legomena) and its reception of the Old Testament (primarily the Massoretic Text, but also knowledge of the LXX), cf. Bauckham, *Jude* 6–8.

16.6–15; CD 2.17–3.12; 3 Macc. 2.4–7; TestNaph. 3.4–5. Jude 6 stands in the long series of Jewish interpretations of Gen. 6.1–4, with comparable texts being found in 1 Enoch 10.4–6, 11–13; 12.4–13.1. In Jude 7 there are reflections on the destiny of Sodom and Gomorrah as in numerous Jewish and Christian texts (cf. 3 Macc. 2.5; Jub. 16.6; 20.5; 22.22; TestAsh. 7.1; Jos. *War* 5.566; Matt. 10.15; 11.24; Luke 10.12; 17.29). Apocryphal traditions about Moses are taken up in Jude 9,[164] and the reference to Cain, Balaam, and Korah come into focus only against the background of the way these figures were interpreted in Jewish tradition.[165] In Jude 14b–15 the author cites 1 Enoch 1.9,[166] in order to emphasize the godlessness of the opponents and the necessity of the imminent judgment on them.

The quotations, allusions, and the technique of scriptural argumentation in the Letter of Jude show how deeply the author thought and lived in the traditions of ancient Judaism.

7.3.8 History-of-religions Standpoint

In which stream of early Christianity can the opponents of Jude be placed? Two explanatory models dominate the research: (1) The opponents are advocates of a libertinistic early form of gnosticism.[167] The following arguments for this identification are usually introduced: (a) According to Jude 4 the opponents deny the lordship of Jesus Christ, demoting him to an intermediate heavenly being; (b) Jude 12 documents the opponents massive individualistic and sacramental approach to salvation; (c) their slander of celestial beings in Jude 8, 10 has a gnostic motivation; (d) In Jude 19 the typical gnostic distinction between pneumatics and psychics is found; (e) The opponents manifest an extreme consciousness of their freedom (Jude 4, 7, 8, 10, 13). Against this chain of arguments may be objected:[168] The information provided by Jude is not specific enough to permit unambiguous inferences. A protological dualism as *the* characteristic of gnostic systems (see below 8.5.8) cannot be proven from Jude. Enthusiastic or libertinistic tendencies are by no means *eo ipso* an expression of

---

[164] On possible sources, cf. Paulsen, *Judasbrief* 66–67.

[165] Cf. here Heiligenthal, *Zwischen Henoch und Paulus* 42–61.

[166] For details, cf. Paulsen, *Judasbrief* 74ff.

[167] So e.g. (with differences in their individual arguments) Kümmel, *Introduction* 426–427; Vielhauer, *Urchristliche Literatur* 590; Schenke and Fischer, *Einleitung* II 316; Schrage, *Judasbrief* 224. A variation of the general gnostic thesis is represented by the supposition that the opponents were advocates of an 'early' gnosticism; cf. for this interpretation Schelkle, *Judasbrief* 230–234; Grundmann, *Judasbrief* 17–19; Hahn, 'Randbemerkungen' 213; Paulsen, *Judasbrief* 49 (with reservations).

[168] Cf. on this, following F. Maier especially Heiligenthal, 'Judasbrief' 122; and *Zwischen Henoch und Paulus* 128–134.

gnostic thought. The antithesis ψυχικός/πνεῦμα (πνευματικός) ('natural instincts'/spirit) in Jude 19 is not documented prior to Paul (cf. 1 Cor. 2.14; 15.44, 46).[169] It has its roots not in gnosticism, but in Jewish-Hellenistic wisdom thought.

(2) The opponents belong, as does the author of Jude himself, within the spectrum of debates about the inheritance of Pauline theology.[170] The following observations speak in favor of this thesis: (a) The motif of disdain for angelic beings[171] as a central charge against the opponents (Jude 8) refers to 1 Cor. 6.3 ('do you not know that we are to judge angels?'), 1 Cor. 13.1 (speaking in the 'language of angels') and Col. 2.18–19 ('do not let anyone disqualify you, insisting on self-abasement and worship of angels . . .'). In the post-Pauline period there was obviously a debate about the legitimacy of veneration of angels, with an appeal to Paul's authority. Col. 2.18–19 and Jude incidentally document a connection between 'legal prescriptions and veneration of angels on the one hand, antinomianism and disdain for angels on the other side.'[172] (b) The antithesis ψυχικός/πνεῦμα ('natural instincts'/spirit) in Jude 19 has recourse to 1 Cor. 2.14 (15.44, 46), documented only in these two places in the New Testament. The author labels the opponents as mere psychics (cf. also Jude 10b) and thus stands on its head their claim to an exalted spiritual status. (c) Both Jude 5 and 1 Cor. 10.1ff. bring into play the motif of the failure and destruction of the majority of the chosen people in the wilderness (Num. 14), in order in each case to warn the opponents against feelings of superiority. (d) Jude 4 charges the opponents with perverting the χάρις (grace) of God into ἀσέλγεια (excess). Here we have an echo of the Pauline terminology of justification (cf. Rom. 3.23–24; Eph. 2.7–9), and the problem named by Paul in Rom. 3.8 could stand in the background: antinomianism as the result of a misunderstood χάρις θεοῦ (grace of God).[173] (e) As in the Deuteropaulines the tradition principle (cf. Jude 3, 17, 20) serves as a defense against the opponents.[174] (f) 2 Peter, dependent on Jude, documents debates concerning the right understanding of Paul (2 Pet. 3.15–16). The connections with Pauline/Deuteropauline theology speak for the supposition that the opponents of Jude (possibly with an appeal to Paul) advocated a doctrine (and practice) of spirit-enthusiasm. They disdained

---

[169] Cf. Gerhard Sellin, *Streit um die Auferstehung der Toten* (see above 2.5.1) 181–189.

[170] So, with (considerable) differences in their individual arguments, e.g. Müller, *Zur frühchristlichen Theologiegeschichte* (see above 5) 23–26; Bauckham, *Jude* 12; Sellin, 'Häretiker' 224–225; Knoch, *Judasbrief* 154–157; Heiligenthal, *Zwischen Henoch und Paulus* 128ff.

[171] Cf. on this point Sellin, 'Häretiker' 219–222.

[172] *Ibid.* 222.

[173] Cf. *ibid.* 209–212.

[174] Cf. Hahn, 'Randbemerkungen' 209ff.

the angelic powers, regarded themselves as spiritual beings, and felt themselves to be exalted above the observance of traditional boundaries.

7.3.9 Basic Theological Ideas

The Letter of Jude is written to help a church striving to *clarify its own identity* by defining its boundaries. In this process the concept of tradition assumes a fundamental role. The church struggles for the faith 'that was once for all entrusted to the saints' (Jude 3). This faith is identical with the words 'previously spoken' by the apostles (Jude 17), and forms the foundation of the community of faith (Jude 20). The endangering of the community by false teaching is a challenge to formulate the tradition and put it into effect throughout the church! This tradition is rooted primarily in Jewish thought, with an essential element of it coming from the Enoch tradition. To be sure, the concept of tradition is not established as a formal principle, but the community knows that it is obligated to its heritage. At the center of Jude's Christology stands the expectation of the coming Kyrios, who will appear with his angels for judgment (Jude 14, 15). Christ will reveal himself as merciful to the community of faith (Jude 21), but the opponents will be punished for their godless works. In Jude's church the veneration of angels was taken for granted, and Jewish ideas of purity appear to have been significant for its ethics (cf. Jude 8, 12, 23).

7.3.10 Tendencies of Recent Research

For a long time the Letter of Jude led a shadowy existence in New Testament exegesis. One factor that played no trifling role was E. Käsemann's classification of the writing as a typical advocate of early catholicism: 'For we have reached a stage when it is not enough for the Spirit to be effective in and through the process of tradition: the spirit is now dissolved *into* tradition. The *ecclesia docens* has now acquired proprietary rights over the "Spirit of Ministry." Every unauthorized exegesis and interpretation of scripture can now be prohibited; the *locus classicus* for this is 2 Pet. 1.20'[175] (103). W. Schrage adopts Käsemann's evaluation and explicitly declares that the shadow existence Jude has had in the church has not been unjustified.[176]

Most recently these disqualifying evaluations have given way to a more

---

[175] Ernst Käsemann, 'The Canon of the New Testament and the Unity of the Church,' *Essays on New Testament Themes* (London: SCM Press Ltd., 1964) 103.

[176] Cf. Schrage, *Judasbrief* 223.

careful interpretation that attempts to locate the precise place of Jude in the history of early Christian theology. F. Hahn classifies the concept of tradition in Jude in a manner that is not simply negative, but explicitly acknowledges it to be a positive principle in the debate with heresy. Historically Jude stands between James and 2 Peter: 'In dependence on the Palestinian tradition of his time, the author wants to establish the lasting valid basis of the apostolic tradition of the faith for his own time and for future generations, and by this means, as well as by casting the false teachers in a typical role, facilitate an effective resistance to heresy.'[177] G. Sellin takes the analysis further and locates the false teachers within the history of early Christian theology: they were wandering teachers oriented toward spiritual phenomena who in continuity with the theology of Colossians and Ephesians disdained angels and by appealing to Paul advocated an antinomian position. R. Heiligenthal has attempted a new interpretation of Jude: 'From the point of view of tradition history, the Letter of Jude is to be explained primarily from Jewish traditions. Its proximity to the Enoch literature is so close that it could be described as the "Christianized part of the Enoch literature".'[178] For Heiligenthal, Jude shows 'that the common basis of Christianity and Judaism was broad and conciliatory.'[179] Jude is then an important witness in the Jewish-Christian dialogue and should be used and taken seriously in this function.

7.4 The Second Letter of Peter

7.4.1 Literature

Commentaries

Windisch, Hans (Preisker, Herbert). *Die Katholischen Briefe*, HNT 15. Tübingen: J. C. B. Mohr (Paul Siebeck), 1951[3]; Grundmann, Walter. *Der Brief des Judas und der Zweite Brief des Petrus*, ThHK 15. Berlin: Evangelische Verlagsanstalt, 1979[2]; Schrage, Wolfgang. *Die Katholischen Briefe*, NTD 10. Göttingen: Vandenhoeck and Ruprecht, 1980[2]; Bauckham, Richard J. *Jude, 2 Peter*, WBC 50. Waco: Word, 1983; Fuchs, Erich and Reymond, Pierre. *La Deuxième Épître de Saint Pierre, L' Épître de Saint Jude*, CNT 13b. Paris: Delachaux et Niestle, 1988[2]; Knoch, Otto. *Der Erste Petrusbrief, Der Zweite Petrusbrief, Der Judasbrief*, RNT. Regensburg: Pustet, 1990; Paulsen, Henning. *Der Zweite Petrusbrief und der Judasbrief*, KEK XII/2. Göttingen: Vandenhoeck & Ruprecht, 1992; Schelkle, Karl H. *Die Petrusbriefe, Der Judasbrief*, HThK XIII 2. Freiburg: Herder, 1994; Vögtle, Anton. *Der Judasbrief, Der Zweite Petrusbrief*, EKK XXII. Neukirchen: Neukirchener Verlag, 1994.

---

[177] Hahn, 'Randbemerkungen' 218.
[178] Heiligenthal, *Zwischen Henoch und Paulus* 156.
[179] *Ibid.* 166.

Monographs

Spitta, Friedrich. *Der zweite Brief des Petrus und der Brief des Judas* (see above 7.3.1); Werdermann, H. *Die Irrlehrer des Judas und des 2. Petrusbriefes* (see above 7.3.1); Fornberg, Tord. *An Early Church in a Pluralistic Society. A Study of 2 Peter*, CB.NT 9, Lund, 1977.

Articles

Käsemann, Ernst. 'An Apologia for Primitive Christian Eschatology.' *Essays on New Testament Themes.* London: SCM Press, 1964, 169–195; Cavallin, H.C.C. 'The False Teachers of 2 PT as Pseudo-Prophets,' NT 21 (1979) 263–270; Neyrey, Jerome H. 'The Form and Background of the Polemic in 2 Peter,' JBL 99 (1980) 407–431; Vögtle, Anton. 'Petrus und Paulus nach dem Zweiten Petrusbrief,' in *Kontinuität und Einheit* (FS F. Mußner), ed. P.G. Müller and W. Stenger. Freiburg: Herder, 1981, 223–239; Berger, Klaus. 'Streit um Gottes Vorsehung. Zur Position der Gegner im 2 Petrusbrief,' in *Tradition and Re-Interpretation in Jewish and Early Christian Literature* (FS J.C.H. Lebram), StPB 36. Leiden: E. J. Brill, 1986, 121–135; Dschulnigg, Peter. 'Der theologische Ort des Zweiten Petrusbriefes,' BZ 33 (1989) 161–177; Vögtle, Anton. 'Christo-logie und Theo-logie im zweiten Petrusbrief,' in *Anfänge der Christologie* (FS F. Hahn) ed. Cilliers Breytenbach and Henning Paulsen. Göttingen: Vandenhoeck & Ruprecht, 1991, 383–398.

Histories of Research

Richard J. Bauckham, '2 Peter: An Account of Research,' *ANRW* 25.5. Berlin: Walter de Gruyter, 1988, 3713–3752.

7.4.2 Author

The Second Letter of Peter represents itself as the final testament of the apostle Simon Peter (2 Pet. 1.1, 13–15). So also the allusion to the trans-figuration of Jesus (2 Pet. 1.18), the reference to 1 Peter as a previous letter (cf. 2 Pet. 3.1), and the picture of Paul presented in 2 Pet. 3.15–16 are intended to strengthen this impression. Some of the arguments already presented in 7.2.2 already speak against the historicity of this claim,[180] as do especially three observations about 2 Peter itself: (a) 2 Peter takes over almost the entire content of the Letter of Jude (see 7.4.7 below). Such a procedure for the apostle Peter is excluded on material and chronological grounds. (b) In 2 Pet. 3.4 the author breaks through the fictive literary world he has created: the 'fathers' have already fallen asleep, so that now

---

[180] The language of 2 Peter is to be especially noted. There are 49 hapax legomena (cf. Kurt Aland, *Vollständige Konkordanz* [see above 5.5.2] 459). In proportion to its length 2 Peter has more hapax legomena than any other New Testament writing. For details, cf. Bauckham, *Second Peter* 135–138.

doubts on the parousia have arisen. Peter himself belongs to these (dead) 'fathers'! (c) Second Peter is so fundamentally different from 1 Peter[181] that both letters cannot be from the same author. Even if 1 Peter were taken to be authentic, 2 Peter would still have to be considered *pseudepigraphical*! So the developed doctrine of inspiration of 2 Pet. 1.20–21 and the disputed reception that 2 Peter experienced in the ancient church (see below 7.4.3) are also indications that the work was written in a later time.[182]

The author of 2 Peter was an educated Hellenistic (Jewish-) Christian,[183] who wanted to provide his church with a helpful approach to dealing with the problem posed by the (delay of) the parousia.

7.4.3 *Place and Time of Composition*

Only conjectures may be offered concerning the time and place of composition of 2 Peter. Some indications derive from the (disputed) history of the letter's reception in the ancient church, for it belongs to the broad range of Petrine literature of the second century CE.[184] Thus the *Apocalypse of Peter*, probably written in Egypt about 135 CE, presupposes 2 Peter.[185] The incorporation of the Letter of Jude provides a *terminus a quo* (see above 7.4.7), the collection of Pauline letters presupposed in 3.15–16 and the problem posed by the delay of the parousia comparable to 1 Clem. 23–37 likewise point to the *period around 110 CE* as the time of composition.[186] The

---

[181] Cf. Schelkle, *2 Petrusbrief* 179ff.

[182] No recent commentary argues for the authenticity of 2 Peter. One may mention as examples only Schelkle, *2 Petrusbrief* 181; Grundmann, *2 Petrusbrief* 58; Bauckham, *2 Peter* 158–162; Knoch, *2 Petrusbrief* 215–218; Paulsen, *2 Petrusbrief* 93. The arguments for Petrine authorship can be found in Zahn, *Introduction to the New Testament* (see above 2.9.3) 2.194ff.

[183] It is striking that the religious-philosophical terminology is presupposed as familiar to the readers and is used in an unselfconscious manner: ἐπίγνωσις (knowledge), γνῶσις (knowledge), εὐσέβεια (godliness), ὑπομονή (endurance), ἐγκράτεια (self-control), ἀρετή (virtue), ἐπόπτης (eyewitness), θεία δύναμις (divine power). For an analysis of the foundational catalogue of virtues in 2 Pet 1.3–7, cf. Fornberg, *Early Church* 87–101.

[184] In addition to the foundational articles in Wilhelm Schneemelcher, *New Testament Apocrypha* Vol. 1 *Gospels and Related Writings* (Louisville: Westminster/John Knox Press, rev. ed., 1991); Vol. 2 *Writings Related to the Apostles; Apocalypses and Related Subjects* (Philadelphia: Westminster Press, 1964), see especially Rudolf Pesch, *Simon Petrus*, Stuttgart: Katholisches Bibelwerk, 1980; Klaus Berger, 'Unfehlbare Offenbarung. Petrus in der gnostischen und apokalyptischen Offenbarungsliteratur,' in *Kontinuität und Einheit* (FS F. Mußner), ed. P.G. Müller and W. Stenger (Freiburg: Herder, 1981) 261–326.

[185] Cf. C. D. G. Müller, 'Apocalypse of Peter,' in *New Testament Apocrypha* II, ed. Wilhelm Schneemelcher, 663ff.; R. J. Bauckham, *2 Peter* 149.

[186] Cf. Schelkle, *2 Peter* 179 (end of the first or beginning of the second century); Knoch, *2 Petrusbrief* 213; Paulsen, *2 Petrusbrief* 94 (first quarter of the second century). Bauckham, *2 Peter* 158, dates 2 Peter in the period 80–90; a later date extending perhaps to the second half of the second century is advocated by Jülicher and Fascher, *Einleitung* 224 (between 100–180); Grundmann, *2 Petrusbrief* 65 (110–150 at the earliest); Kümmel, *Introduction* 434 (125–150); Vielhauer, *Urchristliche Literatur* 599 (150–200).

acceptance of 2 Peter into the canon was long disputed. It is missing from the Muratorian Canon and Origen still lists it among the 'disputed' writings (cf. Eusebius HE 6.25.8; additionally 3.25.3).

The place of composition remains shrouded in darkness. Egypt and Rome are often named in recent discussion. The (disputed) history of the letter's reception in the ancient church speaks in favor of Egypt,[187] while the connection with Peter and Paul speaks in favor of Rome.[188]

7.4.4 Intended Readership

The introduction of the pseudonym 'Simon Peter' and the conscious association with 1 Peter would lead one to suppose that 2 Peter is written to the same churches of Asia Minor named in 1 Pet. 1.1.[189] Gentile-Christian churches with a significant Jewish-Christian element would also be suggested by the Hellenistic conceptuality[190] and the kinds of threats presupposed. The churches are characterized by a confusion about ethics (cf. 2 Pet. 1.5, 10; 2.2; 3.14 and elsewhere), and controversies about the interpretation of Scripture (cf. 2 Pet. 1.20–21), but especially by doubts about the traditional expectation of the parousia (see 7.4.8 below). The author responds to these uncertainties with a comprehensive re-emphasis on the dependability of the promises of God (see 7.4.9 below).

7.4.5 Outline, Structure, Form

1.1–2	Salutation [Prescript]	— Letter beginning
1.3–11	Introduction [Proemium]	
1.12–21	The Departure of the Apostle and the Power of Memory	
2.1–22	The Advent of False Teachers	— Letter body
3.1–13	The Certainty of the Lord's Return	
3.14–18a	Closing Parenesis	— Letter closing
3.18b	Doxology	

---

[187] Cf. Paulsen, *2 Petrusbrief* 95 (Alexandria).

[188] Cf. Knoch, *2 Petrusbrief* 213 (a balanced presentation of all arguments!).

[189] Cf. Knoch, *2 Petrusbrief* 199.

[190] Fornberg, *Early Church* 112ff., concludes from the sophisticated Greek of 2 Peter that the churches addressed were in an urban culture.

Indications of careful composition can be discerned in Second Peter. Already in 2 Pet. 1.4 the theme 'precious and very great promises' emerges. The certainty of these promises is vouched for by the departing Peter (1.18–19), to whom the false teachers are placed in antithetical contrast (2.1ff.). The author meets the doubts of the false prophets about the coming of the Lord by reasserting the faithfulness of God. God has not gone back on his promises, but has only postponed the judgment on the basis of his patience and kindness (cf. 2 Pet. 3.9). The letter concludes with brief admonitions.

Second Peter combines the formal elements of both epistolary and testamentary genres.[191] Letter characteristics include salutation, letter opening, reference to a concrete historical situation, and concluding admonitions. To the genre 'testament'[192] belong the reference to the imminent death of Peter (2 Pet. 1.13–14) and the situation of bidding farewell which this evokes, the Apostle's 'reminding' (2 Pet. 1.12–13; 3.1) and his 'knowledge' of things that will appear in the 'future' (1.20; 3.3). In the situation of saying good-bye, an authorized bearer of the tradition communicates binding instruction to a community of faith that has had its confidence shaken by a series of crises.

The dominance of epistolary over testamentary traits is clear on the form-critical plane,[193] so that 2 Peter is properly described as a *letter*.[194]

7.4.6 Literary Integrity

The literary integrity of 2 Peter is uncontested in exegetical research.

7.4.7 Traditions, Sources

There are a series of close contacts between 2 Peter and the Letter of Jude:

Jude	2 Peter
2	1.2
4	2.1–3
5a	1.12

---

[191] Cf. here especially Otto Knoch, *Die 'Testamente' des Petrus und Paulus*, SBS 62 (Stuttgart: Katholisches Bibelwerk, 1973) 65–81; and *2 Petrusbrief* 251–254.

[192] Cf. E. v. Nordheim, *Die Lehre der Alten* I.II, ALGHL XIII.XVIII, (Leiden: E. J. Brill, 1980, 1985).

[193] Cf. Paulsen, *2 Petrusbrief* 90.

[194] Cf. Fornberg, *Early Church* 19ff.; François Vouga, 'Apostolische Briefe' (see above 7.3.5) 208 ('apostolic letter'); Paulsen, *2 Petrusbrief* 89. Knoch, *2 Petrusbrief* 202, speaks of a fictive 'apostolic office;' Vielhauer, *Urchristliche Literatur* 595, of a 'testament in letter form.'

Jude	2 Peter
6	2.4
7	2.6, 10a
8	2.10b
9	2.11
10	2.12
11	2.15
12	2.13
12f.	2.17
16	2.18
17	3.2
18	3.3

It is clear that the Letter of Jude has been almost entirely incorporated in 2 Peter. This suggests the literary–critical hypothesis that the intention is to promote the acceptance of Jude by including it in 2 Peter.[195] Second Peter tightens up the material in Jude and places it in a changed historical situation. The texts and allusions in Jude from the Jewish pseudepigrapha were not taken over (cf. the omission of Jude 14–15 and the archangel Michael in Jude 9). Nor does 2 Peter take up the warning example of the wilderness generation [cf. Jude 5b]. The key verse 19 in Jude's polemic is omitted by 2 Peter, since the problematic concerning the Spirit is not central to his controversy with his opponents. Nevertheless, how heavily dependent 2 Peter is on Jude is seen in the numerous details of subject matter and vocabulary as well as in the similarities in the structure of the two letters: after the introductory greeting both authors remind their churches of the faith transmitted in the tradition, a faith that now must be preserved in view of the threats of the false teachers. Then follows a description of the heretical teachers, to which are joined admonitions to hold firmly to the right faith and to be vigilant.

The goal of this intentional new interpretation of Jude is not to replace it,[196] but rather to interpret it and make it serviceable to the author's own interests.

The contacts between 2 Peter and the Gospel of Matthew are striking.[197] In addition to the transfiguration story pericope (cf. esp. 2 Pet. 1.17/

---

[195] Cf. most recently the comprehensive presentation of evidence in Fornberg, *Early Church* 33–59; further Grundmann, *2 Petrusbrief* 102–107. The opposite hypothesis (dependence of Jude on 2 Peter) was argued especially by Spitta, *Der zweite Brief des Petrus und der Brief des Judas* 381–470.

[196] Contra Paulsen, *2 Petrusbrief* 99.

[197] Cf. the comprehensive listing in Dschulnigg, 'Der theologische Ort' 168–176. According to Dschulnigg the author of 2 Peter is at home in the Jewish Christianity of the Gospel of Matthew, 'whose theology he defends all along the line' (*Ibid.* 177).

Matt. 17.5) and their common interest in the figure of Peter, one can also name such examples as 2 Pet. 2.6/Matt. 10.15 (Sodom and Gomorrah), 2 Pet. 2.21/Matt. 21.32 ('the way of righteousness'), and 2 Pet. 2.22/Matt. 7.6 (dogs and swine).

The author of 2 Peter takes up traditional Jewish-Christian eschatological expectations. The connection between flood, final judgment with water as the means of punishment, and fire in 2 Pet. 3.5–7, 10, 12, 13 has parallels in the *Life of Adam and Eve* 49.3; Josephus *Antiquities* 1.70–71; *SibOr* 4.172ff.; 5.155ff., 512ff.; 1 Enoch 83.3–5. In dependence on Hab. 2.1–4 an apologetic for the delay of the parousia is developed (cf. 2 Pet. 3.9 and e.g. 1QpHab. 7.1–14), which points to the divine patience especially in connection with the judgment of God that is still sure to come.[198]

7.4.8 History-of-religions Standpoint

The categorization of the opponents encountered in 2 Peter from the point of view of the history of religions is a disputed issue among scholars. If one allows for the typical character of the polemic against the writer's opponents,[199] the following picture emerges: (1) The opponents advocate their own approach to interpreting Scripture (2 Pet. 1.20–21), and are therefore described explicitly as ψευδοδιδάσκαλοι (false teachers) (2 Pet. 2.1). Included among the 'misinterpreted' Scriptures are letters of Paul (2 Pet. 3.15–16). (2) Obviously the opposed teachers reject essential elements of traditional eschatological doctrine (angels, parousia, final judgment, end of the world), to which their dominant attitude is not only skepticism but ridicule (cf. 2 Pet. 1.16; 3.3–5, 9). (3) The opponents 'deny' the Lord (2 Pet. 2.1), they 'blaspheme' and 'despise' the truth and the heavenly powers (2 Pet. 2.2, 10). They are proud, arrogant, and proclaim a false doctrine of freedom (2 Pet. 2.18a, 19). (4) The opponents have 'gluttonous carousings' in broad daylight (2 Pet. 2.13), and from the perspective of 2 Peter lead an impure life (cf. 2 Pet. 2.10, 18b, 20).

The correlation of these elements to a doctrinal system advocated by the opponents can succeed only provisionally.[200] For the most part the opponents are still categorized as 'Gnostics,'[201] which means that a particular

---

[198] On this cf. August Strobel, *Untersuchungen zum eschatologischen Verzögerungsproblem* (see above 5.4.8).

[199] Cf. the listing of typical motifs in Berger, 'Streit um Gottes Vorsehung' 122.

[200] The insight has rightly prevailed in recent exegesis of 2 Peter that the opponents of 2 Peter are not simply to be identified with those of Jude; note the omission of Jude 19 in 2 Peter.

[201] Cf. Kümmel, *Introduction* 432; Vielhauer, *Urchristliche Literatur* 597; Schenke and Fischer, *Einleitung* II, 323–324.

picture of Gnosticism is presupposed and then read into the texts.[202] But the dualism constitutive of the Gnostic system is missing from 2 Peter's description. More vague, and paradoxically yet more precise, are all the attempts to see the opponents as '*gnostic-like*,' without designating them as Gnostics.[203] Obviously the death of the 'fathers' and the delay of the parousia formed the basis for a widespread skepticism at the beginning of the second century (cf. 1 Clem. 23.3–4; 2 Clem. 11.2–4)[204] that regarded Jewish and/or Jewish-Christian ideas of redemption and eschatology as obsolete (cf. 2 Pet. 2.1 for atonement Christology and 2 Pet. 1.16 for the traditional concepts of the parousia as μῦθος [myth]).[205] The opponents appeal to Paul's letters as justification for their position,[206] and proclaim a knowledge of God guided by reason (cf. the emphatic use of γνῶσις [knowledge] in 2 Pet. 1.5, 6; 3.18; and of ἐπίγνωσις [knowledge] in 2 Pet. 1.2, 3, 8; 2.20), and an understanding of the life of faith oriented to the concept of freedom.

7.4.9 Basic Theological Ideas

The Second Epistle of Peter meets the fundamental critique of its opponents on different levels. The choice of the pseudonym 'Simon Peter' already signals the standpoint and intention of the author: he understands himself as the spokesperson for the 'orthodox' church and claims for it the correct interpretation of Scripture. So too the incorporation of elements of the testamentary genre serves the current debate, for 'last words' possess an uncontested authority. They can be neither taken back nor changed. On the fictive level of the letter, Peter claims to possess the προφητικὸς λόγος (prophetic word) (2 Pet. 1.19), and thus to be able to guarantee the certainty of the 'day of the Lord.' In order to place equal emphasis on both the unshakable hope in the Lord's parousia and the futility of trying to calculate its date, he utilizes the idea of the typological correspondence of the judgment of the earth by the flood and the eschatological judgment (2 Pet. 3.5–7), Ps 90.4 (2 Pet. 3.8 'with the Lord one day is like a thousand years, and a thousand years are like one day'), and the motif of the thief

---

[202] For a critique cf. Berger, 'Streit um Gottes Vorsehung' 121; Paulsen, *2 Petrusbrief* 95–96.

[203] Cf. this approach in Grundmann, *2 Petrusbrief* 59–64; Knoch, *2 Petrusbrief* 208–212.

[204] For the pagan realm cf. the references (especially Plutarch, *SerNumVind*) in Berger, 'Streit um Gottes Vorsehung' 124–125. The position of the opponents is explained primarily from the pagan context by Fornberg, *Early Church* 119–120; Neyrey, 'Form and Background'; Bauckham, *2 Peter* 154–157; Berger, 'Streit um Gottes Vorsehung' *passim*.

[205] Vögtle, 'Christo-logie und Theo-logie' 384, rightly supposes that the author of 2 Peter here takes up an objection of the opponents and turns it against them (cf. also 2 Pet. 2.3, 18).

[206] A listing of possible passages is given in Knoch, *2 Petrusbrief* 210–211.

(2 Pet. 3.10; cf. 1 Thess. 5.2; Matt. 24.29ff., 43; Rev. 3.3; 16.15). The basis
for the failure of the parousia to appear so far is named in 2 Pet. 3.9: God's
patience[207] still allows the possibility of repentance. God as Lord of
creation and history not only has a different perspective on time than that
of earthlings, but it is in fact his kindness that is mocked by the
opponents. Thereby they reveal their true nature, that they live in self-
deception and sins (cf. 2 Pet. 1.9; 2.10–12, 14, 18), and do not recognize
that God's righteous judgment will overtake them (cf. 2 Pet. 2.3b, 12–13).

The Second Letter of Peter aims at the right 'knowledge of Jesus Christ,
the Lord and Savior' (cf. 2 Pet. 1.1–2). He is the self-revelation of God (2
Pet. 1.17); he is now the Lord of history (cf. 2 Pet. 3.8–10, 15a, 18).[208] The
divine nature of Jesus is highlighted by the author (cf. 2 Pet. 1.3–4; 3.18;
as well as 1.1, 11), for participation in the θεία φύσις (divine nature) is the
goal of the Christian life (2 Pet. 1.4). The strong christological orientation
of 2 Peter is also seen in the double title 'our Lord and Savior Jesus Christ'
(2 Pet. 1.11; 2.20; 3.18) and in the correspondence between the introduction and conclusion of the letter: the praise of the κύριος (lord) and σωτὴρ
Ἰησοῦς Χριστός (savior Jesus Christ) brackets the writing (cf. 2 Peter
1.1–2; 3.18).

7.4.10 *Tendencies of Recent Research*

Like the Letter of Jude, so also Second Peter stood for a long time under
the verdict of being theologically insignificant. Ernst Käsemann summarized the theology of 2 Peter as follows: 'The conception of an apostle
has therefore changed. The messenger of the Gospel has become the
guarantor of the tradition, the witness of the resurrection has become the
witness of the *historia sacra*, the bearer of the eschatological action of God
has become a pillar of the institution which dispenses salvation, the man
who is subject to the eschatological temptation has become the man who
brings *securitas*.'[209] Käsemann cavils at the lack of christological orientation
in 2 Peter's eschatology,[210] considers the letter to be a mere medley of
didactic topoi and evaluates 2 Peter as 'the clearest testimony to the onset
of early catholicism.'[211] This verdict was widely adopted; it was especially
influential on the exposition of W. Schrage. For him, the acceptance of 2

---

[207] On μακροθυμία (patience) cf. R. Stuhlmann, *Das eschatologische Maß im Neuen Testament*,
FRLANT 132 (Göttingen: Vandenhoeck & Ruprecht, 1983) 85ff.

[208] Especially in 2 Pet 3 the judgment of God and the parousia of the κύριος come together;
cf. Vögtle, 'Christo-logie und Theo-logie' 392ff.

[209] Käsemann, 'Apology' 177.

[210] *Ibid.* 183.

[211] *Ibid.* 195.

Peter into the canon raised a fundamental question: 'In fact its place and rank in the New Testament canon poses a continuing problem for Protestant theology and for the Protestant Church. It cannot be denied that the document contains theological views that by virtue of their unqualified absolutism are in unavoidable competition both with the center of New Testament affirmations and with fundamental positions of Protestant theology.'[212]

Recent exegetical study has freed itself from such value judgments that tend to dismiss 2 Peter, and attempts to uncover the historical necessity and theological legitimacy of its argument. T. Fornberg rejects the concept of 'early catholicism' as a category for evaluating 2 Peter and attempts to locate the document in its historical Hellenistic context. From this perspective, ethics turns out to be a central key to understanding the writing, for extensive sections of 2 Peter are nothing but parenesis. O. Knoch's circumspect exegetical work points out that in 2 Peter there is no reference at all to the teaching authority of authorized ecclesiastical offices. As in the Deuteropauline letters, the only claim to authority is that made for the apostles. The Second Letter of Peter teaches us to take seriously the patience of God, in order that as many as possible might be saved. It directs our view 'to the recognition of the development of the "apostolic" to the "catholic" church in the full sense of the word, and to the earnest concern that the church preserve all legitimate Christian traditions in the church and to allow them to play their proper role.'[213] H. Paulsen's exegesis joins the critique of Ernst Käsemann on the one hand, but on the other hand he also distinguishes himself sharply from it: 'Critical study of 2 Peter (and Jude!) may not abstract itself from the factual situation that formed the historical context within which the text came into being.'[214] For Paulsen, 2 Peter represents the transition to the early catholic church, because the constant element in theology now becomes the hermeneutic of the past.

---

[212] Schrage, *2 Petrusbrief* 122.
[213] Knoch, *2 Petrusbrief* 231.
[214] Paulsen, *2 Petrusbrief* 102.

8

The Writings of the Johannine School

8.1 The Johannine School

8.1.1 Literature

Culpepper, R. Alan. *The Johannine School*, SBLDS 26. Missoula: Scholars Press, 1975; Cullmann, Oscar. *The Johannine Circle*, tr. John Bowden. Philadelphia: Westminster, 1976; Schüssler Fiorenza, Elisabeth. 'The Quest for the Johannine School: The Apocalypse and the Fourth Gospel,' NTS 23 (1977) 402–427; Brown, Raymond E. *The Community of the Beloved Disciple*. NY: Paulist Press, 1979; Strecker, Georg. 'Die Anfänge der johanneischen Schule,' NTS 32 (1986) 31–47; Taeger, Jens W. *Johannesapokalypse und johanneischer Kreis* (see below 9.1); Vouga, François. 'The Johannine School: A Gnostic Tradition in Primitive Christianity?' Bib 69 (1988) 371–385; Hengel, Martin. *The Johannine Question* (see below 8.5.1) 8off., 11off.; Schnelle, Udo. *Antidocetic Christology in the Gospel of John* (see below 8.5.1) 41–63; Hengel, Martin. *Die johanneische Frage* (see below 8.5.1) 219ff., 275ff.

8.1.2 Criteria for Determining the Existence of a Johannine School

(1) In the first place, the existence of a Johannine school[1] is indicated by the *theological agreements* between the three Johannine letters and the Gospel of John. Only a few central ideas need be mentioned here: (a) the unity of Father and Son (e.g. 2 John 9; 1 John 1.3; 2.22ff.; 4.14; John 5.20; 10.30, 38; 14.10 and others); (b) the incarnation of Jesus Christ (2 John 7; 1 John 4.2; John 1.14); (c) the dualism between God and the world (2 John 7; 1 John 2.15–17; 4.3–6; John 14–17); (d) 'begotten/born of God' (1 John 2.29; 3.9; 4.7; John 1.13; 3.3ff.); (e) the 'knowledge of God' (e.g. 1 John 2.3–5, 13–14; 3.1, 6; 4.6–8; John 1.10; 8.55; 14.7; 16.3 and others); (f) 'abiding' in God, in Jesus, in the truth, and in the teaching (2 John 2, 9; 1 John 2.6, 24, 27; 4.12–15; John 8.31; 14.10, 17; 15.4–10); (g) water and blood of Jesus Christ (1 John 5.6–8; John 19.34–35); (h) the command to love (2 John 4–6; 1 John 2.7–8; 3.11; John 13.34–35); (i) 'being of the truth,' 'knowing the

---

[1] On the history of research cf. Elisabeth Schüssler Fiorenza, 'Johannine School' 406–410; Jens W. Taeger, *Johannesapokalypse* 11–20.

truth' (2 John 1; 3 John 3, 8; 1 John 2.21; 3.19; John 8.32; 18.37); (j) 'being from God' (3 John 11; 1 John 3.10; 4.1–6; John 8.47); (k) keeping the commandments (1 John 2.3–4; 3.22, 24; 5.2–3; John 14.15, 21, 23; 15.10).

(2) The second indication that must be considered as evidence for a Johannine school is the *common linguistic elements* between the three Johannine letters and the Gospel.[2] They point beyond the distinctive vocabulary of single author to a common vocabulary shared by the Johannine school. Persuasive evidence is provided by the list of favorite words that occur very often in the Letters and the Gospel, but are documented much less often in the other writings of the New Testament.[3] Just as instructive is the absence or rare use of words in the Johannine writings that occur in the rest of the New Testament with great frequency.[4]

(3) John 21 provides clear evidence of the existence of a Johannine school. In v. 24b with the words καὶ οἴδαμεν ὅτι ἀληθὴς αὐτοῦ ἡ μαρτυρία ἐστίν (and we know that his testimony is true) we hear the words of the authors of the secondary epilogue, and perhaps even the *editor/publisher* of the whole Gospel. They make the 'Beloved Disciple' into the author of the Gospel and provide a new determination of his relationship to Peter. The presence of this appendix and the plural 'we' of 24b,[5] which is by no means to be understood merely as the literary *Plural communicis*, is in itself sufficient evidence of a Johannine school.

(4) So also the *ecclesiological terms* in the Johannine letters and the Gospel point to a Johannine school. In 3 John 15 the presbyter chooses οἱ φίλοι (the friends) as the self-description for his community and likewise uses the title for the addressees (cf. further John 11.11; 15.14–15). A usual address within the Johannine school was τεκνία or τέκνα (θεοῦ) (little children/children [of God]); on τεκνία cf. 1 John 2.1, 12, 28; 3.7, 18; 4.4; 5.21; John 13.33; for τέκνα (θεοῦ) cf. 2 John 1, 4, 13; 3 John 4; 1 John 3.1,

---

[2] The formation of Johannine concepts must be understood as the expression of a specifically Johannine 'way of seeing;' cf. Franz Mußner, *Sehweise* (see below 8.5.1) 8off.

[3] Thus for example ἀγαπάω (love), ἀλήθεια (truth), ἀληθής (true), γεννάω (beget/bear), γινώσκω (know), ἐντολή (commandment), ζωή (life), κόσμος (world), μαρτυρέω (testify), μένω (remain), μισέω (hate), πιστεύω (believe), τηρέω (keep).

[4] Here may be named ἀπόστολος (apostle), γραμματεύς (scribe), δέχομαι (receive), δύναμις (power), ἐλπίς (hope), ἐπαγγελία (promise), εὐαγγελίζομαι (preach good news), εὐαγγέλιον (gospel), κηρύσσω (proclaim), παραβολή (parable), παρακαλέω (exhort), πίστις (faith), πιστός (faithful), προσέρχομαι (approach), πρόσωπον (face), σοφία (wisdom).

[5] On this cf. Adolf von Harnack, 'Das "Wir" in den Johanneischen Schriften,' in *Kleine Schriften zur Alten Kirche* (Leipzig 1980 [= 1923]) 642–643. In his debate with Th. Zahn, Harnack demonstrates that the 'we' in the Johannine writings is not an indication that the author is an eyewitness, but that it can be understood only on the basis of the existence of a Johannine school in Asia Minor.

2, 10; 5.2; John 1.12; 11.52). An additional honorary description used in the Johannine school is ἀδελφός (brother/sister) (cf. 3 John 3.5, 10; John 20.17; 21.23).

(5) The *ethical affirmations*[6] in the Letters and in the Gospel likewise speak for the existence of a Johannine school, for they are to be understood predominately not as universalistic, but as oriented to the in-group of the Johannine churches themselves. Thus the commandment of 'brotherly love' stands clearly in the center of the Johannine ethic (cf. 2 John 5–6; 1 John 2.7–11; John 13.34–35).

(6) A further index for the existence of a Johannine school is the presentation of Jesus as '*Teacher.*'[7] In no other Gospel is Jesus addressed so frequently as ῥαββί (rabbi) (John 9x; Mark 3x; Matthew 2x), and Jesus' activity as a teacher is often reported (John 6.59; 7.14, 28; 8.20; 18.20). Nicodemus names Jesus as a 'teacher who has come from God.' God himself teaches Jesus (8.26, 28), his teaching is ἐκ θεοῦ (from God) (John 7.16, 17). Jesus teaches his friends all that he has received from the Father (John 15.15; cf. 17.26), so that the Johannine school appears as the place in which the revelation of the Father to the Son is nourished and handed on.

8.1.3 The Writings of the Johannine School

From the common linguistic and theological elements found in the three Johannine Letters and the Gospel of John we may conclude that they all belong to the same Johannine school. Whether the Revelation of John also belongs in this group is a disputed issue among scholars. While Revelation is not usually considered a member of the Johannine school in a direct sense, J. W. Taeger votes for a close relationship between Revelation and the Johannine circle of writings. He sees firm lines of connection between Revelation and a 'deutero-Johannine' form of thought seen in the Letters and in the redactional layer of the Gospel. In his view, the deutero-Johannine two-stage eschatology oriented toward the future (cf. John 5.28–29; 6.39, 40, 44, 54; 12.48; 1 John) and the Apocalypse concur in a conception 'which expands the emphasis on the present aspect of life given in the Johannine tradition to include a future aspect, and binds both

---

[6] As an introduction to the difficult problems of the Johannine ethic cf. Rudolf Schnackenburg, *Die sittliche Botschaft des Neuen Testaments*, HThK.S II/2 (Freiburg: Herder, 1988) 148–192. There is no disagreement among scholars that the primary orientation of the Johannine ethic is to the group itself. The only questions are whether the Johannine conception includes concrete ethical directions and whether it has any openness to the world, however these are conceived.

[7] Cf. Culpepper, *Johannine School* 273ff.

together.'[8] Taeger recognizes additional common elements between the Apocalypse and the deutero-Johannine thought in the statements of judgment, the concept of the antichrist, the Logos motif, and the victory theme. The Apocalypse, however, is not to be classified as proto-Johannine or deutero-Johannine, but '– taking into consideration the development that has already occurred very strongly in the Apocalypse – trito-Johannine.'[9] The basis in the text for this sort of wide-ranging conclusions is very small, however, and the presuppositions of Taeger's line of argument are also problematic. Taeger orients himself tendentiously to the explanatory model for the Gospel of John proposed by Rudolf Bultmann that is very disputed in recent scholarship. What functions as a presupposition for Taeger must rather be regarded as a central problem: do the affirmations of futuristic eschatology in the Gospel point to a 'deutero-Johannine' redactional layer, or can they be integrated into the theological conception of the evangelist himself? In addition, there are important distinctions in the language, view of history, understanding of the significance of the Old Testament, Christology, anthropology, ecclesiology, as well as the whole structure of thought, between Revelation on the one side and the Gospel and Letters on the other side (see below 9.2). These differences suggest that it makes more sense not to include Revelation directly in the Johannine school, but to regard it as having an indirect connection with the other Johannine writings by means of which the common elements can also be explained.[10]

---

[8] Taeger, *Johannesapokalypse* 133.

[9] *Ibid* 207.

[10] For this understanding cf. Ulrich B. Müller, *Offenbarung* (see below 9.1) 46–52; Jürgen Roloff, *Offenbarung* (see below 9.1) 19–20; Eduard Lohse, 'Wie christlich ist die Offenbarung des Johannes?' NTS 34 (1988) 326. Schüssler Fiorenza, 'Johannine School' 410–418, works out the linguistic and material connections between Revelation and the Fourth Gospel, confirms that there are points of contact in the history of the tradition, but then still speaks of two independent school traditions. In contrast, Otto Böcher sees both contacts between Revelation and the other Johannine writings in the use of common traditional elements as well as literary contacts; 'Das Verhältnis der Apokalypse des Johannes zum Evangelium des Johannes,' in *L'Apocalypse*, ed. Jan Lambrecht (see below 9.1) 289–301 and 'Johanneisches in der Apokalypse des Johannes,' NTS 27 (1981) 310–321. Cf. further with this perspective Heinrich Kraft, *Offenbarung* (see below 9.1) 10; Pierre Prigent, *L'Apocalypse* (see below 9.1) 369–371; Jörg Frey, 'Erwägungen' (see below 9.1) 415ff.

8.1.4 The Location of the School

The Johannine school was probably located in *Ephesus*.[11] In the area around
Ephesus there were different Johannine congregations (cf. 2–3 John), with
the main congregation settled in Ephesus. This probability can be supported by three lines of evidence:

(1) According to ancient church tradition, the Gospel of John originated
in Ephesus. About 180 CE Irenaeus transmitted the tradition that the
apostle John, the Lord's Beloved Disciple, wrote the Fourth Gospel in
Ephesus in his old age during the time of the emperor Trajan.[12] He
appealed to the presbyters who had assembled around the Lord's disciple
John, but especially to Polycarp and Papias, whom he considered to be disciples of John.[13] Papias, as the oldest witness of an Asia Minor Johannine
tradition, presumably refers both to the apostle John and to a presbyter
John, but knows nothing about either of them having written the Fourth
Gospel.[14] The early stage of Johannine tradition in Asia Minor was thus
not connected with the question of the authorship of the Fourth Gospel,
which increases the credibility of this tradition.

(2) The history of the influence of the Fourth Gospel (*Wirkungsgeschichte*), as represented by the Alogoi, Montanists, Acts of John, and its
reception in gnosticism, points clearly to Asia Minor and the western part
of the Empire.[15] 1 John is documented in Asia Minor soon after its composition (cf. Polycarp Phil. 7.1).

(3) The theological agreements between Pauline and Johannine theology
(see below 8.5.7) point to Ephesus as the common setting for the Pauline
and Johannine schools. It was probably here that elements of Pauline and
Johannine theology were combined during the history of their respective
traditions.

(4) Finally, as indirect witnesses for Ephesus we may also regard the
messages to the seven churches in Rev. 2–3 and the Letters of Ignatius, for
they are directed to churches in the orbit of the Johannine school.

---

[11] Cf. also Raymond E. Brown, *The Epistles of John* (see below 8.2.1) 102–103, Udo Schnelle,
'Paulus und Johannes,' *EvTh* 47 (1987) 225–26; Georg Strecker, *Johannine Letters* (see below
8.2.1) xl–xli; Taeger, *Johannesapokalypse* 22; Rudolf Schnackenburg, 'Ephesus: Entwicklung
einer Gemeinde von Paulus zu Johannes,' BZ 35 (1991) 60; Martin Hengel, *Die johanneische Frage*
302; *Johannine Question* (see below 8.5.1) 123 and passim.

[12] Cf. Irenaeus, *Haer* 3.1.1 (= Eusebius, HE 5.8.4); 2.22.5 (= Eusebius, HE 3.23.3).

[13] Cf. Irenaeus, *Haer* 5.33.3–4; Eusebius, HE 5.20.4–6; 3.39.1. Analysis of the texts in 8.5.2
below.

[14] Cf. Eusebius, HE 3.39.4; analysis of the text in section 8.2.2.

[15] On the history of the influence (*Wirkungsgeschichte*) cf. especially Hengel (see below 8.5.1)
Die johanneische Frage 9–95; *Johannine Question* 1–23, 136–160.

8.1.5 The Chronology of the Johannine Writings

The order of Johannine writings here presupposed (2 John, 3 John, 1 John, Gospel of John) is based on considerations that were current in the nineteenth[16] and first half of the twentieth centuries.[17] Four main arguments may be brought forward for this order:[18]

(1) The two brief Johannine Letters are not insignificant products of the late phase of the Johannine school, but as writings of the πρεσβύτερος Ἰωάννης are original documents from its beginning period.

(2) Since 3 John 9 refers to 2 John, 2 John stands at the beginning of the Johannine literature.

(3) 1 John refers to no recognizable passage in the Gospel of John. It is engaged in a polemical debate with docetic false teachers, that come into view for the first time in 2 John 7.

(4) The Gospel of John presupposes the current controversy with the docetic false teachers, and comprehensively works through the subject of the theological conflict associated with them.

8.2 The Second Letter of John

General Bibliography for the Johannine Letters.

Wendt, Hans H. *Die Johannesbriefe und das johanneische Christentum.* Halle: Waisenhaus, 1925; Bultmann, Rudolf. 'Johannesbriefe,' *RGG*³ III (1959) 836–839; Haenchen, Ernst. 'Neuere Literatur zu den Johannesbriefen,' in *Die Bibel und Wir.* ed. E. Haenchen. Tübingen: J. C. B. Mohr (Paul Siebeck) 1968, 235–311 (history of research!); Thyen, Hardwig. 'Johannesbriefe,' *TRE* 17 (1987) 186–200; Beutler, Johannes. 'Die Johannesbriefe in der neuesten Literatur,' *ANRW* 25.5. Berlin: Walter de Gruyter 1988, 3773–3790; Wengst, Klaus. 'Probleme der Johannesbriefe,' *ANRW* 25.5. Berlin: Walter de Gruyter 1989, 3753–3772.

---

[16] Cf. Johann E. Huther, *Die drei Briefe des Johannes*, KEK XIV (Göttingen: Vandenhoeck & Ruprecht, 1880⁴) 34–35; Friedrich Bleek, *Einleitung in das Neue Testament* (Berlin 1866²) 588; Otto Pfleiderer, 'Beleuchtung der neuesten Johannes-Hypothese,' ZWTh 12 (1869) 419ff.; Adolf Hilgenfeld, *Einleitung in das Neue Testament* (Leipzig 1875) 737; Bernhard Weiß, *Die drei Briefe des Apostels Johannes*, KEK XIV (Göttingen: Vandenhoeck & Ruprecht, 1899²) 8–9.

[17] Cf. Hans H. Wendt, *Die Johannesbriefe und das johanneische Christentum* (see below 8.2) 1–7; Friedrich Büchsel, *Die Johannesbriefe*, ThHK 17 (Leipzig: Deichert, 1933) 7; Heinrich Appel, *Einleitung in das Neue Testament* (Leipzig 1922) 197; Hermann Strathmann, 'Johannesbriefe,' EKL II (1958) 364.

[18] For the detailed evidence cf. the following section.

8.2.1 Literature

Commentaries

Windisch, Hans (Herbert Preisker). *Die katholischen Briefe*, HNT 15. Tübingen: J. C. B. Mohr (Paul Siebeck), 1951[3]; Bultmann, Rudolf. *The Johannine Epistles*, tr. R. Philip O'Hara et al. Philadelphia: Fortress, 1973; Wengst, Klaus. *Der erste, zweite und dritte Briefe des Johannes*, ÖTK 16. Gütersloh: Gütersloher Verlagshaus, 1978; Balz, Horst. *Die 'Katholischen' Briefe. Die Briefe des Jakobus, Petrus, Johannes und Judas*, NTD 10. Göttingen: Vandenhoeck & Ruprecht, 1980[2]; Brown, Raymond E. *The Epistles of John*, AncB 30. Garden City: Doubleday, 1982; Schunack, Gerd. *Die Briefe des Johannes*, ZBK 17. Zürich: Theologischer Verlag, 1982; Smalley, Stephen S. *1, 2, 3 John*, WBC 51. Waco: Word, 1984; Vouga, François. *Die Johannesbriefe*, HNT 15/III. Tübingen: J. C. B. Mohr (Paul Siebeck), 1990; Klauck, Hans-Joseph. *Der Zweite und Dritte Johannesbrief*, EKK XXIII/2. Neukirchen: Neukirchener Verlag, 1992; Schnackenburg, Rudolf. *The Johannine Epistles*. New York: Crossroad, 1992; Vogler, Werner. *Die Briefe des Johannes*, ThHK 17. Leipzig: Evangelische Verlagsanstalt, 1993; Strecker, Georg. *The Johannine Letters*. Minneapolis: Fortress, 1996.

Articles

Bergmeier, Roland. 'Zum Verfasserproblem des II. und III. Johannesbriefes,' ZNW 57 (1966) 93–100; Funk, Robert W. 'The Form and Structure of II. and III. John,' JBL 86 (1967) 424–430; Käsemann, Ernst. 'Ketzer und Zeuge', in *Exegetische Versuche und Besinnungen* I, ed. E. Käsemann. Göttingen: Vandenhoeck & Ruprecht, 1970[6], 168–187; Bornkamm, Günther. 'πρεσβύτερος', TDNT 6, 651–683; Taeger, Jens W. 'Der konservative Rebell. Zum Widerstand des Diotrephes gegen den Presbyter,' ZNW 78 (1987) 267–287; Bonsack, Bernhard. 'Der Presbyteros des dritten Briefes und der geliebte Jünger des Evangeliums nach Johannes,' ZNW 79 (1988) 45–62.

History of Research

Klauck, Hans-Joseph. *Die Johannesbriefe*, EdF 276. Darmstadt: Wissenschaftliche Buchgesellschaft, 1991.

8.2.2 Author

The superscript of the prescripts of both 2 John and 3 John indicate that they were written by ὁ πρεσβύτερος (the elder).[19] The word itself first suggests the meaning 'the elder' in the sense of 'the old man,' one who had attained a special status on the basis of his long life and experience.[20] To be sure, the debate between the elder and his opponents gives no indication

---

[19] A critical analysis of the problem as well as a discussion of the solutions proposed by Adolf von Harnack, Walter Bauer, and Ernst Käsemann is presented by Haenchen, 'Neuere Literatur' 282–311. In addition cf. the history of research surveyed by Brown, *The Epistles of John* 648–651.

[20] The advanced age of the presbyter is emphasized especially by Wendt, *Johannesbriefe* 7–8.

that his authority rests on his great age.[21] Thus ὁ πρεσβύτερος can mean the bearer of a particular congregational office, one who receives his authority by virtue of the office he holds. This thesis has been advocated especially by E. Käsemann,[22] but against it must be said that in early Christianity the office of the presbyter only functioned within the context of a college of presbyters (cf. e.g. Acts 11.30; 14.23; 1 Tim. 4.14; Titus 1.5), in addition to the fact that it would be unique to have the designation 'the Presbyter' in an official sense without giving the person's name. We cannot be sure that either the elder or his counterpart Diotrephes mentioned in 3 John 9 held any official position. Thus ὁ πρεσβύτερος is probably an honorary title for 'a well-known and unmistakable personage.'[23] The presbyter must have been an outstanding figure within the Johannine school, probably even its founder, for only in this way can we account for the preservation of 2 John and 3 John and their admission into the canon.[24] Nothing speaks against the identification of the presbyter of 2 John and 3 John with ὁ πρεσβύτερος Ἰωάννης set forth by Papias as one of the guarantors of his tradition, a figure he clearly distinguishes from John the son of Zebedee (Eusebius, *HE* 3.39.4: 'But if I met with any one who had been a follower of the elders anywhere, I made it a point to inquire what were the declarations of the elders: what Andrew or Peter had said, what Philip, Thomas, James, John, Matthew, or any other of the disciples of the Lord had said, what Aristion and the presbyter John and the disciples of the Lord were saying'). Both the presbyter of the Johannine letters and the presbyter John in Papias are bearers of the tradition, not holders of an office.[25] As bearer and/or founder of the Johannine tradition, the presbyter of 2 John and 3 John enjoyed great respect, and appears also in Papias as the bearer of a special tradition.

Papias preserves the oral traditions from disciples of the presbyters, a tradition that he himself values very highly. The chain of tradition would be: apostle – presbyter (= disciples of the apostles) – disciples of the presbyters – Papias.[26] We can now hardly determine the relation between the first

---

[21] Cf. Bornkamm, 'πρεσβύτερος,' *TDNT* 6. 670.

[22] Käsemann, 'Ketzer und Zeuge' 177, sees the presbyter as a man who 'has become leader of a congregation and missionary group and is very active in church politics, who is attempting to establish supporting links for his organization in other congregations.' For a critique of Käsemann's view see Bornkamm, *ibid.* 671 note 121.

[23] Bornkamm, *ibid.* 671; cf. in addition Schnackenburg, *Johannine Epistles* 278.

[24] Cf. Thyen, 'Johannesbriefe' 195.

[25] Cf. Philipp Vielhauer, *Urchristliche Literatur* 763, who sets forth the view that Papias understood the bearers of tradition to include the πρεσβύτεροι.

[26] Cf. Wilhelm Heitmüller, 'Zur Johannes-Tradition,' *ZNW* 15 (1914) (189–209) 195; Ernst Haenchen, *John* I (see below 8.5.1) 9–10.

group (the apostles) and the second group of 'the Lord's disciples' (Aristion and the presbyter John). The different verbal tenses used (εἶπεν for the apostles, λέγουσιν for Aristion and the presbyter John) permit us to infer that Aristion and the presbyter John were still alive at the time of Papias, so that it must be asked whether Papias might actually have known both of them. Eusebius explicitly affirms this (HE 3.39.7), in order thereby to secure the credibility of the Papias tradition he himself hands on (cf. HE 3.39.15–17). This also seems to be suggested by the Papias citation itself, for in the second relative clause the indirect question expressed by the interrogative τί is taken up by the relative pronoun ἅ, while on the other hand τέ and the new predicate λέγουσιν mark the beginning of a new clause. In this case Papias would have received traditions directly from Aristion and the presbyter John and would be regarded as their disciple.[27]

8.2.3 Place and Time of Composition

If the author of 2–3 John as founder of the Johannine school is identical with the presbyter John mentioned by Papias, then nothing speaks against regarding the two small Johannine letters as the *oldest documents* of the Johannine school.[28] Of the two small Johannine letters, the temporal priority must be given to 2 John, for 3 John 9 obviously refers to 2 John.

The objection is often raised against this view that 3 John 9 must refer to a letter of recommendation for wandering missionaries, but 2 John is not such a letter.[29] But from the expression ἔγραψά τι τῇ ἐκκλησίᾳ (I have written something to the church) we only learn, of course, that the presbyter had already written to the church. Only in v. 10b does the subject return to the wandering missionaries, so that Diotrophes' rejection (v. 9b) can refer to the presbyter and his theological position set forth in 2 John, and the claim to authority inherent in it.[30]

---

[27] This possibility would also be supported by the absolute ἀλήθεια-concept in Eusebius HE 3.39.3 ('. . .For I have never, like many, delighted to hear those who tell many things, but those that teach the truth. . .'), which is reminiscent of the language of 2 John and 3 John.

[28] Cf. for this interpretation (with distinctions within their individual lines of argument) Wendt, *Johannesbriefe* 1–7; Strecker, *Johannine Letters* xli–xlii; Schnelle, *Antidocetic Christology* (see below 8.5.1) 52–53; Thyen, 'Johannesbrief' 195; Martin Hengel, *Die johanneische Frage* 123, 156; *Johannine Question* (see below 8.5.1) 34, 48.

[29] Cf. e.g., Schnackenburg, *Johannine Epistles* 296; Kümmel, *Introduction* 449; Bultmann, *Johannine Epistles* 100; Wengst, *Johannesbriefe* 248.

[30] That 3 John 9 refers to 2 John is argued by e.g. Th. Zahn, *Introduction to the New Testament* (see above 2.9.3) 3.378; Wendt, *Johannesbriefe* 23; Martin Dibelius, 'Johannesbriefe,' RGG² (1929) 3.348; Jülicher and Fascher, *Einleitung* 235; Strecker, *Johannine Letters* 253–254, 263; Vouga, *Johannesbriefe* 18; Vogler, *Johannesbriefe* 30; Hengel, *Die johanneische Frage* 132; *Johannine Question* 38.

The earliest attestation of 2 John is found in Polycarp (cf. Polycarp, Phil. 7.1 with 2 John 7). 2 John was probably written *around* 90 CE.

8.2.4 Intended Readership

In 2 John 1 the expression ἐκλεκτὴ κυρία (elect lady) does not refer to an individual person, but the local congregation addressed by the letter.[31] The presbyter is thereby making use of a metaphorical style derived from the Old Testament (cf. Jer. 4.31; 31.21; Zeph. 3.14), just as elsewhere in the New Testament other writings can describe the church as the 'bride of Christ' (cf. 2 Cor. 11.2; Rev. 12.17; 19.7; 21.2, 9). The whole body of believers are 'elect' (cf. 1 Peter 1.1; Rev. 17.4), and also an individual congregation can be designated as 'elect' (cf. 1 Pet. 5.13).[32] The church is described as κυρία (lady), because by its election it participates in the kingship exercised by the κύριος (Lord) Jesus Christ. 2 John 13 confirms the ecclesiological interpretation of κυρία, for it is not the author of the letter who confers greetings, but 'the children of your elect sister,' i.e. a sister congregation. Here the organizational structure of the Johannine school may be seen: autonomous congregations form an association, send greetings to one another, maintain contact with one another and offer mutual support. The presbyter has a good relation with the congregation (2 John 3), and would like to visit it soon in order to discuss problems with it face to face (2 John 12). At the same time, the presbyter warns the congregation against false teachers that are agitating in the congregations of the Johannine school (2 John 7–8). This obviously refers to wandering preachers that visit individual congregations; the presbyter warns against receiving them (2 John 10).

8.2.5 Outline, Structure, Form

1–2	Prescript	
3	Salutation	— Introduction
4	Thanksgiving	

---

[31] For this understanding cf. Bultmann, *Johannine Epistles* 107–108; Schnackenburg, *Johannine Epistles* 278; Wengst, *Johannesbriefe* 236; Strecker, *Johannine Letters* 220; Vouga, *Johannesbriefe* 80.

[32] In classical Greek κυρία ἐκκλησία described an important meeting of a commonwealth in which the central issues of provisions and security were discussed and decided; cf. Hans-Joseph Klauck, 'κυρία ἐκκλησία in Bauers Wörterbuch und die Exegese des zweiten Johannesbriefes,' ZNW 81 (1990) 135–138.

5–6	The love command	
7–9	The false teachers	— Body
10–11	No hospitality for false teachers	

12	Apostolic parousia	— Conclusion
13	Greetings	

2 John is to be regarded as a *real letter*, manifesting all the characteristics of the ancient personal letter: superscription, adscription, salutation, proemium, epistolary request with ἐρωτάω (ask), announcement of a planned visit, and concluding greetings.[33] The formulation ἐρωτῶ σε (I ask you) typical of a certain type of Hellenistic letters, distinguishes 2 John as a letter of request. The hypothesis that the letter form of 2 John is fictive[34] is not persuasive. Both the structure and the length (one sheet of papyrus) corresponds to ancient personal letters. The character of the document as a real letter is further documented by its dealing with concrete questions, going into congregational problems and the announcement of an impending visit. From a rhetorical point of view the following outline of 2 John emerges:[35] exordium v. 4 (vv. 1–3); narratio v. 5; probatio vv. 6–11; peroratio v. 12 (v. 13).

8.2.6 Literary Integrity

The literary integrity of 2 John is not disputed.

8.2.7 Traditions, Sources

The author of 2 John does not incorporate and edit traditions or sources.

---

[33] As parallels, cf. the letters printed in Adolf Deissmann, *Light from the Ancient East* (see above 2.3.1) 149ff.

[34] So especially Bultmann, *Johannine Epistles* 107–108; Jürgen Heise, *Bleiben. Menein in den Johanneischen Schriften*, HUTh 8 (Tübingen: J. C. B. Mohr [Paul Siebeck], 1967) 164–170; G. Schunack, *Johannesbriefe* 108–9; U. H. J. Körtner, *Papias von Hierapolis* (see above 3.4.2) 197–201.

[35] Cf. Duane F. Watson, 'A Rhetorical Analysis of 2 John according to Greco-Roman Convention,' NTS 35 (1989) 104–130; Hans-Joseph Klauck, 'Zur rhetorischen Analyse der Johannesbriefe,' ZNW 81 (1990) 217ff.

8.2.8 History-of-religions Standpoint

In 2 John 7 the presbyter warns against the agitations of false teachers who travel from congregation to congregation, teachers who do not confess Ἰησοῦν Χριστὸν ἐρχόμενον ἐν σαρκί (Jesus Christ coming in the flesh). The opponents obviously deny the continuing significance of the story and person of Jesus Christ. As in 1 John 4.2 they thereby deny the substantial meaning of Christ's incarnation,[36] the unity between the earthly Jesus and the heavenly Christ and the fundamental soteriological significance of the sacraments. Thus the Christology they advocate (as described in 1 John 4.2) can be described as *docetic* (see below 8.4.8). In 2 John 7b the presbyter identifies the false teachers with the antichrist. The obvious change from the plural to the singular makes clear that for the presbyter πλάνος (deceiver)[37] and ἀντίχριστος (antichrist) (cf. 1 John 2.18, 22; 4.3)[38] are two familiar figures of the end time. For the presbyter, the antichrist who was to emerge in the last days has already appeared in the figure of the opponents. A further mark of the false teachers is named in 2 John 9: they 'go ahead' (= 'progress') and do not remain in the doctrine about Christ that had been handed on previously. As already in 2 John 5, the presbyter thereby introduces the concept of tradition as a means of opposing the false teachers. The essence of the false teaching lies precisely in its departure from the teaching that had been the foundation of the community and that has been preserved by it.

8.2.9 Basic Theological Ideas

Central to 2 John is the concept of ἀλήθεια, which already appears five times in the first four verses.[39] The elect community has recognized the truth, and the truth will remain with it forever (2 John 2). Truth here denominates the reality of God, truth that is present and active in the community. To walk in the truth (2 John 4a) is realized in living by the love

---

[36] Cf. Schnackenburg, *Johannine Epistles* 284–286; Brown, *Epistles of John* 685–686; Wengst, *Johannesbriefe* 240; Carsten Colpe, 'Gnosis II,' *RAC* 11 (1981) 611; Martin Hengel, *Die johanneische Frage* 140ff.; *Johannine Question* (see below 8.5.1) 39ff. Strecker, *Johannine Letters* 232ff., differs; he understands ἐρχόμενον (coming) in a future sense and thinks the presbyter advocated a chiliastic doctrine that was rejected by the 'innovators.'

[37] Πλάνος (deceiver) is only here in the Johannine writings; cf. otherwise πλανάω (deceive) 1 John 1.8; 2.26; 3.7; John 7.12, 47, and πλάνη (deceit) in 1 John 4.6.

[38] Cf. Strecker, *Johannine Letters* 236–241.

[39] On the concept of truth in the two smaller Johannine letters cf. on the one hand Bergmeier, 'Zum Verfasserproblem des II. und III. Johannesbriefe,' and on the other hand Rudolf Schnackenburg, 'Zum Begriff der "Wahrheit" in den beiden kleinen Johannesbriefen,' *BZ* 11 (1967) 253–258.

command (cf. 2 John 4b–6). Whoever lives by this command received from the Father at the same time walks in the truth; for only the one who is in the realm of truth is also in the realm of love, only the one in the realm of love is also in the realm of truth. In contrast, the false teachers are characterized by dissolving this close connection between theological doctrine and ethics. They negate the teaching of the tradition as embodied in the presbyter and do not remain in the doctrine of Christ (2 John 9); their προάγειν ('going ahead', 'progress') sets aside both truth and love. By abandoning the fundamental faith as it had been transmitted and introducing a new doctrine in the community, they place themselves outside the community, and no longer have the Father and the Son. It is consistent with this that the false teachers should no longer be received, that they should not even be greeted, since this would mean participation in their evil works (2 John 10–11). Thus the *concept of tradition* represented by the presbyter, which binds together the realms of theology and ethics, is constitutive for the theology of 2 John. In no statement does the presbyter appeal to 1 John or the Gospel of John to support this tradition;[40] there is neither quotation nor allusion from either the Gospel or 1 John. Rather, the presbyter appeals to the traditions of the Johannine school he himself had founded, traditions that lead into the truth of the confession of Jesus Christ and to love for the brothers and sisters of the Christian community. This does not mean, however, that the position of the presbyter can be described as 'early catholic,' for both the concept of tradition and the critical function of doctrine are found already in Paul (cf. e.g. 1 Cor. 15.1–3a; Gal. 1.12; Rom. 6.17; 16.17).[41]

8.2.10 Tendencies of Recent Research

Until recently, 2 John has attracted little scholarly attention due to its brevity and its seemingly unimportant theological content. But if the presbyter John mentioned by Papias as the author of the letter is the founder of the Johannine school, then 2 John is very significant as an *original document* from the earliest period of Johannine theology. The dualism that is determinative for the thought of the Gospel of John appears in 2 John only in a rudimentary form. On the other hand, the close connection between truth and love and the concept of tradition associated therewith belong to the fundamental elements of Johannine theology. To live in truth and love means both to walk according to the Father's command and to remain in

---

[40] Contra Vouga, *Johannesbriefe* 16ff., who claims that the presbyter appeals to the authority of the Gospel and 1 John.

[41] Cf. Strecker, *Johannine Letters* 244–249.

the doctrine of Christ; the foundational function of the concept of tradition for the presbyter's theology becomes visible in this combination. Among recent scholars, for example G. Strecker, U. Schnelle, H. Thyen and M. Hengel have seen in the two small Johannine letters the oldest documents of the Johannine school. In contrast, for example K. Wengst, R. E. Brown, R. Schnackenburg and F. Vouga interpret 2 John as later than the Gospel and 1 John, and in their light.

While the epistolary form of 2 John can be regarded as established in recent scholarship, the question of the presbyter's opponents continues to be debated. Most scholars proceed on the assumption of a united front, based on the agreements between 1 John 2.22; 4.2, and 2 John 7, but the opposition is thought of in a variety of ways (gnostics: K. Wengst; docetics: U. Schnelle, M. Hengel; Jews: H. Thyen). In contrast, G. Strecker does not identify the false teachers opposed in 2 John with the opponents of 1 John. He regards the presbyter as a chiliast, i.e. as the advocate of the view that a thousand year messianic reign must be established on earth before the final end comes. This view is found in the New Testament only in Revelation 20.1–10, though it does appear frequently in the post-New Testament period (Justin, Dialogue; Barnabas 15.4ff. [?]; Cerinthus [cf. Eusebius, HE 3.28.2]; Papias [cf. Eusebius, HE 3.39.12]; Irenaeus; Tertullian). If the presbyter were a chiliast, then the 'innovators' would be those who reject this doctrine. To be sure, Strecker's futuristic interpretation of the participle ἐρχόμενον (coming) in 2 John 7 is possible, but the agreement between 2 John 7 and 1 John 2.22; 4.2 makes it more likely that the same group of opponents is in view in both cases.

8.3. The Third Letter of John

8.3.1 Literature

See above 8.2.1.

8.3.2 Author

3 John designates its sender as ὁ πρεσβύτερος (the elder), precisely as does 2 John. The extensive agreements between 2 John and 3 John in the letter form and language permit the conclusion that the presbyter John was also the author of 3 John.

8.3.3 *Place and Time of Composition*

3 John 9 refers to 2 John, so that 3 John must be the second writing from the presbyter. A more precise determination of the period between the two writings is not possible, though there seems to be no reason to posit a lengthy interval between them. The composition would thus be located a short time *after 90 CE*. The place of composition is the same as for 2 John, namely Asia Minor, possibly in *Ephesus*.[42]

8.3.4 *Intended Readership*

3 John is addressed to a certain Gaius, who is otherwise unknown. He is called a 'beloved brother' in 3 John 2, 5, 11, and is thus a Christian to whom the elder has a very good relationship. According to 3 John 4, Gaius is numbered among the presbyter's 'children,' i.e. he was either converted by the presbyter or baptized by him. In 3 John 3–6 the presbyter praises Gaius, who shows hospitality to traveling members of the Johannine community and thus walks in truth and love. Whether Gaius belongs to the same congregation as the Diotrephes mentioned in 3 John 9 must remain an open question. At least, Gaius did not belong to the leadership of this congregation, for otherwise the presbyter would not have found it necessary to inform him of his earlier writing and the conflict with Diotrephes (3 John 9ff.). By means of the present letter the presbyter wishes to secure the support of Gaius and attain influence in Diotrephes' congregation despite the difficulties in doing this, so that there must be some connection between Gaius and Diotrephes' congregation. The Demetrius mentioned in 3 John 12 is possibly the middleman between the presbyter and Diotrephes' congregation. In the absence of the presbyter, he could represent the opposition to Diotrephes in his congregation. Gaius is to support him and thereby strengthen the position of the presbyter, until he himself can come to Gaius (3 John 13–14). Although he has failed in his previous attempt, the presbyter wants to try again to gain influence in Diotrephes' congregation.

8.3.5 *Outline, Structure, Form*

1	Prescript	
2	Salutation	Introduction
3–4	Thanksgiving	

---

[42] Cf. Vogler, *Johannesbriefe* 33.

5–8	Continued support of the missionaries by Gaius	
9–10	The conflict with Diotrephes	Body
11–12	Admonition to Gaius and recommendation of Demetrius	
13–14	Apostolic parousia	
15a	Farewell (Eschatokoll)	
15b	Greetings from others	Conclusion
15c	His own greeting	

Like 2 John, so also 3 John has the form and length of the usual *ancient personal letter*. Following the prescript comes a stereotyped wish for good health and a thanksgiving. Within the body of the letter, the central element is the information concerning the presbyter's relation to Diotrephes. That the letter falls within the category of a letter of recommendation is indicated by v. 12.[43] The conclusion introduces the announcement of a planned visit, an element found often in ancient letters. Greetings form the conclusion. From a rhetorical point of view the following division is suggested: exordium, vv. 2–4 (v. 1); narratio, vv. 5–6; probatio, vv. 7–12; peroratio, vv. 13–14 (v. 15).[44]

8.3.6 Literary Integrity

The literary integrity of 3 John is undisputed.

8.3.7 Traditions, Sources

The author of 3 John does not incorporate and edit traditions or sources.

8.3.8 History-of-religion Standpoint

3 John contains no information regarding the conflict between the presbyter and Diotrephes and his group that illuminates their setting from the viewpoint of the history of religions. For this question we are mostly dependent on the presumed connection between the opponents mentioned

---

[43] Cf. Vouga, *Johannesbriefe* 4.
[44] Cf. Duane F. Watson, 'A Rhetorical Analysis of 3 John: A Study in Epistolary Rhetoric,' *CBQ* 51 (1989) 479–501; Klauck, 'Zur rhetorischen Analyse der Johannesbriefe' (see above 8.2.8) 217ff.

in 2 John and how the conflict between the presbyter and Diotrephes is evaluated (see below 8.3.9/8.3.10).

8.3.9 Basic Theological Ideas

As in 2 John, the central concepts are 'truth' (3 John 1, 3, 4, 8, 12) and 'love' (3 John 1, 2, 5, 6, 11). Gaius walks in the truth and in love, since he receives the traveling missionaries associated with the presbyter. Demetrius too receives testimony from the truth and is thus recommended to Gaius by the presbyter (3 John 12). It is difficult to determine the content of the truth-concept in 3 John, but it obviously has an essential connection with how one responds to the traveling missionaries associated with the presbyter.

The presbyter's church is carrying on an extensive (Gentile) mission (3 John 7), for which they are dependent on support from the other congregations of the Johannine school. While Gaius provides this necessary support to the traveling missionaries, Diotrephes does not receive these missionaries, and hinders others from doing so (3 John 10). The presbyter describes Diotrephes' conduct as an imitation or following of evil (3 John 11). From the perspective of the presbyter, Diotrephes is thus imprisoned by evil, and has not 'seen God' (3 John 11). The motives for Diotrephes' conduct are not clearly visible. What is clear is that he does acknowledge the authority of the presbyter. He wants to be 'the first' in his congregation, and he has authority to expel others in the congregation who do receive the presbyter's missionaries (3 John 10b). The information provided by 3 John does not permit us to infer differing conceptions of church law, a conflict between orthodoxy and heresy, or a contrast between Spirit and office as the cause of the conflict between the presbyter and Diotrephes. The only cause for dispute indicated in 3 John is the response to the presbyter's missionaries. Is the arrival of these missionaries the occasion that initiates the conflict, or is the response to them merely the result of a conflict on another level? 3 John 7, 8 suggests that one might see *differing understandings of the church's mission* as a/the cause for the conflict between the presbyter and Diotrephes. While the presbyter's church carries on a comprehensive mission that directs them to receive support from the individual Johannine congregations, Diotrephes rejects such a concept of mission. He obviously advocates a particularist ecclesiological conception concentrated within the local congregation, while the presbyter probably pursued a universalistic ecclesiological conception. This is based on 3 John 8: whoever supports the traveling missionaries is not only testified to by the truth, but becomes a co-worker with the truth.

8.3.10 Tendencies of Recent Research

Current study of 3 John has focused on the occasion, background, and content of the dispute between the elder and Diotrephes.[45] Two explanatory models have been of fundamental importance: (1) the controversy was a matter of church law; (2) the conflict between the presbyter and Diotrephes has theological-dogmatic causes. The church law model was thoroughly explored in the work of A. von Harnack. In his view the presbyter was the leader of a comprehensive missionary organization in the province of Asia Minor that sent out missionaries and provided leadership to local congregations. Diotrephes' congregation protested against this form of organization and the claim to authority of the presbyter inherent in it. 'It is the struggle of the old patriarchal and provincial missions organization against the individual local congregation. Such congregations wanted to consolidate themselves by developing their own monarchial episcopate and then withdrawing from external control.'[46] On this model Diotrephes is thus the first known monarchial bishop.

The theological-dogmatic explanatory model is advocated by W. Bauer. In his view the conflict between the presbyter and Diotrephes is a further reflection of the conflict between orthodoxy and heresy. Bauer sees in the presbyter the advocate of orthodoxy, who is placed on the defensive by the influence of the heretical leader Diotrephes. Diotrephes has succeeded in repressing the influence of the presbyter in his congregation, who now attempts in 3 John to regain the lost ground.[47] E. Käsemann reverses the thesis of W. Bauer, regarding Diotrephes as the monarchial bishop, while the author of 2–3 John as a presbyter who has been excommunicated because of his gnostic false teaching. Käsemann also considers the presbyter to be the author of the Gospel of John, who as a Christian gnostic had the courage to write a Gospel within a gnostic environment. From the perspective of orthodoxy, the Gospel of John contained a heretical gnostic false doctrine that had led to the presbyter's excommunication. 'It is not as a sectarian leader, but as monarchial bishop who sees himself as confronted with a false teacher and acts accordingly, that Diotrephes exercises ecclesiastical disciplinary action against the presbyter and his disciples including those in his own congregation.'[48]

In the course of the history of research, individual elements of the

---

[45] For history of the research, cf. Ernst Haenchen, 'Neuere Literatur zu den Johannesbriefen' (see above 8.2) 282ff.

[46] Adolf von Harnack, *Über den 3. Johannesbrief*, TU XV/3b (Leipzig 1897) 21.

[47] Cf. Walter Bauer, *Orthodoxy and Heresy in Earliest Christianity* (see above 5.5.3) 96–97.

[48] Käsemann, 'Ketzer und Zeuge' 173–74.

church-law and theological-dogmatic explanatory models have often been combined. While R. Bultmann adopted the more theological-dogmatic explanation of E. Käsemann,[49] R. Schnackenburg emphasized the church-law dimension of the dispute between the presbyter and Diotrephes. Diotrephes is already the sole leader of the congregation, but is not yet a monarchial bishop, for 'we are in a period of transition; the monarchial episcopate . . . is in the process of being established.'[50] Like Harnack, K. Wengst sees in Diotrephes the first known monarchial bishop. 'And indeed an orthodox one, not a heretic!'[51] By his claim, Diotrephes brings into question the existing church structure of the Johannine circle which was not hierarchical. R. Brown sees the matter similarly to R. Schnackenburg, regarding Diotrephes as the leader not only of a local- or house church, but 'Diotrephes is on his way to become a presbyter-bishop in the style of the Pastorals.'[52] J. W. Taeger portrays Diotrephes as a conservative member of the Johannine school, who rebels against the presbyter because he is appropriating to himself a kind of authority that does not correspond to the traditional understanding of the church in Johannine tradition. 'The genuinely Johannine view is that the Spirit is the acting subject in church order; the Spirit is the leader and teacher of the community, which thereby stands under the lordship of Christ alone, for the exalted Lord is present in the Spirit/Paraclete (John 14.16–17, 25–26).'[53] His concern for the continuing existence of the Johannine churches leads the presbyter to find himself on the way to the monarchial episcopate, and is opposed by Diotrephes, who wants to save the authentic Johannine conception. Like E. Käsemann, G. Strecker sees the presbyter as more on the heretical side, for as a chiliast he advocates a doctrine that obviously was rejected by Diotrephes.[54]

The course of the history of research clearly illustrates the difficulties in trying to delineate exactly the cause of the controversy between the presbyter and Diotrephes. If 3 John were our only text, then we might say that differing ecclesiological conceptions concerning the role of traveling missionaries had led to the quarrel. But if 2 John is taken into consideration and Diotrephes is numbered among the πλάνοι (deceivers) of 2 John 7, then the *presbyter* is to be counted on the side of *orthodoxy* and *Diotrephes* on the side of *heresy*. To be sure, these value judgments from the later

---

[49] Cf. Bultmann, *Johannine Epistles* 100–101.
[50] Schnackenburg, *Johannine Epistles* 299.
[51] Wengst, *Johannesbriefe* 233.
[52] Brown, *Epistles of John* 738.
[53] Taeger, 'Der konservative Rebell' 286.
[54] Cf. Strecker, *Johannine Letters* 261–263.

writing of church history are inadequate for properly evaluating the historical state of affairs in 2–3 John, for they are witnesses to the debate concerning the right understanding of Christ in a time when generally binding dogmatic decisions had not yet been made. So also, church-law structures cannot yet be discerned behind the letters, for neither letter speaks of either an excommunication of the presbyter by Diotrephes or of a monarchial bishop. The presbyter as founder of the Johannine school obviously understood himself as protector of the true tradition that was being threatened by the 'progressives' and their leader Diotrephes.

8.4. The First Letter of John

8.4.1 Literature

Commentaries

Windisch, Hans (Herbert Preisker). *Die katholischen Briefe*, HNT 15. Tübingen: J. C. B. Mohr (Paul Siebeck), 1951³; Dodd, Charles H. *The Johannine Epistles*, MNTC. London: Hodder and Stoughton, 1961⁴; Bultmann, Rudolf. *The Johannine Epistles*, tr. R. Philip O'Hara et al. Philadelphia: Fortress, 1973; Wengst, Klaus. *Der erste, zweite und dritte Briefe des Johannes*. ÖTK 16. Gütersloh: Gütersloher Verlagshaus, 1978, 227–252; Balz, Horst. *Die 'Katholischen' Briefe. Die Briefe des Jakobus, Petrus, Johannes und Judas*, NTD 10. Göttingen: Vandenhoeck & Ruprecht, 1980²; Brown, Raymond E. *The Epistles of John*, AncB 30. Garden City: Doubleday, 1982; Schunack, Gerd. *Die Briefe des Johannes*, ZBK 17. Zürich: Theologischer Verlag, 1982; Smalley, Stephen S. *1, 2, 3 John*, WBC 51. Waco: Word, 1984; Vouga, François. *Die Johannesbriefe*, HNT 15/III. Tübingen: J. C. B. Mohr (Paul Siebeck), 1990; Klauck, Hans-Joseph. *Der Erste Johannesbrief*, EKK XXIII/1. Neukirchen: Neukirchener Verlag, 1991; Schnackenburg, Rudolf. *The Johannine Epistles*. New York: Crossroad, 1992; Vogler, Werner. *Die Briefe des Johannes*, ThHK 17. Leipzig: Evangelische Verlagsanstalt, 1993; Strecker, Georg. *The Johannine Letters*. Minneapolis: Fortress, 1996.

Monographs

Wurm, Alois. *Die Irrlehrer im ersten Johannesbrief.* Freiburg: Herder, 1903; Nauck, Wolfgang. *Die Tradition und der Charakter des ersten Johannesbriefes*, WUNT 3. Tübingen: J. C. B. Mohr (Paul Siebeck), 1957; Wengst, Klaus. *Häresie und Orthodoxie im Spiegel des 1. Johannesbriefes*. Neukirchen-Vluyn: Neukirchener Verlag, 1976; Bogart, J. *Orthodox and Heretical Perfectionism in the Johannine Community as Evident in the First Epistle of John*, SBLDS 33. Missoula: Scholars Press, 1977; Rusam, Dieter. *Die Gemeinschaft der Kinder Gottes*, BWANT 133. Stuttgart: Kohlhammer, 1993.

Articles

Bultmann, Rudolf. 'Analyse des ersten Johannesbriefes,' in *Exegetica*, ed. E. Dinkler. Tübingen: J. C. B. Mohr (Paul Siebeck) 1967, 105–123; Bultmann, Rudolf. 'Die kirchliche Redaktion des ersten Johannesbriefes,' in *Exegetica*, ed. E. Dinkler. Tübingen: J. C. B. Mohr (Paul Siebeck), 1967, 381–393; Klein, Günter. '"Das wahre Licht scheint schon",' ZThK 68 (1971) 261–326; Conzelmann, Hans. 'Was von Anfang war', in *Theologie als Schriftauslegung*, ed. Hans Conzelmann, BEvTh 65. Munich: Kaiser, 1974, 207–214; Venetz, Hermann Josef. 'Durch Wasser und Blut gekommen (1 Joh 5, 6)' in *Die Mitte des Neuen Testaments* (FS E. Schweizer), ed. Ulrich Luz and Hans Weder (Göttingen: Vandenhoeck & Ruprecht, 1983) 345–361; Blank, Josef. 'Die Irrlehrer des ersten Johannesbriefes,' Kairos 26 (1984) 166–193; Stegemann, Ekkehard. '"Kindlein hütet euch vor den Götzenbildern",' ThZ 41 (1985) 284–294.

8.4.2 Author

In contrast to 2 and 3 John, the author of 1 John does not identify himself. Whether he is to be identified with the author of the two smaller Johannine letters and/or the author of the Gospel is a disputed point. The author of 1 John is considered to be the presbyter of 2–3 John by, among others, Hans Windisch, C. H. Dodd, Rudolf Schnackenburg, Raymond E. Brown, E. Ruckstuhl, H. J. Klauck, W. Vogler and Martin Hengel.[55] Their main argument is the common style manifested by all three Johannine letters. However, the agreements in style can derive from the 'sociolect' of the Johannine school, and it is also to be noted that there are differences in language and style between 2–3 John on the one side and 1 John on the other.

The expression ἐχάρην λίαν (I was overjoyed) is found only in 2 John 4/3 John 3 (cf. Phil. 4.10), and περιπατεῖν ἐν ἀληθείᾳ (walking in the truth) only in 2 John 4/3 John 3, 4. The expressions ἐκλεκτῇ κυρίᾳ (elect lady) (2 John 1), τὴν ἀλήθειαν τὴν μένουσαν ἐν ἡμῖν (the truth that abides in you) (2 John 2), παρὰ Ἰησοῦ Χριστοῦ τοῦ υἱοῦ τοῦ πατρός (from Jesus Christ the Son of the Father) (2 John 3), ἐν ἀληθείᾳ καὶ ἀγάπῃ (in truth and love) (2 John 3) and βλέπετε ἑαυτούς (be on your guard) (2 John 8) are found exclusively in 2 John. The *hapax legomena* within the Johannine school are in the two smaller Johannine letters: μέλαν (ink) (2 John 12/3 John 13, so elsewhere only 2 Cor. 3.3); κάλαμος (pen) (3 John 13); ἔλεος (mercy) (2 John 3); μισθός (reward) (2 John 8), ἀγαθοποιέω, κακοποιέω (doing good, doing evil) (3 John 11), εὐοδόομαι (go well with) (3 John 2). *Hapax legomena* for the whole NT are φιλοπρωτεύων (likes to be first) (3 John 9) and χάρτης (paper) (2 John 12).

---

[55] Cf. Windisch, *Johannesbriefe* 143; Dodd, *Johannine Epistles* lxviii–lxix; Schnackenburg, *Johannine Epistles* 268–269; Brown, *Epistles of John* 19; E. Ruckstuhl and P. Dschulnigg, *Stilkritik und Verfasserfrage* (see below 8.5.1) 45–46; Hans-Joseph Klauck, *2/3 John* (see above 8.2.1) 21, 23; Vogler, *Johannesbriefe* 6; Martin Hengel, *Die johanneische Frage* 151; *Johannine Question* (see below 8.5.1) 46.

If 1 John is from the presbyter, an additional difficult item to be explained is why no indication of the writer's identity appears in this letter. The author of 2–3 John obviously intentionally introduces the honored title ὁ πρεσβύτερος (the elder) in the sense of a special bearer of the tradition in his dispute with his opponents. The title functions to express his dignity and to validate his statements as authoritative. Why should the presbyter decide not to use the honored description to which he is entitled precisely in 1 John, where the dispute with his opponents reaches its zenith? So also the form of 1 John speaks against the presbyter as the author, since while both 2 and 3 John follow the appropriate form for ancient personal letters written to an individual or a single congregation, 1 John lacks the essential characteristics of a letter. Finally, the Johannine dualism is found in 2–3 John only in a rudimentary form, and there are shifts in the way various subjects are treated: (1) In 2 John 4–6 the love commandment is not a new command, but what was given 'from the beginning.' In contrast, 1 John 2.7–11 describes the love commandment dialectically as given 'from the beginning' and as a new commandment. In addition, only 1 John 2.10–11 speaks explicitly of the command to love the brother or sister. (2) The concept ἀντίχριστος appears in 2 John 7 in the singular, but in 1 John 2.18 alongside the singular the historicizing plural ἀντίχριστοι (antichrists) appears. The linguistic independence of 2–3 John, their form as ancient personal letters, the identification of the sender as ὁ πρεσβύτερος, and the differences in content point to *different authors* for 2–3 John and 1 John.[56]

The issue of whether the Gospel of John and 1 John are from the same author is of great importance for understanding the Johannine school. The first category of evidence against this view is the linguistic phenomena, since important terms in the Gospel are missing from the letter (γραφή [scripture], δόξα [glory], δοξάζω [glorify], ζητέω [seek], κρίνω [judge], κύριος [lord], νόμος [law)], πέμπω [send], προσκυνέω [worship], σῴζω [save], χάρις [grace]). On the other hand, central theological terms of the letter are not found in the Gospel (ἀντίχριστος [antichrist], ἐλπίς [hope], ἱλασμός [atoning sacrifice], κοινωνία [participation], σπέρμα [θεοῦ] [seed (of God)], χρῖσμα [anointing]). The linguistic independence of the letter is also found in sentence construction and style,[57] so that the conclusion is

---

[56] Among those who argue for different authors for 1 John and the 2–3 John are Bultmann, *Johannine Epistles* 1–2; Balz, *Johannesbriefe* 59; Wengst, *Johannesbriefe* 230–231; Strecker, *Johannine Letters* 3ff.

[57] Cf. the extensive evidence in Heinrich J. Holtzmann, 'Das Problem des ersten johanneischen Briefes in seinem Verhältnis zum Evangelium II,' JPTh 8 (1882) (128–143) 135ff.; Dodd, *Johannine Epistles* xlviiff. A critical review of research is presented by Ernst Haenchen, 'Neuere Literatur zu den Johannesbriefen' (see above 8.2) 238–242.

permitted: 'Despite the many echoes of the Gospel, the language of the letter leads one to suppose there was a different author.'[58]

In addition, there are specific theological ideas found exclusively in the letter. Only in 1 John 2.1 is Jesus Christ identified with the Paraclete. Although futuristic eschatology is not to be eliminated from the Gospel, statements affirming present eschatology clearly predominate. In contrast, futuristic eschatology dominates in 1 John (cf. only 1 John 2.28; 3.3). Only 1 John 2.2 and 4.10 designate Jesus as ἱλασμός (atoning sacrifice) (cf. further the statements about his atoning death in 1 John 1.7, 9; 3.5), and in the whole New Testament χρῖσμα is spoken of only in 1 John 2.20, 27. In contrast to the Gospel, which cites the Old Testament 19 times, not a single quotation from the Old Testament is found in 1 John; in fact the reference to Cain in 1 John 3.12 is the only allusion to the Old Testament in the letter. So too, the central ethical problem of the sinlessness of Christ (cf. 1 John 1.8–10; 3.4–10; 5.16–18) is not found at all in the Gospel. Finally, 1 John presupposes a different situation than that of the Gospel. It struggles vehemently against false christological teaching that originated in its own community (cf. 1 John 2.19), while the Fourth Gospel gives no indication of an *acute* conflict.

Language, the world of theological concepts presupposed, and the different situation point to the conclusion that 1 John and the Gospel are *by different authors.*[59]

8.4.3 Place and Time of Composition

As a rule, 1 John is read from the point of view of the Gospel. The letter is then regarded as one of the 'Johannine Pastorals,' which presuppose the theology of the Fourth Gospel and interpret and apply it in a changed historical situation.[60] It is precisely the shifts in content when compared with the Gospel that are taken as evidence that the letter is only to be understood on the basis of the Gospel. This model, of course, is unable to

---

[58] Haenchen, 'Neuere Literatur' 242

[59] Among those who argue for different authors are Holtzmann, 'Problem' 136ff.; Bultmann, *Johannine Epistles*, 1; Schnackenburg, *Johannine Epistles* 34–38; Haenchen, 'Neuere Literatur' 282; Conzelmann, 'Was von Anfang war' 211; Klein, 'Das wahre Licht scheint schon' passim; Wengst, *Johannesbriefe* 24–25; Dodd, *Johannine Epistles* vi; Balz, *Johannesbriefe* 160; Brown, *Epistles of John* 30; Strecker, *Johannine Letters* 5–6; Klauck, *1 John* 45; Vogler, *Johannesbriefe* 6–10. The same author for 1 John and the Gospel is argued by, among others, Kümmel, *Introduction* 445; Wikenhauser and Schmid, *Einleitung* 623; G. Schunack, *Johannesbriefe* 108; Martin Hengel, *Die johanneische Frage* 49; *Johannine Question* (see below 8.5.1) 48; Ruckstuhl and Dschulnigg, *Stilkritik und Verfasserfrage* (see below 8.5.1) 46–54.

[60] For this understanding in recent literature, cf. for example Conzelmann, 'Was von Anfang war,' passim; Vouga, *Johannesbriefe* 11ff.; Klauck, *Johannesbriefe* (see above 8.2.1) 46–47.

explain why it is that not a single citation from the Gospel appears in the letter. The agreements and points of contact between the letter and the Gospel could be a reflection of the literary knowledge of the Gospel by the author of the letter, but they could just as well go back to the common tradition of the Johannine school. In favor of the latter possibility is the fact that the author of the letter can be shown neither to have made a literary use of the Gospel, nor even to have known it. The prologue to the letter 1 John 1.1–4 is often seen as a clear reference to the prologue of the Gospel. The use of ἀρχή (beginning) in the prologue of the letter is clearly differentiated, however, from its use in the prologue to the Gospel. In the whole Johannine corpus, ἐν ἀρχῇ appears only in John 1.1–2, where it designates the being of the preexistent Logos with God in the absolute beginning before the creation of the world. In contrast, the ἀπ' ἀρχῆς in 1 John 1.1 describes the whole salvation-event in its significance for the community, in which there is no reference to creation, suggesting that the word might have been used in a different sense previous to the Gospel. The obvious emphasis on the visibility and reality of the saving event is here already directed against the opponents resisted in 1 John 2.22–23; 4.1–3. As in 1 John 2.24 so also the ἀπ' ἀρχῆς at the beginning of the letter appeals to the Johannine tradition as the critical authority against the false teachers. The prologues of both letter and Gospel are rooted in common elements in the tradition of the Johannine school, but John 1.1–18 is not the literary source and model for 1 John 1.1–4.[61]

So also, the Paraclete concept common to Gospel and letter may not be used as evidence for the temporal priority of Gospel to letter. On the contrary, it supports the earlier composition of the letter. If 1 John 2.1 identifies the Paraclete exclusively with Jesus Christ, in the Gospel we find a broadening out of the Paraclete concept (cf. John 14.17, 26; 15.26; 16.13). If 1 John had been written after the Gospel and presupposing it, then it would be difficult to explain why the author of the letter does not take up the ecclesiological functions of the Paraclete, even though the letter then would mark the entrance of the Johannine school into the extended time that became church history. Finally, in John 14.16 we have in fact a reflection of 1 John 2.1, for Jesus prays for the Father to send ἄλλος παράκλητος (another Paraclete) and thus describes himself indirectly as (a) Paraclete.

---

[61] Cf. Udo Schnelle, *Antidocetic Christology* (see below 8.5.1) 52–55; Strecker, *Johannine Letters* 8ff.; Martin Hengel, *Die johanneische Frage* 157; *Johannine Question* (see below 8.5.1) 49. The dependence of the letter's prologue on John 1.1–18 is argued by, among others, Bultmann, *Johannine Epistles* 7–8; Schnackenburg, *Johannine Letters* 50; Balz, *Johannesbriefe* 167; Brown, *Epistles of John* 176ff.; Michael Theobald, *Die Fleischwerdung des Logos* (see below 8.5.1) 400–437.

Often the difference in the eschatology between the Gospel and the letter is taken as evidence for the earlier composition of the Gospel. In the Gospel one sees the 'genuine' Johannine construction of a present eschatology and can then only recognize in the 're-apocalypticizing' of 1 John an accommodation to the dominant future eschatology of early Christianity.[62] Against this view a fundamental methodological objection is to be raised: a real contradiction between the eschatological affirmations of the Gospel and of 1 John only exists if, following R. Bultmann and others, most of the futuristic eschatological texts in the Gospel are explained as secondary additions. But that would be begging the question, since an interpretation of the Gospel that is disputed, to say the least, would be made into the basis for evaluating the eschatology of 1 John.

The possible reference to an earlier writing in 1 John 2.14 does not refer to the Gospel of John, since here only a letter can be intended. Perhaps 1 John 2.14 refers to 2 John, as H. H. Wendt already supposed.[63]

The arguments presented in the literature for the temporal priority of the Gospel to 1 John are not convincing. 1 John contains no quotation from the Gospel, and the shifts in theological emphasis often claimed are either not actually present or rest on a particular interpretation of the Gospel that prejudices the discussion in the direction of the desired result. Thus it is also the case that the conflict with docetic false teachers does not speak in favor of the temporal priority of the Gospel, but on the contrary one can perceive here an indication that the letter was written prior to the Gospel. As the refutation of his opponents views, the author of 1 John holds up what is in his eyes the legitimate doctrinal tradition of the Johannine school (cf. in 1 John 1.1–4; 2.7–8; 3.11) – not the Gospel of John! In contrast, the Gospel obviously presupposes the acute debate reflected in the letter as already present and reworks it theologically.[64] Thus John 6.60–71 obviously refers to the schism of 1 John 2.19, for in both texts the soteriological significance of the incarnation in Jesus has become the occasion of a split among the disciples.[65] In the broadly structured and based argumen-

---

[62] An excellent example of this view is provided by Klein, 'Das wahre Licht scheint schon' 287 and often.

[63] Cf. Hans H. Wendt, 'Die Beziehung unseres ersten Johannesbriefes auf den zweiten,' ZNW 21 (1922) 140–146.

[64] To this extent one can speak of a reception-history of 1 John in the Gospel; contra Vouga, *Johannesbriefe* 11–13, who proceeds on the basis of a reception-history of the Gospel in 1 John and resolves the problem of the missing citations as follows: 'In 1 John it is presupposed merely that the addressees are familiar with the Gospel, but not necessarily that they regard it as a formal authority' (*ibid*. 12).

[65] Cf. Ludger Schenke, 'Das johanneische Schisma und die "Zwölf" (Johannes 6,60–71),' NTS 38 (1992) 105–121, who, however, does not regard the schismatics as docetists. A variation of the view that the letters are to be dated *before* the Gospel, reintroduced into the recent dis-

tation of the evangelist against a docetic Christology is revealed a temporal distance and difference in substance from the acute controversy in which the letter is embroiled. The letter designates the problem; a theological answer, however, is first found in the Gospel.

1 John was thus probably written *before* the Gospel, but *after* 2–3 John. We may take the time of writing to be ca. *95 CE*,[66] and again consider *Ephesus*,[67] the locus of the Johannine school as its probable point of origin. Papias knew 1 John (cf. Eusebius HE 3.39.17), which is documented for the first time in Polycarp (cf. 1 John 4.2 and Polycarp Phil. 7.2).

8.4.4 Intended Readership

In contrast to 2 John, which is addressed to a congregation and 3 John, which is addressed to an individual, 1 John lacks all the external charac-teristics of a real letter. On the other hand, the readers are addressed by the author with τεκνία (little children) (cf. 1 John 2.1, 12, 28; 3.7, 18; 4.4; 5.21) or ἀγαπητοί (beloved) (cf. 1 John 2.7; 3.2, 21; 4.1, 7, 11). So too the frequent γράφω (I write) appears to suggest the situation of a letter (cf. 1 John 1.4; 2.1, 7–8, 12–14, 21, 26; 5.13). According to 1 John 5.13 the readers of the document are those 'who believe in the name of the Son of God.' Thus 1 John is not directed to a particular congregation of the Johannine school, but the whole [Johannine] church is addressed.[68] 1 John is not to be understood as either a letter occasioned by some particular situation nor as an abstract theological tract or meditation unrelated to its historical circumstances, but rather as a writing that contains doctrinal and parenetic passages for the purpose of instructing the community on issues fundamental to its life. The author thus engages concrete problems of his hearer/readers: (1) The question of the sinlessness of Christians obviously represented an acute theological and ethical problem (cf. 1 John 1.8ff.; 3.4ff.; 5.16ff.). 1 John makes it clearly evident that different standpoints on this issue were advocated within the Johannine school, and presents the author's perspective on a possible solution. (2) As in 2 John, so also in 1

---

cussion by Georg Strecker and Udo Schnelle, is advocated by Martin Hengel, *Die johanneische Frage* 158 note 18; *The Johannine Question* (see below 8.5.1) 176–177. The Gospel 'was already a long time in the making, and indeed a good deal of it may already have been fixed when the letters were written, but it was only edited and circulated by pupils some time after the letters— soon after the death of the author, in my view along with the letters.'

[66] Those who place the letter after the Gospel usually date it about 100–110 CE, for example Wengst, *Johannesbriefe* 30; Klauck, *1 Johannesbrief* 49.

[67] Cf. e.g. Wengst, *Johannesbriefe* 30 (western Asia Minor); Brown, *Epistles of John* 102–3; S. S. Smalley, *1, 2, 3 John* xxxii; Klauck, *1 Johannesbrief* 49.

[68] On the church structure presupposed by the letter, cf. Rusam, *Gemeinschaft der Kinder Gottes* 210ff.

John a central theme is the debate with false teachers that have arisen within the community itself (cf. 1 John 2.22–23; 4.2ff.; 5.6ff.). The extent of this polemic against false teachers shows that the influence of the opponents within the Johannine school had by no means receded, but still represented a serious danger. (3) The constant exhortation to 'brotherly love,' in connection with calls for concrete social help for suffering brothers and sisters in 1 John 3.17–18, points to real social distinctions within the Johannine community. The author of 1 John attempts to solve, or at least relieve, this problem by his constant exhortation to 'brotherly love' that works itself out in actual deeds of social and economic support.

8.4.5 Outline, Structure, Form

1.1–4	Prologue: the word of life
1.5–2.17	Parenesis: fellowship with God realized in freedom from sin and in love of the brothers and sisters
2.18–27	Doctrinal arguments: the denial of Jesus as the Christ by the 'antichrists'
2.28–3.24	Parenesis: the coming of the Lord and the keeping of the commandments
4.1–6	Doctrinal arguments: on distinguishing truth and error
4.7–5.4a	Parenesis: God's love requires love of the brothers and sisters
5.4b–12	Doctrinal arguments: the testimony of water, blood, and Spirit
5.13–21	Epilogue: the power of prayer

The uniform manner in which the author thinks and writes makes it difficult to discern of any outline in 1 John.[69] Clear structural markers on the macro-level can hardly be recognized, but the document is characterized by the alternation of doctrinal and parenetical sections. The content of faith and the execution of faith in life belong inseparably together for the author, conditioning each other. The prologue in 1 John 1.1–4 has foundational significance, since it formulates the claim of the writing and is composed with the debate with the false teachers already in view.

In distinction from 2–3 John, 1 John lacks the essential characteristics of a letter (epistolary prescript and concluding greetings). On the other hand, there are certain marks of the letter style, such as the juxtaposition of writer and addressees, the repeated direct address to the readers already mentioned, the engagement with congregational problems, the formula 'I

---

[69] For the history of research on this issue cf. Klauck, *Johannesbriefe* (see above 8.2.1) 59–68, who presents all the major models (from two to seven sections). Klauck himself votes for a tripartite division of the body of the letter: 1.5–2.17; 2.18–3.24; 4.1–5.12.

write this to you,' and the reference to joy in 1 John 1.4, which could have replaced the usual introductory prayer for a letter's recipients. These data, somewhat in tension with each other, have led scholars to quite different judgments as to the genre of the document. Thus 1 John has been described as an 'official letter,'[70] as 'official missive,'[71] as a 'religious tract,'[72] as a 'letter-like homily,'[73] as a 'literary handshake,'[74] and as a 'parenetic or letter.'[75]

In view of the lack of important characteristics of a letter, and the manner in which the whole communication is structured within a doctrinal/parenetic framework, it makes sense to describe 1 John as a *letter-like homily.*'

8.4.6 Literary Integrity

In recent exegesis the question of the literary unity of 1 John has concentrated on the letter's conclusion in 1 John 5.14–21.[76] Arguments for the secondary character of 1 John 5.14–21 are: (1) The document already comes to a conclusion in 1 John 5.13. (2) The distinction between a 'mortal sin' and a 'sin that is not mortal' contradicts the letter's previous statements. (3) The section 1 John 5.14–21 contains several *hapax legomena* and ideas foreign to the rest of the letter. Against these arguments is to be objected: In 1 John 5.13 we have no real conclusion, but in this verse the author looks back over his previous writing and introduces the concluding section.[77] The statements distinguishing two kinds of sins in 1 John 5.14–21 stand in no fundamental tension with 1 John 1.8ff., 3.4ff., for they are the resolution, from the author's point of view, of a conflict within the Johannine school about whether Christians are subject to sin (see below 8.4.9). Here too pointing to *hapax legomena* cannot prove the secondary character of 1 John 5.14–21, for important *hapax legomena* are also found within the corpus of the letter that do not form the basis for inferences that

---

[70] Cf. Nauck, *Die Tradition und der Charakter des ersten Johannesbriefes* 126–127.

[71] Schnackenburg, *Johannine Epistles* 6.

[72] Windisch, *Johannesbriefe* 107.

[73] Strecker, *Johannine Letters* 3.

[74] Vogler, *Johannesbriefe* 24.

[75] Vouga, *Johannesbriefe* 5.

[76] Rudolf Bultmann, 'Die kirchliche Redaktion des ersten Johannesbriefes,' in *Exegetica*, ed. E. Dinkler (Tübingen: J. C. B. Mohr [Paul Siebeck] 1967 [= 1951]) 381–393, assigns not only the concluding section but also the apocalyptic statements (e.g. 1 John 2.28; 3.2; 4.17) and the christological statements affirming atonement (1 John 1.7c; 2.4; 4.10) to his 'ecclesiastical redactor.'

[77] Cf. Strecker, *Johannine Letters* 197ff. Agreements in vocabulary and structure exist between John 20.31 and 1 John 5.13, but there are also differences that indicate that it is not a matter of literary dependence.

they are secondary passages.[78] 1 John 5.14–21 does not simply bring the previous composition to an end, but the solution offered to the problem of sin and the warning against apostasy have the character of an appeal that is constitutive for the understanding of 1 John as a whole.

8.4.7 Traditions, Sources

Rudolf Bultmann presented a model for the origin of 1 John comparable to his literary analysis of the Gospel of John.[79] According to Bultmann's model the author of 1 John utilized a pagan-gnostic source document comprised of antithetical twenty-six units of two lines each, a document that in both form and content resembles the 'revelatory discourse source' postulated by Bultmann for the Gospel. The extent and order of the posited source is as follows: 1 John 1.5–10; 2.4, 5, 9, 10, 11, 29; 3.4, 6–10, 14, 15, 24; 4.7, 8, 12, 16; 5.1, 4; 4.5, 6; 2.23; 5.10, 12; 2 John 9. This analysis originally proposed by Bultmann in 1927[80] was later expanded and revised in numerous ways. Thus he supposed that the original edition of 1 John ended at 2.27, the following sections containing no new ideas but merely representing variations of the preceding material. Bultmann wavered in his efforts to determine the character of 1 John 2.28–5.12. He conjectured that it might represent a collection of sketches or meditations, perhaps even the minutes of seminar sessions that were then added to the original document by the original author 'or by his students, from his literary bequest after his death.'[81] After the original document had thus been expanded with authentic material, editorial expansions and modifications were made by the 'ecclesiastical redactor.'

These hypotheses regarding the process by which 1 John came into being were not convincing to many others, since it is not possible to establish behind our present composition a connected source document supposedly consisting of units structured on a uniform pattern of parallelism. In addition, Bultmann's guiding methodological principle for his reconstruction, the originality of the pure form, is nowadays considered very doubtful.[82] So too it cannot be shown that the original document concluded at 1 John 2.27, since new themes do emerge in the section that

---

[78] Cf. Strecker, *Johannine Letters* 199 note 6.

[79] For the history of research cf. Vogler, *Johannesbriefe* 33–38.

[80] Cf. Rudolf Bultmann, 'Analyse des ersten Johannesbriefes,' in *Exegetica*, ed. E. Dinkler (Tübingen: J. C. B. Mohr [Paul Siebeck], 1967 [= 1927]) 105–123; cf. previously Ernst v. Dobschütz, 'Johanneische Studien,' ZNW 8 (1907) 1–8.

[81] Bultmann, *Johannine Epistles* 43–44.

[82] For a thorough critique, cf. Ernst Haenchen, 'Neuere Literatur zu den Johannesbriefen' (see above 8.2) 250ff.

begins at 2.28 (e.g. futuristic eschatology, sacraments, and mortal sins). But the subsiding of source theories does not necessarily mean that the author of 1 John did not make use of oral traditions and texts that were formulated in the Johannine school. Thus the prologue (1 John 1.1–4) and the ethical-catechetical instructions in 1 John 2.12–14 could derive from tradition already formulated in the Johannine school. The differing statements about the relation of the Christian to sin in 1 John 1.8ff., 3.4ff., and 5.15ff. could go back to discussions within the Johannine school concerning this central problem.

8.4.8 History-of-religions Standpoint

The central question here is how the opponents against which 1 John struggles are to be categorized in terms of the history of religion. They had previously belonged to the Johannine community (cf. 1 John 2.19), and in the view of the author of 1 John had denied the soteriological identity between the earthly Jesus and the heavenly Christ (cf. 1 John 2.22: Ἰησοῦς οὐκ ἔστιν ὁ Χριστός; cf. further the statements of identity in 1 John 4.15; 5.1, 5).[83] Obviously for the opponents only God the Father and the heavenly Christ were relevant for salvation, not, however the life and death of the historical Jesus of Nazareth. But for the author of 1 John, whoever does not have the Father will give false teaching about the works of the Son.

The affirmation of the incarnation in 1 John 4.2 (cf. 1 John 1.2; 3.8b) gives an additional indication that the opponents denied that the preexistent Christ had actually become flesh.[84] The passion of the historical Jesus of Nazareth (cf. 1 John 5.6b), and thus his atoning death (cf. 1 John 1.9; 2.2; 3.16; 4.10), had no salvific importance for them. They made a strict distinction between the heavenly Christ who alone was relevant for salvation,

---

[83] Cf. Bultmann, *Johannine Epistles* 38–39; Balz, *Johannesbriefe* 183; Wengst, *Johannesbriefe* 112; Brown, *Epistles of John* 352; Strecker, *Johannine Letters* 67–68; Windisch, *Johannesbriefe* 127–128; E. Haenchen, 'Neuere Literatur zu den Johannesbriefen' 274. If one considers 1 John 2.22 in isolation, then the Jewish denial that Jesus was the Messiah could also be meant, but this is of course excluded by 1 John 2.19; contra Konrad Weiß, 'Die 'Gnosis' im Hintergrund und im Spiegel der Johannesbriefe,' in *Gnosis und Neues Testament*, ed. Karl W. Tröger (Berlin: Evangelische Verlagsanstalt, 1973) 343, who considers the specific item denied by the opponents to be that Jesus was the Son of God. Hartwig Thyen, 'Johannesbriefe' (see above 8.2) 194, follows A. Wurm in describing the opponents as 'orthodox Jews' who deny the necessity of a heavenly revealer in order to have an authentic knowledge of God.

[84] Cf. Bultmann, *Johannine Epistles* 62ff.; Strecker, *Johannine Letters* 134–135; Dodd, *Johannine Epistle* xix. According to Schnackenburg, *Johannine Letters* 201; Paul Minear, 'The Idea of Incarnation in First John,' *Interpretation* 24 (1970) 300–301; Vouga, *Johannesbriefe* 47, there is no statement about the incarnation in 1 John 4.2.

and the earthly Jesus who only appeared to have a fleshly body during his time on earth. This interpretation is also supported by 1 John 4.3, where καὶ πᾶν πνεῦμα, ὃ λύει τὸν Ἰησοῦν ἐκ τοῦ θεοῦ οὐκ ἔστιν (and every spirit that annuls Jesus is not from God) is the original reading.[85] The opponents 'eliminate Jesus from their doctrine and deny the human side of the Redeemer.'[86]

Ignatius likewise directs his letters against a docetic Christology. He charges his opponents with denying the bodily reality of Jesus Christ. They do not confess that the Lord had a body (IgnSmy. 5.2). In opposition to their teaching Ignatius emphasizes that Jesus Christ was really born from the virgin Mary, was baptized by John, and under Pontius Pilate was in the flesh really nailed to the cross for us (IgnSmy. 1.1; cf. IgnTrall. 9.1). In the opponents' view, Jesus Christ had only appeared to suffer (cf. IgnTrall. 10; cf. IgnSmy. 2; 4.2). In contrast Ignatius points explicitly to the suffering and death of Jesus Christ (cf. IgnEph. 7.2; 20.1; IgnTrall. 9.1; 11.2; IgnRom. 6.1; IgnSmy. 1.2; 6.2). If Jesus Christ appeared on earth only 'τὸ δοκεῖν' (in appearance), he did not really suffer, and so the opponents must also deny the resurrection. This is the only explanation for the vehemence with which Ignatius, with his opponents teaching in view, emphasizes the resurrection of Jesus Christ in the flesh (cf. IgnSmy. 1.2; 3.1; 7.1; IgnTrall. 9.2; IgnEph. 20.1; IgnMagn. 11). When the opponents deny the resurrection, then the eucharist is emptied of meaning and the grace of Christ is made ineffective (IgnSmy. 6.2), so that it is only consistent with their teaching when the opponents no longer participate in the eucharistic celebration (cf. IgnSmy. 7.1, as well as IgnSmy. 6.2). Since the opponents dispute the real, fleshly existence of Jesus Christ, and thus the suffering and resurrection of the Crucified One, from which they infer conclusions for their understanding of the eucharist, and the keyword 'τὸ δοκεῖν' (to appear to be) occurs in the discussion, this doctrine can be properly described as docetism.[87] Obviously the whole earthly existence of Jesus Christ is understood as a δόκησις (appearance),[88] and Jesus Christ, who was never really born as a human being, only seemed to appear on earth.

[85] Among those who argue that λύει is the original reading are Schnackenburg, *Johannine Letters* 201–202 (with extensive evidence and arguments); Bultmann, *Johannine Epistles* 62; Brown, *Epistles of John* 494–96; Peter Weigandt, *Der Doketismus im Urchristentum und in der theologischen Entwicklung des zweiten Jahrhunderts*, Diss. theol., Heidelberg 1961, 104; Wengst, *Häresie und Orthodoxie* 17 note 14; Martin Hengel, *Die johanneische Frage* 171ff.; *The Johannine Question* (see below 8.5.1) 57ff.; differently e.g. Klauck, *1 Johannesbrief* 234–237.
[86] Weigandt, *Doketismus* 105.
[87] Cf. only Walter Bauer, *Die Briefe des Ignatius von Antiochien und der Polykarpbrief*, HNT.EB II (Tübingen: J. C. B. Mohr [Paul Siebeck], 1920) 239–240; Weigandt, *Doketismus* 57–58; Walter Bauer and Henning Paulsen, *Die Briefe des Ignatius* (see above 2.9.6) 64–65; William R. Schoedel, *Ignatius of Antioch*, Hermeneia (Philadelphia: Fortress Press, 1985) 238ff.
[88] Cf. Bauer, *IgnTrall* 239.

It is only this form of monophysite Christology, in which the redeemer himself is exclusively of a divine nature and thus it is not he himself, but only his δόκησις that appears on earth, that can be named docetism.[89] Docetism so defined, the consequence of which is a complete emptying of the earthly being of Jesus Christ, is found not only in the letters of Ignatius, but in Saturinus, Cerdo, Marcion, and the Acts of John.[90]

Especially the parallels between 1 John and the opponents resisted in Ignatius and Polycarp (cf. PolPhil. 7.1) confirm that the opponents of 1 John taught a *docetic Christology*.[91] In each case it is the incarnation of the Son of God in a human body that is disputed. Only the heavenly Christ is relevant for salvation, with no soteriological function being attributed to the existence of the earthly Jesus. The author of 1 John, however, opposes the false teachers with what is in his eyes the legitimate doctrinal tradition of the Johannine school (cf. ἀπ' ἀρχῆς in 1 John 1.1–4; 2.7–8, 3.11), not by citing the Gospel of John! While in practice the opponents allow the

---

[89] Cf. Weigandt, *Doketismus* 16, 18. It is likely that docetism was influenced particularly by the Platonic understanding of reality with its opposition of δοκεῖν – εἶναι (appearance/being) (cf. *Republic* 2 361b, 362a and often). Real being is the spiritual-ideal being (οὐσία [being)], ὄντως ὄν [real being)], ὃ ἔστιν ὄν [that which is]), while the world of perceptions (from the docetic perspective including the bodily existence of Jesus) is subjected to mere 'appearance' (δοκέω, δόκησις). Thus the valid point of view was expressed: 'The relation of truth to faith is the same relation as that of being to becoming' (Plato, *Timaeus* 29c). How a Hellenistic Jew influenced by Plato would understand the being of God is illustrated very nicely by Philo, *Sacr* 101: 'Separate, therefore, my soul, all that is created, mortal, profane, from the conception of God the uncreated, the unchangeable, the immortal, the holy and solely blessed.' Docetism and gnosticism are by no means identical: 'But docetism is one of the presuppositions for the gnostic doctrine of the Redeemer . . .' (Carsten Colpe, 'Gnosis, II,' RAC 11 [1981] 611); cf. also the distinction made by Weigandt, *Doketismus* 4–19; in addition Schoedel, *Ignatius* 242; Norbert Brox, 'Doketismus – eine Problemanzeige', ZKG 95 (1984) 312ff.

[90] Cf. Weigandt, *Doketismus* 28, 82–86. The Christology of the opponents is often associated with, or even identified with, the theology of Cerinthus (cf. esp. Wengst, *Häresie und Orthodoxie* 24ff.; Brown, *Epistles of John* 65ff.). Agreements between the doctrine of Cerinthus (cf. Irenaeus *Haer* 1.26.1) and the supposed Christology of the opponents in 1 John may not be denied (separating the heavenly Christ and the earthly Jesus, placing great importance on the baptism of Jesus). There are also considerable differences, however: cosmology was obviously constitutive for the system of Cerinthus, for which there is no indication in the case of 1 John's opponents. So too, the distinction between a spiritual Christ incapable of suffering and the human being Jesus who served as the *temporary receptacle* for the spiritual Christ is not to be inferred from 1 John 2.22; 5.6.

[91] Cf. Heinrich J. Holtzmann, *Johanneische Briefe*, HC IV (Freiburg ²1893) 236–237; Windisch, *Johannesbriefe* 127 (Cerinthus); Bultmann, *Johannine Epistles* 62; Balz, *Johannesbriefe* 157 (related to docetism); Dodd, *Johannine Epistles* xix; Weigandt, *Doketismus* 193ff.; Brown, *Epistles of John* 65ff. (Cerinthus); Bogart, *Orthodox and Heretical Perfectionism* 28–29; Ulrich B. Müller, *Die Geschichte der Christologie in der johanneischen Gemeinde*, SBS 77 (Stuttgart: Katholisches Bibelwerk, 1975) 59–63; Carsten Colpe, 'Gnosis II' *RAC* 11 611; Schunack, *Johannesbriefe* 75 (preliminary stages of distinct docetic concepts); Strecker, *Johannine Letters* 69–76; Martin Hengel, *Die johanneische Frage* 185, 192 and often; *The Johannine Question* (see below 8.5.1) 64, 67 and often. A history of research is presented by Klauck, *1 John* 34–42, who does not attempt to give a concrete historical location of the opponents.

figure of the redeemer to dissolve, the author of 1 John emphasizes the soteriological unity of the earthly Jesus and the heavenly Christ (cf. 1 John 2.22; 4.2, 9, 15; 5.1, 5). The false teaching is set over against the confession of the Johannine community. If the bodily appearance of the redeemer is ultimately irrelevant for the opponents, for the author of 1 John it is the essential statement of the community's faith (cf. 1 John 2.6; 3.3–4; 4.17). Over against the pneumatic self-confidence of the dissidents, 1 John places the anointing of the community (cf. 1 John 2.20, 27) that instructs those who have received it about what is true and what is false.

8.4.9 Basic Theological Ideas

As in the case of the Prologue to the Gospel, so also the letter prologue 1 John 1.1–4 functions to orient the reader to the proper understanding of the whole. By using the confessional and witnessing 'we' and the grammatically past forms ἀκηκόαμεν, ἑωράκαμεν, ἐθεασάμεθα (we have heard, seen, beheld) the author emphasizes immediately at the beginning of his composition the real incarnation of the Logos and thereby the reality and historicity of the saving event. This *theology of the incarnation* determines the whole of 1 John. It characterizes the debate with the docetists in 1 John 2.22–23; 4.2–3; 5.6–8; the antichrists and false teachers are revealed by their denial of the real incarnation of the Son of God, Jesus Christ. The community infers from the arrival of the antichrists that the end time has already begun, that it is now the last hour (1 John 2.18), that Jesus' parousia stands immediately before them (1 John 2.28). With an eager expectation of the coming End, the community hopes for the revelation of Jesus Christ, for then the reservations of the eschatological time will be removed. Believers will become like Jesus, and will see him as he is (1 John 3.1–3). This dominance of futuristic eschatology is to be counted among the special features of 1 John.

Like the Gospel of Matthew and the Letter to the Hebrews, 1 John documents a vigorous debate within early Christianity on the issues of whether a baptized Christian can sin, and how the church is to relate to sinners in its midst.[92] In 1 John 1.8–10 the author confirms the fact that sin continues to exist in his church, and engages in polemic against church leaders who obviously deny the reality of sin within the church. They make Jesus into a liar, for in him the community has an advocate with God, one who has died as the sin-offering for our sins (1 John 2.1–2). A completely

---

[92] For analysis of the texts, cf. I. Goldhahn-Müller, *Grenze der Gemeinde* (see above 6.4) 27–75.

different statement is found in 1 John 3.9, which now affirms the impossibility of sin for the Christian. Because God is the origin and ground of Christian existence, sin appears as an impossible possibility. 1 John 5.16–17 points to the resolution of this supposed contradiction, where the author distinguishes between a sin 'unto death' and a sin that is 'not unto death.' By speaking of a 'sin unto death,' 1 John holds fast to the conviction that a Christian life cannot be combined with continuing to sin. Whoever sins is not in the realm of Spirit and life, but belongs to the realm of death. On the other hand, the author of 1 John takes account of the reality of life within the church when he speaks of sins that are 'not mortal.' For these sins the fellow Christian may ask God for forgiveness.

The ethic of 1 John is determined throughout by the command of love for the brothers and sisters of the Christian community. Jesus Christ is presented as the one who both originally practiced this love himself and is the model for Christians. Just as he lived, so Christians should also live (cf. 1 John 2.6b). Indicative and imperative are coordinated in a reflective form comparable to Paul (cf. 1 John 4.19: ἡμεῖς ἀγαπῶμεν, ὅτι αὐτὸς πρῶτος ἠγάπησεν ἡμᾶς, 'we love because he first loved us'; further 1 John 2.7–11; 4.10). The concept of love in 1 John is oriented primarily to the brothers and sisters of the Christian community, but does not exclude the love of [the non-Christian] neighbor.[93] This is documented in 1 John 2.6, 3.3, 7, 16, where the paradigmatic act of Jesus calls for a corresponding conduct on the part of the disciples. Finally, the demand for concrete social action in response to needy brothers and sisters (1 John 3.17, 18) prevents John's ethic from being understood in the sense of an ethic that is valid only within the narrow confines of the Christian community or an ethic that can be reduced only to interior attitudes.

This ethic already indicates that there can be no talk of hostility to the world in 1 John, and this is confirmed by the statements about the cosmos. The world is not evaluated in 1 John as essentially inferior, for it is only one's faith that decides whether one belongs to the realm of the world or to the realm of God. God sent his son because of his love for the world (cf. 1 John 4.9, 14); Jesus is the σωτήρ τοῦ κόσμου (savior of the world) (cf. 1 John 2.2; 4.14). The world first becomes a realm hostile to God where unbelief determines a person's being and action. The author of 1 John does not demand distance from the world, but an overcoming of the cosmos as the place of unbelief while living within the world (cf. 1 John 5.4–5).

---

[93] Differently Martin Rese, 'Das Gebot der Bruderliebe in den Johannesbriefen,' ThZ 41 (1985) 44–58.

8.4.10 *Tendencies of Recent Research*

Influenced by Bultmann's interpretation of the Johannine documents, for a long time questions of literary criticism and source analysis stood in the foreground of research on 1 John. A fundamental change has taken place on this point, since only occasionally are written sources now thought to lie behind 1 John, and the only serious literary-critical problem is represented by the conclusion of the letter. The relation of 1 John to the Gospel of John has formed a central focus of recent discussion. Hans Conzelmann's classifying 1 John as a 'Johannine Pastoral Epistle' has had great influence. For him, the author of 1 John already had the Gospel before him, which he regarded as a fixed authority. For Conzelmann, the theological shifts between 1 John and the Gospel emerged from the changed church situation to which the letter was directed. The church reorients itself in a new situation, reaches back to its origins, and transposes the eschatological self-understanding 'onto the historical reality of society.'[94] The interpretations of 1 John by G. Klein, R. Schnackenburg, R. E. Brown, F. Vouga, and H. J. Klauck also have their point of departure the assumption that the author of 1 John and his community had received the Gospel of John as part of their authoritative tradition. G. Strecker advocates a different line of interpretation. Here, 1 John does not appear as an appendix or readers' guide to the Gospel, but as an independent witness of the Johannine theology prior to the composition of the Gospel. The theory that in 1 John, Johannine theology suffered decline by accommodating itself more and more to the emerging institutional church is still oriented to the Protestant idea of a falling away from the original teaching, which in this case can be seen in the Gospel once it has been purified from later accretions. In contrast, Strecker numbers the concept of tradition, futuristic eschatology, the doctrine of the atoning death and the emphasis on the sacraments among the theological themes that were dominant in the Johannine school from the beginning.[95]

The identification of the opponents against which 1 John struggled continues to be a focus of research. Just as in the case of 2 John, the suggestions here range from Jewish Christians to gnostics and docetists. The majority of exegetes regard the false teachers as docetists or gnostics, whose doctrine is similar to that of the false teachers opposed by Ignatius, a teaching that results in emptying the earthly existence of Jesus of all soteriological significance. A major dispute rages around 1 John's ethical

---

[94] Conzelmann, 'Was von Anfang war' 213.

[95] Cf. also Georg Strecker, 'Chiliasmus und Doketismus in der Johanneischen Schule,' KuD 38 (1992) 30–46.

concept related to the key word 'brotherly [and sisterly] love.' While, in connection with E. Käsemann's interpretation of the Gospel of John[96] the ethic of 1 John can be described as 'the narrowed ethic of a conventicle' by W. Schrage,[97] M. Rese, W. Marxsen,[98] and others, G. Strecker emphasizes the universal tendencies of the Johannine ἀγάπη-concept.[99] The evaluation of this problematic topic is closely bound to the categorization of the Johannine community as a 'sect.' The adoption of an exclusively negative concept of the cosmos and of an ethical conception centered on the group itself does suggest the label 'sectarian mentality.'[100] In any case, the textual data presented here resists such a categorization, for the Johannine letters too 'in no case permit the church to withdraw into a sectarian conventicle.'[101]

8.5 The Gospel of John

8.5.1 Literature

Commentaries

Bauer, Walter. *Das Johannes - Evangelium*, HNT 6. Tübingen: J. C. B. Mohr (Paul Siebeck), 1933³; Brown, Raymond. *The Gospel According to John*, AncB 29 AB. Garden City: Doubleday, 1966, 1970; Bultmann, Rudolf. *The Gospel of John*, 2nd edition, tr. G. R. Beasley-Murray. Philadelphia: Westminster, 1971; Lindars, Barnabas. *The Gospel of John*, NCeB. London: Oliphants, 1972; Barrett, C. K. *The Gospel According to St. John*. Philadelphia: Westminster, 1978²; Blank, Josef. *Das Evangelium nach Johannes*, GSL.NT 4.1-3. Düsseldorf: Patmos, 1977–1981; Schnackenburg, Rudolf. *The Gospel According to John*, 3 Vols. New York: Herder and Herder, 1968, I; Crossroad 1982, II, III; Gnilka, Joachim. *Johannesevangelium*, NEB. Würzburg: Echter, 1983; Haenchen, Ernst. *John 1-2. A Commentary on the Gospel of John*, ed. Ulrich Busse and tr. Robert W. Funk. Philadelphia: Fortress Press, 1984; Beasley-Murray, G. R. *John*, WBC 36. Waco: Word, 1987; Schulz, Siegfried. *Das Evangelium nach Johannes*, NTD 4. Göttingen: Vandenhoeck & Ruprecht, 1987⁵; Schneider, Johannes. *Das Evangelium nach Johannes*, ThHK (Sonderband). Berlin: Evangelische

---

[96] Cf. Ernst Käsemann, *The Testament of Jesus. A Study of the Gospel of John in the Light of Chapter 17* (see below 8.5.1) 56–73.

[97] Cf. Wolfgang Schrage, *The Ethics of the New Testament*, trans. David E. Green (Edinburgh: T & T Clark, 1988) 295–319.

[98] Cf. Willi Marxsen, *New Testament Foundations for Christian Ethics*, tr. O. C. Dean, Jr. (Minneapolis: Fortress Press, 1989) 308, who thinks it is established 'that the brotherly [and sisterly] love of the Johannine school is bought with a lovelessness that is unparalleled in the New Testament scriptures.'

[99] Cf. Strecker, *Johannine Letters* 144–148.

[100] So for example Walter Rebell, *Gemeinde als Gegenwelt* (see below 8.5.1) 112–123.

[101] Siegfried Schulz, *Neutestamentliche Ethik* (see above 2.4.9) 525

Verlagsanstalt, 1989⁴; Becker, Jürgen. *Das Evangelium nach Johannes*, ÖTK 4.1–2. Gütersloh: Gütersloher Verlagshaus (Gerd Mohn), 1991³; Carson, D.A. *The Gospel according to John*. Leicester: Inter-Varsity/Grand Rapids: Wm. B. Eerdmans, 1992.

Monographs

Dodd, Charles H. *The Interpretation of the Fourth Gospel*. Cambridge: Cambridge University Press, 1953; Wilkens, Wilhelm. *Die Entstehungsgeschichte des vierten Evangeliums*. Zürich: Evangelischer Verlag, 1958; Blank, Josef. *Krisis*. Freiburg: Herder, 1964; Mußner, Franz. *Die johanneische Sehweise*, QD 28. Freiburg: Herder, 1965; Käsemann, Ernst. *The Testament of Jesus: A Study of the Gospel of John in the Light of Chapters 17*, tr. Gerhard Krodel. Philadelphia: Fortress, 1968; Fortna, Robert. *The Gospel of Signs*, SNTSMS 11. Cambridge: Cambridge University Press, 1970; Schottroff, Luise. *Der Glaubende und die feindliche Welt*, WMANT 37. Neukirchen-Vluyn: Neukirchener Verlag, 1970; Bühner, Jan-Adolf. *Der Gesandte und sein Weg im 4. Evangelium*, WUNT 2.2. Tübingen: J. C. B. Mohr (Paul Siebeck), 1977; Langbrandtner, Wolfgang. *Weltferner Gott oder Gott der Liebe*, BET 6. Frankfurt: Lang, 1977; Smalley, Stephen S. *John. Evangelist and Interpreter*. Exeter: Paternoster Press, 1978; Martyn, J. Louis. *History and Theology in the Fourth Gospel*. Nashville: Abingdon, 1979²; Culpepper, R. Alan. *Anatomy of the Fourth Gospel*. Philadelphia: Fortress Press, 1983; Onuki, Takashi. *Gemeinde und Welt im Johannesevangelium*, WMANT 56. Neukirchen-Vluyn: Neukirchener Verlag, 1984; Grundmann, Walter. *Der Zeuge der Wahrheit*. Berlin: Evangelische Verlagsanstalt, 1985; Kohler, Herbert. *Kreuz und Menschwerdung im Johannesevangelium*, AThANT 72. Zürich: Theologischer Verlag, 1987; Rebell, Walter. *Gemeinde als Gegenwelt. Zur soziologischen und didaktischen Funktion des Johannesevangeliums*, BET 20. Frankfurt: Lang, 1987; Ruckstuhl, Eugen. *Die literarische Einheit des Johannesevangeliums*, NTOA 5. Göttingen: Vandenhoeck & Ruprecht, 1987²; Fortna, Robert. *The Fourth Gospel and its Predecessor. From Narrative Source to Present Gospel*. Philadelphia: Fortress, 1988; Theobald, Michael. *Die Fleischwerdung des Logos*, NTA 20. Münster: Aschendorff, 1988; Hengel, Martin. *The Johannine Question*. tr. John Bowden, London: SCM Press, 1989; Ashton, John. *Understanding the Fourth Gospel*. Oxford: Oxford University Press, 1991; Painter, John. *The Quest for the Messiah*. Edinburgh: T. & T. Clark, 1991; Ruckstuhl, Eugen and Dschulnigg, Peter. *Stilkritik und Verfasserfrage im Johannesevangelium*, NTOA 17. Göttingen: Vandenhoeck & Ruprecht, 1991; Bull, Klaus Michael. *Gemeinde zwischen Integration und Abgrenzung*, BET 24. Frankfurt: Lang, 1992; Loader, William, *The Christology of the Fourth Gospel*, BET 23. Frankfurt: Lang, 1992²; Schenke, Ludger. *Das Johannesevangelium*. Stuttgart: Kolhammer, 1992; Schmithals, Walter. *Johannesevangelium und Johannesbriefe. Forschungsgeschichte und Analyse*, BZNW 64. Berlin: Walter de Gruyter, 1992; Schnelle, Udo. *Antidocetic Christology in the Gospel of John*, tr. Linda M. Maloney. Minneapolis: Fortress Press, 1992; Wengst, Klaus. *Bedrängte Gemeinde und verherrlichter Christus*. München: Kaiser, 1992; Hengel, Martin. *Die johanneische Frage*, WUNT 67. Tübingen: J. C. B. Mohr (Paul Siebeck), 1993.

Articles

Bornkamm, Günther. 'Zur Interpretation des Johannes-Evangeliums,' in *Geschichte und Glaube* I. , ed. G. Bornkamm, BEvTh 48. München: Kaiser, 1968, 104–121; Fischer, Karl Martin. 'Der johanneische Christus und der gnostische Erlöser,' in *Gnosis und Neues Testament*, ed. Karl Wolfgang Tröger. Berlin: Evangelische Verlagsanstalt, 1973, 245–266; Richter, Georg. *Studien zum Johannesevangelium*, BU 13. Regensburg: Pustet, 1977 (important collection of essays); Thyen, Hartwig. 'Entwicklungen innerhalb der johanneischen Theologie und Kirche im Spiegel von Joh 21 und der Lieblingsjüngertexte des Evangeliums,' in *L'Évangile de Jean*. BETL 44, ed. Martinus de Jonge. Leuven: Leuven University Press, 1977, 259–299; Martyn, J. Louis. *The Gospel of John in Christian History*. New York: Paulist Press, 1978 (collection of essays); Gnilka, Joachim. 'Zur Christologie des Johannesevangeliums,' in *Christologische Schwerpunkte*, ed. Walter Kasper. Düsseldorf: Patmos, 1980, 92–107; Smith, D. Moody. *Johannine Christianity*. Columbia: University of South Carolina Press, 1984 (Collection of Essays); Klaiber, Walter. 'Die Aufgabe einer theologischen Interpretation des 4. Evangeliums,' ZThK 82 (1985) 300–324; Weder, Hans. 'Die Menschwerdung Gottes,' ZThK 82 (1985) 325–360; Thyen, Hartwig. 'Johannesevangelium,' *TRE* 17 (1987) 200–225; Schnelle, Udo. 'Johanneische Ekklesiologie,' NTS 37 (1991) 37–50; Denaux, Adelbert, ed. *John and the Synoptics*, BETL 101. Leuven: Leuven University Press, 1992 (important collection of essays).

History of Research / Bibliographies

Malatesta, Edward. *St. John's Gospel.1920–1965*, AB 32. Rome: Pontifical Biblical Institute, 1967; Kysar, Robert. *The Fourth Evangelist and His Gospel*. Minneapolis: Augsburg, 1975; Thyen, Hartwig. 'Aus der Literatur zum Johannesevangelium,' ThR 39 (1974) 1–69, 222–252, 289–330; ThR 42 (1977) 211–270; ThR 43 (1978) 328–359; ThR 44 (1979) 97–134; Becker, Jürgen. 'Aus der Literatur zum Johannesevangelium,' ThR 47 (1982) 279–301, 305–347; ThR 51 (1986) 1–78; Belle, Gilbert van. *Johannine Bibliography 1966–1985*, BETL LXXXII. Leuven: Leuven University Press, 1988. Schmithals, Walter. *Johannesevangelium und Johannesbriefe* (see above) 1–214.

8.5.2 Author

About 180 CE Irenaeus transmitted a tradition about the authorship of the Gospel of John that had originated previously in Asia Minor[102] and by ca. 200 CE had attained general acceptance: 'Afterwards John, the disciple of the Lord who also leaned upon his chest, he too published a gospel while residing in Ephesus' (Irenaeus, *Against Heresies* 3.1.1 = Eusebius HE 5.8.4). In another passage Irenaeus comments about the age of John: 'And all the presbyters who had gathered about John, the disciple of the Lord,

---

[102] On the reception of the Gospel of John in the second century, cf. Walther v. Loewenich, *Das Johannes-Verständnis im zweiten Jahrhundert*, BZNW 13. (Berlin 1932). The Fourth Gospel was rejected by the Alogoi (Epiphanius, *Heresies* 51).

testify that John has given us this. For he remained with them until the time of Trajan' (Irenaeus, *Against Heresies* 2.22.5 = Eusebius, HE 3.23.3).[103] For his tradition Irenaeus appeals to the presbyters who gathered around John the Lord's disciple in Asia Minor, but especially to Polycarp and Papias, whom he regards as disciples of John.[104] Irenaeus says about Papias: 'Papias, one who heard John, a friend of Polycarp, a man of the ancient period, gives us written testimony in his fourth book' (Irenaeus, *Against Heresies* 5.33.4 = Eusebius, HE 3.39.1).

Papias, as the oldest witness of an Asia Minor Johannine tradition probably did mention the apostle John and a presbyter John, but says nothing about either of these having written the Gospel of John (cf. Eusebius HE 3.39.4). He cannot therefore be regarded as a representative of the traditions handed on by Irenaeus.[105] Irenaeus reports about Polycarp (died ca. 156 CE): 'Polycarp was not only instructed by apostles and conversant with many who had seen the Lord, but was appointed by apostles to serve in Asia as Bishop of Smyrna. I myself saw him in my early years, for he lived a long time and was very old indeed when he laid down his life by a glorious and most splendid martyrdom. At all times he taught the things which he had learnt from the apostles, which the Church transmits, which alone are true. These facts are attested by all the churches of Asia and by the successors of Polycarp to this day – and he was a much more trustworthy and dependable witness to the truth than Valentinus and Marcion and all other wrong-headed persons. In the time of Anicetus he stayed for a while in Rome, where he won over many from the camp of those heretics to the Church of God, proclaiming that the one and only truth he had received from the apostles was the truth transmitted by the Church. And there are people who heard him describe how John, the Lord's disciple when at Ephesus went to take a bath, but seeing Cerinthus inside rushed out of the building without taking a bath, crying, "Let us get out of here, for fear the place falls in, now that Cerinthus, the enemy of truth, is inside!"' (Irenaeus, *Against Heresies* 3.3.4 = Eusebius HE 4.14.3–4, 6, Williamson/Penguin trans.).

In his letter to Florinus Irenaeus says the following about his contact with Polycarp: 'I can describe the place where the blessed Polycarp sat and

---

[103] Cf. also Irenaeus, *Against Heresies* 3.3.4 = Eusebius, HE 3.23.4: 'Also the church founded by Paul in Ephesus, in which John lived into the days of Trajan, is a truthful witness of the apostolic tradition.'

[104] On the interpretation of these texts cf. also Haenchen, *John* 1.2–19; Schmithals, *Johannesevangelium und Johannesbriefe* 2–5; Hengel, *Die johanneische Frage* 13–25; *Johannine Question* 2–5.

[105] Whether Papias knew the Fourth Gospel remains an open question. The late Armenian Papias tradition presupposes that he did; cf. Folker Siegert, 'Unbeachtete Papiaszitate' (see above 3.6.2) 607–609.

talked, his goings out and comings in, the character of his life, his personal appearance, his addresses to crowded congregations. I remember how he spoke of his intercourse with John and with the others who had seen the Lord; how he repeated their words from memory; and how the things that he had heard them say about the Lord, His miracles and His teaching' (Eusebius, HE 5.20.6, Williamson/Penguin trans, 228–229). The direct chain of tradition claimed by Irenaeus between himself and the apostle John, with Polycarp forming a principal link in the chain of tradition, finds no support in the few writings that have come to us from Polycarp himself. It is also remarkable that Ignatius, in his letter to the church in Ephesus written around 110, makes no reference to a residence of the apostle John in that city.[106] Thus the tradition that John the son of Zebedee, the Beloved Disciple, published his Gospel in Ephesus when he was at advanced age during the time of Trajan (89–117 CE) is not documented prior to the time of Irenaeus himself. But Irenaeus himself is certainly not the creator of this tradition,[107] though he is the tradent who gave it normative status. The historical credibility of this tradition must then be evaluated in the light of the internal testimony of the Gospel itself.

Can the Fourth Gospel be understood as the writing of an eyewitness of the life of Jesus? The portrayal of the life of Jesus departs considerably from the Synoptic model. In contrast to the Synoptics (cf. Mark 11.15–17), the cleansing of the temple (John 2.14–22) stands at the beginning and not at the end of the public ministry of Jesus. In John, Jesus makes at least three trips to Jerusalem (cf. John 2.13; 5.1; 7.10), which cannot be harmonized with the Markan portrayal of only one trip to Jerusalem at the end of his ministry. So too the message of Jesus in the Gospel of John speaks against the assumption that the Gospel was composed by an eyewitness. In the Synoptic Gospels, at the center of Jesus' proclamation stands the approaching kingdom of God that is also already present in the person of Jesus (cf. e.g. Luke 11.20; 17.21). In contrast, the kingdom of God plays only a very subordinate role in Jesus' message as presented in the Fourth Gospel, the expression βασιλεία τοῦ θεοῦ (kingdom of God) appearing only in John 3.3, 5. In the Gospel of John, Jesus himself is the content of his message (cf. e.g., the ἐγώ εἰμι [I am . . .] sayings in John 6.35a; 8.12; 10.7, 11; 11.25; 14.6; 15.1). The revelatory discourses of the Fourth Gospel have no real parallel in the Synoptics. Similarly, there is nothing in the Synoptics comparable to the Johannine dualism and the Christology of the

---

[106] Cf. Barrett, *Gospel According to St. John* 117.

[107] If 𝔓[66] is dated in the middle of the second century (so e.g. Johannes B. Bauer, 'Zur Datierung des Papyrus Bodmer II [P 66],' BZ 12 [1968] 121–122), then at least the title documents the attribution of the Gospel to John (the Apostle).

Sent One. As the Gospel of John is dominated by present-tense eschatology (cf. e.g. John 5.25; 11.25–26), so future-tense eschatology prevails in
the preaching of the Synoptic Jesus.

The different way in which the life of Jesus is portrayed, the independent theology, the numerous special traditions and the thought world
explicitly oriented to the post-Easter perspective point to the conclusion
that the Fourth Gospel was not composed by an eyewitness of the life of
Jesus.[108] He was a *theologian of the later period* who, on the basis of comprehensive traditions, rethought the meaning of Jesus' life, and interpreted
and presented it in his own way.[109]

In the secondary appendix John 21 the group that published the Gospel
(οἴδαμεν [we know] 21–24) made the Beloved Disciple into its author. This
is a secondary identification, for in John 1–20 the Beloved Disciple, while
he is the guarantor for the validity of the Johannine tradition, is not the
author of the Gospel. So too it is no accident that the sons of Zebedee James
and John appear only in John 21.2. The editors of the appended chapter 21
suggest the conclusion that is first documented in Irenaeus, that it was John
son of Zebedee, the Lord's Beloved Disciple, who is also the author of the
Fourth Gospel.

---

[108] Among recent commentaries the case for apostolic authorship is made especially by Leon
Morris, *The Gospel according to John*, NIC. (Grand Rapids: Eerdmans, 1971) 8–30. Often it is
acknowledged that the apostle (son of Zebedee, Beloved Disciple) was not the actual author, but
was its spiritual composer. Rudolf Schnackenburg, *John* 1.102 distinguishes the apostle John and
the evangelist, 'the evangelist would have been both the spokesman who transmitted the tradition and the preaching of the apostle John, and a theologian in his own right and teacher of the
readers whom he addressed' (similarly Brown, *John* xcvii–cii. On the later position of Schnackenburg, cf. Thyen, 'Forschungsbericht' [ThR 42] 239ff.). According to Barrett, *Gospel According to
St. John* 148, John emigrated from Palestine and lived in Ephesus, where he
gathered a group of disciples around himself. One of these disciples, a 'keen thinker,' equally at
home in Judaism and Hellenism, 'brought forth John 1–20.' For Oscar Cullmann, *The Johannine
Circle* (see above 8.1.1) 63–85, the anonymous Beloved Disciple is the author of the Gospel. He
belonged to the wider circle of Jesus' disciples and is also to be considered an eyewitness in a
limited sense.

Martin Hengel, *Die johanneische Frage* 306–325; *Johannine Question* 124–135, regards the
Presbyter John mentioned by Papias as the author of the Gospel and the three Letters. After the
death of this Jewish Christian, who originally came from the upper stratum of Jerusalem society
and later lived in Ephesus, the Presbyter John's work was published by his disciples, who at the
same time identified the Presbyter with the Beloved Disciple. To be sure, Hengel does not regard
the Presbyter as John son of Zebedee, but still thinks 'that as a young man he in some way came
into close contact with Jesus and was deeply impressed by him' (*Die johanneische Frage* 321).

[109] That the Gospel was written by an unknown author named John is also argued by Schulz,
Johannesevangelium 2; Lindars, *Gospel of John* 33; Becker, *John* 1.62–64. Ernst Haenchen speaks
of three 'authors,' *John* 1A, 35–39 (1. author of a 'miracle Gospel.' 2. The 'Evangelist.' 3. An
ecclesiastical redactor). H. Thyen, *Entwicklungen* 267 and elsewhere, regards the author of John
21 as the 'real' Evangelist.

8.5.3 Place and Time of Composition

The determination of the place of composition is closely dependent on one's understanding of the Gospel of John as a whole. If the Fourth Gospel is interpreted as standing within the context of gnosticizing streams of early Christianity, then Syria is often suggested as its place of composition.[110] Supporting arguments related to the content of the Gospel are its contacts with Mandean literature, the Odes of Solomon, and the points of similarity to the letters of Ignatius of Antioch. So also the debate with Judaism and the Baptist movement are frequently introduced as pointing to a Syrian origin. The Gospel of John is often located in the area of Palestine, whether in Transjordan[111] or in the southern parts of the territory of King Agrippa II, especially in the region of Gaulanitis and Batanaea in the northern section of Palestine east of the Jordan.[112] K. Wengst sees behind the Gospel a Greek speaking, predominately Jewish Christian community that lives as a minority in an environment where Jews are the prevailing cultural and religious group, a community that had not yet separated from the synagogue but now suffers under the decisions about exclusion from the synagogue made at Jamnia and reflected in John 9.22; 12.42; 16.2. The church traditions already mentioned regarding authorship are also witnesses for Asia Minor as the place of the Fourth Gospel's composition. Other indications of an Asia Minor origin are the Johannine letters, the history of the influence and reception of the Johannine theology, and the nearness to Pauline theology. A comprehensive hypothesis that embraces all the serious proposals is advocated by Rudolf Schnackenburg: 'The Johannine tradition, whose roots lie in Palestine, has also gone through the medium of Syrian influence, before it gained a firm foothold in Asia Minor (Ephesus), where it became a firmly fixed tradition and was finally edited.'[113]

Of all these possibilities, *Asia Minor (Ephesus)* is the most like place for the composition of the Gospel of John. In favor of this conclusion is the tradition of the ancient church, which at its earliest stage (Papias!) was not yet connected with the issue of authorship! So also the anti-docetic orientation of the Gospel of John and the history of its influence (Alogoi,

---

[110] Cf. e.g., Bauer, *Johannesevangelium* 244, Rudolf Bultmann, 'Johannesevangelium,' *RGG*³ (1959) 3.849 (original Gospel composed in Syria; final redaction made in Asia Minor); Kümmel, *Introduction* 246–247; Vielhauer, *Urchristliche Literatur* 460; Koester, *Introduction* 2.178; Becker, *John* 1.64.

[111] Cf. Cullmann, *Johannine Circle* 98–99.

[112] Cf. Wengst, *Bedrängte Gemeinde* 183–184. Günter Reim, 'Zur Lokalisierung der johanneischen Gemeinde,' *BZ* 32 (1988) 72–86, develops Wengst's position by arguing that the Johannine community was located not far from Bethsaida and Capernaum.

[113] Schnackenburg, *Gospel of John* 152.

Montanists) point to Asia Minor. Ephesus could well have been the place where Pauline and Johannine theology came in contact with each other (see below 8.5.7). Finally, the explanation of Jewish practices in John 2.6; 11.55; 18.20, 28b and the comment on the relation of Jews and Samaritans in John 4.9 point to readers who were not in the immediate vicinity of Palestine. The argument frequently made in older scholarship and still sometimes found in recent exegesis, that Johannine theology has close contacts with gnosticism, no longer is valid (see below 8.5.8), so that a principal reason for seeing Syria as the place of composition of the Fourth Gospel has now fallen away. The debate with the Jews presupposed by the Gospel by no means necessarily points to Syria, but makes just as much sense in the context of the significant Jewish communities of Asia Minor.[114] The location of the Johannine community adopted by K. Wengst and G. Reim is improbable, because the evangelist is not interested in these geographical areas and because ἀποσυνάγωγος (put out of the synagogue) in John 9.22; 12.42; 16.2 does not refer to the introduction of the *Birkat Ha-Minim* (the blessing [curse] against the heretics/separatists) in the Eighteen Benedictions (see below 8.5.4).[115] There is no evidence for R. Schnackenburg's thesis either in the Gospel itself or in the ancient church tradition, so that it must be eliminated as an elegant, but historically unlikely possibility.

The terminus a quo for the dating of the Fourth Gospel is provided by John 11.48, where the destruction of Jerusalem in 70 CE is presupposed. It cannot be proven that the Christian writers of the first half of the second century CE (Ignatius of Antioch, Polycarp of Smyrna, the Letter of Barnabas, the Shepherd of Hermas) knew the Gospel of John, though possibly Justin Martyr was acquainted with it (compare *Apology* 61.4–5 with John 3.3–5). The commentary of Heracleon, a disciple of Valentinus, from the second half of the second century CE, must be regarded as the first positive documentation for the history of the reception of the Gospel of John.[116] A possible terminus ad quem for the dating of the Gospel of John

---

[114] Philo, *Leg* 245, mentions Asia Minor and Syria in the same breath as the two areas where Jews are found in great numbers in every city. On the Jews in Asia Minor, cf. Emil Schürer, *The History of the Jewish People in the Age of Jesus Christ* III/1, ed. G. Vermes – F. Millar (Edinburgh: T. & T. Clark, 1986) 17–36 (22–23: Ephesus); Paul R. Trebilco, *Jewish Communities in Asia Minor*, (SNTSMS 69. Cambridge: Cambridge University Press, 1991). According to Josephus, *Apion* 2.39, Jews had lived in Ephesus since the early Hellenistic period.

[115] For a critique of Wengst's view see also Hengel, *Die johanneische Frage* 290–291; *Johannine Question* 114–115. On the *Birkat ha-Minim* see Boring, Berger, Colpe *Hellenistic Commentary to the New Testament* (Nashville: Abingdon, 1995) §470, 301–302.

[116] Cf. Kurt Rudolph, *Gnosis: The Nature and History of Gnosticism* (San Francisco: Harper & Row, Publishers, 1977) 17.

is provided by the manuscript tradition (cf. 𝔓⁵², 𝔓⁹⁰, 𝔓⁶⁶),[117] for 𝔓⁵² with John 18.31–33, 37–38 is generally dated around 125 CE[118] To be sure, this dating is no longer established beyond all doubt,[119] but nonetheless both the history of the reception and the MS tradition of the Gospel of John suggest it originated between 100 and 110 CE.[120]

8.5.4 Intended Readership

The Evangelist's predominately Gentile Christian community[121] was influenced and shaped during the course of its history by the debate with the disciples of John the Baptist, Jews, and docetic false teachers within the Johannine school itself.

The initial competitive situation with the *Baptist community*[122] is seen throughout in the demotion of John the Baptist to a mere witness to the Christ event (cf. John 1.6–8, 15, 19ff.; 3.28ff.; 5.33–35; 10.40–42). Obviously, the Johannine school had succeeded in winning over some adherents of the Baptist community (cf. John 1.35ff.), and in surpassing the Baptist community in its mission work. This is the only way that the remarkable statements about Jesus' own baptizing activity can be under-

---

[117] On this cf. Kurt Aland, 'Der Text des Johannesevangeliums im 2. Jahrhundert,' in *Studien zum Text und zur Ethik des Neuen Testaments* (FS Heinrich Greeven), ed. Wolfgang Schrage, BZNW 47 (Berlin: Walter de Gruyter, 1986) 1–10.

[118] Cf. Kurt and Barbara Aland, *The Text of the New Testament* 99.

[119] Colin H. Roberts, *An Unpublished Fragment of the Fourth Gospel in the John Ryland's Library* (Manchester 1935) 14–15,16ff., 23, emphasizes very strongly in his dating of 𝔓⁵² the family resemblance to 𝔓 Egerton 2, adopting the dating of which ca. 150 CE. Now another fragment of 𝔓 Egerton 2 in Cologne has been identified that points to the third century as its date (alternatively around 200), since here an apostrophe is found between consonants; cf. Michael Gronewald, 'Unbekanntes Evangelium oder Evangelienharmonie (Fragment aus dem 'Evangelium Egerton'),' in *Kölner Papyri* Vol. 6 (RWA Sonderreihe Papyrologica Coloniensia Vol VII) (Opladen 1987) 136–145. Cf. A. Schmidt, 'Zwei Anmerkungen zu P. Ryl. III 457,' APF 35 (1989) 11–12, who dates 𝔓⁵² in the period around 170 CE (+/– 25) on the basis of a comparison with 𝔓 Chester Beatty X, and thus excludes an early dating around ca. 125 for 𝔓⁵²! The result for the dating of 𝔓⁵² is that the 125 CE period, usually given with extraordinary certitude, must now be stated with some doubt. One must at least allow a margin of 25 years, so that one could think of a dating around 150.

[120] In recent research the Gospel of John is mostly dated in the last decade of the first century, or around 100 CE. Cf. e.g., Barrett, *Gospel According to St. John* 143; Brown, *John* 1.lxxxiii; Becker, *John* 1.66; Schneider, *Johannesevangelium* 45; Thyen, 'Johannesevangelium' 215; Kümmel, *Introduction* 246; Vielhauer, *Urchristliche Literatur* 460. An earlier dating is advocated by e.g., Schenke and Fischer, *Einleitung* 2.197 (75–85 CE); Beasley-Murray, *John* lxxviii (ca. 80 CE). A later dating (ca. 140 CE) is now postulated again by Schmithals, *Johannesevangelium und Johannesbriefe* 422.

[121] Cf. Hengel, *Die johanneische Frage* 300–305; *The Johannine Question* 121–124.

[122] On the Baptist texts in the Fourth Gospel, cf. most recently Knut Backhaus, *Die 'Jüngerkreise' des Täufers Johannes*, PaThSt 19 (Paderborn: Schöningh, 1991) 230–265, 345–366; Martin Stowasser, *Johannes der Täufer im Vierten Evangelium*, ÖBS 12 (Klosterneuburg: Österreichisches Katholisches Bibelwerk, 1992).

stood, which picture him as more successful in baptizing than was John the Baptist himself (cf. John 3.22ff.; 4.1). The reference to disciples of John the Baptist in Ephesus (cf. Acts 19.1–7)[123] shows that within a brief period the Baptist movement spread from east of the Jordan to Asia Minor. Both the Christian movement and the Baptist movement appeared to outsiders to be similar, which explains the competitive situation.

Throughout the text, the issue of Jesus' messiahship determines the debate of the Johannine community with *Judaism*. There is no continuity in the history of salvation between Moses and Jesus; Christians stand under grace and truth, not under the Law (John 1.17). The Law belongs to the Jewish side (cf. John 7 .19; 8.17; 10.34), for Christians have long since left the stage of legal religion behind them (cf. John 4.20ff.). The Law even testifies of Jesus (cf. John 7.19, 23; 8.17; 10.31–39; 15.25). Likewise, Moses bears witness to Jesus' messiahship (cf. John 5.45–47), and Abraham would have rejoiced, if he could have seen this day (cf. John 8.56ff.).

By rejecting Jesus, the Jews finally turn against God, and therefore have the devil as their father (cf. John 8.37–45). For John, the Law can be understood only from the point of view of faith in Jesus, who is at one and the same time the content, goal, and the Lord of the Law and the Scripture (cf. John 2.22; 5.39; 7.38, 42; 10.35; 17.12; 19.24, 28, 36–37; 20.9). If the characteristic indication of Jewish-Christian theology is keeping the Law alongside the confession of Christ, [124] then the Gospel of John, due to its understanding of the Law, cannot be regarded as a Jewish Christian Gospel. In addition to its understanding of the Law, the distance of the Gospel from Judaism is seen in its translation of Hebrew or Aramaic vocabulary as foreign words (cf. John 1.38, 41, 42; 4.25; 5.2; 9.7; 11.16; 19.13, 17; 20.16, 24)[125] and the distancing manner of speech about the Jewish festivals and practices (cf. John 2.13; 5.1; 6.4; 7.2, 11; 11.55). The distance from Judaism also becomes clear in the Johannine use of 'Ιουδαῖος ('Jews,' 'Jewish leaders').[126]

One cannot proceed, however, on the basis of a presumed uniform (negative) Johannine linguistic practice, for in the Fourth Gospel the Jews are not simply a *massa damnata* as such. Jesus is a Jew (John 4.9), and salvation comes from the Jews (John 4.22). Nicodemus (John 3.1ff.; 7.50;

---

[123] For analysis of the text cf. Hermann Lichtenberger, 'Täufergemeinden und frühchristliche Täuferpolemik im letzten Drittel des 1. Jahrhunderts,' ZThK 84 (1987) 47–51.

[124] Cf. the definition by Georg Strecker, 'Judenchristentum,' *TRE* 17 (1988) 311.

[125] The language of the Gospel of John belongs to the non-literary Koine. Cf. Haenchen, *John* 1.52–66; Ruckstuhl and Dschulnigg, *Stilkritik und Verfasserfrage*, passim.

[126] Cf. here the survey in Horst Kuhli, *EWNT* 2.479–480.

19.39) and Joseph of Arimathea (John 19.38) are sympathizers of the Jesus movement among the Jews, and many Jews believe in Jesus (cf. John 8.30–31; 11.45; 12.11). Nevertheless, it is characteristic that almost half of the cases of Jesus' conflict with his opponents involve 'the Jews.' They complain about Jesus (John 6.41; 7.12), persecute him (John 5.16), attempt to kill him (John 5.18; 7.1, 19; 8.22–24), want to stone him (John 8.59; 10.31–33, 11.8), and emerge as decisive opponents in his trial (John 18.36, 38; 19.7, 12, 20). The main charge against Jesus is that he makes himself equal to God (John 5.18; 10.33; 19.7). The disciples (John 20.19), Nicodemus (John 3.2), the parents of the man born blind (John 9.22) and Joseph of Arimathea (John 19.38) are all afraid of the Jews, who are finally described not as children of Abraham (cf. John 8.33–40) or God (cf. John 8.41–43, 45–47), but as sons of the devil (John 8.44).[127]

Interpreters have always noticed the agreements between John's portrayal of 'the Jews' with his statements about the cosmos.[128] The 'world' rejects Jesus (John 1.10; 3.19) and hates him (John 7.7). It is not capable of recognizing and acknowledging him (John 17.25), and cannot receive the Spirit of truth (John 14.17). Like Jesus (John 8.23), so also the disciples are not ἐκ τοῦ κόσμου (of the world) (John 15.19; 17.14, 16), and must therefore endure the world's hatred (John 15.18–19; 17.14; cf. further John 16.20, 33). Finally, the cosmos is the realm of the Adversary's rule (ἄρχων τοῦ κόσμου [ruler of the world] John 12.31; 14.30; 16.11), whose power is already fundamentally broken, but still has an effect. The correspondence between οἱ Ἰουδαῖοι (the Jews) and ὁ κόσμος (the world) is also clearly seen in John 14–17, where 38 of the 78 references to the cosmos are found, but Ἰουδαῖος is not found at all. The function of the Ἰουδαῖοι (Jews) in the life of Jesus on the level internal to the text is now taken over in the farewell discourses by the cosmos for the hearers and readers external to the text. What happens to Jesus at the story level at the hands of 'the Jews' is now suffered in the present by the church at the hands of 'the world.' 'The Jews' serve John at the level of the story primarily as a paradigm for the crisis of the world confronted by the revelatory event.[129]

---

[127] On this point cf. Schnackenburg, *John* 2.213–215.

[128] Cf. among others, Bultmann, *John* 239; Blank, *Krisis* 231ff.; Erich Grässer, 'Die anti-jüdische Polemik im Johannesevangelium,' in *Der Alte Bund im Neuen*, ed. E. Grässer (Tübingen: J. C. B. Mohr [Paul Siebeck], 1985) 150–151; Günther Baumbach, 'Gemeinde und Welt im Johannesevangelium,' *Kairos* 14 (1972) 123–124.

[129] On this point cf. especially Bultmann, *John* 86 and *Theology of the New Testament* (see above 2) 2.26ff.; Grässer, 'Polemik' 152–153; Bauer, *Johannesevangelium* 28–29. On the problem of the purported 'anti-Judaism' in John, cf. the balanced reflections in Franz Mußner, *Traktat über die Juden* (München: Kaiser, 1979) 281ff.; Ferdinand Hahn, '"Die Juden" im Johannesevangelium,' in *Kontinuität und Einheit* (FS F. Mußner), eds. P. G. Müller and W. Stenger (Freiburg: Herder, 1981) 430–438.

Doubtless there were conflicts with the Jewish environment in the history of the Johannine school, which find their deposit in the texts of the Gospel of John as elements of the life of Jesus (cf. e.g., John 9; 16.1–4; 19.38). But these debates no longer play a decisive role for the Johannine school at the *current* situation when the Gospel of John was composed.[130] The process of disengagement of Christianity from Judaism had already begun in a comprehensive way with the Pauline mission to the Gentiles, and is already reflected in the oldest New Testament traditions (cf. Luke 6.22–23; 1 Thess. 2.14–16). The Fourth Gospel looks back on this painful separation.[131] The Letters of John confirm this state of affairs, for they lack any polemic against the unbelieving Jews, the term Ἰουδαῖος in fact being entirely missing.[132]

Weighty objections may be made to the idea that there was a direct connection between the ἀποσυνάγωγος (put out of the synagogue) in John 9.22; 12.42; 16.2 and (בִּרְכַּת הַמִּינִים) and its insertion into the Eighteen Benedictions by Samuel the Small, which is supposed to have happened at the so-called Synod of Jamnia between 85 and 90 CE:[133] (1) The events at Jamnia cannot be precisely dated. (2) The text of the Birkat ha-minim can no longer be reconstructed. (3) The term מִינִים ('heretics') does not refer primarily to Jewish Christians. (4) The introduction of the term נוֹצְרִים (Jewish Christians) happened only at a later period.[134] Very likely the inser-

---

[130] Cf. M. Hengel, *The Johannine Question* 121: 'The immediate controversy with the Jews has long ceased to be the main theme of the school.'

[131] Hengel, *Die johanneische Frage* 298; *Johannine Question* 119 rightly emphasizes that the Johannine school had been separate from the synagogue for a long time. 'The "expulsion" lies quite far in the past and was not dependent on one historical act of excommunication . . .'

[132] This observation retains its importance even if the Letters were written after the Gospel. How is one to imagine the history of Johannine theology, if ca. 10 years after the composition of the Gospel the theme that is supposed to have dominated it appears to have vanished from sight?

[133] One need only refer to Brown, *John* 1.lxxxv; 35ff. (first edition of the Gospel around 80 CE, before the emergence of the decree of excommunication); Lindars, *John* 35; Becker, *John* 1.56–57; Smalley, *John* 83; Schnackenburg, *John* 2. 250; Schulz, *Johannesevangelium* 145; Barrett, *John* 108; Martyn, *History and Theology* 31ff.; Wengst, *Bedrängte Gemeinde* 75ff.; R. Leistner, *Antijudaismus im Johannesevangelium* (Frankfurt: Lang, 1974) 50–51; Severino Pancaro, *The Law in the Fourth Gospel*, NT.S 42 (Leiden: E. J. Brill, 1975) 245ff.; Wolfgang Trilling, 'Gegner Jesu – Widersacher der Gemeinde – Repräsentanten der "Welt". Das Johannesevangelium und die Juden,' in *Studien zur Jesusüberlieferung*, ed. W. Trilling. SBAB 1 (Stuttgart: Katholisches Bibelwerk, 1988) (209–131) 218–219; Onuki, *Gemeinde und Welt* 31ff.; Wolfgang Wiefel, 'Die Scheidung von Gemeinde und Welt im Johannesevangelium auf dem Hintergrund der Trennung von Kirche und Synagoge,' ThZ 35 (1979) (213–227) 226; Grässer, 'Polemik' 148; Rodney A. Whitacre, *Johannine Polemic*, SBLDS 67 (Chico: Scholars Press, 1982) 7ff.

[134] The reference to נוֹצְרִים is not considered original by e.g., Gustav Hoennicke, *Das Judenchristentum* (Berlin: Trowitzsch & Sohn, 1908) 388–389; Moriz Friedländer, *Die religiösen Bewegungen innerhalb des Judentums im Zeitalter Jesu* (Berlin: Georg Reimer, 1905) 223; Michael Avi-Yonah, *Geschichte der Juden im Zeitalter des Talmud* (Berlin: Walter de Gruyter, 1962) 141–142; Johann Maier, *Jüdische Auseinandersetzung mit dem Christentum in der Antike*, EdF 177

tion of the Birkat ha-minim was an inner-Jewish event, directed against all groups that posed a danger to the unity of the Jewish community, and so must be understood as primarily an act within Judaism.[135]

It is not therefore the influence of contemporary debates with Jews, but Christological interests and dramatic strategy that influence the way 'the Jews' are characterized in the Johannine presentation. While in John 1–4 the Jews are characterized in a positive or neutral manner, with chapter five there begins a debate between Jesus and the Jews that constantly escalates, that finally finds its climax in John 11.47–53. Each of these lines of the story is taken up again in the passion narrative. Here the Jews emerge again as Jesus' opponents (cf. John 18.36; 19.7, 12, 38b), while at the same time Jesus is for John in a profoundly true sense the 'King of the Jews' (cf. John 19.3, 14, 19, 21–22).

The conflict with *docetic false teachers* documented in the Johannine letters (see above 8.4.8) also shapes the central features of the Christology of the Gospel of John.[136] The evangelist begins with a clearly anti-docetic accent with his emphasis on the incarnation of the preexistent Logos in John 1.14. The miracles are real deeds of the Revealer in the world, deeds that cannot be overlooked. John emphasizes the factuality of the saving act in baptism (John 3.3, 5) and eucharist (John 6.51c–58; 19, 34b, 35), that presuppose the reality of Jesus' own incarnation and suffering. For John, the cross is the place where salvation occurs (John 19.28–30); for John, Jesus' way stands under the perspective of the cross from the very beginning (see below 8.5.5). As the docetists separate the earthly Jesus from the

---

(Darmstadt: Wissenschaftliche Buchgesellschaft, 1982) 137ff.; Peter Schäfer, 'Die sogenannte Synode von Jabne,' *Jud* 31 (1975) (54–64, 116–124) 60; and in *Geschichte der Juden in der Antike* (Stuttgart – Neukirchen 1983) 54; R. Kimelman, '"Birkat-Ha-Minim" and the Lack of Evidence for an Anti-Christian Jewish Prayer in Late Antiquity", in *Jewish and Christian Self-Definition*, ed. E. P. Sanders et al. (Philadelphia: Fortress, 1981) 232ff.; Stephen T. Katz, 'Issues in the Separation of Judaism and Christianity after 70 CE: A Reconsideration,' JBL 103 (1984) 63–68, 74; David Flusser, 'Das Schisma zwischen Judentum und Christentum,' EvTh 40 (1980) 229–230; Karl M. Fischer, *Das Urchristentum* (see above 7.2.3) 131.

[135] Schäfer, 'Synode,' 60; Günter Stemberger, 'Die sogenannte "Synode von Jabne" und das frühe Christentum,' *Kairos* 19 (1977) 18; Maier, *Auseinandersetzung* 140.

[136] On the anti-docetic tendency of the Fourth Gospel, cf. Edwyn C. Hoskyns (- F.N. Davey), *The Fourth Gospel* (London: Faber and Faber 1947²) 48–57; Lindars, *John* 61–63; Eduard Schweizer, 'Jesus der Zeuge Gottes. Zum Problem des Doketismus im Johannesevangelium,' in *Studies in John* (FS J.N. Sevenster), NT.S 24 (Leiden: E. J. Brill, 1970) 161–168; Carsten Colpe, 'Gnosis' II, *RAC* 11 (1981) 611; Schnelle, *Antidocetic Christology* passim; Schmithals, *Johannesevangelium und Johannesbriefe* 431–432; Roland Deines, *Jüdische Steingefäße und pharisäische Frömmigkeit*, WUNT 2.52 (Tübingen: J. C. B. Mohr [Paul Siebeck], 1993) 249, 274–275; Hengel, *Die johanneische Frage* 183 note 91, 194, 265 and often; *The Johannine Question* 63 notes 50, 68, 103 and often. An anti-docetic perspective in John is disputed by e.g., Ulrich B. Müller, *Die Menschwerdung des Gottessohnes*, SBS 140 (Stuttgart: Katholisches Bibelwerk, 1990) 62–83; Becker, *John* 2.745–752.

heavenly Christ, so the evangelist insists on the identity of the historical Jesus with the heavenly Christ (John 20.31). John explicitly emphasizes the unity of the Christian community (cf. e.g., John 17.11, 21) that is endangered by the work of the false teachers (cf. 1 John 2.19).

But the situation of the Johannine community cannot be adequately explained only in terms of the fronts on which it was engaged with opponents. The self-understanding of the Johannine Christians is primarily shaped and characterized by its confession of Christ (see below 8.5.9). The Gospel of John originated in the *post-Easter anamnesis* of the Christ event (cf. John 2.17, 22; 12.16; 13.7) under the leadership of the Paraclete (cf. John 14.26).[137] Just as the Paraclete determines the present of the community and reveals the future to it, the 'Beloved Disciple' uniquely connects the community with the past of the earthly work of Jesus.[138] He testifies to the reality of Jesus' death on the cross (John 19.34b–35) and becomes the first witness of the Easter event (John 20.2–10). He is Jesus' hermeneut and the spokesperson for the circle of disciples (John 13.23–26a). In the time of turmoil and doubt, he remains true to his master (John 18.15–18), and thus becomes the true witness beneath the cross and the true disciple of Jesus (John 19.25–27).

The literary figure of the Beloved Disciple probably represents the founder of the Johannine school, the presbyter of 2–3 John who is also identical with the presbyter John mentioned by Papias (see above 8.2.2). When after Easter the evangelist makes the founder of the Johannine school into the faithful eyewitness and guarantor of the tradition, the tradition comes full circle: with the 'Beloved Disciple' and the Paraclete John achieves a double meshing of the temporal levels with regard to both past and future, in which Easter serves respectively as midst and beginning point. Thus the Johannine community knows itself to be related in a special way to both the earthly Jesus and the exalted Lord; the Johannine Christians are διδακτοὶ θεοῦ (taught of God) (John 6.45). It is from this self-awareness and self-understanding that the Johannine Christians carry out their mission (cf. John 4.5–42; 7.35–36; 12.20–22; 17.18, 20, 21; 20.22)[139], celebrate the sacraments (John 3.5; 6.51c–58; 19.34b–35) and put the love command into effect in their midst (cf. John 13.34–35).

---

[137] On Johannine pneumatology cf. Gary M. Burge, *The Anointed Community* (Grand Rapids: Wm. B. Eerdmans, 1987).

[138] On the Beloved Disciples texts, cf. Thorwald Lorenzen, *Der Lieblingsjünger im Johannesevangelium*, SBS 55 (Stuttgart: Katholisches Bibelwerk, 1971); Joachim Kügler, *Der Jünger, den Jesus liebte*, SBB 16 (Stuttgart: Katholisches Bibelwerk, 1988).

[139] Cf. Miguel Rodriguez Ruiz, *Der Missionsgedanke des Johannesevangeliums*, FzB 55 (Würzburg: Echter, 1987).

8.5.5 Outline, Structure, Form

1.1–18	Prologue: Jesus the Logos

1.19–12.50	The ministry of the revealer in the world

1.19–51	The testimony of the Baptist and the first disciples
2.1–4.54	The Cana ring–composition
	2: The wine miracle at Cana, cleansing the temple
	3: Nicodemus: testimony of the Baptist
	4: The Samaritan woman, the second miracle at Cana
5.1–47	Jesus' first debate with the Jews
6.1–71	Jesus in Galilee (feeding the 5000, walking on the water, bread of life, Peter's confession)
7.1–11.54	Increasing conflict with the Jews
	7: Discourse at Feast of Tabernacles (in Jerusalem temple)
	8: Light of the world, children of Abraham
	9: Healing blind man on the Sabbath
	10: The good shepherd, Jesus as Son of God
	11: The raising of Lazarus
11.55–12.50	The final Passover in Jerusalem and Jesus' imminent suffering (anointing in Bethany, procession into Jerusalem)

13.1–20.29	Jesus' revelation to his own; passion; exaltation and appearances of the Risen One

13.1–17.26	The revelation to the disciples
	13.1–30 Footwashing, Jesus' last meal, naming the betrayer, the new commandment of love, Peter's denial announced
	13.31–14.31: First farewell discourse
	15.1–16.33: Second farewell discourse
	17: Jesus' prayer to the Father
18.1–20.29	Passion and Easter
	18: Jesus' arrest, Peter's denial, Jesus before Annas, Jesus before Pilate
	19: Torture, sentencing, crucifixion, death, burial of Jesus
	20: The empty tomb, Jesus' appearances to Mary Magdalene, the disciples, and Thomas

20.30–31	Epilogue: understanding the Gospel

Supplements.

21.1–23	Appearance of the Risen One at the Sea of Tiberias
21.24–25	Second conclusion

The Prologue functions as a programmatic opening text, serving as preliminary direction for the reader, by preparing for and anticipating the
reading of what follows in the manner intended by the evangelist. There is
a clear correspondence between John 1.1–18 and John 20.30–31, where the
evangelist names the goal of his composition of the Gospel: awakening and
renewing faith in Jesus as the Son of God. In this way the readers are introduced to the work, and at the conclusion they may be sure that they have
understood if they can affirm the fundamental confession of faith made at
John 20.31. At the macro-level the Gospel is clearly divided into two major
sections. The portrayal of the ministry of the Revealer in the world (John
1.19–12.50) is followed by the revelation of Jesus to his own including the
appearance of the Risen One (John 13.1–20.29). The numerous references
to the coming passion provide a pervasive structural element throughout
the Gospel as a whole: John 1.29, 36 point to the passion of Jesus, just as do
John 2.1a, 4c. By the scene in which Jesus cleanses the temple (John
2.14–22) the evangelist consciously places the ministry of Jesus from the
very beginning under the perspective of the cross. A further distinctive
feature in comparison with the Synoptics is provided by the trips to
Jerusalem in John 2.13; 5.1; 7.10 where Jesus' destiny is to be fulfilled. In
John 7–10 the evangelist pictures the constantly escalating dispute between
Jesus and the Jews, in dramatic scenes[140] that reach their climax in the raising of Lazarus and the consequent final decision by the Jewish leaders to put
Jesus to death (cf. John 11.1–44, 45–54). Paradoxically, the greatest miracle
in the New Testament becomes the occasion of the decision to kill Jesus.

The footwashing (John 13.1–21) is a key scene in the structure of the
Fourth Gospel, since it functions as the prologue to the second main part
of the composition. John 13.1 takes up the preceding references to the
passion and directs the view of the reader definitively to Jesus' imminent

---

[140] Schenke, *Das Johannesevangelium* 202–223, understands the whole Fourth Gospel as a
drama. Prologue: Setting the mood and perspective (1.1–18); Act I: Exposition (1.19–3.21); Act
II: Repetition, the plot thickens (3.22–5.46); Act III: Climax (6.1–10.39); Act IV: Peripetie
(Journeys) (10.40–12.36); Epilogue I: the balance-sheet of unbelief (12.37–50); Act V:
Departure/catastrophe (13.1–20.29); Epilogue II: the balance-sheet of faith (20.30–31); Postlude:
Future perspective (21.1–24); Conclusion of the book 21.25. Cf. previously e.g., Emanuel
Hirsch, *Das vierte Evangelium* (Tübingen: J. C. B. Mohr [Paul Siebeck], 1936) 83–91, who sees
the Gospel of John as a drama in seven acts.
   Against this classification is to be objected that in the Gospel of John almost throughout the
entire text dramatic *and* epic stylistic elements are combined in a tensive unity. The evangelist
makes use of a rich repertoire of narrative devices (e.g., dialogue, monologue, reporting sections,
commentary, flashbacks, dramatic intensifications, differing temporal perspectives), which he
effectively applies especially by the constant interweaving of perspectives from the story level
internal to the text and the readers' perspective external to the text. The Gospel of John is not
constructed so as to build up to a resolution of the 'drama' at the end of the story, but the resolution is always present to the reader from the first verse on.

suffering and death. At the same time, the footwashing scene ties together the characteristic themes of the farewell discourses: Jesus' love for his own and the resulting love of the disciples for each other (cf. John 13.15). Already in Luke 22.14–38 the reader can recognize the tendency to expand the brief account of Jesus' presence with his disciples at the last supper (cf. Mark 14.17–21) into a farewell discourse. John takes up this tendency and elaborates the farewell discourses into a central complex of his Gospel as a whole. The farewell discourses do not appear in the comprehensive structure of the Gospel without preparation, for the central keyword ὑπάγω (go away) (cf. John 7.33–34; 8.14, 21–22; 13.3, 33, 36; 14.4–5, 28; 16.5, 10, 17) has already taken hold of this theme early on. As the farewell discourses find their appropriate conclusion in Jesus' high-priestly prayer in John 17, the Johannine passion story of 18.1–20.29 thus follows immediately.

Like Mark, so also John lets his presentation of the ministry of Jesus modulate into the literary genre 'gospel.' As in the case of Mark, so also John encloses his portrayal of Jesus' person and work within the framework of the cross and resurrection. Each evangelist, in differing ways, makes this central theological concept the undergirding motif of the composition of their respective Gospels. Both the ministry of the Logos in the world and the return of the Logos to the Father is placed by John under the perspective of the cross.

8.5.6 Literary Integrity

Modern exegetical work on the Gospel of John has raised strong questions against its literary integrity.[141] Primarily under the influence of the Johannine exegesis of Rudolf Bultmann, it has been supposed even to the present day that the original order of the text of the Fourth Gospel has been disarranged and that there is a secondary editorial layer that has been imposed upon it. Bultmann's considerations proceeded from the hypothesis that the original text of the Fourth Gospel had suffered dislocations and mutilation[142] and was brought into its present arrangement by a redactor who not only sought to restore it to a coherent order, but also provided it with annotations in order to domesticate some of its theological assertions that in his eyes were too radical.

Bultmann did not think, of course, that the redactor had succeeded in

---

[141] A concentrated history of research is given by Haenchen, *John* 1.44–51. For recent summaries, cf. Herbert Kohler, *Kreuz und Menschenwerdung* 85–124.

[142] Cf. Bultmann, *John* 222 note 2. Bultmann also reckons with damage and loss to the original text (cf. *John* 315), and with dislocation of pages; cf. Rudolf Bultmann, 'Hirschs Auslegung des Johannes-Evangeliums,' EvTh 4 (1937) 119. For a critique of the theory of dislocated pages, cf. especially Haenchen, *John* 1.44–51.

restoring the original order, so as an exegete he had to assume this responsibility himself. Thus it is not the final form of the Gospel that is the object of his interpretation, but a hypothetical form of the text purified from all tensions and placed in the presumed original order. This procedure has rightly been considered problematic on the methodological level, since it must be asked whether this original form of the Gospel in fact ever existed, a form of the text reconstructed primarily by source analysis. The claim that the restored text makes more sense and the exploitation of tensions in the order of the text revealed by source analysis are by no means sufficient to justify rearranging the text. Nor can supposed secondary passages be excluded in order to attain the presumed original form of the text. The reconstruction of the original order is dominated by the subjective feelings of the exegete and his delight in reconstructing and recombining, by his theological evaluation of the whole, as documented by the numerous, complicated, and in part contradictory theories of how the Gospel of John originated. Methodologically, a new arrangement of the text is therefore only justified when the *impossibility* of the order of the traditional text can be demonstrated on both the source critical and theological levels.[143] It is with this presupposition that the original order of the text in John 4–7 and John 13–17, and the possibility of smaller additions of a later redactor are to be discussed.

(1) The order of the texts in John 4–7: When it is said in John 6.1 that Jesus went to the other side of the sea, then he must first have been on the opposite side. But in chapter five he is in Jerusalem! On the other hand, chapter six would join well to chapter four, where Jesus is already in Galilee. Likewise, chapter seven follows well after chapter five, since 7.1 presupposes a stay in Judea. 'The original order was then most likely: chapters 4, 6, 5, 7.'[144] In view of this logic must the present order then be

---

[143] What Reinhard Wonneberger, *Redaktion*, FRLANT 156. (Göttingen: Vandenhoeck & Ruprecht, 1992) 95, says about tensions within Old Testament texts applies also to the New Testament: 'That contradictions were not usually ironed out can only be satisfactorily explained when one acknowledges that individual textual units retained a strong life of their own even after having been edited together into larger compositions. That means that the goal of the redaction cannot be seen as producing a united and continuous story, but as a kind of "connected series of pericopes." If one proceeds on the basis that the redactional process was guided by an attempt at a "meaningful connection," then the individual units need not at all be smoothed out to harmonize with each other, since such a "meaningful connection" is not constituted at the level of the sagas and historical materials, and thus is not constituted by mere retelling. This "meaningful connection" requires an actively engaged interpretation, as revealed by the many inserted interpretive comments, and is thus to be located on a higher level of abstraction.' In the Fourth Gospel, the one responsible for this higher level of abstraction in the composition of the various elements in the text and the interpretation connected with it is the redactor John, not an anonymous later editor!

[144] Bultmann, *John* 209. Bultmann's argument is followed with individual modifications by e.g. Schnackenburg, *John* 2.5–9 and Becker, *Johannesevangelium* 1.35.

seen as nonsense? The transition from chapter four to chapter five presents no problems, since the evangelist only mentions the festival in 5.1 in order to bring Jesus to Jerusalem where the miracle and following speech take place. John 2.12–13 shows that jumpy transitions are not exceptional in the Gospel of John (cf. further John 4.3, 43; 7.9, 10; 10.40; 11.54ff.), and that it is obviously possible for the evangelist to have Jesus in Galilee in one verse and in Judea in the next. The Johannine trips to the festivals in Jerusalem are, like several of his instances of setting the scene in unidentifiable locations, 'only a literary medium without historical or chronological value.'[145] They thus do not always require preparation in the context. This is what is illustrated by the very abrupt transition from chapter five to chapter six, but it still does not justify switching the order of the chapters, since John 6.2 clearly presupposes the traditional order of the chapters.[146] John 6.2b refers to both of the miracles narrated in John 4.46–54; 5.1–9ab, and derives from the evangelist (cf. John 2.23b; 4.45; 11.45), to whom the present order of the chapters is to be credited. Besides, the placing of chapter six immediately after chapter four still does not produce a smooth order, for John 6.1 presupposes that Jesus is staying on the west bank of the sea of Gennesaret – more particularly, in Capernaum, to which he returns after John 6.17, 24 – but according to John 4.46 he is in Cana and according to John 4.54 merely in Galilee. So also John 7.1–14 is to be attributed to the evangelist,[147] who with this Galilean episode not only connects chapters six and seven, but ultimately brings Jesus to Jerusalem, where on a very solemn festival day he again declares his commission from God and is rejected.

The present order of the chapters in John 4–7 is accordingly not to be seen as the unhappy effort of a later redactor to reconstruct a work that had fallen into disorder, nor is it the unpersuasive, problematic new composition of such a later redactor, but is the order intended by the evangelist John, whose goal was to bring Jesus repeatedly to Jerusalem where he carries on his debate with the unbelieving cosmos and where he will fulfill his destiny.[148]

---

[145] Haenchen, *John* 1.243; cf. further Bauer, *Johannesevangelium* 251.

[146] Bultmann, *John* 211 note 4 regards v. 2 as probably an addition of the evangelist, but thinks that it refers only to John 4.46–54 as an example of Jesus' miracles. However, in my opinion the plural formulation in John 6.2 must be understood as presupposing John 4.46–54 *and* 5.1–9ab.

[147] Cf. Schnackenburg, *John* 136ff. Probably Jesus leaves Jerusalem once again in connection with the raising of Lazarus (cf. John 10.40–42; 11.54; 12.12), but this does not change the function of the trip to the Feast of Booths.

[148] This tendency is taken up and sharpened in John 7–10; cf. Ludger Schenke, 'John 7–10: Eine dramatische Szene,' ZNW 80 (1989) 172–192.

(2) The order of chapters 13–17.[149] An additional crucial point of Johannine literary criticism is the way in which John 14.31c and 18.1 fit neatly together, along with the awkward transition between John 14.31c and 15.1. Two models have emerged as important in the effort to explain the present form of the text: (1) Solution of the problems by rearrangements of the text. Thus Bultmann reckons with the original order John 13.1–30; 17.1–26; 13.31–35; 15.1–16.33; 13.36–14.31.[150] Apart from methodological considerations, the chief objection to be posed against Bultmann's procedure is that it does not succeed in reconstructing a 'better' text. This approach shatters against John 17, which forms the high point and meaningful conclusion of the Farewell Discourses. As Jesus has been speaking with his disciples, now in the hour of his departure he turns in prayer to his Father. (2) The second attempt at a solution regards chapters 15–17 as the supplement of a later redactor. This hypothesis, advocated by R. Schnackenburg[151] and J. Becker[152] among others, shatters on the editorial procedure of the redactor that must be presupposed. By unskillfully adding John 15–17 between John 14.31 and 18.1 he would have created all the problems that have occupied exegesis in this century. The only way he could have avoided all these difficulties would have been by placing chapters 15–17 before John 14.30, thereby constructing a 'satisfying' order. Finally, the post–Johannine character of chapters 15–17 cannot be proven.

On the other hand, the procedure of the evangelist himself becomes clear when one attends to the tradition he has taken up. Beside John 14.31c there is a series of references that John knows from the passion traditions also taken over and edited by Mark (see below 8.5.7). Since in John 14.30b he obviously makes reference to Mark 14.42b, and in John 14.31c to Mark 14.42a, the supposition that the evangelist also knew the tradition of Jesus' arrest (Mark 14.43ff.) is not beside the point, for this tradition presupposes the preceding narrative.[153] Not only is it the case that a close connection to v. 42 is established by the introductory expression ἔτι αὐτοῦ λαλοῦντος (while he was still speaking) in Mark 14.43, but with these words the pre-Markan tradition shows that Jesus had said something else before the encounter with Judas. Linguistically, the present participle portrays quite

---

[149] On this cf. Udo Schnelle, 'Die Abschiedsreden im Johannesevangelium,' ZNW 80 (1989) 64–79.

[150] Cf. Bultmann, *John* 457–461.

[151] Cf. Schnackenburg, *John* 3.89–91.

[152] Cf. J. Becker, *Johannesevangelium* 2.572–573.

[153] Cf. Joachim Gnilka, *Markusevangelium* (see 3.4.1) 2.266–267; Rudolf Pesch, *Markusevangelium* (see above 3.4.1) 2.397.

precisely an event happening at the same time as the main verb, and is by no means to be referred to what had been said previously. The pre-Markan tradition thus knew of words of Jesus on the way to the encounter with those who would arrest him. Thus for the Fourth evangelist a literary location was already provided by the tradition into which additional traditions from his school as well as texts he had composed himself could be integrated into the narrative line of his Gospel. Psychological considerations about the length of the way or of Jesus' speech are not appropriate, since the literary procedure under consideration here is not at all unusual for the evangelist. Abrupt transitions are not unusual for John, especially since he is acquainted with the literary technique of taking up again the narrative thread once it has been temporarily placed aside (cf. e.g., John 2.1–11 with 4.46; 7.14 with 7.25–30; John 9 with John 10.21; John 11.1–45 with 12.9; John 12.15, 16 with 18.33ff.), a technique also present in 18.1. There is also a sense in which a certain parallel to the procedure of the evangelist in John 14.31c; 15.1; 18.1 is provided by the trips to Jesus to the Jerusalem festivals (John 2.13; 5.1; 7.10), which are also without preparation in their contexts and serve only the one goal of bringing Jesus to the place of his enemies. The insertion of John 15–17 between John 14.31 and 18.1 can thus be understood as a literary procedure that has a point of contact in the report in the pre-Johannine tradition that Jesus said something to his disciples after his command to depart from the table but before his encounter with Judas at the arrest.

This procedure of the evangelist is significant at not only the internal plane of the story, but also the external plane of the reader, and thus for the Johannine community: the command of Jesus in John 14.31c has the character of a signal, since for the post-Easter community of Johannine readers, the events that follow Jesus' command are already present for the readers, so that the strong ethical and ecclesiological orientation of John 15–17 is appropriate. Jesus' departure from the table signals the situation that first arrived after the death and resurrection of the Son of God, the situation of the hearers and readers of the Gospel of John themselves. The thoroughly parenetic character of John 15–17 thus represents an appropriate continuation of John 14, in that now the community is addressed under the presupposition of the revelatory event (cf. the indicative in John 5.3, 9) concerning the appropriation and testing of salvation in their own experience.[154]

---

[154] Cf. Onuki, *Gemeinde und Welt* 125ff. Contra Schnackenburg, *John* 3.106ff. and Becker, *Johannesevangelium* 2.572ff., who regard this change of perspective as their main argument that chapters 15–17 are to be attributed to a later redactor.

(3) Secondary additions: A relative consensus exists among scholars on the secondary character of John 21. Linguistic and stylistic peculiarities cannot prove that John 21 is secondary,[155] but the numerous arguments based on content are compelling. In chapter 21 the previously-lacking epiphanies in Galilee are added, but in such a way that the appearance of Jesus to his disciples in John 20.19–29 is ignored. After the conferral of the Holy Spirit upon them and their commissioning (John 20.21–22) the disciples return to their old job of fishing, which has not previously been mentioned in the Gospel at all. In addition, John 20.29 excludes any subsequent appearance, for from now on the principle of believing-without-seeing applies. That chapter 21 is a later addition is also indicated by the enumeration in v. 14, since the two previous appearances in John 20.19–23, 24–29 are presupposed and supplemented. The sons of Zebedee appear in John 21.2, and it must be asked why the reader here learns for the first time that Nathanael comes from Cana. Furthermore, in John 21.24–25 the authors of chapter 21 and possibly the editors of the whole Gospel identify themselves. Their testimony about the Beloved Disciple stands in a double tension with John 1–20: (1) only in the appendix does the Beloved Disciple become the author of the whole Gospel; (2) John 21 corrects the relation between Peter and the Beloved Disciple. In John 1–20 Peter has no particular significance, is not the first one called (cf. John 1.40ff.: Andrew brings him to Jesus); he is only one of several disciples. The appearance stories in John 20 report nothing of a first appearance to Peter. But now in chapter 21, Peter is clearly exalted above the Beloved Disciple, Jesus installs him in the office of shepherd, and thereby constitutes him his earthly representative (John 21.15–17; contrast John 19.25–27!). Finally, in John 20.30–31 the proper conclusion of the book has already been presented, which clearly shows that the second conclusion in John 21.24–25 is secondary.[156] In John 21.24 the editors of the present Gospel themselves

---

[155] Important *hapax legomena* are παιδία (children) in 21.5 as address to the disciples and ἀδελφοί (brothers and sisters) in 21.23 as a descriptive term for Christians.

[156] Representative of those who regard John 21 as secondary: Bultmann, *John* 700ff.; Haenchen, *John* 2.218ff.; Becker, *Johannesevangelium* 2.758ff.; Schneider, *Johannesevangelium* 327; Barrett, *John* 551ff.; Wengst, *Bedrängte Gemeinde* 25–26; Michael Lattke, 'Joh 20,30f als Buchschluß,' ZNW 78 (1978) 288–292, who sees in Tertullian, *Adversus Praxean* 25.4, documentation 'that the Fourth Gospel apparently circulated for some time without the "Epilogue"' (*ibid.* 289). Examples of those who consider John 21 to be original are Bauer, *Johannesevangelium* 234–235; Brown, *John* 2.1077ff. (Epilogue); Paul S. Minear, 'The Original Function of John 21,' JBL 102 (1983) 85–98; Günter Reim, 'Johannes 21 – Ein Anhang?,' in *Studies in New Testament Language and Text* (FS Kilpatrick), NT.S XLIV (Leiden: E. J. Brill, 1976) 330–337. Thyen, 'Johannesevangelium' 210 and often, elevates the 'Epilogue' of John 21 to become the key for understanding the whole Fourth Gospel; for him all the threads of the narrative come together here.

distinguish between their contribution (John 21) and the preceding text (John 1–20).

In recent exegesis the issue of secondary editorial contributions within the Fourth Gospel is no longer dealt with under the easily-misunderstood category of an 'ecclesiastical redactor,' but there is still interest in identifying texts that belong to a post-Gospel redaction. From the point of view of content and literary criticism, some texts that are still to be considered serious candidates for such a secondary redactional layer are 5.28–29; 6.39, 40, 44, 54; 12.48 (futuristic eschatology) and John 6.51c–58; 19.34b–35 (eucharist).

The question of whether statements of future eschatology in the Fourth Gospel are original is, taken strictly, not a problem of literary criticism, but depends primarily on how the theology of the Gospel is evaluated (see below 8.5.9). The eucharistic section John 6.51c–58 stands out from the preceding traditional discourse on the bread of life[157] by the new level of argumentation. The bread from heaven is now Jesus' flesh and blood with the bodily reality of the redeemer standing clearly as the central focus. Thus on the one hand John develops the theme of the bread of life further, while at the same time placing an anti-docetic accent on it with his emphasis on the incarnation of Jesus Christ and the believer's eucharistic participation in his suffering. Recourse to a post-Johannine redaction is not necessary to explain either the literary form or the theological intention of John 6.51c–58.

Neither is the absence of the concept of faith in John 6.51c–58 an indication of the secondary character of this passage. Rather, the evangelist obviously presupposes that participants in the eucharist are believers in Jesus as the Christ. Moreover, the composition of John 6 actually reaches its high point in this eucharistic section. The redactional verses 26–29 prepare for the subject of the pre-Johannine bread-of-life discourse (John 6.30–51ab) and the eucharist section (6.51c–58) shaped by the evangelist, and at the same time bind the two major sections of the chapter together (6.1–25, 30–58).[158] Neither can John 19.34b–35 be attributed to a post-

---

[157] On this point cf. Schnelle, *Antidocetic Christology* 201–202.

[158] John 6.51c–58 is regarded as a meaningful continuation of the bread of life discourse on the plane of the evangelist by, among others, Ruckstuhl, *Einheit* 243ff.; Eduard Schweizer, 'Das johanneische Zeugnis vom Herrenmahl,' in *Neotestamentica*, ed. E. Schweizer (Zürich: Zwingli, 1963) 371–396; Peder Borgen, *Bread from Heaven*, NT.S X (Leiden: E. J. Brill, 1981²); Ludger Schenke, 'Die formale und gedankliche Struktur von John 6,26–58,' BZ 24 (1980) 21–41; and 'Die literarische Vorgeschichte von John 6,26–58,' BZ 29 (1985) 68–89; Schnelle, *Antidocetic Christology* 194–208 (extensive and detailed grounding!); Schmithals, *Johannesevangelium und Johannesbriefe* 355. John 6,51c–58 is included among texts that point to a post-Johannine redaction, according to R. Bultmann, *John* 161–161; Richter, *Studien* 105ff.; Becker, *Johannesevangelium* I 263ff.

Johannine redaction,[159] for both stylistic and thematic considerations point to the evangelist as the author of this section. At the conclusion of the passion narrative the evangelist in 19.34b–35 once more formulates his anti-docetic understanding of the death of Jesus, claims the testimony of the Beloved Disciple as the acknowledged guarantor of the Johannine tradition, and thereby validates the sacramental practice of his church.

John 1–20 can be understood as a literary unity, except for the passages that are clearly secondary from the point of view of text criticism (5.3b–4; 7.53–8.11 and the gloss at John 4.2).[160] The evangelist presents himself in John 20.30–31 as an author who selects his material critically and shapes it according to theological reflections, and who wrote his Gospel on the basis of numerous traditions he had at his disposal.

8.5.7 Traditions, Sources

The agenda for the discussion of sources and/or traditions used by the Gospel of John was determined for a long time by the source theories of Rudolf Bultmann. On the basis of stylistic and linguistic characteristics and such phenomena as the enumeration of miracles in John 2.11 and 4.54, Bultmann postulated a 'Signs Source,' a source of 'Revelation Discourses,' and a source for the passion story.[161]

Today it is generally acknowledged that John 18.1–19.30 forms the basis of the Johannine *passion story*. It is composed primarily of the special traditions of the Johannine school, which probably lay before the evangelist in written form and were edited by him.[162] Among the redactional supplements to the pre-Johannine passion traditions we may identify the following: John 18.4–9, 13b, 14, 15b, 16, 19b–21, 23, 24, 28b, 29, 32, 33a, 34–38a; 19.4, 5, 7–11, 20–22, 23a, 26–28a.[163] Similarly, the Johannine portrayal of the crucifixion, burial of Jesus (John 19.30–42), and the resurrection and appearance stories in John 20 have their basis in pre-Johannine traditions. We may here list as redaction of the evangelist: John 19.31c, 34b, 35, 39, 40c, 42b; 20.2, 3b, 4, 5b, 6, 8, 10, 11a, 12, 13, 14a, 17b,

---

[159] For detailed arguments and analysis, cf. Schnelle, *Antidocetic Christology* 208–210.

[160] Hengel, *Die johanneische Frage* 224–264; *Johannine Question* 83–101 also votes for the unity of John 1–20.

[161] The Greek texts of the 'sources' postulated by Bultmann are printed in D. Moody Smith, *The Composition and Order of the Fourth Gospel* (New Haven: Yale; London: 1965) 23–34 ('revelatory discourses'), 38–44 ('signs source). 48–51 ('passion source').

[162] For evidence and rationale, cf. Udo Schnelle, 'Johannes und die Synoptiker,' in *The Four Gospels* (FS F. Neirynck), ed. Franz Van Segbroeck et al., BETL 100 (Leuven: Leuven University Press, 1992) 1799–1814.

[163] On this point cf. the reconstruction (varying in details) in Anton Dauer, *Die Passionsgeschichte im Johannesevangelium*, StANT 30 (München: Kösel, 1972) 334.

21, 24–29. There can be no talk of a comprehensive connected pre-Johannine passion story. John had at his disposal passion traditions, some of which were very old and reliable, but he has thoroughly reworked them, integrated them into central themes of his theology, and in dependence on Mark has inserted them into the compositional framework he himself has constructed. The will of the evangelist to shape the story according to his own literary and theological intention is just as present in John 18–20 as in the other parts of the Gospel.

R. Bultmann's thesis of a 'revelatory discourse source' in the Gospel of John has rightly not been widely accepted among scholars.[164] Bultmann localized this source in a gnosticizing context and reconstructed it on the basis of certain stylistic features.[165] In his view the speeches were not composed in a prosaic style, but as poetry, their principal stylistic feature being (antithetic) parallelism. In Bultmann's view the original Gospel manuscript suffered some sort of partial damage, and was then later edited and rearranged by the 'ecclesiastical redactor,' so that the individual texts of the 'revelatory discourse source' are now found widely separated from each other. But the religious location of the 'revelatory discourse source' posited by Bultmann as well as the reconstruction he presupposed must be regarded as problematic. The literary parallels proposed by Bultmann (Odes of Solomon, Mandean literature, as well as others) are all very much later than the Gospel of John and thus are out of the question for a meaningful comparison. In the reconstruction of the 'source' with the help of stylistic analysis Bultmann was operating in a methodological and hermeneutical circle. Formal and material parallels are lacking outside the Gospel, so that there are no external controls.[166] The methodological problematic of his procedure is seen clearly when the text of the 'source' and the evangelist's own style cannot be distinguished, which Bultmann must admit in several passages.

In recent exegesis the existence of a *'Semeia Source'* has been vigorously disputed. Bultmann supposed that the 'Semeia Source' originated in the propaganda for the Christian faith by former disciples of John the

---

[164] Recently Hans M. Schenke has argued again for a 'revelatory discourse source' in 'Die Rolle der Gnosis in Bultmanns Kommentar zum Johannesevangelium' 58ff. (see above 2.5.8).

[165] The 'revelatory discourse source' is supposed to have included the following texts: 1.1–5, 9–12, 14, 16; 3.6, 8, 11–13, 18, 20, 21, 31–36; 7.37, 38; 4.13, 14, 23, 24; 6.27, 35, 33, 48, 47, 44, 45, 37; 5.17, 19–21, 24–26; 11.25, 26; 5.30–32, 37, 39, 40; 7.16–18; 5.41–44; 8.14, 16, 19; 7.6, 7, 28, 29, 33, 34; 8.50, 54, 55, 43, 42, 44, 47, 45, 46, 51; 8.12; 12.44, 45; 9.39; 12.47–49; 8.50, 23, 28, 29; 9.5, 4; 11.9, 10; 12.35, 36; 10.11, 12, 1–4, 8, 10, 14, 15, 27–30, 9; 12.27–29, 31, 32; 8.31, 32, 34, 35, 38; 17.1, 4–6, 9–14, 16, 17, 20–23; 13.31, 32; 15.1–2, 4–6, 9, 10, 14, 16, 18–20, 22, 24, 26; 16.8, 12–14, 16, 20–24, 28; 14.1–4, 6, 7, 9, 10, 12, 14, 16–19, 26, 27; 18.37.

[166] For a critique of Bultmann's view, see especially Haenchen, 'Literatur zum Johannesevangelium' 305–306 and Schnackenburg, *John* 1.51–52.

Baptist.[167] This source is supposed to have shown 'Jesus as the θεῖος ἄνθρωπος (divine man), whose miraculous knowledge overwhelms those who meet him.'[168] For a long time the assumption of a pre-Johannine 'semeia source' was the uncontested basis of the interpretation of the Gospel of John, with Robert T. Fortna even expanding the 'source' into a 'Signs Gospel.' In recent exegesis, however, the existence of a 'semeia source' or 'Signs Gospel' has rightly been seen as problematic.[169] The enumeration in John 2.11 and 4.54 has been regarded as an essential indication of the existence of a 'signs source.' Accordingly, the 'source' contained an enumeration of miracles, which, however, has only been preserved in the case of the first two miracles. But why does the enumeration break off after the first two miracles? The advocates of the existence of a 'semeia source' cannot give a satisfactory answer to this obvious question. In addition, an analysis of the language of John 2.11 and 4.54 makes it clear that both these verses and the enumeration derive from the evangelist himself. He numbers the two miracles of Jesus in *Cana*, in order to emphasize them as the beginning and end of the first public activity of Jesus. No contradiction to this enumeration is presented by John 2.23 or 4.45, for they give summary reports of miracles in Jerusalem. This means that the primary indication of a Johannine miracle source disappears.

Closely related to the enumeration of miracles is the text John 20.30–31, which is often regarded as the conclusion of the 'semeia source.' Here too

---

[167] Cf. Bultmann, *John* 108 note 6. For a history of research on the 'semeia source,' cf. Gilbert v. Belle, *The Signs Source in the Fourth Gospel*, BETL 106 (Leuven: Leuven University Press, 1994). For arguments supporting the hypothesis of a 'signs source' in addition to Fortna, *The Gospel of Signs*, cf. especially W. Nicol, *The Semeia in the Fourth Gospel*, NT.S 32 (Leiden: E. J. Brill, 1972); Becker, *Johannesevangelium* 1.134–142. According to Becker, the original form of the following texts belong to the 'semeia source:' John 1.19–34; 1.35–51; 2.1–12; 3.22–30; 4.1–42; 4.43–54; 6.1–21; 7.1–13; 5.1–18; 9.1–34; 10.40–42; 11.1–44, 54; 12.37–43; 20.30–31. A variation of the usual thesis is presented by Hans Peter Heekerens, *Die Zeichen-Quelle der johanneischen Redaktion*, SBS 113 (Stuttgart : Katholisches Bibelwerk, 1984). He counts only John 2.1–11, 12; 4.46–54; 21.1–14 as belonging to a common source, incorporated into the Gospel of John by the editor-author of John 21.

[168] Bultmann, *John* 106.

[169] Cf. Schnelle, *Antidocetic Christology* 87–194 (extensive argument and detailed evidence!); Wolfgang J. Bittner, *Jesu Zeichen im Johannesevangelium*, WUNT 2.26 (Tübingen: J. C. B. Mohr [Paul Siebeck], 1987); Daniel Marguerat, 'La "source des signes" existe-t-elle? Reception des recits de miracle dans l'évangile de Jean,' in *La communaute johannique et son histoire*, ed. J. D. Kaestli, J. M. Poffet and J. Zumstein (Geneva 1990) 69–93; Barrett, *John* 36–37; Ruckstuhl and Dschulnigg, *Stilkritik und Verfasserfrage im Johannesevangelium* 238–241; Frans Neirynck, 'The Signs Source in the Fourth Gospel. A Critique of the Hypothesis,' in *Evangelica*, BETL XCIX (Leuven: Leuven University Press, 1991) 2.651–678; Thyen, 'Johannesevangelium' 207; Georg Strecker, *History of New Testament Literature* (see above 1.2) 163; Painter, *Quest for the Messiah* 80–87; Bull, *Gemeinde* 87; Schmithals, *Johannesevangelium und Johannesbriefe* 124–126; Hengel, *Die johanneische Frage* 246–247; *Johannine Question* 91–92; François Vouga, *Geschichte des frühen Christentums* (Tübingen: J. C. B. Mohr [Paul Siebeck], 1993) 10; with some hesitation, now also Schnackenburg, *Jesus in the Gospels* (see above 3.4.9) 240.

analysis of the language shows that these verses certainly go back to the evangelist himself. He uses the σημεῖον concept in order to bring concisely to expression the revelatory quality of Jesus' ministry that evokes faith as pictured in the preceding Gospel narrative, while at the same time characterizing the 'grasping' of the Resurrected One granted to Thomas as a miracle.

Often the supposed tensions, contradictions, and contrasts between the theology of the evangelist and the christological conception of the 'semeia source' are regarded as evidence for its actual existence, with John 4.48 most often pointed out as a key illustration.[170] But here we find no Johannine critique of miracles and the faith based on them in principle, but Jesus at first rejects the mere demand for a miracle, as he does in John 2.4, only to go ahead and accomplish it on his own initiative (cf. the rejection of the demand for signs in Mark 8.11–12; Matt. 12.39–42; 16.1–2, 4; Luke 11.16, 29–32).

Furthermore, the variety of traditions and backgrounds of the pre-Johannine miracle stories, from the viewpoint of the history of religions, makes it difficult to assign them to one consistent tradition, and this speaks against the existence of a 'signs source.' Likewise, the reconstruction of a 'semeia source' is not made possible by the analysis of literary style, since a style distinct from that of the evangelist on the one hand and that of several pericopes of the 'semeia source' does not exist.[171] Finally, there are no parallels to a 'semeia source,' nor is there a recognizably distinctive coherent theology or Christology of the 'semeia source.'

Rather, it is the case that the evangelist John himself integrates a variety of types of miracle stories into his Gospel. Thus the number of miracle stories adopted by John is not accidental, for according to Genesis 2.2 seven is the number of fullness and completion. In addition, the Revelation of John shows that the number seven was significant in the circles within which the Gospel of John was written (cf. Rev. 1.4, 12; 5.1; 8.2; 10.3–4; 12.3). Obviously the number seven is a factor in the Johannine composition, in order to underscore the fullness of Jesus' revelation in the miracle stories. The individual miracle stories are distributed over the public

---

[170] Cf. in exemplary fashion Schottroff, *Der Glaubende und die feindliche Welt* 263ff. In contrast, Bittner, *Jesus Zeichen* 128–134, suggests a new interpretation of John 4.48. He understands v. 48 as a positive rule, formulated on the occasion of the father's request that Jesus heal his son. Jesus 'formulates this saying as a general insight, which was known and acknowledged as a general rule: "If you do not see signs and wonders, you will not believe." In this moment Jesus formulates this saying because he recognizes that the path by which human beings come to faith leads through the experience of σημεῖα (signs)' (*ibid.* 134).

[171] Cf. Ruckstuhl, 'Sprache und Stil im johanneischen Schrifttum,' in *Die literarische Einheit* 304–331.

ministry of Jesus according to a definite plan, and embedded in the constantly intensifying dispute with the Jews, which attains its high point in John 11. The author took up both prominent special traditions of his own school (cf. John 2.1–11; 5.1–9ab; 9; 11) and miracle stories dependent on the Synoptic tradition (John 4.46–54; 6.1–25), which he integrated into his own specific theology in a number of different ways.

The evangelist had at his disposal a collection of *Paraclete sayings* and '*I am' sayings*. The collection of 'I am' sayings probably included the motifs of the seven images of the bread of life (John 6.35a), the light of the world (John 8.12), the door (John 10.7), the shepherd (John 10.11), the resurrection and the life (John 11.25), the way, the truth, and the life (John 14.6), and the vine (John 15.1). The collection of Paraclete sayings is found in John 14.16–17; 14.26; 15.26; 16.7–11; 16.13–15.

Alongside the numerous individual traditions of the Johannine school, the *Old Testament* forms one of the substructures of the Johannine Gospel's composition. Identification-quotations and delimitation-quotations from the Old Testament are found in John 1.23; 1.51; 2.17; 6.31; 6.45; 10.34; 12.13, 15, 27, 38, 40; 13.18; 15.25; 16.22; 19.24, 28, 36, 37; 20.28; in addition, cf. John 3.13; 7.18, 38, 42; 17.12. Among the numerous additional references to the Old Testament, it is frequently the case that no clear distinction can be made between citation, allusion, and reference.[172] An analysis of the quotations shows that as a rule John uses the LXX, but occasionally refers to the Hebrew text. A noticeable feature is the different introductory formulae used in the two main parts of the Gospel. While in the first part of the Gospel the participle γεγραμμένον (written) is used five times in connection with ἐστίν (is) (cf. John 2.17; 6.31; 6.45; 10.34; 12.14),[173] the new introductory formulae in the second main part (from John 12.38) speak explicitly of the fulfillment of God's will in the passion of Jesus Christ. From the point of view of the history of traditions, the Old Testament forms the background for numerous speeches in the Gospel of John (cf. e.g., John 10; 15), which shows that the Old Testament was obviously used as an authority within the Johannine school and by the evangelist himself.

An additional source for the Gospel's composition is represented by the *Synoptic Gospels*. The following points of agreement exist between the Fourth Gospel and the Synoptics:

---

[172] Cf. on this point Günter Reim, *Studien zum alttestamentlichen Hintergrund des Johannesevangeliums*, SNTSMS 22 (Cambridge: Cambridge University Press, 1974) 97–190 and Bruce C. Schuchard, *Scripture within Scripture*, SBL.DS 133 (Atlanta: Scholars Press, 1992).

[173] Cf. further καθὼς εἶπεν (just as he said) in John 1.23; 7.38.

(a) Common narrative texts

John 1.29–34/Mark 1.9–11/Matt. 3.13–17/Luke 3.21–22: Baptism of Jesus

John 2.14–22/Mark 11.15–17/Matt. 21.12–13/Luke 19.45–46: Cleansing of the temple

John 4.46–54/Matt. 8.5–13/Luke 7.1–10: Official at Capernaum

John 5.8, 9/Mark 2.11, 12/Matt. 9.6b–8/Luke 5.24b, 25: Command to the paralytic

John 6.1–15/Mark 6.32–44/Matt. 14.19–21/Luke 9.10b–17: Feeding the 5000

John 6.16–21/Mark 6.45–52/Matt. 14.22–23: Walking on the water

John 6.22–25/Mark 6.53–54; 8.10/Matt. 14.34–35: Crossing the sea

John 6.26/Mark 8.11–13/Matt. 16.1–4; 12.38–39/Luke 11.16; 11.29; 12.54–56: Demand for a sign

John 6.66–71/Mark 8.27–30/Matt. 17.13–20/Luke 9.18–21: Peter's confession

John 12.1–8/Mark 14.3–9/Matt. 26.6–13/Luke 7.36–50; 10.38–42: The anointing in Bethany

John 12.12–19/Mark 11.1–10/Matt. 21.1–9/Luke 19.28–40: The entry into Jerusalem

John 18.3–12/Mark 14.43–50/Matt. 26.47–56/Luke 22.47–53: Jesus' arrest

John 18.25–27/Mark 14.66–72/Matt. 26.69–75/Luke 22.56–62: Peter's denial

John 18.39–40/Mark 15.6–14/Matt. 27.15–23/Luke 23.17–23: Amnesty at Passover

John 19.1–3/Mark 15.16–20a/Matt. 27.27–31a: Jesus is mocked

John 19.16b–19/Mark 15.20b–26/Matt. 27.31–37/Luke 23.33–34: Jesus' crucifixion

John 19.24b–27/Mark 15.40–41/Matt. 27.55–56/Luke 23.49: The witnesses beneath the cross

John 19.38–42/Mark 15.42–46/Matt. 27.57–60/Luke 23.50–54: Jesus' burial

John 20.19–29/Luke 24.36–49: Jesus appears to the disciples

(John 20.2–10, 11–18/Luke 24.12; 24.4: Race to the tomb; appearance of the angel)

(John 21.1–19/Luke 5.1–11: The miraculous draught of fish)

(b) Agreements in the sayings tradition

John 1.27/Mark 1.7/Matt. 3.11b, c/Luke 3.16c, d: 'The one who comes after me . . .'

John 1.33b/Mark 1.8/Matt. 3.11d/Luke 3.16e: 'The one baptizing with the Holy Spirit . . .'

John 1.34/Mark 1.11/Matt. 3.17/Luke 3.22: The heavenly voice

John 1.43/Mark 3.16b/Matt. 16.17/Luke 6.14a: Simon's new name

John 2.19/Mark 14.58/Matt. 26.61; Mark 15.29b/Matt. 27.40a; Acts 6.14: The temple logion

John 4.44/Mark 6.4/Matt. 13.57/Luke 4.24: The prophet not accepted in his own town

John 5.23b/Luke 10.16b: 'Whoever denies me . . . '

John 6.42/Mark 6.3/Matt. 13.55/Luke 4.22: Jesus' parents

John 10.14/Matt. 11.27/Luke 10.22: The mutual knowledge of Father and Son

John 11.27/Matt. 16.16: You are the Christ, the Son of God

John 12.25/Mark 8.35/Matt. 16.25/Luke 9.24: Loving and hating one's life

John 12.27/Mark 14.34ff./Matt. 26.38ff./Luke 22.42: Jesus' distress on the Mount of Olives

John 13.16;15.20/Matt. 10.24/Luke 6.40: The servant is not greater than the master

John 13.20/Mark 9.37b/Luke 9.48b/Matt. 10.40/Luke 10.16: 'Whoever receives the one I send . . . '

John 15.21/Mark 13.13/Matt. 10.22a; 24.9/Luke 21.17: 'For the sake of my name . . . '

John 16.32/Mark 14.27/Matt. 26.31: The scattering of the disciples

John 20.23/Matt. 18.18: Binding and loosing

c) Additional points of contact

John 11.1/Luke 10.38–39: Mary and Martha

John 12.2/Luke 10.40: Martha who serves

John 9.6/Mark 8.23: πτύω (spit) only here in the New Testament

John 11.47, 53/Matt. 26.3–4: The Jewish leaders condemn Jesus to death

John 14.16/Luke 24.49: Jesus sends the Spirit/power from on high

d) Analogical compositions

John 6.1–15/Mark 6.32–44: feeding; John 6.16–21/Mark 6.45–52: walking on the water; John 6.22–25/Mark 6.53–54; 8.10: crossing the sea; John 6.26/Mark 8.11–13: demand for a sign; John 6.66–71/Mark 8.27–33: Peter's confession, John 18.3–12/Mark 14.43–50: arrest; John 18.13–14/Mark 14.53: delivering Jesus to the High Priests; John 18.15–18/Mark 14.54: Peter's denial, part 1; John 18.19–22/Mark 14.55ff.: hearing before the High Priests; John 18.25–27/Mark 14.66–72: Peter's denial, part 2; John 18.28/Mark 15.1: delivery to Pilate 'in the early morning'; John 18.33–38a/Mark 15.2–5: hearing before Pilate; John 18.38b–40/Mark 15.6–12, 15: offer of amnesty; John 19.1–5/Mark 15.15–20: scourging and mocking.

Research on the Gospels[174] has developed four models that have been
used for discussing the relation of the Gospel of John to the Synoptics:
(1) Neither the evangelist John nor his sources nor the later redactional
layers of his Gospel know any Synoptic Gospel.[175] This hypothesis explains
affinities in individual cases in terms of the taking up of individual units of
oral tradition 'from the wide stream'[176] of traditions from and about Jesus.
(2) The evangelist John himself presupposes no Synoptic Gospel, but
the pre-Johannine tradition does manifest a knowledge and reception of
material from the Synoptic Gospels.[177] It is not direct literary dependence,
but the flowing together of a variety of traditions (including Synoptic traditions) at the pre-Johannine level that explains the points of contact evident
in our present texts. (3) The final editorial layer that had thoroughly
reworked the earlier versions of the Gospel of John knew the Synoptic
Gospels and made use of them.[178] The final form of the Gospel of John
(including John 21) cannot be understood independently of the Synoptic
Gospels. (4) The evangelist John (John 1–20) composed his Gospel with an
awareness of the Gospels of Mark and Luke. He chose the new literary
genre 'gospel' as the framework for his life of Jesus and in the process
directly adopted traditions from the Synoptic Gospels and/or Synoptic
traditions reworked by himself and/or his school.[179]

While the obvious agreements between John and details of the Synoptic
Gospels are always open to different possibilities of explanation, John's
adoption of the gospel genre and the compositional analogies speak in favor
of John's knowledge of the Synoptics. If the Fourth Gospel came into
being completely independently of Mark, then within the Johannine circle
the gospel genre must have been invented for the second time. 'He (sc.
John) was thus a second Mark.'[180] Historically, however, it is very improbable that about thirty years after the creation of the gospel genre, and about
ten to twenty years after its adoption by Matthew and Luke, a second theologian reinvented the gospel genre without any awareness of the Gospel of

---

[174] Basic to recent research on this subject is Percival Gardner-Smith, *Saint John and the
Synoptic Gospels* (Cambridge: Cambridge University Press, 1938), who argues for the independence of John from the Synoptics. For the history of research, cf. Josef Blinzler, *Johannes und die
Synoptiker*, SBS 5 (Stuttgart: Katholisches Bibelwerk, 1965); Anton Dauer, *Johannes und Lukas*,
FzB 50 (Würzburg: Echter, 1984) 15–37; Frans Neirynck, 'John and the Synoptics: 1975–1990,'
in Adelbert Denaux (ed.), *John and the Synoptics* 3–62.
[175] Cf. e.g., Becker, *Johannesevangelium* 1.41ff.
[176] *Ibid.* 45.
[177] Cf. e.g., Dauer, *Die Passionsgeschichte im Johannesevangelium* 121, 164 and often; *Johannes
und Lukas* 297 and often.
[178] Cf. e.g. Thyen, 'Johannesevangelium' 208.
[179] Cf. e.g. Barrett, *John* 59–71.
[180] Becker, *Johannesevangelium* 1.47.

Mark. This is the reason why it is often supposed that John already knew some sort of 'basic gospel' or 'basic document' or a 'signs gospel,' which he took up and elaborated.[181] But the pre-Johannine combination of a 'signs source' and the passion story that is necessary for this theory cannot be demonstrated.[182] Moreover, the existence of a 'signs source' has rightly become more and more problematic, so that a 'signs gospel' as a preliminary stage of the Gospel of John evaporates. So also, other preliminary forms such as a 'basic document' can neither be reconstructed with any precision in terms of source analysis nor persuasively classified in terms of form criticism. The grasping after hypothetical sources is unable to solve the problem, but simply shifts it into the twilight zone of lost literature. Rather, the uniqueness and originality of the gospel genre point to Mark as the only extant model for John. Moreover, John takes over from Mark the two constitutive elements of the gospel genre: (1) Jesus Christ as the speaking and acting subject of the gospel (cf. Mark 1.1; 1.14; for John, the Paraclete sayings and the 'I am' sayings); (2) the cross and resurrection as the optical vanishing point of the composition of a gospel (see above 3.4.5/8.5.5).

The compositional analogies between the Markan and Johannine passion stories are very significant:[183]

In the Fourth Gospel, the real decision to put Jesus to death was already made in John 11.47–53, to which the evangelist explicitly refers in John 18.13b–14. This is the reason he does not take over the report of the trial from Mark 14.55–56, especially since the issue there was Jesus' claim to Messiahship, and this had already been answered long before in John's own presentation (cf. John 10.24–25, 33, 36). This also corresponds to the literary procedure observed in John 2.14–22; 12.27–28, in which central elements of the Synoptic passion story are placed earlier in the narrative. Moreover, John also had available the special tradition of a hearing before Annas which he could now work into his portrayal. The Annas/Caiaphas connection immediately before the first account of Peter's denial was probably derived by John from Mark 14.53–54. The comment in v. 53, 'and all the chief priests were assembled' (πάντες οἱ ἀρχιερεῖς), offered the evangelist the possibility of combining his tradition about a hearing before Annas with the reference to Caiaphas, which then is continued in John 18.24 with the delivery of Jesus to Caiaphas. By dividing the scene of Peter's

---

[181] Thus e.g., Fortna, *The Fourth Gospel and its Predecessor* 206, describes his 'Gospel of Signs' as the first Christian gospel, 'purer, simpler, and thus almost certainly earlier than Mark.'

[182] Cf. on this point James M. Robinson, 'The Johannine Trajectory,' in H. Koester and J. M. Robinson, *Trajectories through Early Christianity* (Philadelphia: Fortress Press, 1971); Schnelle, *Antidocetic Christology* 171–177.

[183] Cf. Schnelle, 'Johannes und die Synoptiker' 1805–1813.

denial, John obviously orients his presentation to the two-fold scene of Mark 14.54/14.66–72. John 18.15a takes up Mark 14.54a and John 18.18c corresponds to Mark 14.54b. John extends the three acts of Peter's denial beyond the Markan portrayal (John 18.17, 25–26, 27). With the scene of the hearing before Annas, John fulfills the demand made by Nicodemus for a hearing of Jesus by the Jewish authorities (cf. John 7.50–51). The adoption of Mark 14.65c in John 18.22 shows that the evangelist was aware of the original location and function of the report of the trial in Mark 14.55–65, which he has omitted. In its place he now emphasizes in a summary (John 18.20–21) the public nature of Jesus' preaching and underscores the innocence of the Messiah. With the temporal notice ἦν δὲ πρωΐ (now it was early) in John 18.28 the evangelist makes contact with Mark 15.1, after which he basically stays with the narrative line of the Markan composition.

The brief and inconspicuous Markan scene of the hearing before Pilate (Mark 15.2–5) is elaborated by John into a central section of his passion story. This again lets us see a typical Johannine literary procedure: the composition of comprehensive scenes from individual Synoptic logia (compare John 20.3–10 with Luke 24.12). John obviously adopts the royal motif from Mark 15.2 and formulates the interrogation by Pilate into a high point of his passion story. But here too there are clear indications of adoption of the Markan order: hearing before Pilate (Mark 15.2–5/John 18.33–38a), the offer of amnesty (Mark 15.6–12, 15a/John 18.38b–40), flogging and mocking (Mark 15.15b–20/John 19.1–5). John distinguishes the scenes clearly from each other and thereby increases the dramatic element. While in Mark the demand for crucifixion is the concluding part of the Barabbas scene (Mark 15.13–14), in John it is clearly the Jewish leaders (not the people) who, after the flogging and mocking, respond to the presentation of their king before them with the demand for crucifixion (John 19.6). It is not until John 19.15 that the people then take up the call for Jesus' crucifixion, since in 19.7–15a John has placed the scene he has composed of Jesus' second hearing before Pilate (John 19.8–11) along with special traditions of his school. So too the text sequences that follow John 19.15 manifest agreements between John and Mark. The following points of correspondence are to be noted: the procession to Golgotha and the crucifixion (Mark 15.20b, 22, 24/John 19.17b, 18a), the crucifixion with two other prisoners (Mark 15.27/John 19.18b), the title on the cross (Mark 15.26/John 19.19), the dividing of the garments (Mark 15.24/John 19.23b, 24), the women beneath the cross (Mark 15.40/John 19.25), the offer of a drink to Jesus on the cross (Mark 15.36/John 19.28–29) and Jesus' death (Mark 15.37/John 19.30). To be noted in addition is the adoption of the Markan ἐπεὶ ἦν παρασκευή ('since it was Friday') from Mark 15.42 in John 19.31, for Matthew and Luke omit this temporal signal.

It is obvious that John has shaped central sections of his passion story in dependence on the Markan sequence of pericopes. The differences may be accounted for by the incorporation of pre-Johannine special traditions, redactional passages, and the particular theological intentions of the evangelist. The evangelist may also have known the Gospel of Luke, for the numerous agreements point to lines of connection between the pre-Lucan and pre-Johannine level of tradition. If the Gospel of Luke was known within the Johannine school, then no persuasive reason can be given why the evangelist should not have known it as well. But to be sure, this does not mean that John used either the Gospel of Mark or the Gospel of Luke as sources in the manner in which the Synoptic Gospels are related to each other. The evangelist's procedure was not a wholesale incorporation of material, but intentional adoption of individual traditions corresponding to the goal declared in John 20.30–31. John had numerous special traditions of his school at his disposal, so he did not find it necessary to make extensive use of Mark and Luke as sources.[184]

There is no indication of John's use of authentic letters of Paul, but numerous agreements suggest that there was a connection between Pauline and Johannine traditions in *the Pauline and Johannine schools* in Ephesus.[185]

There are important points of agreement in the realm of Pauline and Johannine Christology (the sending of the pre-existent Son of God, Jesus' death as a giving of himself because of his love, the cross as the place of God's saving act). Like Paul before him, John is the advocate of an exclusive monotheism in a binitarian form. The worship of the one God is

---

[184] Various arguments have also been advanced in recent times for John's knowledge of one or more of the Synoptic Gospels by: Frans Neirynck, 'John and the Synoptics,' in *L'Évangile de Jean*, ed. Marinus de Jonge, BETL 44 (Leuven: University Press, 1977) 73–106; Maurits Sabbe, 'The Arrest of Jesus in Jn 18,1–11 and its Relation to the Synoptic Gospels,' in *L'Évangile de Jean*, ed. Marinus de Jonge, 203–234; Wolfgang Schenk, *Der Passionsbericht nach Markus* (Gütersloh: Gütersloher Verlagshaus [Gerd Mohn], 1974) 127ff.; Wengst, *Bedrängte Gemeinde* 182; Peter Stuhlmacher, 'The Theme: The Gospel and the Gospels,' in *The Gospel and the Gospels*, ed. P. Stuhlmacher (Grand Rapids: William B. Eerdmans, 1991) 15; Rosel Baum-Bodenbender, *Hoheit in Niedrigkeit*, FzB 49 (Würzburg: Echter, 1984) 199–200, 350; Till A. Mohr, *Markus- und Johannespassion*, AThANT 70 (Zürich: Theologischer Verlag, 1982) 250; E. Stegemann, 'Zur Tempelreinigung im Johannesevangelium,' in *Die Hebräische Bibel und ihre zweifache Nachgeschichte* (FS R. Rendtorff), ed. Erhard Blum et al. (Neukirchen: Neukirchener Verlag, 1990) 507; Schmithals, *Johannesevangelium und Johannesbriefe* 123; Hartwig Thyen, 'Johannes und die Synoptiker,' in *John and the Synoptics*. ed. Adelbert Denaux, 81–107 (in addition cf. in this volume the contributions of Frans Neirynck, Charles K. Barrett, René Kieffer, François Vouga, Ulrich Busse, Maurits Sabbe); Hengel, *Die johanneische Frage* 208–209; *Johannine Question* 74–75.

[185] On this point cf. Dieter Zeller, 'Paulus und Johannes,' BZ 27 (1983) 167–182; Schnackenburg, 'Paulinische und johanneische Christologie,' in *John* 4.102–118; Udo Schnelle, 'Paulus und Johannes' (see above 8.1.4); Rudolf Schnackenburg, 'Ephesus: Entwicklung einer Gemeinde von Paulus zu Johannes' (see above 8.1.4).

extended to his only Son.[186] In both Paul and John, in contrast to other New Testament authors, one meets a highly developed concept of the κόσμος (world). In neither Paul nor John does the world have an inherently inferior status, but the power of sin first actualizes the alienation of the world and the perversion of the will of the creator. Paul and John both determine the being of the believer in the world as dialectic existence: the believer lives in the world, not however from the world, but 'from God' or 'in Christ.' Major agreements can also be seen in the realm of anthropology. No metaphysical dualism separates human beings from God, but human beings are historical beings, each of whom is set before the decision of whether to continue to be subject to the powers of flesh and sin that dominate the world, or to accept the liberating Christ event as determinative for his or her life. For both Paul and John, faith is the central means by which the saving event is appropriated. In the Gospel of John, πιστεύω (believe) occurs 98 times (1 John 9 times, πίστις [faith] only 1 John 5.4), but in Matthew only 11 times, in Mark 14 times and in Luke 9 times.[187] Only in Paul do we find 'faith' playing a comparable role: the verb πιστεύω is found 54 times, the noun πίστις 142 times. The object of faith is the saving event accomplished by God in Jesus Christ, which is actualized for human beings as salvation when they accept the Christian message (as illustrations, cf. only Rom. 10.9; 1 Cor. 1.21; Gal. 2.16; John 1.12; 20.31). Both the Pauline and the Johannine ethic are characterized by the reflective connection between indicative and imperative (cf. Gal. 5.25; Rom. 6.2, 12; Phil. 2.12–13; John 13.15, 34–35; 15.9, 10; 1 John 4.19). The imperative as the actualization of a new existence is both based on and results from the indicative of the divine act for the human being. Both Paul and John agree in the way in which they describe the extremely close relationship between the believer and Jesus Christ or God as a mutual 'indwelling.' For Paul, the believer is placed by baptism in the realm of the spiritual Christ (cf. 2 Cor. 5.17), he or she is now ἐν Χριστῷ (in Christ). Corresponding to this, Jesus Christ or God work in the believer as the Spirit (cf. 2 Cor. 13.5; Gal. 2.20a; Rom. 8.9–11). For

---

[186] By no means is Jewish monotheism thereby surrendered, but rather the mediator figures in ancient Judaism (Moses, Enoch, Old Testament heroes, angels, Wisdom, Logos) form the background for this development in the realms of the history of tradition and the history of religion; cf. Larry Hurtado, *One God, One Lord. Early Christian Devotion and Ancient Jewish Monotheism* (Philadelphia: Fortress Press, 1988).

[187] On the understanding of faith in the Synoptic Gospels, cf. the contributions of Georg Strecker, Hans Klein, Ferdinand Hahn, Wolfgang Schenk in *Glaube im Neuen Testament* (FS H. Binder), ed. Ferdinand Hahn and Hans Klein, BThS 7 (Neukirchen: Neukirchener Verlag, 1982). The best discussion of the Pauline and Johannine understanding of faith is still found in Bultmann's *Theology of the New Testament* (see above 2) §28–31, 49–50. For the more recent discussion cf. Ferdinand Hahn, 'Das Glaubensverständnis im Johannesevangelium,' in *Glaube und Eschatologie* (FS W.G. Kümmel), ed. Erich Grässer and Otto Merk (Tübingen: J. C. B. Mohr [Paul Siebeck], 1985) 51–69; U. Schnelle, *The Human Condition* (see above 2.8.9), 49–54, 118–124.

John this means that just as God is in Christ and Christ is in God (cf. John 14.10), the believer abides in Christ (cf. John 6.56; 15.4–7) and Christ abides in the believer (cf. John 15.4–7). In both Paul and John, the Law is no longer a means of salvation, but a witness to the Christ event and an ethical norm (cf. e.g. Rom. 3.21; 10.4; John 1.17). That which Paul struggled against with his critique of the Law is already presupposed by John. This is the explanation for the differences in the linguistic expression used by each in their respective critique of the Law. Since he now found himself in a different situation, John did not find it necessary to adopt Paul's particular form of polemic, which had been strongly affected by his particular circumstances. Nonetheless, he took over the Pauline critique of the Law with a remarkable persistency and sharpness: with the arrival of the Christ event, the Law was no longer an independent witness to divine revelation relevant to salvation. The numerous points of agreement between Pauline and Johannine theology permit the conclusion that, at least at the level of oral tradition, John was aware of Pauline theology.

Study of the Gospel of John reveals a very complex background in terms of the history of traditions. In his composition the evangelist took up many of the traditions of the Johannine school, he obviously found in the Old Testament a witness and confirmation for the Christ event, he appropriated materials from the Gospels of Mark and Luke in varying degrees, and adopted ideas from Pauline theology. The abundance and multiplicity of materials made a selection necessary (cf. John 20.30), and he names the criterion for his selection in John 20.31. He integrated into his Gospel those traditions that in his opinion were appropriate for furthering the understanding of the Christ event and the faith in Jesus Christ as the incarnate Son of God. This process of reception reveals the theological and literary competence of the Fourth Evangelist. Though he did it by reformulating previous traditions and redactions, John brought into being something genuinely new in terms of both narrative and theology.

8.5.8 History-of-religions Standpoint

From the point of view of the history of religion, the main issue in Johannine research in this century has been the question of the relation of the Fourth Gospel to *gnosticism*. Thus Walter Bauer had an extensive discussion of the relevance of the Mandean texts, which had been newly edited in his own time, for the interpretation of the Gospel of John, and Rudolf Bultmann interpreted John against the background of the gnostic myth. So also recent Johannine scholarship has emphasized the proximity of Johannine theology to gnostic views. Thus L. Schottroff states: 'When the Gospel of John was included in the canon, the gnostic understanding of salvation came along with it.'[188] J. Becker describes the Johannine perspective on the whole as 'borderline gnostic' and speaks of a 'gnosticizing theology.'[189] An appropriate treatment of the theme first requires that one attend to chronological issues.[190] Patristic reports do in fact illustrate the history of the reception of the Gospel of John among Christian gnostics (cf. e.g., the commentary on John by Heracleon), but do not permit one to draw any conclusions regarding the relation of gnosticism to the Fourth Gospel's point of origin.

On the significance of Manichaeism, the judgment of A. Böhlig may be taken as representative: 'The New Testament is not to be interpreted from Mani, but Mani from the New Testament.'[191] The Mandean literature was brought together in the seventh and eighth centuries CE in Babylonia. Essential elements were already present in the third and fourth centuries CE, and the oldest components of the Mandean literature (the hymns) could go back as far as the second century CE.[192] Of course the tracing back of traditions through several centuries is burdened with great uncertainty, so that all analyses of the history of the traditions related to Mandean literature that proceed on the basis of locating their themes earlier than the middle of the second century CE must be considered entirely hypothetical. The same applies to the Nag Hammadi texts, which are for the most part to be dated in the midst of the fourth century CE. For many Nag Hammadi texts a lengthy history of tradition and redaction may legitimately be posited, a history that sometimes extends to the middle of the second century CE.

Two documents from the Nag Hammadi corpus are of particular significance for interpreting the Gospel of John: the 'Apocryphon of John' (BG 2; NHC 2.1; 3.1; 4.1) and the 'Trimorphic Protennoia' (NHC 13). In each case, the oldest layer probably originated in the middle of the second century CE, but there is no evidence that Johannine thought was influenced by these or other Nag Hammadi texts. To be sure, there are remarkable parallels between the Protennoia document and the Prologue to the Gospel

---

[188] Schottroff, *Der Glaubende und die feindliche Welt* 295.

[189] Becker, *Johannesevangelium* 1.55; cf. further Schenke and Fischer, *Einleitung* 2.188ff.; Schmithals, *Johannesevangelium und Johannesbriefe* 149, who understand the Fourth Gospel as a witness to Christian gnosticism.

[190] M. Hengel emphatically makes this point in *The Son of God. The Origin of Christology and the History of Jewish-Hellenistic Religion* tr. John Bowden (London: SCM Press, 1976) 33–34.

[191] Alexander Böhlig, 'Neue Initiativen zur Erschließung der koptisch-manichäischen Bibliothek von Medinet Madi,' ZNW 80 (1989) (240–260) 255.

[192] On the chronology of Mandean texts cf. Kurt Rudolph, *Die Mandäer* I, FRLANT 74 (Göttingen: Vandenhoeck & Ruprecht, 1964) 53–58.

of John,[193] but it is out of the question that the Protennoia could have been a source for the Johannine Prologue.[194] Both the reception of the Gospel of John by Heracleon and in the Nag Hammadi writings (Gospel of Truth, Gospel of Philip, Apocryphon of James) and the similarity in content of other Nag Hammadi texts to the Gospel of John (cf. 'The Thunder, Perfect Mind' [NHC 7.2] and 'The Second Treatise of the Great Seth' [NHC 6.2]) indicate that rather than John's having been influenced by preliminary forms of these writings, the Fourth Gospel itself influenced writings in gnostic circles, where it was subjected to a very arbitrary interpretation.[195] Probably early Christianity and gnosticism at first developed independently of each other,[196] until they made contact about the end of the first century CE (cf. 1 Tim. 6.20), which then led to a partial synthesis between Christianity and gnosticism in the first quarter of the second century CE. According to the current state of research on gnosticism it is no longer possible to interpret the Gospel of John on the basis of a fully developed myth of the gnostic redeemer for which Philo could be presented as evidence, as done by Bultmann.[197] According to Bultmann, this myth had the following form:

> From the world of light a divine figure was sent down to the earth that was dominated by demonic powers in order to free the sparks of light that had originated in the world of light, and had been banished to live in human bodies as the result of a primeval fall. The Sent One takes human form and accomplishes on earth the works assigned him by the Father, but in the process he is not 'cut off' from the Father. He reveals himself in his discourses ('I am the shepherd,' etc.), and thus effects a separation between those who see and those who are blind, to whom he appears as a stranger. Those who are his own hear him, and he awakens in them the memory of their true homeland in the world of light, teaches them to recognize their true self, and instructs them in the way back to their heavenly homeland, the way which he himself ascends as the redeemed Redeemer.[198]

---

[193] Cf. the listing in Carsten Colpe, 'Heidnische, jüdische und christliche Überlieferung in den Schriften von Nag Hammadi III,' *JAC* 17 (1974) (109–125) 123.

[194] Cf. Kurt Rudolph, 'Die Nag Hammadi-Texte und ihre Bedeutung für die Gnosisforschung,' ThR 50 (1985) (1–40) 20–21.

[195] To be sure, there can be no talk of a widespread reception of the Gospel of John among the gnostics; cf. Wolfgang G. Röhl, *Die Rezeption des Johannesevangeliums in christlich-gnostischen Schriften aus Nag Hammadi*, EHS 32.428 (Frankfurt: Lang, 1991).

[196] Gnosticism was at first an independent religious phenomenon. On this point cf. Karl W. Tröger, *Das Christentum im zweiten Jahrhundert* (Berlin: Evangelische Verlagsanstalt, 1988) 116–128.

[197] Cf. Christoph Markschies, 'Gnosis/Gnostizismus,' *NBL* I (1991) 869: 'It is not likely that a pre-Christian gnosticism ever existed. No extant sources indicate that it did.'

[198] Rudolf Bultmann, 'Johannesevangelium,' *RGG*³ III (1959) 847.

If for Bultmann the pre-Christian gnostic redeemer myth was still the hermeneutical and historical key to the interpretation of the Gospel of John, current scholarship proceeds on the basis that the correlation of individual elements of the Gospel of John first occurred in the Christian period.[199] To be sure, individual elements of gnostic speculation could already have been formed in the pre-Christian period, but the formation of a comprehensive syncretistic myth did not happen until later in the Christian period, primarily from the second century CE on.[200] It is thus no longer possible to leap over the chronological problems involved in the relationship of early Christianity and gnosticism by referring to a pre-Christian or early Christian redeemer myth.

For a long time the parallels in language, content, and motifs between the Gospel of John and gnostic writings – parallels that are not to be doubted – were regarded as evidence for the proximity of the Gospel of John to gnostic thought. Thus for example both Walter Bauer[201] and Rudolf Bultmann[202] interpreted the two central discourses in John 10.1–18 and 15.1–8, 9–17 against a gnostic background and depreciated the comparable material in the Old Testament. In contrast, one may point out that both speeches are characterized by ideas taken from the Old Testament (for John 10, cf. e.g., Ezek. 34,[203] for John 15, Jer. 2.21 and Isa. 5.1–7a[204]), so that it is not at all necessary to introduce into the discussion the considerably later gnostic texts to explain the Johannine world of images and concepts. No concept or image in the Gospel of John necessarily points to a gnostic origin, but rather parallels may be found throughout to the Old Testament, ancient Judaism, and the writings of early Christianity.[205]

The proximity of the Gospel of John to gnosticism depends to a considerable degree on how gnosticism is defined. Hans Jonas' definition of gnosticism as a specific understanding of existence current in antiquity has been very influential.[206] This broad definition of gnosticism has caused very

---

[199] Cf. Carsten Colpe, 'Gnosis II,' *RAC* 11 (1981) 542.

[200] Thyen, 'Johannesevangelium' 220 appropriately comments: 'It can probably be said that the gnostic redeemer myth was not a deep structure behind the Gospel of John, but was something still in the future when the Gospel of John was written.'

[201] Cf. Bauer, *Johannesevangelium* 143–144, 189–190.

[202] Cf. Bultmann, *Johannesevangelium* 373–374, 378, 530–531 note 5.

[203] Cf. here Michael Rodriguez Ruiz, 'El Discurso del buen Pastor (Jn 10,1–18),' EstB XLVIII (1990) 5–45; Johannes Beutler and Robert T. Fortna, *The Shepherd Discourse of John 10 and its Context*, SNTSMS 67 (Cambridge: Cambridge University Press, 1991).

[204] On this cf. Rainer Borig, *Der wahre Weinstock*, StANT 16 (München: Kösel, 1967).

[205] Cf. as a methodological rule Klaus Berger, 'Gnosis/Gnostizismus I,' *TRE* 13 (1984) 520: 'One may not project a gnostic worldview or a developed gnostic myth on the basis of individual concepts. On the contrary, there is no unified gnostic terminology.'

[206] Cf. Hans Jonas, *Gnosis und spätantiker Geist* I, FRLANT 51 (Göttingen: Vandenhoeck & Ruprecht, 1964³) 12ff.

different movements in late antiquity to be subsumed under the major heading of 'gnosticism,' which has impeded concrete research in the field of the history of religions. At the Messina Conference of 1966 the suggestion was made that 'Gnostizismus' and 'Gnosis' be distinguished. 'Gnostizismus' was accordingly to be used for a specific 'group of systems of the second century CE . . .. In contrast, "Gnosis" was to refer to a "knowledge of divine mysteries reserved for an elite."'[207] But this interpretation did not advance the discussion, since in fact one term was simply exchanged for another: what had previously been called 'Gnosis' is now supposed to be called 'Gnostizismus.' The only innovative suggestions are thus those definitions that precisely designate which fundamental conceptions must be present in order to speak of 'gnosticism.' G. Sellin thus proposes as a definition: 'The world (and human beings as earthly beings) is the creation of a being who has fallen from the world of light (a demiurge) and is therefore the product of a force hostile to God.'[208] If one applies this precise definition of Gnostizismus/Gnosis to the Gospel of John, then the difference between Johannine and gnostic thought stands out clearly. The Prologue already speaks of an anteriority of the good, the creation owes its existence to the work of the preexistent Logos, through whom everything was created (cf. John 1.1–4). It was God's love for the world that sent his Son into the world in order to save those who believe in Jesus Christ (John 3.16; 1 John 4.9). Jesus appears as the σωτὴρ τοῦ κόσμου (savior of the world) (John 4.42, cf. 1 John 2.2), he is the 'Bread of Life' (John 6.30–50) and the 'Light of the World' (John 8.12). Moreover, the Fourth Gospel stands in contrast to gnostic thought by its orientation to the theology of the cross. It anchors salvation in a once-for-all historical event and is thus radically different from the gnostic understanding of human existence in

---

[207] Cf. Carsten Colpe, 'Vorschläge des Messina-Kongresses von 1966 zur Gnosis-Forschung,' in *Christentum und Gnosis*, ed. Walter Eltester, BZNW 37 (Berlin: Walter de Gruyter, 1969) 129–130. [Translator's note: this pair of words is difficult to render consistently into English, but something like 'Gnostic' with a capital 'G' and 'gnosticizing' with a small 'g' perhaps catches the distinction. No attempt has been made in the preceding to emphasize this distinction, as Schnelle does not utilize it.]

[208] Gerhard Sellin, *Der Streit um die Auferstehung der Toten* (see above 2.5.1), 200. A different definition is presented by Carsten Colpe, 'Gnosis II,' *RAC* 11 (1981) 559: 'Gnosis is the function of an organ of cognition, which is a substance, a function that is dualistically divided into two hypostases and is reunited by gnosis.' Chr. Markschies, 'Gnosis/Gnostizismus' 870 names as characteristic motifs of gnosis: (1) the experience of a completely transcendent highest God; (2) the introduction of other divine figures; (3) the evaluation of the world and matter as an evil creation; (4) the introduction of a lower creator god; (5) the explanation of the present negative situation by means of a mythological drama; (6) the revelation of this situation by a transcendent revealer figure; (7) redemption through knowledge; (8) previous determination of classes of human beings; (9) a pronounced dualism at every level.

the world and salvation out of the world.[209] The potential 'gnosticization'
of Johannine images and concepts and their use in later gnostic writings is
not the same as a purported 'gnosticism' in the Gospel of John!

The location of the Gospel of John in its context in the history of
religion may no more be explained in terms of a single factor than can its
context in the history of traditions. It is rooted in the Old Testament and
in the wisdom literature of *Hellenistic Judaism* (cf. e.g., John 1.1–18; 3.16),
while at the same time having indications of a certain proximity to the
thought world of Qumran and the Testaments of the Twelve Patriarchs
(dualism),[210] while individual elements have parallels in Hellenistic philosophy[211] and later gnostic texts, but not in a way that lines of direct
dependence may be constructed.

8.5.9 Basic Theological Ideas

In the Fourth Gospel, the unfolding of the Christ event occurs as post-
Easter anamnesis effected by the Spirit (cf. John 2.17, 22; 12.16; 13.7;
20.9).[212] The presence of the Paraclete (cf. John 14.26) facilitates a
deepened grasp of the meaning of the incarnation, the earthly work,
suffering, exaltation and glorification of Jesus Christ. At the same time, the
Paraclete provides that memory of the work and words of Jesus of which
the Gospel of John is the literary deposit. The Paraclete[213] leads the
community as its helper, hermeneut, teacher, advocate, legal counselor,
representative and witness to Jesus (cf. John 14.15–17, 26; 15.26; 16.7–11,
13–15), and contemporizes the once-for-all saving event. Thus Johannine
thought derives from the consciousness of the Johannine Christians that
they are led by the Paraclete to bring the faith in Jesus Christ to expression
in a distinctive and appropriate manner.

The basis of Johannine thought is the *unity of Father and Son* (cf. John

---

[209] On this point cf. Karl W. Tröger, *Ja oder Nein zur Welt. War der Evangelist Johannes Christ
oder Gnostiker?*, TheolVers VII (Berlin: Evangelische Verlagsanstalt, 1976) 61–80.; Kohler, *Kreuz
und Menschwerdung* 137–139.

[210] On this point cf. Otto Böcher, *Der johanneische Dualismus im Zusammenhang des
nachbiblischen Judentums* (Gütersloh: Gütersloher Verlagshaus Gerd Mohn, 1965); *John and
Qumran* ed. James H. Charlesworth (London: Geoffrey Chapman, 1972); Roland Bergmeier,
Glaube als Gabe bei Johannes, BWANT 112 (Stuttgart: Kohlhammer, 1980).

[211] On Logos philosophy in antiquity, cf. Bernhard Jendorff, *Der Logosbegriff*, EHS R. XX,
Vol. 19 (Frankfurt: Lang, 1976); on the concept of spiritual worship of God not bound to any
particular locality, cf. John 4.21–24 und Seneca, *Epistles* 41.1–2; cf. further Dieter Zeller, 'Jesus
und die Philosophen vor dem Richter (zu Joh 19,8–11),' BZ 37 (1993) 88–92.

[212] Cf. Mußner, *Sehweise* 45ff.; Udo Schnelle, 'Perspektiven der Johannesexegese,' SNTU 15
(1990) (59–72) 61ff.

[213] For the background of the Paraclete concept in the history of religions, cf. Ulrich B.
Müller, 'Die Parakletvorstellung im Johannesevangelium,' ZThK 71 (1975) 31–77.

10.30; 17.21 and often), as its center is the *incarnation* of God in Jesus Christ.[214] This fundamental feature oriented to the incarnation is already seen in the Prologue (John 1.14), which functions as a programmatic opening text to tilt the understanding of the Gospel as a whole in a certain direction. As the narrative of the Gospel proceeds, the revelatory path of the Logos among human beings is developed and the saving significance of Jesus Christ is reflected upon. In the process of this development it is clear that for the Gospel of John too, the work of Jesus in the world stands under the perspective of the cross from the very beginning (cf. John 1.29, 36). Compositionally, the placing of the cleansing of the temple at the beginning of the public ministry of Jesus (John 2.14–22) emphatically underscores the salvific significance of the cross and resurrection. Allusions to the passion permeate the whole Gospel (cf. John 2.1, 4c; 10.11, 15, 17; 11.13; 12.16, 32–33; 13.1–3, 7, 37; 15.13; 17.19; 18.32) in order to make it clear that the Incarnate One is none other than the Crucified One. Incarnation and cross are equally movements of condescending love, just as is the foot washing (John 13.1–20) by which Jesus introduces his own into the new existence of familial love, in that he himself lives it out before them and makes it possible by his cross. Thus also in the Gospel of John the revelatory event reaches its goal on the cross; it is here that the Son fulfills the will of his Father (cf. John 13.1, 32; 14.31; 17.5; 19.11a and often), fulfills the Scripture (John 19.28), and the incarnate Christ speaks the concluding τετέλεσται (it is finished) (19.30). John rests everything on the identity of the Preexistent and Incarnate One with the Crucified and Exalted One, as the Thomas pericope John 20.24–29 makes absolutely plain. The one who suffered such a shameful death on the cross has been exalted by God and is the living Word of God. In John, the exaltation of the Son occurs on the cross (cf. John 12.27–33); the cross remains the place of salvation (not being superseded by the resurrection and ascension).

The *dualism* constitutive for Johannine thought must likewise be understood from the post-Easter remembrance and re-experiencing of the Christ event. John thinks of the decision human beings must make as they confront the incarnate Logos in the categories of rejection and acceptance.[215]

---

[214] Cf. Weder, 'Die Menschwerdung Gottes' 352; additionally Marianne M. Thompson, *The Humanity of Jesus in the Fourth Gospel* (Philadelphia: Fortress Press, 1988). According to W. G. Röhl, *Rezeption des Johannesevangeliums* (see above 8.5.8), the reason that the Fourth Gospel received only a limited acceptance among the Gnostics was its theology of the incarnation: 'The Gnostics wanted nothing to do with this "Christ according to the flesh," since to them the flesh—the bodyliness of human existence—was only the expression of the opposite pole of salvation, something that was to be overcome' (*ibid.* 209–210).

[215] On this point in addition to Onuki, *Gemeinde und Welt*, cf. esp. Franz Mußner, 'Die "semantische Achse" des Johannesevangeliums. Ein Versuch,' in *Vom Urchristentum zu Jesus* (FS J. Gnilka), ed. Hubert Frankemölle and Karl Kertelge (Freiburg: Herder, 1989) 246–255.

The believers are ἐκ θεοῦ (of God) (cf. John 1.13, 8.47), they hear God's word (cf. John 5.24; 6.45) and do the will of God (cf. John 3.21; 13.15; 15.14). They are children of light (John 12.36a) and are of the truth (John 18.37). In contrast, unbelief is imprisoned by the world, unbelievers are from the world and have the devil as their father. Thus John is not the advocate of a protological dualism; rather, for him the transition from being imprisoned in the world to the realm of God happens in the act of believing, i.e. it is a historical act. It is by faith that one enters the realm of God's saving act, faith that is bound to the person of Jesus Christ. In the Gospel of John, faith in Jesus means faith in the God who reveals himself in the sending of Jesus (cf. John 5.24; 6.29; 11.42; 12.44; 17.8). It is precisely as the saving event that faith for John is not inconsequential, for faith mediates the saving reality of eternal life (cf. John 3.15–16; 5.24; 6.47; 11.25–26). For believers, the judgment already belongs to the past, and faith saves one from the wrath of the judgment to come (cf. John 3.18). Thus the life and death decision is the decision of faith, it is faith that reveals the human situation as it really is. John's understanding of the cosmos also speaks against a protological dualism. The primacy and anteriority of the good is seen already in the creation (cf. John 1.1–4), with the dualistic antithesis light/darkness first appearing after the creation (cf. John 1.5). It is love that causes God to send his Son into the world (cf. John 3.16; 10.36). Jesus Christ gives life to the cosmos as the bread that has come down from heaven (John 6.33), he is the light of the world (John 9.5). Jesus came to save the world (cf. John 3.17; 4.42; 12.47).

There is a causal relation between the post-Easter anamnesis, Johannine dualism, and the spatial aspects of Johannine thought.[216] The realms that were kept separate in the ancient world, the divine 'above' and the earthly 'below,' are united in Jesus Christ. The Revealer is 'from above' (John 8.23), he comes from heaven and is above all (cf. John 3.31; 6.38). Heaven is open above the Incarnate One, as ascending and descending Son of Man he is bound to the heavenly world, in him heaven and earth are united (cf. John 1.51; 3.13). Human beings are by nature oriented to the 'lower' world (cf. John 8.23), and thus must be born 'anew' and that means 'from above' (John 3.3, 5, 7).

This interweaving of spatial realms corresponds in John to the interweaving of temporal realms, so that events traditionally located in the future already reach back into the present (cf. John 5.25). The eschatological events have a present reality, the future determines the present (cf.

---

[216] On this cf. Jan-Adolf Bühner, 'Denkstrukturen im Johannesevangelium,' TheolBeitr 13 (1982) 224–231.

John 3.18). In the present encounter with the word of the Revealer the eschatological judgment already takes place, the future decision is already made in the present (cf. John 8.51 and often). Because the saving reality of eternal life is already present in faith, the step from life to death does not happen in the future, but for the believer already lies in the past (cf. John 5.24).

While affirmations about the present are predominant in the Gospel of John they do not, however, represent the whole spectrum of Johannine eschatology. It is rather the case that the distinctive Johannine approach also requires sayings with a future eschatology. The post-Easter anamnesis takes place in a certain interval, so that seen from the perspective internal to the Gospel narrative the Johannine Christians find themselves already in the future and the future-eschatological statements of the narrative refer to what is already their present. Faith does not abolish time, but gives it a new quality and orientation.

John develops this theme particularly in the farewell discourses, whose real addressee is the post-Easter congregation of readers and hearers. Thus John 14.2–3 looks to Christ's parousia, just as the expected return of Christ is also the theme of John 14.18–21, 28; 16.13e, 16. So also the announcement of an eschatological resurrection of the dead in John 5.28, 29; 6.39, 40, 44, 54 is directed to the community of hearers and readers external to the text. The decision about the future is made in the present, but this does not mean that the resurrection happens when one believes – the Johannine concept of life does not exclude physical death. Rather, it is the case that the resurrection happens as the re-awakening or new creation of life in the encounter with Jesus, to whom the Father has given the authority and power to raise the dead (cf. John 5.21). At the level internal to the text this is illustrated by the Lazarus pericope, in which Jesus appears as Lord of life and death (cf. John 11.1–44).

On the other hand, the Johannine community finds itself in a completely different situation. Jesus is back with the Father, and the believers will not meet him until the parousia. Then he will actualize what has already been decided in the present, but has not yet happened: the resurrection of the dead. Present and future eschatology are not alternatives for John, but supplement each other. That which is already firmly written in history also endures into the eschatological future. This does not mean that the affirmations of salvation as already present are relativized, but are made more specific from the perspective of the lived reality of the church.[217]

---

[217] Among those who argue that the subject matter of Johannine eschatology requires future statements are Barrett, *John* 83–86; Werner Georg Kümmel, *The Theology of the New Testament. According to Its Major Witnesses, Jesus—Paul—John* (Nashville & New York: Abingdon Press,

8.5.10 Tendencies of Recent Research

At the center of research on the Fourth Gospel still stands the issue of its literary genesis. The theories of Rudolf Bultmann continue to be significant, namely that the present text of the Gospel is to be explained by two theories of tradition and redaction, each of which has three layers. The evangelist John and the 'ecclesiastical redactor' are responsible for the present form of the text, which they composed from three sources: revelatory discourses, a semeia (signs) source and a passion source. In recent exegesis the interpretations of S. Schulz and J. Becker in their commentaries on John are close to Bultmann's own view. W. Wilkens also reckons on successive stages in the formation of the Gospel, and supposes 'that the Gospel was developed in successive stages from the original nucleus to its present form by the hand of one and the same evangelist.'[218] In dependence on Wilkens, R. E. Brown affirms a five-stage process for the origin of the Gospel of John: the collection of early traditional material, its reformation by the Johannine community in its distinctive idiom, the composition of these materials into a first outline of the Gospel, a reworking by the evangelist, and a final editing by a redactor.[219] R. Schnackenburg argues that a disciple of John son of Zebedee who had received a Hellenistic education composed the Fourth Gospel, with a later redactor adding chapter 21 and brief glosses. The later redaction is also responsible for the disjunctions in the text of John 3; 4–7; 14–17, by subsequent insertion of notes and compositions of the evangelist into his work. The old thesis already proposed by Julius Wellhausen[220] and Eduard Schwarz of a Johannine 'core document' (*Grundschrift*) has experienced a renaissance. G. Richter sees the oldest layer of the Fourth Gospel in a 'Jewish Christian *Grundschrift*,' which was then adopted by the evangelist, edited and expanded, until finally an antidocetic redactor edited it once again. H. Thyen and W. Langbrandtner regard the author of John 21 as the 'real' Fourth Evangelist, who reworked a '*Grundschrift*' that was independent of the Synoptics so thoroughly and comprehensively that he alone deserves the

---

1973) 293–294; Leonhard Goppelt, *Theologie des Neuen Testaments*, ed. Jürgen Roloff, (Göttingen: Vandenhoeck & Ruprecht, 1978³) 640–643; Joachim Gnilka, *Neutestamentliche Theologie*, NEB (Würzburg: Echter, 1989) 140–141. The clearest statement of the alternative to Bultmann's interpretation of Johannine eschatology continues to be that of Gustav Stählin, 'Zum Problem der johanneischen Eschatologie,' ZNW 33 (1934) 225–259.

[218] Wilhelm Wilkens, *Zeichen und Werke. Ein Beitrag zur Theologie des vierten Evangeliums in Erzählungs- und Redestoff*, AThANT 55 (Zürich: Zwingli Verlag, 1969) 9; cf. his previous work *Die Entstehungsgeschichte des vierten Evangeliums*.

[219] Cf. Brown, *John* 1.xxxivff.

[220] Cf. Julius Wellhausen, *Die Evangelium Johannis* (Berlin: Georg Reimer, 1908) 100–102.

title 'evangelist.'[221] For M. Theobald, the Prologue (1.1–18) was added, together with other texts, to the original beginning of the Gospel (1.19ff.) to form the present composition. The original form of the Gospel is supposed to have existed without a prologue, so that it was thoroughly re-edited at the beginning (John 1) and at the end (John 21). W. Schmithals distinguishes a 'core gospel' (*Grundevangelium*) that derived from the situation of being expelled from the synagogue (ἀποσυνάγωγος, John 9.22; 12.42; 16.2), from the composition of the evangelist, who was engaged in a debate with docetic Christians. The 'beloved disciple' texts were added by a Montanist redaction about 170 CE in order to facilitate the acceptance of the Gospel into the canon.[222] The problem with these approaches oriented to an extensive source analysis of the Fourth Gospel lies in the plausibility of their presuppositions and the logic of their arguments. Neither individual source documents (e.g. a 'semeia source') nor a 'core document' or a comprehensive 'core gospel' can be reconstructed with methodological precision. Since there are no parallel traditions,[223] all the evidence must be found internal to the document itself. Linguistic[224] or theological[225] characteristics of purported 'sources' cannot be convincingly excavated, so that the subjective judgment of the exegete plays a role without methodological controls. The acceptance of secondary redactional layers likewise rests on advance decisions of the exegete that then determine from case to case what must be considered compatible and what is incompatible, and where redactors have been at work.[226] These methodological inadequacies of an extensive source analytical approach[227] suggest

---

[221] More recently Thyen has backed away from the 'core gospel' hypothesis. He continues to hold fast, however, to the view that the author of John 21 should be regarded as the real 'evangelist.' All the texts about the 'beloved disciple' and Peter derive from him, and he is the one who created the intentional correspondence between the Prologue and the Epilogue (John 21), and is himself the architect of the literary world of the Fourth Gospel. Cf. most recently Hartwig Thyen, 'Johannes und die Synoptiker,' in *John and the Synoptics*, ed. Adelbert Denaux, 81–107.

[222] Cf. Schmithals, *Johannesevangelium und Johannesbriefe* 220–259.

[223] Therefore the two-source theory cannot be called in to support the plausibility of extensive Johannine source analysis, as Jürgen Becker repeatedly suggests; cf. ThR 47 (1982) 295; ThRev. 84 (1988) 370.

[224] On this cf. Ruckstuhl, 'Sprache und Stil im johanneischen Schrifttum,' in *Die literarische Einheit* 304–331.

[225] On the purported 'theology' of a 'semeia source,' cf. Schnelle, *Antidocetic Christology* 163–164.

[226] A classic example is provided by the Johannine farewell discourses (John 13.31–17.26). On the one side cf. Jürgen Becker, 'Die Abschiedsreden im Johannesevangelium,' ZNW 61 (1970), 215–246, on the other side Udo Schnelle, 'Die Abschiedsreden im Johannesevangelium' (see above 8.5.6).

[227] I do not thereby reject a source analysis that attempts to identify traditions taken over by the author and works on the premise of the compositional and theological unity of the Gospel. On the contrary, this form of a source analysis applied primarily to defined textual units is the indispensable presupposition of a redaction–critical method that takes up the issues of history of

that the procedure of analyzing the history of tradition and redaction as the key to unraveling the Johannine question is a false path. The beginning point should rather be the awareness that the Gospel of John in its present literary and theological form is not the result of a more or less unfortunate redactional conglomeration, but is the direct expression of an imposing theological intention expressed in its manner of expression and the form of the whole.[228]

Most of the source hypotheses are associated with particular historical and theological models of interpretation. With varying arguments from case to case, the Gospel of John is located in the neighborhood of gnostic currents by W. Bauer, R. Bultmann, E. Käsemann, L. Schottroff, J. Becker and W. Langbrandtner. In contrast, among those who see the Fourth Gospel as representing an intensive debate with Judaism are J. L. Martyn, K. Wengst, L. Schenke and H. Thyen. For them, it is precisely the origin of the Johannine community from within Judaism and the trauma of exclusion from the synagogue that to a considerable degree determines the theology of the evangelist. Another reading of the evidence relates the conflict with the Jews to an earlier phase of the Johannine school and sees the current problem at the time of the composition of the Fourth Gospel as a dispute about the soteriological relevance of the incarnation and Jesus' death on the cross (U. Schnelle, M. Hengel). In any case, the issue of the Johannine theology of the cross has been drawn more and more to the center of the debate on the theological orientation of the Fourth Gospel. While E. Käsemann,[229] J. Becker and U. B. Müller[230] either deny the existence of a Johannine theology of the cross outright or refuse to grant it any real function, others such as H. Kohler, U. Schnelle, K. Wengst,[231] M.

---

religions, history of traditions, and form criticism, integrates them, and carries them forward. Differently Hartwig Thyen, 'Johannes 10 im Kontext des vierten Evangeliums,' in Beutler and Fortna, *The Shepherd Discourse* (see above 8.5.8) 116–134, who not only regards John 1.1–21.25 as a coherent literary text, but also declares that the question of the pre- or post-history of a text is irrelevant, since 'only its current use and its structural tonal value and difference from other parts of the text on the synchronic plane of the work as a whole decide anything about its meaning and significance' (*ibid.* 117).

[228] This is a good point at which to be reminded of the outstanding but unfortunately neglected interpretation of the Gospel of John by Hermann Strathmann, *Das Evangelium nach Johannes*, NTD 4 (Göttingen: Vandenhoeck & Ruprecht, 1959⁴) 8: 'Thus the structure of the Gospel is for the most part intentionally arranged by a superior intellect and bears throughout the character of a literary work of art that comes to light in the choice of material, structure, and formation.'

[229] Cf. Käsemann, *Testament of Jesus* 62.

[230] Cf. Ulrich B. Müller, 'Die Bedeutung des Kreuzestodes Jesu im Johannesevangelium,' KuD 21 (1975) 49–71.

[231] Cf. Wengst, *Bedrängte Gemeinde* 199–219.

Hengel[232] and Th. Knöppler[233] regard the theology of the cross as a central concern of Johannine theology.

The literary relation of the Fourth Gospel to the Synoptics is facing a new evaluation. While a few years ago most scholars were of the view that John was independent of the Synoptics, today the dominant view is that there were literary contacts between John and the Gospels of Mark and Luke. Another focus of recent research is the narrative analysis of the Fourth Gospel. The narrative world created by the text is communicated by the manner in which the characters are presented, the planes of time and space with which the narrative works, geographical data, cultural and religious value judgments inherent in the text, and by the dynamic of the event represented in the conflict of belief and unbelief. 'The plot of the gospel is propelled by conflict between belief and unbelief as responses to Jesus.'[234]

---

[232] Cf. Martin Hengel, 'Die Schriftauslegung des 4. Evangelisten auf dem Hintergrund der urchristlichen Exegese,' JBTh 4 (1989) (249–288) 271ff.

[233] Cf. Thomas Knöppler, *Die theologia crucis des Johannesevangeliums*, WMANT 69 (Neukirchen: Neukirchener Verlag, 1994).

[234] Culpepper, *Anatomy* 97; cf. further Schenke, *Das Johannesevangelium*; Mark W. G. Stibbe, *John as Storyteller*, SNTSMS 73 (Cambridge: Cambridge University Press, 1992), as well as the narrative commentary by Francis J. Moloney, *Belief in the Word. Reading John 1–4* (Minneapolis: Fortress Press, 1993).

9

The Revelation of John

9.1 Literature

Commentaries

Bousset, Wilhelm. *Die Offenbarung Johannis*, KEK 16. Göttingen: Vandenhoeck & Ruprecht, 1906[6]; Charles, R. H. *The Revelation of St. John* I. II., ICC. Edinburgh: T. & T. Clark, 1920; Hadorn, Wilhelm. *Die Offenbarung des Johannes*, ThHK 18. Leipzig: Deichert, 1928; Lohmeyer, Ernst. *Die Offenbarung des Johannes*. HNT 16. Tübingen: J. C. B. Mohr (Paul Siebeck), 1953[2]; Caird, George B. *A Commentary on the Revelation of St. John the Divine*, Harper's New Testament Commentaries. New York & Evanston: Harper & Row, 1966; Kraft, Heinrich. *Die Offenbarung des Johannes*, HNT 16a. Tübingen: J. C. B. Mohr (Paul Siebeck), 1974; Sweet, J. P. M. *Revelation*, Westminster Pelican Commentaries. Philadelphia: Westminster Press, 1979; Prigent, P. *L'Apocalypse de Saint Jean*, CNT 14. Lausanne: Delachaux & Niestlé, 1981; Müller, Ulrich. B. *Die Offenbarung des Johannes*, ÖTK 19. Gütersloh: Gütersloher Verlagshaus (Gerd Mohn), 1984; Boring, M. Eugene. *Revelation*, Interpretation. A Bible Commentary for Teaching and Preaching. Louisville: Westminster/John Knox, 1988; Lohse, Eduard. *Die Offenbarung des Johannes*, NTD 11. Göttingen: Vandenhoeck & Ruprecht, 1988[7]; Schüssler Fiorenza, Elisabeth. *Revelation: Vision of a Just World*, Proclamation Commentaries. Minneapolis: Fortress Press, 1991; Roloff, Jürgen. *The Revelation of John*, tr. John E. Alsup. Minneapolis: Fortress Press, 1993; Aune, David E. *Revelation*. WBC 52ABC. Dallas: Word Books, 1997–1998.

Monographs

Schütz, R. *Die Offenbarung des Johannes und Kaiser Domitian*, FRLANT 32. Göttingen: Vandenhoeck & Ruprecht, 1933; Rissi, Mathias. *Time and History. A Study on the Revelation*. Richmond: John Knox Press, 1966; Satake, Akiru. *Die Gemeindeordnung in der Johannesapokalypse*, WMANT 21. Neukirchen: Neukirchener Verlag, 1966; Holtz, Traugott. *Die Christologie der Apokalypse des Johannes*, TU 85. Berlin: Akademie Verlag, 1971[2]; Jörns, Klaus Peter. *Das hymnische Evangelium. Untersuchungen zu Aufbau, Funktion und Herkunft der hymnischen Stücke in der Johannesoffenbarung*, StNT 5. Gütersloh: Gütersloher Verlagshaus (Gerd Mohn), 1971; Müller, Ulrich. B. *Messias und Menschensohn in jüdischen Apokalypsen und in der Offenbarung des Johannes*, StNT 6. Gütersloh: Gütersloher Verlagshaus (Gerd Mohn), 1972; Schüssler Fiorenza, Elisabeth. *Priester für Gott. Studien zum Herrschafts- und Priestermotiv in der Apokalypse*, NTA 7. Münster: Aschendorff, 1972; Collins, Adela Yarbro. *The Combat Myth in the*

Book of Revelation, Harvard Dissertations in Religion, Number 9. Missoula: Scholars Press, 1976; Günther, H. W. *Der Nah- und Enderwartungshorizont in der Apokalypse des heiligen Johannes*, FzB 41. Würzburg: Echter, 1980; Hemer, Colin J. *The Letters to the Seven Churches of Asia in their Local Setting*, JSNT. SS 11. Sheffield: JSOT Press, 1986; Collins, Adela Yarbro. *Crisis and Catharsis. The Power of the Apocalypse*. Philadelphia: Westminster Press, 1984; Karrer, Martin. *Die Johannesoffenbarung als Brief*, FRLANT 140. Göttingen: Vandenhoeck & Ruprecht, 1986; Taeger, Jens W. *Johannesapokalypse und johanneischer Kreis*, BZNW 51. Berlin: Walter de Gruyter, 1988; Thompson, Leonard. L. *The Book of Revelation*. Oxford: Oxford University Press, 1990; Bauckham, Richard. *The Climax of Prophecy. Studies on the Book of Revelation*. Edinburgh: T. &T. Clark, 1993; Bauckham, Richard. *The Theology of the Book of Revelation*. Cambridge: Cambridge University Press, 1993.

Articles

Delling, Gerhard. 'Zum gottesdienstlichen Stil der Johannes-Apokalypse,' in *Studien zum Neuen Testament und zum hellenistischen Judentum*, ed. Gerhard Delling. Göttingen: Vandenhoeck & Ruprecht, 1970, 425–450; Hahn, Ferdinand. 'Die Sendschreiben der Johannesapokalypse,' in *Tradition und Glaube* (FS K. G. Kuhn) ed. Gerd Jeremias, H. W. Kuhn and H. Stegemann. Göttingen: Vandenhoeck & Ruprecht, 1971, 357–394; Strobel, August. 'Apokalypse des Johannes,' *TRE* 3 (1978) 174–189; Georgi, Dieter. 'Die Visionen vom himmlischen Jerusalem in Apk 21 und 22,' in *Kirche* (FS G. Bornkamm) ed. Dieter Lührmann and Georg Strecker. Tübingen: J. C. B. Mohr (Paul Siebeck), 1980, 351–372; Lambrecht, Jan, ed. *L'Apocalypse johannique et l'Apocalyptique dans le Nouveau Testament*, BETL 53. Gembloux: Duculot; Leuven: Leuven University Press, 1980; Satake, Akiru. 'Kirche und feindliche Welt,' in *Kirche* (FS G. Bornkamm) ed. Dieter Lührmann and Georg Strecker. Tübingen: J. C. B. Mohr (Paul Siebeck), 1980, 329–349; Fischer, Karl Martin. 'Die Christlichkeit der Offenbarung des Johannes,' ThLZ 106 (1981) 165–172. Lampe, Peter. 'Die Apokalyptiker – ihre Situation und ihr Handeln,' in *Eschatologie und Friedenshandeln*, SBS 101. Stuttgart: Katholisches Bibelwerk, 1981, 59–114; Wolff, Christian. 'Die Gemeinde des Christus in der Apokalypse des Johannes,' NTS 27 (1981) 186–197; Böcher, Otto. *Kirche in Zeit und Endzeit. Aufsätze zur Offenbarung des Johannes*, Neukirchen-Vluyn: Neukirchener Verlag, 1983 (important collection of essays); Müller, Ulrich, B. 'Literarische und formgeschichtliche Bestimmung der Apokalypse des Johannes als einem Zeugnis frühchristlicher Apokalyptik,' in *Apocalypticism in the Mediterranean World and the Near East* ed. D. Hellholm. Tübingen: J. C. B. Mohr (Paul Siebeck), 1983, 599–619; Boring, M. Eugene. 'The Theology of Revelation. "The Lord our God the Almighty Reigns",' *Interpretation* 50 (1986) 257–269; Collins, John J., ed. *Semeia* 36 (1986) (important collection of essays); Schüssler Fiorenza, Elisabeth. *The Book of Revelation*. Philadelphia: Fortress Press, 1989² (important collection of essays); Roloff, Jürgen. 'Neuschöpfung in der Offenbarung des Johannes,' in *Jahrbuch für Biblische Theologie* 5. Neukirchen-Vluyn: Neukirchener Verlag, 1990, 119–138; Klauck, Hans-Joseph. 'Das Sendschreiben nach Pergamon und der Kaiserkult in der Johannesoffenbarung,' Bib 72 (1991) 183–207; Boring, M. Eugene. 'Narrative Christology in the Apocalypse,' CBQ 54 (1992)

702–723; Boring, M. Eugene. 'The Voice of Jesus in the Apocalypse of John,' NT 34 (1992) 334–359; Frey, Jörg. 'Erwägungen zum Verhältnis der Johannesapokalypse zu den übrigen Schriften des Corpus Johanneum,' in *Die johanneische Frage*, ed. Martin Hengel, WUNT 67. Tübingen: J. C. B. Mohr (Paul Siebeck), 1993 326–429; Boring, M. Eugene, 'Revelation 19–21: End without Closure,' in *The Princeton Seminary Bulletin, Supplementary Issue*, No. 3 (1994) 57–84.

History of Research

Kraft, Heinrich. 'Zur Offenbarung des Johannes,' ThR 38 (1974) 81–98; Taeger, Jens W. 'Einige neue Veröffentlichungen zur Apokalypse des Johannes,' VF 29 (1984) 50–75; Böcher, Otto, ed. *Die Johannesapokalypse*, EdF 41. Darmstadt: Wissenschaftliche Buchgesellschaft, 1988³; Wainwright, Arthur W. *Mysterious Apocalypse: Interpreting the Book of Revelation*. Nashville: Abingdon Press, 1993.

9.2 Author

According to its own claim, the Apocalypse derives from Jesus Christ, and through him its ultimate author is God (Rev. 1.1a; cf. 22.16). The δοῦλος Ἰωάννης (servant John) functions as transmitter of the content (Rev. 1.1b). He testifies to the truth of what he has heard and seen (Rev. 1.2; 22.8), and in Rev. 1.4 addresses the congregations of Asia Minor as a leader with authority. Nonetheless, he claims no special official or functional titles, but by means of the predicates ἀδελφός (brother) and συγκοινωνός (fellow participant) joins himself to the communities he addresses (Rev. 1.9). The seer John characterizes his message repeatedly as προφητεία (prophecy) (Rev. 1.3; 19.10; 22.7, 10, 18, 19), and in Rev. 10.11 the angels explicitly charge John: 'You must prophesy again about many peoples and nations and languages and kings.' John clearly understands himself to be a prophet; according to Rev. 22.9 he is the leading member of a circle of early Christian prophets (cf. Rev. 22.6).[1]

To these prophets Jesus grants insight into the historical acts of God that are set forth in Revelation (Rev. 22.16), in order to strengthen the congregations. The broad extent of the communities to which the document is addressed indicates that the seer John had previously worked as a wandering prophet in the congregations named, and now turns to them in the situation of threatened persecution.[2] In the history of early Christian theology parallels are found in the context of Syrian Christianity; both Matthew (cf. Matt. 10.41; 23.34) and the Didache (cf. Did 11.1–12; 13;

---

[1] Cf. Roloff, *Revelation* 11.
[2] Cf. Müller, *Offenbarung* 50.

15.1) presuppose the existence of such wandering prophets.[3] The history-of-tradition connections to the Syrian-Palestinian stream of tradition and the semitizing Greek (see below 9.7) likewise point to Syria/Palestine as the homeland of the seer. One may readily suppose that after the Jewish War (66–73/74 CE.) John left Palestine and worked in Asia Minor, as did other Jewish Christians (cf. Eusebius, HE 3.31.3).[4]

In the tradition of the ancient church, it was Justin (*Dialogue* 81.4) who first identified John the seer with the son of Zebedee.[5] Irenaeus traced the Revelation, as well as the Gospel and Letters of John, back to John the disciple of Jesus (cf. *Against Heresies* 2.22.5; 3.1.2; 3.3.4; 3.11.7; 5.30.1, 3). By around 200 CE the Revelation was generally acknowledged in the west, but was vigorously rejected by the Alogoi and Dionysius of Alexandria (Eusebius, HE 6.25).[6] Eusebius too remained uncertain in his own judgment, stating that within the apostolic writings 'one could also include the Revelation of John, if one is so inclined, though there is a wide spectrum of opinions' (HE 3.25.2). The testimony of the book itself does not support the dominant tradition of the ancient church, for in Rev. 18.20 and 21.14 the apostles appear to be a group of past history, to which the author of Revelation, as a prophet, does *not* belong. The identification of the apocalyptist of Asia Minor with the son of Zebedee, John the apostle, is also prohibited by the historical context in which the Revelation apparently originated, for in that case a very old man (ca. 90) would have composed this powerful writing.[7] It is also unlikely that John the seer may be identified with the πρεσβύτερος (presbyter, elder) of Papias (see above 8.2.2),[8] since this honorary title is not used by the author of Revelation of himself,[9]

---

[3] Cf. Müller, *Theologiegeschichte* (see 7.3.8 above) 36–37.

[4] Cf. Müller, *Offenbarung* 51–52; Roloff, *Revelation* 11. The seer was not, however, an advocate of a strict Jewish Christianity, for the Gentile mission is presupposed (cf. Rev. 7.9–10; 5.9), and he designates the Jews the 'synagogue of Satan' (see 9.8 below). On this, cf. the reflections of Bousset, *Offenbarung* 139–140.

[5] It is probable that Papias knew the Revelation (cf. Eusebius HE 3.39.12), but whom he regarded as its author has not been preserved.

[6] Cf. the analysis of the most important texts by Bousset, *Offenbarung* 19–34; Wikenhauser and Schmid, *Einleitung* 643–648.

[7] Others who reject apostolic authorship of Revelation are Bousset, *Offenbarung* 35–36; Lohmeyer, *Offenbarung* 203; Kraft, *Offenbarung* 9; Lohse, *Offenbarung* 6; Böcher, *Johannes-apokalypse* 35; Schenke and Fischer, *Einleitung* 2.298–299; Müller, *Offenbarung* 46; Roloff, *Revelation* 11. Those who hold fast to apostolic authorship include: Hadorn, *Offenbarung* 225; Ethelbert Stauffer, *New Testament Theology*, tr. John Marsh (London: SCM Press Ltd, 1963) 40–41; W. Michaelis, *Einleitung* (see above 5.5.2) 314–315.

[8] This view was advocated by Bousset, *Offenbarung* 43–44, 49; Lohmeyer, *Offenbarung* 203.

[9] Πρεσβύτερος (elder) in Rev. 4.4, 10; 5.5–6, 8, 11, 14; 7.11, 13; 11.16; 14.3; 19.4 refers exclusively to the twenty-four heavenly Elders, which are not modeled on an earthly presbytery; cf. Satake, *Gemeindeordnung* 149.

and πρεσβύτερος refers to the role of an early Christian teacher, not to a prophet.[10]

What is the relationship between the seer John and the authors of the Gospel and Letters of John? The first remarkable datum is that the name Ἰωάννης (John) appears only in the text of Revelation (1.1, 4, 8; 22.8).[11] Thematic points of contact between Revelation and the Fourth Gospel are found in the motif of 'living water' (Rev. 7.16–17; 21.6; 22.1, 17 /John 4.10, 13–14; 7.37–39); in Rev. 19.13 the Jesus Christ who returns is described as ὁ λόγος τοῦ θεοῦ (the word of God) (cf. John 1.1), and the concept of Christ as 'lamb of God' is central to the Christology of both Revelation (τὸ ἀρνίον 29x) and the Gospel of John (ὁ ἀμνὸς τοῦ θεοῦ in John 1.29, 36; different Greek words for 'lamb' in Revelation and the Gospel). Clearly, the concept of 'conquering, victory' is in the foreground of both documents (νικάω, conquer 17x in Rev., 7x in the Johannine corpus, of 24 occurrences in the New Testament; νίκη [victory] is found only in 1 John 5.4).[12] So too the witness/testimony motif (μαρτυρέω, testify 76x NT; μαρτυρία, testimony 37x NT) is found in extraordinary frequency in both documents (Revelation: μαρτυρέω 4x; μαρτυρία 9x); in the writings of the Johannine school (μαρτυρέω 43x; μαρτυρία 21x). These lines of contact do not permit certain conclusions concerning the relationship of the documents themselves, however, since both the purely linguistic statistics and the common motifs, when examined individually, manifest either theological concepts that differ widely from each other,[13] or the agreements may be attributed to derivation from a comparable stock of traditions in their respective backgrounds.[14]

---

[10] Cf. Kraft, *Offenbarung* 9; Müller, *Offenbarung* 47; Böcher, *Johannesapokalypse* 35.

[11] Frey, 'Erwägungen' 425ff. attributes the insertion of the name to a redactional layer and categorizes the Apocalypse as pseudepigraphical.

[12] Cf. further: ὄψις (face) only in John 7.24; 11.44; Rev. 1.16; σφάζειν (slay, kill) only in 1 John 3.12; Rev. 5.6, 9, 12; 6.4, 9; 13.3, 8; 18.24. For an analysis of thematic connections and points of contact between the Revelation and the Johannine corpus in the history of the traditions they respectively used, cf. also Frey 'Erwägungen' 385–415, who however would like to reverse the usual understanding of direction in which the materials flowed: 'the evidence taken as a whole speaks for the higher age of the apocalyptic traditions and the "more developed" character of the elaboration of the corresponding motifs in the Fourth Gospel.' (*ibid.* 414)

[13] On the 'conquering/victory' motif: In 1 John νικάω (conquer) denotes the victory of faith in Christ as the (already accomplished) overcoming of the world. By contrast, in Revelation the dominant idea associated with the term is the struggle and victory of the Lamb (cf. Rev. 12.11; 17.14), or the preservation of Christians in the world as the place of struggle (cf. Rev. 2.7, 11, 17, etc.). On the 'witness' motif: In the Gospel and Letters of John the witness refers primarily to the person of Jesus, but in Revelation, to what is seen in the vision.

[14] On the motif of 'living water,' cf. Ferdinand Hahn, 'Die Worte vom lebendigen Wasser im Johannesevangelium,' in *God's Christ and His People* (FS N. A. Dahl), ed. Jacob Jervell and Wayne A. Meeks (Oslo, Bergen, Tromsö: Universitetsforlaget, 1977) 51–70.

In addition there are serious differences in language, Christology, ecclesiology, and eschatology.

1. Language: The semitizing Greek of Revelation has been considered a compelling argument against the thesis that Revelation and the Fourth Gospel were written by the same author since the time of W. Bousset and R. H. Charles.[15] A few peculiarities of the 'Semitic idiom' of Revelation may be mentioned:[16]

a. Neglecting the correspondence of cases (cf. Rev. 1.5; 2.13, 20; 3.12; 4.1; 5.11–12; 11.15; and many others).

b. Introducing sentences with καί (and, also, even) analogous to w-consecutive (cf. Rev. 3.20; 6.12; 10.7; 14.9–10).

c. The tenses are used with great freedom, so that e.g., past, present, and future can stand in the same sentence, even though they all refer to the same time (cf. Rev. 4.9–11; 6.15–17; 11; 14.2–3; 16.21; 20.7–8).

d. The substitution of a finite verb by an infinitive (cf. Rev. 12.7; 13.10) or a participial clause (cf. Rev. 10.2; 12.2; 19.12; 21.12, 14).

e. Unusual use of prepositions (e.g. ἐπί, upon).[17]

2. Christology: At the center of the Christology of the Fourth Gospel and the Letters of John stands the concept of the incarnation. It is based on the essential unity of Father and Son, so that the incarnate one is none other than the pre-existent and exalted one (see above 8.5.9). In contrast, in Revelation the Lamb, i.e. the Son, is clearly subordinate to God (cf. e.g. Rev. 3.5; 5.6–7, 13; 6.16; 7.10; 14.14; 15.3; 20.11–15). It is not the incarnation of the Son of God (υἱὸς τοῦ θεοῦ only in Rev. 2.18), but the idea of the installation of Christ as Lord of the world and history that determines the Christology of Revelation.[18]

3. Ecclesiology: Already in the messages to the seven churches the dominance of ecclesiology is signaled (ἐκκλησία [church] in Revelation 15x in chapters 2–3).[19] The seer John struggles against an accommodation of the church to the political ideology of his time. For him the key issue is the

---

[15] Cf. Bousset, *Offenbarung* 159–177; Charles, *Revelation* 1.cxvii–clix ('A Short Grammar of the Apocalypse'). Cf. further G. Mussies, *The Morphology of Koine Greek as Used in the Apocalypse of St. John*, NT.S 27 (Leiden: E. J. Brill, 1971); Steven Thompson, *The Apocalypse and Semitic Syntax*, SNTSMS 52 (Cambridge: Cambridge University Press, 1985); Frey, 'Erwägungen' 336–382, concludes his own thorough linguistic comparison between Revelation and the Fourth Gospel with the assessment that 'the composition of both works by the same author is extremely improbable, in fact appears to be virtually excluded' (*ibid.* 381).

[16] The question of the author's original language of Revelation may no longer be clearly answered. Thompson, *Apocalypse and Semitic Syntax* 106–108, considers Hebrew and Aramaic to be equally possible.

[17] Cf. Bousset, *Offenbarung* 165–166.

[18] Cf. Roloff, *Revelation* 11–12.

[19] Cf. Roloff, *Kirche* (see above 3.5.4) 169–189.

right relationship between church and society, which finds its expression in the vision of the New Jerusalem (Rev. 21). These determinative universal components are lacking in the Fourth Gospel and in the Johannine letters. There state and society come into view only in rudimentary ways or not at all.

4. Eschatology: Revelation sets forth strongly indicative accents (cf. e.g., Rev. 1.5–6), which are hardly comparable with the dominance of present eschatology in the Fourth Gospel. Rather, it is the future that receives the primary emphasis in Revelation – a future determined by the present. It directs its view, with eager anticipation, to the mighty appearance of Jesus Christ (compare Rev. 1.3 with Rev. 22.20; further 1.7; 19.11ff.; 22.7, 17), who as Judge of the world will render to each one according to his or her works (Rev. 22.12). Millennial views are as foreign to the Gospel of John as the idea of an eschatological new creation (cf. Rev. 21.5). In addition, essential elements of the Johannine dualism (light/darkness; life/death; truth/lie) are missing from Revelation.

The authors of Revelation and of the other Johannine writings are not the same (see above 8.1.3). The author of Revelation is a Jewish-Christian *wandering prophet* who has worked for a long time in the area of Paul's previous mission in Asia Minor, who now attempts to give them a new orientation in view of the mass of troubles he sees approaching.[20] He emerges as a Spirit-endowed spokesman for the Christ who is living and present to his churches, and discloses both present and future to them.[21]

9.3 Place and Time of Composition

When he received his vision, the seer John was on the Aegean island of Patmos (Rev. 1.9), one day by ship from the west coast of Asia Minor. His residence there was 'because of the word of God and the testimony of Jesus.' Probably he had been banned to this island because of his resistance to the Caesar cult (see below. 9.8).[22] Whether John was still on Patmos at

---

[20] The description of the messages to the seven churches as 'John's pastoral letters' is thoroughly appropriate. Cf. Paul Anton, *Exegetische Abhandlung der Paulinischen Pastoral-Briefe* (see above 5.5) 513.

[21] On the origin of the prophet John, cf. especially Müller, *Zur frühchristlichen Theologiegeschichte* 46–50 (see section 5. above).

[22] Cf. Roloff, *Revelation* 32; Müller, *Offenbarung* 81; Bousset, *Offenbarung* 191–192. This understanding is supported by the preposition διά, which in Revelation when used with the accusative always means the reason, not the goal; cf. especially Rev. 6.9; 20.4. In contrast, Kraft, *Offenbarung* 40–42 supposes that the seer's residence on Patmos was part of his prophetic vocation, i.e. he withdrew into isolation in order to receive revelations. For a critique of this hypothesis cf. Karrer, *Johannesoffenbarung als Brief* 187 note 213.

the time he composed the Revelation remains unclear. The aorist ἐγενόμην (was, Rev. 1.9) points to his stay there as already in the past.[23]

The time of composition is derived from the situation presupposed in the churches (see below 9.4, 9.8). The intensification of the Caesar cult and the conflicts associated with it at the end of the reign of Domitian form the historical context of Revelation, which probably was written between 90 and 95 CE.[24] The picture of the (Pauline) churches of Asia Minor supports this dating, since the critical symptoms of internal drowsiness and the threat of heresy is confirmed by the Deuteropauline Letters.

9.4 Intended Readership

The churches of Asia Minor to whom the Revelation is addressed obviously stand in the Pauline tradition, to which the seer consciously alludes by his adoption of the Pauline greeting formula in 1.4–5. The textual world of Revelation suggests that the recipients belonged primarily to the non-Jewish Hellenistic population, though one must also think of a strong Jewish-Christian minority.[25] One can only make vague statements about the social structure of the churches. The congregation in the commercial city Laodicea considers itself to be rich both spiritually and materially (Rev. 3.17–18), while in contrast the economically poor congregation of Smyrna is truly rich (Rev. 2.9). Possibly Christians were included in the merchants attacked in Rev. 18.11ff. They engage in business with the harlot Babylon and become rich. But they must bear the mark of the beast in order to be able to buy and sell at all (Rev. 13.16–18).[26] These indications seem to confirm the picture of the socially stratified post-Pauline Christianity in Asia Minor (see above 5.5.4).

The Christians are exposed to a wide range of troubles. From within false teachers (see below 9.8) threaten the identity of the churches (cf. Rev.

---

[23] Cf. Bousset, *Offenbarung* 192; Müller, *Offenbarung* 81.

[24] Cf. already Irenaeus (*Against Heresies* 5.30.3; Eusebius HE 5.8.6–7). Cf. further Bousset *Offenbarung* 133–134 (93 CE); Charles, *Revelation* 1.xci; Schütz, *Offenbarung*, passim; Ethelbert Stauffer, *Christ and the Caesars: Historical Sketches* (Philadelphia: Westminster) 175; Kümmel, *Introduction* 469; Vielhauer, *Urchristliche Literatur* 503; Lohse, *Offenbarung* 7; Böcher, *Johannesapokalypse* 41; A. Y. Collins, 'Dating the Apocalypse of John,' BR 26 (1981) 41–43; Roloff, *Revelation* 10–11; Müller, *Offenbarung* 41–42; Hemer, *Letters* 2–12; Klauck, 'Sendschreiben nach Pergamon' 161; Thompson, *Book of Revelation* 15. Earlier dates are advocated by (among others) Hadorn, *Offenbarung* 221 (before 70 CE); Albert A. Bell, 'The Date of John's Apocalypse,' NTS 25 (1979) 93–102 (68/69 CE). A later dating is advocated by (among others) Kraft, *Offenbarung* 10, 222 (97/98 CE); Taeger, *Johannesapokalypse* 22 (time of Trajan, 98–117 CE).

[25] Cf. Karrer, *Johannesoffenbarung als Brief* 151.

[26] Cf. Klauck, 'Sendschreiben nach Pergamon' 178–179.

2.2, 6, 15; 2.14, 20ff.). But there is also talk of 'lukewarmness' in the faith (2.4–5; 3.15–16), some congregations are weak (Rev. 3.8) and 'dead' (Rev. 3.1). From outside, the churches are not only pressed by the danger of war (Rev. 6.2–4),[27] inflation (Rev. 6.5–6)[28] and repressions from the Jewish side (Rev. 2.9–10; 3.9), but in Asia Minor the dominant power is the loathsome beast, the Roman emperor (Rev. 12.18–13.10), and with him the second beast, the imperial priesthood (Rev. 13.11–17; 16.13–14; 19.20). They propagate the Caesar cult as an obligatory loyalty test for all citizens/ residents. Numerous institutions devoted to the ruler cult are located in the seven cities of the addressees.[29] In the Caesar temple in Ephesus stood an enormous statue of Domitian, four times life-size,[30] in Pergamon a temple to Zeus towered over the city,[31] and Smyrna too was a center of the Caesar cult.

The Christian community sees itself exposed to the exalted claims to sacral and political power of the Roman Empire, which it portrays in an elaborate language of symbols and images. In mythological terms the seer describes the wrath of the Beast (Rev. 13, 17, 18); the messages to the seven churches clarify the historical background.[32] Christians are harassed (Rev. 2.9), thrown into prison (Rev. 2.10), and one witness has already been martyred (Antipas in Rev. 2.13; cf. Rev. 6.9–11). The hour of testing is coming on the whole earth (3.10).[33]

Domitian (born 51 CE, emperor 81–96 CE),[34] who since 85 CE had insisted on being addressed as '*dominus et deus noster*' ('our Lord and God,' Suetonius, *Domitian* 13.2) (cf. Rev. 4.11!), increased the pressure on his opposition near the end of his reign (cf. Suetonius, *Domitian* 14.4; 10.5; 11.1–3). For years he executed his opponents at every opportunity (cf. Dio Cassius 67.31.1), and in 93 CE he expelled all philosophers from Rome (Suetonius, *Domitian*

---

[27] Rev. 6.2 could refer to Parthian raids (cf. Rev. 9.13ff.; 16.12), Rev. 6.3–4 on internal disputes within the Empire; cf. Müller, *Offenbarung* 167; Roloff, *Revelation* 6.

[28] Cf. here Bousset, *Offenbarung* 135–136.

[29] Cf. S. R. F. Price, *Rituals and Power: The Roman Imperial Cult in Asia Minor* (Cambridge: Cambridge University Press, 1984). To the point is the comment of Walter Burkert, 'Griechische Religion,' TRE 14 (1985) 248: 'The entire political organization of Asia Minor was centered in the Caesar cult.'

[30] Cf. W. Elliger, *Ephesos* 96–99 (see above 2.2.2).

[31] This temple is interpreted by Adolf Deissmann, *Light from the Ancient East* (see above 2.3.1) 281 note 3, and Lohmeyer, *Offenbarung* 25, as the 'throne of Satan' of Rev. 2.13. Others argue for a shrine sacred to the Caesar cult, e.g. Müller, *Offenbarung* 110; Klauck, 'Sendschreiben nach Pergamon' 161; on the religious 'infrastructure' of Pergamon, cf. *ibid.* 157–159.

[32] The reference to persecutions or killings in Rev. 11.7–9; 13.15; 17.6; 18.24; 20.4 is in the context of the mythological imagery not clearly a reference to historical events.

[33] Cf. Horatio E. Lona, 'Treu bis zum Tod,' in *Neues Testament und Ethik* (FS R. Schnackenburg) ed. Helmut Merklein (Freiburg: Herder, 1989) 442–461.

[34] A historical portrait of Domitian is given by Thompson, *Book of Revelation* 96–115.

10.3; Dio Cassius 67.13.1ff.). In 95 he had his cousin T. Flavius Clemens executed and his wife Flavia Domitilla exiled.[35] Both were probably Christians.[36] It must, however, remain questionable whether Domitian ever initiated a major persecution of Christians.[37] His biographers were as a rule oriented toward the Senate (Suetonius, Tacitus), and intentionally present a demeaning picture of the emperor.[38] Probably the intensification of the Caesar cult in the area to which Revelation is addressed led to individual cases of local repressions.[39] Refusal to participate in the Caesar cult could result in the repressive measures that Pliny reports and presupposes in part already for the time of Domitian (see above 7.2.4).[40] Christians were anonymously charged (e.g. by the propagandizers for the Caesar cult) (Letter 10.96.4–5). They had to invoke the gods, offer a sacrifice before the statue of the emperor, and curse Christ (Letter 10.96.5). If they refused and held fast to their Christian confession, execution was a possible result (Letter 10.96.3).

The manner in which Christians distanced themselves from the worship of Hellenistic gods and the Caesar cult may have been only one basis for the danger in which the churches found themselves. In the eyes of the seer, the way in which the silent accommodation to the forms in which pagan religion was expressed (see below 9.8) was just as problematical as the overt persecution. They constituted a challenge to the purity of the eschatological community, so that assimilation to pagan forms appeared as a subtle form of apostasy.[41]

---

[35] Cf. Dio Cassius 67.14.1–2: 'In the same year Domitian had, with many others, also the Consul Flavius Clemens executed, although he was his cousin and was married to Flavia Domitilla, who was related to him [Domitian]. Both were charged with atheism (ἀθεότης), which is why many others who were inclined to Jewish practices (τὰ τῶν Ἰουδαίων ἤθη) were also executed. Others only lost their possessions, and Domitilla was only banned to Pandateria.' On the analysis of this text cf. Peter Lampe, *Die stadrömischen Christen* (see 2.8.1 above) 166–172. He concludes that only Domitilla was a Christian, and that Flavius Clemens was executed as father of a possible successor of Domitian, [since he was his cousin]. (cf. Suetonius, *Domitian* 15.1).

[36] Cf. Rudolf Hanslik, 'Domitian,' *KP* 2.124.

[37] Cf. Rudolf Freudenberger, 'Christenverfolgungen,' *TRE* 8 (1981) 25; Kurt Aland, 'Das Verhältnis von Kirche und Staat in der Frühzeit,' *ANRW* 2. 23.1 (Berlin: Walter de Gruyter, 1979) 224; Collins, *Crisis and Catharsis* 69ff. The classical argument to the contrary is advocated by Stauffer, *Christ and the Caesars* (see above 9.3) 176: 'We may read the book of Revelation with new understanding when we see it as the apostolic reply to the declaration of war by the divine emperor in Rome.'

[38] Cf. Hanslik, 'Domitian,' *KP* 2. 125

[39] Cf. Müller, *Offenbarung* 260.

[40] In addition to Letter 10.96.6 (twenty years previously some who were denounced had recanted their faith), Letter 10.96.5 can also be mentioned. Here Pliny refers to his demands that the accused do things 'that committed Christians, as they are called, would never let themselves be forced to do.' This presupposes that such a procedure had already been practiced in Asia Minor for some time!

[41] Cf. Müller, *Offenbarung* 113 and elsewhere; Klauck, 'Sendschreiben nach Pergamon' 181–182.

9.5 Outline, Structure, Form

1.1–3	Opening Words
1.4–8	Epistolary Introduction
1.9–20	The Commissioning Vision
2.1–3.22	The Messages to the Seven Churches
4.1–5.14	The Throneroom Vision
6.1–8.1	The Vision of the Seven Seals
8.2–11.19	The Vision of the Seven Trumpets
12.1–13.18	The Adversary of God
14	The Lamb and the Redeemed
15.1–16.21	The Vision of the Seven Bowls
17.1–19.10	The Harlot Babylon
19.11–22.5	Final Visions
22.6–21	Conclusion

In 1.19 the seer gives a clear indication of the structure of his work:[42] 'Now write what you have seen, what is, and what is to take place after this.' 'What you have seen' refers to the call vision of 1.9–20, 'what is' refers to the messages to the seven churches of chapters two and three, and 'what is to take place after this' is the theme of chapters four to the end. The conscious allusion to 1.19 in 4.1 confirms this understanding of John's structure, so that on the macro level one can speak of a two-fold main structure (messages to the seven churches/apocalyptic section),[43] to which 1.9–20 is the introduction.[44]

While the messages to the seven churches have a clear common structure, the literary construction of the main apocalyptic section is difficult to determine. The number seven also functions here as a structural principle, as indicated by the three great visionary series (seals, trumpets, bowls). The action of a heavenly figure (the Lamb or an angel) actuates the release of sevenfold plagues on the earth (cf. Rev. 6.1–8.1; 8.2–11.19; 15.1–16.21). The explicit mention of the *last* seven plagues in Rev. 15.1 likewise shows

---

[42] Cf. Müller, *Offenbarung* 29; opposed by Elisabeth Schüssler Fiorenza, 'The Composition and Structure of Revelation,' in *The Book of Revelation* 173, who refers 1.19 only to the messages to the seven churches.

[43] Cf. Ferdinand Hahn, 'Zum Aufbau der Johannesoffenbarung,' in *Kirche und Bibel* (FS E. Schick) (Paderborn: Schöningh, 1979) 149: Rev. 1.9–3.20; 4.1–22.5. In contrast, an argument for a three-fold structure on the macro-level is made by Karrer, *Johannesoffenbarung als Brief* 227: Rev. 4–11; 12.1–19.10; 19.11–22.5. Cf. most recently Norbert Baumert, 'Ein Ruf zur Entscheidung: Aufbau und Botschaft der Offenbarung des Johannes,' in *Die Freude an Gott— unsere Kraft* (FS O. Knoch), ed. Johannes Degenhardt (Stuttgart: Katholisches Bibelwerk, 1991) 197–210.

[44] Cf. Müller, *Offenbarung* 30.

that a compositional principle is involved.[45] At the same time, it is clear
that the heptad principle in itself is not adequate to explain the structural
principles of the Apocalypse. Rather, one must inquire after the intention
implicit in the arrangement of the materials, which is identical with the
guideline provided for the reader.[46]

A key role is played by the throneroom vision of 4.1–5.14,[47] the theme of
which is the reality of the reign of Christ, a reign that has already broken
into this world. On the basis of this encouraging announcement of salvation, the Christian community can view the revelation of what is to come.
The opening of the seven seals of Rev. 6.1–8.1 introduces the presentation
of the conquering power of the Lamb. A first break comes after the vision
of the first six trumpets between Rev. 9.21 and 10.1, then follow less
structured complexes of material, before Rev. 11.15–19 resumes a clear
concluding order. After 12.1, the woman, the dragon, and other new
characters are the powerful agents that determine the plot of the following
scenes. The vision of the beast in Rev. 13 is conceived as the counterpart of
the saving figure of the Lamb in Rev. 5. The vision of redemption in
chapter 14 and the following series of plagues of Rev. 15.1–16.21
correspond to the order in Rev. 7 and Rev. 8–9. The Babylon complex Rev.
17–18 is concluded by the celebration of the demonstration of God's
sovereign power in Rev. 19.1–10.

Another new section begins in Rev. 19.11 and extends through Rev.
22.5, providing the ultimate series of eschatological visions: the universal
world judgment, the gathering of the elect and the eschatological act of
God the Creator. The vision of the heavenly Jerusalem thus corresponds
to the throneroom vision of Rev. 4. The conclusion of the book in Rev.
22.6–21 finally returns to the beginning, attributing the message of the
book once again to the exalted Jesus, and leads into the eucharistic worship
of the Christian community as the setting in which the visions of the book
and the reality of the church's life are merged.[48] The structure of the
Apocalypse as a whole is determined by its movement toward its final goal:
God's kingdom finally comes despite the plagues and the eschatological
adversary.

Determination of the literary form of the whole begins with the epistolary framework. After the incipit of Rev. 1.1–3[49] there follows in Rev. 1.4–6
the epistolary prescript, which is both oriented to the form made con-

---

[45] Cf. *ibid.*

[46] On this, cf. especially Karrer, *Johannesoffenbarung als Brief* 224–248.

[47] Cf. Roloff, *Revelation* 68, who regards this text as the theological center of the Apocalypse.
Müller, *Offenbarung* 30, incorrectly reduces Rev. 4 to a 'prelude.'

[48] Cf. Roloff, *Revelation* 249.

[49] For an analysis, cf. Karrer, *Johannesoffenbarung als Brief* 86–108.

ventional by the Pauline letters and bears the accent of John's own independent style.[50] It includes *superscriptio* and *adscriptio* (v. 4a), an expanded *salutatio* (v. 4b, 5a), and a doxology (vv. 5b–6), which stands in the place of the customary thanksgiving. So too, the concluding greeting in Rev. 22.21 is formulated on the Pauline model (cf. 1 Thess. 5.28; 1 Cor. 16.23; Phil. 4.23). Corresponding to the liturgically oriented line of thought characteristic of the Apocalypse, the book concludes with a prayer for the coming of the Lord (Rev. 22.21) and the responsorial pronouncement of grace (cf. 1 Cor. 16.22–23).[51] The epistolary form of Revelation must be understood as the direct expression of the way in which the message of the whole book is directed to the particular situation of the addressees. The seer addresses congregations in the Pauline tradition and facilitates the reception of his message by the conscious utilization of the Pauline epistolary convention. The formulation of his message as a letter is clearly seen in the messages to the seven churches. The seer stylizes them according to the epistolary form of communication:[52] the naming of the addressees, a statement about the sender, the command to write, and the sender's 'knowing' of the church situation (cf. 1 Thess. 1.3ff.) point in this direction. The messages to the seven churches are structured according to a fixed scheme:[53] (1) command to write; (2) messenger formula; (3) portrayal of the situation; (4) call to alertness (5) saying about 'conquering.' John obviously is dependent on the model of the prophetic letter genre (cf. Jer. 29.4, 31; 2 Chron 21.12). Like the apostolic letters, so also the prophetic letters stand in the place of the absent writer and mediate his influence on the current congregational situation. In addition, individual thematic elements in the messages to the churches already point ahead to the following visionary section.[54] Here additional formal elements alongside the hymns (see below 9.7) are found, especially the prophetic visions, the series of plagues and the numerical speculations.[55]

Revelation's literary form as a whole can be properly determined when its typically apocalyptic elements (picture language, visions, numerical mysteries) as well as the untypical elements (no pseudepigraphical traits) are conceived as a meaningful whole within the comprehensive epistolary form of the work. Revelation will then be rightly seen as an apocalypse stylized in the form of a (circular) letter that is intended to be read in the

---

[50] Documented by Karrer, *ibid.* 66–83.
[51] Cf. Roloff, *Revelation* 253–54.
[52] Cf. Karrer, *Johannesoffenbarung als Brief* 160; Müller, *Offenbarung* 91–92.
[53] Cf. Hahn, 'Sendschreiben' 366ff. (does not however include the command to write in his analysis); Müller, *Offenbarung* 91–96.
[54] Cf. Roloff, *Revelation* 46.
[55] Cf. the analysis of Müller, 'Literarische und formgeschichtliche Bestimmung' 608–618.

worship of the church (cf. 1 Thess. 5.27; Col. 4.16; 2ApocBaruch 86.1–2; Paraleipomena Jerimiou) 7.19.[56] The author's reason for writing determined the form he chose and corresponds to the goal of his communication.

9.6 Literary Integrity

The apparent lack of connections between the messages to the seven churches of Rev. 2–3 and the main apocalyptic section Rev. 4–22 has repeatedly led to attempted solutions along the lines of source analysis and the literary prehistory of the document. From this approach the messages to the seven churches are regarded either as a later addition,[57] or as the earliest section of Revelation.[58] The essential argument in both cases is the differing perspectives of the messages to the churches and the apocalyptic body of the work: in the former only local persecution, while the latter pictures a time of universal distress. However, the numerous points of contact between the two sections in both composition and content (see 9.5 above) speak against the hypothesis that the Revelation originated in a series of separate stages.

The kind of source hypotheses that flourished around the turn of the century has found little acceptance in recent exegesis.[59] The theory that a redactor had taken up an earlier Jewish apocalyptic document and edited it from a Christian point of view has now been generally abandoned. The only such hypothesis that attained any lasting influence has been that of W. Bousset, who advocated a 'fragments hypothesis.' 'We do not accept the idea of an original document that was gradually expanded, nor was there a collection of original sources edited by a mechanical redactor. Rather, there

---

[56] Cf. Müller, *Offenbarung* 92. Roloff, *Revelation* 8, makes the key statement: 'Revelation is a prophetic writing that contains numerous apocalyptic motifs and elements of style, but whose form is chiefly characterized by the purpose of epistolary communication.' In the opinion of Schüssler Fiorenza, 'The Composition and Structure of Revelation' 176, 'the author intended to write a work of prophecy in the form of the apostolic letter.' Karrer, *Johannesoffenbarung als Brief* 302–303, 305, emphasizes the literary independence of Revelation, describes it as a 'circular letter' and characterizes it as an epistolary text of revelatory literature, 'that in its communication procedure integrates both Jewish as well as Greek-Hellenistic and Roman-imperial revelatory traditions, presented through the means of a letter.' The narrative dimensions of Revelation is rightly emphasized by Boring, 'Narrative Christology' 703, "apocalypse' as a genre of revelatory literature has a narrative framework.'

[57] So Martin Dibelius, 'Rom und die Christen im ersten Jahrhundert,' in *Botschaft und Geschichte* II, ed. Günther Bornkamm (Tübingen: J. C. B. Mohr [Paul Siebeck], 1956) 223–225; Kraft, *Offenbarung* 14–15.

[58] So Charles, *Revelation* I.xciv.

[59] On the history of research cf. Bousset, *Offenbarung* 108ff., 234ff.; Böcher, *Johannesapokalypse* 11ff.

was an apocalyptic author, but an author who at several points did not compose freehand, but reworked older apocalyptic fragments and traditions, the prehistory of which remain tentative and obscure.'[60] This model takes the complex history of traditions in the background of the Apocalypse seriously (see 9.7 above), and stands apart from the hypothesis of an original document with later editing by its flexibility and openness.[61] More plausible is the view that apparent tensions originated from the heterogeneous (and partly written)[62] materials and the redactional tendencies of the author.[63] 'As far as its composition as a whole is concerned, Revelation should be seen as a uniform, consistently–constructed work that from beginning to end reflects the theological intention of its author.'[64]

9.7 Traditions, Sources

The seer's major source is provided by the Old Testament. His work is characterized by an enormous number of allusions and by echoes of extensive passages.[65] Fragmentary citations and even by direct quotations[66] from the Old Testament are found in Rev. 1.7; 2.27; 4.8; 6.16; 7.16, 17; 11.11; 14.5; 15.3, 4; 19.15; 20.9; 21.4, 7. Quotations and allusions are influenced in part by the LXX or other later translations, but often reflect the author's own knowledge of Hebrew or Aramaic texts.[67] Continual reference is made to Ezekiel, Isaiah, Jeremiah, Daniel, and the Psalms.

The second great source of tradition used in the Apocalypse is the worship of the early Christian community. The liturgical orientation of the work emerges clearly in Rev. 1.10 and 22.20: the seer receives his vision on the Lord's Day and refers to the Eucharist, in order to involve the listening congregation directly in the revelatory event (cf. Rev. 4.20). The hymnic elements of Revelation[68] are mostly composed as antiphons (cf.

---

[60] Bousset, *Offenbarung* 129.

[61] Bousset's suggestion has received a positive response from (among others) Kümmel, *Introduction* 464; Vielhauer, *Urchristliche Literatur* 500; Schenke and Fischer, *Einleitung* 2.294, 312.

[62] Traditional elements may stand behind Rev. 11.1–14; 12.1–5, 14–16; 14.6–20; 17.8–18; 18.1–24.

[63] Cf. Müller, *Offenbarung* 38–39.

[64] Roloff, *Revelation* 13.

[65] According to Wikenhauser and Schmid *Einleitung* 643, the Apocalypse contains about 580 allusions to the Old Testament.

[66] The comment of Kümmel, *Introduction* 464, that 'there is not a single word-for-word quotation' of the Old Testament in the Apocalypse, is incorrect. Verbatim citations are found in Rev. 4.8; 15.4; 19.15, and 20.9. [67] On this cf. Charles, *Revelation* 1.lxvi–lxxxii.

[68] Cf. Delling, 'Zum gottesdienstlichen Stil' *passim*; Jörns, *Das hymnische Evangelium passim*; R. Deichgräber, *Gotteshymnus und Christushymnus* (see above 5.2.7) 44–59.

Rev. 4.9/11; 5.9b–10/12; 7.10b/12; 11.15b/17f; 16.5b–6/7b; 19.1b–8a). Of traditional forms are found, among others, (a) doxologies (Rev. 1.6; 4.9; 5.13; 7.12); (b) the Trishagion (Rev. 4.8c) (c) 'worthy art thou' acclamations (Rev. 4.11; 5.9b–10; 5.12); (d) prayers of thanksgiving (Rev. 11.17–18); (e) doxologies of judgment (Rev. 16.5–7); (f) titular predications of God, in nominal style (Rev. 4.8, 11; 15.3; 16.7; 19.6) and participial style (Rev. 4.9; 5.13; 7.10; 11.17; 16.5); (g) *parallelismus membrorum* (Rev. 4.11; 5.9–10; 11.15, 17; 12.11, 12; 13.4; 15. 3–4; 16.6); (h) laments of the martyrs (Rev. 6.10); (i) victory cries (Rev. 7.10; 12.10; 19.1); (j) declarations of praise grounded with a ὅτι-clause (Rev. 4.11; 5.9; 11.17; 12.10; 15.4; 16.5; 18.20; 19.2, 6).

The hymnic pieces stand mostly in exposed locations (cf. Rev. 4.8ff.; 5.9ff.; 11.15ff.; 15.3–4; 16.5–6; 19.1ff.). They praise God for the preceding or following events and thus steer the hearer/readers' view from the earthly ordeals to the glory of God.[69] Most scholars see the hymnic texts as reflections of actual liturgical events. As evidence for this one might, in addition to the forms named above, educe the responsorial elements in Revelation (strophes, antiphonal verses, ἀμήν [amen] in Rev. 5.14; 7.12a; 19.4, and 'Hallelujah' in Rev. 19.1, 3, 4, 6). Of course all this does not provide data from which an actual order of service can be reconstructed.[70]

Recent scholarship has not attained a consensus on the issue of whether the seer used (a limited amount of) fixed written sources, or drew from oral traditions. Consideration is given for example by U. B. Müller to Rev. 11–12[71] and by J. Roloff to Rev. 10.1–11; 11.1–14; 14.6–20; 17.8–18 and 18.1–24.[72]

9.8 History-of-religions Standpoint

In the messages to the seven churches the seer engages in intensive polemics with the internal movements within the congregations and attacks opposing tendencies.[73] The use of διδαχή (teaching) (Rev. 2.14, 15, 24) and διδάσκω (teach) (Rev. 2.14, 20) indicate that doctrinal disputes form the background of the controversy. In the congregation at Pergamon there

---

[69] According to Delling, 'Zum gottesdienstlichen Stil' 448, the liturgical elements in Revelation interpret the apocalyptic event; differently Jörns, *Das himmlische Evangelium* 175–178, who points to the proleptic character of the hymns.

[70] Cf. Jörns, *ibid.* 180ff.

[71] Müller, *Revelation* 13.

[72] Roloff, *Revelation* 14.

[73] The opponents addressed in Smyrna and Philadelphia do not belong to this category, for here the dominant problem is the tensions between the Christian and the Jewish congregations (cf. Rev. 2.9–10; 3.9).

are Christians who hold to the teaching of Balaam; the seer designates this as eating food sacrificed to idols and practicing immorality (Rev. 2.14). Balaam also appears in Jude 22 and 2 Pet. 2.15–16 as the prototype of the greedy teacher of false doctrine. Both places reflect the negative picture of Balaam that had developed in Jewish tradition.[74] The teaching of the Nicolaitans (Rev. 2.6) is paralleled in Rev. 2.15 to the views previously attacked by the use of οὕτως and ὁμοίως (thus . . . likewise; NRSV 'also').

In Thyatira a prophetess ('Jezebel')[75] emerged, who likewise misleads the members of the congregations to eat food sacrificed to idols and to immorality (Rev. 2.20). John is apparently engaged in conflict with an opposition group relatively similar to the 'Balaamites' in Pergamon.[76] Led by a group of male and female prophets, the groups in different ways gained influence in the churches of Ephesus, Pergamon, and Thyatira.[77] John disqualifies them by labeling them with the names of enemies of the people of God taken from his Bible,[78] and makes the question of whether one may eat food sacrificed to idols into a central issue of the dispute. Only those who keep their distance from the earthly sacral meals of the pagan culture will eat of the hidden heavenly manna (cf. Rev. 2.17).

In the ancient world, in the normal course of life it was hardly possible to avoid eating meat that had been dedicated to an idol, and this had already led to conflicts within the community during Paul's own lifetime (cf. 1 Cor. 8–10). The decisive difference between the seer and his opponents may be seen in Rev. 2.24–25, where in striking similarity to the Apostolic Decree (Acts 15.28–29)[79] the church in Thyatira is told, 'I do not lay on you any other burden; only hold fast what you have until I come.' As in Acts 15.28, βάρος (burden) in Rev. 2.24 describes the minimal lawful expectation, which applies to Gentiles. Probably the teaching of the seer's opponents rejects even this minimum of obedience to a legal norm, and appeal to special revelatory insights (cf. the 'deep things of Satan' in Rev. 2.24 with 1 Cor. 2.10). The confession of faith in one true God (cf. 1 Cor. 8.4, 6) makes uninhibited contact with pagan society possible for them, which was in the seer's eyes a false readiness to compromise and a dangerous strategy of adjusting to the pagan environment. In contrast, he

---

[74] The positive picture of Num 22–24 had already changed in Num 31.16. Cf. further Philo, *Life of Moses* 1.296–299; Josephus, *Antiquities* 4.129–130.

[75] Cf. 1Kgs 16.29–33; 18.19; 19.2.

[76] Cf. Müller, *Offenbarung*, 112, 118; Klauck, 'Sendschreiben nach Pergamon' 166.

[77] The false teaching also seems to have had an influence in Sardis (Rev. 3.4).

[78] According to Roloff, *Revelation* 51–52, the expression 'teaching of Balaam' derives from the opponents themselves.

[79] Cf. Müller, *Zur frühchristlichen Theologiegeschichte* (see above 7.3.8) 17–21. I cannot share the skepticism of Karrer, *Johannesoffenbarung als Brief* 201–202, regarding this line of interpretation.

called for a minimal standard of observance of distance over against the pagan state and its multiform religious practice in order to avoid actual idolatry.

Where can this opposing group be located in the history of earliest Christianity? One bit of evidence is provided by the name 'Nicolaitans.' The proselyte Nicolaus (Acts 6.5) fits well into the gallery of ancestral portraits of a radicalized post-Pauline Christianity that appealed to the earliest beginnings of the church in Jerusalem to validate its position. The Nicolaitans denied that the Old Testament law was binding in any sense, and based this on their special knowledge of God. They also set themselves forth as traveling apostles and prophets (cf. Rev. 2.2, 20),[80] and successfully propagated their views of an open participation in the pagan world, its institutions, and its meaningless rituals. This stance is by no means the expression of a Gnostic self-consciousness,[81] but is to be explained in terms of a charismatic post-Pauline stream of Christianity[82] that was on the way toward the Gnosticism of the second century.[83]

9.9 Basic Theological Ideas

The seer John composes his work in the horizon of the kingdom of God that has already broken in and is proceeding toward its consummation. The function of God as king and judge determines his thinking, so that world history is interpreted in terms of its end. God's pre-temporal creative act (cf. Rev. 4.11; 10.6; 14.7) corresponds to his eschatological act, of which it is appropriately said, 'See, I am making all things new' (Rev. 21.5). The devil in his earthly form of the dragon (Rev. 12.12–13) is permitted to afflict the church for a short time, for God is coming (cf. Rev. 1.4, 8; 4.8; 22.6–7). As παντοκράτωρ (Almighty) (Rev. 1.8; 4.8; 11.17; 15.3; 16.7, 14; 19.6, 15; 21.22), God will through his 'just and true judgment' (Rev. 15.3;

---

[80] Cf. Müller, *Offenbarung* 101.

[81] Contra among others Roloff, *Revelation* 45, 52 and Karrer, *Johannesoffenbarung als Brief* 99, 102, who speak of Gnosticism or gnosticizing tendencies, without defining 'Gnosticism.' So also Schüssler Fiorenza, 'Apocalyptic and Gnosis in Revelation and in Paul,' in *Book of Revelation* 115–117. At least gnosticizing tendencies are seen by Kraft, *Offenbarung* 87–94 (the Nicolaitans can be equated with the docetists of the letters of Ignatius); Helmut Koester, *Introduction* 2.253; Strobel, 'Apokalypse' 187; Roman Heiligenthal, 'Wer waren die "Nikolaiten"?,' ZNW 82 (1991) 133–137, argues that the 'Nicolaitans' are never understood solely as Gnostics in the anti-heretical literature of the church fathers.

[82] For an exemplary argument, cf. Müller, *Offenbarung* 96–99. Heiligenthal, 'Wer waren die "Nikolaiten"?' 136–137, while he sees the Nicolaitans as in the Pauline stream of tradition, proposes that their background was also a skepticism related to the pagan enlightenment that had rejected the concept of cultic purity (as also in the case of the views opposed in Jude).

[83] Cf. Klauck, 'Sendschreiben nach Pergamon' 169; Boring, 'Theology of Revelation.'

16.5–7) destroy the satanic figure of the Roman Empire and all the godless. The fundamentally theocentric orientation[84] of Revelation follows consistently from its identification of God as the One characterized as the almighty king and judge.

The foundation of Revelation's Christology is the saving act of God in Christ. This act establishes eschatological salvation and saves from the world's realm of power (cf. e.g., Rev. 1.5b, 6; 5.9–10; 7.15; 12.11). The distinctive christological dignity of Jesus is expressed in the title ἀρνίον (lamb, used 28x as a title in Rev.),[85] which at one and the same time expresses Jesus' giving himself for his own and his exaltation as Lord (Rev. 5.6).[86] The exaltation of the Lamb is based on his humiliation (cf. Rev. 5.9, 12); the firstborn of the dead (Rev. 1.5) is the slaughtered lamb. Jesus acts as God's authorized agent who in Rev. 5 is explicitly portrayed as being commissioned to accomplish God's plan of eschatological salvation.[87] In contrast to the Gospel of John, Revelation has no concept of an essential equality between God and Christ, but does picture them in terms of a 'functional unity.'[88] Christ executes the saving and judging act of God in the struggle with the anti-God forces. For the church, Christ is the present Lord (cf. Rev. 2–3), who addresses the church directly in words of warning and encouragement. Already in the present Christ, by his sacrificial death, has made the believing community into priests who participate in his lordship (Rev. 1.6; 5.10), but it is only the future that will make this manifest to all (cf. Rev. 20.6; 22.5). In reality the power of the world is already broken, but only at the parousia will the ultimate realization of the kingdom of God become visible to all through the renewing of the heavens and the earth (cf. Rev. 19.11ff.). In the meantime, Christians bear the seal of the living God (cf. Rev. 7.1–8; 3.12), while the godless are exposed to the temptations of Satan without the protection provided by this seal (Rev. 9.4). A fundamental conviction expressed in the Christology of Revelation is thus that Christ is at the same time the present Lord and the One to come in the future.

The eschatological affirmations of the Apocalypse also point to the reality of the presence of salvation, as the basis of eschatology is provided by the affirmations of the presence of salvation in Rev. 1.5b–6; 5.9–10; 14.3–4 that Christians, by the sacrificial death of the Lamb, are already

---

[84] Cf. Traugott Holtz, 'Gott in der Apokalypse' in Lambrecht, *L'Apocalypse* 247–265.

[85] Cf. Holtz, *Christologie* 78–80; Müller, *Offenbarung* 160–162.

[86] Cf. Böcher, *Johannesapokalypse* 47, who prefers to translate ἀρνίον with 'ram,' in order to express the juxtaposition of weakness and power of the heavenly Messiah.

[87] On Rev. 5 cf. especially Holtz, *Christologie* 27–54.

[88] Müller, *Offenbarung* 55, argues that traits of subordination are undeniably present. One only needs to note Rev. 1.13; 14.14, as well as 'his anointed' in 11.15; 12.10; 20.4, 6.

participants in the kingdom of God (Rev. 1.9).[89] It is not the future events that bring about the fundamental turning point of history; they are rather the crucial test and demonstration of God's power.[90] Because in reality the Lamb has already defeated the dragon, Christ can say to the community, 'I am coming soon' (Rev. 3.11; cf. 1.7; 2.16; 3.11, 20; 4.8; 22.7, 12, 17, 20). The events that are breaking in on them cannot overwhelm the community if they hold fast and recognize God's decisive acts in history that are now coming to their ultimate fulfillment. The conviction of the present reality of future salvation grounded in the death of the Lamb permeates the eschatology of Revelation. Despite the opposition of the world, the victory of God that John is permitted to see as perfected in the heavenly world has already begun in this world.

The basis of the Christian ethic is formulated by the seer in Rev. 1.5: the saving act of God in Jesus Christ has delivered Christians from their past sins. This indicative is the basis for the radical imperative.[91] The seer calls for a clear boundary between believers and the pagan world, a boundary that must be visible in the life and work of the church, for they will be judged according to their works (cf. Rev. 2.23; 20.12–13). These 'works' for John are the appropriate response to the saving work of God received in Jesus Christ,[92] and are never related to the Jewish law (νόμος is not found in Revelation!). In the 'conqueror' sayings (2.7, 11, 17, 26; 3.5, 12, 21) the seer's concept of ethics emerges clearly: the promise of the future fulfillment of the kingdom of God is the motivation for faithful endurance in the face of the testings of the present. The steadfastness and sufferings of Christians is seen as the counterpart of the steadfastness and suffering of Christ (cf. Rev. 2.3; 6.9). The positive counterpart is then the sharing of Christians in the rulership of God at the end of time (cf. Rev. 3.21; 20.4).

The ecclesiology of the seer bears the imprint of the conviction that the church is composed of those who are brothers and sisters in one family of God. John describes himself as a fellow brother (Rev. 1.9; 19.10; 22.9) who participates in the present distress of the church. All members of the community are servants/slaves (δοῦλοι; cf. Rev. 2.20; 7.3; 19.2, 5; 22.3). Even the angels are fellow-δοῦλοι (cf. Rev. 22.9).[93] Even Christ will act in

---

[89] Cf. Holtz, *Christologie* 70: 'The redemption of the community is already a present reality; it has in its possession what was once promised to the community of the Old Covenant as eschatological possession.'

[90] Cf. Karrer, *Johannesoffenbarung als Brief* 136.

[91] On the connection between Rev. 1.5–6 and 5.1–14 see Holtz, *Christologie* 70–71.

[92] Cf. Traugott Holtz, 'Die "Werke" in der Johannesapokalypse,' *Neues Testament und Ethik* (FS R. Schnackenburg), ed. H. Merklein (Freiburg: Herder, 1989) 426–441.

[93] According to Karrer, *Johannesoffenbarung als Brief* 169–186, the seer intentionally reduces the status and function of angels, because the addressees are too inclined to reverence them as independent powers.

a brotherly manner in sharing his throne with Christians (Rev. 3.21; 20.6; 21.17). This basic conception explains the noticeable silence about official church structures that are to be presupposed for the churches in Asia Minor at the end of the first century (cf. the Pastorals and letters of Ignatius).[94] The only church 'office' John mentions is that of the prophet, without however considering it to be institutionalized. From an ecumenical perspective he takes seriously the problems of the local congregations, because they will be decisive for the destiny of the whole church. On the whole, the Apocalypse is concerned with 'demonstrating the validity and certainty of the kingdom that belongs to God and to Jesus his Anointed One, the Lamb, who grant and guarantee salvation to those that belong to them.'[95] It is this concern that is expressed in the mythological language and conceptuality: 'The that, not the what or how is the focus of John's concern.'[96] This basic perspective is not grasped by a linear historical perception oriented to the end time, but by a concentric interpretation that regards the exaltation of Jesus as Lord that has already happened as the central element of the seer's theology.

9.10 Tendencies of Recent Research

Scholarship has reached a consensus on the question of authorship: practically all scholars regard the Revelation as not written by the apostle John the son of Zebedee. There is continuing dispute, however, on the relationship of Revelation to the writings of the Johannine school. While J. Roloff, U. B. Müller, E. Schüssler Fiorenza and E. Lohse emphasize the relative independence of Revelation, O. Böcher and especially J. W. Taeger place the Apocalypse in greater proximity to the other Johannine writings (see above 8.1.3). 'The idea that the Apocalypse belongs to the Johannine circle of writings is not a mere supposition, but there is enough solid evidence to keep the question open.'[97] While Taeger interprets Revelation within the framework of the later influence of the Fourth Gospel, G. Strecker sees the chiliast or apocalyptic views as traditional material that was present in the Johannine school from its beginnings.[98]

---

[94] Müller, *Zur Frühchristlichen Theologiegeschichte* (see above 5) 33–34, supposes that John intentionally ignores these structures, and that this is the reason he addresses the angel of each church as its heavenly representative.

[95] Karrer, *Johannesoffenbarung als Brief* 247.

[96] Boring, 'Narrative Christology in the Apocalypse' 718.

[97] Taeger, *Johannesapokalypse* 206.

[98] Cf. Georg Strecker, *History of New Testament Literature* (see above 1.2), 220; further, Frey, 'Erwägungen' 414ff.

Most scholars continue to regard the final years of Domitian's reign as the historical background against which the Apocalypse must be read. The acceptance of a general persecution of Christians under Domitian has become increasingly problematic in recent study, and is being replaced by an understanding of local conflicts between the Christian congregations and their pagan surroundings (U. B. Müller, J. Roloff, H. J. Klauck). The chief problem for John was not the (rarely demanded) offering of sacrifice before the image of Caesar. 'The apocalyptic author considered the much more dangerous situation that of the 'soft' imperial cult, for example when someone was incidentally present at a pagan festival or participated in a social club that had religious overtones, because he believed that for economic and professional reasons he could not exclude himself from them, and since they did not see them as touching on his Christian commitments anyway.'[99] In addition, the seer's polemic against internal streams of the church points to a controversy in the churches over accommodation and distance to Hellenistic-Roman society. Here two different lines of interpretation are precipitated out of the discussion: the seer's opponents are seen either in the context of early Christian Gnosticism (E. Schüssler Fiorenza, J. Roloff, M. Karrer) or as continuing developments within the stream of Pauline theology (U. B. Müller).

The issue of the literary genre of the document as a whole has become a central issue in recent study of apocalyptic. After E. Schüssler Fiorenza, U. B. Müller, and J. Roloff had already worked out the epistolary structure of Revelation, M. Karrer emphasized: the whole work 'is written as a letter relevant to a particular situation.'[100] This approach based on an aesthetics of reception can be sustained for Rev. 1–3, but the evidence has not yet been provided for the visionary part.[101]

There is agreement that the theological purpose of Revelation is the strengthening of the present assurance of salvation for the harassed and tempted community. Its primary concern, however, does not lie in the consolation of the community,[102] but in the decisive challenge to grasp both present and future in the horizon of the powerful saving act of God.

---

[99] Klauck, 'Sendschreiben nach Pergamon' 181. On pragmatic grounds present in the text, Klauck sees the primary concern of the author expressed in the demand, 'Come out of her, my people' (Rev. 18.4; cf. pp. 176–180 of his essay).

[100] Karrer, *Johannesoffenbarung als Brief* 30.

[101] It is hardly accidental that Karrer gives the main section of Revelation only a summary treatment, *Johannesoffenbarung als Brief* 220–281.

[102] Differently, e.g., Kümmel, *Introduction* 462, who describes Revelation as a 'book of consolation.'

Index of Biblical References

References to a document within the chapter dealing with that document are not included.

Index of Modern Authors

Index of Ancient Persons and Texts